THE NEW OXFORD BOOK OF SEVENTEENTH-CENTURY VERSE

THE NEW OXFORD BOOK OF SEVENTEENTH CENTURY VERSE

Edited by

ALASTAIR FOWLER

Oxford New York

OXFORD UNIVERSITY PRESS

1991

Oxford University Press, Walton Street, Oxford OX2 6DP

Oxford New York Toronto
Delhi Bombay Calcutta Madras Karachi
Petaling Jaya Singapore Hong Kong Tokyo
Nairobi Dar es Salaam Cape Town
Melbourne Auckland

and associated companies in
Berlin Ibadan

Oxford is a trade mark of Oxford University Press

British Library Cataloguing in Publication Data

The New Oxford book of seventeenth-century verse.
1. Poetry in English, 1625–1702. Anthologies
I. Fowler, Alastair
821.408

ISBN 0–19–214164–3

Library of Congress Cataloging in Publication Data

The New Oxford book of seventeenth-century verse/edited by Alastair Fowler.
p. cm.
Includes index.
1. English poetry—Early modern, 1500–1700. I. Fowler, Alastair.
PR1209.N49 1991 821'.408–dc20 90–22290

ISBN 0–19–214164–3

Printed in Great Britain by
The Bath Press Ltd.
Bath, Avon

CONTENTS

CONTENTS

CONTENTS

CONTENTS

CONTENTS

CONTENTS

CONTENTS

CONTENTS

CONTENTS

CONTENTS

ABBREVIATIONS

Ault	*Seventeenth-Century Lyrics*, ed. N. Ault (1928).
Blunden and Mellor	*Wayside Poems of the Seventeenth Century*, ed. E. Blunden and B. Mellor (Hong Kong, 1963).
Bowers	*The Dramatic Works in the Beaumont and Fletcher Canon*, gen. ed. F. Bowers, 10 vols. (Cambridge, 1966–).
Cutts	*Seventeenth Century Songs and Lyrics*, ed. J. P. Cutts (New York, 1969).
Doughtie	*Lyrics from English Airs 1596–1622*, ed. E. Doughtie (Cambridge, Mass., 1970).
Fellowes	*English Madrigal Verse 1588–1632*, ed. E. H. Fellowes: 3rd edn., rev. F. W. Sternfeld and D. Greer (Oxford, 1967).
Greer	*Kissing the Rod: An Anthology of Seventeenth-Century Women's Verse*, ed. G. Greer *et al.* (1988).
Kerr	*Restoration Verse 1660–1715*, ed. W. Kerr (1930).
Love	*The Penguin Book of Restoration Verse*, ed. H. Love (1968).
Marshall	*Rare Poems of the Seventeenth Century*, ed. L. B. Marshall (Cambridge, 1936).
Meserole	*Seventeenth-Century American Poetry*, ed. H. T. Meserole (New York, 1972).
Saintsbury	*Minor Poets of the Caroline Period*, ed. G. Saintsbury, 3 vols. (Oxford, 1968).
STS	*Scottish Text Society.*
a.	acted.
d.	died.
wr.	written.

INTRODUCTION

THE seventeenth century has a special fascination for us, in that it saw a decisive stage in the transition away from the divine cosmos of the Middle Ages towards our own very different world. Yet for that very reason it is a difficult period to get in focus. This is true even of its literature. Confused critical ideas of seventeenth-century poetry abound, and scholars' stories that cover only some of the facts. One misconception needs to be dismissed at the outset: that there was a great revolution early in the century, whereby Donne and his new army of Metaphysical poets overthrew Tudor conventionality, and introduced a style of concrete sensuous particularity. So far as sensuous particularity is concerned, the seventeenth century began well before 1600: many poems of the early 1590s (such as John Donne's 'The Calm') had plenty of it. Fulke Greville was a contemporary of Sir Philip Sidney, yet he used Metaphysical conceits; Nicholas Breton and Thomas Campion survived well into the seventeenth century, yet had the limpid 'golden' quality often regarded as characteristically Elizabethan. Moreover, Donne was in many ways a conventional, traditional, even a retrospective poet. In fact, there are literary and learned writers in all periods, as well as 'natural' writers. Walter Benjamin's idea of the seventeenth century as bookish may have some truth in it; but when you think of the freshness of Charles Cotton or Anne Bradstreet, of Edmund Waller or Sir William Davenant, it seems at best a very partial view.

Not that my predecessors Herbert Grierson and Geoffrey Bullough, editors of *The Oxford Book of Seventeenth-Century Verse* (1934), were altogether wrong to characterize the century's verse in terms of 'the intrusion of the intellect, and spirit of enquiry impatient of traditional, conventional sentiment'. They were justifiably concerned to correct Victorian distortions—partiality for lyric and relegation of Metaphysical difficulty. But this need no longer be the anthologist's chief anxiety. Over the last century the Metaphysicals have suffered almost anything but neglect. Indeed, critics interested in a balanced view have felt it necessary to press the parallel claims of Ben Jonson and the poetry of passionate simplicity. But offsetting the 'School of Donne' with the 'Tribe of Ben' may still be taking too narrow a view, for there was at least one other 'school' or grouping, that of Michael Drayton. Just as Donne had his following of associates and imitators (Thomas Carew, John Cleveland, Abraham Cowley, George and Edward Herbert, Andrew Marvell, and many university wits), and Jonson had his (Carew again, Mildmay Fane, Robert Herrick, John Denham, Sir

Edmund Waller, and many Cavalier lyrists), so Drayton can be regarded as the centre of a circle that included William Browne of Tavistock, William Drummond of Hawthornden, John Davies of Hereford, George Sandys, Joshua Sylvester, and George Wither.

Period ideas are abstractions more or less distant from the real diversity of the past. And in any case, when tastes change, anthologies of old verse cannot afford to be fully representative—if they were, they would be intolerable. Nevertheless, some representations are less untrue than others, and I have tried to make this one more representative than its excellent predecessor. It does not emulate the high seventeenth-century proportions of religious poetry, poetry of patronage, nor satiric and political forms with their obscure topicalities. But I have attempted to avoid the falsifications attendant on adhering to a fixed idea of the selection's 'dominant character' (as Grierson and Bullough ingenuously put it). A representative selection has meant more Drayton (second only to Spenser in *England's Parnassus* in 1600); more Cowley and Marvell; more Oldham and Strode; and many more female poets. It has meant including marginal figures such as the waterman Taylor, the alcoholic Brathwait, and the lunatic Carkesse. It has meant, in fact, including some 'subliterary' verse, and some very minor poets. If literature is the nation's memory, forgotten verse may contain things we need to know.

On this more inclusive, less tidy view, what happened in seventeenth-century poetry? What directions did it actually take? There are many themes, and many stories could be made of them. A main plot is certainly the success of the Metaphysical style. In part this was the personal triumph of Donne, whose brilliance illuminated or challenged most of his contemporaries. In part, it was a fashion for a particular manneristic rhetoric, in which imagery was not supposed to seem 'naturally' appropriate. Instead, it had to seem startlingly inapposite at first, and 'made good' only after much argument or witty justification. Embracing lovers, say, were no longer to be likened to Hermaphrodites, but rather to something quite unlikely—pairs of compasses, perhaps. Whether the style was often metaphysical in a philosophical sense may be questioned, but there can be no doubting Donne's intellectual acuity. And some at least of his followers were ready to meet the challenge of waning essentialism and visionary new sciences. The Metaphysical fashion began in the 1590s, and reached an early peak. Fulke Greville and Edward Herbert, learned academics and frivolous cavaliers: all clothed deep and light thoughts alike in Metaphysical gowns. Some, however, like Thomas Carew, mixed Donne with Jonson; and the 1630s were in many ways Drayton's decade. When Metaphysical wit revived at the mid-century, it was applied differently from before, and especially to the re-envisioning of nature—whether through science (Cowley) or emblematic interpretation (Marvell).

Recovery of classical genres like elegy and satire might be another story—a longer one, for it was to change the whole subsequent history of English poetry. Most Elizabethan poets had been classical enough in their (often mythological) content; but they seem to have apprehended ancient forms but vaguely. Jonson and his tribe shared a sharper idea of the classical genres, and worked towards viable naturalized versions, or modern variants. This programme affected how poets interacted. Elizabethan poets might occasionally compete in addressing the same subject, but seventeenth-century poets were more likely to emulate one another by taking up the same sub-genre—valediction, perhaps, or funeral elegy. Clearly understood genres encouraged sustained, closely articulated efforts, and improved both the communicative effectiveness and the quality of verse. Jonson's example was fruitful in this way, as were his individual poems: 'To Penshurst', for example, prompted many estate poems, by Carew, Herrick, Marvell, and others. And Drayton and Denham and Dryden were similarly influential in setting up definitive models.

No recovered genre was more significant historically than epigram, that is, the compressed short poem built round a single idea and culminating in a witty closure or 'point'. Indeed, the most important literary change of the century could be seen as the pervasive tendency whereby epigram merged with and transformed almost every other kind. (Thus, Donne's love poems are epigrammatic love elegies, and Dryden's satires contain many inset satiric epigrams.) The epigrammatic shift was important because it put an end to the loose divagations and formulaic padding of earlier tradition, so that all poetry (retrospective gothicism apart) became more compressed. It brought a lasting change of scale: even now we take for granted that every word in a poem must count. Before the seventeenth century, however, single words rarely released their potentiality; Shakespeare's 'incarnadine' was one of the first to do so. But Herrick's epigrams have many such foregrounded words—'transshifting', for example, and 'liquefaction'. Epigram also affected poetic syntax; as when the pursuit of 'points' led to compressed 'strong lines', so full of wit that the chains of discourse became difficult to follow. (Think how many strands of meaning there are in Cleveland's couplet 'Women commence by Cupid's dart,/ As a king's hunting dubs a hart'.) But possibly the largest consequence of the epigram shift lay in another feature of the genre altogether, its freedom of subject. This made it well suited to a period of information explosion, when discoveries and literary topics rapidly accrued, and the appetite for novelty was sharp.

Among longer forms, the one of special value for a period of expanding knowledge was georgic. For this term extended, beyond formal manuals of husbandry, to 'arts', didactic verse essays, and digressive description generally. Although in theory georgic contrasted with pastoral, the two frequently mingled—British pastoral had never been very 'pure', either in the sense of free from knowledge, or from detailed sensuous description. Nevertheless, during the century georgic gradually displaced pastoral, becoming latterly a dominant genre. This was for several reasons a momentous change. For one thing, it re-established the possibility of serious poetry in the poet's own voice. For another, it brought in the oblique, hidden subject. Who can say exactly what John Denham's *Cooper's Hill*, or Marvell's 'Upon Appleton House', is really 'about'? Again, georgic poets—teaching by example, as it were—cultivated local mimetic and implicit effects that have subsequently been generalized throughout literature. And it was in georgic that poets like Wither expressed unaristocratic values, such as that of labour. Above all, georgic introduced detailed sensuous description and the poetry of landscape. In these respects direct filiations run from Drayton through Denham and Cowley to Pope, James Thomson, and other Augustan georgic poets.

Landscape description was but part of a larger concern: the new sciences demanded a fundamental reordering of the experience of nature in general. For a century of discoveries, both from exploration and from quasi-experimental research, had aroused keen interest in astronomy, geography, physics, and natural history, all of which were pursued with a new freedom of speculation. To some, like Cowley, this meant enlightened reflection—revision of ideas about man's relation to nature. For others, the world of given meanings and found emblems continued, even if emblematic thinking might take a fresh empirical or sceptical turn, as in Marvell and Denham. For others again, like Mildmay Fane or Henry Vaughan, nature was a matter for religious meditation. Meditation of all varieties, from mystical to self-interested, was practised throughout the period, and gave rise to some of its most familiar literature. The century's religious verse, even when written by amateurs or by such as the modestly endowed Thomas Flatman, often expresses doubts, depressions, and melancholy fears of death with a touchingly simple, open sincerity that would be hard to match in earlier, and not all that easy in later, periods. But it could still achieve triumphs of faith and vision like those of Richard Crashaw and Edward Taylor. In short, the period was one of a pristine individuality of experience, as well as, at times, individual oddity.

Individualism helped to shape even the poetry of love, that most conventional of subjects. At the outset, the assumptions of love poetry were mostly Petrarchist (or, what is much the same thing, anti-Petrarchist). This is especially true of the countless sonnets (by

Drayton, Drummond, Ayton, Wroth, and others) that continued, contrary to received opinion, well into the century. But already in some of these, and later in the Cavalier poets, in Cowley, and in the female poets and libertines of the Restoration, more varied attitudes emerged. For, as narcissistic Metaphysical paradox gave way to preposterous fancy, and display of wit to witty exchanges, love poetry too became more exploratory in a social direction. The inner-directed visions of the sonneteers were replaced by more externalized and reciprocal colloquies; the beloved, from being the mute subject of rhetoric, emerged as an active adversary in debates of love. Innumerable poems for or against 'platonic love', or 'fruition', in effect discussed how sexual relations should be reordered; contributing to the broader controversies implied by the revisionist marriage contracts in Dryden's *Marriage à la Mode* and Congreve's *The Way of the World*. Considering the enormous quantity of seventeenth-century love poetry, the quality, both of songs and epigrams, seems remarkably high. The variety of the achievement is particularly striking; ranging as it does from different sorts of wit in Donne, Edward Herbert, and Dryden, through the lyric serenity of Drummond and Milton, and the passion of Wroth, to the tellingly simple directness of 'Ephelia'.

Reflections and effectuations of social change are no less perceptible in satire, a genre gradually re-established on the ancient models of Martial, Juvenal, and Horace. The Juvenalian Joseph Hall showed the way, and Donne, with his satyr-rough, half-spoken dramatic monologues. But Donne's satires (or 'satyrs') lack penetration of social structure; satire became more effective when a political dimension was added by the royalist Cleveland and by Marvell the Commonwealth man. And satiric wit became sharper in the Earl of Rochester's radical critiques, its obliquities more outrageous in Samuel Butler (who often hit more targets than one). At length John Oldham's closer imitation of classical satire brought force, economy, and subtlety effectively together. Foundations were laid by Oldham and Dryden on which the work of the Augustan satirists would be raised.

In all these developments can be traced filiations or poetic lineages of influence and appropriation. One obvious line of wit runs from Donne to Oldham and Dryden; to Rochester; and ultimately to Pope, who put Donne's *Satires* into correct verse. Another connects the same *termini*, but through Cowley and the Metaphysical epigones. Or one might follow a georgic line, from Drayton and Jonson, through Denham, Marvell, and Cotton, to the Pope of *Windsor-Forest* and *An Essay on Criticism*. And a Jonsonian tradition of social verse, varied by the Cavalier poets, plainly descends to the Augustans through Waller and Davenant. But these are all relatively local connections. Dryden, our first great critic, took a longer view, and saw other dynasties altogether:

'Milton was the poetical son of Spenser, and Mr Waller of Fairfax'; the Elizabethans being 'great masters in our language, and who saw much further into the beauties of our numbers [rhythms] than those who immediately followed them'. (Old versification is soon forgotten; the Augustans themselves thought Donne's spoken rhythms impossibly rough, and John Upton, Spenser's first editor, did not know that 'compassion' had once been tetrasyllabic.) Dryden's tradition of art might be thought of as handed down by Spenser and the Continental masters to Fairfax, Drayton, and Drummond; to Milton; to Waller and Denham; to Dryden himself; to Pope; and later to James Thomson. And taking a larger view still, one might link Martial and Jonson, Herrick and his Victorian admirers. But which is the main line, the true canon?

That depends on many factors: movements of taste, availability of editions, representation of values (whether congenial or challenging), and criteria of judgement, to mention a few. A criterion of moral seriousness, or religious intensity, might seem to us to call for promoting Jonson and Milton, Herbert and Edward Taylor. One of social consciousness might select Jonson and Milton, Wither and Oldham. And one of art, surely, Jonson and Milton, Lovelace and Dryden. But who can say which of these changes the canon of the next age may not reverse? Nevertheless, some revaluations are so long overdue as to have seemed inevitable in making the present selection. Rochester, long repudiated for immorality and unavailability, now takes a more prominent place; and I have responded to growing recognition of the art of Drayton and Cowley, Lovelace and Strode, Ayton and Davenant, and Oldham. Finally, a number of female poets, such as Emilia Lanier, Lady Mary Wroth, Margaret Cavendish, Duchess of Newcastle, and Anne Finch, Countess of Winchilsea, have displaced a larger number of minor male poets.

EDITORIAL PRINCIPLES

Coverage

The 'Verse' of the title may be taken to mean 'Verse in English'; so that my inclusion of American, Irish, Scottish, and Welsh poets writing in English need not be thought anomalous. Where my predecessors' selection could not be bettered, I have aimed at alternative choices, so that *The New Oxford Book of Seventeenth Century Verse* and *The Oxford Book of Seventeenth Century Verse* are to some extent complementary volumes. Even their coverage is not quite equivalent, since I have included far more female authors, and some popular ones like John Taylor the Water Poet. In determining eligibility, dates of publication have generally been decisive. In consequence, the work of several poets whose active lives extended beyond the century's ends has been divided between volumes in the present series: much of Shakespeare, Campian, and Samuel Daniel, for example, will be found in *The New Oxford Book of Sixteenth Century Verse*. But, in a century when manuscript circulation was still widespread, publication dates cannot always be regarded as the most significant. A few inconsistencies, therefore, will be encountered, such as the exclusion of Shakespeare's *Sonnets* (printed in 1609 but assigned to the sixteenth century), or the inclusion of Finch's poems (not published until the eighteenth century, but probably written before 1689).

Dates

Each item is accompanied by the date of its first early printed publication (if any), even where the text follows a later revision or version. Where known, a probable date of composition or performance may also be given, particularly if very different from that of publication: '(1713; wr. ?1689)'. The arrangement of items within an author selection is generally chronological; but where many dates are uncertain I have allowed myself some latitude in the interest of variety, arrangement by genre, or (as with the large Donne selection) have for convenience followed alphabetic order of titles. The sequence of poets agrees with that of their birth-dates, where known; otherwise, with that of their *floruits*, adjusted on an arbitrary assumption of publication at the age of 30.

Texts

Usually a poet's latest revisions are followed, although the date given is that of the earliest printed version. A little work has been done among the countless printed and manuscript miscellanies of the seventeenth century, so that in some cases it has been possible to advance the date of earliest publication. Occasionally, as with Walter Pope's 'The Wish', an earlier (and perhaps less familiar) version has been printed. No attempt has been made to give alternative readings: this is not a textual edition. Nevertheless I have ventured a few emendations, as in Donne's 'The Autumnal', line 7 (Were her first years the Golden Age; that's true] Were her first years the Golden Age? That's true). And I have corrected some long-accepted readings, such as Norman Ault's 'angels' cry' (for 'angels' key') in Paman's 'On Christmas Day'. My preference is for complete items; but with a century of many long poems, excerpting has been inevitable. Titles invented on this account, or because they were omitted originally, are signalized by square brackets.

In an edition such as this, old spelling would raise unnecessary difficulties. As a rule, therefore, orthography (including conventions of capitalization and italicization) has been modernized. Thus, it has not been possible to retain the visual patterning of capitals and italics that some seventeenth-century poets (or their printers) cultivated. Occasionally, however, old spellings or word segmentations are retained, if a rhyme or some other reason demands it. And I have kept a few contraction marks, where they help with difficult scansion. Since many words were once stressed differently from modern expectations, three diacritic marks have been introduced: 'armèd' indicates that *-ed* is sounded; 'conjúre', that the *u* is stressed; and the dieresis, that an extra syllable is to be sounded, as in 'contemplatïon' (five syllables) or 'entïre' (three syllables, vocalic *r*). Old inflections are left; so that, for example, plural subject commonly agrees with singular verb, as in Cavendish 'The Hunting of the Hare', line 49, where 'think' would in modern English be 'thinks'.

Modernization of old punctuation is more necessary still, but harder to accomplish without loss. I have replaced many parentheses with modern commas, and many colons with modern semicolons. Very often, too, commas have been omitted between verb and object, and where they merely underline the interlinear pause (as in Marvell's 'Bermudas', lines 19–20) or indicate caesuras (as in Donne's 'The Relic': 'Then, he that digs us up, will bring / Us, to the bishop, and the king,'). But, because much seventeenth-century punctuation was rhetorical rather than grammatical, exact modern equivalents can be hard to find. And sometimes, especially where the heavy old pointing indicated emphasis or inversion, it may prove undesirable to disturb it. While aiming, therefore, at a rather light punctuation, I have modernized conservatively, and left some old points alone where they were not misleading.

Selection

The author selections should not be thought proportioned in all cases by my ideas of relative merit. Too many constraining factors have entered in, for that—suitability, length, genre, accessibility, obscurity, and others. Nevertheless, I have tried to keep the sizes of the selections roughly proportionate in the case of major authors. The most fully represented, Milton, seems to me also the best—in terms of quality alone, indeed, he might have filled most of the volume. No anthology can do justice to poets like Milton or Dryden or Cowley, who run to length. In the case of female poets, however, discriminated against during the last century and virtually ignored in Oxford Books of Verse before the present series, I have tried to do some belated justice, by unashamedly practising positive discrimination; as also with a few revalued male poets, such as Strode and Ayton. In the main this is meant as an anthology—flowers rather than weeds—but I have included several items mainly for their historical or human interest.

ACKNOWLEDGEMENTS

A volume such as this is largely built on debts of one sort or another. Mine are to colleagues at Edinburgh University, Oxford University, and the University of Virginia; to librarians at the Alderman Library, the Bodleian Library, the British Library, Edinburgh University Library, and the National Library of Scotland; to my tutors and students and friends; to critics and scholars and bibliographers and (especially) other anthologists. Debts so innumerable can only be consolidated and inadequately gestured at by this single acknowledgement. I can at least express, however, particular thanks for the generous help of those who suggested items (Lyndy Abram, Jonquil Bevan, Lynne Brown, Howard Erskine-Hill, Tony Gibbs, David Levin and Michael Wilding); those who answered specific queries (Bridget Cusack, Michael Phillips, Leighton D. Reynolds, and Alex Crampton Smith); and those who made practical contributions such as library searches and photocopying (Mark Ray Clinton, Don Simonton, Tanya Stanciu, Sheila Strathdee, and, above all, my wife). I owe much to the staff of Oxford University Press, who made valuable suggestions at each stage of the work. And I am grateful to the Carnegie Trust for the Universities of Scotland, who awarded a generous grant for library studies, without which this book would not have been possible.

ELIZABETH, LADY TANFIELD?
fl. 1565–1628

1 ### [*Epitaph for Sir Lawrence Tanfield*]

HERE shadow lie:
  Whilst life is sad,
Still hopes to die
  To him she had.
In bliss is he
  Whom I loved best:
Thrice happy she
  With him to rest.
So shall I be
  With him I loved,
And he with me
  And both us blessed.
Love made me poet,
  And this I writ;
My heart did do it,
  And not my wit.

(wr. 1625?)

FULKE GREVILLE, LORD BROOKE
1554–1628

from *Caelica* (2–6)

2 ### *Sonnet LVI*

ALL my senses, like beacon's flame,
Gave alarum to desire
To take arms in Cynthia's name,
And set all my thoughts on fire:
Furies' wit persuaded me
Happy love was hazard's heir,
Cupid did best shoot and see
In the night where smooth is fair;

1 Still] Ever

Up I start believing well,
To see if Cynthia were awake.
Wonders I saw, who can tell?
And thus unto myself I spake:
'Sweet god Cupid, where am I,
That by pale Diana's light
Such rich beauties do espy
As harm our senses with delight?
Am I borne up to the skies?
See where Jove and Venus shine,
Showing in her heavenly eyes
That desire is divine:
Look where lies the Milken Way,
Way unto that dainty throne
Where, while all the gods would play,
Vulcan thinks to dwell alone.
Shadowing it with curious art,
Nets of sullen golden hair:
Mars am I, and may not part,
Till that I be taken there.'
Therewithal I heard a sound,
Made of all the parts of love,
Which did sense delight and wound;
Planets with such music move.
Those joys drew desires near.
The heavens blushed, the white showed red,
Such red as in skies appear
When Sol parts from Thetis' bed.
Then unto myself I said
'Surely I Apollo am;
Yonder is the glorious maid
Which men do Aurora name,
Who for pride she hath in me
Blushing forth desire and fear,
While she would have no man see,
Makes the world know I am there.
I resolve to play my son
And misguide my chariot fire,
All the sky to overcome
And inflame with my desire.'
I gave reins to this conceit;
Hope went on the wheel of lust;
Fancy's scales are false of weight,
Thoughts take thought that go of trust.

Shadowing] (1) shading; (2) adumbrating Thetis'] the sea's (Latin mythology) Aurora] Morning conceit] fancy

I stept forth to touch the sky,
I a god by Cupid dreams;
Cynthia, who did naked lie,
Runs away like silver streams,
Leaving hollow banks behind,
Who can neither forward move
Nor, if rivers be unkind,
Turn away or leave to love.
There stand I, like Arctic pole,
Where Sol passeth o'er the line,
Mourning my benighted soul,
Which so loseth light divine.
There stand I like men that preach
From the execution place,
At their death content to teach
All the world with their disgrace:
He that lets his Cynthia lie,
Naked on a bed of play,
To say prayers ere she die,
Teacheth time to run away.
Let no love-desiring heart
In the stars go seek his fate:
Love is only nature's art;
Wonder hinders love and hate.
None can well behold with eyes
But what underneath him lies.

(1633)

3

Sonnet LXXXVII

WHENAS man's life, the light of human lust,
In socket of his earthly lanthorn burns,
That all this glory unto ashes must,
And generation to corruption turns;
Then fond desires that only fear their end
Do vainly wish for life, but to amend.

But when this life is from the body fled,
To see itself in that eternal glass
Where time doth end and thoughts accuse the dead,
Where all to come is one with all that was;
Then living men ask how he left his breath,
That while he livèd never thought of death.

(1633)

3 Whenas] Seeing that

4 *Sonnet LXXXVIII*

MAN, dream no more of curious mysteries,
As what was here before the world was made,
The first man's life, the state of paradise,
Where heaven is, or hell's eternal shade.
  For God's works are like him, all infinite;
  And curious search, but crafty sin's delight.

The Flood that did, and dreadful fire that shall,
Drown and burn up the malice of the Earth,
The divers tongues and Babylon's downfall,
Are nothing to the man's renewèd birth;
  First let the Law plough up thy wicked heart,
  That Christ may come and all these types depart.

When thou hast swept the house that all is clear,
When thou the dust hast shaken from thy feet,
When God's all-might doth in thy flesh appear,
Then seas with streams above thy sky do meet;
  For goodness only doth God comprehend,
  Knows what was first and what shall be the end.

(1633)

5 *Sonnet XCIX*

DOWN in the depth of mine iniquity,
That ugly centre of infernal spirits
Where each sin feels her own deformity
In these peculiar torments she inherits,
  Deprived of human graces and divine,
  Even there appears this saving God of mine.

And in this fatal mirror of transgression
Shows man as fruit of his degeneration,
The error's ugly infinite impression,
Which bears the faithless down to desperation;
  Deprived of human graces and divine,
  Even there appears this saving God of mine.

In power and truth, almighty and eternal,
Which on the sin reflects strange desolation,
With glory scourging all the sprites infernal
And uncreated hell with unprivation;
  Deprived of human graces, not divine,
  Even there appears this saving God of mine.

4 types] prefigurations   dust . . . shaken] (Mark 6: 11)

For on this spiritual cross condemnèd lying,
To pains infernal by eternal doom,
I see my saviour for the same sins dying
And from that hell I feared, to free me, come;
  Deprived of human graces, not divine,
  Thus hath his death raised up this soul of mine.

(1633)

6

Sonnet CV

THREE things there be in man's opinion dear:
Fame, many friends, and fortune's dignities;
False visions all, which in our sense appear,
To sanctify desire's idolatries.

For what is fortune but a watery glass?
Whose crystal forehead wants a steely back,
Where rain and storms bear all away that was,
Whose ship alike both depths and shallows wrack.

Fame again, which from blinding power takes light,
Both Caesar's shadow is and Cato's friend,
The child of humour, not allied to right,
Living by oft exchange of wingèd end.

And many friends, false strength of feeble mind,
Betraying equals, as true slaves to might,
Like echoes still send voices down the wind,
But never in adversity find right.

Then man, though virtue of extremities
The middle be, and so hath two to one,
By place and nature constant enemies,
And against both these no strength but her own,
  Yet quit thou for her, friends, fame, fortune's throne;
  Devils, there many be, and Gods but one.

(1633)

doom] judgement

6 forehead] front   wrack] wreck

7 from *A Treaty of Human Learning*

THE mind of man is this world's true dimension,
And knowledge is the measure of the mind;
And as the mind in her vast comprehension
Contains more worlds than all the world can find,
So knowledge doth itself far more extend
Than all the minds of men can comprehend.

A climbing height it is without a head,
Depth without bottom, way without an end,
A circle with no line environèd;
Not comprehended, all it comprehends;
Worth infinite, yet satisfies no mind
Till it that infinite of the Godhead find.

This knowledge is the same forbidden tree
Which man lusts after to be made his maker;
For knowledge is of power's eternity,
And perfect glory, the true image-taker;
So as what doth the infinite contain
Must be as infinite as it again.

No marvel, then, if proud desire's reflection
By gazing on this sun do make us blind,
Nor if our lust, our centaur-like affection,
Instead of nature fathom clouds and wind;
So adding to original defection,
As no man knows his own unknowing mind,
And our Egyptian darkness grows so gross
As we may easily in it feel our loss.

For our defects in nature who sees not?
We enter first things present not conceiving,
Not knowing future, what is past forgot:
All other creatures instant power receiving
To help themselves, man only bringeth sense
To feel and wail his native impotence.

Which sense, man's first instructor, while it shows
To free him from deceit, deceives him most;
And from this false root that mistaking grows,
Which truth in human knowledges hath lost,

Treaty] Treatise   dimension] measure   affection] passion; emotion   defection] falling away; fall   Egyptian darkness] darkness of sin (Exod. 10: 21)   shows] pretends   deceit] deception

So that by judging sense herein perfection
Man must deny his nature's imperfection.

Which to be false, even sense itself doth prove,
Since every beast in it doth us exceed;
Besides, these senses, which we thus approve,
In us as many diverse likings breed
As there be different tempers in complexions,
Degrees in healths, or age's imperfections.

Again, change from without no less deceives
Than do our own debilities within;
For th' object, which in gross our flesh conceives
After a sort, yet when light doth begin
These to retail and subdivide—or sleaves
Into more minutes—then grows sense so thin
As none can so refine the sense of man
That two, or three, agree in any can.

Yet these racked up by wit excessively
Make fancy think she such gradations finds
Of heat, cold, colours, such variety
Of smells and tastes, of tunes such diverse kinds
As that brave Scythian never could descry,
Who found more sweetness in his horses naying
Than all the Phrygian, Dorian, Lydian playing.

(1633)

from *Mustapha*

8 *Chorus primus of bashaws or cadis*

THE mufti and their spiritual jurisdictions
By course succeed these other guilt-inflictions;
Conscience annexing to our crescent star
All freedoms that in man's frail nature are,
By making doctrines large, strict, mild, severe,
As power intends to stir up hope, or fear;
Which heavenly shadow, with Earth-centres fixed,
Rack men by truth and untruths, strangely mixed;
And prove to thrones such a supporting cause
As finely gives law to all other laws.

complexions] temperaments retail] itemize sleaves] separates into filaments minutes] minute parts racked up] stretched; cleared up

8 *bashaws*] pashas cause] case

Thus, like the wood that yields helves for the axe
Upon itself to lay an heavy tax,
We silly bashaws help power to confound,
With our own strength exhausting our own ground.
An art of tyranny, which works with men
To make them beasts, and high-raised thrones their den,
Where they that mischief others may retire
Safe with their prey, as lifting tyrants higher.
By which enthralling of ourselves with others,
Prove we not both confusion's heirs, and mothers?
Far unlike Adam, putting civil names
Upon those errors which the whole world blames.
For if power ravine more than is her own,
'People,' we say, 'are checkers to a throne.'
Again, if she to rise up will pull down,
'Creation,' we say, 'still inheres the crown.'
If good men chance to interrupt this way,
'Too much in virtue oft there is,' we say;
Since each inferior limb must from the head
Receive his standard and be balancèd.
If people grudge their freedom, thus made thrall,
Power is their body, they but shadows all.

(1633)

from *A Treatise of Monarchy* (9–10)

9 from *Of Nobility*

FOR as the harmony which sense admires
Of discords (yet concording) is compounded,
And as each creature really aspires
Unto that unity which all things founded,
So must the throne and people both affect
Discording tones, united with respect.

By which consent of disagreeing movers
There will spring up aspécts of reverence,
Equals and betters quarrelling like lovers
Yet all confessing one omnipotence,
And therein each estate to be no more
Than instruments out of their maker's store.

8 mischief] harm   checkers] (1) pawns; (2) exchequer-men   inheres] is an attribute of

From whence nobility doth of creation
A secret prove to kings and tyranny;
For as the stamp gives bullion valuation,
So these fair shadows of authority
Are marks for people to look up unto
And see what princes with our earth can do.

In whom it is great wisdom to reward
Unequal worth with inequality;
Since it doth breed a prosperous regard,
As well to princes as to tyranny,
When people shall see those men set above
That more with worth than fortune seem in love.

Yet must this brave magnificence be used
Not really to dispossess the Crown
Either of power or wealth, but so infused
As it may rather raise than pull it down;
Which frugal majesty in growing Rome
Gave her above all states a lasting doom.

(1670)

10 from *Of Peace*

PEACE is the next in order, first in end,
As the most perfect state of government,
Where art and nature, each to other friend,
Enlarge the Crown by giving men content,
And what, by laws within and leagues without,
Leaves nothing but prosperity to doubt;

So that in her orb there is left for kings
Great undertakings, far beyond the flight
Or pitch of any lower feathered wings;
The charge, care, counsel being infinite,
As undertaking range of time and seas,
Which tyrantlike to ruin else finds ways.

Ordering of boats and bridges to be placed
Upon advantage for the trade of men;
Rebuilding monuments or towns defaced;
Cleansing of havens; draining dry of fens;
Fitting out brooks and meres for navigation:
All works of princely art, charge, reputation.

Such was the cleansing of the Egyptian sluices,
Which got Augustus ornament and food
For his praetorian bands' and peoples' uses;
In this kind proved their Appian highway good
Those public works which active states bring forth,
Showing the stranger maps of wealth and worth.

* * * * *

The base of great works, and the majesty,
Is when the workers power and wisdom show
Both in the use and possibility;
So over Ister Trajan's bridge did go.
Amasis and Cheops how can time forgive,
Who in their useless pyramids would live?

Next, and of more refinèd policy,
The founding is of these sweet nurseries
Where knowledge and obedience multiply
The fame and sinews of great monarchies—
As schools, which finely do, between the sense
And nature's large forms, frame intelligence.

(1670)

ANNE HOWARD?
1557–1630

11 from *The Good Shepherd's Sorrow for the Death of His Beloved Son*

In sad and ashy weeds
I sigh, I pine, I grieve, I mourn;
My oats and yellow reeds
I now to jet and ebon turn.
My urgèd eyes,
Like winter skies,
My furrowed cheeks o'erflow.
All heaven knows why
Men mourn as I,
And who can blame my woe?

In sable robes of night
My days of joy appareled be:
My sorrows see no light:
My light through sorrows nothing see;

11 urgèd] burning

For now my son
His date hath run,
And from his sphere doth go
To endless bed
Of folded lead;
And who can blame my woe?

My flocks I now forsake,
That silly sheep my griefs may know,
And lilies loathe to take
That since his fall presumed to grow.
I envy air,
Because it dare
Still breathe, and he not so;
Hate earth, that doth
Entomb his youth;
And who can blame my woe?

Not I, poor lad alone
(Alone how can this sorrow be?):
Not only men make moan,
But more than men make moan with me:
The gods of greens,
The mountain queens,
The fairy circle's row,
The Muses nine,
The nymphs divine,
Do all condole my woe.

(1631)

GEORGE CHAPMAN
1559–1634

from Euthymiae Raptus (12–15)

12 [*Peace Discovers the Poet*]

THOU wretched man, whom I discover, born
To want and sorrow and the vulgars' scorn:
Why hauntst thou freely these unhaunted places
Empty of pleasures? Empty of all graces,
Fashions, and riches; by the best pursued
With broken sleep, toil, love, zeal, servitude;

With fear and trembling, with whole lives and souls?
While thou breakst sleeps, digst under earth, like moles
To live, to seek me out, whom all men fly;
And thinkst to find light in obscurity,
Eternity in this deep vale of death:
Lookst ever upwards, and liv'st still beneath;
Fillst all thy actions with strife, what to think,
Thy brain with air, and scatterst it in ink:
Of which thou mak'st weeds for thy soul to wear,
As out of fashion as the bodies are.

(1608)

13 [*Justice*]

WRETCHED estate of men by fortune blessed,
That being ever idle, never rest;
That have goods ere they earn them, and for that,
Want art to use them. To be wondered at
Is justice, for proportion, ornament;
None of the Graces is so excellent.
Vile things adorn her: methought once I saw
How by the sea's shore she sat giving law
Even to the streams and fish (most loose and wild),
And was (to my thoughts) wondrous sweet and mild;
Yet fire flew from her that dissolvèd rocks;
Her looks to pearl turned pebble, and her locks
The rough and sandy banks to burnished gold;
Her white left hand did golden bridles hold,
And with her right she wealthy gifts did give,
Which with their left hands men did still receive.
Upon a world in her chaste lap did lie
A little ivory book that showed mine eye
But one page only; that, one verse contained,
Where all arts were contracted and explained:
All policies of princes, all their forces;
Rules for their fears, cares, dangers, pleasures, purses;
All the fair progress of their happiness here,
Justice converted and composèd there.
All which I thought on, when I had expressed
Why great men, of the great states they possessed,
Enjoyed so little; and I now must note
The large strain of a verse I long since wrote,

13 still] ever

Which, methought, much joy to men poor presented:
God hath made none, that all might be, contented.

(1608)

14

[*Learning*]

So learned men in controversies spend
(Of tongues, and terms, readings, and labours penned)
Their whole lives' studies: glory, riches, place
In full cry, with the vulgar giving chase;
And never with their learning's true use strive
To bridge strifes within them, and to live
Like men of peace whom art of peace begat;
But, as their deeds are most adulterate,
And show them false sons to their peaceful mother
In those wars, so their arts are proved no other.
And let the best of them a search impose
Upon his art; for all the things she knows
(All being referred to all to her unknown)
They will obtain the same proportion
That doth a little brook that never ran
Through summer's sun, compared with th' ocean.
But, could he oracles speak, and write to charm
A wild of savages; take nature's arm,
And pluck into his search the circuit
Of Earth and heaven, the seas' space and the spirit
Of every star, the powers of herbs and stones,
Yet touch not at his perturbations,
Nor give them rule and temper to obey
Imperial reason, in whose sovereign sway
Learning is wholly used and dignified,
To what end serves he? Is his learning, tried,
That comforting and that creating fire
That fashions men? or that which doth inspire
Cities with civil conflagrations,
Countries and kingdoms? that art that atones
All opposition to good life, is all;
Live well, yet learned, and all men ye enthral.

(1608)

14 place] social position, office perturbations] disorders sway] power (poetic)

15 [*The Peace of Death*]

PEACEFUL and young, Herculean silence bore
His craggy club, which up aloft he held;
With which and his forefinger's charm he stilled
All sounds in air, and left so free mine ears
That I might hear the music of the spheres
And all the angels singing out of heaven,
Whose tunes were solemn, as to passion given;
For now, that justice was the happiness there
For all the wrongs to right, inflicted here.
Such was the passion that Peace now put on;
And on, all went; when suddenly was gone
All light of heaven before us, from a wood
Whose sight foreseen (now lost) amazed we stood,
The sun still gracing us; when now (the air
Inflamed with meteors) we discovered, fair,
The skipping Goat; the Horse's flaming mane;
Bearded and trainèd comets; stars in wane;
The burning Sword; the Firebrand, flying Snake;
The Lance; the Torch; the licking Fire; the Drake;
And all else meteors, that did ill abode.
The thunder chid; the lightning leaped abroad;
And yet, when Peace came in, all heaven was clear;
And then did all the horrid wood appear,
Where mortal dangers more than leaves did grow;
In which we could not one free step bestow,
For treading on some murdered passenger,
Who thither was by witchcraft forced to err,
Whose face the bird hid that loves humans best;
That hath the bugle eyes and rosy breast,
And is the yellow autumn's nightingale.
Peace made us enter here secure of all . . .

(1608)

from *Homer's Iliads* (16–23)

16 [*Homer's Gift of Fame*]

THROUGH all the pomp of kingdoms still he shines
And graceth all his gracers. Then let lie
Your lutes and viols, and more loftily

15 Drake] (1) the constellation Draco; (2) fire-drake, fiery meteor   abode] bode   passenger] wayfarer   err] wander   bugle] beady

Make the heroic of your Homer sung;
To drums and trumpets set his angel's tongue;
And with the princely sport of hawks you use
Behold the kingly flight of his high Muse,
And see how like the phoenix she renew
Her age and starry feathers in your sun—
Thousands of years attending, every one
Blowing the holy fire and throwing in
Their seasons, kingdoms, nations that have been
Subverted in them; laws, religions, all
Offered to change and greedy funeral,
Yet still your Homer lasting, living, reigning,
And proves how firm truth builds in poet's feigning.
  A prince's statue, or in marble carved
Or steel or gold, and shrined (to be preserved)
Aloft on pillars or pyrámides,
Time into lowest ruins may depress;
But, drawn with all his virtues in learned verse,
Fame shall resound them on oblivion's hearse
Till graves gasp with her blasts and dead men rise.
No gold can follow where true poesy flies.
  Then let not this divinity in earth,
Dear Prince, be slighted as she were the birth
Of idle fancy, since she works so high,
Nor let her poor disposer (learning) lie
Still bedrid. Both which being in men defaced,
In men (with them) is God's bright image raced;
For, as the sun and moon are figures given
Of his refulgent deity in heaven,
So learning and her lightener, poesy,
In Earth present his fiery majesty.

(1611)

17 [*Proposition and Invocation*]

ACHILLES' baneful wrath resound, O goddess, that imposed
Infinite sorrows on the Greeks, and many brave souls loosed
From breasts heroic—sent them far, to that invisible cave
That no light comforts; and their limbs to dogs and vultures gave.
To all which Jove's will gave effect; from whom first strife begun
Betwixt Atrides, king of men, and Thetis' godlike son.

Subverted] Overthrown feigning] fiction or] either disposer] director learning] wisdom gained in meditation raced] rased; erased

17 invisible cave] Hades Thetis' . . . son] Achilles

What god gave Eris their command, and oped that fighting vein?
Jove's and Latona's son, who, fired against the king of men
For contumely shown his priest, infectious sickness sent
To plague the army; and to death, by troops, the soldiers went.
Occasioned thus: Chryses, the priest, came to the fleet to buy,
For presents of unvalued price, his daughter's liberty—
The golden sceptre and the crown of Phoebus in his hands
Proposing—and made suit to all, but most to the commands
Of both th' Atrides, who most ruled. 'Great Atreus' sons,' said he,
'And all ye well-greaved Greeks, the gods, whose habitations be
In heavenly houses, grace your powers with Priam's razèd town,
And grant ye happy conduct home! To win which wished renown
Of Jove, by honouring his son, far-shooting Phoebus, deign
For these fit presents to dissolve the ransomable chain
Of my loved daughter's servitude.' The Greeks entirely gave
Glad acclamations, for sign that their desires would have
The grave priest reverenced, and his gifts of so much price embraced.
The general yet bore no such mind, but viciously disgraced
With violent terms the priest, and said: 'Dotard, avoid our fleet,
Where lingering be not found by me, nor thy returning feet
Let ever visit us again, lest nor thy godhead's crown
Nor sceptre save thee. Her thou seekst I still will hold mine own
Till age deflower her. In our court at Argos, far transferred
From her loved country, she shall ply her web, and see prepared
(With all fit ornaments) my bed. Incense me then no more,
But, if thou wilt be safe, begone.'

(1598)

18 [*Hector's Defiance*]

'POLYDAMAS, your depth in augury
I like not, and know passing well thou dost not satisfy
Thyself in this opinion, or, if thou thinkst it true,
Thy thoughts the gods blind, to advise and urge that as our due
That breaks our duties, and to Jove, whose vow and sign to me
Is passed directly for our speed; yet light-winged birds must be
(By thy advice) our oracles, whose feathers little stay
My serious actions. What care I if this or th' other way
Their wild wings sway them—if the right, on which the sun doth rise,
Or to the left hand, where he sets? 'Tis Jove's high counsel flies

Eris] Strife Latona's son] Apollo commands] authority entirely] unanimously avoid] get out of

18 passing well] well enough speed] success

With those wings that shall bear up us—Jove's, that both Earth and
heaven,
Both men and gods, sustains and rules. One augury is given
To order all men best of all: fight for thy country's right.
But why fearst thou our further charge? For though the dangerous
fight
Strew all men here about the fleet, yet thou needst never fear
To bear their fates; thy wary heart will never trust thee where
An enemy's look is, and yet fight; for, if thou dar'st abstain
Or whisper into any ear an abstinence so vain
As thou advisest, never fear that any foe shall take
Thy life from thee, for 'tis this lance.' This said, all forwards make,
Himself the first; yet before him exulting clamour flew,
And thunder-loving Jupiter from lofty Ida blew
A storm that ushered their assault and made them charge like him.

(1609?)

19 [*Sarpedon's Speech*]

As ye see a mountain lion fare,
Long kept from prey, in forcing which his high mind makes him dare
Assault upon the whole full fold, though guarded never so
With well-armed men and eager dogs—away he will not go,
But venture on and either snatch a prey or be a prey:
So fared divine Sarpedon's mind, resolved to force his way
Through all the fore-fights and the wall. Yet, since he did not see
Others as great as he in name, as great in mind as he,
He spake to Glaucus: 'Glaucus, say why are we honoured more
Than other men of Lycia in place—with greater store
Of meats and cups, with goodlier roofs, delightsome gardens, walks,
More lands and better, so much wealth that court and country talks
Of us and our possessions and every way we go
Gaze on us as we were their gods? This where we dwell is so:
The shores of Xanthus ring of this; and shall not we exceed
As much in merit as in noise? Come, be we great in deed
As well as look, shine not in gold but in the flames of fight,
That so our neat-armed Lycians may say: "See, these are right
Our kings, our rulers: these deserve to eat and drink the best;
These govern not ingloriously; these thus exceed the rest,
Do more than they command to do." O friend, if keeping back
Would keep back age from us, and death, and that we might not
wrack

19 forcing] pursuing place] rank wrack] undergo shipwreck

In this life's human sea at all, but that deferring now
We shunned death ever—nor would I half this vain valour show,
Nor glorify a folly so, to wish thee to advance;
But, since we must go though not here, and that, besides the chance
Proposèd now, there are infinite fates of other sort in death
Which (neither to be fled nor scaped) a man must sink beneath—
Come, try we if this sort be ours, and either render thus
Glory to others or make them resign the like to us.'

(1609?)

20 [*Neptune Goes to the Greeks*]

BUT this security in Jove the great sea-rector spied,
Who sat aloft on th' utmost top of shady Samothrace
And viewed the fight. His chosen seat stood in so brave a place
That Priam's city, th' Achive ships, all Ida did appear
To his full view, who from the sea was therefore seated there.
He took much ruth to see the Greeks by Troy sustain such ill,
And (mightily incensed with Jove) stooped straight from that steep hill,
That shook as he flew off, so hard his parting pressed the height.
The woods and all the great hills near trembled beneath the weight
Of his immortal moving feet. Three steps he only took
Before he far-off Aegas reached, but with the fourth it shook
With his drad entry. In the depth of those seas he did hold
His bright and glorious palace built of never-rusting gold;
And there arrived, he put in coach his brazen-footed steeds,
All golden-maned and paced with wings; and all in golden weeds
He clothed himself. The golden scourge (most elegantly done)
He took and mounted to his seat, and then the god begun
To drive his chariot through the waves. From whirlpits every way
The whales exulted under him and knew their king: the sea
For joy did open, and his horse so swift and lightly flew
The under-axletree of brass no drop of water drew.
And thus these deathless coursers brought their king to th' Achive ships.

Twixt th' Imber cliffs and Tenedos a certain cavern creeps
Into the deep sea's gulfy breast, and there th' earth-shaker stayed
His forward steeds, took them from coach and heavenly fodder laid
In reach before them. Their brass hooves he girt with gyves of gold,
Not to be broken nor dissolved, to make them firmly hold

nor] neither sort] fate

20 sea-rector] Neptune brave] magnificent stooped] swooped drad] dread (archaic) paced . . . wings] having a gait appropriate to their wings whirlpits] whirlpools

A fit attendance on their king—who went to th' Achive host
Which (like to tempests or wild flames) the clustering Troyans tossed,
Insatiably valorous: in Hector's like command,
High sounding, and resounding, shouts; for hope cheered every hand
To make the Greek fleet now their prize and all the Greeks destroy.
But Neptune, circler of the earth, with fresh heart did employ
The Grecian hands.

(1611?)

21 [*Hector Arms*]

WHEN he whose empire is in clouds saw Hector bent to wage
War in divine Achilles' arms, he shook his head, and said:
'Poor wretch, thy thoughts are far from death, though he so near hath
laid
His ambush for thee. Thou putst on those arms as braving him
Whom others fear, hast slain his friend and from his youthful limb
Torn rudely off his heavenly arms, himself being gentle, kind
And valiant. Equal measure then thy life in youth must find.
Yet since the justice is so strict that not Andromache
(In thy denied return from fight) must ever take of thee
Those arms in glory of thy acts, thou shalt have that frail blaze
Of excellence that neighbours death—a strength even to amaze.'
To this his sable brows did bow, and he made fit his limb
To those great arms, to fill which up the war god entered him,
Austere and terrible: his joints and every part extends
With strength and fortitude; and thus to his admiring friends
High clamour brought him. He so shined that all could think no less
But he resembled every way great-souled Aeacides.

(1611?)

22 [*The Shield of Achilles*]

THE queen of martials
And Mars himself conducted them, both which, being forged of gold,
Must needs have golden furniture, and men might so behold
They were presented deities. The people Vulcan forged
Of meaner metal. When they came where that was to be urged
For which they went, within a vale close to a flood, whose stream
Used to give all their cattle drink, they there enambushed them,

21 limb] any part of the body

22 queen] Minerva martials] soldiers furniture] armour, accoutrements urged] done cattle] livestock enambushed] placed themselves in ambush

And sent two scouts out to descry when th' enemy's herds and sheep
Were setting out. They straight came forth, with two that used to keep
Their passage always; both which piped and went on merrily,
Nor dreamed of ambuscados there. The ambush then let fly,
Slew all their white fleeced sheep and neat, and by them laid their guard.
When those in siege before the town so strange an uproar heard
Behind, amongst their flocks and herds (being then in council set)
They then start up, took horse, and soon their subtle enemy met,
Fought with them on the river's shore, where both gave mutual blows
With well-piled darts. Amongst them all perverse contention rose,
Amongst them tumult was enraged, amongst them ruinous fate
Had her red finger; some they took in an unhurt estate,
Some hurt yet living, some quite slain—and those they tugged to them
By both the feet, stripped off and took their weeds, with all the stream
Of blood upon them that their steels had manfully let out.
They fared as men alive indeed, drew dead indeed about.
  To these the fiery artisan did add a new-eared field,
Large and thrice ploughed, the soil being soft and of a wealthy yield;
And many men at plough he made that drave earth here and there
And turned up stitches orderly; at whose end when they were,
A fellow ever gave their hands full cups of luscious wine,
Which emptied, for another stitch the earth they undermine,
And long till th' utmost bound be reached of all the ample close.
The soil turned up behind the plough, all black like earth arose,
Though forged of nothing else but gold, and lay in show as light
As if it had been ploughed indeed, miraculous to sight.
  There grew by this a field of corn, high, ripe, where reapers wrought,
And let thick handfuls fall to earth, for which some other brought
Bands, and made sheaves. Three binders stood and took the handfuls reaped
From boys that gathered quickly up, and by them armfuls heaped.
Amongst these at a furrow's end the king stood pleased at heart,
Said no word, but his sceptre showed. And from him, much apart,
His harvest bailifs underneath an oak a feast prepared,
And, having killed a mighty ox, stood there to see him shared.
Which women for their harvest folks (then come to sup) had dressed,
And many white wheat-cakes bestowed, to make it up a feast.
  He set near this a vine of gold that cracked beneath the weight
Of bunches black with being ripe; to keep which, at the height,

ambush] troops in ambush   neat] cattle   well-piled] well pointed, barbed   steels] weapons   fiery artisan] Vulcan   new-eared] newly ploughed   stitches] ridges   close] field; enclosed space of the shield   Bands] ropes of straw or rushes   bestowed] laid out

A silver rail ran all along, and round about it flowed
An azure moat, and to this guard a quick-set was bestowed
Of tin, one only path to all, by which the press-men came
In time of vintage: youths and maids, that bore not yet the flame
Of manly Hymen, baskets bore of grapes and mellow fruit.
A lad that sweetly touched a harp, to which his voice did suit,
Centred the circles of that youth, all whose skill could not do
The wanton's pleasure to their minds, that danced, sung, whistled too.

(1611?)

23 [*Priam and Achilles*]

THE king then left his coach
To grave Idaeus, and went on, made his resolved approach
And entered in a goodly room, where with his princes sate
Jove-loved Achilles at their feast; two only kept the state
Of his attendance, Alcimus and Lord Automedon.
At Priam's entry a great time Achilles gazed upon
His wondered-at approach, nor eat: the rest did nothing see
While close he came up, with his hands fast holding the bent knee
Of Hector's conqueror, and kissed that large man-slaughtering hand
That much blood from his sons had drawn. And as in some strange land
And great man's house, a man is driven (with that abhorred dismay
That follows wilful bloodshed still, his fortune being to slay
One whose blood cries aloud for his) to plead protection
In such a miserable plight as frights the lookers on:
In such a stupefied estate Achilles sate to see,
So unexpected, so in night, and so incredibly,
Old Priam's entry. All his friends one on another stared
To see his strange looks, seeing no cause. Thus Priam then prepared
His son's redemption: 'See in me, O godlike Thetis' son,
Thy aged father, and perhaps even now being outrun
With some of my woes, neighbour foes (thou absent) taking time
To do him mischief, no mean left to terrify the crime
Of his oppression; yet he hears thy graces still survive
And joys to hear it, hoping still to see thee safe arrive
From ruined Troy. But I (cursed man) of all my race shall live
To see none living. Fifty sons the deities did give

quick-set] hedge planted from slips   press-men] men operating the winepress
flame . . . Hymen] the *cereus* or wedding taper

23 frights] frightens   estate] state   mean] means   terrify] deter from

My hopes to live in—all alive when near our trembling shore
The Greek ships harboured—and one womb nineteen of those
  sons bore.
Now Mars a number of their knees hath strengthless left, and he
That was (of all) my only joy and Troy's sole guard, by thee
(Late fighting for his country) slain, whose tendered person now
I come to ransom. Infinite is that I offer you,
Myself conferring it, exposed alone to all your odds,
Only imploring right of arms. Achilles, fear the gods,
Pity an old man like thy sire—different in only this,
That I am wretcheder, and bear that weight of miseries
That never man did, my cursed lips enforced to kiss that hand
That slew my children.' This moved tears; his father's name did stand
(Mentioned by Priam) in much help to his compassion,
And moved Aeacides so much he could not look upon
The weeping father. With his hand, he gently put away
His grave face; calm remission now did mutually display
Her power in either's heaviness. Old Priam, to record
His son's death and his deathsman see, his tears and bosom poured
Before Achilles. At his feet he laid his reverend head.
Achilles' thoughts now with his sire, now with his friend, were fed.
Betwixt both sorrow filled the tent. But now Aeacides,
Satiate at all parts with the ruth of their calamities,
Start up, and up he raised the king. His milk-white head and beard
With pity he beheld, and said: 'Poor man, thy mind is scared
With much affliction. How durst thy person thus alone
Venture on his sight that hath slain so many a worthy son,
And so dear to thee? Thy old heart is made of iron. Sit
And settle we our woes, though huge, for nothing profits it.
Cold mourning wastes but our lives' heats. The gods have destinate
That wretched mortals must live sad. 'Tis the immortal state
Of deity that lives secure. Two tuns of gifts there lie
In Jove's gate, one of good, one ill, that our mortality
Maintain, spoil, order; which when Jove doth mix to any man,
One while he frolics, one while mourns. If of his mournful can
A man drinks only, only wrongs he doth expose him to.
Sad hunger in th' abundant earth doth toss him to and fro,
Respected nor of gods nor men. The mixed cup Peleus drank;
Even from his birth heaven blessed his life; he lived not that could thank
The gods for such rare benefits as set forth his estate.
He reigned among his Myrmidons most rich, most fortunate,
And, though a mortal, had his bed decked with a deathless dame.
And yet with all this good, one ill god mixed, that takes all name

tendered] (1) had in tender regard; (2) offered in fulfilment of an obligation Aeacides] Achilles deathsman] executioner Start] Started scared] shorn; reduced in power

From all that goodness—his name now (whose preservation here
Men count the crown of their most good) not blessed with power to bear
One blossom but myself, and I shaken as soon as blown.
Nor shall I live to chear his age and give nutrition
To him that nourished me. Far off my rest is set in Troy,
To leave thee restless and thy seed. Thyself, that did enjoy
(As we have heard) a happy life—what Lesbos doth contain
(In times past being a blessed man's seat), what the unmeasured main
Of Hellespontus, Phrygia, holds, are all said to adorn
Thy empire, wealth and sons enow—but, when the gods did turn
Thy blessed state to partake with bane, war and the bloods of men
Circled thy city, never clear. Sit down and suffer then.
Mourn not inevitable things; thy tears can spring no deeds
To help thee, nor recall thy son: impatience ever breeds
Ill upon ill, makes worst things worse. And therefore sit.'

(1611?)

from *Eugenia*

24 [*Death Described by His True Effects*]

EAT what you wish; I'll teach ye all to die:
If ye believe, express it in your lives,
That best appear in death, gainst whom who strives
Would faithless and most reasonless deny
All laws of nature and necessity.
No frail thing simply is; no flesh nor blood
Partakes with essence; all the flitting flood
Of nature's mortal; birth and death do toss
Upwards and downwards, ever at a loss;
Human births ever are, and never stay,
Still in mutation; we die every day:
Ridiculous are we then, in one death flying,
That dead so often are; and ever dying.
Ye fear your own shades; they are fools that make
Death's form so ugly, and remembrance take
Of their dissolving by so foul a sight,
When death presents the fair of heavenly light.
The ghostly form, that in this world we leave
When death dissolves us, wise men should conceive

enow] enough   spring] produce, set going

24 Still] Continually   in one] unanimously   fair] beauty

Shows well what life is; far from figuring death.
Am I this trunk? It is my painted sheath:
As brave young men think they are what they wear,
So these encourage men with what they fear.
  Make death an angel, scaling of a heaven,
And crown him with the Asterism of Seven,
To show he is the death of deadly sins:
A rich spring make his robe, since he begins
Our endless summer: let his shoulders spring
Both the sweet Cupids for his either wing;
Since love, and joy in death, to heaven us bring.
Hang on the ivory brawn of his right arm
A bunch of golden keys; his left a swarm
Of thrifty bees, in token we have done
The year, our life's toil, and our fruits have shone
In honey of our good works laboured here:
Before his flaming bosom, let him wear
A shining crystal; since through him we see
The lovely forms of our felicity.
His thighs make both the heaven-supporting poles,
Since he sustains heaven, storing it with souls.
His left hand, let a plenty's horn extend:
His right, a book to contemplate our end.
  This form, conceive death bears; since truly this
In his effects informs us what he is.
Who, in life, flies not to inheritance given?
And why not then, in death, t' inherit heaven?
Wrestlers for games know they shall never be
(Till their strife end, and they have victory)
Crowned with their garlands, nor receive their game;
And in our heaven's strife know not we the same?
Why strive we, not being certain to obtain
If we do conquer; and because we gain
Conquest in faith, why faint we?—since therein
We lose both strife and conquest? Who will win
Must lose in this strife; in death's easy lists
Who yields subdues, he's conquered that resists.

(1614)

brave] finely dressed, showy scaling] mounting Asterism] constellation
spring (l.28)] cause to appear Cupids] Eros and Anteros brawn] muscle
horn] cornucopia game] prize

from *Homer's Odyssey* (25–28)

25 [*Homer and the Brazen Head of Rumour*]

. . . SUCH men as sideling ride the ambling Muse,
Whose saddle is as frequent as the stews,
Whose raptures are in every pageant seen,
In every wassail rhyme and dancing green—
When he that writes by any beam of truth
Must dive as deep as he past shallow youth.
Truth dwells in gulfs, whose deeps hide shades so rich
That night sits muffled there in clouds of pitch,
More dark than nature made her, and requires,
To clear her tough mists, heaven's great fire of fires,
To whom the sun itself is but a beam.
For sick souls then (but rapt in foolish dream)
To wrestle with these heaven-strong mysteries
What madness is it—when their light serves eyes
That are not worldly in their least aspéct,
But truly pure, and aim at heaven direct.
Yet these none like but what the brazen head
Blatters abroad, no sooner born but dead.

* * * * *

Homer, three thousand years dead, now revived
Even from that dull death that in life he lived,
When none conceited him, none understood
That so much life in so much death as blood
Conveys about it could mix. But when death
Drunk up the bloody mist that human breath
Poured round about him (poverty and spite
Thick'ning the hapless vapour), then truth's light
Glimmered about his poem; the pinchèd soul
(Amidst the mysteries it did enroll)
Brake powerfully abroad. And, as we see
The sun, all hid in clouds, at length got free
Through some forced covert, over all the ways
Near and beneath him shoots his vented rays
Far off and sticks them in some little glade,
All woods, fields, rivers left besides in shade:
So your Apollo, from that world of light
Closed in his poem's body shot to sight

sideling] sidelong, obliquely frequent] frequented brazen] (alluding to the omniscient brazen head of romance) Blatters] Chatters volubly conceited] fancied; apprehended forced] penetrated by force

Some few forced beams, which near him were not seen
(As in his life or country), fate and spleen
Clouding their radiance, which, when death had cleared,
To far-off regions his free beams appeared—
In which all stood and wondered, striving which
His birth and rapture should in right enrich.

(1614)

26 [*Ulysses Insults over the Cyclops*]

'CYCLOP! if any ask thee who imposed
Th' unsightly blemish that thine eye enclosed,
Say that Ulysses (old Laertes' son,
Whose seat is Ithaca, and who hath won
Surname of City-racer) bored it out.'
At this he brayed so loud that round about
He drave affrighted echoes through the air,
And said: 'O beast! I was premonished fair,
By aged prophecy in one that was
A great and good man, this should come to pass;
And how 'tis provèd now! Augur Telemus,
Surnamed Eurymides (that spent with us
His age in augury and did exceed
In all presage of truth) said all this deed
Should this event take, authored by the hand
Of one Ulysses; who I thought was manned
With great and goodly personage, and bore
A virtue answerable, and this shore
Should shake with weight of such a conqueror;
When now a weakling came, a dwarfy thing,
A thing of nothing, who yet wit did bring
That brought supply to all, and with his wine
Put out the flame where all my light did shine.
Come, land again, Ulysses! that my hand
May guest-rites give thee. . . .'

(1614?)

27 [*Ulysses Invokes the Dead*]

ARRIVED now at our ship, we launched, and set
Our mast up, put forth sail, and in did get

25 spleen] grudging ill-will

26 enclosed] closed brayed] uttered a loud cry of pain premonished] forewarned manned] endowed with manly qualities answerable] corresponding

Our late-got cattle. Up our sails, we went,
My wayward fellows mourning now th' event.
A good companion yet, a foreright wind
Circe (the excellent utterer of her mind)
Supplied our murmuring consorts with, that was
Both speed and guide to our adventurous pass.
All day our sails stood to the winds, and made
Our voyage prosperous. Sun then set, and shade
All ways obscuring, on the bounds we fell
Of deep Oceanus, where people dwell
Whom a perpetual cloud obscures outright,
To whom the cheerful sun lends never light,
Nor when he mounts the star-sustaining heaven,
Nor when he stoops Earth and sets up the even;
But night holds fixed wings, feathered all with banes,
Above those most unblest Cimmerians.
Here drew we up our ship, our sheep withdrew,
And walked the shore till we attained the view
Of that sad region Circe had foreshowed.
And then the sacred offerings, to be vowed,
Eurylochus and Perimedes bore;
When I my sword drew, and earth's womb did gore
Till I a pit digged of a cubit round,
Which with the liquid sacrifice we crowned:
First, honey mixed with wine, then sweet wine neat,
Then water poured in, last the flour of wheat.
Much I importuned then the weak-necked dead,
And vowed, when I the barren soil should tread
Of cliffy Ithaca, amidst my hall
To kill a heifer, my clear best of all,
And give in offering on a pile composed
Of all the choice goods my whole house enclosed—
And to Tiresias himself alone
A sheep coal-black and the selectest one
Of all my flocks. When to the powers beneath,
The sacred nation that survive with Death,
My prayers and vows had done devotions fit,
I took the offerings, and upon the pit
Bereft their lives. Out gushed the sable blood,
And round about me fled out of the flood
The souls of the deceased. There clustered then
Youths and their wives, much suffering aged men,

Up our sails] Our sails set   foreright] favourable; on course   pass] passage   stood] applied themselves manfully   Nor (l.15)] Neither   stoops Earth] (1) descends to; (2) lowers Earth like a sail   banes] (1) deadly agencies; (2) bones   withdrew] disembarked   vowed (l.22)] sacrificed   Death] i.e. Hades

Soft tender virgins that but new came there
By timeless death, and green their sorrows were.
There men at arms, with armours all imbrued,
Wounded with lances and with falchions hewed,
In numbers up and down the ditch did stalk,
And threw unmeasured cries about their walk,
So horrid that a bloodless fear surprised
My daunted spirits. Straight then I advised
My friends to flay the slaughtered sacrifice,
Put them in fire, and to the deities,
Stern Pluto and Persephone, apply
Exciteful prayers. Then drew I from my thigh
My well-edged sword, stepped in, and firmly stood
Betwixt the press of shadows and the blood,
And would not suffer anyone to dip
Within our offering his unsolid lip
Before Tiresias, that did all control.
His body in the broad-wayed earth as yet
Unmourned, unburièd by us, since we sweat
With other urgent labours. Yet his smart
I wept to see, and rued it from my heart,
Enquiring how he could before me be
That came by ship?

(1614?)

28 [*Ulysses Reunited with Penelope*]

AND now Eurynome had bathed the king,
Smoothed him with oils, and he himself attired
In vestures royal. Her part then inspired
The goddess Pallas: decked his head and face
With infinite beauties, gave a goodly grace
Of stature to him, a much plumper plight
Through all his body breathed. Curls soft and bright
Adorned his head withal, and made it show
As if the flowery hyacinth did grow
In all his pride there, in the general trim
Of every lock and every curious limb.
Look how a skilful artisan, well seen
In all arts metalline, as having been

timeless] untimely green] fresh imbrued] bloodstained Straight] Immediately exciteful] hopefully exciting to action control] dominate broad-wayed] frequented

28 inspired] infused, imparted plight] condition, health curious limb] beautifully shaped part metalline] metallic

Taught by Minerva and the god of fire,
Doth gold with silver mix so that entire
They keep their self-distinction, and yet so
That to the silver from the gold doth flow
A much more artificial lustre than his own,
And thereby to the gold itself is grown
A greater glory than if wrought alone,
Both being stuck off by either's mixtion:
So did Minerva hers and his combine;
He more in her, she more in him did shine.
Like an immortal from the bath he rose,
And to his wife did all his grace dispose,
Encountering thus her strangeness: 'Cruel dame
Of all that breathe, the gods past steel and flame
Have made thee ruthless. Life retains not one
Of all dames else that bears so overgrown
A mind with abstinence, as twenty years
To miss her husband, drowned in woes and tears,
And at his coming keep aloof, and fare
As of his so long absence and his care
No sense had seized her. Go, nurse, make a bed,
That I alone may sleep; her heart is dead
To all reflection.' To him thus replied
The wise Penelope: 'Man half deified,
'Tis not my fashion to be taken straight
With bravest men—nor poorest use to slight.
Your mean apparence made not me retire,
Nor this your rich show makes me now admire,
Nor moves at all. For what is all to me,
If not my husband?'

(1615)

from *The Georgics of Hesiod*

29

[*Winter*]

WHEN air's chill north his noisome frosts shall blow
All over Earth, and all the wide sea throw
At heaven in hills, from cold horse-breeding Thrace;
The beaten earth and all her sylvan race
Roaring and bellowing with his bitter strokes.
Plumps of thick fir-trees and high-crested oaks

stuck off] shown to advantage   mixtion] mixture   strangeness] coldness   ruthless] pitiless   overgrown] grown over; overburdened; too big   apparence] appearance

Torn up in valleys, all air's flood let fly
In him at earth, sad nurse of all that die;
Wild beasts abhor him, and run clapping close
Their sterns betwixt their thighs; and even all those
Whose hides their fleeces line with highest proof,
Even ox-hides, also want expulsive stuff,
And bristled goats, against his bitter gale:
He blows so cold he beats quite through them all.
Only with silly sheep it fares not so;
For they, each summer fleeced, their fells so grow,
They shield all winter, crushed into his wind.
He makes the old man trudge for life, to find
Shelter against him; but he cannot blast
The tender and the delicately-graced
Flesh of the virgin: she is kept within
Close by her mother, careful of her skin,
Since yet she never knew how to enfold
The force of Venus swimming all in gold;
Whose snowy bosom choicely washed and balmed
With wealthy oils, she keeps the house, becalmed
All winter's spite. When in his fireless shed
And miserable roof still hiding head,
The boneless fish doth eat his feet for cold,
To whom the sun doth never food unfold,
But turns above the black men's populous towers,
On whom he more bestows his radiant hours
Than on th' Hellenians. Then all beasts of horn,
And smooth-browed, that in beds of wood are born,
About the oaken dales that north wind fly,
Gnashing their teeth with restless misery;
And everywhere that care solicits all
That, out of shelter, to their coverts fall,
And caverns eaten into rocks; and then
Those wild beasts shrink; like tame three-footed men
Whose backs are broke with age, and foreheads driven
To stoop to earth, though born to look on heaven;
Even like to these those tough-bred rude ones go,
Flying the white drifts of the northern snow.
  Then put thy body's best munition on,
Soft waistcoats, weeds that th' ankles trail upon;
And with a little linen weave much wool
In forewoven webs, and make thy garments full.

(1618)

proof] impenetrability　　expulsive] impervious　　silly] simple
balmed] anointed　　boneless fish] cuttle; octopus　　Hellenians] Greeks

SIR JOHN HARINGTON
1561–1612

30 *Epigram IV. v: Of Treason*

TREASON doth never prosper—what's the reason?
For if it prosper, none dare call it treason.

(1615)

SAMUEL DANIEL
1563?–1619

31 *To the Lady Margaret, Countess of Cumberland*

HE that of such a height hath built his mind,
And reared the dwelling of his thoughts so strong
As neither fear nor hope can shake the frame
Of his resolvèd powers, nor all the wind
Of vanity or malice pierce to wrong
His settled peace, or to disturb the same;
  What a fair seat hath he, from whence he may
  The boundless wastes and wilds of man survey!

And with how free an eye doth he look down
Upon these lower regions of turmoil!
Where all the storms of passions mainly beat
On flesh and blood; where honour, power, renown
Are only gay afflictions, golden toil;
Where greatness stands upon as feeble feet
  As frailty doth, and only great doth seem
  To little minds, who do it so esteem.

He looks upon the mightiest monarchs' wars
But only as on stately robberies,
Where evermore the fortune that prevails
Must be the right; the ill-succeeding mars
The fairest and the best-faced enterprise:
Great pirate Pompey lesser pirates quails:

31 mainly] violently   quails] overpowers; daunts

Justice, he sees, as if seducèd, still
Conspires with power, whose cause must not be ill.

He sees the face of right t'appear as manifold
As are the passions of uncertain man,
Who puts it in all colours, all attires,
To serve his ends and make his courses hold:
He sees that, let deceit work what it can,
Plot and contrive base ways to high desires,
That the all-guiding providence doth yet
All disappoint, and mocks this smoke of wit.

Nor is he moved with all the thunder-cracks
Of tyrants' threats, or with the surly brow
Of power, that proudly sits on others' crimes,
Charged with more crying sins than those he checks;
The storms of sad confusion, that may grow
Up in the present for the coming times,
Appal him not, that hath no side at all
But of himself, and knows the worst can fall.

Although his heart, so near allied to earth,
Cannot but pity the perplexèd state
Of troublous and distressed mortality,
That thus make way unto the ugly birth
Of their own sorrows, and do still beget
Affliction upon imbecillity;
Yet, seeing thus the course of things must run,
He looks thereon, not strange, but as foredone.

And whilst distraught ambition compasses
And is encompassèd; whilst as craft deceives
And is deceived; whilst man doth ransack man,
And builds on blood, and rises by distress;
And th' inheritance of desolation leaves
To great expecting hopes; he looks thereon
As from the shore of peace with unwet eye,
And bears no venture in impiety.

Thus, Madam, fares that man that hath prepared
A rest for his desires, and sees all things
Beneath him, and hath learned this book of man,
Full of the notes of frailty, and compared
The best of glory with her sufferings;
By whom I see you labour all you can

side] view ransack] visit with violence

To plant your heart, and set your thought as near
His glorious mansion as your powers can bear.

Which, Madam, are so soundly fashionèd
By that clear judgement that hath carried you
Beyond the feeble limits of your kind,
As they can stand against the strongest head
Passion can make, inured to any hue
The world can cast, that cannot cast that mind
Out of her form of goodness, that doth see
Both what the best and worst of earth can be.

Which makes that, whatsoever here befalls,
You in the region of yourself remain,
Where no vain breath of th' impudent molests,
That hath secured within the brazen walls
Of a clear conscience, that without all stain
Rises in peace, in innocency rests;
Whilst all what malice from without procures
Shows her own ugly heart, but hurts not yours.

And whereas none rejoice more in revenge
Than women use to do, yet you well know
That wrong is better checked by being contemned
Than being pursued; leaving to him t' avenge
To whom it appertains; wherein you show
How worthily your clearness hath condemned
Base malediction, living in the dark,
That at the rays of goodness still doth bark.

Knowing the heart of man is set to be
The centre of this world, about the which
These revolutions of disturbances
Still roll, where all th' aspécts of misery
Predominate; whose strong effects are such
As he must bear, being powerless to redress;
And that unless above himself he can
Erect himself, how poor a thing is man!

And how turmoiled they are that level lie
With earth, and cannot lift themselves from thence;
That never are at peace with their desires,
But work beyond their years, and even deny
Dotage her rest, and hardly will dispense
With death: that when ability expires,

kind] nature still] ever

Desire lives still, so much delight they have
To carry toil and travel to the grave.

Whose ends you see, and what can be the best
They reach unto, when they have cast the sum
And reckonings of their glory; and you know
This floating life hath but this port of rest,
A heart prepared, that fears no ill to come;
And that man's greatness rests but in his show,
The best of all whose days consumèd are
Either in war, or peace conceiving war.

This concord, Madam, of a well-tuned mind
Hath been so set, by that all-working hand
Of heaven, that though the world hath done his worst
To put it out by discords most unkind,
Yet doth it still in perfect union stand
With God and man, nor ever will be forced
From that most sweet accord, but still agree
Equal in fortune's inequality.

And this note, Madam, of your worthiness
Remains recorded in so many hearts
As time nor malice cannot wrong your right
In th' inheritance of fame you must possess:
You that have built you by your great deserts,
Out of small means, a far more exquisite
And glorious dwelling for your honoured name
Than all the gold that leaden minds can frame.

(1601)

32

ARE they shadows that we see?
And can shadows pleasure give?
Pleasures only shadows be
Cast by bodies we conceive,
And are made the things we deem,
In those figures which they seem.

But these pleasures vanish fast,
Which by shadows are expressed:
Pleasures are not, if they last;
In their passing is their best.
Glory is most bright and gay
In a flash, and so away.

31 travel] trouble inequality] injustice

Feed apace then greedy eyes
On the wonder you behold.
Take it sudden as it flies,
Though you take it not to hold;
  When your eyes have done their part,
  Thought must length it in the heart.

(1610)

SIR JOHN STRADLING
1563–1637

from *Divine Poems in Seven Several Classes*

33 ### [*Abraham's Sacrifice of Isaac*]

YET once again heaven's king, and Earth's great lord,
Saith thus: my servant Abraham's faith I'll prove;
He worships me, by him I am adored:
I must try out the assurance of his love.
  'Give me', saith God, 'thy son in sacrifice,
  Isaac, that son so precious in thine eyes.'

This was indeed a trial to the quick,
A feat whereby sound friendship should be known:
It would have made the strongest heart half sick,
To spill the blood much dearer than his own.
  Excuses fair and many might he feign,
  If not to avoid it quite, yet time to gain:

'My God, this is the child by thee assigned,
To bring thy faithful promise to effect:
How can I be so rash, or so unkind,
By killing him, to see that promise checked?
  Give me some time to pause upon the matter:
  There is no haste, it may be done hereafter.

'If not by prayer, or by long persuasion,
A pardon for his life may be obtained
(As once I got for Sodom, wicked nation,
Had ten been found from filthy lust unstained):
  Be it so; when I perceive no remedy,
  Thy will shall be fulfilled, the lad shall die.'

length] lengthen

33 feat] deed; course of action   unkind] unnatural

(And did not once our Lord's apostle prime
Dissuade his master: near in such a case?
'Twas kindness to his Lord that movèd him;
Yet Christ rebuked him sharply to his face.
There's nothing wherewith God is better paid
Than when his will is readily obeyed.)

The arch-patriarch used no such glozing trick;
His heart unto his God was firmly knit:
Early next morn he rose, bestirred him quick,
And for performance gets all that was fit.
Fire, wood, and knife he took, with full intent
To execute the deed about which he went.

'Twere sin to think that good and holy man
Ran rudely to the work without some stay:
We must conceive he told to Isaac, then,
What moved him so to do; taught him to pray,
And yield himself to God's good will and pleasure.
Some such short shrift he used, as served his leisure.

His son then bound and on the altar laid,
Meek as a lamb, prepared himself to die.
The knife ta'en up in hand, he never stayed
Till God from heaven stopped him with a cry.
God took that thing as done which was intended:
A ram did serve the turn, and so it ended.

(1625)

MICHAEL DRAYTON
1563–1631

from *Idea* (34–41)

34 *To the Reader of These Sonnets*

INTO these loves who but for passion looks,
At this first sight here let him lay them by,
And seek elsewhere, in turning other books,
Which better may his labour satisfy.

prime] first (St Peter)

34 passion] (genre term for passionate poem)

No far-fetched sigh shall ever wound my breast;
Love from mine eye a tear shall never wring;
Nor in *ah me* s my whinning sonnets dressed
(A libertine) fantasticly I sing.
My verse is the true image of my mind,
Ever in motion, still desiring change;
And, as thus to variety inclined,
So in all humours sportively I range:
My Muse is rightly of the English strain,
That cannot long one fashion entertain.

(1599)

35 *Sonnet I*

LIKE an adventurous seafarer am I,
Who hath some long and dang'rous voyage been,
And called to tell of his discovery,
How far he sailed, what countries he had seen;
Proceeding from the port whence he put forth,
Shows by his compass how his course he steered,
When east, when west, when south, and when by north,
As how the pole to every place was reared,
What capes he doubled, of what continent,
The gulfs and straits that strangely he had passed,
Where most becalmed, where with foul weather spent,
And on what rocks in peril to be cast!
Thus, in my love, time calls me to relate
My tedious travels and oft-varying fate.

(1619)

36 *Sonnet VI*

HOW many paltry, foolish, painted things,
That now in coaches trouble every street,
Shall be forgotten, whom no poet sings,
Ere they be well wrapped in their winding sheet!
Where I to thee eternity shall give,
When nothing else remaineth of these days,
And queens hereafter shall be glad to live
Upon the alms of thy superfluous praise.

fantasticly] fantastically: (1) according to my fancy; (2) fictitiously

35 reared] raised geometrically, in calculating latitude by the pole star doubled] rounded

36 things] women (contemptuous)

Virgins and matrons reading these my rhymes
Shall be so much delighted with thy story
That they shall grieve they lived not in these times,
To have seen thee, their sex's only glory:
So shalt thou fly above the vulgar throng,
Still to survive in my immortal song.

(1619)

37 *Sonnet VIII*

THERE'S nothing grieves me but that age should haste,
That in my days I may not see thee old;
That where those two clear sparkling eyes are placed
Only two loop-holes then I might behold.
That lovely archèd, ivory, polished brow
Defaced with wrinkles, that I might but see;
Thy dainty hair, so curled and crispèd now
Like grizzled moss upon some agèd tree;
Thy cheek, now flush with roses, sunk and lean;
Thy lips, with age as any wafer thin;
Thy pearly teeth out of thy head so clean
That, when thou feedst, thy nose shall touch thy chin.
These lines that now thou scornst, which should delight thee,
Then would I make thee read, but to despite thee.

(1619)

38 *Sonnet IX*

As other men, so I myself do muse
Why in this sort I wrest invention so,
And why these giddy metaphors I use,
Leaving the path the greater part do go.
I will resolve you. I am lunatic,
And ever this in madmen you shall find:
What they last thought of, when the brain grew sick,
In most distraction they keep that in mind.
Thus talking idly in this bedlam fit,
Reason and I, you must conceive, are twain;
'Tis nine years now since first I lost my wit:
Bear with me, then, though troubled be my brain.
With diet and correction, men distraught
(Not too far past) may to their wits be brought.

(1600)

37 crispèd] put into short wavy folds flush] flushed

38 giddy] mad, foolish most distraction] the worst mental derangement

39 *Sonnet XXXI: To the Critic*

METHINKS I see some crooked mimic jeer,
And tax my Muse with this fantastic grace;
Turning my papers, asks 'What have we here?'—
Making withal some filthy antic face.
I fear no censure, nor what thou canst say,
Nor shall my spirit one jot of vigour lose.
Think'st thou my wit shall keep the pack-horse way
That every dudgen low invention goes?
Since sonnets thus in bundles are impressed,
And every drudge doth dull our satiate ear,
Think'st thou my love shall in those rags be dressed,
That every dowdy, every trull doth wear?
  Up to my pitch no common judgement flies:
  I scorn all earthly dung-bred scarabees.

(1599)

40 *Sonnet LIII: Another to the River Ankor*

CLEAR Ankor, on whose silver-sanded shore
My soul-shrin'd saint, my fair Idea lies,
O blessèd brook, whose milk-white swans adore
Thy crystal stream refinèd by her eyes,
Where sweet myrrh-breathing Zephyr in the spring
Gently distils his nectar-dropping showers,
Where nightingales in Arden sit and sing
Amongst the dainty dew-empearlèd flowers;
Say thus, fair brook, when thou shalt see thy queen:
Lo, here thy shepherd spent his wandering years,
And in these shades, dear nymph, he oft hath been,
And here to thee he sacrificed his tears.
  Fair Arden, thou my Tempe art alone,
  And thou, sweet Ankor, art my Helicon.

(1594)

fantastic] quaint, eccentric, arbitrarily devised   antic] grotesquely distorted
dudgen] mean, homely   impressed] printed   scarabees] beetles (Spenserian)

40 Zephyr] West Wind, initiator of spring   Tempe] valley near Olympus, the classical earthly paradise   Helicon] the Muses' mountain haunt (or, by common error, spring)

41 Sonnet LXI

SINCE there's no help, come let us kiss and part—
Nay, I have done: you get no more of me;
And I am glad, yea glad with all my heart,
That thus so cleanly I myself can free.
Shake hands for ever, cancel all our vows,
And when we meet at any time again,
Be it not seen in either of our brows
That we one jot of former love retain.
Now at the last gasp of love's latest breath,
When, his pulse failing, passion speechless lies,
When faith is kneeling by his bed of death,
And innocence is closing up his eyes,
  Now if thou wouldst, when all have given him over,
  From death to life thou mightst him yet recover.

(1619)

from *Odes* (42–49)

42 *To the New Year*

RICH statue double-faced,
With marble temples graced,
  To raise thy god-head higher,
In flames where altars shining,
Before thy priests divining,
  Do od'rous fumes expire.

Great Janus, I thy pleasure,
With all the Thespian treasure,
  Do seriously pursue;
To th' passèd year returning,
As though the old adjourning,
  Yet bringing in the new.

Thy ancient vigils yearly
I have observèd clearly,
  Thy feasts yet smoking be;
Since all thy store abroad is,
Give something to my goddess,
  As hath been used by thee.

cleanly] completely

42 statue double-faced] (Janus Bifrons, ancient god of beginnings) expire] exhale Thespian] poetic, Heliconian

Give her th' Eoan brightness
Winged with that subtile lightness
   That doth transpierce the air;
The roses of the morning
The rising heaven adorning,
   To mesh with flames of hair.

Those ceaseless sounds, above all,
Made by those orbs that move all,
   And ever swelling there,
Wrapped up in numbers flowing,
Them actually bestowing
   For jewels at her ear.

O rapture great and holy,
Do thou transport me wholly,
   So well her form to vary
That I aloft may bear her,
Whereas I will ensphere her
   In regions high and starry.

And in my choice composures
The soft and easy closures
   So amorously shall meet
That ev'ry lively ceasure
Shall treat a perfect measure,
   Set on so equal feet.

That spray to fame so fertile,
The lover-crowning myrtle,
   In wreaths of mixèd boughs,
Within whose shades are dwelling
Those beauties most excelling,
   Enthroned upon her brows.

Those parallels so even,
Drawn on the face of heaven,
   That curious art supposes,
Direct those gems, whose clearness
Far off amaze by nearness,
   Each globe such fire encloses.

Eoan] morning, eastern (from Eos, Greek goddess of dawn)   sounds] (music of the spheres)   numbers] rhythm   composures] poetic compositions; human constitutions   ceasure] caesura   gems] (1) jewels; (2) sprays, shoots

Her bosom full of blisses,
By nature made for kisses,
 So pure and wond'rous clear,
Whereas a thousand Graces
Behold their lovely faces,
 As they are bathing there.

O thou self-little blindness,
The kindness of unkindness,
 Yet one of those divine;
Thy brands to me were liefer,
Thy fascia and thy quiver,
 And thou this quill of mine.

This heart so freshly bleeding,
Upon it own self feeding,
 Whose wounds still dropping be;
O love, thyself confounding,
Her coldness so abounding,
 And yet such heat in me.

Yet if I be inspirèd,
I'll leave thee so admirèd
 To all that shall succeed,
That were they more than many,
'Mongst all there is not any
 That time so oft shall reed.

Nor adamant engraved,
That hath been choicely'st saved,
 Idea's name out-wears;
So large a dower as this is,
The greatest often misses,
 The diadem that bears.

(1606)

43 *The Heart*

If thus we needs must go,
What shall our one heart do,
This one made of our two?

42 Graces] putti brands] weapons fascia] bandolier; bond of love reed] (1) read; (2) rede (guide)

MICHAEL DRAYTON

Madam, two hearts we brake,
And from them both did take
The best, one heart to make.

Half this is of your heart,
Mine in the other part,
Joined by our equal art.

Were it cemented, or sewn,
By shreds or pieces known,
We each might find our own.

But 'tis dissolved, and fixed,
And with such cunning mixed
No diff'rence that betwixt.

But how shall we agree
By whom it kept shall be,
Whether by you or me?

It cannot two breasts fill;
One must be heartless still,
Until the other will.

It came to me today,
When I willed it to say,
With whether it would stay?

It told me, in your breast,
Where it might hope to rest:
For if it were my guest,

For certainty it knew
That I would still anew
Be sending it to you.

Never, I think, had two
Such work, so much to do,
A unity to woo.

Yours was so cold and chaste,
Whilst mine with zeal did waste,
Like fire with water placed.

brake] broke equal] just, equitable known] told apart still] invariably
With whether] With which

How did my heart entreat,
How pant, how did it beat,
Till it could give yours heat!

Till to that temper brought,
Through our perfection wrought,
That blessing either's thought.

In such a height it lies
From this base world's dull eyes
That heaven it not envies.

All that this Earth can show
Our heart shall not once know,
For it too vile and low.

(1619)

44 *The Sacrifice to Apollo*

PRIESTS of Apollo, sacred be the room
For this learn'd meeting: let no barbarous groom,
How brave soe'er he be,
Attempt to enter;
But of the Muses free,
None here may venture;
This for the Delphian prophets is prepared:
The profane vulgar are from hence debarred.

And since the feast so happily begins,
Call up those fair nine, with their violins;
They are begot by Jove:
Then let us place them
Where no clown in may shove,
That may disgrace them:
But let them near to young Apollo sit;
So shall his foot-pace over-flow with wit.

temper] temperament, adjustment That ... thought] That each blessed the other

44 Apollo] (see endnote) groom] fellow (contemptuous) But] Except Delphian prophets] prophets of Apollo; poets nine] Muses clown] ignorant boor, Philistine foot-pace] hearth

Where be the Graces, where be those fair three?
In any hand they may not absent be:
        They to the gods are dear,
        And they can humbly
        Teach us ourselves to bear,
        And do things comely:
They and the Muses rise both from one stem;
They grace the Muses and the Muses them.

Bring forth your flagons (filled with sparkling wine)
Whereon swollen Bacchus, crownèd with a vine,
        Is graven; and fill out,
        It well bestowing,
        To ev'ry man about,
        In goblets flowing:
Let not a man drink, but in draughts profound;
To our god Phoebus let the health go round.

Let your jests fly at large; yet therewithal
See they be salt, but yet not mixed with gall:
        Not tending to disgrace,
        But fairly given,
        Becoming well the place,
        Modest, and even;
That they with tickling pleasure may provoke
Laughter in him on whom the jest is broke.

Or if the deeds of heroes ye rehearse,
Let them be sung in so well-ordered verse
        That each word have his weight,
        Yet run with pleasure;
        Holding one stately height
        In so brave measure
That they may make the stiffest storm seem weak,
And damp Jove's thunder, when it loud'st doth speak.

And if ye list to exercise your vein,
Or in the sock, or in the buskined strain,
        Let art and nature go
        One with the other;
        Yet so, that art may show
        Nature her mother,

hand] skill   bear] carry   salt] pungent, stinging   gall] bitterness
Jove's] Jupiter's—ruler of the Roman pantheon   Or] Either   the sock] comedy
buskined strain] tragedy

The thick-brained audience lively to awake,
Till with shrill claps the theatre do shake.

Sing hymns to Bacchus then, with hands upreared,
Offer to Jove, who most is to be feared:
From him the Muse we have,
From him proceedeth
More than we dare to crave:
'Tis he that feedeth
Them, whom the world would starve; then let the lyre
Sound, whilst his altar's endless flames expire.

(1619)

45 *To the Virginian Voyage*

You brave heroic minds
Worthy your country's name,
That honour still pursue,
Go, and subdue,
Whilst loit'ring hinds
Lurk here at home with shame.

Britons, you stay too long:
Quickly aboard bestow you,
And with a merry gale
Swell your stretch'd sail
With vows as strong
As the winds that blow you.

Your course securely steer,
West and by south forth keep:
Rocks, lee-shores, nor shoals,
When Aeolus scowls,
You need not fear,
So absolute the deep.

And cheerfully at sea,
Success you still entice,
To get the pearl and gold,
And ours to hold,
Virginia,
Earth's only paradise,

45 hinds] rustics, servants   Aeolus] ruler of the winds (classical mythology)
absolute] untrammelled

Where nature hath in store
Fowl, venison and fish,
    And the fruitfull'st soil
    Without your toil
Three harvests more,
All greater than your wish.

And the ambitious vine
Crowns with his purple mass
    The cedar reaching high
    To kiss the sky,
The cypress, pine
And useful sassafras.

To whose, the golden age
Still nature's laws doth give,
    No other cares that tend,
    But them to defend
From winter's age,
That long there doth not live.

Whenas the luscious smell
Of that delicious land
    Above the seas that flows
    The clear wind throws,
Your hearts to swell
Approaching the dear strand.

In kenning of the shore
(Thanks to God first given),
    Oh you, the happiest men,
    Be frolic then,
Let cannons roar,
Frighting the wide heaven.

And in regions far
Such heroes bring ye forth
    As those from whom we came,
    And plant our name
Under that star
Not known unto our north.

To whose] To whose age   Whenas] And then   kenning of] discerning
frolic] merry

And as there plenty grows
Of laurel everywhere,
  Apollo's sacred tree,
  You it may see
A poet's brows
To crown, that may sing there.

Thy voyages attend,
Industrious Hakluit,
  Whose reading shall enflame
  Men to seek fame,
And much commend
To after times thy wit.

(1606)

46 *An Ode Written in the Peak*

THIS while we are abroad,
  Shall we not touch our lyre?
Shall we not sing an ode?
  Shall that holy fire,
In us that strongly glowed,
  In this cold air expire?

Long since the summer laid
  Her lusty bravery down,
The autumn half is wayed
  And Boreas 'gins to frown,
Since now I did behold
  Great Brute's first builded town.

Though in the utmost Peak
  A while we do remain,
Amongst the mountains bleak
  Exposed to sleet and rain,
No sport our hours shall break,
  To exercise our vain.

Apollo] the ancient Greek god of poetry Hakluit] (see endnote)

46 bravery] finery, splendour wayed] (1) gone; (2) weighed Boreas] the north wind of winter Brute] (legendary founder of London) vain] (1) vein, genius, characteristic style; (2) vain (noun), vanity

What though bright Phoebus' beams
  Refresh the southern ground,
And though the princely Thames
  With beauteous nymphs abound,
And by old Camber's streams
  Be many wonders found;

Yet many rivers clear
  Here glide in silver swathes,
And what of all most dear,
  Buckston's delicious baths,
Strong ale and noble cheer,
  T' assuage breme winter's scathes.

Those grim and horrid caves,
  Whose looks affright the day,
Wherein nice nature saves
  What she would not bewray,
Our better leisure craves,
  And doth invite our lay.

In places far or near,
  Or famous, or obscure,
Where wholesome is the air,
  Or where the most impure,
All times, and everywhere,
  The Muse is still in ure.

(1606)

47 *His Defence Against the Idle Critic*

THE rhyme nor mars, nor makes,
Nor addeth it, nor takes,
  From that which we propose;
Things imaginary
Do so strangely vary
  That quickly we them lose.

46 Camber] Wales (Cambria), famous for the virtuous River Dee breme] stormy, raging, rough (Spenserian, medieval) nice] shy bewray] reveal; divulge prejudicially Or] Either ure] use; practice

And what's quickly begot
As soon again is not,
  This do I truly know:
Yea, and what's born with pain,
That sense doth long'st retain,
  Gone with a greater flow.

Yet this critic so stern,
But whom none must discern
  Nor perfectly have seeing,
Strangely lays about him,
As nothing without him
  Were worthy of being.

That I my self betray
To that most public way,
  Where the world's old bawd,
Custom, that doth humour
And by idle rumour
  Her dotages applaud

That whilst she still prefers
Those that be wholly hers,
  Madness and ignorance,
I creep behind the time,
From spirtling with their crime,
  And glad too with my chance.

O wretched world the while,
When the evil most vile
  Beareth the fairest face,
And inconstant lightness
With a scornful slightness
  The best things doth disgrace.

Whilst this strange knowing beast,
Man, of himself the least,
  His envy declaring,
Makes virtue to descend,
Her title to defend,
  Against him, much preparing.

Gone . . . flow] That fluent expression would have failed to fix   But] Without   Strangely] Extremely; in an unusual sense   time] fashion   From spirtling] To obviate being spattered   glad] rejoice

Yet these me not delude,
Nor from my place extrude,
By their resolvèd hate;
Their vileness that do know,
Which to myself I show,
To keep above my fate.

(1606)

48

The Crier

GOOD folk, for gold or hire,
But help me to a crier;
For my poor heart is run astray
After two eyes that passed this way.
Oyes, oyes, oyes,
If there be any man
In town or country can
Bring me my heart again,
I'll please him for his pain;
And by these marks I will you show
That only I this heart do owe.
It is a wounded heart,
Wherein yet sticks the dart;
Every piece sore hurt throughout it,
Faith and troth writ round about it;
It was a tame heart, and a dear,
And never used to roam;
But having got this haunt, I fear
'Twill hardly stay at home.
For God's sake, walking by the way,
If you my heart do see,
Either impound it for a stray,
Or send it back to me.

(1619)

49

To His Coy Love: A Canzonet

I PRAY thee leave, love me no more,
Call home the heart you gave me:
I but in vain that saint adore,
That can, but will not save me:

48 hire] reward eyes] (punning perhaps on 'eyas', hawk) owe] own heart] (punning on 'hart') dear] (punning on 'deer')

These poor half kisses kill me quite;
  Was ever man thus servèd?
Amidst an ocean of delight,
  For pleasure to be starvèd.

Show me no more those snowy breasts
  With azure riverets branchèd,
Where whilst mine eye with plenty feasts,
  Yet is my thirst not stanchèd.
O Tantalus, thy pains ne'er tell,
  By me thou art prevented;
'Tis nothing to be plagued in hell,
  But thus in heaven tormented.

Clip me no more in those dear arms,
  Nor thy life's comfort call me;
O, these are but too pow'rful charms,
  And do but more enthral me.
But see how patient I am grown,
  In all this coil about thee;
Come nice thing, let thy heart alone,
  I cannot live without thee.

(1619)

from *Poly-Olbion* (50–54)

50 from *Song I*

THOU Foy, before us all,
By thine own namèd town made famous in thy fall,
As Low, amongst us here; a most delicious brook
With all our sister nymphs that to the noon-stead look,
Which, gliding from the hills upon the tinny ore
Betwixt your high-reared banks, resort to this our shore:
Loved streams, let us exult and think ourselves no less
Than those upon their side, the setting that possess.
  Which, Camell overheard; but what doth she respect
Their taunts, her proper course that loosely doth neglect?
As frantic, ever since her British Arthur's blood
By Mordred's murderous hand was mingled with her flood.

servèd] treated; gratified riverets] surface veins stanchèd] quenched Tantalus] see endnote prevented] outdone Clip] Clasp coil] disturbance nice] shy

50 noon-stead] sun's noon position what] in what respect

For, as that river best might boast that conqueror's breath,
So sadly she bemoans his too untimely death;
Who, after twelve proud fields against the Saxon fought,
Yet back unto her banks by fate was lastly brought,
As though no other place on Britain's spacious earth
Were worthy of his end, but where he had his birth;
And, careless ever since how she her course do steer,
This muttereth to herself, in wandering here and there:
Even in the agèdest face, where beauty once did dwell
And nature (in the least) but seemèd to excel,
Time cannot make such waste but something will appear,
To show some little tract of delicacy there.
Or some religious work, in building many a day,
That this penurious age hath suffered to decay:
Some limb or model, dragged out of the ruinous mass,
The richness will declare in glory whilst it was.
But time upon my waste committed hath such theft
That it of Arthur here scarce memory hath left.

(1612)

51 from *Song II*

MARCH strongly forth, my Muse, whilst yet the temperate air
Invites us easily on to hasten our repair.
Thou powerful god of flames (in verse divinely great)
Touch my invention so with thy true genuine heat
That high and noble things I slightly may not tell,
Nor light and idle toys my lines may vainly swell;
But, as my subject serves, so high or low to strain,
And to the varying earth so suit my varying vein,
That, nature, in my work thou mayst thy power avow;
That, as thou first foundst art and didst her rules allow,
So I, to thine own self that gladly near would be,
May herein do the best, in imitating thee.
As thou hast here a hill, a vale there, there a flood,
A mead here, there a heath, and now and then a wood,
These things so in my song I naturally may show:
Now as the mountain high, then as the valley low;
Here fruitful as the mead, there as the heath be bare;
Then, as the gloomy wood, I may be rough, though rare.

(1612)

in the least] at the lowest estimate limb] part; edge, moulding model] structural design; image The richness . . . was] Will declare the richness the work had, while it was in glory

51 repair] going; restoration toys] trifles foundst] (1) discovered; (2) foundedst, instituted rare] (1) splendid; (2) infrequently

52 from *Song II*

THEN Frome (a nobler flood) the Muses doth implore
Her mother Blackmore's state they sadly would bewail,
Whose big and lordly oaks once bore as brave a sail
As they themselves that thought the largest shades to spread;
But man's devouring hand, with all the earth not fed,
Hath hewed her timber down. Which wounded, when it fell,
By the great noise it made, the workmen seemed to tell
The loss that to the land would shortly come thereby,
Where no man ever plants to our posterity:
That when sharp winter shoots her sleet and hardened hail,
Or sudden gusts from sea the harmless deer assail,
The shrubs are not of power to shield them from the wind.

(1612)

53 from *Song III*

WHERE she, of all the plains of Britain that doth bear
The name to be the first, renownèd every where,
Hath worthily obtained that Stonendge there should stand:
She, first of plains, and that, first wonder of the land.
She Wansdike also wins, by whom she is embraced,
That in his agèd arms doth gird her ampler waist:
Who (for a mighty mound sith long he did remain
Betwixt the Mercians' rule and the West-Saxons' reign,
And therefore of his place himself he proudly bare)
Had very oft been heard with Stonendge to compare;
Whom for a paltry ditch when Stonendge pleased t'upbraid,
The old man taking heart thus to that trophy said:
Dull heap, that thus thy head above the rest dost rear,
Precisely yet not knowst who first did place thee there;
But traitor basely turned to Merlin's skill does fly,
And with his magics dost thy maker's truth belie:
Conspirator with time, now grown so mean and poor,
Comparing these his spirits with those that went before;
Yet rather art content thy builder's praise to lose
Than passèd greatness should thy present wants disclose.
Ill did those mighty men to trust thee with their story,
That hast forgot their names who reared thee for their glory:
For all their wondrous cost, thou that hast served them so,
What 'tis to trust to tombs by thee we easily know.

* * * * *

53 Stonendge] Stonehenge   sith] since   wants] shortcomings

When in behalf of plains thus gloriously she spake:
  Away ye barbarous woods; how ever ye be placed
On mountains or in dales, or happily be graced
With floods or marshy fells, with pasture, or with earth
By nature made to till, that by the yearly birth
The large-bayed barn doth fill, yea though the fruitfullest ground.
For, in respect of plains, what pleasure can be found
In dark and sleepy shades, where mists and rotten fogs
Hang in the gloomy thicks, and make unsteadfast bogs
By dropping from the boughs, the o'er-grown trees among,
With caterpillars' kells and dusky cobwebs hung?
  The deadly screech-owl sits in gloomy covert hid;
Whereas the smooth-browed plain as liberally doth bid
The lark to leave her bower, and on her trembling wing
In climbing up towards heaven her high-pitched hymns to sing
Unto the springing day, when 'gainst the sun's arise
The early dawning strews the goodly eastern skies
With roses every where: who scarcely lifts his head
To view this upper world but he his beams doth spread
Upon the goodly plains, yet at his noonstead's height
Doth scarcely pierce the brake with his far-shooting sight.
  The gentle shepherds here survey their gentler sheep;
Amongst the bushy woods luxurious satyrs keep.
To these brave sports of field who with desire is won
To see his greyhound course, his horse (in diet) run,
His deep mouthed hound to hunt, his long winged hawk to fly,
To these most noble sports his mind who doth apply,
Resorts unto the plains. And not a foughten field,
Where kingdoms' rights have lain upon the spear and shield,
But plains have been the place, and all those trophies high
That ancient times have reared to noble memory;
As Stonendge, that to tell the British princes slain
By those false Saxons' fraud here ever shall remain.
It was upon the plain of Mamre (to the fame
Of me and all our kind) whereas the angels came
To Abraham in his tent, and there with him did feed;
To Sara his dear wife then promising the seed
By whom all nations should so highly honoured be,
In which the son of God they in the flesh should see.
But forests, to your plague there soon will come an age,
In which all damnèd sins most vehemently shall rage.

cost] expenditure of time, labour, etc. gloriously] proudly, boastfully fells] fens; 'boggy places. A word frequent in Lancashire' (D.) thicks] thickets kells] cocoons keep] live in diet] ?at a meet foughten field] battlefield Mamre] (Gen. 18–19)

An age! What have I said! Nay, ages there shall rise,
So senseless of the good of their posterities
That of your greatest groves they scarce shall leave a tree
(By which the harmless deer may after sheltered be),
Their luxury and pride but only to maintain,
And for your long excess shall turn ye all to pain.

(1612)

54 from *Song XIII*

WITH solitude what sorts, that here's not wondrous rife?
Whereas the hermit leads a sweet retirèd life,
From villages replete with ragg'd and sweating clowns
And from the loathsome airs of smoky citied towns.
Suppose twixt noon and night the sun his half-way wrought
(The shadows to be large by his descending brought)
Who with a fervent eye looks through the twiring glades,
And his dispersèd rays commixeth with the shades,
Exhaling the milch dew, which there had tarried long,
And on the ranker grass till past the noon-stead hong;
When as the hermit comes out of his homely cell,
Where from all rude resort he happily doth dwell:
Who in the strength of youth a man at arms hath been;
Or one who, of this world the vileness having seen,
Retires him from it quite, and with a constant mind
Man's beastliness so loathes that, flying human kind,
The black and darksome nights, the bright and gladsome days
Indifferent are to him, his hope on God that stays.
Each little village yields his short and homely fare:
To gather wind-fallen sticks his great'st and only care;
Which every agèd tree still yieldeth to his fire.
  This man, that is alone a king in his desire,
By no proud ignorant lord is basely overawed,
Nor his false praise affects, who grossly being clawed
Stands like an itchy moyle; nor of a pin he weighs
What fools, abusèd kings and humorous ladies raise.
His free and noble thought ne'er envies at the grace
That often times is given unto a bawd most base,
Nor stirs it him to think on the imposter vile,
Whom seeming what he's not, doth sensually beguile

54 twiring] winking; being twired (peeped through) with light milch dew] dew exuding like milk noon-stead] south hong] hung stays] sustains, comforts clawed] flattered, fawned on moyle] mule; hornless cow abusèd] deceived, misguided humorous] capricious, fanciful envies at] feels a grudge towards

The sottish purblind world; but, absolutely free,
His happy time he spends the works of God to see,
In those so sundry herbs which there in plenty grow:
Whose sundry strange effects he only seeks to know.
And in a little maund, being made of osiers small,
Which serveth him to do full many a thing withal,
He very choicely sorts his simples got abroad.

(1612)

55 from *Noah's Flood*

By this the sun had sucked up the vast deep,
And in gross clouds like cisterns did it keep;
The stars and signs by God's great wisdom set
By their conjunctions waters to beget
Had wrought their utmost, and even now began
Th'Almighty's justice upon sinful man:
From every several quarter of the sky
The thunder roars and the fierce lightnings fly
One at another, and together dash,
Volley on volley: flash comes after flash:
Heaven's lights look sad, as they would melt away;
The night is com'n i'th' morning of the day:
The cardinal winds he makes at once to blow,
Whose blasts to buffets with such fury go
That they themselves into the centre shot,
Into the bowels of the earth, and got,
Being condensed and strongly stiffened there,
In such strange manner multiplied the air,
Which turned to water, and increased the springs
To that abundance that the earth forth brings
Water to drown herself, should heaven deny
With one small drop the deluge to supply;
That through her pores, the soft and spungy earth,
As in a dropsy or unkindly birth,
A woman, swollen, sends from her fluxive womb
Her oozy springs, that there was scarcely room
For the waste waters which came in so fast,
As though the earth her entrails up would cast.

maund] woven basket with handle(s) simples] medicinal herbs abroad] here and there; as he freely moved about

55 sad] dismal-looking, calamitous; dark, dull com'n] comen, come centre] i.e. of Earth got] generated deny] refuse unkindly] unnatural fluxive] flowing

But these seemed yet but easily let go,
And from some sluice came softly in, and slow;
Till God's great hand so squeezed the boisterous clouds
That from the spouts of heaven's embattled shrouds,
Even like a flood-gate plucked up by the height,
Came the wild rain, with such a ponderous weight
As that the fierceness of the hurrying flood
Removed huge rocks and rammed them into mud:
Pressing the ground with that impetuous power,
As that the first shock of this drowning shower
Furrowed the earth's late plump and cheerful face
Like an old woman, that in little space
With rivelled cheeks and with bleared blubbered eyes
She wistly looked upon the troubled skies.
Up to some mountain as the people make,
Driving their cattle till the shower should slake,
The flood o'retakes them, and away doth sweep
Great herds of neat; and mighty flocks of sheep
Down through a valley as one stream doth come,
Whose roaring strikes the neighbouring eccho dumb:
Another meets it, and, whilst there they strive
Which of them two the other back should drive,
Their dreadful currents they together dash,
So that their waves like furious tides do wash
The head of some near hill, which falleth down
For very fear, as it itself would drown.
Some back their beasts, so hoping to swim out,
But by the flood encompassèd about
Are overwhelmed; some clamber up to towers,
But these and them the deluge soon devours:
Some to the top of pines and cedars get,
Thinking themselves they safely there should set;
But the rude flood that over all doth sway
Quickly comes up and carrieth them away.
The roe's much swiftness doth no more avail
Nor help him now than if he were a snail;
The swift-winged swallow and the slow-winged owl,
The fleetest bird and the most flagging fowl,
Are at one pass: the flood so high hath gone
There was no ground to set a foot upon.
Those fowl that followed moistness now it fly,
And leave the wet land to find out the dry;
But by the mighty tempest beaten down
On the blank water they do lie and drown.

shrouds] screens, coverings, defences impetuous] having impetus; violent
rivelled] wrinkled wistly] intently back] mount sway] (1) go; (2) rule

The strong-built tower is quickly overborne,
The o're-grown oak out of the earth is torn:
The subtile shower the earth hath softened so,
And with the waves the trees tossed to and fro,
That the roots loosen and the tops down sway,
So that whole forests quickly swim away.
Th'offended heaven had shut up all her lights:
The sun nor moon make neither days nor nights.
The waters so exceedingly abound
That in short time the sea itself is drowned:
That by the freshness of the falling rain
Neptune no more his saltness doth retain,
So that those scaly creatures used to keep
The mighty wastes of the immeasured deep,
Finding the general and their natural brack,
The taste and colour every where to lack,
Forsake those seas wherein they swam before,
Strangely oppressèd with their watery store.
The crookèd dolphin on those mountains plays
Whereas before that time not many days
The goat was grazing; and the mighty whale
Upon a rock out of his way doth fall,
From whence before one easily might have seen
The wandering clouds far under to have been.
The grampus and the whirlpool, as they rove,
Lighting by chance upon a lofty grove
Under this world of waters, are so much
Pleased with their wombs each tender branch to touch
That they leave slime upon the curled sprays,
On which the birds sung their harmonious lays.
As huge as hills still waves are wallowing in,
Which from the world so wondrously do win
That the tall mountains which on tiptoe stood,
As though they scorned the force of any flood,
No eye of heaven of their proud tops could see
One foot, from this great inundation free.
As in the chaos ere the frame was fixed
The air and water were so strongly mixed,
And such a bulk of grossness do compose,
As in those thick clouds which the globe enclose
Th'all-working spirit were yet again to wade,
And heaven and Earth again were to be made.

(1630)

used to keep] accustomed to inhabit   general] largest part   natural] natural habitat   brack] brackish   Whereas] Where   grampus] dolphinlike blowing mammal   whirlpool] large blowing whale   wombs] stomachs   sung] sang

JOSHUA SYLVESTER
1563–1618

from *The Divine Weeks of du Bartas*

56 [*The Zodiac*]

He that to number all the stars would seek
Had need invent some new arithmetic,
And who to cast that reck'ning takes in hand
Had need for counters take the ocean's sand;
Yet have our wise and learned elders found
Four dozen figures in the heavenly round,
For aid of memory, and to our eyes
In certain houses to divide the skies.
Of those are twelve in that rich girdle graffed
Which God gave nature for her New-Year's gift
(When making all, his voice almighty-most
Gave so fair laws unto heaven's shining host),
To wear it bias, buckled overthwart her,
Not round about her swelling waist to girt her.
This glorious baldric of a golden tinge,
Embossed with rubies, edged with silver fringe,
Buckled with gold, with a bend glistering bright,
Heav'n bias-wise environs day and night:
For from the period where the Ram doth bring
The day and night to equal balancing,
Ninety degrees towards the north it wends;
Thence just as much toward mid-heav'n it bends;
As many thence toward the south; and thence
Toward th' year's portal, the like difference.
Nephelian crook-horn with brass cornets crowned,
Thou buttest bravely 'gainst the New-Year's bound,
And richly clad in thy fair golden fleece
Dost hold the first house of heaven's spacious mese.
Thou spiest anon the Bull behind thy back,
Who lest that fodder by the way he lack,
Seeing the world so naked, to renew 't
Coats th' infant Earth in a green gallant suit,

cast] sum up houses] sectors of the heavens (astrology) graffed] inserted, implanted girdle, baldric] zodiac bias] slanting, obliquely bend] band, ribbon environs] encircles period] spring equinox mid-heav'n] the zenith Nephelian] Of Nephele (who to save her children gave them to a golden ram) cornets] horns (Latinism) bound] boundary mese] messuage, dwelling site

And without plough or yoke doth freely fling
Through fragrant pastures of the flowery spring.
The Twins, whose heads, arms, shoulders, knees and feet
God filled with stars to shine in season sweet,
Contend in course, who first the Bull shall catch,
That neither will nor may attend their match.
Then summer's guide, the Crab, comes rowing soft
With his eight oars through the heaven's azure loft,
To bring us yearly in his starry shell
Many long days, the shaggy Earth to swell.
Almost with like pace leaps the Lion out,
All clad with flames, bristled with beams about,
Who, with contagion of his burning breath,
Both grass and grain to cinders withereth.
The Virgin next, sweeping heav'n's azure globe
With stately train of her bright golden robe,
Mild-proudly marching, in her left hand brings
A sheaf of corn, and in her right hand wings.
After the Maiden shines the Balance bright,
Equal divider of the day and night,
In whose gold beam with three gold rings there fastens,
With six gold strings, a pair of golden basins.
The spiteful Scorpion next the Scale addressed
With two bright lamps covers his loathsome breast,
And fain from both ends with his double sting
Would spet his venom over every thing;
But that the brave half-horse Phylirean scout,
Galloping swift the heavenly belt about,
Aye fiercely threats with his flame-feathered arrow
To shoot the sparkling starry Viper thorough;
And th' hoary Centaur during all his race
Is so attentive to this only chase
That, dreadless of his dart, heaven's shining Kid
Comes jumping light, just at his heels unspied.
Meanwhile the Skinker from his starry spout,
After the Goat, a silver stream pours out;
Distilling still out of his radiant fire
Rivers of water (who but will admire?),
In whose clear channel mought at pleasure swim
Those two bright Fishes that do follow him,

course] running attend] pay attention to loft] sky corn . . . wings] (attributes of Astraea) Equal] (1) Just; (2) Equal Scale] Balance spet] spit Phylirean scout] the centaur Chiron, son of Philyra and Saturn; Sagittarius belt] zodiac Viper] venomous creature (Scorpio) Kid] Capricorn Skinker] Tapster (Aquarius) Distilling still] Constantly flowing mought] might (archaic)

But that the torrent slides so swift away
That it outruns them ever, even as they
Outrun the Ram, who ever them pursues,
And by returning yearly all renews.

(1605)

57

Aestas

WHEN summer's heat hath done his part,
The husband hath a gladsome heart;
Sith golden treasures of the plains
Make large amends for all his pains.
  But th' idle lubber, labour-loathing,
Walking, talking, wishing store,
Sowing naught but wind before,
  Shall, but wind behind, reap nothing.

(1621)

58

Of a Husbandman

GOOD morrow bids the cock, th' owl bids good night
To country cares; I bid, God speed them right.

(1621)

59

Variable

VARY, re-vary; tune and tune again
  (Anon to this string, and anon to that;
  Base, treble, tenor; swift, slow, sharp and flat)
Thy one same subject in a sundry strain,
To represent, by thy so diverse ditties,
  The dying world's so diverse alterations:
  Yet will the world have still more variations;
And, past thy verse, thy various subject yet is.

57 husband] husbandman   store] plenty

WILLIAM SHAKESPEARE
1564–1616

60

Song

HARK, hark! the lark at heaven's gate sings,
  And Phoebus gins arise,
His steeds to water at those springs
  On chaliced flowers that lies;
And winking Mary-buds begin to ope their golden eyes.
With everything that pretty is, my lady sweet, arise:
    Arise, arise!

(1623; a. *c.*1609)

61

Song

FEAR no more the heat o' th' sun,
  Nor the furious winter's rages:
Thou thy worldly task hast done,
  Home art gone and ta'en thy wages.
Golden lads and girls all must,
As chimney-sweepers, come to dust.

Fear no more the frown o' th' great,
  Thou art past the tyrant's stroke;
Care no more to clothe and eat:
  To thee the reed is as the oak;
The sceptre, learning, physic, must
All follow this and come to dust.

Fear no more the lightning flash,
  Nor th' all-dreaded thunder-stone.
Fear not slander, censure rash:
  Thou hast finished joy and moan.
All lovers young, all lovers must
Consign to thee and come to dust.

gins] begins to   Mary-buds] marigolds

61 physic] physicians   thunder-stone] thunderbolt   Consign to] Cosign the same contract with

No exorciser harm thee!
Nor no witchcraft charm thee!
Ghost unlaid forbear thee!
Nothing ill come near thee!
Quiet consummation have,
And renownèd be thy grave!

(1623; a. *c.*1609)

62

COME unto these yellow sands,
And then take hands;
Curtsied when you have and kissed—
The wild waves whist—
Foot it featly here and there,
And, sweet sprites, bear
The burden. Hark, hark!
Bow-wow.
The watch-dogs bark.
Bow-wow.
Hark, hark! I hear
The strain of strutting Chanticleer:
Cry: 'Cock-a-diddle-dow.'

(1623; a. 1611)

63

Ariel's Song

FULL fathom five thy father lies;
Of his bones are coral made;
Those are pearls that were his eyes:
Nothing of him that doth fade,
But doth suffer a sea-change
Into something rich and strange.
Sea-nymphs hourly ring his knell:
Ding-dong
Hark! now I hear them.
Ding-dong, bell.

(1623; a. 1611)

WILLIAM SHAKESPEARE?

64

[*Bridal Song*]

ROSES, their sharp spines being gone,
Not royal in their smells alone,
But in their hue;
Maiden pinks, of odour faint,
Daisies smell-less, yet most quaint,
And sweet thyme true;

Primrose, firstborn child of Ver,
Merry springtime's harbinger,
With harebells dim;
Oxlips in their cradles growing,
Marigolds on death-beds blowing,
Larks' heels trim:

All dear nature's children sweet,
Lie fore bride and bridegroom's feet,
Blessing their sense.
Not an angel of the air,
Bird melodious, or bird fair,
Is absent hence.

The crow, the slanderous cuckoo, nor
The boding raven, nor chough hoar,
Nor chattering pie,
May on our bride-house perch or sing,
Or with them any discord bring,
But from it fly.

(1634; wr. before 1611?)

Ver] Spring

KING JAMES VI OF SCOTLAND AND I OF ENGLAND

1566–1625

65 [*Lady Cicely Wemyss*]

NOT oriental Indus' crystal streams;
Nor fruitful Nilus that no banks can thole;
Nor golden Tagus, where bright Titan's beams
Are headlong'st hurled to view the Antarctic pole;
Nor Ladon (which sweet Sidney doth extol)
While it the Arcadian beauties did embrace—
All these cannot thee, nameless thee, control,
But with good right must render and give place.
For, whilst sweet she vouchsafest to show her face,
And with her presence honours thee ilk day,
Thou, sliding, seemst to have a slower pace,
Against thy will, as if thou went away,
And, loath to leave the sight of such a one,
Thou still imparts thy plaints to every stone.

(1911; wr. 1600–06?)

JOHN HOSKYNS

1566–1638

66 *An Epitaph: On a Man for Doing Nothing*

HERE lies the man was born and cried,
Told three score years, fell sick and died.

(1605)

67 *To His Son Benedict Hoskyns*

SWEET Benedict, whilst thou art young
And knowst not yet the use of tongue,
Keep it in thrall whilst thou art free:
Imprison it or it will thee.

(1672)

65 Titan's] the sun's control] overcome render] submit ilk] each

SIR WILLIAM ALEXANDER, EARL OF STIRLING

1567?–1640

from *Aurora* (68–69)

68 *Sonnet LI*

I DREAMED the nymph that o'er my fancy reigns
Came to a part whereas I paused alone,
Then said, 'What needs you in such sort to moan?
Have I not power to recompense your pains?
Lo, I conjúre you, by that loyal love
Which you profess, to cast those griefs apart.
It's long, dear love, since that you had my heart,
Yet I was coy your constancy to prove;
But having had a proof, I'll now be free:
I am the eccho that your sighs resounds;
Your woes are mine, I suffer in your wounds,
Your passions all they sympathize in me.'
  Thus whilst for kindness both began to weep,
  My happiness evanished with the sleep.

(1604)

69 *An Echo*

AH, will no soul give ear unto my moan? *one*
Who answers thus so kindly when I cry? *I*
What fostered thee that pities my despair? *air*
Thou blabbing guest, what knowst thou of my fall? *all*
What did I when I first my fair disclosed? *losed*
Where was my reason, that it would not doubt? *out*
What canst thou tell me of my lady's will? *ill*
Wherewith can she acquit my loyal part? *art*
What hath she then with me to disaguise? *aguise*
What have I done, since she gainst love repined? *pined*
What did I when I her to life preferred? *erred*
What did mine eyes, whilst she my heart restrained? *rained*
What did she whilst my Muse her praise proclaimed? *claimed*
And what? And how? This doth me most affright. *of right*
What if I never sue to her again? *gain*

69 *losed*] wasted time disaguise] disguise *aguise*] dress

And what when all my passions are repressed? *rest*
But what thing will best serve t' assuage desire? *ire*
And what will serve to mitigate my rage? *age*
I see the sun begins for to descend. *end*

(1604)

THOMAS CAMPIAN
1567?–1619

70

FOLLOW thy fair sun, unhappy shadow.
  Though thou be black as night,
  And she made all of light,
Yet follow thy fair sun, unhappy shadow.

Follow her whose light thy light depriveth.
  Though here thou liv'st disgraced,
  And she in heaven is placed,
Yet follow her whose light the world reviveth.

Follow those pure beams whose beauty burneth,
  That so have scorchèd thee
  As thou still black must be
Till her kind beams thy black to brightness turneth.

Follow her while yet her glory shineth.
  There comes a luckless night,
  That will dim all her light;
And this the black unhappy shade divineth.

Follow still, since so thy fates ordainèd.
  The sun must have his shade,
  Till both at once do fade,
The sun still proud, the shadow still disdainèd.

(1601)

71

  FOLLOW your saint, follow with accents sweet;
  Haste you, sad notes, fall at her flying feet.
  There wrapped in cloud of sorrow, pity move,
And tell the ravisher of my soul I perish for her love.
  But if she scorns my never-ceasing pain,
Then burst with sighing in her sight, and ne'er return
  again.

All that I sung still to her praise did tend.
Still she was first, still she my songs did end.
Yet she my love and music both doth fly,
The music that her echo is, and beauty's sympathy.
Then let my notes pursue her scornful flight;
It shall suffice that they were breathed and died for her delight.

(1601)

72

ROSE-CHEEKED Laura, come,
Sing thou smoothly with thy beauty's
Silent music, either other
Sweetly gracing.

Lovely forms do flow
From concent divinely framed;
Heaven is music, and thy beauty's
Birth is heavenly.

These dull notes we sing
Discords need for helps to grace them;
Only beauty purely loving
Knows no discord,

But still moves delight
Like clear springs renewed by flowing,
Ever perfect, ever in them-
Selves eternal.

(1602)

73

[*Winter Nights*]

Now winter nights enlarge
The number of their hours,
And clouds their storms discharge
Upon the airy towers.
Let now the chimneys blaze
And cups o'erflow with wine;
Let well-tuned words amaze
With harmony divine.

Still] Ever

72 concent] harmony, concord

Now yellow waxen lights
Shall wait on honey love,
While youthful revels, masques, and courtly sights
Sleep's leaden spells remove.

This time doth well dispense
With lovers' long discourse:
Much speech hath some defence,
Though beauty no remorse.
All do not all things well:
Some measures comely tread,
Some knotted riddles tell,
Some poems smoothly read.
The summer hath his joys,
And winter his delights.
Though love and all his pleasures are but toys,
They shorten tedious nights.

(*c.*1618)

74

THERE is a garden in her face,
Where roses and white lilies grow;
A heavenly paradise is that place,
Wherein all pleasant fruits do flow.
There cherries grow which none may buy,
Till 'cherry-ripe' themselves do cry.

Those cherries fairly do enclose
Of orient pearl a double row,
Which when her lovely laughter shows,
They look like rosebuds filled with snow.
Yet them nor peer nor prince can buy,
Till 'cherry-ripe' themselves do cry.

Her eyes like angels watch them still,
Her brows like bended bows do stand,
Threatening with piercing frowns to kill
All that attempt, with eye or hand,
Those sacred cherries to come nigh,
Till 'cherry-ripe' themselves do cry.

(*c.*1617)

74 orient] shining

SIR HENRY WOTTON
1568–1639

75 *A Hymn to My God in a Night of My Late Sickness*

O THOU great power, in whom I move,
For whom I live, to whom I die,
Behold me through thy beams of love,
Whilst on this couch of tears I lie;
And cleanse my sordid soul within
By thy Christ's blood, the bath of sin.

No hallowed oils, no grains I need,
No rags of saints, no purging fire,
One rosy drop from David's seed
Was worlds of seas, to quench thine ire.
O precious ransom! which once paid,
That *Consummatum est* was said:

And said by him that said no more,
But sealed it with his sacred breath.
Thou then, that has dispunged my score,
And dying, wast the death of death,
Be to me now, on thee I call,
My life, my strength, my joy, my all.

(1651)

76 *On His Mistress, the Queen of Bohemia*

YOU meaner beauties of the night,
That poorly satisfy our eyes
More by your number than your light:
You common people of the skies,
What are you when the sun shall rise?

You curious chanters of the wood,
That warble forth Dame Nature's lays,
Thinking your voices understood
By your weak accents: what's your praise
When Philomel her voice shall raise?

grains] grains of paradise; spice *Consummatum est*] It is finished (John 19: 30)
dispunged] deleted

76 Philomel] the nightingale

You violets that first appear,
  By your pure purple mantles known,
Like the proud virgins of the year,
  As if the spring were all your own:
  What are you when the rose is blown?

So when my mistress shall be seen
  In form and beauty of her mind,
By virtue first, then choice, a queen,
  Tell me, if she were not designed
  The eclipse and glory of her kind?

(1651)

77 *Upon the Sudden Restraint of the Earl of Somerset, Then Falling from Favour*

DAZZLED thus with height of place,
Whilst our hopes our wits beguile,
No man marks the narrow space
'Twixt a prison and a smile.

Then since fortune's favours fade,
You that in her arms do sleep,
Learn to swim and not to wade;
For the hearts of kings are deep.

But if greatness be so blind
As to trust in towers of air,
Let it be with goodness lined,
That at least the fall be fair.

Then though darkened you shall say,
When friends fail and princes frown,
Virtue is the roughest way,
But proves at night a bed of down.

(1651)

78 *The Character of a Happy Life*

HOW happy is he born and taught,
That serveth not another's will?
Whose armour is his honest thought,
And simple truth his utmost skill?

Whose passions not his masters are,
Whose soul is still prepared for death,
Untied unto the world by care
Of public fame or private breath.

Who envies none that chance doth raise;
Nor vice hath ever understood,
How deepest wounds are given by praise;
Nor rules of state, but rules of good.

Who hath his life from rumours freed,
Whose conscience is his strong retreat;
Whose state can neither flatterers feed,
Nor ruin make oppressors great.

Who God doth late and early pray,
More of his grace than gifts to lend,
And entertains the harmless day
With a religious book or friend.

This man is freed from servile bands
Of hope to rise or fear to fall;
Lord of himself, though not of lands,
And having nothing yet hath all.

(1651)

79 *On a Bank as I Sat a Fishing: A Description of the Spring*

AND now all nature seemed in love:
The lusty sap began to move,
New juice did stir th' embracing vines,
And birds had drawn their valentines.
The jealous trout, that low did lie,
Rose at a well-dissembled fly:
There stood my friend, with patient skill
Attending of his trembling quill.
Already were the eaves possessed
With the swift pilgrims' daubèd nest.
The groves already did rejoice
In Philomel's triúmphing voice.
  The showers were short, the weather mild,
The morning fresh, the evening smiled.

state (l.15)] splendour

79 quill] float   Philomel's] the nightingale's

Joan takes her neat-rubbed pail, and now
She trips to milk the sand-red cow;
Where for some sturdy football swain,
Joan strokes a sillabub or twain.
The fields and gardens were beset
With tulip, crocus, violet;
And now, though late, the modest rose
Did more than half a blush disclose.
Thus all looked gay, all full of cheer,
To welcome the new-liveried year.

(1651)

80 De Morte

MAN'S life's a tragedy: his mother's womb
(From which he enters) is the tiring room;
This spacious earth the theatre; and the stage
That country which he lives in: passions, rage,
Folly and vice are actors: the first cry
The prologue to th' ensuing tragedy.
The former act consisteth of dumb shows;
The second, he to more perfection grows;
I'th third he is a man, and doth begin
To nurture vice and act the deeds of sin:
I'th fourth declines; i'th fifth diseases clog
And trouble him; then death's his epilogue.

(1651)

81 *To J[ohn] D[onne] from Mr H[enry] W[otton]*

'TIS not a coat of gray or shepherd's life,
'Tis not in fields or woods remote to live,
That adds or takes from one that peace or strife
Which to our days such good or ill doth give:
It is the mind that makes the man's estate
For ever happy or unfortunate.

Then first the mind of passions must be free,
Of him that would to happiness aspire,
Whether in princes' palaces he be
Or whether to his cottage he retire;

neat-rubbed] cow-worn strokes] milks into (to make it froth)
80 De Morte] Of Death tiring room] dressing-room I'th] In the

For our desires that on extremes are bent
Are friends to care and traitors to content.

Nor should we blame our friends, though false they be,
  Since there are thousands false for one that's true,
But our own blindness, that we cannot see
  To choose the best although they be but few;
For he that every feignèd friend will trust
Proves true to friend, but to himself unjust.

The faults we have are they that make our woe;
  Our virtues are the motives of our joy.
Then is it vain if we to deserts go,
  To seek our bliss or shroud us from annoy:
Our place need not be changèd, but our will;
For everywhere we may do good or ill.

But this I do not dedicate to thee
  As one that holds himself fit to advise,
Or that my lines to him should precepts be,
  That is less ill than I, and much more wise;
But 'tis no harm mortality to preach,
For men do often learn when they do teach.

(1911)

SIR FRANCIS HUBERT
1568 or 1569–1629

82 from *The Life and Death of Edward II*

THIS highest scholar in the school of sin,
This centaur, half a man and half a beast,
This pleasing siren so my soul did win
That he was dear to me above the rest.
Look, what he said was gospel at the least.
  Look, what he did I made my precedent.
  So soon we learn what we too late repent.

This angel-devil thus shrined in my heart,
This dragon having got the golden fruit,
My very soul to him I did impart,
Nor was I ever deaf unto his suit.
He acted all, I was a silent mute;

81 motives] causes, promoters   annoy] pain   ill] bad

My being seemed to be in him alone.
Plantagenet was turned to Gaveston.

And having seized me thus into his hands
(For fear belike lest he should be diseased),
He thought to tie me still in straiter bands
By praising that wherewith my sense was pleased;
Affirming that our lives were to be eased
Of many cumbers which the curious wise
Had laid on men, the more to tyrannize.

For what are laws but servile observations
Of this or that, what pleased the maker's mind?
The self-conceited-sown imaginations
Of working brains, which did in freedom find
Our human state, which they forsooth would bind
To what they liked; what liked not was forbidden.
So horse and mule with bit and spur are ridden.

(1628)

SIR ROBERT AYTON
1569–1638

83 [*Sonnet: On Loss*]

Lo how the sailor in a stormy night
Wails and complains, till he the star perceive
Whose situation and assurèd height
Should guide him through the strong and watery cave.
As many motives, wretched soul, I have
For to regret, as few for to rejoice
In seeing all things, once this sight I crave,
Since I the lodestar of my life did lose.
And which is worse, amidst those many woes,
Amidst my pains which passes all compare,
No help, no hope, no comfort, no repose,
No sun appears to clear those clouds of care,
Save this, that fortune neither may nor dare
Make my mishaps more hapless than they are.

(1844; wr. 1600–5?)

82 diseased] inconvenienced bands] bonds cumbers] troubles self-conceited] overweening working] restless, disturbed

84 [*Sonnet: On the River Tweed*]

FAIR famous flood, which sometime did divide,
But now conjoins, two diadems in one,
Suspend thy pace and some more softly slide,
Since we have made thee trinchman of our moan.
And since none's left but thy report alone
To show the world our captain's last farewell,
That courtesy I know, when we are gone
Perhaps your lord the sea will it reveal.
And you again the same will not conceal,
But straight proclaim't through all his bremish bounds,
Till his high tides these flowing tidings tell,
And so will send them with his murmuring sounds
  To that religious place whose stately walls
  Does keep the heart which all our hearts enthrals.

(1844; wr. 1603–5?)

85 *To His Coy Mistress*

WHAT others doth discourage and dismay
Is unto me a pastime and a play.
I sport in her denials and do know
Women love best that does love least in show.
Too sudden favours may abate delight;
When modest coyness sharps the appetite,
I grow the hotter for her cold neglect,
And more inflamed when she shows least respect.
Heat may arise from rocks, from flints so fire:
So from her coldness I do strike desire.
She, knowing this perhaps, resolves to try
My faith and patience, offering to deny
Whate'er I ask of her, that I may be
More taken with her, for her slighting me.
When fishes play with baits, best, anglers say,
To make them bite, is draw the bait away:
So dallies she with me till, to my smart,
Both bait and hook sticks fastened in my heart.

84 trinchman] spokesman bremish] (1) loudly current (of rumours); (2) raging; rugged bounds] boundaries religious place] Melrose Abbey (where Robert the Bruce's heart was buried)

And now I am become her foolish prey;
And, that she knows I cannot break away,
Let her resolve no longer to be free
From Cupid's bonds, and bind herself to me.
Nor let her vex me longer with despair
That they be cruel that be young and fair:
It is the old, the creasèd, and the black
That are unkind and for affection lack.
I'll tie her eyes with lines, her ears with moans;
Her marble heart I'll pierce with hideous groans
That neither eyes, ears, heart shall be at rest
Till she forsake her sire to love me best;
Nor will I raise my siege nor leave my field
Till I have made my valiant mistress yield.

(1960)

86

THERE is none, no none but I,
None but I so full of woe,
That I cannot choose but die,
Or else beg physic from my foe.
Now what hopes she shall be moved
To revive my hopes forlorne!
She that loves for to be loved,
Yet pays her lovers' hopes with scorn;
Whose deserts inflames desire,
Whose disdains strikes comfort dead,
In whose eyes lies all love's fire,
From whose heart all love is fled.
Lovely eyes and loveless heart,
Why do you so disagree?
How can sweetness cause such smart,
Or smarting so delightful be?
No, fair eyes—no, no more so:
Cruel eyes and full of guile;
You are only sweet in show,
And never kill but when you smile.
Yet, fair eyes, this I must say:
Though you should be still unkind,
He whose heart is not your prey
Must either be a fool or blind.

(1844)

that she knows] so that she may know creasèd] wrinkled

86 physic] medical treatment

87 [*Valediction*]

THEN will thou go and leave me here?
Ah do not so my dearest dear.
The sun's departure clouds the sky;
But thy departure makes me die.

Thou canst not go but with my heart,
Even that which is my chiefest part:
Then with two hearts thou shall be gone,
And I shall rest behind with none.

Prevent the danger of this ill,
Go not away, stay with me still:
I'll bathe thy lips with kisses then,
Expecting increase back again.

And if thou needs will go away,
Ah, leave one heart with me to stay;
Take mine, let thine in pawn remain,
That thou will quickly come again.

Meantime, my part shall be to mourn,
To tell the hours till thou return;
My eyes shall be but eyes to weep,
And neither eyes to see nor sleep.

And if perchance their lids I close
To ease them with some false repose,
Yet still my longing dreams shall be
Of nothing in the world but thee.

(1844)

88 *Upon Love*

THERE is no worldly pleasure here below
Which by experience doth not folly prove,
But amongst all the follies that I know
The sweetest folly in the world is love.

But not that passion which with fools' consent
Above the reason bears imperious sway,
Making their lifetime a perpetual Lent,
As if a man were born to fast and pray.

No, that is not the humour I approve,
As either yielding pleasure or promotion:
I like a mild and lukewarm zeal in love,
Although I do not like it in devotion.

For it hath no coherence with my creed
To think that lovers die as they pretend:
If all that say they die had died indeed,
Sure long ere now the world had had an end.

Besides, we need not love unless we please:
No destiny can force man's disposition;
And how can any die of that disease
Whereof himself may be his own physician?

But some seems so distracted of their wits
That I would think it but a venial sin
To take some of those innocents that sits
In Bedlam out, and put some lovers in.

And some men, rather than incur the slander
Of true apostates, will false martyrs prove;
But I am neither Iphis nor Leander:
I'll neither drown nor hang myself for love.

Methinks a wise man's actions should be such
As always yields to reason's best advice:
Now, for to love too little or too much
Are both extremes, and all extremes are vice.

Yet have I been a lover by report,
Yea, I have died for love as others do;
But, praised be God, it was in such a sort
That I revived within an hour or two.

Thus have I lived, thus have I loved till now,
And finds no reason to repent me yet;
And whosoever otherwise will do,
His courage is as little as his wit.

(1844)

humour] sentiment coherence] agreement Iphis] (low-born lover of Anaxerete: rejected, he hanged himself) Leander] (drowned crossing the Hellespont to Hero)

89 [*A Song: On His Mistress*]

DEAR, why do you say you love,
When indeed you careless prove?
Reason better can digest
Earnest heat, than love in jest.
Wherefore do your smiling eyes
Help your tongue to make sweet lies?
Leave to statesman tricks of state,
Love doth politicians hate.
You perhaps presume to find
Love of some chameleon kind;
But be not deceived, my fair,
Love will not be fed on air.
Love's a glutton of his food,
Surfeit makes his stomach good.
Love whose diet grows precise
Sick of some consumption dies.
Then, dear love, let me obtain
That which may true love maintain;
Or if kind you cannot prove,
Prove true, say you cannot love.

(1844 wr. by 1633)

90 [*Song*]

WHAT means this strangeness now of late
  Since time doth truth approve?
Such distance may well stand with state,
  It cannot stand with love.
It's either cunning or distrust
  That doth such ways allow;
The first is base, the last's unjust,
  Let neither blemish you.
If you intend to draw me on,
  You overact your part,
And if you mean to send me gone,
  You need not half this art.
Speak but the word, or do but cast
  A look which seems to frown:
I'll give you all the love that's past,
  The rest shall be my own.

89 precise] strict

And such a fair and efald way
On both sides none can blame,
Since everyone is bound to play
The fairest of his game.

(1659)

91 [*The Rejection*]

SHALL fear to seem untrue
To vows of constant duty
Make me disgest disdains undue
From an inconstant beauty?
No, I do not affect
In vows to seem so holy
That I would have the world to check
My constancy with folly.
Let her call breach of vow
What I call just repentance:
I count him base, and brainsick too,
That dotes on coy acquaintance.
Thus if out of her snare
At last I do unfold me,
Accuse herself that caught me there
And knew not how to hold me.
And if I rebel prove,
Against my will I do it;
Yet can I hate as well as love
When reason binds me to it.

(1844)

92 [*Upon His Unconstant Mistress*]

WHY did I wrong my judgement so
As to affect where I did know
There was no hold for to be taken?
That which her heart thirsts after most,
If once of it her hope can boast,
Straight by her folly is forsaken.

efald] simple, honest

91 disgest] digest   check] reproach; taunt   coy] disdainful

92 affect] aspire to

Thus while I still pursue in vain,
Methinks I turn a child again
And of my shadow am a chasing;
For all her favours are to me
Like apparitions which I see,
Yet never can come near t'embracing.

Oft have I wished that there had been
Some almanac whereby to have seen
When love with her had been in season;
But I perceive there is no art
Can find the epact of a heart
That loves by chance and not by reason.

Yet will I not for this despair
But time her humour may prepare
To love him who is now neglected;
For what unto my constancy
Is now denied, one day may be
From her inconstancy expected.

(1641)

93

The Answer

THOU that loved once now loves no more
For fear to show more love than brain,
With heresy unhatched before
Apostasy thou dost maintain.
   Can he have either brain or love
   That doth inconstancy approve?
   A choice well made no change admits,
   All changes argue afterwits.

Say that she had not been the same:
Should thou therefore another be?
What thou in her as vice did blame,
Can that take virtue's name in thee?
   No, thou in this her captive was,
   And made thee ready by her glass;
   Example led revenge astray,
   When true love should have kept the way.

93 afterwits] second thoughts; coming to one's senses

True love hath no reflecting end;
The object, good, sets it at rest,
And noble breasts will freely lend
Without expecting interest.
'Tis merchant love, 'tis trade for gain,
To barter love for love again;
'Tis usury, yea worse than this,
For self idolatry it is.

Then let her choice be what it will,
Let constancy be thy revenge:
If thou retribute good for ill
Both grief and shame shall check her change.
Thus mayst thou laugh when thou shall see
Remorse reclaim her home to thee,
And where thou begst of her before,
She now sits begging at thy door.

(1660)

94 *On the Prince's Death, to the King*

DID you ever see the day
When blossoms fell in midst of May?
Rather, did you ever see
All the blossoms on the tree
Grow to ripe fruit? Some must fall.
Nature says so, though not all.
Though one be fallen, we have store:
The tree is fresh, and may have more.

And for our comfort this we know,
The soil is good, and you may sow.
What would we more? More seed cast on,
For so have thriving husbands done.
And though the first crop fail, they find
A fruitful earth will still be kind.
And, sir, your patience is but just,
For live we may but die we must.

But this was the first? 'Tis true
God should be first served, then you.
He that made the sun to shine
Said, the first fruit shall be mine.

94 husbands] (1) farmers; (2) husbands

And think it not a heavy doom,
For he that gives all, may take some.
  God's will is done, and yet to you
  His will ordains a blessing too.

A man begets a man; the king
Did more, begat a holy thing,
An angel, that ne'er knew offence,
Such privilege hath innocence.
The king then cannot make complaint
When the king's first born is a saint,
  Nay more, an angel heavenly blest:
  So let our heavenly angel rest.

(1963; wr. 1629)

95 *Upon Platonic Love: To Mistress Cicely Crofts, Maid of Honour*

Oh that I were all soul, that I might prove
  For you as fit a love
As you are for an angel; for I vow,
None but pure spirits are fit loves for you.

You're all ethereal, there is in you no dross
  Nor any part that's gross;
Your coarsest part is like the curious lawn
O'er vestal relicts for a covering drawn.

Your other part, part of the purest fire
  That e'er heaven did inspire,
Makes every thought that is refined by it
A quintessénce of goodness and of wit.

Thus do your raptures reach to that degree
  In love's philosophy
That you can figure to yourself a fire
Void of all heat, a love without desire.

Nor in divinity do you go less:
  You think and you profess
That souls may have a plenitude of joy,
Although their bodies never meet t'enjoy.

doom] judgement

95 curious] fine, delicate; fastidious

But I must needs confess I do not find
   The motions of my mind
So purified as yet, but at their best
My body claims in them some interest.

I hold a perfect joy makes all our parts
   As joyful as our hearts;
My senses tell me, if I please not them,
My love is but a dotage or a dream.

How shall we then agree? You may descend,
   But will not to my end.
I fain would tune my fancy to your key,
But cannot reach to that abstracted way.

There rests but this, that, while we sojourn here,
   Our bodies may draw near,
And when our joys they can no more extend,
Then let our souls begin where they did end.

(1659; wr. 1630–3?)

96 [*A Posy*]

DEAR love, I am resolved with thee to live,
Though with my smock thy pains for to relieve.
Thus she replied: Dear sir if it be so,
Without my smock through a world with thee I'll go.

(1960)

EMILIA LANIER
1569?–1645

97 *To the Lady Arabella*

GREAT learnèd lady, whom I long have known,
And yet not known so much as I desired;
Rare phoenix, whose fair feathers are your own,
With which you fly, and are so much admired;
True honour, whom true fame hath so attired

97 *Arabella*] Arabella Stuart

In glittering raiment shining much more bright
Than silver stars in the most frosty night:

Come like the morning sun new out of bed,
And cast your eyes upon this little book.
Although you be so well accompanied
With Pallas and the Muses, spare one look
Upon this humbled king, who all forsook,
That in his dying arms he might embrace
Your beauteous soul, and fill it with his grace.

(1611)

98 from *To the Lady Anne, Countess of Dorset*

To you I dedicate this work of grace,
This frame of glory which I have erected;
For your fair mind I hold the fittest place
Where virtue should be settled and protected:
If highest thoughts true honour do embrace,
And holy wisdom if of them respected,
Then in this mirror let your fair eyes look,
To view your virtues in this blessèd book.

Blessed by our Saviour's merits, not my skill,
Which I acknowledge to be very small.
Yet if the least part of his blessèd will
I have performed, I count I have done all:
One spark of grace sufficient is to fill
Our lamps with oil, ready when he doth call
To enter with the bridegroom to the feast,
Where he that is the greatest may be least.

Greatness is no sure frame to build upon,
No worldly treasure can assure that place;
God makes both even, the cottage with the throne:
All worldly honours there are counted base.
Those he holds dear, and reckoneth as his own,
Whose virtuous deeds by his especial grace
Have gained his love, his kingdom, and his crown,
Whom in the book of life he hath set down.

Pallas] Athena, goddess of wisdom (Greek mythology)

98 frame] base

Titles of honour which the world bestows
To none but to the virtuous doth belong;
As beauteous bowers where true worth should repose,
And where his dwelling should be built most strong.
But when they are bestowed upon her foes,
Poor virtue's friends endure the greatest wrong;
  For they must suffer all indignity,
  Until in heaven they better gracèd be.

What difference was there when the world began;
Was it not virtue that distinguished all?
All sprang but from one woman and one man;
Then how doth gentry come to rise and fall?
Or who is he that very rightly can
Distinguish of his birth, or tell at all
  In what mean state his ancestors have bin,
  Before some one of worth did honour win?

Whose successors, although they bear his name,
Possessing not the riches of his mind,
How do we know they spring out of the same
True stock of honour, being not of that kind?
It is fair virtue gets immortal fame;
'Tis that doth all love and duty bind:
  If he that much enjoys doth little good,
  We may suppose he comes not of that blood.

Nor is he fit for honour or command
If base affections overrules his mind,
Or that self-will doth carry such a hand
As worldly pleasures have the power to blind,
So as he cannot see nor understand
How to discharge that place to him assigned:
  God's stewards must for all the poor provide,
  If in God's house they purpose to abide.

To you as to God's steward I do write,
In whom the seeds of virtue have been sown
By your most worthy mother, in whose right
All her fair parts you challenge as your own;
If you, sweet lady, will appear as bright
As ever creature did that time hath known,
  Then wear this diadem I present to thee,
  Which I have framed for her eternity.

(1611)

gracèd] favoured   bin] been   carry . . . hand] treat in such a way (*OED* 34)

99 *from* Salve Deus Rex Judaeorum

Now Pontius Pilate is to judge the cause
Of faultless Jesus, who before him stands,
Who neither hath offended prince nor laws;
Although he now be brought in woeful bands.
O noble governor, make thou yet a pause:
Do not in innocent blood imbrue thy hands,
But hear the words of thy most worthy wife,
Who sends to thee, to beg her Saviour's life.

Let barbarous cruelty far depart from thee,
And in true justice take affliction's part;
Open thine eyes, that thou the truth mayst see:
Do not the thing that goes against thy heart;
Condemn not him that must thy Saviour be,
But view his holy life, his good desert.
Let not us women glory in men's fall,
Who had power given to overrule us all.

Till now your indiscretion sets us free
And makes our former fault much less appear:
Our mother Eve, who tasted of the tree,
Giving to Adam what she held most dear,
Was simply good, and had no power to see;
The aftercoming harm did not appear.
The subtile serpent that our sex betrayed
Before our fall so sure a plot had laid

That undiscerning ignorance perceived
No guile or craft that was by him intended;
For had she known of what we were bereaved,
To his request she had not condescended.
But she, poor soul, by cunning was deceived:
No hurt therein her harmless heart intended;
For she alleged God's word, which he denies,
That they should die, but even as gods be wise.

But surely Adam cannot be excused:
Her fault though great, yet he was most to blame;
What weakness offered, strength might have refused.
Being lord of all, the greater was his shame:
Although the serpent's craft had her abused,
God's holy word ought all his actions frame;

cause] case   bands] bonds   bereaved] deprived, dispossessed
condescended] yielded; lowered herself   alleged] cited

For he was lord and king of all the Earth
Before poor Eve had either life or breath.

Who being framed by God's eternal hand,
The perfect'st man that ever breathed on Earth;
And from God's mouth received that strait command,
The breath whereof he knew was present death:
Yea, having power to rule both sea and land,
Yet with one apple won to lose that breath
Which God had breathèd in his beauteous face,
Bringing us all in danger and disgrace.

And then to lay the fault on patience' back,
That we, poor women, must endure it all!
We know right well he did discretion lack,
Being not persuaded thereunto at all.
If Eve did err, it was for knowledge' sake;
The fruit being fair persuaded him to fall:
No subtle serpent's falsehood did betray him;
If he would eat it, who had power to stay him?

Not Eve, whose fault was only too much love,
Which made her give this present to her dear,
That what she tasted he likewise might prove,
Whereby his knowledge might become more clear:
He never sought her weakness to reprove
With those sharp words which he of God did hear.
Yet men will boast of knowledge, which he took
From Eve's fair hand, as from a learnèd book.

If any evil did in her remain,
Being made of him, he was the ground of all:
If one of many worlds could lay a stain
Upon our sex, and work so great a fall
To wretched man by Satan's subtile train,
What will so foul a fault amongst you all?
Her weakness did the serpent's words obey,
But you in malice God's dear Son betray.

Whom, if unjustly you condemn to die,
Her sin was small to what you do commit;
All mortal sins that do for vengeance cry
Are not to be compared unto it:
If many worlds would altogether try
By all their sins the wrath of God to get,
This sin of yours surmounts them all as far
As doth the sun, another little star.

prove] experience train] procedure

Then let us have our liberty again,
And challenge to yourselves no sovereignty:
You came not in the world without our pain;
Make that a bar against your cruelty.
Your fault being greater, why should you disdain
Our being your equals, free from tyranny?
  If one weak woman simply did offend,
  This sin of yours hath no excuse nor end.

To which, poor souls, we never gave consent;
Witness thy wife, O Pilate, speaks for all;
Who did but dream, and yet a message sent,
That thou shouldst have nothing to do at all
With that just man; which, if thy heart relent,
Why wilt thou be a reprobate with Saul?
  To seek the death of him that is so good,
  For thy soul's health to shed his dearest blood.

(1611)

SAMUEL ROWLANDS
1570?–1630?

100

Prologue

UNDER the shadow of the gloomy night,
When silent sleep arrests each mortal wight,
When fairy Oberon and his night queen
In Cynthia's honour frisks o'er every green,
Sleep, parting from me, gave invention light
To find some subject for my pen to write;
When, musing how the world I best might fit,
I saw how poets humoured out their wit.
Nay then, thought I: write all of what they list,
Once in my days I'll prove a humorist.
When on a sudden, as I thought the thing,
I was encountered by the fairy king.
'Mortal', quoth he, 'I charge thee to engage
Thy pen to scourge the humours of this age.
Thou shalt not need to make a long relation,
What thou canst get by tedious observation.

100 humorist] (1) person given to fancies; (2) humoralist (believer in the pathology of humours)   tedious] long; painful

Fairies have left their low infernal places,
The several forms of humours in their faces.
Take what and where thou list while it is night;
But send them home before the day be light.'

(1605)

101 *Epigram XXIX*

A GENTLEWOMAN of the dealing trade
Procured her own sweet picture to be made;
Which being done, she from her word did slip,
And would not pay full due for workmanship.
The painter swore she ne'er should have it so:
She bade him keep it, and away did go.
He, choleric and mighty discontent,
Straight took his pencil, and to work he went,
Making the dog she held a grim cat's face;
And hung it in his shop, to her disgrace.
Some of her friends, that saw it, to her went
In jesting manner, asking what she meant,
To have her picture hang where gazers swarm,
Holding a filthy cat within her arm?
She, in a shameful heat, in haste did hie,
The painter to content and satisfy,
Right glad to give a French crown for his pain,
To turn her cat into a dog again.

(1600)

THOMAS DEKKER

1572?–1632

from *The Sun's Darling* (102–103)

102 *Song*

HAYMAKERS, rakers, reapers and mowers,
  Wait on your summer queen;
Dress up with musk-rose her eglantine bowers,
  Daffadils strew the green;

100 humours] temperaments

102 Procured] Commissioned pencil] brush

Sing, dance and play:
'Tis holy day.
  The sun does bravely shine
  On our ears of corn.
Rich as a pearl
Comes every girl,
  This is mine, this is mine, this is mine;
Let us die, ere away they be borne.

Bow to the sun, to our queen, and that fair one
  Come to behold our sports;
Each bonny lass here is counted a rare one,
  As those in princes' courts.
    These and we
    With country glee
      Will teach the woods to resound,
      And the hills with echoes hollow:
    Skipping lambs
    Their bleating dams
      'Mongst kids shall trip it round,
    For joy thus our wenches we follow.

Wind, jolly huntsmen, your neat bugles shrilly,
  Hounds make a lusty cry;
Spring up, you falconers, the partridges freely,
  Then let your brave hawks fly.
    Horses amain
    Over ridge, over plain,
      The dogs have the stag in chase;
      'Tis a sport to content a king.
    So ho ho, through the skies
    How the proud bird flies,
      And sousing kills with a grace;
    Now the deer falls, hark how they ring.

(1656; a. 1624)

103 [*Folly's Song*]

I WILL roar and squander,
  Cozen, and be drunk too;
I will maintain my pander,
  Keep my horse, and punk too;

Spring] Cause to rise from cover So ho ho] hunting-call sousing] swooping

103 punk] prostitute

Brawl and scuffle,
Shift and shuffle,
Swagger in my potmeals:
Damn-me's rank with,
Do mad prank with
Roaring boys and oatmeals.

Pox, a time, I care not,
Being past 'tis nothing:
I'll be free and spare not.
Sorrows are life's loathing:
Melancholy
Is but folly,
Mirth and youth are plotters.
Time go hang thee,
I will bang thee
Though I die in totters.

(1656; a. 1624)

JOHN DONNE
1572–1631

104 *Elegy IX: The Autumnal*

No spring nor summer beauty hath such grace
As I have seen in one autumnal face.
Young beauties force your love, and that's a rape;
This doth but counsel, yet you cannot scape.
If 'twere a shame to love, here 'twere no shame:
Affections here take reverence's name.
Were her first years the Golden Age? That's true;
But now she's gold oft tried, and ever new.
That was her torrid and inflaming time,
This is her tolerable tropic clime.

Fair eyes, who asks more heat than comes from hence,
He in a fever wishes pestilence.

Shift] Devise a stratagem potmeals] drinking bouts Damn-me's] Lords Roaring boys] Insolent bloods oatmeals] swaggerers a time] at times bang] defeat totters] tatters

104 *Autumnal*] Past the prime torrid] equatorial tolerable . . . clime] climate at the temperate edge of the torrid zone

Call not these wrinkles, graves; if graves they were,
  They were Love's graves; or else he is no where.
Yet lies not Love dead here, but here doth sit
  Vowed to this trench like an anachorit.
And here, till hers, which must be his death, come,
  He doth not dig a grave, but build a tomb.
Here dwells he: though he sojourn everywhere,
  In progress, yet his standing house is here.
Here, where still evening is, not noon, nor night;
  Where no voluptuousness, yet all delight.
In all her words, unto all hearers fit:
  You may at revels, you at council, sit.
This is Love's timber, youth his underwood;
  There he, as wine in June, enrages blood,
Which then comes seasonabliest, when our taste
  And appetite to other things is past.
Xerxes' strange Lydian love, the platan tree,
  Was loved for age, none being so large as she,
Or else because, being young, nature did bless
  Her youth with age's glory, barrenness.
If we love things long sought, age is a thing
  Which we are fifty years in compassing.
If transitory things, which soon decay,
  Age must be loveliest at the latest day.
But name not winter-faces, whose skin's slack;
  Lank, as an unthrift's purse; but a soul's sack;
Whose eyes seek light within, for all here's shade;
  Whose mouths are holes, rather worn out than made;
Whose every tooth to a several place is gone,
  To vex their souls at Resurrection;
Name not these living death's-heads unto me,
  For these, not anciénts, but antiques be.
I hate extremes; yet I had rather stay
  With tombs than cradles, to wear out a day.
Since such love's natural lation is, may still
  My love descend, and journey down the hill;
Not panting after growing beauties, so,
  I shall ebb on with them, who homeward go.

(1633)

anachorit] anchorite   In progress] On state visits or tours   standing house] permanent dwelling   youth his] youth's   underwood] brushwood, quickly burnt out   Xerxes' ... love] (see endnote)   being] although   anciénts] seniors, elders   antiques] ancients, people of ancient times   lation] movement (astrological)

105 *Antiquary*

IF, in his study, he hath so much care
To hang all old strange things, let his wife beware.

(1633)

106 *The Bait*

COME live with me, and be my love,
And we will some new pleasures prove
Of golden sands and crystal brooks,
With silken lines and silver hooks.

There will the river whispering run
Warmed by thy eyes, more than the sun.
And there the'enamoured fish will stay,
Begging themselves they may betray.

When thou wilt swim in that live bath,
Each fish, which every channel hath,
Will amorously to thee swim,
Gladder to catch thee, than thou him.

If thou, to be so seen, be'st loth,
By sun, or moon, thou darkenest both,
And if myself have leave to see,
I need not their light, having thee.

Let others freeze with angling reeds,
And cut their legs with shells and weeds,
Or treacherously poor fish beset,
With strangling snare or windowy net:

Let coarse bold hands, from slimy nest
The bedded fish in banks out-wrest,
Or curious traitors, sleavesilk flies
Bewitch poor fishes' wandering eyes.

For thee, thou need'st no such deceit,
For thou thyself art thine own bait:
That fish, that is not catched thereby,
Alas, is wiser far than I.

(1633)

106 windowy net] trammel-net   curious] artful   sleavesilk flies] flies made of sleaved (unravelled) silk

107

The Canonization

FOR God's sake hold your tongue, and let me love;
  Or chide my palsy, or my gout,
My five grey hairs or ruined fortune flout,
With wealth your state, your mind with arts improve,
  Take you a course, get you a place,
  Observe his honour, or his grace,
Or the king's real, or his stampèd face
  Contémplate; what you will, approve,
    So you will let me love.

Alas, alas, who's injured by my love?
  What merchant's ships have my sighs drowned?
Who says my tears have overflowed his ground?
When did my colds a forward spring remove?
  When did the heats which my veins fill
  Add one more to the plaguy bill?
Soldiers find wars, and lawyers find out still
  Litigious men, which quarrels move,
    Though she and I do love.

Call us what you will, we're made such by love;
  Call her one, me another fly:
We're tapers too, and at our own cost die.
And we in us find the eagle and the dove;
  The phoenix riddle hath more wit
  By us: we two being one, are it;
So to one neutral thing both sexes fit.
  We die and rise the same, and prove
    Mysterious by this love.

We can die by it, if not live by love,
  And if unfit for tombs and hearse
Our legend be, it will be fit for verse;
And if no piece of chronicle we prove,
  We'll build in sonnets pretty rooms;
  As well a well wrought urn becomes
The greatest ashes, as half-acre tombs;
  And by these hymns, all shall approve
    Us canonized for love.

Take . . . course] Follow a purposeful line of advancement   Observe . . . grace] Court a secular or ecclesiastical patron   real] (1) real; (2) royal; (3) Spanish coin   approve] try   plaguy bill] list of plague victims   still] always   fly] moth   die] climax (believed life-curtailing)   phoenix] mythical unique bird, periodically regenerated from its own ashes   live] make a living   rooms] (playing on Italian *stanza*, 'room')

And thus invoke us: 'You whom reverend love
Made one another's hermitage;
You, to whom love was peace, that now is rage;
Who did the whole world's soul contract, and drove
Into the glasses of your eyes
(So made such mirrors, and such spies,
That they did all to you epitomize)
Countries, towns, courts: beg from above
A pattern of your love!'

(1633)

108 *The Damp*

When I am dead, and doctors know not why,
And my friends' curiosity
Will have me cut up to survey each part,
When they shall find your picture in my heart,
You think a sudden damp of love
Will through all their senses move,
And work on them as me, and so prefer
Your murder, to the name of massacre.

Poor victories! But if you dare be brave,
And pleasure in your conquest have,
First kill th' enormous giant, your disdain;
And let th' enchantress honour next be slain;
And like a Goth and Vandal rise,
Deface records, and histories
Of your own arts and triumphs over men,
And without such advantage kill me then.

For I could muster up as well as you
My giants, and my witches too,
Which are vast constancy, and secretness;
But these I neither look for, nor profess.
Kill me as woman, let me die
As a mere man: do you but try
Your passive valour, and you shall find then,
Naked you have odds enough of any man.

(1633)

rage] passion contract] condense; concentrate

108 damp] noxious vapour prefer] promote Goth . . . Vandal] the barbarians that at Rome's fall erased records of triumphs Kill . . . die] (the sexual *double entendre* was commonplace) passive valour] courage under attack

109 *The Good Morrow*

I WONDER by my troth, what thou and I
Did, till we loved? Were we not weaned till then,
But sucked on country pleasures, childishly?
Or snorted we in the seven sleepers' den?
'Twas so; but this, all pleasures fancies be.
If ever any beauty I did see,
Which I desired, and got, 'twas but a dream of thee.

And now good morrow to our waking souls,
Which watch not one another out of fear;
For love, all love of other sights controls,
And makes one little room, an every where.
Let sea-discoverers to new worlds have gone,
Let maps to others, worlds on worlds have shown:
Let us possess one world, each hath one, and is one.

My face in thine eye, thine in mine appears,
And true plain hearts do in the faces rest:
Where can we find two better hemispheres
Without sharp north, without declining west?
Whatever dies, was not mixed equally;
If our two loves be one, or, thou and I
Love so alike that none do slacken, none can die.

(1633)

110 *The Indifferent*

I CAN love both fair and brown,
Her whom abundance melts, and her whom want betrays,
Her who loves loneness best, and her who masks and plays,
Her whom the country formed, and whom the town,
Her who believes, and her who tries,
Her who still weeps with spongy eyes,
And her who is dry cork, and never cries;
I can love her, and her, and you and you,
I can love any, so she be not true.

country pleasures] (1) infantile pleasures of being wet-nursed in the country; (2) crude sexual pleasures   seven sleepers' den] see endnote   but this] except for this   sharp . . . west] (the angle of declination, acute towards the north pole, declines to the west)   mixed equally] (life depended on proportionate mixture of the four elements)

110 masks] takes part in masquerades   plays] flirts   tries] tests

Will no other vice content you?
Will it not serve your turn to do, as did your mothers?
Have you old vices spent, and now would find out others?
Or doth a fear, that men are true, torment you?
Oh we are not, be not you so,
Let me, and do you, twenty know.
Rob me, but bind me not, and let me go.
Must I, who came to travail thorough you,
Grow your fixed subject, because you are true?

Venus heard me sigh this song,
And by love's sweetest part, variety, she swore,
She heard not this till now; and it should be so no more.
She went, examined, and returned ere long,
And said, 'Alas, some two or three
Poor heretics in love there be,
Which think to stablish dangerous constancy.
But I have told them, "Since you will be true,
You shall be true to them, who're false to you." '

(1633)

111 *Lovers' Infiniteness*

If yet I have not all thy love,
Dear, I shall never have it all;
I cannot breathe one other sigh, to move,
Nor can entreat one other tear to fall.
And all my treasure, which should purchase thee,
Sighs, tears, and oaths, and letters, I have spent,
Yet no more can be due to me
Than at the bargain made was meant.
If then thy gift of love were partial,
That some to me, some should to others fall,
Dear, I shall never have it all.

Or if then thou gavest me all,
All was but all which thou hadst then;
But if in thy heart, since, there be or shall
New love created be, by other men,

travail] (1) work hard; (2) trouble; (3) travel stablish] establish

111 gift . . . partial] transference of property in specific parts (legal)

Which have their stocks entire, and can in tears,
  In sighs, in oaths, and letters outbid me,
This new love may beget new fears,
  For this love was not vowed by thee.
And yet it was, thy gift being general:
The ground, thy heart, is mine; whatever shall
    Grow there, dear, I should have it all.

Yet I would not have all yet:
  He that hath all can have no more,
And since my love doth every day admit
  New growth, thou shouldst have new rewards in store;
Thou canst not every day give me thy heart,
  If thou canst give it, then thou never gav'st it:
Love's riddles are, that though thy heart depart,
  It stays at home, and thou with losing sav'st it:
But we will have a way more liberal,
Than changing hearts, to join them, so we shall
    Be one, and one another's all.

(1633)

112 *Love's Growth*

I SCARCE believe my love to be so pure
  As I had thought it was,
  Because it doth endure
Vicissitude, and season, as the grass;
Methinks I lied all winter, when I swore
My love was infinite, if spring make it more.
But if this medicine, love, which cures all sorrow
With more, not only be no quintessénce,
But mixed of all stuffs, paining soul, or sense,
And of the sun his working vigour borrow,
Love's not so pure and abstract as they use
To say, which have no mistress but their Muse,
But as all else, being elemented too,
Love sometimes would contémplate, sometimes do.

gift ... general] transference of the entire property   liberal] generous   changing] exchanging

112 doth ... season] suffers seasonal change (unlike unmixed things)   cures ... more] i.e. by homeopathy   quintessénce] pure unmixed essence, above the four elements

And yet not greater, but more eminent,
Love by the spring is grown;
As, in the firmament,
Stars by the sun are not enlarged, but shown,
Gentle love deeds, as blossoms on a bough,
From love's awakened root do bud out now.
If, as in water stirred more circles be
Produced by one, love such additions take,
Those like so many spheres, but one heaven make;
For, they are all concentric unto thee,
And though each spring do add to love new heat,
As princes do in times of action get
New taxes, and remit them not in peace,
No winter shall abate the spring's increase.

(1633)

113 *A Nocturnal upon S. Lucy's Day, Being the Shortest Day*

'TIS the year's midnight, and it is the day's,
Lucy's, who scarce seven hours herself unmasks;
The sun is spent, and now his flasks
Send forth light squibs, no constant rays;
The world's whole sap is sunk:
The general balm th' hydroptic earth hath drunk,
Whither, as to the bed's-feet, life is shrunk,
Dead and interred; yet all these seem to laugh,
Compared with me, who am their epitaph.

Study me then, you who shall lovers be
At the next world, that is, at the next spring:
For I am a very dead thing,
In whom love wrought new alchemy.
For his art did express
A quintessénce even from nothingness,
From dull privations, and lean emptiness:
He ruined me, and I am re-begot
Of absence, darkness, death; things which are not.

enlarged . . . shown] (some thought stars reflected sunlight, rather than being 'enlarged' by it) spheres] celestial spheres (in whose circumferences planets moved but] only

113 *S. Lucy's Day*] (see endnote) year's midnight] winter solstice balm] preservative essence of a living body (medical) hydroptic] unnaturally thirsty, as with dropsy new alchemy] alchemy in reverse express] extract

All others, from all things, draw all that's good,
Life, soul, form, spirit, whence they being have;
  I, by love's limbeck, am the grave
  Of all that's nothing. Oft a flood
    Have we two wept, and so
Drowned the whole world, us two; oft did we grow
To be two chaoses, when we did show
Care to aught else; and often absences
Withdrew our souls, and made us carcases.

But I am by her death (which word wrongs her)
Of the first nothing, the elixir grown;
  Were I a man, that I were one,
  I needs must know; I should prefer,
    If I were any beast,
Some ends, some means; yea plants, yea stones detest,
And love; all, all some properties invest;
If I an ordinary nothing were,
As shadow, a light, and body must be here.

But I am none; nor will my sun renew.
You lovers, for whose sake the lesser sun
  At this time to the Goat is run
  To fetch new lust and give it you,
    Enjoy your summer all;
Since she enjoys her long night's festival,
Let me prepare towards her, and let me call
This hour her vigil, and her eve, since this
Both the year's, and the day's deep midnight is.

(1633)

114 *The Paradox*

No lover saith, I love, nor any other
  Can judge a perfect lover;
He thinks that else none can, nor will agree
  That any loves but he:
I cannot say I loved, for who can say
  He was killed yesterday?
Love with excess of heat, more young than old,
  Death kills with too much cold;

Life . . . spirit] (see endnote) limbeck] alembic (gourd-shaped retort, for alchemic distillation) Of . . . elixir] extract or principle of nothing, in the new alchemy prefer] promote stones . . . love] experience affinity or repulsion (as early scientists believed) Goat] Capricorn (which Sol entered at the solstice)

114 else none] no one else

We die but once, and who loved last did die,
He that saith twice, doth lie:
For though he seem to move, and stir a while,
It doth the sense beguile.
Such life is like the light which bideth yet
When the light's life is set,
Or like the heat, which fire in solid matter
Leaves behind, two hours after.
Once I loved and died; and am now become
Mine epitaph and tomb.
Here dead men speak their last, and so do I;
Love-slain, lo, here I lie.

(1633)

115 *The Prohibition*

TAKE heed of loving me:
At least remember, I forbade it thee;
Not that I shall repair my' unthrifty waste
Of breath and blood upon thy sighs and tears,
By being to thee then what to me thou wast;
But, so great joy our life at once outwears.
Then, lest thy love, by my death, frustrate be,
If thou love me, take heed of loving me.

Take heed of hating me,
Or too much triumph in the victory.
Not that I shall be mine own officer,
And hate with hate again retaliate;
But thou wilt lose the style of conqueror,
If I, thy conquest, perish by thy hate.
Then, lest my being nothing lessen thee,
If thou hate me, take heed of hating me.

Yet, love and hate me too,
So, these extremes shall ne'er their office do:
Love me, that I may die the gentler way;
Hate me, because thy love's too great for me;
Or let these two, themselves, not me decay;
So shall I live, thy stage not triumph be.
Lest thou thy love and hate and me undo,
To let me live, Oh love and hate me too.

(1633)

115 officer] executioner; constable lose ... conqueror] not have a defeated prisoner to accompany your triumph die . . . way] (1) die by excess of joy; (2) climax

116 *The Relic*

WHEN my grave is broke up again
  Some second guest to entertain,
  (For graves have learned that woman-head
  To be to more than one a bed)
      And he that digs it, spies
A bracelet of bright hair about the bone,
      Will he not let us alone,
And think that there a loving couple lies,
Who thought that this device might be some way
To make their souls, at the last busy day,
Meet at this grave, and make a little stay?

  If this fall in a time, or land,
  Where mis-devotion doth command,
  Then he that digs us up will bring
  Us to the Bishop and the King
      To make us relics; then
Thou shalt be a Mary Magdalen, and I
      A something else thereby;
All women shall adore us, and some men;
And since at such time, miracles are sought,
I would have that age by this paper taught
What miracles we harmless lovers wrought.

  First, we loved well and faithfully,
  Yet knew not what we loved, nor why;
  Difference of sex no more we knew
  Than our guardian angels do;
      Coming and going, we
Perchance might kiss, but not between those meals;
      Our hands ne'er touched the seals
Which nature, injured by late law, sets free:
These miracles we did; but now alas,
All measure and all language I should pass,
Should I tell what a miracle she was.

(1633)

woman-head] womanliness; womanhood   bright] fair   mis-devotion] misdirected devotion (a term D. used for prayers to saints)   something else] i.e. Jesus Christ   harmless] innocent; innocuous

117

Song

Go, and catch a falling star,
   Get with child a mandrake root,
Tell me where all past years are
   Or who cleft the Devil's foot,
Teach me to hear mermaids singing
   Or to keep off envy's stinging,
         And find
         What wind
Serves to advance an honest mind.

If thou be'st born to strange sights,
   Things invisible to see,
Ride ten thousand days and nights,
   Till age snow white hairs on thee,
Thou, when thou return'st, wilt tell me
All strange wonders that befell thee,
         And swear
         No where
Lives a woman true, and fair.

If thou findst one, let me know:
   Such a pilgrimage were sweet;
Yet do not, I would not go,
   Though at next door we might meet,
Though she were true when you met her,
And last till you write your letter,
         Yet she
         Will be
False, ere I come, to two, or three.

(1633)

118

The Sun Rising

Busy old fool, unruly sun,
      Why dost thou thus
Through windows and through curtains call on us?
Must to thy motions lovers' seasons run?

mandrake] forked plant (thought to scream when uprooted)

Saucy pedantic wretch, go chide
Late schoolboys and sour prentices;
Go tell court huntsmen that the king will ride;
Call country ants to harvest offices:
Love, all alike, no season knows, nor clime,
Nor hours, days, months, which are the rags of time.

Thy beams, so reverend and strong
Why shouldst thou think?
I could eclipse and cloud them with a wink,
But that I would not lose her sight so long:
If her eyes have not blinded thine,
Look, and tomorrow late tell me
Whether both th' Indias of spice and mine
Be where thou leftst them, or lie here with me.
Ask for those kings whom thou sawst yesterday,
And thou shalt hear, all here in one bed lay.

She's all states, and all princes, I;
Nothing else is.
Princes do but play us; compared to this,
All honour's mimic; all wealth alchemy.
Thou, sun, art half as happy as we,
In that the world's contracted thus;
Thine age asks ease, and since thy duties be
To warm the world, that's done in warming us.
Shine here to us, and thou art everywhere:
This bed thy centre is, these walls, thy sphere.

(1633)

119 *The Triple Fool*

I AM two fools, I know:
For loving, and for saying so
In whining poetry.
But where's that wise man that would not be I,
If she would not deny?
Then as th' earth's inward narrow crookèd lanes
Do purge sea water's fretful salt away,
I thought, if I could draw my pains
Through rhyme's vexation, I should them allay.
Grief brought to numbers cannot be so fierce,
For he tames it that fetters it in verse.

country ants] prudent industrious farmers   Indias . . . mine] East Indies (source of spice) and West (of gold)   alchemy] pursuit of wealth

119 numbers] poetic form

But when I have done so,
Some man, his art and voice to show,
Doth set and sing my pain,
And, by delighting many, frees again
Grief, which verse did restrain.
To love and grief tribute of verse belongs
(But not of such as pleases when 'tis read:
Both are increasèd by such songs);
For both their triumphs so are publishèd,
And I, which was two fools, do so grow three:
Who are a little wise, the best fools be.

(1633)

120 *A Valediction: Forbidding Mourning*

As virtuous men pass mildly away,
And whisper to their souls to go,
Whilst some of their sad friends do say,
The breath goes now, and some say, no:

So let us melt, and make no noise,
No tear-floods, nor sigh-tempests move,
'Twere profanation of our joys
To tell the laity our love.

Moving of th' Earth brings harms and fears,
Men reckon what it did and meant;
But trepidation of the spheres,
Though greater far, is innocent.

Dull sublunary lovers' love
(Whose soul is sense) cannot admit
Absence, because it doth remove
Those things which elemented it.

But we by a love so much refined
That ourselves know not what it is,
Inter-assurèd of the mind,
Care less, eyes, lips, and hands to miss.

120 *Valediction*] (see endnote) melt] vanish Moving . . . Earth] An earthquake trepidation] movement invented to account for precession of the equinoxes, in the Ptolemaic planetary system sublunary] i.e. mortal and corruptible Those . . . elemented it] things of the body with its four elements) refined] (alchemically, to quintessential purity)

Our two souls therefore, which are one,
   Though I must go, endure not yet
A breach, but an expansion,
   Like gold to aery thinness beat.

If they be two, they are two so
   As stiff twin compasses are two;
Thy soul the fixed foot makes no show
   To move, but doth, if th'other do.

And though it in the centre sit,
   Yet when the other far doth roam
It leans, and hearkens after it,
   And grows erect as that comes home.

Such wilt thou be to me, who must
   Like th' other foot obliquely run;
Thy firmness makes my circle just,
   And makes me end where I begun.

(1633)

121 *A Valediction: Of Weeping*

LET me pour forth
My tears before thy face, whilst I stay here;
For thy face coins them, and thy stamp they bear,
And by this mintage they are something worth,
For thus they be
Pregnant of thee.
Fruits of much grief they are, emblems of more:
When a tear falls, that thou falls which it bore;
So thou and I are nothing then, when on a diverse shore.

On a round ball
A workman that hath copies by can lay
An Europe, Afric, and an Asia,
And quickly make that which was nothing, all;
So doth each tear,
Which thee doth wear,
A globe, yea world, by that impression grow,
Till thy tears mixed with mine do overflow
This world, by waters sent from thee, my heaven dissolvèd so.

stiff] (1) hard to move; (2) steadfast, constant   compasses] dividers (emblem of constancy)   makes . . . begun] (see endnote)

121 stamp] reflected image   all] the speaker's whole world   impression] (1) atmospheric disturbance; (2) stamping of printed world-images in manufacture of terrestrial globes

O more than moon,
Draw not up seas to drown me in thy sphere;
Weep me not dead in thine arms, but forbear
To teach the sea what it may do too soon;
Let not the wind
Example find,
To do me more harm than it purposeth:
Since thou and I sigh one another's breath,
Whoe'er sighs most is cruellest, and hastes the other's death.

(1633)

122 *Woman's Constancy*

Now thou hast loved me one whole day,
Tomorrow, when thou leav'st, what wilt thou say?
Wilt thou then antedate some new made vow?
Or say that now
We are not just those persons, which we were?
Or, that oaths made in reverential fear
Of Love and his wrath, any may forswear?
Or, as true deaths, true marriages untie,
So lovers' contracts, images of those,
Bind but till sleep, death's image, them unloose?
Or, your own end to justify,
For having purposed change and falsehood, you
Can have no way but falsehood to be true?
Vain lunatic, against these scapes I could
Dispute, and conquer, if I would;
Which I abstain to do,
For by tomorrow I may think so too.

(1633)

123 *To the Countess of Bedford*

Madam,
Reason is our soul's left hand, faith her right:
By these we reach divinity, that's you;
Their loves, who have the blessing of your light,
Grew from their reason, mine from far faith grew.

Draw ... sphere] Do not use your power over tear-floods to draw them up to your orbit

122 scapes] loopholes in the contract

123 Reason ... grew] I love you, without our meeting

But as, although a squint lefthandedness
  Be ungracious, yet we cannot want that hand,
So would I, not to increase, but to express
  My faith, as I believe, so understand.

Therefore I study you first in your saints,
  Those friends whom your election glorifies;
Then in your deeds, accesses, and restraints,
  And what you read, and what yourself devise.

But soon, the reasons why you are loved by all
  Grow infinite, and so pass reason's reach;
Then back again to implicit faith I fall,
  And rest on what the catholic voice doth teach,

That you are good: and not one heretic
  Denies it: if he did, yet you are so.
For rocks which high-topped and deep-rooted stick
  Waves wash, not undermine nor overthrow.

In everything there naturally grows
  A balsamum to keep it fresh and new,
If 'twere not injured by extrinsic blows;
  Your birth and beauty are this balm in you.

But you of learning and religion,
  And virtue, and such ingredients, have made
A mithridate, whose operation
  Keeps off or cures what can be done or said.

Yet, this is not your physic but your food,
  A diet fit for you; for you are here
The first good angel, since the world's frame stood,
  That ever did in woman's shape appear.

squint lefthandedness] (1) awkwardness; (2) sceptical reliance on reason   cannot want] need   election] selection as an elect (theological)   accesses] favours granted   restraints] reserves; prohibitions   devise] invent; write   balsamum] individual balm preserving each living creature from decay (Paracelsian medicine)   extrinsic blows] infection from without   mithridate] antidote   physic] medicine

Since you are then God's masterpiece, and so
  His factor for our loves, do as you do,
Make your return home gracious; and bestow
  This life on that; so make one life of two.
    For so God help me, I would not miss you there
    For all the good which you can do me here.

(1633; wr. 1609–14?)

124 *An Hymn to the Saints, and to Marquis Hamilton*

Whether that soul which now comes up to you
Fill any former rank or make a new,
Whether it take a name named there before
Or be a name itself, and order more
Than was in heaven till now; (for may not he
Be so, if every several angel be
A kind alone?) what ever order grow
Greater by him in heaven, we do not so;
One of your orders grows by his access;
But, by his loss grow all our orders less;
The name of father, master, friend, the name
Of subject and of prince, in one are lame;
Fair mirth is damped, and conversation black,
The household widowed, and the garter slack;
The Chapel wants an ear; Council a tongue;
Story, a theme; and music lacks a song.
Blessed order that hath him, the loss of him
Gangrened all orders here; all lost a limb.
Never made body such haste to confess
What a soul was; all former comeliness
Fled in a minute, when the soul was gone,
And, having lost that beauty, would have none:
So fell our monasteries, in one instant grown
Not to less houses but to heaps of stone;
So sent this body that fair form it wore
Unto the sphere of forms, and doth (before

factor] agent home] i.e. to heaven make . . . two] (1) add your earthly life to the eternal; (2) unite your own life with mine

124 order] rank in the angelic hierarchy (which included saints) access] admittance; addition household] i.e. royal household garter] order of Garter knights Council] Privy Council confess] testify one instant] i.e. after Henry VIII dissolved the English monasteries sphere of forms] the celestial threshold of life, where souls awaited incarnation soul . . . stone] fame must fill the grave (the body's fair form having ascended)

His soul shall fill up his sepulchral stone)
Anticipate a resurrectïon;
For, as in his fame, now, his soul is here,
So in the form thereof his body's there.
And if, fair soul, not with first innocents
Thy station be, but with the penitents
(And who shall dare to ask then when I am
Dyed scarlet in the blood of that pure Lamb
Whether that colour which is scarlet then
Were black or white before in eyes of men?),
When thou rememberest what sins thou didst find
Amongst those many friends now left behind,
And seest such sinners as they are, with thee
Got thither by repentance, let it be
Thy wish to wish all there, to wish them clean;
Wish him a David, her a Magdalen.

(1633)

125 from *The First Anniversary: An Anatomy of the World*

AND new philosophy calls all in doubt,
The element of fire is quite put out;
The sun is lost, and th' Earth, and no man's wit
Can well direct him where to look for it.
And freely men confess that this world's spent,
When in the planets and the firmament
They seek so many new: they see that this
Is crumbled out again t' his atomies.
'Tis all in pieces, all coherence gone;
All just supply, and all relation:
Prince, subject, father, son, are things forgot,
For every man alone thinks he hath got
To be a phoenix, and that there can be
None of that kind, of which he is, but he.
This is the world's condition now, and now
She that should all parts to reunion bow,
She that had all magnetic force alone,
To draw and fasten sundered parts in one;
She whom wise nature had invented then
When she observed that every sort of men
Did in their voyage in this world's sea stray,
And needed a new compass for their way;

124 first innocents] those who died before committing actual sin David . . . Magdalen] (penitent sinners)

She that was best, and first original
Of all fair copies; and the general
Steward to fate; she whose rich eyes and breast
Gilt the West Indies, and perfúmed the East;
Whose having breathed in this world did bestow
Spice on those isles, and bade them still smell so;
And that rich Indie which doth gold inter
Is but as single money coined from her:
She to whom this world must itself refer,
As suburbs, or the microcosm of her:
She, she is dead; she's dead: when thou knowst this,
Thou knowst how lame a cripple this world is.

(1611)

from *The Second Anniversary: Of the Progress of the Soul* (126–127)

126 WE now lament not, but congratulate.
She, to whom all this world was but a stage,
Where all sat hearkening how her youthful age
Should be employed, because in all she did,
Some figure of the Golden Times was hid;
Who could not lack, whate'er this world could give,
Because she was the form that made it live;
Nor could complain that this world was unfit
To be stayed in, then when she was in it;
She that first tried indifferent desires
By virtue, and virtue by religious fires,
She to whose person paradise adhered,
As courts to princes, she whose eyes ensphered
Star-light enough to' have made the south control
(Had she been there) the star-full northern pole,
She, she is gone; she's gone; when thou knowst this,
What fragmentary rubbish this world is
Thou knowst, and that it is not worth a thought;
He honours it too much that thinks it naught.
Think then, my soul, that death is but a groom
Which brings a taper to the outward room,
Whence thou spiest first a little glimmering light,
And after brings it nearer to thy sight:

single money] small change

126 hearkening] waiting to know figure] symbol, type Golden Times] the Golden Age before the Fall form] soul tried] separated, selected indifferent] morally neutral ensphered] had on their surfaces; were the orbits of control] excel; dominate

For such approaches doth heaven make in death.
Think thyself labouring now with broken breath,
And think those broken and soft notes to be
Division, and thy happiest harmony.
Think thee laid on thy death-bed, loose and slack;
And think that but unbinding of a pack,
To take one precious thing, thy soul, from thence.
Think thyself parched with fever's violence,
Anger thine ague more, by calling it
Thy physic: chide the slackness of the fit.
Think that thou hearst thy knell, and think no more,
But that, as bells called thee to church before,
So this, to the Triumphant Church calls thee.
Think Satan's sergeants round about thee be,
And think that but for legacies they thrust;
Give one thy pride, to another give thy lust:
Give them those sins which they gave thee before,
And trust th' immaculate blood to wash thy score.
Think thy friends weeping round, and think that they
Weep but because they go not yet thy way.
Think that they close thine eyes, and think in this
That they confess much in the world amiss,
Who dare not trust a dead man's eye with that
Which they from God and angels cover not.
Think that they shroud thee up, and think from thence
They reinvest thee in white innocence.
Think that thy body rots, and (if so low,
Thy soul exalted so, thy thoughts can go)
Think thee a prince, who of themselves create
Worms which insensibly devour their state.
Think that they bury thee, and think that rite
Lays thee to sleep but a Saint Lucy's night.

(1612)

127 WE see in authors, too stiff to recant,
A hundred controvérsies of an ant;
And yet one watches, starves, freezes, and sweats,
To know but catechisms and alphabets

Division] (1) Melody of short notes; (2) Separation (of soul from body) physic] medicine slackness] (1) remissness; (2) weakness Triumphant Church] Church in glory white] sinless so low] i.e. as an earthly prince create] invest with rank state] (1) realm's prosperity; (2) dignity; (3) physical constitution Saint . . . night] (longest of the year)

127 stiff] obstinate

Of unconcerning things, matters of fact;
How others on our stage their parts did act;
What Caesar did, yea, and what Cicero said.
Why grass is green, or why our blood is red,
Are mysteries which none have reached unto.
In this low form, poor soul, what wilt thou do?
When wilt thou shake off this pedantery,
Of being taught by sense and fantasy?
Thou lookst through spectacles; small things seem great
Below; but up unto the watch-tower get,
And see all things despoiled of fallacies:
Thou shalt not peep through lattices of eyes,
Nor hear through labyrinths of ears, nor learn
By circuit or collections to discern.
In heaven thou straight knowst all, concerning it,
And what concerns it not, shalt straight forget.

(1612)

from *Divine Meditations* (128–139)

128 *Sonnet I*

THOU hast made me, and shall thy work decay?
Repair me now, for now mine end doth haste,
I run to death, and death meets me as fast,
And all my pleasures are like yesterday,
I dare not move my dim eyes any way,
Despair behind, and death before doth cast
Such terror, and my feeble flesh doth waste
By sin in it, which it towards hell doth weigh;
Only thou art above, and when towards thee
By thy leave I can look, I rise again;
But our old subtle foe so tempteth me
That not one hour I can myself sustain;
Thy Grace may wing me to prevent his art,
And thou like adamant draw mine iron heart.

(1635)

unconcerning] indifferent low form] inferior state of ignorance (as of schoolchildren in a low class) fantasy] the faculty that interpreted sense data circuit] roundabout process; reasoning collections] (1) inferences; (2) summaries (of tradition)

128 prevent] forestall adamant] (1) lodestone, magnet; (2) diamond (emblem of faith)

129 *Sonnet VII*

AT the round Earth's imagined corners, blow
Your trumpets, angels, and arise, arise
From death, you numberless infinities
Of souls, and to your scattered bodies go,
All whom the flood did, and fire shall o'erthrow,
All whom war, dearth, age, agues, tyrannies,
Despair, law, chance, hath slain, and you whose eyes
Shall behold God, and never taste death's woe.
But let them sleep, Lord, and me mourn a space,
For, if above all these my sins abound,
'Tis late to ask abundance of thy grace
When we are there; here on this lowly ground
Teach me how to repent; for that's as good
As if thou' hadst sealed my pardon with thy blood.

(1633)

130 *Sonnet X*

DEATH be not proud, though some have callèd thee
Mighty and dreadful, for thou art not so;
For those whom thou thinkst thou dost overthrow
Die not, poor death, nor yet canst thou kill me;
From rest and sleep, which but thy pictures be,
Much pleasure, then from thee, much more must flow,
And soonest our best men with thee do go,
Rest of their bones, and soul's delivery.
Thou art slave to fate, chance, kings, and desperate men,
And dost with poison, war, and sickness dwell;
And poppy or charms can make us sleep as well
And better than thy stroke; why swellst thou then?
One short sleep past, we wake eternally,
And death shall be no more: death thou shalt die.

(1633)

imagined] i.e. in maps, and in Rev. 7: 1

130 swellst] be arrogant

131 *Sonnet XIII*

WHAT if this present were the world's last night?
Mark in my heart, O soul, where thou dost dwell,
The picture of Christ crucified, and tell
Whether that countenance can thee affright:
Tears in his eyes quench the amazing light,
Blood fills his frowns, which from his pierced head fell,
And can that tongue adjudge thee unto hell,
Which prayed forgiveness for his foes' fierce spite?
No, no; but as in my idolatry
I said to all my profane mistresses,
Beauty, of pity, foulness only is
A sign of rigour: so I say to thee,
To wicked spirits are horrid shapes assigned,
This beauteous form assures a piteous mind.

(1633)

132 *Sonnet XIV*

BATTER my heart, three-personed God; for you
As yet but knock, breathe, shine, and seek to mend;
That I may rise, and stand, o'erthrow me, and bend
Your force, to break, blow, burn, and make me new.
I, like an usurped town to another due,
Labour to admit you, but oh, to no end:
Reason your viceroy in me, me should defend,
But is captived, and proves weak or untrue;
Yet dearly'I love you, and would be loved fain,
But am betrothed unto your enemy:
Divorce me, untie, or break that knot again,
Take me to you, imprison me, for I
Except you enthral me, never shall be free,
Nor ever chaste, except you ravish me.

(1633)

amazing] dreadful adjudge] sentence assures] guarantees

132 knock] (1) test by tapping; (2) beat the breast in contrition due] belonging by right untie . . . again] annul or dissolve our bond enthral] enslave

133 *Sonnet XVII*

SINCE she whom I loved hath paid her last debt
To nature, and to hers and my good is dead,
And her soul early into heaven ravishèd,
Wholly in heavenly things my mind is set.
Here the admiring her my mind did whet
To seek thee God; so streams do show the head;
But though I have found thee, and thou my thirst hast fed,
A holy thirsty dropsy melts me yet.
But why should I beg more love, when as thou
Dost woo my soul for hers, offering all thine:
And dost not only fear lest I allow
My love to saints and angels, things divine,
But in thy tender jealousy dost doubt
Lest the world, flesh, yea devil put thee out.

(1894)

134 *Sonnet XVIII*

SHOW me, dear Christ, thy spouse so bright and clear.
What, is it she which on the other shore
Goes richly painted? or which robbed and tore
Laments and mourns in Germany and here?
Sleeps she a thousand, then peeps up one year?
Is she self truth and errs? now new, now outwore?
Doth she, and did she, and shall she evermore
On one, on seven, or on no hill appear?
Dwells she with us, or like adventuring knights
First travail we to seek and then make love?
Betray kind husband thy spouse to our sights,
And let mine amorous soul court thy mild dove,
Who is most true and pleasing to thee then
When she' is embraced and open to most men.

(1899)

she . . . loved] D.'s wife Ann (d. 1617) paid . . . nature] died to hers . . . dead] dead to her own good, since she can do no more head] source (Christ, the fountain of grace) melts me] touches my feelings Dost . . . thine] Offer Christ as dowry, to secure D. as son-in-law put . . . out] outdo God in securing D.

134 spouse] the Church clear] (1) free from confusion; (2) pure she . . . painted] the Church of Rome tore] torn peeps up] re-emerges reformed (as certain Protestants claimed) outwore] outworn, discarded like an outmoded fashion one] Moriah (2 Chron. 3: 1, site of Solomon's temple) seven] i.e. hills of Rome no hill] no special place (as Protestants held, rejecting local devotions) open] (1) universal; (2) easily available

135 *Sonnet XIX*

OH, to vex me, contraries meet in one:
Inconstancy unnaturally hath begot
A constant habit; that when I would not
I change in vows, and in devotïon.
As humorous is my contritïon
As my profane love, and as soon forgot:
As riddlingly distempered, cold and hot,
As praying, as mute; as infinite, as none.
I durst not view heaven yesterday; and today
In prayers and flattering speeches I court God:
Tomorrow I quake with true fear of his rod.
So my devout fits come and go away
Like a fantastic ague: save that here
Those are my best days, when I shake with fear.

(1899)

136 *Good Friday, 1613. Riding Westward*

LET man's soul be a sphere, and then, in this,
The intelligence that moves, devotion is;
And as the other spheres, by being grown
Subject to foreign motions, lose their own,
And being by others hurried every day,
Scarce in a year their natural form obey:
Pleasure or business, so, our souls admit
For their first mover, and are whirled by it.
Hence is't that I am carried towards the west
This day, when my soul's form bends to the east.
There I should see a sun by rising set,
And by that setting endless day beget;
But that Christ on this cross did rise and fall,
Sin had eternally benighted all.
Yet dare I' almost be glad I do not see
That spectacle of too much weight for me.

distempered] unbalanced none] non-existent fantastic ague] irregular fever

136 *Westward*] (to Sir Edward Herbert at Montgomery) sphere] celestial sphere intelligence] guiding spirit foreign motions] outside forces by . . . hurried] accelerated by other motions natural form] complete circular shape first mover] outermost celestial sphere (revolving east–west once a day and carrying the others with it) whirled] (1) rotated, urged; (2) distracted; (3) 'world' soul's form] essential principle sun] Christ, sun of righteousness and Son of God rising] (on to the cross)

Who sees God's face, that is self life, must die;
What a death were it then to see God die?
It made his own lieutenant nature shrink,
It made his footstool crack, and the sun wink.
Could I behold those hands which span the poles,
And turn all spheres at once, pierced with those holes?
Could I behold that endless height which is
Zenith to us, and our antipodes,
Humbled below us? or that blood which is
The seat of all our souls, if not of his,
Made dirt of dust, or that flesh which was worn
By God, for his apparel, ragged and torn?
If on these things I durst not look, durst I
Upon his miserable mother cast mine eye,
Who was God's partner here, and furnished thus
Half of that sacrifice which ransomed us?
Though these things, as I ride, be from mine eye,
They are present yet unto my memory,
For that looks towards them; and thou lookst towards me,
O Saviour, as thou hangst upon the tree;
I turn my back to thee but to receive
Corrections, till thy mercies bid thee leave.
Oh think me worth thine anger, punish me,
Burn off my rusts and my deformity,
Restore thine image so much, by thy grace,
That thou mayst know me, and I'll turn my face.

(1633)

137 *A Hymn to Christ, at the Author's Last Going into Germany*

IN what torn ship soever I embark,
That ship shall be my emblem of thy ark;
What sea soever swallow me, that flood
Shall be to me an emblem of thy blood;
Though thou with clouds of anger do disguise
Thy face, yet through that mask I know those eyes,
Which, though they turn away sometimes,
They never will despise.

self life] life itself shrink] recoil (Matt. 27: 51–4) footstool crack] Earth quake wink] close his eyes (in eclipse) seat] place of residence dirt . . . dust] lowest of the low from . . . eye] eastward, behind him Corrections] Punishments leave] leave off know] (1) recognize; (2) acknowledge

137 *Germany*] (see endnote) torn] split

I sacrifice this island unto thee,
And all whom I loved there, and who loved me;
When I have put our seas 'twixt them and me,
Put thou thy sea betwixt my sins and thee.
As the tree's sap doth seek the root below
In winter, in my winter now I go,
  Where none but thee, th' eternal root
    Of true love I may know.

Nor thou nor thy religion dost control
The amorousness of an harmonious soul;
But thou wouldst have that love thyself. As thou
Art jealous, Lord, so I am jealous now:
Thou lov'st not, till from loving more thou free
My soul; who ever gives, takes liberty:
  O, if thou car'st not whom I love
    Alas, thou lov'st not me.

Seal then this bill of my divorce to all
On whom those fainter beams of love did fall;
Marry those loves, which in youth scattered be
On fame, wit, hopes (false mistresses), to thee.
Churches are best for prayer, that have least light:
To see God only, I go out of sight:
  And to scape stormy days, I choose
    An everlasting night.

(1633)

138 *Hymn to God My God, in My Sickness*

SINCE I am coming to that holy room,
  Where, with thy choir of saints for evermore,
I shall be made thy music; as I come
  I tune the instrument here at the door,
  And what I must do then, think here before.

control] restrain   loving more] more than yourself   who . . . liberty] giving freedom to love other things takes away freedom from entanglements   out of sight] (1) of his countrymen; (2) of humankind

138 music] (1) harmony (of his risen nature); (2) company of musicians; (3) black note

Whilst my physicians by their love are grown
  Cosmographers, and I their map, who lie
Flat on this bed, that by them may be shown
  That this is my south-west discovery
  Per fretum febris, by these straits to die,

I joy that in these straits I see my west;
  For though their currents yield return to none,
What shall my west hurt me? As west and east
  In all flat maps (and I am one) are one,
  So death doth touch the resurrection.

Is the Pacific Sea my home? Or are
  The eastern riches? Is Jerusalem?
Anyan, and Magellan, and Gibraltar,
  All straits, and none but straits, are ways to them,
  Whether where Japhet dwelt, or Cham, or Shem.

We think that paradise and Calvary,
  Christ's cross and Adam's tree, stood in one place:
Look, Lord, and find both Adams met in me;
  As the first Adam's sweat surrounds my face,
  May the last Adam's blood my soul embrace.

So, in his purple wrapped receive me Lord,
  By these his thorns give me his other crown;
And as to others' souls I preached thy word,
  Be this my text, my sermon to mine own,
  Therefore that he may raise the Lord throws down.

(1635)

south-west discovery] (hotter than the north-west passage to 'eastern riches') *Per fretum febris*] Through fever's (1) raging heat, (2) straits straits] (1) tight places; narrow waterway; (2) sufferings west] death east] Christ, the rising sun and resurrecting Son flat maps] projections eastern . . . Jerusalem] heaven Anyan] (see endnote) Japhet . . . Shem] Europe, Asia, or Africa (Noah's sons shared the world between them) one place] (1) the Holy Land, vaguely; (2) (as in the Golden Legend) the same spot exactly both Adams] Christ and his type the first Adam purple] blood-coloured (poetical): (1) Christ's blood; (2) his imperial robe; (3) the red of fever thorns] sufferings (like those of Christ's crown of thorns) Therefore] In order

139 *A Hymn to God the Father*

WILT thou forgive that sin where I begun,
  Which is my sin, though it were done before?
Wilt thou forgive that sin through which I run,
  And do run still, though still I do deplore?
    When thou hast done, thou hast not done,
      For I have more.

Wilt thou forgive that sin which I have won
  Others to sin? and made my sin their door?
Wilt thou forgive that sin which I did shun
  A year or two, but wallowed in, a score?
    When thou hast done, thou hast not done,
      For I have more.

I have a sin of fear, that when I have spun
  My last thread, I shall perish on the shore;
Swear by thyself, that at my death thy son
  Shall shine as he shines now and heretofore;
    And, having done that, thou hast done,
      I fear no more.

(1633)

BEN JONSON
1572?–1637

from *Epigrams* (140–158)

140 *Epigram XIV: To William Camden*

CAMDEN, most reverend head, to whom I owe
All that I am in arts, all that I know
(How nothing's that?), to whom my country owes
The great renown, and name wherewith she goes:
Than thee the age sees not that thing more grave,
More high, more holy, that she more would crave.
What name, what skill, what faith hast thou in things!
What sight in searching the most ántique springs!

sin . . . begun] original sin   begun] began   sin . . . run] actual sin   not done] (1) not finished; (2) not Donne

140 *Camden*] (see endnote)   name (l.4)] (see endnote)   things] facts

What weight, and what authority in thy speech!
Man scarce can make that doubt, but thou canst teach.
Pardon free truth, and let thy modesty,
Which conquers all, be once overcome by thee.
Many of thine this better could than I;
But for their powers accept my piety.

(1616)

141 *Epigram XXII: On My First Daughter*

HERE lies, to each her parents' ruth,
Mary, the daughter of their youth:
Yet, all heaven's gifts being heaven's due,
It makes the father less to rue.
At six months' end she parted hence
With safety of her innocence;
Whose soul heaven's queen (whose name she bears),
In comfort of her mother's tears,
Hath placed amongst her virgin train:
Where, while that severed doth remain,
This grave partakes the fleshly birth;
Which cover lightly, gentle earth.

(1616)

142 *Epigram XLV: On My First Son*

FAREWELL, thou child of my right hand, and joy;
My sin was too much hope of thee, loved boy.
Seven years thou wert lent to me, and I thee pay,
Exacted by thy fate, on the just day.
Oh, could I lose all father, now! For why
Will man lament the state he should envy?
To have so soon scaped world's and flesh's rage,
And, if no other misery, yet age!
Rest in soft peace, and, asked, say here doth lie
Ben Jonson his best piece of poetry;
For whose sake, henceforth, all his vows be such,
As what he loves may never like too much.

(1616)

free] (1) uninhibited; (2) generous thine] your pupils for] instead of

141 ruth] grief while . . . remain] while the soul is in heaven, separated until the body's resurrection partakes . . . birth] enjoys its share of the mortal body

142 *Son*] Benjamin (d. 1603) child . . . hand] i.e. the sense of 'Benjamin' (Gen. 35: 18): fortunate lose all father] relinquish all paternal feelings

143 *Epigram LII: To Censorious Courtling*

COURTLING, I rather thou shouldst utterly
Dispraise my work than praise it frostily:
When I am read thou feignst a weak applause,
As if thou wert my friend, but lackedst a cause.
This but thy judgement fools: the other way
Would both thy folly and thy spite betray.

(1616)

144 *Epigram LXII: To Fine Lady Would-Be*

FINE Madam Would-be, wherefore should you fear,
That love to make so well, a child to bear?
The world reputes you barren; but I know
Your 'pothecary, and his drug says no.
Is it the pain affrights? That's soon forgot.
Or your complexion's loss? You have a pot
That can restore that. Will it hurt your feature?
To make amends, you're thought a wholesome creature.
What should the cause be? Oh, you live at court:
And there's both loss of time, and loss of sport
In a great belly. Write, then, on thy womb:
Of the not born, yet buried, here's the tomb.

(1616)

145 *Epigram LXIV: To the Same [Robert, Earl of Salisbury] Upon the Accession of the Treasurership to Him*

NOT glad, like those that have new hopes or suits
With thy new place, bring I these early fruits
Of love, and what the Golden Age did hold
A treasure, art: contemned in th'age of gold;
Nor glad as those that old dependants be,
To see thy father's rights new laid on thee;
Nor glad for fashion; nor to show a fit
Of flattery to thy titles; nor of wit.

cause] case   thy . . . fools] makes a fool of your judgement

144 love to make so well] so much enjoy making children   says no] (1) says you are not barren; (2) says no to pregnancy by inducing an abortion

145 *Accession . . . Treasurership*] 6 May 1608   age of gold] mercenary age   thy father's rights] offices of Lord Burghley, an earlier Lord Treasurer

But I am glad to see that time survive
Where merit is not sepulchred alive;
Where good men's virtues them to honours bring,
And not to dangers; when so wise a king
Contends to have worth enjoy, from his regard,
As her own conscience, still the same reward.
These, noblest Cecil, laboured in my thought,
Wherein what wonder, see, thy name hath wrought:
That whilst I meant but thine to gratulate,
I've sung the greater fortunes of our state.

(1616)

146 *Epigram LXVI: To Sir Henry Cary*

THAT neither fame nor love might wanting be
To greatness, Cary, I sing that, and thee;
Whose house, if it no other honour had,
In only thee might be both great and glad;
Who, to upbraid the sloth of this our time,
Durst valour make almost, but not a crime.
Which deed I know not whether were more high
Or thou more happy, it to justify
Against thy fortune: when no foe that day
Could conquer thee but chance, who did betray.
Love thy great loss, which a renown hath won
To live when Broick not stands, nor Ruhr doth run.
Love honours, which of best example be
When they cost dearest and are done most free;
Though every fortitude deserves applause,
It may be much or little in the cause.
He's valiant'st that dares fight, and not for pay;
That virtuous is when the reward's away.

(1616)

147 *Epigram LXX: To William Roe*

WHEN nature bids us leave to live, 'tis late
Then to begin, my Roe: he makes a state
In life that can employ it, and takes hold
On the true causes ere they grow too old.

gratulate] congratulate

146 *Cary*] (see endnote) crime] (see endnote) justify] maintain legally loss] (see endnote) Broick . . . Ruhr] 'The castle and river near where he was taken' (J).

147 *Roe*] (see endnote) makes . . . state] achieves an admirable condition

Delay is bad, doubt worse, depending worst;
Each best day of our life escapes us first.
Then, since we (more than many) these truths know,
Though life be short, let us not make it so.

(1616)

148 *Epigram LXXVI: On Lucy, Countess of Bedford*

THIS morning, timely rapt with holy fire,
I thought to form unto my zealous muse
What kind of creature I could most desire
To honour, serve and love, as poets use.
I meant to make her fair, and free, and wise,
Of greatest blood, and yet more good than great;
I meant the day-star should not brighter rise,
Nor lend like influence from his lucent seat.
I meant she should be courteous, facile, sweet,
Hating that solemn vice of greatness, pride;
I meant each softest virtue there should meet,
Fit in that softer bosom to reside.
Only a learnèd and a manly soul
I purposed her, that should, with even powers,
The rock, the spindle and the shears control
Of destiny, and spin her own free hours.
Such when I meant to feign and wished to see,
My Muse bad, *Bedford* write, and that was she.

(1616)

149 *Epigram LXXXV: To Sir Henry Goodyere*

GOODYERE, I'm glad and grateful to report
Myself a witness of thy few days' sport,
Where I both learned, why wise men hawking follow,
And why that bird was sacred to Apollo:
She doth instruct men by her gallant flight
That they to knowledge so should tower upright,
And never stoop but to strike ignorance;
Which, if they miss, they yet should readvance

148 *Lucy*] (see endnote) use] are accustomed to do free] noble day-star] morning-star lucent] shining, luminous (playing on the derivation of 'Lucy') facile] easy, approachable rock . . . shears] (attributes of the Fates) rock] distaff

149 *Goodyere*] (see endnote) that bird] i.e. the hawk (emblem of intellect) tower] soar (falconry) stoop] swoop (falconry)

To former height, and there in circle tarry
Till they be sure to make the fool their quarry.
Now, in whose pleasures I have this discerned,
What would his serious actions me have learned?

(1616)

150 *Epigram LXXXIX: To Edward Alleyn*

IF Rome so great, and in her wisest age,
Feared not to boast the glories of her stage,
As skilful Roscius and grave Aesop, men
Yet crowned with honours as with riches then,
Who had no less a trumpet of their name
Than Cicero, whose every breath was fame:
How can so great example die in me,
That, Alleyn, I should pause to publish thee?
Who both their graces in thyself hast more
Outstripped, than they did all that went before;
And present worth in all dost so contract,
As others speak, but only thou dost act.
Wear this renown. 'Tis just that who did give
So many poets life, by one should live.

(1616)

151 *Epigram CI: Inviting a Friend to Supper*

TONIGHT, grave sir, both my poor house and I
Do equally desire your company:
Not that we think us worthy such a guest,
But that your worth will dignify our feast
With those that come; whose grace may make that seem
Something, which else could hope for no esteem.
It is the fair acceptance, sir, creates
The entertainment perfect, not the cates.
Yet shall you have, to rectify your palate,
An olive, capers, or some better salad
Ushering the mutton; with a short-legged hen,
If we can get her, full of eggs, and then

learned] taught

150 *Alleyn*] (see endnote) Roscius . . . Aesop] (famous Roman actors, comic and tragic, respectively) Cicero] (the great Roman orator) publish thee] proclaim your qualities publicly As] That act] (1) perform on the stage; (2) do (playing on the proverb 'deeds, not words')

151 cates] food rectify] purify

Lemons, and wine for sauce; to these, a cony
Is not to be despaired of, for our money;
And though fowl now be scarce, yet there are clerks,
The sky not falling, think we may have larks.
I'll tell you of more, and lie, so you will come:
Of partridge, pheasant, woodcock, of which some
May yet be there; and godwit, if we can;
Knat, rail and ruff, too. Howsoe'er, my man
Shall read a piece of Virgil, Tacitus,
Livy, or of some better book to us,
Of which we'll speak our minds, amidst our meat;
And I'll profess no verses to repeat;
To this, if aught appear which I not know of,
That will the pastry, not my paper, show of.
Digestive cheese and fruit there sure will be;
But that which most doth take my Muse and me
Is a pure cup of rich Canary wine,
Which is the Mermaid's now, but shall be mine;
Of which had Horace or Anacreon tasted,
Their lives, as do their lines, till now had lasted.
Tobacco, nectar, or the Thespian spring
Are all but Luther's beer to this I sing.
Of this we will sup free, but moderately;
And we will have no Poley or Parrot by;
Nor shall our cups make any guilty men,
But at our parting we will be as when
We innocently met. No simple word
That shall be uttered at our mirthful board
Shall make us sad next morning, or affright
The liberty that we'll enjoy tonight.

(1616)

152 *Epigram CV: To Mary, Lady Wroth*

MADAM, had all antiquity been lost,
All history sealed up and fables crossed;
That we had left us, nor by time nor place,
Least mention of a nymph, a Muse, a Grace,

sky . . . larks] playing on the proverb 'if the sky falls, we shall have larks' godwit] curlew-like marsh bird knat] knot, bird of snipe family rail] corncrake ruff] bird of the sandpiper family Mermaid's] (famous Cheapside tavern frequented by poets) Horace . . . Anacreon] (Latin and Greek poets, praisers of wine) Thespian spring] (Boeotian fountain sacred to the Muses) Luther's beer] weak Continental hop beer Poley] (government spy, present at Marlowe's murder) Parrot] an informer

152 *Mary*] (see endnote) crossed] crossed out

But even their names were to be made anew:
Who could not but create them all from you?
He that but saw you wear the wheaten hat
Would call you more than Ceres, if not that;
And, dressed in shepherd's 'tire, who would not say
You were the bright Oenone, Flora, or May?
If dancing, all would cry the Idalian queen
Were leading forth the Graces on the green;
And, armèd to the chase, so bare her bow
Diana alone, so hit, and hunted so.
There's none so dull that for your style would ask
That saw you put on Pallas' plumèd casque;
Or, keeping your due state, that would not cry
There Juno sat, and yet no peacock by.
So are you nature's index, and restore
In yourself all treasure lost of the age before.

(1616)

153 *Epigram CX: To Clement Edmonds, on His* Caesar's Commentaries *Observed, and Translated*

NOT Caesar's deeds, nor all his honours won
In these west parts; nor when that war was done,
The name of Pompey for an enemy,
Cato's to boot, Rome and her liberty
All yielding to his fortune; nor, the while,
To have engraved these acts with his own style,
And that so strong and deep as't might be thought
He wrote with the same spirit that he fought;
Nor that his work lived in the hands of foes,
Unargued then, and yet hath fame from those:
Not all these, Edmonds, or what else put to,
Can so speak Caesar as thy labours do.
For, where his person lived scarce one just age,
And that midst envy and parts, then fell by rage:
His deeds too dying, but in books (whose good
How few have read, how fewer understood!)

wheaten] straw Ceres] (Roman goddess of corn) Oenone] (a nymph of Mt Ida, with the gift of prophecy) Flora] (Roman goddess of flowers and gardens) May] Maia, May (mother of Mercury by Jupiter) Idalian queen] Venus Pallas'] Pallas Athene's, the ancient Greek goddess of wisdom and arts peacock] (attribute of Juno, and emblem of vanity)

153 *Edmonds*] (see endnote) style] (1) manner; (2) stylus put to] added parts] factions

Thy learnèd hand and true Promethean art
(As by a new creation) part by part,
In every counsel, stratagem, design,
Action, or engine worth a note of thine,
To all future time not only doth restore
His life, but makes that he can die no more.

(1609)

154 *Epigram CXV: On the Town's Honest Man*

YOU wonder who this is, and why I name
Him not aloud that boasts so good a fame.
Naming so many, too! But this is one
Suffers no name, but a description:
Being no vicious person, but the Vice
About the town; and known too, at that price.
A subtle thing that doth affections win
By speaking well of the company it's in.
Talks loud and bawdy, has a gathered deal
Of news and noise, to strew out a long meal.
Can come from Tripoli, leap stools, and wink,
Do all that 'longs to the anarchy of drink,
Except the duel. Can sing songs and catches,
Give everyone his dose of mirth; and watches
Whose name's unwelcome to the present ear,
And him it lays on; if he be not there,
Tells of him all the tales itself then makes;
But, if it shall be questioned, undertakes
It will deny all, and forswear it, too:
Not that it fears, but will not have to do
With such a one. And therein keeps its word.
'Twill see its sister naked, ere a sword.
At every meal where it doth dine or sup,
The cloth's no sooner gone but it gets up
And, shifting of its faces, doth play more
Parts than the Italian could do with his door.
Acts old Iniquity, and in the fit
Of miming gets the opinion of a wit.

Promethean] (alluding to Prometheus' creation of man from clay and fire) engine] device

154 *Honest*] Candid, open (see endnote) it] he (contemptuous) strew out] ?intersperse with come ... Tripoli] tumble like a monkey lays on] attacks Italian ... door] ?a Zanni actor who did quick-change impressions from behind a door Iniquity] the Vice, an amusing stock character in the interludes

Executes men in picture. By defect,
From friendship, is its own fame's architect.
An engineer in slanders of all fashions,
That, seeming praises, are yet accusations.
Described, it's thus; defined would you it have?
Then, the town's honest man's her arrant'st knave.

(1616)

155 *Epigram CXVII: On Groin*

Groin, come of age, his 'state sold out of hand
For his whore: Groin doth still occupy his land.

(1616)

156 *Epigram CXX: Epitaph on S[alomon] P[avy], a Child of Q[ueen] El[izabeth's] Chapel*

Weep with me all you that read
  This little story;
And know, for whom a tear you shed,
  Death's self is sorry.
'Twas a child that so did thrive
  In grace and feature,
As heaven and nature seemed to strive
  Which owned the creature.
Years he numbered scarce thirteen
  When Fates turned cruel,
Yet three filled zodiacs had he been
  The stage's jewel;
And did act (what now we moan)
  Old men so duly
As, sooth, the Parcae thought him one,
  He played so truly.
So, by error, to his fate
  They all consented;
But viewing him since (alas, too late)
  They have repented,

engineer] (1) schemer; (2) designer arrant'st] most notorious, unmitigated

155 occupy] (1) inhabit; (2) cohabit with

156 *Salomon Pavy*] (d.1602) Parcae] Fates

And have sought (to give new birth)
In baths to steep him;
But, being so much too good for Earth,
Heaven vows to keep him.

(1616)

157 *Epigram CXXIV: Epitaph on Elizabeth, L. H.*

Wouldst thou hear what man can say
In a little? Reader, stay.
Underneath this stone doth lie
As much beauty as could die;
Which in life did harbour give
To more virtue than doth live.
If at all she had a fault,
Leave it buried in this vault.
One name was Elizabeth,
The other let it sleep with death:
Fitter where it died to tell,
Than that it lived at all. Farewell.

(1616)

158 from *Epigram CXXXIII: On the Famous Voyage*

By this time had they reached the Stygian pool
By which the masters swear when, on the stool
Of worship, they their nodding chins do hit
Against their breasts. Here several ghosts did flit
About the shore, of farts but late departed,
White, black, blue, green, and in more forms outstarted
Than all those *atomi* ridiculous
Whereof old Democrite and Hill Nicholas,
One said, the other swore, the world consists.
These be the cause of those thick frequent mists
Arising in that place, through which who goes
Must try the unused valour of a nose:
And that ours did. For yet no nare was tainted,
Nor thumb nor finger to the stop acquainted,
But open and unarmed encountered all.
Whether it languishing stuck upon the wall,

baths] i.e. revivifying baths (such as Jupiter used to restore the young Pelops)

157 *Elizabeth L. H.*] (unidentified)

158 Stygian] of the Styx (river of the ancient underworld) Democrite] Democritus, the ancient Greek atomic theorist Hill Nicholas] (see endnote) nare] nostril

Or were precipitated down the jakes,
And after swom abroad in ample flakes,
Or that it lay heaped like an usurer's mass,
All was to them the same: they were to pass,
And so they did, from Styx to Acheron,
The ever-boiling flood, whose banks upon
Your Fleet Lane Furies and hot cooks do dwell,
That with still-scalding steams make the place hell.
The sinks ran grease, and hair of measled hogs,
The heads, houghs, entrails, and the hides of dogs:
For, to say truth, what scullion is so nasty
To put the skins and offal in a pasty?
Cats there lay divers had been flayed and roasted
And, after mouldy grown, again were toasted;
Then selling not, a dish was ta'en to mince 'em,
But still, it seemed, the rankness did convince 'em.
For here they were thrown in wi' the melted pewter,
Yet drowned they not. They had five lives in future.

(1616)

from *The Forest* (159–162)

159 *II: To Penshurst*

THOU art not, Penshurst, built to envious show,
Of touch or marble, nor canst boast a row
Of polished pillars, or a roof of gold;
Thou hast no lantern whereof tales are told,
Or stair, or courts; but standst an ancient pile,
And these grudged at, art reverenced the while.
Thou joy'st in better marks, of soil, of air,
Of wood, of water; therein thou art fair.
Thou hast thy walks for health as well as sport:
Thy Mount, to which the dryads do resort,
Where Pan and Bacchus their high feasts have made
Beneath the broad beech and the chestnut shade;
That taller tree, which of a nut was set
At his great birth, where all the Muses met.

jakes] privy   Acheron] another river of the classical underworld   Fleet Lane] (running past Fleet prison, along the Fleet, a common sewer flowing into the Thames at Blackfriars)   measled] spotty   convince] convict

159 *Penshurst*] (home of Sir Robert Sidney, Viscount Lisle, near Tonbridge, Kent) touch] touchstone; any black stone   lantern] glazed structure on the top of a building (then fashionable)   marks] features   Pan] Greek god of the country and fertility Bacchus] Roman god of wine and vegetation

There, in the writhèd bark, are cut the names
Of many a sylvan, taken with his flames;
And thence the ruddy satyrs oft provoke
The lighter fauns to reach thy lady's oak.
Thy copse, too, named of Gamage, thou hast there,
That never fails to serve thee seasoned deer
When thou wouldst feast or exercise thy friends.
The lower land, that to the river bends,
Thy sheep, thy bullocks, kine and calves do feed;
The middle grounds thy mares and horses breed.
Each bank doth yield thee conies, and the tops,
Fertile of wood, Ashour and Sidney's copse,
To crown thy open table, doth provide
The purpled pheasant with the speckled side;
The painted partridge lies in every field,
And for thy mess is willing to be killed.
And if the high-swoll'n Medway fail thy dish,
Thou hast thy ponds that pay thee tribute fish:
Fat, agéd carps, that run into thy net;
And pikes, now weary their own kind to eat,
As loth the second draught or cast to stay,
Officiously, at first, themselves betray;
Bright eels, that emulate them, and leap on land
Before the fisher, or into his hand.
Then hath thy orchard fruit, thy garden flowers,
Fresh as the air and new as are the Hours:
The early cherry, with the later plum,
Fig, grape and quince, each in his time doth come;
The blushing apricot and woolly peach
Hang on thy walls, that every child may reach.
And though thy walls be of the country stone,
They're reared with no man's ruin, no man's groan;
There's none that dwell about them wish them down,
But all come in, the farmer and the clown,
And no one empty-handed, to salute
Thy lord and lady, though they have no suit.
Some bring a capon, some a rural cake,
Some nuts, some apples; some that think they make
The better cheeses, bring them; or else send
By their ripe daughters, whom they would commend
This way to husbands; and whose baskets bear
An emblem of themselves, in plum or pear.
But what can this (more than express their love)
Add to thy free provisions, far above

draught] (1) drawing of the net; (2) draft; section of the poem Officiously] Dutifully; without being asked Hours] Horae (representing the three classical seasons) plum] emblem of fidelity or inaccessibility) pear] (emblem of accessibility)

The need of such? whose liberal board doth flow,
With all that hospitality doth know!
Where comes no guest but is allowed to eat
Without his fear, and of thy lord's own meat;
Where the same beer and bread and self-same wine
That is his lordship's shall be also mine;
And I not fain to sit (as some, this day,
At great men's tables) and yet dine away.
Here no man tells my cups, nor, standing by,
A waiter, doth my gluttony envy,
But gives me what I call, and lets me eat;
He knows below he shall find plenty of meat,
Thy tables hoard not up for the next day.
Nor, when I take my lodging, need I pray
For fire or lights or livery: all is there,
As if thou then wert mine, or I reigned here;
There's nothing I can wish, for which I stay.
That found King James, when, hunting late this way
With his brave son, the prince, they saw thy fires
Shine bright on every hearth, as the desires
Of thy Penates had been set on flame
To entertain them; or the country came
With all their zeal to warm their welcome here.
What (great, I will not say, but) sudden cheer
Didst thou then make them! And what praise was heaped
On thy good lady then! who therein reaped
The just reward of her high huswifery:
To have her linen, plate, and all things nigh,
When she was far; and not a room but dressed
As if it had expected such a guest!
These, Penshurst, are thy praise, and yet not all.
Thy lady's noble, fruitful, chaste withal;
His children thy great lord may call his own,
A fortune in this age but rarely known.
They are and have been taught religion; thence
Their gentler spirits have sucked innocence.
Each morn and even they are taught to pray
With the whole household, and may every day
Read in their virtuous parents' noble parts
The mysteries of manners, arms and arts.
Now, Penshurst, they that will proportion thee
With other edifices, when they see
Those proud, ambitious heaps, and nothing else,
May say, their lords have built, but thy lord dwells.

(1616)

Penates] household guardian spirits sudden] prompt mysteries] skills; truths

160 *VI: To the Same [Celia]*

KISS me, sweet: the wary lover
Can your favours keep and cover,
When the common courting jay
All your bounties will betray.
Kiss again: no creature comes.
Kiss, and score up wealthy sums
On my lips, thus hardly sundered,
While you breathe. First give a hundred,
Then a thousand, then another
Hundred, then unto the t'other
Add a thousand, and so more.
Till you equal with the store
All the grass that Romney yields,
Or the sands in Chelsea fields,
Or the drops in silver Thames,
Or the stars that gild his streams
In the silent summer nights,
When youths ply their stol'n delights:
That the curious may not know
How to tell 'em as they flow,
And the envious, when they find
What their number is, be pined.

(1607)

161 *IX: Song: To Celia*

DRINK to me only with thine eyes,
  And I will pledge with mine;
Or leave a kiss but in the cup,
  And I'll not look for wine.
The thirst that from the soul doth rise
  Doth ask a drink divine;
But might I of Jove's nectar sup,
  I would not change for thine.
I sent thee late a rosy wreath,
  Not so much honouring thee
As giving it a hope that there
  It could not withered be.

jay] impertinent chatterer Romney] (on the east coast of Kent: rich in grazing land) Chelsea fields] (Thames riverside area: derived from the tidal 'chesel' of sand and pebbles) pined] vexed

161 Jove's] Jupiter's

But thou thereon didst only breathe,
  And sentst it back to me:
Since when it grows, and smells, I swear,
  Not of itself, but thee.

(1616)

162 *XV: To Heaven*

GOOD and great God, can I not think of thee,
But it must straight my melancholy be?
Is it interpreted in me disease
That, laden with my sins, I seek for ease?
Oh, be thou witness, that the reins dost know
And hearts of all, if I be sad for show;
And judge me after, if I dare pretend
To aught but grace, or aim at other end.
As thou art all, so be thou all to me,
First, midst, and last; converted one and three;
My faith, my hope, my love; and in this state,
My judge, my witness, and my advocate.
Where have I been this while exiled from thee?
And whither rapt, now thou but stoopst to me?
Dwell, dwell here still: oh, being everywhere,
How can I doubt to find thee ever here?
I know my state, both full of shame and scorn,
Conceived in sin, and unto labour born,
Standing with fear, and must with horror fall,
And destined unto judgment, after all.
I feel my griefs too, and there scarce is ground
Upon my flesh to inflict another wound.
Yet dare I not complain, or wish for death
With holy Paul, lest it be thought the breath
Of discontent; or that these prayers be
For weariness of life, not love of thee.

(1616)

162 Good ... be?] Can I not have pious thoughts without being called morbid? converted] turned into (mathematics) stoopst] (1) condescend; (2) swoop, to seize on scorn] object of scorn ground] (1) space; (2) cause

from *The Underwood* (163–170)

163

from *I: Poems of Devotion*
ii: A Hymn to God the Father

HEAR me, O God!
  A broken heart
  Is my best part:
Use still thy rod,
  That I may prove
  Therein thy love.

If thou hadst not
  Been stern to me,
  But left me free,
I had forgot
  Myself and thee.

For sin's so sweet,
  As minds ill bent
  Rarely repent,
Until they meet
  Their punishment.

Who more can crave
  Than thou hast done?
  That gav'st a Son,
To free a slave
  First made of nought;
  With all since bought.

Sin, death, and hell
  His glorious name
  Quite overcame,
Yet I rebel,
  And slight the same.

But I'll come in,
  Before my loss
  Me farther toss,
As sure to win
  Under his cross.

(1616)

from *II: A Celebration of Charis in Ten Lyric Pieces*

164 *i: His Excuse for Loving*

LET it not your wonder move,
Less your laughter, that I love.
Though I now write fifty years,
I have had, and have, my peers;
Poets, though divine, are men:
Some have loved as old again.
And it is not always face,
Clothes, or fortune gives the grace,
Or the feature, or the youth;
But the language, and the truth,
With the ardour and the passion,
Gives the lover weight and fashion.
If you then will read the story,
First prepare you to be sorry
That you never knew till now,
Either whom to love, or how;
But be glad as soon with me,
When you know that this is she,
Of whose beauty it was sung,
She shall make the old man young,
Keep the middle age at stay,
And let nothing high decay,
Till she be the reason why
All the world for love may die.

(1640)

165 *iv: Her Triumph*

SEE the chariot at hand here of Love,
  Wherein my lady rideth!
Each that draws is a swan or a dove,
  And well the car Love guideth.
As she goes, all hearts do duty
    Unto her beauty;
And enamoured, do wish, so they might
    But enjoy such a sight,
That they still were to run by her side,
Through swords, through seas, whither she would ride.

feature] figure   high] advanced; exalted

165 *Triumph*] (1) Victory; (2) Victory procession   swan . . . dove] i.e. birds sacred to Venus   whither] wherever

Do but look on her eyes, they do light
All that Love's world compriseth!
Do but look on her hair, it is bright
As Love's star when it riseth!
Do but mark, her forehead's smoother
Than words that soothe her!
And from her arched brows, such a grace
Sheds itself through the face,
As alone there triumphs to the life
All the gain, all the good, of the elements' strife.

Have you seen but a bright lily grow,
Before rude hands have touched it?
Have you marked but the fall o' the snow
Before the soil hath smutched it?
Have you felt the wool o' the beaver?
Or swan's down ever?
Or have smelt o' the bud o' the briar?
Or the nard in the fire?
Or have tasted the bag o' the bee?
Oh so white! Oh so soft! Oh so sweet is she!

(1640)

166 *XI: The Dream*

Or scorn, or pity on me take,
I must the true relation make:
I am undone tonight;
Love in a subtle dream disguised
Hath both my heart and me surprised,
Whom never yet he durst attempt awake;
Nor will he tell me for whose sake
He did me the delight,
Or spite,
But leaves me to inquire,
In all my wild desire
Of sleep again, who was his aid;
And sleep so guilty and afraid
As, since, he dares not come within my sight.

(1640)

165 smutched] dirtied, stained

167 *XXIII: An Ode. To Himself*

WHERE dost thou careless lie,
Buried in ease and sloth?
Knowledge that sleeps doth die;
And this security,
It is the common moth,
That eats on wits, and arts, and oft destroys them both.

Are all the Aonian springs
Dried up? Lies Thespia waste?
Doth Clarius' harp want strings,
That not a nymph now sings?
Or droop they, as disgraced
To see their seats and bowers by chattering pies defaced?

If hence thy silence be,
As 'tis too just a cause,
Let this thought quicken thee:
Minds that are great and free
Should not on fortune pause;
'Tis crown enough to virtue still, her own applause.

What though the greedy fry
Be taken with false baits
Of worded balladry,
And think it poesy?
They die with their conceits,
And only piteous scorn upon their folly waits.

Then take in hand thy lyre,
Strike in thy proper strain;
With Japhet's line, aspire
Sol's chariot for new fire
To give the world again;
Who aided him, will thee, the issue of Jove's brain.

And since our dainty age
Cannot endure reproof,
Make not thyself a page
To that strumpet, the stage;
But sing high and aloof,
Safe from the wolf's black jaw, and the dull ass's hoof.

(1640)

security] carefree recklessness Aonian springs] Boeotian springs, sacred to the Muses Thespia] town near Mt Helicon, haunt of the Muses Clarius'] Apollo's pies] magpies worded] wordy Japhet's line] Prometheus aspire] mount up to issue . . . brain] Minerva, born from Jupiter's head

168 *XXXIV: An Epigram. To the Small-Pox*

ENVIOUS and foul disease, could there not be
One beauty in an age, and free from thee?
What did she worth thy spite? Were there not store
Of those that set by their false faces more
Than this did by her true? She never sought
Quarrel with nature, or in balance brought
Art, her false servant; nor, for Sir Hugh Platt
Was drawn to practise other hue than that
Her own blood gave her; she ne'er had, nor hath
Any belief in Madam Bawd-be's bath,
Or Turner's oil of talc; nor ever got
Spanish receipt to make her teeth to rot.
What was the cause, then? Thoughtst thou in disgrace
Of beauty so to nullify a face
That heaven should make no more; or should amiss
Make all hereafter, hadst thou ruined this?
Ay, that thy aim was: but her fate prevailed;
And, scorned, thou hast shown thy malice, but hast failed.

(1640)

169 *LXX: To the Immortal Memory and Friendship of That Noble Pair, Sir Lucius Cary and Sir H. Morison*

THE TURN

BRAVE infant of Saguntum, clear
Thy coming forth in that great year
When the prodigious Hannibal did crown
His rage with razing your immortal town.
Thou, looking then about,
Ere thou wert half got out,
Wise child, didst hastily return,
And mad'st thy mother's womb thine urn.
How summed a circle didst thou leave mankind
Of deepest lore, could we the centre find!

Platt] (writer on cosmetics) practise] devise by artifice bath] sweating-bath for complexion Turner's . . . talc] cleansing lotion

169 *Cary . . . Morison*] (see endnote) TURN . . . COUNTER-TURN . . . STAND] sections of a Greek choral ode Saguntum] Roman town destroyed by Hannibal clear] noble (Latin *clarus*) summed] complete circle] emblem of perfection

THE COUNTER-TURN

Did wiser nature draw thee back
From out the horror of that sack?
Where shame, faith, honour, and regard of right
Lay trampled on; the deeds of death and night
Urged, hurried forth, and hurled
Upon the affrighted world:
Sword, fire, and famine with fell fury met,
And all on utmost ruin set;
As, could they but life's miseries foresee,
No doubt all infants would return like thee.

THE STAND

For what is life, if measured by the space,
Not by the act?
Or maskèd man, if valued by his face
Above his fact?
Here's one outlived his peers,
And told forth fourscore years;
He vexèd time, and busied the whole state;
Troubled both foes and friends,
But ever to no ends;
What did this stirrer, but die late?
How well at twenty had he fallen or stood!
For three of his four score he did no good.

THE TURN

He entered well by virtuous parts,
Got up and thrived with honest arts;
He purchased friends and fame and honours then,
And had his noble name advanced with men;
But weary of that flight,
He stooped in all men's sight
To sordid flatteries, acts of strife,
And sunk in that dead sea of life
So deep, as he did then death's waters sup,
But that the cork of title buoyed him up.

THE COUNTER-TURN

Alas, but Morison fell young!
He never fell: thou fallst, my tongue.
He stood, a soldier to the last right end,
A perfect patriot, and a noble friend;

fact] deeds   one] probably the statesman Sir Edward Coke   stirrer] trouble-maker   parts] qualities

But most a virtuous son.
All offices were done
By him so ample, full, and round,
In weight, in measure, number, sound,
As, though his age imperfect might appear,
His life was of humanity the sphere.

THE STAND

Go now, and tell out days summed up with fears;
And make them years;
Produce thy mass of miseries on the stage,
To swell thine age;
Repeat of things a throng,
To show thou hast been long,
Not lived; for life doth her great actions spell
By what was done and wrought
In season, and so brought
To light: her measures are, how well
Each syllabe answered, and was formed, how fair;
These make the lines of life, and that's her air.

THE TURN

It is not growing like a tree
In bulk, doth make man better be;
Or standing long an oak, three hundred year,
To fall a log at last, dry, bald, and sere:
A lily of a day
Is fairer far, in May,
Although it fall and die that night;
It was the plant and flower of light.
In small proportions we just beauty see,
And in short measures life may perfect be.

THE COUNTER-TURN

Call, noble Lucius, then for wine,
And let thy looks with gladness shine:
Accept this garland, plant it on thy head;
And think, nay know, thy Morison's not dead.
He leapt the present age,
Possessed with holy rage
To see that bright eternal day,
Of which we priests and poets say

round] complete sphere] ideal form summed up] completed spell] scan measures] (1) criteria; (2) verse metres syllabe] syllable lines] (1) lineaments; (2) verses; (3) Fates' threads air] (1) manner; (2) melody rage] passion, *furor*

Such truths as we expect for happy men;
And there he lives with memory, and Ben.

THE STAND

Jonson, who sung this of him, ere he went
Himself to rest,
Or taste a part of that full joy he meant
To have expressed
In this bright asterism;
Where it were friendship's schism
(Were not his Lucius long with us to tarry)
To separate these twi-
Lights, the Dioscuri;
And keep the one half from his Harry.
But fate doth so altérnate the design,
Whilst that in heaven, this light on earth must shine.

THE TURN

And shine as you exalted are;
Two names of friendship, but one star:
Of hearts the union. And those not by chance
Made, or indentured, or leased out to advance
The profits for a time.
No pleasures vain did chime,
Of rhymes, or riots, at your feasts,
Orgies of drink, or feigned protests:
But simple love of greatness, and of good;
That knits brave minds and manners, more than blood.

THE COUNTER-TURN

This made you first to know the why
You liked; then after to apply
That liking; and approach so one the t'other,
Till either grew a portion of the other:
Each stylèd by his end,
The copy of his friend.
You lived to be the great surnames
And titles by which all made claims
Unto the virtue. Nothing perfect done,
But as a Cary, or a Morison.

asterism] constellation twi-Lights] twin lights Dioscuri] Castor and Pollux (who became the constellation Gemini) altérnate] reverse that . . . shine] the twin stars were supposed not to appear simultaneously

THE STAND
And such a force the fair example had,
As they that saw
The good and durst not practise it, were glad
That such a law
Was left yet to mankind;
Where they might read and find
Friendship in deed was written, not in words;
And with the heart, not pen,
Of two so early men
Whose lines her rolls were, and records.
Who, ere the first down bloomèd on the chin,
Had sowed these fruits, and got the harvest in.

(1640)

170 from *LXXXIV: Eupheme: iii: The Picture of the Body*

SITTING, and ready to be drawn,
What makes these velvets, silks, and lawn,
Embroideries, feathers, fringes, lace,
Where every limb takes like a face?

Send these suspected helps to aid
Some form defective, or decayed;
This beauty without falsehood fair
Needs naught to clothe it but the air.

Yet something, to the painter's view,
Were fitly interposed; so new,
He shall, if he can understand,
Work with my fancy his own hand.

Draw first a cloud, all save her neck,
And out of that make day to break;
Till, like her face it do appear,
And men may think all light rose there.

Then let the beams of that disperse
The cloud, and show the universe;
But at such distance as the eye
May rather yet adore than spy.

170 new] inexperienced Work ... hand] Direct his hand according to my imagination

The heaven designed, draw next a spring,
With all that youth or it can bring:
Four rivers branching forth like seas,
And paradise confining these.

Last, draw the circles of this globe,
And let there be a starry robe
Of constellations 'bout her hurled;
And thou hast painted beauty's world.

But, painter, see thou do not sell
A copy of this piece, nor tell
Whose 'tis: but if it favour find,
Next sitting we will draw her mind.

(1640)

171 *To the Memory of My Beloved, the Author Mr William Shakespeare: And What He Hath Left Us*

To draw no envy, Shakespeare, on thy name,
Am I thus ample to thy book and fame;
While I confess thy writings to be such
As neither man nor Muse can praise too much:
'Tis true, and all men's suffrage. But these ways
Were not the paths I meant unto thy praise:
For silliest ignorance on these may light,
Which, when it sounds at best, but echoes right;
Or blind affection, which doth ne'er advance
The truth, but gropes, and urgeth all by chance;
Or crafty malice might pretend this praise,
And think to ruin where it seemed to raise.
These are as some infamous bawd or whore
Should praise a matron: what could hurt her more?
But thou art proof against them, and indeed
Above the ill fortune of them, or the need.
I therefore will begin. Soul of the age!
The applause, delight, the wonder of our stage!
My Shakespeare, rise: I will not lodge thee by
Chaucer or Spenser, or bid Beaumont lie
A little further, to make thee a room;
Thou art a monument without a tomb,

170 confining] bordering on   hurled] whirled

And art alive still while thy book doth live,
And we have wits to read, and praise to give.
That I not mix thee so, my brain excuses;
I mean with great, but disproportioned, Muses:
For if I thought my judgement were of years
I should commit thee surely with thy peers:
And tell how far thou didst our Lyly outshine,
Or sporting Kyd, or Marlowe's mighty line.
And though thou hadst small Latin, and less Greek,
From thence to honour thee I would not seek
For names, but call forth thundering Aeschylus,
Euripides, and Sophocles to us,
Pacuvius, Accius, him of Cordova dead,
To life again, to hear thy buskin tread,
And shake a stage; or, when thy socks were on,
Leave thee alone for the comparison
Of all that insolent Greece or haughty Rome
Sent forth, or since did from their ashes come.
Triumph, my Britain, thou hast one to show,
To whom all scenes of Europe homage owe.
He was not of an age, but for all time!
And all the Muses still were in their prime
When like Apollo he came forth to warm
Our ears, or like a Mercury to charm!
Nature herself was proud of his designs,
And joyed to wear the dressing of his lines,
Which were so richly spun and woven so fit
As, since, she will vouchsafe no other wit.
The merry Greek, tart Aristophanes,
Neat Terence, witty Plautus, now not please,
But antiquated and deserted lie
As they were not of nature's family.
Yet must I not give nature all: thy art,
My gentle Shakespeare, must enjoy a part.
For though the poet's matter nature be,
His art doth give the fashion. And that he
Who casts to write a living line must sweat
(Such as thine are) and strike the second heat
Upon the Muses' anvil: turn the same
(And himself with it) that he thinks to frame;

of years] mature commit] match (Latinism) him of Cordova] Seneca buskin] tragic actor's boot socks] comic actor's footwear Apollo] (Greek god of poetry) Mercury] (Roman god of eloquence) Aristophanes] Greek satiric dramatist Neat] Pithy Terence ... Plautus] Roman comic dramatists fashion] making; form casts] intends, plans

Or for the laurel he may gain a scorn:
For a good poet's made, as well as born;
And such wert thou. Look how the father's face
Lives in his issue: even so, the race
Of Shakespeare's mind and manners brightly shines
In his well-turnèd, and true-filèd lines:
In each of which he seems to shake a lance,
As brandished at the eyes of ignorance.
Sweet swan of Avon! What a sight it were
To see thee in our waters yet appear,
And make those flights upon the banks of Thames
That so did take Eliza, and our James!
But stay, I see thee in the hemisphere
Advanced, and made a constellation there!
Shine forth, thou star of poets, and with rage,
Or influence chide or cheer the drooping stage;
Which, since thy flight from hence, hath mourned like night,
And despairs day, but for thy volume's light.

(1623)

from Plays and Masques (172–178)

from *Cynthia's Revels* (172–173)

172 [*Echo's Song*]

SLOW, slow, fresh fount, keep time with my salt tears;
Yet slower yet, oh faintly, gentle springs;
List to the heavy part the music bears:
Woe weeps out her division when she sings.
Droop, herbs and flowers,
Fall, grief, in showers;
Our beauties are not ours:
Oh, I could still,
Like melting snow upon some craggy hill,
Drop, drop, drop, drop,
Since nature's pride is now a withered daffodil.

(1601)

race] (1) offspring; (2) liveliness; (3) movement, flow   shake a lance] gesture chivalrously (playing on 'Shakespeare')

172 division] rapid melody

173 [*Hymn to Cynthia*]

QUEEN and huntress, chaste and fair,
Now the sun is laid to sleep,
Seated in thy silver chair,
State in wonted manner keep:
  Hesperus entreats thy light,
  Goddess excellently bright.

Earth, let not thy envious shade
Dare itself to interpose;
Cynthia's shining orb was made
Heaven to clear, when day did close:
    Bless us then with wishèd sight,
    Goddess excellently bright.

Lay thy bow of pearl apart,
And thy crystal-shining quiver;
Give unto the flying hart
Space to breathe, how short soever:
    Thou that mak'st a day of night,
    Goddess excellently bright.

(1601)

174 from *The Masque of Queens*

HELP, help all tongues, to celebrate this wonder:
The voice of Fame should be as loud as thunder.
    Her house is all of echo made,
      Where never dies the sound;
    And as her brows the clouds invade,
      Her feet do strike the ground.
Sing then good Fame, that's out of Virtue born,
For who doth Fame neglect doth Virtue scorn.

(1609)

173 *Cynthia*] Diana   Hesperus] Evening

from *Epicoene*

175 [*Clerimont's Song*]

STILL to be neat, still to be dressed,
As you were going to a feast;
Still to be powdered, still perfúmed:
Lady, it is to be presumed,
Though art's hid causes are not found,
All is not sweet, all is not sound.

Give me a look, give me a face,
That makes simplicity a grace;
Robes loosely flowing, hair as free:
Such sweet neglect more taketh me
Than all the adulteries of art:
They strike mine eyes, but not my heart.

(1616; a. 1609)

from *Pleasure Reconciled to Virtue*

176 [*Hymn to Comus*]

ROOM, room, make room for the bouncing belly!
First father of sauce, and deviser of jelly:
Prime master of arts and the giver of wit,
That found out the excellent engine, the spit,
The plough and the flail, the mill and the hopper,
The hutch and the bolter, the furnace and copper:
The oven, the bavin, the malkin and peel,
The hearth and the range, the dog and the wheel.
He, he first invented both hogshead and tun,
The gimlet and vice, too, and taught 'em to run.
And since, with the funnel, an hippocras bag
He's made of himself, that now he cries swag.
Which shows, though the pleasure be but of four inches,
Yet he is a weezle, the gullet that pinches,

Still] Always dressed ... feast] (then a possible rhyme) As] As if

176 hutch] kneading trough bolter] sifter, sieve bavin] brushwood bundle for an oven fire malkin] mop for baker's oven peel] baker's shovel dog ... wheel] i.e. means of driving the spit gimlet] (1) hole for tap; (2) tool for (illicit) tapping vice] (1) tap; (2) viciousness hippocras bag] conical wine strainer cries swag] boasts his pot belly weezle] windpipe

Of any delight; and not spares from the back
Whatever, to make of the belly a sack.
Hail, hail, plump paunch! O the founder of taste
For fresh meats or powdered or pickle or paste;
Devourer of broilèd, baked, roasted or sod,
And emptier of cups, be they even or odd.
All which have now made thee so wide i' the waist
As scarce with no pudding thou art to be laced:
But eating and drinking until thou dost nod,
Thou breakst all thy girdles, and breakst forth a god.

(1641; a. 1618)

from *The New Inn*

177 [*Vision of Beauty*]

IT was a beauty that I saw
So pure, so perfect, as the frame
Of all the universe was lame;
To that one figure, could I draw,
Or give least line of it a law!

A skein of silk without a knot!
A fair march made without a halt!
A curious form without a fault!
A printed book without a blot!
All beauty, and without a spot!

(1631; a. 1629)

from *The Gypsies Metamorphosed*

178 [*Dinner for the Devil*]

COCKLOREL would needs have the devil his guest,
  And bade him once into the Peak to dinner,
Where never the fiend had such a feast,
  Provided him yet at the charge of a sinner.

sod] boiled   pudding] (1) haggis: sheep's stomach stuffed with minced meat; (2) cordage binding to support ship's mast (nautical); (3) fortified with spirits (culinary)   laced] (1) compressed at the waist; (2) tied in   breakst forth] (1) emerges; (2) farts

178 Cocklorel] Arch-rogue

His stomach was queasy (he came thither coached)
    The jogging had caused some crudities rise:
To help it he called for a puritan poached,
    That used to turn up the eggs of his eyes.

And so recovered unto his wish,
    He sat him down, and he fell to eat;
Promoter in plum broth was the first dish—
    His own privy kitchen had no such meat.

Yet though with this he much were taken,
    Upon a sudden he shifted his trencher,
As soon as he spied the bawd and the bacon,
    By which you may note the devil's a wencher.

Six pickled tailors sliced and cut,
    Sempsters and tirewomen fit for his palate,
With feathermen and perfúmers put
    Some twelve in a charger to make a great salad.

A rich fat usurer stewed in his marrow,
    And by him a lawyer's head and green sauce;
Both which his belly took up like a barrow,
    As if till then he had never seen sauce.

Then carbonadoed and cooked with pains,
    Was brought up a cloven sergeant's face:
The sauce was made of his yeoman's brains,
    That had been beaten out with his own mace.

Two roasted sherriffs came whole to the board
    (The feast had been nothing without 'em)
Both living and dead they were foxed and furred,
    Their chains like sausages hung about 'em.

The very next dish was the mayor of a town,
    With a pudding of maintenance thrust in his belly,
Like a goose in the feathers, dressed in his gown,
    And his couple of hench-boys boiled to a jelly.

crudities] undigested food   Promoter] Informer   bawd] (1) hare; (2) procurer   bacon] (1) pig; (2) rustic   tirewomen] lady's maids; dressmakers   feathermen] dealers in plumes   carbonadoed] slashed so as to expose the flesh   pains] (1) messes suitable for side dishes (culinary); (2) sufferings   mace] (1) staff of office; (2) spice   foxed] (1) trimmed with fox fur; (2) drunk   hench-boys] pages of honour

A London cuckold hot from the spit,
    And when the carver up had broken him,
The devil chopped up his head at a bit,
    But the horns were very near like to choke him.

The chine of a lecher too there was roasted,
    With a plump harlot's haunch and garlic,
A pandar's pettitoes, that had boasted
    Himself for a captain, yet never was warlike.

A large fat pasty of a midwife hot,
    And for a cold baked meat into the story,
A reverend painted lady was brought,
    And coffined in crust till now she was hoary.

To these, an over-grown justice of peace,
    With a clerk like a gizzard trussed under each arm;
And warrants for sippits laid in his own grease,
    Set over a chafing dish to be kept warm.

The jowl of a gaoler served for fish,
    A constable soused with vinegar by;
Two aldermen lobsters asleep in a dish,
    A deputy tart, a churchwarden pie.

All which devoured, he then for a close
    Did for a full draught of Derby call;
He heaved the huge vessel up to his nose,
    And left not till he had drunk up all.

Then from the table he gave a start,
    Where banquet and wine were nothing scarce,
All which he flirted away with a fart,
    From whence it was called the Devil's Arse.

(1640; a. 1621)

pettitoes] pigs' trotters   coffined] enclosed in pastry   sippits] croutons   churchwarden pie] (on the analogy of warden pie, made with baking pears)   Derby] i.e. Derby ale   flirted] gusted

ANONYMOUS

fl. 1603

179

WEEP you no more, sad fountains;
  What need you flow so fast?
Look how the snowy mountains
  Heaven's sun doth gently waste.
But my sun's heavenly eyes
  View not your weeping,
  That now lies sleeping
Softly, now softly lies
    Sleeping.

Sleep is a reconciling,
  A rest that peace begets:
Doth not the sun rise smiling
  When fair at even he sets?
Rest you, then, rest sad eyes,
  Melt not in weeping,
  While she lies sleeping
Softly, now softly lies
    Sleeping.

(1603)

THOMAS HEYWOOD

1574?–1641

180

The Author to His Book

THE world's a theatre, the Earth a stage,
Which God and nature doth with actors fill:
Kings have their entrance in due equipage,
And some their parts play well and others ill.
The best no better are, in this theatre,
Where every humour's fitted in his kind:
This a true subject acts, and that a traitor,
The first applauded and the last confined;

180 equipage] state; military array   kind] nature

This plays an honest man and that a knave,
A gentle person this, and he a clown;
One man is ragged and another brave:
All men have parts, and each man acts his own.
She a chaste lady acteth all her life,
A wanton courtesan another plays.
This covets marriage love, that, nuptial strife:
Both in continual action spend their days:
Some citizens, some soldiers born to adventure,
Shepherds and seamen. Then our play's begun
When we are born, and to the world first enter;
And all find *exits* when their parts are done.
If then the world a theatre present,
As by the roundness it appears most fit,
Built with star-galleries of high ascent,
In which Jehove doth as spectator sit
And chief determiner to applaud the best,
And their endeavours crown with more than merit;
But by their evil actions dooms the rest
To end disgraced whilst others praise inherit,
    He that denies then theatres should be,
    He may as well deny a world to me.

(1612)

JOHN WEBSTER
*c.*1575?–1634 or 1638

181 from *The White Devil*

CALL for the robin redbreast and the wren,
Since o'er shady groves they hover,
And with leaves and flowers do cover
The friendless bodies of unburied men.
Call unto his funeral dole
The ant, the field-mouse and the mole,
To rear him hillocks, that shall keep him warm
And (when gay tombs are robbed) sustain no harm.
But keep the wolf far thence, that's foe to men,
For with his nails he'll dig them up again.

(1612)

clown] peasant He . . . me] 'No theatre, no world' (H.)
181 dole] rites

182

from *The Devil's Law Case*

ALL the flowers of the spring
Meet to perfúme our burying;
These have but their growing prime,
And man does flourish but his time.
Survey our progress from our birth:
We are set, we grow, we turn to earth.
Courts adieu, and all delights,
All bewitching appetites;
Sweetest breath, and clearest eye,
Like perfúmes go out and die;
And consequently this is done,
As shadows wait upon the sun.
Vain the ambition of kings,
Who seek by trophies and dead things
To leave a living name behind,
And weave but nets to catch the wind.

(1623)

ANONYMOUS
fl. before 1605

183

[*Epitaph*]

MY friend, judge not me;
Thou seest I judge not thee:
Betwixt the stirrup and the ground,
Mercy I asked, mercy I found.

(1605)

182 consequently] consistently

ROBERT BURTON
1577–1640

184 *The Author's Abstract of Melancholy, Διαλογικῶς*

WHEN I go musing all alone,
Thinking of divers things foreknown,
When I build castles in the air,
Void of sorrow and void of fear,
Pleasing myself with phantasms sweet,
Methinks the time runs very fleet.
All my joys to this are folly,
Naught so sweet as melancholy.
When I lie waking all alone,
Recounting what I have ill done,
My thoughts on me then tyrannize:
Fear and sorrow me surprise;
Whether I tarry still or go,
Methinks the time goes very slow.
All my griefs to this are jolly,
Naught so sad as melancholy.
When to myself I act and smile,
With pleasing thoughts the time beguile
By a brook side or wood so green,
Unheard, unsought for, or unseen,
A thousand pleasures do me bless,
And crown my soul with happiness.
All my joys besides are folly,
None so sweet as melancholy.
When I lie, sit, or walk alone,
I sigh, I grieve, making great moan,
In a dark grove or irksome den
With discontents and Furies, then
A thousand miseries at once
Mine heavy heart and soul ensconce.
All my griefs to this are jolly,
None so sour as melancholy.
Methinks I hear, methinks I see,
Sweet music, wondrous melody,
Towns, palaces and cities fine,
Here now, then there; the world is mine;

Διαλογικῶς] in a dialogue

Rare beauties, gallant ladies shine,
Whate'er is lovely or divine.
    All other joys to this are folly,
    None so sweet as melancholy.
Methinks I hear, methinks I see
Ghosts, goblins, fiends; my fantasy
Presents a thousand ugly shapes:
Headless bears, black men and apes,
Doleful outcries and fearful sights
My sad and dismal soul affrights.
    All my griefs to this are jolly,
    None so damned as melancholy.
Methinks I court, methinks I kiss,
Methinks I now embrace my mistress.
Oh blessed days, oh sweet content,
In paradise my time is spent.
Such thoughts may still my fancy move:
Let me not die, but live in love.
    All my joys to this are folly,
    Naught so sweet as melancholy.
When I recount love's many frights,
My sighs and tears, my waking nights,
My jealous fits, oh mine hard fate,
I now repent, but 'tis too late.
No torment is so bad as love,
So bitter to my soul can prove.
    All my griefs to this are jolly,
    Naught so harsh as melancholy.
Friends and companions get you gone,
'Tis my desire to be alone,
Ne'er well but when my thoughts and I
Do domineer in privacy.
No gem, no treasure like to this:
'Tis my delight, my crown, my bliss.
    All my joys to this are folly,
    Naught so sweet as melancholy.
'Tis my sole plague to be alone:
I am a beast, a monster grown;
I will no light nor company,
I find it now my misery.
The scene is turned, my joys are gone,
Fear, discontent and sorrows come.
    All my griefs to this are jolly,
    Naught so fierce as melancholy.

fantasy] faculty of imagination   affrights] frightens

I'll not change life with any king;
I ravished am: can the world bring
More joy than still to laugh and smile,
In pleasant toys times to beguile?
Do not, oh do not trouble me,
So sweet content I feel and see.
    All my joys to this are folly,
    None so divine as melancholy.
I'll change my state with any wretch
Thou canst from gaol or dunghill fetch:
My pains past cure, another hell,
I may not in this torment dwell.
Now desperate I hate my life;
Lend me an halter or a knife.
    All my griefs to this are jolly,
    Naught so damned as melancholy.

(1628)

THOMAS FORDE
fl. 1607–1648

185

THERE is a lady sweet and kind,
Was never face so pleased my mind;
I did but see her passing by,
And yet I love her till I die.

Her gesture, motion, and her smiles,
Her wit, her voice, my heart beguiles;
Beguiles my heart, I know not why,
And yet I love her till I die.

Her free behaviour, winning looks,
Will make a lawyer burn his books.
I touched her not, alas, not I,
And yet I love her till I die.

Had I her fast betwixt mine arms,
Judge, you that think, such sports were harms,
Were 't any harm? No, no, fie, fie!
For I will love her till I die.

184 still] ever

Should I remain confinèd there,
So long as Phebus in his sphere,
I to request, she to deny,
Yet would I love her till I die.

Cupid is wingèd and doth range,
Her country so my love doth change;
But change she earth or change she sky,
Yet will I love her till I die.

(1607)

GEORGE SANDYS
1578–1644

186 from *A Paraphrase upon Job*

AGAIN when all the radiant sons of light
Before his throne appeared, whose only sight
Beatitude infused, th' inveterate foe,
In fogs ascending from the depth below,
Profaned their blest assembly. 'What pretence'
Said God, 'hath brought thee hither? And from whence?'
'I come', said he, 'from compassing the Earth;
Their travails seen who spring from human birth.'
Then God: 'Hast thou my servant Job beheld?
Can his rare piety be paralleled,
His justice equalled? Can alluring vice,
With all her sorceries, his soul entice?
His daily orisons attract our ears;
Who punishment, less than the trespass, fears,
And still his old integrity retains
Through all his woes, inflicted by thy trains.'
When he, whose labouring thoughts admit no rest,
This answer threw out of his Stygian breast:
'Job to himself is next: who will not give
All that he hath, so his own soul may live?
Stretch out thy hand; with aches pierce his bones,
His flesh with lashes; multiply his groans:
Then if he curse thee not, let thy dire curse
Increase my torments, if they can be worse.'

186 pretence] intention trains] snares, deceits Stygian] infernal Job . . . next] Job is out for himself

To whom the Lord: 'Thou instrument of strife,
Enjoy thy cruel wish; but spare his life.'
The soul of envy from his presence went,
And through the burning air made his descent.
To execution falls: the blood within
His veins inflames, and poisons his smooth skin.
Now all was but one sore: from foot to head
With burning carbuncles and ulcers spread
He on the ashes sits; his fate deplores;
And with a potsherd scrapes the swelling sores.
His frantic wife, whose patience could not bear
Such weight of miseries, thus wounds his ear:
'Is this the purchase of thy innocence?
O fool, thy piety is thy offence.'

(1638)

JOHN TAYLOR
1578?–1653

187

Epigram II. vi

FAIR Beatrice tucks her coats up somewhat high,
Her pretty leg and foot cause men should spy.
Says one 'You have a handsome leg, sweet duck.'
'I have two', quoth she, 'or else I had hard luck.'
'There's two indeed: I think they're twins', quoth he.
'They are, and are not, honest friend,' quoth she;
'Their birth was both at once, I dare be sworn,
But yet between them both a man was born.'

(1612)

188

Epigram II. xxxv

THERE chanced to meet together in an inn
Four men that thought that lying was no sin:
The first an old man was in age well entered,
The next a traveller that far had ventured,
The third a poet, in prose and verse attired,
The fourth a painter for his art admired.

188 attired] equipped

These four strived, each other to excel,
Who should in lying bear away the bell.
The old man said that when he was a boy,
To lift nine hundredweight was but a toy;
To jump in plain ground thirty foot at least
Then was accounted but an idle jest.
The traveller replied that he had seen
The king of pygmies and the faerie queen,
And been where triple-headed Cerberus
Did guard the sulphurous gate of Erebus.
The poet he had been at Helicon,
And raked from embers of oblivion
Old Saturn's downfall and Jove's royal rising,
With thousand fictions of his wit's devising;
And for the painter scorns to come behind,
He paints a flying horse, a golden hind,
A sagittary and a grim wild man,
A two-necked eagle, and a coal-black swan.
Now, reader, tell me: which of those four liars
Doth best deserve the whetstone for their hires?

(1612)

189 *Epigram II. xxxii*

LOOK how yon lecher's legs are worn away
With haunting of the whorehouse every day:
He knows more greasy panders, bawds, and drabs,
And eats more lobsters, artichokes, and crabs,
Blue roasted eggs, potatoes muscadine,
Oysters, and pith that grows i'th' ox's chine,
With many drugs, compounds, and simples store;
Which makes him have a stomach to a whore.
But one day he'll give o'er when 'tis too late,
When he stands begging through an iron grate.

(1612)

bell] prize Cerberus] monstrous watchdog (classical mythology) Erebus] Hades Helicon] Boeotian haunt of the Muses sagittary] centaur whetstone] reward of lying (hung round the neck)

189 muscadine] sweetmeat perfumed with musk pith] marrow store] plenty

190 *Epigram III. xii*

A LUSTY wench as nimble as an eel
Would give a gallant leave to kiss and feel;
His itching humour straightway was in hope
To toy, to wanton, dally, buss and grope.
'Hold, sir,' quoth she, 'My word I will not fail,
For you shall feel my hand, and kiss my t—.'

(1614)

191 *Virgo: August*

UNHAPPY Phaeton's splendidious sire
  Left amorous bussing beauteous Climen's lips,
  And all inspired with love's celestial fire
  His globe-surrounding steed amain he whips,
And to the virgin Virgo down doth glide,
  Where, for she entertained him to his pleasure
  He his exchequer coffers opens wide,
  And fills the world with harvest's wished-for treasure,
Now country hinds unto their tools betake,
  The fork, the rake, the scythe, the hook, the cart,
  And all a general expedition make,
  Till nature be left naked by their art.
At last the Virgin, when these things are done,
Till that time twelve-month leaves her love the sun.

(1614)

192 *Libra: September*

THE great all-seeing burning eye of day
  In Libra's Balance restless comes to rest,
  Where equally his way he seems to weigh,
  And day and night with equal hours are dressed:
By these just scales true justice is expressed,
  Which doth to times and places render right,
  Where wealth insults not, nor the poor oppressed,
  But all's even poisèd, like the day and night.

190 buss] kiss

191 Phaeton] son of Apollo   splendidious] magnificent   bussing] kissing
Climen's] Clymene's (Phaeton's mother)   hinds] labourers

And now this lamp of light doth here alight,
Making this Sign his equinoctial inn,
Whilst fruitful trees are overladen quite
(Too great a gracious guerdon for man's sin);
And as in March he gan to do us grace,
So to th' antipodes he now gins show her face.

(1614)

193 *Epigram XXIV: A Supposed Construction*

MARY and *mare*, anagrammatized,
The one is Army, and the other arme;
In both their names is danger moralized,
And both alike do sometimes good, or harm:
Mare's the sea, and *mare*'s arme's a river,
And Mary's army's all for what'll ye give her.

(1614)

194 from *Sir Gregory Nonsense's News from No Place*

IT was in June the eight and thirtieth day
That I embarkèd was on Highgate Hill,
After discourteous friendly taking leave
Of my young father Madge and Mother John;
The wind did ebb, the tide flowed north south-east,
We hoist our sails of coloquintida,
And after thirteen days and seventeen nights
(With certain hieroglyphic hours to boot)
We with tempestuous calms and friendly storms
Split our main top-mast close below the keel.
But I with a dull quick congruity
Took eighteen ounces of the western wind,
And with the pith of the pole artichoke
Sailed by the flaming Coast of Trapezond.
There in a fort of melting adamant,
Armed in a crimson robe as black as jet,
I saw Alcides with a spider's thread
Lead Cerberus to the Pronontic Sea;
Then, cutting further through the marble main,
Mongst flying bulls and four-legged Turkicocks,
A dumb fair-spoken, wellfaced agèd youth,
Sent to me from the stout Stymphalides,

194 Trapezond] Trebizond Alcides] Hercules Stymphalides] mythic vultures destroyed by Hercules

With tongueless silence thus began his speech:
'Illustrious flapjack, to thy hungry doom
Low as the ground I elevate my cause,
As I upon a gnat was riding late,
In quest to parley with the Pleiades,
I saw the Duke of Houndsditch gaping close,
In a green arbour made of yellow starch,
Betwixt two brokers howling madrigals.
A banquet was served in of lampreys' bones,
Well pickled in the tarbox of old time,
When Demogorgon sailed to Islington;
Which I perceiving with nine shads of steel,
Straight flew unto the coast of Pimlico,
To inform great Prester John and the Mogul
What excellent oysters were at Billingsgate.
The Mogul, all enragèd with these news,
Sent a black snail post to Tartaria,
To tell the Irishmen in Saxony
The dismal downfall of old Charing Cross.
With that, nine butter firkins in a flame
Did coldly rise to arbitrate the cause:
Guessing by the synderesis of Wapping,
Saint Thomas Watrings is most ominous.
For though an andiron and a pair of tongs
May both have breeding from one teeming womb,
Yet by the calculation of pickedhatch,
Milk must not be so dear as muscadel.
First shall Melpomene in cobweb lawn
Adorn great Memphis in a mussel boat,
And all the Muses clad in robes of air
Shall dance lavoltas with a whirligig;
Fair Pluto shall descend from brazen Dis,
And Polyphemus keep a seamster's shop;
The Isle of Wight shall like a dive-dapper
Devour the Egyptian proud pyrámides,
Whilst Cassia Fistula shall gourmandize
Upon the flesh and blood of Croydon coal dust.
Then on the banks of Shoreditch shall be seen
What 'tis to serve the great Utopian queen.'

(1622)

synderesis] remorse of conscience St Thomas Watrings] St Thomas a Watering (a small stream on the Old Kent Road) pickedhatch] half-door with spikes Melpomene] Muse of tragedy lawn] very fine linen Dis] Pluto, king of the underworld (ancient mythology) Polyphemus] Cyclops dive-dapper] dabchick; waterfowl Cassia] Cinnamon

JOHN FLETCHER
1579–1625

from *The Faithful Shepherdess* (195–196)

195

[*The River God's Song*]

Do not fear to put thy feet
Naked in the river, sweet:
Think not leach or newt or toad
Will bite thy foot when thou hast trod;
Nor let the water rising high,
As thou wadest in, make thee cry
And sob; but ever live with me,
And not a wave shall trouble thee.

(1609–10?)

196

[*The Satyr's Song*]

Softly gliding as I go,
With this burden full of woe,
Through still silence of the night,
Guided by the glow-worm's light,
Hither am I come at last;
Many a thicket have I passed;
Not a twig that durst deny me,
Nor a bush that durst descry me,
To the little bird that sleeps
On the tender spray; nor creeps
That hardy worm with pointed tail,
But if I be under sail,
Flying faster than the wind,
Leaving all the clouds behind,
But doth hide her tender head
In some hollow tree or bed
Of seeded nettles: not a hare
Can be started from his fare
By my footing, nor a wish
Is more sudden, nor a fish
Can be found, with greater ease
Cut the vast unbounded seas,
Leaving neither print nor sound,
Than I when nimbly on the ground:
I measure many a league an hour.

(1609–10?)

197 from *Henry VIII*

ORPHEUS with his lute made trees,
And the mountain tops that freeze
  Bow themselves when he did sing.
To his music, plants and flowers
Ever sprung, as sun and showers
  There had made a lasting spring.
Everything that heard him play,
Even the billows of the sea,
  Hung their heads, and then lay by.
In sweet music is such art,
Killing care and grief of heart
  Fall asleep, or hearing, die.

(1623)

198 from *The Elder Brother*

  BEAUTY clear and fair,
    Where the air
Rather like a perfume dwells;
  Where the violet and the rose
  The blue veins in blush disclose,
And come to honour nothing else.

  Where to live near,
    And planted there,
Is to live and still live new;
  Where to gain a favour is
  More than light, perpetual bliss—
Make me live by serving you.

  Dear, again back recall
    To this light
A stranger to himself and all;
  Both the wonder and the story
  Shall be yours, and eke the glory:
I am your servant and your thrall.

(1637)

199 from *Love's Cure*

TURN, turn thy beauteous face away,
How pale and sickly looks the day
In emulation of thy brighter beams!
O envious light, fly, fly, be gone;
Come night, and piece two breasts as one;
When what love does, we will repeat in dreams.
Yet, thy eyes open, who can day hence fright,
Let but their lids fall and it will be night.

(1647)

from *Women Pleased*

200 [*To his Sleeping Mistress*]

O FAIR sweet face! O eyes celestial bright,
Twin stars in heaven that now adorn the night!
O fruitful lips, where cherries ever grow,
And damask cheeks, where all sweet beauties blow!
O thou from head to foot divinely fair!
Cupid's most cunning net's made of that hair,
And as he weaves himself for curious eyes,
'Oh me, oh me, I am caught myself!' he cries.
Sweet rest about thee, sweet and golden sleep:
Soft peaceful thoughts your hourly watches keep,
Whilst I in wonder sing this sacrifice,
To beauty sacred, and those angel eyes.

(1647)

from *The Tragedy of Valentinian* (201–202)

201 [*Love's Emblems*]

NOW the lusty spring is seen,
Golden yellow, gaudy blue,
Daintily invite the view
Everywhere, on every green.

199 fright] frighten

201 invite] attract

Roses blushing as they blow
And enticing men to pull,
Lilies whiter than the snow,
Woodbines of sweet honey full:
All love's emblems, and all cry,
Ladies, if not plucked we die.

Yet the lusty spring hath stayed,
Blushing red and purest white:
Daintily to love invite
Every woman, every maid;
Cherries kissing as they grow,
And inviting men to taste;
Apples even ripe below,
Winding gently to the waist:
All love's emblems, and all cry,
Ladies, if not plucked we die.

(1647)

202

[*Sleep Song*]

CARE charming sleep, thou easer of all woes,
Brother to death, sweetly thyself dispose
On this afflicted prince: fall like a cloud
In gentle showers, give nothing that is loud
Or painful to his slumbers; easy, light,
And as a purling stream, thou son of night,
Pass by his troubled senses; sing his pain
Like hollow murmuring winds or silver rain.
Into this prince gently, oh gently slide,
And kiss him into slumbers like a bride.

(1647)

from *Beggar's Bush*

203

The Beggars' Holiday

CAST our caps and cares away
This is beggars' holiday!
At the crowning of our king,
Thus we ever dance and sing.
In the world look out and see:
Where so happy a prince as he?

201 blow] bloom

Where the nation live so free,
And so merry as do we?
Be it peace, or be it war,
Here at liberty we are,
And enjoy our ease and rest:
To the field we are not pressed;
Nor are called into the town,
To be troubled with the gown.
Hang all officers, we cry,
And the magistrate too, by!
When the subsidy's increased,
We are not a penny sessed;
Nor will any go to law
With the beggar for a straw.
All which happiness, he brags,
He doth owe unto his rags.

(1647; a. 1622)

ROBERT HAYMAN
1579?–1631?

from *Owen's Epigrams*

204 *Owen's Bracelet*

OUR senses, without reason, are naught worth;
Nor reason, unless faith do set it forth:
Neither is faith without love to be deemed,
Nor is love without God to be esteemed.

(1628)

205 *Saturn's Three Sons*

DOUBTFUL divines, lawyers that wrangle most,
Nasty physicians: these three rule the roast.

(1628)

203 by] by the bye sessed] assessed

THOMAS MIDDLETON?
1580–1627

206

Melancholy

HENCE, hence, all you vain delights,
As short as are the nights
Wherein you spend your folly;
There's nought in this life sweet,
If men were wise to see 't,
But only melancholy:
  O sweetest melancholy!

Welcome folded arms and fixèd eyes,
A sigh that piercing mortifies,
A look that's fastened to the ground,
A tongue chained up without a sound.
Fountains' heads and pathless groves,
Places which pale passion loves;
Moonlike wakes, when all the fowls
Are warmly housed, save bats and owls;
A midnight knell; a parting groan:
These are the sounds we feed upon.
Then stretch your bones in a still gloomy valley:
There's nothing dainty, sweet, save melancholy.

(1647; a. 1615/16)

JOHN DIGBY, EARL OF BRISTOL
1580–1654

207 GRIEVE not, dear love, although we often part;
  But know that nature gently doth us sever
Thereby to train us up with tender art,
  To brook the day when we must part for ever.

For nature, doubting we should be surprised
  By that sad day whose dread doth chiefly fear us,
Doth keep us daily schooled and exercised,
  Lest that the fright thereof should overbear us.

mortifies] deprives of life   fowls] birds

207 fear] frighten

And this may make both death and absence sweet,
  That wheresoe'er we die, on sea or shore,
A pious life and death will make us meet
  In heavenly joys where we shall part no more.

(1653; wr. before *c.*1640)

THOMAS MORTON
1580–1646

208

[*Epitaph*]

TIME that brings all things to light
Doth hide this thing out of sight;
Yet fame hath left behind a story,
A hopeful race to show the glory;
For underneath this heap of stones
Lieth a parcel of small bones.
What hope at last can such imps have,
That from the womb goes to the grave?

(1637)

LORD NORTH
1581–1666

209

Platonic

PLATONIC is a pretty name,
  But Cupid disavows it;
It hath no body but in fame;
  Disguise alone allows it.

True love cannot divine its end,
  'Twas by some spirit given
That ne'er knew further than a friend:
  Its proper sphere is heaven.

Even she and she may make it as good
  As he and she together:
'Tis little better understood
  Than playing with a feather.
Beyond ideas, love must go,
Or Cupid may break shafts and bow.

(1645)

RICHARD CORBETT
1582–1635

210 *A Proper New Ballad, Intituled the Fairies' Farewell, or God-a-Mercy Will: to be sung or whistled, to the tune of* The Meadow Brow *by the learned, by the unlearned to the tune of* Fortune.

FAREWELL, rewards and fairies,
  Good housewives now may say;
For now foul sluts in dairies
  Do fare as well as they,
And though they sweep their hearths no less
  Than maids were wont to do,
Yet who of late for cleanliness
  Finds sixpence in her shoe?

Lament, lament, old abbeys,
  The fairies lost command;
They did but change priests' babies,
  But some have changed your land;
And all your children sprung from thence
  Are now grown Puritans,
Who live as changelings ever since,
  For love of your demesnes.

At morning and at evening both
  You merry were and glad,
So little care of sleep or sloth
  These pretty ladies had;

210 changed] substituted; transferred; altered changelings] (1) children left by fairies; (2) turncoats

When Tom came home from labour,
  Or Ciss to milking rose,
Then merrily went their tabor,
  And nimbly went their toes.

Witness those rings and roundelays
  Of theirs, which yet remain,
Were footed in Queen Mary's days
  On many a grassy plain;
But since of late Elizabeth,
  And later James, came in,
They never danced on any heath
  As when the time hath been.

By which we note the fairies
  Were of the old profession;
Their songs were Ave Maries,
  Their dances were procession.
But now, alas, they all are dead,
  Or gone beyond the seas,
Or further for religion fled,
  Or else they take their ease.

A tell-tale in their company
  They never could endure,
And whoso kept not secretly
  Their mirth was punished sure:
It was a just and Christian deed
  To pinch such black and blue.
Oh, how the commonwealth doth need
  Such justices as you!

Now they have left our quarters,
  A register they have,
Who can preserve their charters,
  A man both wise and grave;
A hundred of their merry pranks
  By one that I could name
Are kept in store; con twenty thanks
  To William for the same.

roundelays] round dances, carols   old profession] Roman Catholic persuasion   procession] ceremonial; a service book of processional offices   register] recorder, registrar   con] offer

I marvel who his cloak would turn
  When Puck had led him round,
Or where those walking fires would burn
  Where Cureton would be found;
How Broker would appear to be,
  For whom this age doth mourn;
But that their spirits live in thee,
  In thee, old William Chourne.

To William Chourne of Staffordshire
  Give laud and praises due,
Who every meal can mend your cheer
  With tales both old and true.
To William all give audience,
  And pray ye for his noddle,
For all the fairies' evidence
  Were lost, if that were addle.

(1647)

211 *An Elegy upon the Death of His Own Father*

VINCENT Corbett, farther known
By Poynter's name than by his own,
Here lies engagèd till the day
Of raising bones and quickening clay.
Nor wonder, reader, that he hath
Two surnames in his epitaph,
For this one did comprehend
All that two families could lend;
And if to know more arts than any
Could multiply one into many,
Here a colony lies, then,
Both of qualities and men.
Years he lived well-nigh fourscore,
But, count his virtues, he lived more;
And number him by doing good,
He lived the age before the flood.
Should we undertake his story,
Truth would seem feigned, and plainness glory.
Beside, this tablet were too small:
Add too the pillars and the wall.

turn] reverse (as protection against the fairies) walking fires] will o' the wisps Cureton . . . Broker] ?Staffordshire worthies Chourne] (see endnote) addle] confused

211 this . . . comprehend] this man comprehended in himself

Yet of this volume much is found
Written in many a fertile ground,
Where the printer thee affords
Earth for paper, trees for words.
He was nature's factor here,
And ledger lay for every shire,
To supply the ingenious wants
Of soon-sprung fruits and foreign plants.
Simple he was, and wise withal;
His purse nor base nor prodigal;
Poorer in substance than in friends,
Future and public were his ends;
His conscience, like his diet, such
As neither took nor left too much,
So that made laws were useless grown
To him: he needed but his own.
Did he his neighbours bid, like those
That feast them only to enclose,
Or with their roast meat rack their rents,
And cozen them with their consents?
No; the free meetings at his board
Did but one literal sense afford;
No close or acre understood,
But only love and neighbourhood.
His alms were such as Paul defines,
Not causes to be saved, but signs;
Which alms, by faith, hope, love laid down,
Laid up, what now he wears, a crown.
Besides his fame, his goods, his life,
He left a grieved son and a wife;
Strange sorrow, not to be believed,
When the son and heir is grieved.
  Read then, and mourn, whate'er thou art
  That dost hope to have a part
  In honest epitaphs, lest, being dead,
  Thy life be written, and not read.

(1647)

factor] agent   ledger lay] acted as representative   ingenious] honest   enclose] fence in for pasture   rack] raise steeply   cozen] cheat   Paul defines] (1 Cor. 13: 3, 13: all his goods)

212 *On Mr. Rice the Manciple of Christ Church in Oxford*

WHO can doubt, Rice, to which eternal place
Thy soul is fled, that did but know thy face?
Whose body was so light, it might have gone
To heaven without a resurrection.
Indeed thou wert all type: thy limbs were signs,
Thy arteries but mathematic lines;
As if two souls had made thy compound good,
Which both should live by faith, and none by blood.

(1647)

213 *To His Son, Vincent Corbett*

WHAT I shall leave thee none can tell,
But all shall say I wish thee well:
I wish thee, Vin, before all wealth,
Both bodily and ghostly health;
Nor too much wealth, nor wit, come to thee:
Too much of either may undo thee.
I wish thee learning, not for show,
But truly to instruct and know;
Not such as gentlemen require,
To prate at table or at fire.
I wish thee all thy mother's graces,
Thy father's fortunes, and his places.
I wish thee friends, and one at court,
Not to build up but to support:
To keep thee, not in doing many
Oppressions, but from suffering any.
I wish thee peace in all thy ways,
Nor lazy nor contentious days;
And, when thy soul and body part,
As innocent as now thou art.

(1647)

type] symbol compound] (1) composition; (2) union

213 ghostly] spiritual

214 *Upon Fairford Windows*

TELL me, you anti-saints, why glass
With you is longer lived than brass?
And why the saints have scaped their falls
Better from windows than from walls?
Is it because the brethren's fires
Maintain a glass-house at Blackfriars,
Next which the church stands north and south,
And east and west the preachers mouth?
Or is't because such painted ware
Resembles something what you are,
So pied, so seeming, so unsound
In manners, and in doctrine, found,
That, out of emblematic wit,
You spare yourselves in sparing it?
If it be so, then, Fairford, boast
Thy church hath kept what all have lost,
And is preservèd from the bane
Of either war or Puritan,
Whose life is coloured in thy paint:
The inside dross, the outside saint.

(1648)

215 *On the Lady Arabella*

HOW do I thank thee, death, and bless thy power,
That I have passed the guard, and scaped the Tower:
And now my pardon is my epitaph,
And a small coffin my poor carcass hath.
For at thy charge both soul and body were
Enlarged at last, secured from hope and fear.
That amongst saints, this amongst kings is laid;
And what my birth did claim, my death hath paid.

(1648)

pied] particoloured

215 *Arabella*] (see endnote)

LORD HERBERT OF CHERBURY
1582–1648

216 *To One Black, and Not Very Handsome, Who Expected Commendation*

WHAT though your eyes be stars, your hair be night
And all that beauty which adorns your face
Yield in effect but such a sullen light
It hardly serves for to set off that grace
Which every shadow yieldeth in his place:
Yet, more than any other, you delight.

For since I love not with mine eyes but heart,
Your red or white so little could incline,
Whether it came from nature or from art,
I should not think it either yours or mine,
As that which doth but with the skin confine
And with the light that gave it first depart.

Let novices in love themselves address
Unto those parts which superficial be;
Cloris, I must ingeniously confess
Nothing appears a real fair to me
Which at the most but sometimes I do see
But never can at any time possess:

Give me a beauty at such distance set
That all the senses which I would employ,
Being within an even compass met,
Each sense may there such equal share enjoy
That neither one the other shall destroy,
Or force it for to pay its fellow's debt.

So, though with dovelike murmurs I did rest,
Faster enchanted than with any spell,
Lying within your arms upon your breast,
Sipping a nectar kiss whose fragrant smell
My tongue within your lips alone should tell,
I would not think my powers were oppressed.

Expected] Waited for confine] have a common boundary ingeniously] (1) ingenuously, candidly; (2) cunningly

Then leave your simpering, Cloris, and make haste,
Without delighting thus to hear me pray,
That all your sweets I may together taste.
Should I too long on one perfection stay
I might be forced to linger on my way,
Or leave thee with the praise of being chaste.

(1923)

217 *Another [Madrigal]*

DEAR, when I did from you remove,
I left my joy, but not my love;
That never can depart:
It neither higher can ascend
Nor lower bend.
Fixed in the centre of my heart
As in his place,
And lodgèd so, how can it change,
Or you grow strange?
Those are Earth's properties, and base.
Each where, as the bodies divine
Heaven's lights and you to me will shine.

(1665)

218 *Kissing*

COME hither womankind, and all their worth:
Give me thy kisses as I call them forth.
Give me the billing-kiss, that of the dove,
A kiss of love;
The melting-kiss, a kiss that doth consume
To a perfúme;
The extract-kiss, of every sweet a part,
A kiss of art;
The kiss which ever stirs some new delight,
A kiss of might;
The twaching smacking kiss, and when you cease
A kiss of peace;
The music-kiss, crotchet and quaver time,
The kiss of rhyme;
The kiss of eloquence, which doth belong
Unto the tongue;
The kiss of all the sciences in one,
The kiss alone.
So 'tis enough.

(1665)

219 *Ditty*

IF you refuse me once, and think again,
I will complain
You are deceived: love is no work of art;
It must be got and born,
Not made and worn,
Or such wherein you have no part.

Or do you think they more than once can die
Whom you deny?
Who tell you of a thousand deaths a day,
Like the old poets feign,
And tell the pain
They met but in the common way.

Or do you think it is too soon to yield
And quit the field?
You are deceived: they yield who first entreat;
Once one may crave for love,
But more would prove
This heart too little, that too great.

Give me then so much love that we may burn
Past all return,
Who midst your beauties' flames and spirit lives,
So great a light must find
As to be blind
To all but what their fire gives.

Then give me so much love as in one point
Fixed and conjoint
May make us equal in our flames arise,
As we shall never start
Until we dart
Lightning upon the envious eyes.

Then give me so much love that we may move
Like stars of love,
And glad and happy times to lovers bring;
While glorious in one sphere
We still appear,
And keep an everlasting spring.

(1665)

start] flinch; withdraw

220

Sonnet: Made upon the Groves near Merlow Castle

YOU well compacted groves, whose light and shade,
  Mixed equally, produce nor heat nor cold
  Either to burn the young or freeze the old,
But to one even temper being made,
Upon a green embroidering through each glade
  An airy silver and a sunny gold,
  So clothe the poorest that they do behold
Themselves in riches which can never fade:
  While the wind whistles and the birds do sing,
While your twigs clip, and while the leaves do frizz,
  While the fruit ripens which those trunks do bring,
  Senseless to all but love, do you not spring
Pleasure of such a kind as truly is
A self-renewing vegetable bliss?

(1665)

221

Ditty

WHY dost thou hate return instead of love,
      And with such merciless despite
        My faith and hope requite?
      Oh! if the affection cannot move,
      Learn innocence yet of the dove,
And thy disdain to juster bounds confine;
Or if towards man thou equally decline
    The rules of justice and of mercy too,
Thou mayst thy love to such a point refine
    As it will kill more than thy hate can do.

Love, love, Melaina, then, though death ensue;
      Yet if it is a greater fate
        To die through love than hate,
      Rather a victory pursue,
      To beauty's lawful conquest due,
Than tyrant eyes envenom with disdain;
Or if thy power thou wouldst so maintain
    As equally to be both loved and dread,
Let timely kisses call to life again
    Him whom thy eyes have planet-strucken dead.

clip] embrace   frizz] curl   spring] cause, bring forth
221 decline] repudiate

Kiss, kiss, Melaina, then, and do not stay
Until these sad effects appear,
Which now draw on so near,
That didst thou longer help delay,
My soul must fly so fast away
As would at once both life and love divorce:
Or if I needs must die without remorse,
Kiss and embalm me so with that sweet breath
That while thou triúmph'st o'er love and his force,
I may triúmph yet over fate and death.

(1665)

222 La Gialletta Gallante, *Or* *The Sunburned Exotic Beauty*

CHILD of the sun, in whom his rays appear
Hatched to that lustre as doth make thee wear
Heaven's livery in thy skin, what needst thou fear
The injury of air and change of clime,
When thy exalted form is so sublime
As to transcend all power of change or time?

How proud are they that in their hair but show
Some part of thee, thinking therein they owe
The greatest beauty nature can bestow!—
When thou art so much fairer to the sight
As beams each where diffusèd are more bright
Than their derived and secondary light.

But thou art cordial both to sight and taste,
While each rare fruit seems in his time to haste
To ripen in thee, till at length they waste
Themselves to inward sweets, from whence again
They, like elixirs passing through each vein,
An endless circulation do maintain.

How poor are they, then, whom if we but greet
Think that raw juice which in their lips we meet
Enough to make us hold their kisses sweet!—
When that rich odour which in thee is smelt
Can itself to a balmy liquor melt,
And make it to our inward senses felt.

222 Hatched] (1) Inlaid with gold; (2) Incubated by warmth owe] possess cordial] exhilarating, restorative

Leave then thy country soil and mother's home:
Wander a planet this way, till thou come
To give our lovers here their fatal doom;
While if our beauties scorn to envy thine,
It will be just they to a jaundice pine,
And by thy gold show like some copper mine.

(1665)

223 *Platonic Love*

MADAM, your beauty and your lovely parts
Would scarce admit poetic praise and arts,
As they are love's most sharp and piercing darts;
Though, as again they only wound and kill
The more depraved affections of our will,
You claim a right to commendation still.

For as you can unto that height refine
All love's delights as, while they do incline
Unto no vice, they so become divine,
We may as well attain your excellence,
As without help of any outward sense
Would make us grow a pure intelligence.

And as a soul thus being quite abstract
Complies not properly with any act
Which from its better being may detract,
So, through the virtuous habits you infuse,
It is enough that we may like and choose,
Without presuming yet to take or use.

Thus angels in their starry orbs proceed
Unto affection, without other need
Than that they still on contemplation feed:
Though as they may unto this orb descend,
You can, when you would so much lower bend,
Give joys beyond what man can comprehend.

Do not refuse then, madam, to appear,
Since every radiant beam comes from your sphere
Can so much more than any else endear,

doom] judgement

223 intelligence] spirit; rational being   Complies . . . with] Does not of its own nature conform to   comes] that comes

As while through them we do discern each grace,
The multiplièd lights from every place
Will turn and circle with their rays your face.

(1665)

224 *Sonnet of Black Beauty*

Black beauty, which above that common light,
  Whose power can no colours here renew
  But those which darkness can again subdue,
Dost still remain unvaried to the sight,
And like an object equal to the view
  Art neither changed with day nor hid with night;
  When all those colours which the world calls bright,
And which old poetry doth so pursue,
Are with the night so perishèd and gone
  That of their being there remains no mark,
Thou still abidest so entirely one
  That we may know thy blackness is a spark
Of light inàccessible, and alone
  Our darkness which can make us think it dark.

(1665)

PHINEAS FLETCHER
1582–1650

225 from *The Locusts*

The porter to the infernal gate is sin,
A shapeless shape, a foul deformèd thing,
Nor nothing, nor a substance: as those thin
And empty forms, which through the air fling
Their wandering shapes, at length they're fastened in
The crystal sight. It serves, yet reigns as king;
  It lives, yet's death; it pleases, full of pain:
  Monster! Ah who, who can thy being feign?
Thou shapeless shape, live death, pain pleasing, servile reign.

223 turn] return

Of that first woman and th' old serpent bred,
By lust and custom nursed; whom when her mother
Saw so deformed, how fain would she have fled
Her birth, and self! But she her dam would smother,
And all her brood, had not he rescuèd
Who was his mother's sire, his children's brother:
  Eternity, who yet was born and died:
  His own creator, Earth's scorn, heaven's pride,
Who th' deity infleshed, and man's flesh deified.

Her former parts her mother seems resemble,
Yet only seems to flesh and weaker sight;
For she with art and paint could fine dissemble
Her loathsome face: her back parts (black as night)
Like to her horrid sire would force to tremble
The boldest heart; to the eye that meets her right
  She seems a lovely sweet, of beauty rare;
  But at the parting, he that shall compare,
Hell will more lovely deem, the devil's self more fair.

(1627)

226 *To Thomalin*

THOMALIN, since Thirsil nothing has to leave thee,
And leave thee must, pardon me, gentle friend,
If nothing but my love I only give thee;
Yet see how great this nothing is, I send:
  For though this love of thine I sweetest prove,
  Nothing's more sweet than is this sweetest love.

The soldier nothing like his prey esteems;
Nothing tossed sailors equal with the shore;
Nothing before his health the sick man deems;
The pilgrim hugs his country, nothing more;
  The miser hoarding up his golden wares,
  This nothing with his precious wealth compares.

Our thought's ambition only nothing ends;
Nothing fills up the golden-dropsied mind:
The prodigal, that all so lavish spends,
Yet nothing cannot—nothing stays behind;
  The king, that with his life a kingdom buys,
  Than life or crown doth nothing higher prize.

226 prove] experience

Who all enjoys, yet nothing now desires;
Nothing is greater than the highest Jove:
Who dwells in heaven then nothing more requires;
Love, more than honey; nothing more sweet than love:
  Nothing is only better than the best;
  Nothing is sure: nothing is ever blest.

I love my health, my life, my books, my friends,
Thee; dearest Thomalin, nothing above thee;
For when my books, friends, health, life, fainting ends,
When thy love fails, yet nothing still will love me:
  When heaven, and air, the earth and floating mains
  Are gone, yet nothing still untouched remains.

Since then to other streams I must betake me,
And spiteful Chame of all has quite bereft me;
Since Muses selves (false Muses) will forsake me,
And but this nothing, nothing else is left me;
  Take thou my love, and keep it still in store:
  That given, nothing now remaineth more.

(1633)

227 *Against a Rich Man Despising Poverty*

If well thou viewst us with no squinted eye,
No partial judgement, thou wilt quickly rate
Thy wealth no richer than my poverty,
My want no poorer than thy rich estate,
  Our ends and births alike: in this, as I,
  Poor thou wert born and poor again shalt die.

My little fills my little-wishing mind;
Thou having more than much, yet seekest more:
Who seeks, still wishes what he seeks to find;
Who wishes wants, and whoso wants is poor.
  Then this must follow of necessity:
  Poor are thy riches, rich my poverty.

Though still thou getst, yet is thy want not spent,
But as thy wealth, so grows thy wealthy itch;
But with my little I have much content,
Content hath all, and who hath all is rich.
  Then this in reason thou must needs confess:
  If I have little, yet that thou hast less.

226 Chame] Cam, the river and its university

Whatever man possesses, God hath lent,
And to his audit liable is ever,
To reckon how and where and when he spent;
Then this thou bragst, thou art a great receiver:
  Little my debt, when little is my store;
  The more thou hast, thy debt still grows the more.

But seeing God himself descended down
To enrich the poor by his rich poverty—
His meat, his house, his grave, were not his own,
Yet all is his from all eternity—
  Let me be like my head, whom I adore:
  Be thou great, wealthy, I still base and poor.

(1633)

228 *An Hymn*

WAKE, O my soul; awake, and raise
Up every part to sing his praise,
Who from his sphere of glory fell
To raise thee up from death and hell:
See how his soul, vexed for thy sin,
Weeps blood without, feels hell within:
  See where he hangs;
    Hark how he cries:
  Oh bitter pangs!
    Now, now he dies.

Wake, O mine eyes; awake, and view
Those two twin-lights, whence heavens drew
Their glorious beams, whose gracious sight
Fills you with joy, with life, and light:
See how with clouds of sorrow drowned
They wash with tears thy sinful wound;
  See how with streams
    Of spit they're drenched;
  See how their beams
    With death are quenched.

Wake, O mine ear; awake, and hear
That powerful voice, which stills thy fear,
And brings from heaven those joyful news,
Which heaven commands, which hell subdues;

head] i.e. Christ

228 vexed] troubled

Hark how his ears (heaven's mercy-seat)
Foul slanders with reproaches beat:
  Hark how the knocks
    Our ears resound;
  Hark how their mocks
    His hearing wound.

Wake O my heart, tune every string;
Wake O my tongue, awake, and sing:
Think not a thought in all thy lays,
Speak not a word but of his praise.
Tell how his sweetest tongue they drowned
With gall; think how his heart they wound:
  That bloody spout
    Gagged for thy sin,
  His life lets out,
    Thy death lets in.

(1633)

229 from *The Purple Island*

WITH her, her sister went, a warlike maid,
Parthenia, all in steel and gilded arms;
In needle's stead a mighty spear she swayed,
With which in bloody fields and fierce alarms
  The boldest champion she down would bear,
  And like a thunderbolt wide passage tear,
Flinging all to the earth with her enchanted spear.

Her goodly armour seemed a garden green,
Where thousand spotless lilies freshly blew;
And on her shield the lone bird might be seen,
The Arabian bird, shining in colours new:
  Itself unto itself was only mate,
  Ever the same, but new in newer date;
And underneath was writ SUCH IS CHASTE SINGLE STATE.

Thus hid in arms, she seemed a goodly knight
And fit for any warlike exercise;
But when she list lay down her armour bright
And back resume her peaceful maiden's guise,

Gagged] Pricked

229 swayed] wielded   blew] bloomed   Arabian bird] phoenix

The fairest maid she was that ever yet
Prisoned her locks within a golden net,
Or let them waving hang, with roses fair beset.

Choice nymph, the crown of chaste Diana's train,
Thou beauty's lily set in heavenly earth,
Thy fairs unpatterned all perfections stain:
Sure heaven with curious pencil at thy birth
In thy rare face her own full picture drew:
It is a strong verse here to write, but true;
Hyperboles in others are but half thy due.

Upon her forehead love his trophies fits,
A thousand spoils in silver arch displaying;
And in the midst himself full proudly sits,
Himself in awful majesty arraying.
Upon her brows lies his bent ebon bow
And ready shafts: deadly those weapons show;
Yet sweet that death appeared, lovely that deadly blow.

And at the foot of this celestial frame
Two radiant stars, than stars yet better being,
Endued with living fire and seeing flame,
Yet with heaven's stars in this too near agreeing:
They timely warmth, themselves not warm, inspire;
These kindle thousand hearts with hot desire,
And burning all they see, feel in themselves no fire.

Yet matchless stars (yet each the other's match),
Heav'n's richest diamonds set on amel white,
From whose bright spheres all grace the Graces catch,
And will not move but by your lodestars bright,
How have you stolen and stored your armoury
With love's and death's strong shafts, and from your sky
Pour down thick showers of darts to force whole armies fly?

Above those suns two rainbows high aspire,
Not in light shows but sadder liveries dressed:
Fair Iris seemed to mourn in sable tire.
Yet thus more sweet the greedy eye they feast,
And but that wondrous face it well allowed,
Wondrous it seemed that two fair rainbows showed
Above their sparkling suns, without or rain or cloud.

fairs] beauties stain] eclipse, put into the shade pencil] brush amel] enamel aspire] rise sadder] darker Iris] (messenger of the gods; rainbow) tire] dress but] except that

A bed of lilies flower upon her cheek,
And in the midst was set a circling rose,
Whose sweet aspéct would force Narcissus seek
New liveries, and fresher colours choose
  To deck his beauteous head in snowy tire;
  But all in vain: for who can hope to aspire
To such a fair, which none attain but all admire?

Her ruby lips lock up from gazing sight
A troop of pearls which march in goodly row,
But when she deigns those precious bones undight,
Soon heavenly notes from those divisions flow,
  And with rare music charm the ravished ears;
  Daunting bold thoughts, but cheering modest fears:
The spheres so only sing, so only charm the spheres.

Her dainty breasts, like to an April rose
From green silk fillets yet not all unbound,
Began their little rising heads disclose,
And fairly spread their silver circlets round;
  From those two bulwarks love doth safely fight,
  Which swelling easily, may seem to sight
To be enwombèd both of pleasure and delight.

Yet all these stars which deck this beauteous sky,
By force of the inward sun both shine and move:
Throned in her heart sits love's high majesty;
In highest majesty the highest love.
  As when a taper shines in glassy frame,
  The sparkling crystal burns in glittering flame:
So does that brightest love brighten this lovely dame.

(1633)

230 *Ocean of Light*

VAST ocean of light, whose rays surround
The universe, who knowst nor ebb nor shore,
Who lendst the sun his sparkling drop, to store
With overflowing beams heaven, air, ground;
Whose depths beneath the centre none can sound,
Whose heights 'bove heav'n, and thoughts so lofty soar,

undight] undo, open   divisions] (1) separations; (2) modulations
230 centre] Earth

Whose breadth no feet, no lines, no chains, no eyes survey,
Whose length no thoughts can reach, no worlds can bound,
What cloud can mask thy face? Where can thy ray
Find an eclipse? What night can hide eternal day?

Our seas (a drop of thine) with arms dispread
Through all the Earth make drunk the thirsty plains;
Our sun (a spark of thine) dark shadows drains,
Gilds all the world, paints Earth, revives the dead;
Seas (through earth pipes distilled) in cisterns shed,
And power their liver springs in river veins.
The sun peeps through jet clouds, and when his face and gleams
Are masked, his eyes their light through aïrs spread,
Shall dullard Earth bury life-giving streams?
Earth's fogs impound heaven's light? Hell quench heaven-kindling beams?

How miss I then? In bed I sought by night,
But found not him in rest, nor rest without him.
I sought in towns, in broadest streets I sought him,
But found not him where all are lost. Dull sight,
Thou canst not see him in himself: his light
Is masked in light; brightness his cloud about him.
Where, when, how he'll be found, there, then, thus seek thy love:
Thy lamb in flocks, thy food with appetite,
Thy rest on resting days, thy turtle dove
Seek on his cross: there, then, thus love stands nailed with love.

(1633)

SIR JOHN BEAUMONT
*c.*1583–1627

231 *A Description of Love*

LOVE is a region full of fires,
And burning with extreme desires
An object seeks; of which possessed,
The wheels are fixed, the motions rest,
The flames in ashes like oppressed:
This meteor, striving high to rise
(The fuel spent) falls down and dies.

liver] active

231 meteor] fireball (supposed an exhalation from Earth)

Much sweeter and more pure delights
Are drawn from fair alluring sights—
When ravished minds attempt to praise
Commanding eyes like heavenly rays,
Whose force the gentle heart obeys—
Than where the end of this pretence
Descends to base inferior sense.

Why then should lovers (most will say)
Expect so much the enjoying day?
Love is like youth: he thirsts for age,
He scorns to be his mother's page;
But when proceeding times assuage
The former heat, he will complain
And wish those pleasant hours again.

We know that hope and love are twins;
Hope gone, fruition now begins.
But what is this? Unconstant, frail,
In nothing sure, but sure to fail;
Which, if we lose it, we bewail.
And when we have it, still we bear
The worst of passions, daily fear.

When love thus in his centre ends,
Desire and hope, his inward friends,
Are shaken off; while doubt and grief,
The weakest givers of relief,
Stand in his council as the chief;
And now he to his period brought,
From love becomes some other thought.

These lines I write not to remove
United souls from serious love:
The best attempts by mortals made
Reflect on things which quickly fade;
Yet never will I men persuade
To leave affections where may shine
Impressions of the love divine.

(1629)

Expect] Await

232 *Upon a Funeral*

To their long home the greatest princes go
In hearses dressed with fair escutcheons round,
The blazons of an ancient race, renowned
For deeds of valour; and in costly show
The train moves forward in procession slow
Towards some hallowed fane: no common ground,
But the arched vault and tomb with sculpture crowned
Receive the corse, with honours laid below.
Alas! Whate'er their wealth, their wit, their worth,
Such is the end of all the sons of Earth.

(1629)

AURELIAN TOWNSHEND

*c.*1583–*c.*1651

233 Let not thy beauty make thee proud,
  Though princes do adore thee;
Since time and sickness were allowed
  To mow such flowers before thee.

Nor be not shy to that degree
  Thy friends may hardly know thee,
Nor yet so coming or so free
  That every fly may blow thee.

A state in every princely brow
  As decent is required:
Much more in thine, to whom they bow
  By beauty's lightnings fired;

And yet a state so sweetly mixed
  With an attractive mildness,
It may like virtue sit betwixt
  The extremes of pride and vileness.

Then every eye that sees thy face
  Will in thy beauty glory,
And every tongue that wags will grace
  Thy virtue with a story.

(1652)

233 coming] forward

234 *Upon Kind and True Love*

'TIS not how witty, nor how free,
Nor yet how beautiful she be,
But how much kind and true to me.
Freedom and wit none can confine,
And beauty like the sun doth shine,
But kind and true are only mine.

Let others with attention sit,
To listen, and admire her wit:
That is a rock where I'll not split.
Let others dote upon her eyes,
And burn their hearts for sacrifice;
Beauty's a calm where danger lies.

But kind and true have been long tried
A harbour where we may confide
And safely there at anchor ride.
From change of winds there we are free,
And need not fear storm's tyranny,
Nor pirate, though a prince he be.

(1656)

235

THOUGH regions far divided
  And tedious tracts of time,
By my misfortune guided,
  Make absence thought a crime;
Though we were set asunder
  As far as east from west,
Love still would work this wonder,
  Thou shouldst be in my breast.

How slow alas are paces,
  Compared to thoughts that fly
In moment back to places
  Whole ages scarce descry.
The body must have pauses;
  The mind requires no rest.
Love needs no second causes
  To guide thee to my breast.

234 confide] have confidence

Accept in that poor dwelling
  But welcome, nothing great;
With pride no turrets swelling,
  But lowly as the seat;
Where, though not much delighted,
  In peace thou mayst be blest,
Unfeasted yet unfrighted
  By rivals, in my breast.

But this is not the diet
  That doth for glory strive;
Poor beauties seek in quiet
  To keep one heart alive.
The price of his ambition,
  That looks for such a guest,
Is, hopeless of fruition,
  To beat an empty breast.

See then my last lamenting:
  Upon a cliff I'll sit,
Rock constancy presenting
  Till I grow part of it;
My tears a quicksand feeding,
  Whereon no foot can rest,
My sighs a tempest breeding
  About my stony breast.

Those arms, wherein wide open
  Love's fleet was wont to put,
Shall laid across betoken
  That haven's mouth is shut:
Mine eyes no light shall cherish
  For ships at sea distressed,
But darkling let them perish,
  Or split against my breast.

Yet if I can discover
  When thine before it rides,
To show I was thy lover
  I'll smooth my ruggèd sides,
And so much better measure
  Afford thee than the rest,
Thou shalt have no displeasure
  By knocking at my breast.

(1912)

WILLIAM BASSE
1583–1653

236 *The Angler's Song*

As inward love breeds outward talk,
The hounds some praise, and some the hawk;
Some, better pleased with private sport,
Use tennis, some a mistress court:
  But these delights I neither wish
  Nor envy, while I freely fish.

Who hunts, doth oft in danger ride;
Who hawks, lures oft both far and wide;
Who uses games shall often prove
A loser; but who falls in love
  Is fettered in fond Cupid's snare:
  My angle breeds me no such care.

Of recreation there is none
So free as fishing is alone;
All other pastimes do no less
Than mind and body doth possess:
  My hand alone my work can do,
  So I can fish and study too.

I care not, I, to fish in seas,
Fresh rivers best my mind do please,
Whose sweet calm course I contemplate,
And seek in life to imitate:
  In civil bounds I fain would keep,
  And for my past offences weep.

And when the timorous trout I wait
To take, and he devours my bait,
How poor a thing, sometimes I find
Will captivate a greedy mind:
  And when none bite, I praise the wise,
  Whom vain allurements ne'er surprise.

But yet, though while I fish I fast,
I make good fortune my repast,
And thereunto my friend invite,
In whom I more than that delight:

Who is more welcome to my dish
Than to my angle was my fish.

As well content no prize to take,
As use of taken prize to make:
For so our Lord was pleasèd when
He fishers made fishers of men;
Where, which is in no other game,
A man may fish and praise His name.

The first men that our saviour dear
Did choose to wait upon him here,
Blest fishers were; and fish the last
Food that he on Earth did taste:
I therefore strive to follow those
Whom he to follow him hath chose.

(1653)

FRANCIS BEAUMONT
1584 or 1585–1616

237 *The Fourth Song*

YE should stay longer if we durst;
Away, alas that he that first
Gave time wild wings to fly away,
Has now no power to make him stay.
But though these games must needs be played,
I would this pair, when they are laid,
And not a creature nigh them,
Could catch his scythe as he doth pass,
And cut his wings, and break his glass,
And keep him ever by them.

(1613?)

FRANCIS BEAUMONT?

238 *Song in the Wood*

THIS way, this way: come and hear,
You that hold these pleasures dear;
Fill your ears with our sweet sound,
Whilst we melt the frozen ground.

This way come, make haste, O fair,
Let your clear eyes gild the air:
Come and bless us with your sight;
This way, this way, seek delight.

(1647)

WILLIAM DRUMMOND OF HAWTHORNDEN
1585–1649

239 *Sonnet I. ix*

SLEEP, silence' child, sweet father of soft rest,
Prince whose approach peace to all mortals brings,
Indifferent host to shepherds and to kings,
Sole comforter of minds with grief oppressed,
Lo, by thy charming rod all breathing things
Lie slumb'ring, with forgetfulness possessed,
And yet o'er me to spread thy drowsy wings
Thou spares, alas! who cannot be thy guest.
Since I am thine, oh come, but with that face
To inward light which thou art wont to show,
With feignèd solace ease a true-felt woe;
Or if, deaf god, thou do deny that grace,
Come as thou wilt, and what thou wilt bequeath:
I long to kiss the image of my death.

(1614?)

240 *Madrigal I. i*

A DAEDAL of my death,
Now I resemble that subtle worm on Earth,
Which, prone to its own evil, can take no rest;
For with strange thoughts possessed,
I feed on fading leaves
Of hope, which me deceives,
And thousand webs doth warp within my breast.
And thus in end unto myself I weave
A fast-shut prison, no, but even a grave.

(1614?)

241 *Madrigal I. iii*

LIKE the Idalian queen,
Her hair about her eyne,
With neck and breasts ripe apples to be seen,
At first glance of the morn
In Cyprus gardens gathering those fair flowers
Which of her blood were born,
I saw, but fainting saw, my paramours.
The Graces naked danced about the place,
The winds and trees amazed
With silence on her gazed;
The flowers did smile, like those upon her face,
And as their aspen stalks those fingers band,
That she might read my case,
A hyacinth I wished me in her hand.

(1614?)

242 *Sonnet I. xxxix*

SLIDE soft, fair Forth, and make a crystal plain;
Cut your white locks, and on your foamy face
Let not a wrinkle be, when you embrace
The boat that Earth's perfections doth contain.
Winds, wonder; and through wond'ring hold your peace.

240 Daedal] fabricator (from the mythological Daedalus) in end] ultimately

241 Idalian queen] Venus aspen] quivering read] consider case] (1) state; (2) body

Or, if that ye your hearts cannot restrain
From sending sighs, moved by a lover's case,
Sigh, and in her fair hair yourselves enchain;
Or take these sighs which absence makes arise
From mine oppressèd breast, and wave the sails,
Or some sweet breath new brought from paradise.
Floods seem to smile, love o'er the winds prevails,
And yet huge waves arise; the cause is this:
The ocean strives with Forth the boat to kiss.

(1614?)

243 *Sextain I. ii*

SITH gone is my delight and only pleasure,
The last of all my hopes, the cheerful sun
That cleared my life's dark day, nature's sweet treasure,
More dear to me than all beneath the moon,
What resteth now, but that upon this mountain
I weep, till heaven transform me in a fountain?

Fresh, fair, delicious, crystal, pearly fountain,
On whose smooth face to look she oft took pleasure,
Tell me (so may thy streams long cheer this mountain,
So serpent ne'er thee stain, nor scorch thee sun,
So may with gentle beams thee kiss the moon),
Dost thou not mourn to want so fair a treasure?

While she her glassed in thee, rich Tagus' treasure,
Thou envy needed not, nor yet the fountain
In which that hunter saw the naked moon;
Absence hath robbed thee of thy wealth and pleasure,
And I remain like marigold of sun
Deprived, that dies by shadow of some mountain.

Nymphs of the forests, nymphs who on this mountain
Are wont to dance, showing your beauty's treasure
To goat-feet sylvans and the wondering sun,
Whenas you gather flowers about this fountain,
Bid her farewell who placèd here her pleasure,
And sing her praises to the stars and moon.

243 *Sextain*] *Sestina* Sith] Since resteth] remains stain] (1) defile; (2) discolour want] lack her glassed] mirrored herself that hunter] Actaeon (ancient mythology) sylvans] satyr-like country deities

Among the lesser lights as is the moon,
Blushing through scarf of clouds on Latmos' mountain,
Or when her silver locks she looks for pleasure
In Thetis' streams, proud of so gay a treasure,
Such was my fair when she sat by this fountain
With other nymphs, to shun the amorous sun.

As is our Earth in absence of the sun,
Or when of sun deprivèd is the moon;
As is without a verdant shade a fountain,
Or wanting grass, a mead, a vale, a mountain;
Such is my state, bereft of my dear treasure,
To know whose only worth was all my pleasure.

Ne'er think of pleasure, heart; eyes, shun the sun,
Tears be your treasure, which the wandering moon
Shall see you shed by mountain, vale, and fountain.

(1614?)

244 *Sonnet I. xlvi*

ALEXIS, here she stayed; among these pines,
Sweet hermitress, she did alone repair;
Here did she spread the treasure of her hair,
More rich than that brought from the Colchian mines.
She set her by these muscat eglantines,
The happy place the print seems yet to bear;
Her voice did sweeten here thy sugared lines,
To which winds, trees, beasts, birds, did lend their ear.
Me here she first perceived, and here a morn
Of bright carnations did o'erspread her face:
Here did she sigh, here first my hopes were born,
And I first got a pledge of promised grace;
  But, ah! what served it to be happy so,
  Sith passèd pleasures double but new woe?

(1614?)

Latmos] (where the moon goddess loved Endymion) looks] views Thetis] sea-goddess

244 Colchian] (source of the golden fleece) muscat] musk-scented

245 *Madrigal I. vii*

UNHAPPY light,
Do not approach to bring the woeful day,
When I must bid for aye
Farewell to her, and live in endless plight.
Fair moon, with gentle beams
The sight who never mars,
Long clear heaven's sable vault; and you, bright stars,
Your golden locks long glass in Earth's pure streams;
Let Phoebus never rise
To dim your watchful eyes:
Prolong, alas! prolong my short delight,
And if ye can, make an eternal night.

(1614?)

246 *Madrigal II. i*

THIS life which seems so fair
Is like a bubble blown up in the air
By sporting children's breath,
Who chase it everywhere,
And strive who can most motion it bequeath:
And though it sometime seem of its own might,
Like to an eye of gold, to be fixed there,
And firm to hover in that empty height,
That only is because it is so light.
But in that pomp it doth not long appear;
For even when most admired, it in a thought,
As swelled from nothing, doth dissolve in nought.

(1614?)

247 *Sonnet II. viii*

MY lute, be as thou wast when thou didst grow
With thy green mother in some shady grove,
When immelodious winds but made thee move,
And birds on thee their ramage did bestow.

245 glass] (1) glaze; (2) mirror

247 ramage] song

Sith that dear voice which did thy sounds approve,
Which used in such harmonious strains to flow,
Is reft from Earth to tune those spheres above,
What art thou but a harbinger of woe?
Thy pleasing notes be pleasing notes no more,
But orphan wailings to the fainting ear.
Each stop a sigh, each sound draws forth a tear:
Be therefore silent as in woods before;
   Or if that any hand to touch thee deign,
   Like widowed turtle, still her loss complain.

(1614?)

248 *Sonnet II. xii*

As, in a dusky and tempestuous night,
A star is wont to spread her locks of gold,
And while her pleasant rays abroad are rolled,
Some spiteful cloud doth rob us of her sight;
Fair soul, in this black age so shined thou bright,
And made all eyes with wonder thee behold,
Till ugly death, depriving us of light,
In his grim misty arms thee did enfold.
Who more shall vaunt true beauty here to see?
What hope doth more in any heart remain,
That such perfections shall his reason rein,
If beauty, with thee born, too died with thee?
   World, plain no more of love, nor count his harms;
   With his pale trophies death hath hung his arms.

(1614?)

249 *Madrigal II. v*

My thoughts hold mortal strife;
I do detest my life,
And with lamenting cries,
Peace to my soul to bring,
Oft calls that prince which here doth monarchize;
But he, grim-grinning king,
Who caitives scorns, and doth the blest surprise,
   Late having decked with beauty's rose his tomb,
   Disdains to crop a weed, and will not come.

(1614?)

247 spheres] crystalline nested globes, in which planets were placed at musical intervals stop] pressing on the string to raise tone turtle] dove

from *Urania, or Spiritual Poems* (250–251)

250 *Sonnet I*

TRIUMPHING chariots, statues, crowns of bays,
Sky-threat'ning arches, the rewards of worth,
Works heavenly wise in sweet harmonious lays,
Which sprites divine unto the world set forth;
States, which ambitious minds with blood do raise,
From frozen Tanaïs to sun-gilded Gange,
Gigantic frames, held wonders rarely strange,
Like spiders' webs, are made the sport of days.
All only constant is in constant change;
What done is, is undone, and when undone,
Into some other fashion doth it range:
Thus goes the floating world beneath the moon:
Wherefore, my mind, above time, motion, place,
Thee raise, and steps unknown to nature trace.

(1614?)

251 *Madrigal III*

ASTREA in this time
Now doth not live, but is fled up to heaven;
Or if she live, it is not without crime
That she doth use her power,
And she is no more virgin, but a whore,
Whore prostitute for gold:
For she doth never hold her balance even;
And when her sword is rolled,
The bad, injurious, false she not o'erthrows,
But on the innocent lets fall her blows.

(1614?)

252 from *Forth Feasting*

WHAT blust'ring noise now interrupts my sleep,
What echoing shouts thus cleave my crystal deep,
And call me hence from out my watery court?
What melody, what sounds of joy and sport,

250 bays] laurels   Gange] Ganges

251 Astrea] Astraea, goddess of justice (Greek mythology)   rolled] (1) swung; (2) burnished

Be these here hurled from every neighbour spring?
With what loud rumours do the mountains ring,
Which in unusual pomp on tiptoes stand,
And, full of wonder, overlook the land?
Whence come these glittering throngs, these meteors bright,
This golden people set unto my sight?
Whence doth this praise, applause, and love arise?
What lodestar eastward draweth thus all eyes?
Am I awake, or have some dreams conspired
To mock my sense with shadows much desired?
Stare I that living face, see I those looks,
Which with delight wont to amaze my brooks?
Do I behold that worth, that man divine,
This age's glory, by these banks of mine?
Then is it true, what long I wished in vain,
That my much-loving prince is come again?
So unto them whose zenith is the pole,
When six black months are past, the sun doth roll:
So after tempest to sea-tossed wights
Fair Helen's brothers show their cheering lights:
So comes Arabia's marvel from her woods,
And far, far off is seen by Memphis' floods;
The feathered silvans cloudlike by her fly,
And with applauding clangours beat the sky;
Nile wonders, Serap's priests entrancèd rave,
And in Mygdonian stone her shape engrave,
In lasting cedars mark the joyful time
In which Apollo's bird came to their clime.
  Let mother Earth now decked with flowers be seen,
And sweet-breathed zephyrs curl the meadows green;
Let heavens weep rubies in a crimson shower,
Such as on Indies' shores they use to pour,
Or with that golden storm the fields adorn,
Which Jove rained when his blue-eyed maid was born.
May never hours the web of day outweave,
May never night rise from her sable cave.
Swell proud, my billows, faint not to declare
Your joys as ample as their causes are;
For murmurs hoarse sound like Arion's harp,
Now delicately flat, now sweetly sharp.
And you, my nymphs, rise from your moist repair,
Strow all your springs and grots with lilies fair:

pomp] display meteors] luminous appearances (e.g. aurora borealis) Helen's brothers] Castor and Pollux Arabia's marvel] the phoenix Serap's] (Egyptian god) Apollo's bird] the swan maid] Athene Arion's] the Greek lyric poet, saved from drowning by his music Strow] Strew

Some swiftest-footed get her hence and pray
Our floods and lakes come keep this holiday;
Whate'er beneath Albania's hills do run,
Which see the rising or the setting sun,
Which drink stern Grampius' mists, or Ochils' snows;
Stone-rolling Tay, Tyne tortoise-like that flows,
The pearly Don, the Dees, the fertile Spey,
Wild Nevern which doth see our longest day,
Ness smoking sulphur, Leave with mountains crowned,
Strange Lomond for his floating isles renowned,
The Irish Rian, Ken, the silver Ayr,
The snaky Dun, the Ore with rushy hair,
The crystal-streaming Nid, loud-bellowing Clyde,
Tweed which no more our kingdoms shall divide,
Rank-swelling Annan, Lid with curled streams,
The Esks, the Solway where they lose their names:
To every one proclaim our joys and feasts,
Our triumphs; bid all come, and be our guests;
And as they meet in Neptune's azure hall,
Bid them bid sea-gods keep this festival.
This day shall by our currents be renowned,
Our hills about shall still this day resound:
Nay, that our love more to this day appear,
Let us with it henceforth begin our year.
  To virgins flowers, to sunburnt earth the rain,
To mariners fair winds amidst the main,
Cool shades to pilgrims, which hot glances burn,
Please not so much to us as thy return.
That day, dear Prince, which reft us of thy sight—
Day, no, but darkness, and a cloudy night—
Did freight our breasts with sighs, our eyes with tears,
Turned minutes in sad months, sad months in years;
Trees left to flourish, meadows to bear flowers,
Brooks hid their heads within their sedgy bowers;
Fair Ceres cursed our fields with barren frost,
As if again she had her daughter lost;
The Muses left our groves, and for sweet songs
Sat sadly silent, or did weep their wrongs:
Ye know it, meads, ye murmuring woods it know,
Hills, dales, and caves, copartners of their woe;
And ye it know, my streams, which from their eyne
Oft on your glass received their pearlèd brine.
'O naiads dear,' said they, 'napaeas fair,

Albania's] Albany's, Scotland's Grampius'] the Grampians' Nevern] river Naver Leave] Leven Nid] Nith Lid] Liddel Water Ceres] (Roman harvest goddess) daughter] Proserpina napaeas] nymphs of glens

O nymphs of trees, nymphs which on hills repair,
Gone are those maiden glories, gone that state
Which made all eyes admire our hap of late.'
As looks the heaven when never star appears,
But slow and weary shroud them in their spheres,
While Tithon's wife embosomed by him lies,
And world doth languish in a dreary guise;
As looks a garden of its beauty spoiled;
As wood in winter by rough Boreas foiled;
As portraits razed of colours use to be;
So looked these abject bounds deprived of thee.
  While as my rills enjoyed thy royal gleams,
They did not envy Tiber's haughty streams,
Nor wealthy Tagus with his golden ore,
Nor clear Hydaspes, which on pearls doth roar,
Empampered Gange, that sees the sun new born,
Nor Acheloüs with his flowery horn,
Nor floods which near Elyzian fields do fall;
For why? Thy sight did serve to them for all.
No place there is so desert, so alone,
Even from the frozen to the torrid zone,
From flaming Hecla to great Quincy's Lake,
Which thine abode could not most happy make.
All those perfections which by bounteous heaven
To diverse worlds in diverse times were given,
The starry senate poured at once on thee,
That thou exemplar mightst to others be.
  Thy life was kept till the three sisters spun
Their threads of gold, and then it was begun.
With curled clouds when skies do look most fair,
And no disordered blasts disturb the air;
When lilies do them deck in azure gowns,
And new-born roses blush with golden crowns;
To bode how calm we under thee should live,
What halcyonean days thy reign should give,
And to two flowery diadems thy right,
The heavens thee made a partner of the light.
Scarce was thou born, when, joined in friendly bands,
Two mortal foes with other claspèd hands,
With virtue fortune strove, which most should grace

shroud] shelter spheres] crystalline globes Tithon's wife] Aurora (Greek myth) Boreas] north wind (ancient myth) foiled] trampled; overwhelmed; deflowered Hydaspes] river Jhehum Gange] Ganges Acheloüs] Greek river-god Elyzian fields] place of idyllic afterlife (Greek myth) Hecla] Icelandic volcano Quincy's] Hang-chu's sisters] Fates (ancient myth) bands] bonds

Thy place for thee, thee for so high a place;
One vowed thy sacred breast not to forsake,
The other on thee not to turn her back,
And that thou more her love's effects mightst feel,
For thee she rent her sail, and broke her wheel.
When years thee vigour gave, oh then how clear
Did smothered sparkles in bright flames appear!
Amongst the woods to force a flying hart,
To pierce the mountain wolf with feathered dart,
See falcons climb the clouds, the fox ensnare,
Outrun the wind-outrunning daedal hare,
To loose a trampling steed alongst a plain,
And in meand'ring gyres him bring again,
The press thee making place, were vulgar things;
In admiration's air, on glory's wings,
Oh! thou far from the common pitch didst rise,
With thy designs to dazzle envy's eyes:
Thou soughtst to know this all's eternal source,
Of ever-turning heavens the restless course,
Their fixèd eyes, their lights which wandering run,
Whence moon her silver hath, his gold the sun;
If destine be or no, if planets can
By fierce aspécts force the free will of man;
The light and spiring fire, the liquid air,
The flaming dragons, comets with red hair,
Heaven's tilting lances, artillery, and bow,
Loud-sounding trumpets, darts of hail and snow,
The roaring element with people dumb,
The Earth, with what conceived is in her womb,
What on her moves, were set unto thy sight,
Till thou didst find their causes, essence, might:
But unto nought thou so thy mind didst strain,
As to be read in man, and learn to reign,
To know the weight and Atlas of a crown,
To spare the humble, proudlings pester down.
When from those piercing cares which thrones invest,
As thorns the rose, thou wearied wouldst thee rest,
With lute in hand, full of celestial fire,
To the Pierian groves thou didst retire:
There, garlanded with all Urania's flowers,
In sweeter lays than builded Thebees' towers,

flying] fleeing daedal] inventive press] crowd, mob destine] destiny force] press hard upon read] learned Atlas] responsibility (from the Titan supporting the world, Greek myth pester down] obstruct; crowd out Pierian] of the Muses Urania's] Venus' Thebees'] Thebes' (built by Amphion's music)

Or them which charmed the dolphins in the main,
Or which did call Eurydice again,
Thou sungst away the hours, till from their sphere
Stars seemed to shoot, thy melody to hear.
The god with golden hair, the sister maids,
Left nymphal Helicon, their Tempe's shades,
To see thine isle, here lost their native tongue,
And in thy world-divided language sung.

(1617)

from *Flowers of Sion* (253–259)

253

[*Sonnet VI*]

OF this fair volume which we world do name,
If we the sheets and leaves could turn with care,
Of him who it corrects, and did it frame,
We clear might read the art and wisdom rare;
Find out his power which wildest powers doth tame,
His providence extending everywhere,
His justice, which proud rebels doth not spare,
In every page, no, period of the same:
But silly we, like foolish children, rest
Well pleased with coloured vellum, leaves of gold,
Fair dangling ribbons; leaving what is best,
On the great writer's sense ne'er taking hold;
  Or if by chance our minds do muse on aught,
  It is some picture on the margin wrought.

(1623)

254

[*Sonnet VIII*]

RUN, shepherds, run where Bethlem blest appears:
We bring the best of news, be not dismayed;
A saviour there is born, more old than years,
Amidst heaven's rolling heights this Earth who stayed.
In a poor cottage inned, a virgin maid
A weakling did him bear, who all upbears;
There is he poorly swaddled, in manger laid,
To whom too narrow swaddlings are our spheres:

them . . . charmed] Arion's which . . . again] Orpheus' (which almost recalled Eurydice from the dead) god . . . hair] Apollo maids] Muses Helicon] haunt of the Muses Tempe's] paradisiac Thessalian valley's

253 period] sentence

254 stayed] established inned] lodged

Run, shepherds, run, and solemnize his birth.
This is that night—no, day, grown great with bliss,
In which the power of Satan broken is;
In heaven be glory, peace unto the Earth!
  Thus singing, through the air the angels swam,
  And cope of stars re-echoèd the same.

(1623)

255 [*Sonnet XI: For the Baptist*]

THE last and greatest herald of heaven's king,
Girt with rough skins, hies to the deserts wild,
Among that savage brook the woods forth bring,
Which he than man more harmless found and mild:
His food was locusts, and what young doth spring,
With honey that from virgin hives distilled;
Parched body, hollow eyes, some uncouth thing
Made him appear, long since from Earth exiled.
There burst he forth: 'All ye whose hopes rely
On God, with me amidst these deserts mourn;
Repent, repent, and from old errors turn.'
Who listened to his voice, obeyed his cry?
  Only the echoes, which he made relent,
  Rung from their marble caves, 'Repent, repent!'

(1623)

256 [*Madrigal IV*]

THIS world a hunting is,
The prey poor man, the Nimrod fierce is death;
His speedy greyhounds are
Lust, sickness, envy, care,
Strife that ne'er falls amiss,
With all those ills which haunt us while we breathe.
Now, if by chance we fly
Of these the eager chase,
Old age with stealing pace
Casts up his nets, and there we panting die.

(1623)

255 distilled] trickled

256 Nimrod] tyrant hunter (Gen. 10: 9)

257

[*Sonnet XXII*]

THRICE happy he, who by some shady grove,
Far from the clamorous world, doth live his own;
Though solitary, who is not alone,
But doth converse with that eternal love.
Oh how more sweet is birds' harmonious moan,
Or the hoarse sobbings of the widowed dove,
Than those smooth whisperings near a prince's throne,
Which good make doubtful, do the evil approve!
Oh how more sweet is zephyr's wholesome breath,
And sighs embalmed, which new-born flow'rs unfold,
Than that applause vain honour doth bequeath!
How sweet are streams to poison drunk in gold!
The world is full of horrors, troubles, slights,
Woods' harmless shades have only true delights.

(1623)

258

[*Sonnet XXIV*]

AS when it happeneth that some lovely town
Unto a barbarous besieger falls,
Who there by sword and flame himself instals,
And, cruel, it in tears and blood doth drown;
Her beauty spoiled, her citizens made thralls,
His spite yet so cannot her all throw down,
But that some statue, arch, fane of renown
Yet lurks unmaimed within her weeping walls:
So, after all the spoil, disgrace, and wrack,
That time, the world, and death could bring combined,
Amidst that mass of ruins they did make,
Safe and all scarless yet remains my mind:
From this so high transcending rapture springs,
That I, all else defaced, not envy kings.

(1623)

259

[*Sonnet XXV*]

MORE oft than once death whispered in mine ear,
Grave what thou hears in diamond and gold:
I am that monarch whom all monarchs fear,
Who hath in dust their far-stretched pride uprolled;
All, all is mine beneath moon's silver sphere,
And nought, save virtue, can my power withhold:
This, not believed, experience true thee told,
By danger late when I to thee came near.

As bugbear then my visage I did show,
That of my horrors thou right use mightst make,
And a more sacred path of living take:
Now still walk armèd for my ruthless blow,
  Trust flattering life no more, redeem time past,
  And live each day as if it were thy last.

(1630)

260 from *An Hymn of the Fairest Fair*

In those vast fields of light, ethereal plains,
Thou art attended by immortal trains
Of intellectual powers, which thou brought forth
To praise thy goodness and admire thy worth;
In numbers passing other creatures far,
Since most in number noblest creatures are,
Which do in knowledge us no less outrun
Than moon doth stars in light, or moon the sun.
Unlike, in orders ranged and many a band
(If beauty in disparity doth stand),
Archangels, angels, cherubs, seraphins,
And what with name of thrones amongst them shines,
Large-ruling princes, dominations, powers,
All-acting virtues of those flaming towers:
These freed of umbrage, these of labour free,
Rest ravishèd with still beholding thee;
Inflamed with beams which sparkle from thy face,
They can no more desire, far less embrace.
  Low under them, with slow and staggering pace,
Thy handmaid nature thy great steps doth trace,
The source of second causes, golden chain
That links this frame, as thou it dost ordain;
Nature gazed on with such a curious eye
That earthlings oft her deemed a deity.
By nature led, those bodies fair and great,
Which faint not in their course nor change their state,
Unintermixed, which no disorder prove,
Though aye and contrary they always move;
The organs of thy providence divine,
Books ever open, signs that clearly shine,
Time's purpled maskers, then do them advance,
As by sweet music in a measured dance.

bugbear] imaginary terror, bugaboo still] always

260 umbrage] shadow; semblance aye . . . contrary] with opposite rotations

Stars, host of heaven, ye firmament's bright flowers,
Clear lamps which overhang this stage of ours,
Ye turn not there to deck the weeds of night,
Nor, pageant-like, to please the vulgar sight;
Great causes, sure ye must bring great effects,
But who can descant right your grave aspécts?
He only who you made, decipher can
Your notes; heaven's eyes, ye blind the eyes of man.
  Amidst these sapphire far-extending heights,
The never-twinkling, ever-wandering lights
Their fixèd motions keep: one dry and cold,
Deep-leaden coloured, slowly there is rolled;
With rule and line for time's steps measured even,
In twice three lustres he but turns his heaven.
With temperate qualities and countenance fair,
Still mildly smiling, sweetly debonair,
Another cheers the world, and way doth make
In twice six autumns through the zodiac.
But hot and dry, with flaming locks and brows
Enraged, this in his red pavilion glows.
Together running with like speed, if space,
Two equally in hands achieve their race;
With blushing face this oft doth bring the day,
And ushers oft to stately stars the way;
That various in virtue, changing, light,
With his small flame ingems the veil of night.
Prince of this court, the sun in triumph rides,
With the year snake-like in herself that glides:
Time's dispensator, fair life-giving source,
Through sky's twelve posts as he doth run his course,
Heart of this all, of what is known to sense
The likest to his maker's excellence;
In whose diurnal motion doth appear
A shadow, no, true portrait of the year.
The moon moves lowest, silver sun of night,
Dispersing through the world her borrowed light,
Who in three forms her head abroad doth range,
And only constant is in constant change.
  Sad queen of silence, I ne'er see thy face
To wax, or wane, or shine with a full grace,
But straight amazed on man I think, each day
His state who changeth, or, if he find stay,
It is in dreary anguish, cares, and pains,
And of his labours death is all the gains.

one dry] Saturn lustres] five-year periods Another] Jupiter Enraged, this] Mars Two] Venus and Mercury posts] zodiacal signs

Immortal monarch, can so fond a thought
Lodge in my breast, as to trust thou first brought
Here in Earth's shady cloister wretched man,
To suck the air of woe, to spend life's span
'Midst sighs and plaints, a stranger unto mirth,
To give himself his death, rebuking birth?
By sense and wit of crëatures made king,
By sense and wit to live their underling?
And, what is worst, have eaglet's eyes to see
His own disgrace, and know an high degree
Of bliss, the place, if thereto he might climb,
And not live thrallèd to imperious time?
Or, dotard, shall I so from reason swerve,
To deem those lights which to our use do serve—
For thou dost not them need—more nobly framed
Than us that know their course and have them named?
No, I ne'er think but we did them surpass,
As far as they do asterisms of glass,
When thou us made. By treason high defiled,
Thrust from our first estate, we live exiled,
Wand'ring this earth, which is of death the lot,
Where he doth use the power which he hath got,
Indifferent umpire unto clowns and kings,
The súpreme monarch of all mortal things.
  When first this flowery orb was to us given,
It but in place disvalued was to heaven;
These creatures which now our sovereigns are,
And as to rebels do denounce us war,
Then were our vassals; no tumultuous storm,
No thunders, quakings, did her form deform;
The seas in tumbling mountains did not roar,
But like moist crystal whispered on the shore;
No snake did mete her meads, nor ambushed lower
In azure curls beneath the sweet spring flower;
The nightshade, henbane, naple, aconite,
Her bowels then not bare, with death to smite
Her guiltless brood; thy messengers of grace,
As their high rounds, did haunt this lower place.
O joy of joys! with our first parents thou
To cómmune then didst deign, as friends do now:
Against thee we rebelled, and justly thus
Each crëature rebellèd against us;
Earth, reft of what did chief in her excel,

rebuking] repulsing; repressing   asterisms of glass] starlike appearance of light in some crystals   of death the lot] death's share   disvalued] disparaged   denounce] declare upon   mete] measure; traverse   naple] apple

To all became a jail, to most a hell,
In time's full term until thy son was given,
Who man with thee, Earth reconciled with heaven.
  Whole and entire, all in thyself thou art,
All-where diffused, yet of this all no part;
For infinite, in making this fair frame,
Great without quantity, in all thou came,
And filling all, how can thy state admit
Or place or substance to be void of it?
Were worlds as many as the rays which stream
From heaven's bright eyes, or madding wits do dream,
They would not reel in nought, nor wandering stray,
But draw to thee, who could their centres stay;
Were but one hour this world disjoined from thee,
It in one hour to nought reduced should be,
For it thy shadow is; and can they last,
If severed from the substances them cast?
O only blest, and author of all bliss,
No, bliss itself, that all-where wishèd is,
Efficient, exemplary, final good,
Of thine own self but only understood!
Light is thy curtain, thou art light of light,
An ever-waking eye still shining bright,
In-looking all, exempt of passive power
And change, in change since death's pale shade doth lower.
All times to thee are one; that which hath run,
And that which is not brought yet by the sun,
To thee are present, who dost always see
In present act what past is, or to be.
Day-livers, we rememberance do lose
Of ages worn, so miseries us toss
(Blind and lethargic of thy heavenly grace,
Which sin in our first parents did deface,
And even while embryons cursed by justest doom),
That we neglect what gone is, or to come:
But thou in thy great archives scrollèd hast,
In parts and whole, whatever yet hath past,
Since first the marble wheels of time were rolled,
As ever living, never waxing old.
Still is the same thy day and yesterday,
An undivided now, a constant aye.
  O King, whose greatness none can comprehend,
Whose boundless goodness doth to all extend,
Light of all beauty, ocean without ground,

madding wits] frenzied intellectuals   In-looking] Inspecting   Day-livers] Those who live for the day   embryons] embryos

That standing flowest, giving dost abound;
Rich palace, and indweller ever blest,
Never not working, ever yet in rest!
What wit cannot conceive, words say of thee,
Here, where, as in a mirror, we but see
Shadows of shadows, atoms of thy might,
Still owly-eyed when staring on thy light,
Grant that, releasèd from this earthly jail,
And freed of clouds which here our knowledge veil,
In heaven's high temples, where thy praises ring,
I may in sweeter notes hear angels sing.

(1630)

261 *[Against the King]*

AGAINST the king, sir, now why would ye fight?
Forsooth, because he dubbed me not a knight.
And ye, my lords, why arm yet against Charles?
Because of lords he would not make us earls.
Earls, why do ye lead forth these angry bands?
Because we will not quit the Church's lands.
Most holy churchmen, what is your intent?
The king our stipends largely did augment.
Commons, to tumult thus how are ye driven?
Our priests say fighting is the way to heaven.
Are these just cause of war, good brethren, grant?
Him plunder! He ne'er swore our Covenant.
  Give me a thousand Covenants, I'll subscrive
Them all, and more, if more ye can contrive
Of rage and malice; and let everyone
Black treason bear, not bare rebellion.
I'll not be mocked, hissed, plundered, banished hence
For more years standing for a . . . prince.
His castles all are taken, and his crown,
His sword and sceptre, ensigns of renown,
With the lieutenant fame did so extol,
And all led captives to the capitol;
I'll not die martyr for a mortal thing:
It's enough to be confessor for a king.
Will this you give contentment, honest men?
I've written rebels, pox upon the pen!

(1711)

261 subscrive] subscribe to ensigns] symbols (the Scottish regalia) lieutenant] Traquair, Charles I's chief minister capitol] Edinburgh Castle

262 *On Pym*

WHEN Pym last night descended into hell,
Ere he his cups of Lethè did carouse,
'What place is this', said he, 'I pray me tell?'
To whom a devil: 'This is the lower house.'

(1711)

263 *Sextain*

WITH elegies, sad songs, and mourning lays,
While Craig his Kala would to pity move,
Poor brainsick man! he spends his dearest days;
Such silly rhyme cannot make women love.
  Morice, who sight of never saw a book,
  With a rude stanza this fair virgin took.

(1711)

264 *For a Lady's Summons of Non-Entry*

KITE!
Summon not me to enter: there's no doubt
These twice four years and more I have been out,
And I it not deny; I did you wrong
At first, but since could not come in for throng.
Counts, knights, and gentiles so haunted your room,
Then your kinsmen, yeomen, and every groom.
Why should I pressed? What? Should I been there
Where brother-nephew were so familiar?
And that (with his French page) sore-gallèd lord
Whom our east neighbours brought unto accord?
When all are gone and desolate's the place,
Ye will me enter, altered is your case;
Now it no more is like unto that thing
That erst it was than a gate is like a ring.

Pym] (see endnote)   Lethè] river of forgetfulness (Greek mythology)

263 *Sextain*] *Sixain*   Craig, Kala] (see endnote)

264 *Non-Entry*] *Payment due to a feudal superior from a vassal's heir*   gentiles] (1) gentles, gentlemen; (2) heathens   pressed] (have) pushed forward   brother-nephew] (1) brother's nephew; (2) brotherly nephew   sore-galled] (1) chafed with rubbing; (2) affected with swollen sores   case] (1) state; (2) body

Look how a meadow ere that it be shorn
And when its hay with carts and cars all worn
Doth differ from itself; or as a way
Which was untrod, unbarbered yesterday
Is not itself when cattle's feet it gore:
So is not yours the thing it was before;
As is that hole in which to save an host
The valiant Curtius himself madly lost.
Is it not now? Or like that ship of Drake's
That sailed all seas, and now stands full of lakes;
Or like those wells which turn in iron or stone
Any good timber that is in them thrown.
A candlestick, though of silver, when some light
Hath burnt into its socket some dark night,
Doth turn so furious hot that who would try
A new light thereof, needs his light must fry.
Thou something was when lying thee behind
That lord laughed at thy mother breaking wind,
And was surprised; or when thy hand betrayed
Unto thy dildo thy soft maidenhead.
And when thy bloodless husband rode from home,
And some rode after and took up his room.
Unhappy Kite, doth not thy breath stink worse
Than that strong matter which nature doth force
From a turned gut, and though it scent perfúme
That's but some stronger ordure to consume.
And, fool, though thou a bonnet wear of hair,
Is not thy spotted skull as ugly bare
As thy painted cheek? Thy hairs were strongly stout:
Each one did tire a man ere it came out.
Are not the twins now of thy withered breast
(Which sometime like Parnassus raised each crest)
Like sodden haggises, and thy dry skin
Like to those bags that saffron's put within?
Let your geometric footman serve your turn,
Or the porter whom last year ye did burn,
Or your learned children's tutor, who well can
Teach any woman to decline to man,
That will himself a diphthong turn with you:
Pox on them if they tell whate'er ye do.
It's only he alone sees both the poles,
And shall see yours, like to two hills of moles

cars] wagons; hurdles   Curtius] (see endnote)   those wells] i.e. petrifying wells   in iron] into iron   needs] of necessity   strong matter] ambergris   came out] fell out (one for each act of sex, by popular superstition)   Parnassus] twin mountain of the Muses (Greek mythology)   burn] infect

Which are grown one; though late they looked aside,
Now only interjections them divide.
Let me alone, and force me not to enter:
If hell be into Earth, it's in your centre.

(1976)

265 [*No Epitaph*]

If of the dead save good nought should be said,
He'll get no epitaph who here is laid:
He overturnèd churches, did confound
The heaven and Earth, threw monuments to ground,
Disdained and scornèd all memorials
Of antique ages, and for funerals
Of worthy men he suffered not a tomb
To enclose their bones, nor any temple hold
Their sad remembrances; nor would hear told
That husbands and their wives one quire contained;
That sacred places by the saints were stained;
That ravens their corses rather should consume
Ere to church burials they should presume.
He filled the age he lived in with strange dreams;
Now the posterity gives him anathemes,
Detesteth his remembrance, and doth pray
He never rise more in the latter day.

(1976)

GILES FLETCHER
*c.*1586–1623

from *Christ's Victory and Triumph*

266 [*The Enchantress' Song*]

Love is the blossom where there blows
Everything that lives or grows:
Love doth make the heavens to move,
And the sun doth burn in love;

centre] pudenda

265 quire] (1) chancel; (2) sheet saints] Reformers stained] abused anathemes] curses

266 blows] blooms

Love the strong and weak doth yoke,
And makes the ivy climb the oak,
Under whose shadows lions wild,
Softened by love, grow tame and mild.
Love no med'cine can appease,
He burns the fishes in the seas:
Not all the skill his wounds can stench,
Not all the sea his fire can quench.
Love did make the bloody spear
Once a leafy coat to wear,
While in his leaves there shrouded lay
Sweet birds, for love that sing and play;
And of all love's joyful flame,
I the bud and blossom am.
  Only bend thy knee to me,
  Thy wooing shall thy winning be.

See, see the flowers that below
Now as fresh as morning blow,
And of all, the virgin rose,
That as bright Aurora shows
How they all unleafèd die,
Losing their virginity:
Like unto a summer shade,
But now born, and now they fade.
Everything doth pass away,
There is danger in delay,
Come, come gather then the rose:
Gather it, or it you lose.
All the sand of Tagus shore
Into my bosom casts his ore;
All the valley's swimming corn
To my house is yearly borne;
Every grape of every vine
Is gladly bruised to make me wine,
While ten thousand kings, as proud
To carry up my train, have bowed,
And a world of ladies send me
In my chambers to attend me:
All the stars in heaven that shine,
And ten thousand more, are mine:
  Only bend thy knee to me,
  Thy wooing shall thy winning be.

(1610)

stench] stanch shrouded] sheltered Aurora] goddess of dawn (who lost her virginity to Apollo)

267 from *Christ's Triumph after Death*

HERE let my lord hang up his conquering lance
And bloody armour with late slaughter warm,
And looking down on his weak militants,
Behold his saints, midst of their hot alarm,
Hang all their golden hopes upon his arm.
  And in this lower field dispacing wide,
  Through windy thoughts that would their sails misguide
Anchor their fleshly ships fast in his wounded side.

Here may the band, that now in triumph shines,
And that, before they were invested thus,
In earthly bodies carried heavenly minds,
Pitched round about in order glorious
Their sunny tents and houses luminous,
  All their eternal day in songs employing,
  Joying their end, without end of their joying,
While their almighty prince destruction is destroying.

Full, yet without satiety, of that
Which whets and quiets greedy appetite,
Where never sun did rise, nor ever sat,
But one eternal day and endless light
Gives time to those whose time is infinite,
  Speaking with thought, obtaining without fee,
  Beholding him whom never eye could see,
And magnifying him that cannot greater be.

How can such joy as this want words to speak?
And yet what words can speak such joy as this?
Far from the world, that might their quiet break,
Here the glad souls the face of beauty kiss,
Poured out in pleasure on their beds of bliss;
  And drunk with nectar torrents, ever hold
  Their eyes on him whose graces manifold,
The more they do behold, the more they would behold.

Their sight drinks lovely fires in at their eyes;
Their brain sweet incense with fine breath accloys,
That on God's sweating altar burning lies;
Their hungry cares feed on their heavenly noise,

dispacing] wandering (Spenserian) sat] set magnifying] (1) praising; (2) making greater Poured out] Spread out (Latinism) accloys] fills to satiety noise] sound

That angels sing to tell their untold joys;
  Their understanding, naked truth, their wills
  The all and selfsufficient goodness fills,
That nothing here is wanting but the want of ills.

No sorrow now hangs clouding on their brow,
No bloodless malady empales their face,
No age drops on their hairs his silver snow,
No nakedness their bodies doth embase,
No poverty themselves and theirs disgrace,
  No fear of death the joy of life devours,
  No unchaste sleep their precious time deflowers,
No loss, no grief, no change wait on their wingèd hours.

But now their naked bodies scorn the cold,
And from their eyes joy looks, and laughs at pain;
The infant wonders how he came so old,
And old man how he came so young again;
Still resting, though from sleep they still refrain;
  Where all are rich, and yet no gold they owe;
  And all are kings, and yet no subjects know:
All full, and yet no time on food they do bestow.

For things that pass are past, and in this field
The indeficient spring no winter fears,
The trees together fruit and blossom yield,
The unfading lily leaves of silver bears,
And crimson rose a scarlet garment wears;
  And all of these on the saints' bodies grow,
  Not as they wont on baser Earth below:
Three rivers here of milk and wine and honey flow.

About the holy city rolls a flood
Of molten crystal like a sea of glass,
On which weak stream a strong foundation stood;
Of living diamonds the building was,
That all things else, besides itself, did pass.
  Her streets, instead of stones, the stars did pave,
  And little pearls, for dust, it seemed to have,
On which soft-streaming manna like pure snow did wave.

No sorrow now] 'By the amotion [ousting] of all evil' (F.)   empales] makes pale
embase] degrade, humiliate   owe] own   indeficient] unfailing, exhaustless
Three rivers] 'By the access of all good again' (F.)

In midst of this city celestial,
Where the eternal temple should have rose,
Lightened the idea beatifical:
End and beginning of each thing that grows,
Whose self no end nor yet beginning knows,
  That hath no eyes to see, nor ears to hear,
  Yet sees and hears, and is all-eye, all-ear;
That nowhere is contained, and yet is everywhere.

Changer of all things, yet immutable;
Before and after all, the first and last,
That moving all is yet immoveable;
Great without quantity; in whose forecast
Things past are present, things to come are past;
  Swift without motion, to whose open eye
  The hearts of wicked men unbreasted lie;
At once absent and present to them, far and nigh.

It is no flaming lustre made of light,
No sweet concent or well-timed harmony,
Ambrosia for to feast the appetite,
Or flowery odour mixed with spicery,
No soft embrace or pleasure bodily.
  And yet it is a kind of inward feast,
  A harmony that sounds within the breast,
An odour, light, embrace, in which the soul doth rest.

(1610)

JOHN FORD
1586–1639?

268

Oh, no more, no more. Too late
  Sighs are spent; the burning tapers
Of a life as chaste as fate,
  Pure as are unwritten papers,
Are burnt out. No heat, no light
Now remains: 'tis ever night.

267 idea] divine image   beatifical] imparting supreme blessedness (?coinage)
unbreasted] unbosomed   concent] concord

Love is dead. Let lovers' eyes,
Locked in endless dreams,
The extremes of all extremes,
Ope no more; for now love dies,
Now love dies, implying
Love's martyrs must be ever, ever dying.

(1633)

LADY MARY WROTH
*c.*1586–*c.*1652

from *The Countess of Montgomerie's 'Urania'* (269–280)

269

Sonnet VI

OH strive not still to heap disdain on me,
Nor pleasure take your cruelty to show
On hapless me, on whom all sorrows flow,
And biding make, as given, and lost, by thee:
Alas, even grief is grown to pity me;
Scorn cries out gainst itself, such ill to show,
And would give place for joy's delights to flow;
Yet wretched I all tortures bear from thee.
Long have I suffered, and esteemed it dear,
Since such thy will; yet grew my pain more near:
Wish you my end? Say so, you shall it have;
For all the depth of my heart-held despair
Is that for you I feel not death for care;
But now I'll seek it, since you will not save.

(1621)

270

Sonnet IX

BE you all pleased? Your pleasures grieve not me.
Do you delight? I envy not your joy.
Have you content? Contentment with you be.
Hope you for bliss? Hope still, and still enjoy.

269 still] always

Let sad misfortune hapless me destroy,
  Leave crosses to rule me, and still rule free,
  While all delights their contraries employ
  To keep good back, and I but torments see:
Joys are bereaved, harms do only tarry;
  Despair takes place, disdain hath got the hand;
  Yet firm love holds my senses in such band
  As since, despisèd, I with sorrow marry;
Then if with grief I now must coupled be,
Sorrow I'll wed: despair thus governs me.

(1621)

271

Song II

All night I weep, all day I cry, ay me;
I still do wish, though yet deny, ay me;
I sigh, I mourn, I say that still
I only am the store for ill, ay me;

In coldest hopes I freeze, yet burn, ay me;
From flames I strive to fly, yet turn, ay me;
From grief I haste but sorrows hie,
And on my heart all woes do lie, ay me;

From contraries I seek to run, ay me;
But contraries I cannot shun, ay me,
For they delight their force to try,
And to despair my thoughts do tie, ay me;

Whither, alas, then shall I go, ay me,
Whenas despair all hopes outgo? ay me;
If to the forest, Cupid hies,
And my poor soul to his law ties, ay me;

To the court? Oh no. He cries fie, ay me;
There no true love you shall espy, ay me;
Leave that place to falsest lovers,
Your true love all truth discovers, ay me;

Then quiet rest, and no more prove, ay me,
All places are alike to love, ay me,
And constant be in this begun;
Yet say, till life with love be done, ay me.

(1621)

crosses] thwartings rule] go hand] i.e. upper hand band] bond

271 whenas] since prove] test

272 *Sonnet XIV*

Am I thus conquered? Have I lost the powers
That to withstand which joys to ruin me?
Must I be still while it my strength devours,
And captive leads me prisoner, bound, unfree?
Love first shall leave men's fant'sies to them free,
Desire shall quench love's flames, spring hate sweet showers,
Love shall lose all his darts, have sight, and see
His shame, and wishings hinder happy hours:
Why should we not love's purblind charms resist?
Must we be servile, doing what he list?
No, seek some host to harbour thee: I fly
Thy babish tricks, and freedom do profess.
But oh my hurt makes my lost heart confess
I love, and must; so farewell liberty.

(1621)

273 *Sonnet XIX*

Come, darkest night, becoming sorrow best;
Light, leave thy light, fit for a lightsome soul;
Darkness doth truly suit with me oppressed,
Whom absence' power doth from mirth control:
The very trees with hanging heads condole
Sweet summer's parting, and of leaves distressed
In dying colours make a grieffull roll,
So much, alas, to sorrow are they pressed.
Thus of dead leaves her farewell carpet's made:
Their fall, their branches, all their mournings prove,
With leafless, naked bodies, whose hues vade
From hopeful green, to wither in their love:
If trees and leaves for absence mourners be,
No marvel that I grieve, who like want see.

(1621)

babish] babyish

273 control] restrain distressed] plundered grieffull] sorrowful roll] (1) role; (2) roll of pressed leaves prove] experience vade] weaken, fade

274

Sonnet XXII

LIKE to the Indians, scorchèd with the sun,
The sun which they do as their god adore,
So am I used by love: for evermore
I worship him: less favours have I won;
Better are they who thus to blackness run,
And so can only whiteness' want deplore,
Than I who pale and white am with grief's store,
Nor can have hope, but to see hopes undone.
Besides, their sacrifice received 's in sight
Of their chose saint, mine hid as worthless rite.
Grant me to see where I my offerings give;
Then let me wear the mark of Cupid's might
In heart, as they in skin of Phoebus' light;
Not ceasing offerings to love while I live.

(1621)

275

Sonnet XXVII

FIE, tedious hope, why do you still rebel?
Is it not yet enough you flattered me,
But cunningly you seek to use a spell
How to betray? Must these your trophies be?
I looked from you far sweeter fruit to see;
But blasted were your blossoms when they fell,
And those delights expected from hands free
Withered and dead, and what seemed bliss proves hell.
No town was won by a more plotted sleight
Than I by you, who may my fortune write
In embers of that fire which ruined me.
Thus, hope, your falsehoods calls you to be tried.
You're loath, I see, the trial to abide;
Prove true at last, and gain your liberty.

(1621)

276

Sonnet XXXII

HOW fast thou fliest, O time, on love's swift wings
To hopes of joy that flatters our desire,
Which to a lover still contentment brings!
Yet, when we should enjoy, thou dost retire;

Thou stayst thy pace, false time, from our desire,
When to our ill thou hast'st with eagle's wings,
Slow, only to make us see thy retire
Was for despair and harm, which sorrow brings.
Oh! slack thy pace, and milder pass to love;
Be like the bee, whose wings she doth but use
To bring home profit: master's good to prove,
Laden and weary, yet again pursues.
So lade thyself with honey of sweet joy,
And do not me the hive of love destroy.

(1621)

277 *Sonnet XLVIII*

How like a fire doth love increase in me:
The longer that it lasts, the stronger still,
The greater, purer, brighter; and doth fill
No eye with wonder more than hopes still be
Bred in my breast, when fires of love are free
To use that part to their best pleasing will;
And now impossible it is to kill
The heat so great, where love his strength doth see.
Mine eyes can scarce sustain the flames my heart
Doth trust in them, my passions to impart,
And languishingly strive to show my love;
My breath not able is to breathe least part
Of that increasing fuel of my smart;
Yet love I will till I but ashes prove.

(1621)

278 *Song*

Oh me, the time is come to part,
And with it my life-killing smart.
Fond hope, leave me: my dear must go
To meet more joy, and I more woe.

Where still of mirth enjoy thy fill:
One is enough to suffer ill.
My heart so well to sorrow used
Can better be by new griefs bruised;

Thou whom the heavens themselves like made
Should never sit in mourning shade.
No, I alone must mourn, and end,
Who have a life in grief to spend:

276 retire] drawing back

My swiftest pace, to wailings bent,
Shows joy had but a short time lent
To bide in me, where woes must dwell
And charm me with their cruel spell.

And yet, when they their witchcrafts try,
They only make me wish to die;
But ere my faith in love they change,
In horrid darkness will I range.

(1621)

279 *Sonnet VI*

My pain, still smothered in my grievèd breast,
  Seeks for some ease, yet cannot passage find
  To be discharged of this unwelcome guest;
  When most I strive, more fast his burdens bind,
Like to a ship on Goodwins cast by wind:
  The more she strives, more deep in sand is pressed,
  Till she be lost. So am I, in this kind
  Sunk and devoured and swallowed by unrest,
Lost, shipwrecked, spoiled, debarred of smallest hope.
  Nothing of pleasure left, save thoughts have scope,
  Which wander may. Go then, my thoughts, and cry
Hope's perished; love tempest-beaten; joy lost.
  Killing despair hath all these blessings crossed;
  Yet faith still cries, 'Love will not falsify.'

(1621)

280 *Song*

Love, a child, is ever crying:
Please him and he straight is flying,
Give him, he the more is craving,
Never satisfied with having;

His desires have no measure,
Endless folly is his treasure,
What he promiseth he breaketh,
Trust not one word that he speaketh;

He vows nothing but false matter,
And to cozen you he'll flatter:
Let him gain the hand, he'll leave you,
And still glory to deceive you;

279 Goodwins] (treacherous sands)   crossed] thwarted
280 cozen] deceive

He will triumph in your wailing,
And yet cause be of your failing.
These his virtues are, and slighter
Are his gifts, his favours lighter:

Feathers are as firm in staying,
Wolves no fiercer in their preying.
As a child, then, leave him crying,
Nor seek him so given to flying.

(1621)

WILLIAM AUSTIN
1587–1634

281 [*Job 17*] *Verse 13:* 'Sepulchrum Domus Mea Est'

HERE we must rest; and where else should we rest?
Is not a man's own house to sleep in, best?
If this be all our house, they are to blame
That brag of the great houses whence they came,
And evermore their speech thus interlace:
'I, and my father's house.' Alas, alas:
What is my father's house? And what am I?
My father's house is earth, where I must lie;
And I a worm, no man, that fit no room,
Till, like a worm, I crawl into my tomb.
This is my dwelling; this is my truest home:
A house of clay best fits a guest of loam.
Nay, 'tis my house; for I perceive I have
In all my life ne'er dwelt out of a grave.
The womb was first my grave; whence since I rose,
My body, grave-like, doth my soul enclose:
That body (like a corpse) with sheets o'erspread,
Dying each night, lies buried in my bed;
O'er which my spreading tester's large extent,
Borne with carved antiques, makes my monument;
And o'er my head, perchance, such things may stand,
When I am quite run out in dust and sand.
My close low-builded chamber, to mine eye,
Shows like a little chapel, where I lie;

281 'Sepulchrum . . . Est'] The grave is my house   tester's] (1) canopy's; (2) shrine's   antiques] grotesques

While at my window pretty birds do ring
My knell, and with their notes my *obiit*s sing.
Thus, when the day's vain toil my soul hath wearied,
I in my body, bed, and house lie buried.
Then have I little cause to fear my tomb,
When this wherein I live, my grave's become.
Nay, we not only do ourselves entomb,
But make (for others) graves in our own womb:
Creatures of sea and land we in us bury,
And at their funerals are blithe and merry;
Who groan to serve us thus, and die unwilling.
How can we then live long, that live by killing?
Methinks that we should neither eat nor drink,
But straight to dig our graves we should bethink;
For since by their dead bodies we are fed,
I wonder all this while we are not dead.
It is an old-said-saw (yet in request)
When belly's full, then bones would be at rest.
Well have we fed the flesh, and from sin's cup
Have drunk iniquity like water up;
The creatures we have eaten, flayed, and shorn,
The fruits from earth to feed us we have torn:
Are we not satisfied? Oh, sure, 'tis best,
That after all we get us home to rest.
And nowhere can the flesh true slumbers have
But in our truest home, or homely grave.
There we sleep sound, there let the tempest roar:
The world's proud waves shall dash on us no more.
We are at home, and safe, whatever comes:
Let them fight on, we shall not hear their drums.
Let those we doted on, now love, or hate;
It shall not grieve us, though they prove ingrate:
Yea, let them praise or rail, we lie aloof,
Out of their reach; our sleep is cannon-proof.
  And we but sleep; for as we close our eyes
Each night we go to bed, in hope to rise,
So do we die. For when the trump doth blow,
We shall as easily awake, we know.
And as we, after sleep, our bodies find
More fresh in strength, and cheerfully inclined,
So after death our flesh, here dead and dried,
Shall rise immortal, new, and purified.
If this be true, why make we no more haste?
'Tis time to sleep, day fails, night draws on fast:

*obiit*s] epitaphs   womb] stomach

Let's get us home. For as the evening sun
Looking us in the face when day is done
Makes us cast long our shadows, so when death
Looks in our face, through age, and claims our breath,
We cast his shadow long off, from our sight,
Yet may we thereby know 'tis almost night.
And when we see night come, in frowning skies,
What man will not go home, if he be wise?
Here let him come; this house is of such fashion,
The tenant ne'er shall pay for reparation:
There shall the dew not wet him; cold, not harm him;
There shall no sun nor weather overwarm him.
From thence he'll find (when thither he is gone)
A private walk to heaven, for one alone.
Why do we then not go? Are flesh and blood
The hinderers that clog us from this good?
Oh rid thyself at home, and cast off those:
What wise man ever went to bed in's clothes?
Shall we, that know how after this life's end
An everlasting one for us doth tend,
Grieve to lay down these rags, for Earth to keep,
That we awhile may take a nap of sleep?
Then were we worse than children; for but say
That they tomorrow shall have holiday,
They'll straight to bed and put off all apparel.
Then cease, my flesh, with heaven's decree to quarrel,
And with these words reduce thy thoughts that roam:
He that dies first shall only first go home.
But when thy flesh, hither, to sleep repairs,
Say, as when to thy bed thou go'st, thy prayers.
Since he most oft forgets himself in death
That thinks not of his God that gives him breath,
Invoke his mercy ere thy rest thou take;
For as thou fallst asleep, so thou shalt wake.
   This house, of which we have before been telling,
Is but a sleeping-chamber, not a dwelling.
For when thou wak'st, this house no more shall hold thee,
But that whereof the blessed apostle told thee,
Saying: 'If this our earthly house decay,
We have a house not made with hands of clay,
But in the heavens eternal.' Blest is he,
Whom thou, O Lord, admittest there to be:
He in thy courts shall dwell; thy temple's store
Shall in thy house fill him for evermore.

long off] far away   reparation] (1) repair; (2) salvation   rid] disencumber, strip
store] plenty

But stay, my soul. Thou canst not yet come thither;
Thy wings are clogged, and thou more strength must gather.
Meantime, till from this Earth thou getst free scope,
Even in thy grave, thy flesh shall rest in hope.
So farewell world. Here in my house I'll rest:
Sepulchrum enim domus mea est.

(1983)

SIR FRANCIS KYNASTON
1587–1642

282 *To Cynthia*

THERE is no sense that I should write a line
On such a beauty, Cynthia, as thine;
I am no poet, and it is in vain,
Since thou exceedst all worth, to strive to feign:
On my poor lines the Thespian well ne'er dropped,
From me the fount of Helicon is stopped:
I ne'er was so ill bred as to invoke
Apollo, and to sacrifice with smoke
Of coals, or billets, nor yet am I able,
In the west end of Cardinal Wolsey's stable,
To keep a Pegasus, a horse that might
Advance my Muse by his swift nimble flight.
Yet like a man oppressed with grief and cares,
Lawsuits, and troubles, so with me it fares:
If he but take a lusty jovial drink,
Forgets all sorrows; so if I but think
On thee or thy chaste beauty, then my cheer
Is changed, no clouds do in my soul appear;
Thy rare divinest beauty so expels
With joys the horror of ten thousand hells.

(1642)

Sepulchrum . . . est] For the grave is my house

282 Thespian well . . . fount of Helicon] fountains of the Muses   Pegasus] (symbol of inspiration) (classical mythology)

RICHARD BRATHWAIT
1588?–1673

283 *Vandunk's Four Humours, in Quality and Quantity*

I AM mighty melancholy,
  And a quart of sack will cure me;
I am choleric as any,
  Quart of claret will secure me;

I am phlegmatic as may be,
  Peter-see-me must inure me;
I am sanguine for a lady,
  And cool Rhenish shall conjúre me.

(1617)

LUKE WADDING
1588–1657

284 [*Christmas Day*]

CHRISTMAS day is come; let's all prepare for mirth,
  Which fills the heavens and Earth at this amazing birth.
Through both, the joyous angels in strife and hurry fly
  With glory and hosannas: 'All holy' do they cry;
In heaven the Church Triumphant adores with all her choirs,
  The Militant on Earth with humble faith admires.

But why should we rejoice? Should we not rather mourn,
  To see the hope of nations thus in a stable born?
Where are his crown and sceptre, where is his throne sublime,
  Where is his train majestic, that should the stars outshine?
Is there not sumptuous palace, nor any inn at all,
  To lodge his heavenly mother but in a filthy stall?

283 Peter-see-me] a Spanish wine (Pedro Ximines)   conjúre] charm

GEORGE WITHER
1588–1667

285

Epigram VII

WOMEN, as some men say, unconstant be;
'Tis like enough, and so no doubt are men:
Nay, if their scapes we could so plainly see,
I fear that scarce there will be one for ten.
Men have but their own lusts that tempt to ill;
Women have lusts and men's allurements too:
Alas, if their strengths cannot curb their will,
What should poor women, that are weaker, do?
Oh, they had need be chaste and look about them,
That strive 'gainst lust within and knaves without them.

(1612)

from *The Shepherd's Hunting*

286

Sonnet

I THAT erstwhile the world's sweet air did draw,
Graced by the fairest ever mortal saw,
Now closely pent with walls of ruthless stone
Consume my days and nights and all alone.

When I was wont to sing of shepherds' loves,
My walks were fields, and downs, and hills, and groves;
But now, alas, so strict is my hard doom,
Fields, downs, hills, groves, and all's but one poor room.

Each morn, as soon as daylight did appear,
With nature's music birds would charm mine ear,
Which now, instead of their melodious strains,
Hear rattling shackles, gyves, and bolts, and chains.

But though that all the world's delight forsake me,
I have a Muse, and she shall music make me;
Whose airy notes, in spite of closest cages,
Shall give content to me, and after ages.

Nor do I pass for all this outward ill:
My heart's the same, and undejected still;
And, which is more than some in freedom win,
I have true rest, and peace, and joy within.

And then my mind, that spite of prison's free,
Whene'er she pleases anywhere can be:
She's in an hour in France, Rome, Turkey, Spain,
In Earth, in hell, in heaven, and here again.

Yet there's another comfort in my woe:
My cause is spread, and all the world may know
My fault's no more but speaking truth and reason;
Nor debt, nor theft, nor murder, rape, or treason.

Nor shall my foes, with all their might and power,
Wipe out their shame, nor yet this fame of our;
Which when they find, they shall my fate envy,
Till they grow lean, and sick, and mad, and die.

Then, though my body here in prison rot,
And my wronged satires seem awhile forgot,
Yet when both fame and life hath left those men,
My verse and I'll revive, and live again.

So thus enclosed I bear affliction's load,
But with more true content than some abroad;
For whilst their thoughts do feel my scourge's sting,
In bands I'll leap, and dance, and laugh, and sing.

(1615)

from *A Description of Love*

287 *A Love Sonnet*

I LOVED a lass, a fair one,
   As fair as e'er was seen;
She was indeed a rare one,
   Another Sheba queen.
But fool as then I was,
   I thought she loved me too;
But now, alas, she's left me,
   Falero, lero, loo.

286 pass for] care about   bands] bonds; shackles

Her hair like gold did glister,
  Each eye was like a star;
She did surpass her sister,
  Which passed all others far.
She would me honey call;
  She'd, oh she'd kiss me too;
But now, alas, she's left me,
  Falero, lero, loo.

In summer time to Medley
  My love and I would go;
The boatmen there stood ready,
  My love and I to row.
For cream there would we call,
  For cakes, and for prunes too;
But now, alas, she's left me,
  Falero, lero, loo.

Many a merry meeting
  My love and I have had;
She was my only sweeting,
  She made my heart full glad.
The tears stood in her eyes,
  Like to the morning dew;
But now, alas, she's left me,
  Falero, lero, loo.

And as abroad we walkèd,
  As lovers' fashion is,
Oft as we sweetly talkèd
  The sun should steal a kiss.
The wind upon her lips
  Likewise most sweetly blew;
But now, alas, she's left me,
  Falero, lero, loo.

Her cheeks were like the cherry,
  Her skin as white as snow;
When she was blithe and merry,
  She angel-like did show.
Her waist exceeding small,
  The fives did fit her shoe;
But now, alas, she's left me,
  Falero, lero, loo.

Medley] (?near Godstow, Oxfordshire)

In summer time or winter
  She had her heart's desire;
I still did scorn to stint her
  From sugar, sack, or fire.
The world went round about,
  No cares we ever knew;
But now, alas, she's left me,
  Falero, lero, loo.

As we walked home together
  At midnight through the town,
To keep away the weather
  O'er her I'd cast my gown.
No cold my love should feel,
  Whate'er the heavens could do;
But now, alas, she's left me,
  Falero, lero, loo.

Like doves we would be billing,
  And clip and kiss so fast;
Yet she would be unwilling
  That I should kiss the last.
They're Judas-kisses now,
  Since that they proved untrue;
For now, alas, she's left me,
  Falero, lero, loo.

To maidens' vows and swearing
  Henceforth no credit give;
You may give them the hearing,
  But never them believe.
They are as false as fair,
  Unconstant, frail, untrue;
For mine, alas, has left me,
  Falero, lero, loo.

'Twas I that paid for all things,
  'Twas others drank the wine;
I cannot now recall things,
  Live but a fool to pine.
'Twas I that beat the bush,
  The bird to others flew;
For she, alas, hath left me,
  Falero, lero, loo.

sack] imported white wine (often sweetened with sugar)   clip] embrace

If ever that dame Nature,
  For this false lover's sake,
Another pleasing creature
  Like unto her would make,
Let her remember this,
  To make the other true;
For this, alas, hath left me,
  Falero, lero, loo.

No riches now can raise me,
  No want make me despair;
No misery amaze me,
  Nor yet for want I care.
I have lost a world itself,
  My earthly heaven, adieu;
Since she, alas, hath left me,
  Falero, lero, loo.

(1620)

from *Fair Virtue*

288 *Sonnet V*

I WANDERED out a while agone,
And went I know not whither:
But there do beauties many a one
Resort and meet together.
And Cupid's power will there be shown
If ever you come thither.

For like two suns, two beauties bright
I shining saw together,
And tempted by their double light
My eyes I fixed on either;
Till both at once so thralled my sight,
I loved, and knew not whether.

Such equal ⟨sweet⟩ sweet Venus gave,
That I preferred not either,
And when for love I thought to crave
I knew not well of whether.
For one while this I wished to have,
And then I that had liefer.

288 whether] which   liefer] rather

A lover of the curious'st eye
Might have been pleased in either;
And so, I must confess, might I,
Had they not been together.
Now both must love or both deny:
In one enjoy I neither.

But yet at last I scaped the smart
I feared at coming hither;
For seeing my divided heart,
I choosing, knew not whether,
Love angry grew, and did depart:
And now I care for neither.

(1622)

from *A Collection of Emblems* (289–293)

289 *I. xxxv:* [*Planting*]

HE that delights to plant and set
Makes after ages in his debt.

When I behold the havoc and the spoil
Which, even within the compass of my days,
Is made through every quarter of this isle,
In woods and groves, which were this kingdom's praise;
And when I mind with how much greediness
We seek the present gain in everything,
Not caring (so our lust we may possess)
What damage to posterity we bring:
They do, methinks, as if they did foresee
That some of those whom they have cause to hate
Should come in future times, their heirs to be;
Or else why should they such things perpetrate?
For if they think their children shall succeed,
Or can believe that they begot their heirs,
They could not, surely, do so foul a deed
As to deface the land that should be theirs.
What our forefathers planted, we destroy:
Nay, all men's labours, living heretofore,
And all our own, we lavishly employ
To serve our present lusts, and for no more.

289 mind] remember   lust] desire

But let these careless wasters learn to know
That, as vain spoil is open injury,
So planting is a debt they truly owe
And ought to pay to their posterity.
Self love, for none but for itself, doth care,
And only for the present taketh pain;
But charity for others doth prepare,
And joys in that which future time shall gain.
If after ages may my labours bless,
I care not, much, how little I possess.

(1635)

290 *II. xxx:* [*The Spade and the Wreath*]

WHERE labour wisely is employed
Deservèd glory is enjoyed.

Do men suppose, when God's free-giving hand
Doth by their friends, or by inheritance,
To wealth or titles raise them in the land,
That those to lasting glories them advance?
Or can men think such goods or gifts of nature
As nimble apprehensions, memory,
An able body, or a comely feature,
Without improvement, them shall dignify?
May sloth and idleness be warrantable
In us, because our fathers have been rich?
Or are we therefore truly honourable,
Because our predecessors have been such?
When nor our fortunes nor our natural parts
In any measure are improved by us,
Are others bound, as if we had deserts,
With attributes of honour to belie us?
No, no; the more our predecessors left
(Yea, and the more by nature we enjoy),
We of the more esteem shall be bereft,
Because our talents we do misemploy.
True glory doth on labour still attend;
But without labour, glory we have none.
She crowns good workmen when their works have end,
And shame gives payment where is nothing done.
Laborious, therefore, be; but, lest the spade
(Which here doth labour mean) thou use in vain,

290 apprehensions] sensibilities, grasp feature] form warrantable] praiseworthy belie] misrepresent still] ever

The serpent thereunto be sure thou add;
That is, let prudence guide thy taking pain.
  For where a wise endeavour shall be found,
  A wreath of glory will enclose it round.

(1635)

291 *II.xliv:* [*The Husbandman*]

THE husbandman doth sow the seeds,
And then on hope till harvest feeds.

The painful husbandman with sweaty brows
Consumes in labour many a weary day:
To break the stubborn earth, he digs and ploughs,
And then the corn he scatters on the clay.
When that is done he harrows in the seeds,
And by a well cleansed furrow lays it dry:
He frees it from the worms, the moles, the weeds;
He on the fences also hath an eye.
And though he see the chilling winter bring
Snows, floods and frosts, his labours to annoy;
Though blasting winds do nip them in the spring,
And summer's mildews threaten to destroy:
Yea, though not only days but weeks they are
(Nay, many weeks and many months beside)
In which he must with pain prolong his care,
Yet constant in his hopes he doth abide.
For this respect, hope's emblem here you see
Attends the plough, that men beholding it
May be instructed, or else minded be
What hopes continuing labours will befit.
Though long thou toilèd hast, and long attended
About such workings as are necessary;
And oftentimes, ere fully they are ended,
Shalt find thy pains in danger to miscarry:
Yet be not out of hope, nor quite dejected.
For buried seeds will sprout when winter's gone;
Unlikelier things are many times effected;
And God brings help when men their best have done.
  Yea, they that in good works their life employ,
  Although they sow in tears, shall reap in joy.

(1635)

292

IV.i: [*The Marigold*]

WHILST I the sun's bright face may view,
I will no meaner light pursue.

When with a serious musing I behold
The grateful and obsequious marigold:
How duly every morning she displays
Her open breast when Titan spreads his rays;
How she observes him in his daily walk,
Still bending towards him her tender stalk;
How, when he down declines, she droops and mourns,
Bedewed (as 'twere) with tears, till he returns;
And how she vails her flow'rs when he is gone,
As if she scornèd to be lookèd on
By an inferior eye, or did contemn
To wait upon a meaner light than him.
When this I meditate, methinks the flowers
Have spirits far more generous than ours,
And give us fair examples to despise
The servile fawnings and idolatries
Wherewith we court these earthly things below,
Which merit not the service we bestow.
  But, oh my God! though grovelling I appear
Upon the ground (and have a rooting here
Which hales me downward), yet in my desire,
To that which is above me I aspire,
And all my best affections I profess
To him that is the sun of righteousness.
Oh! keep the morning of his incarnation,
The burning noontide of his bitter passion,
The night of his descending, and the height
Of his ascension, ever in my sight;
  That imitating him in what I may,
  I never follow an inferior way.

(1635)

obsequious] dutiful in performing obsequies   Titan] the sun   Still] Always
vails] lowers   sun of righteousness] (Mal. 4: 2)

293 *IV.xxxi: [The Spade]*

A FORTUNE is ordained for thee
According as thy labours be.

The spade, for labour stands. The ball with wings
Intendeth flitting, rolling, worldly things.
This altar stone may serve in setting forth
Things firmer, solid, and of greater worth;
In which, and by the words enclosing these,
You there may read your fortune, if you please.
If you your labour on those things bestow
Which roll and flutter always to and fro,
It cannot be but that which you obtain
Must prove a wavering and unconstant gain;
For he that soweth vanity shall find,
At reaping time, no better fruit than wind.
  Your hours in serious matters if you spend,
Or such as to a lasting purpose tend,
The purchase of your pains will ever last,
And bring you pleasure when the labour's past.
Yea, though in tears your seed-time you employ,
Your harvest shall be fetchèd home with joy.
If much be wrought, much profit will ensue;
If little, but a little meed is due.
Of nothing, nothing comes: on evil deeds
An evil conscience and ill fame succeeds:
An honest life still finds prepared for 't
Sweet hopes in death; and, after, good report.
Of sex, or of degree, there's no regard;
But, as the labour, such is the reward.
  To work aright, O Lord, instruct thou me;
And ground my works and buildings all on thee:
  That, by the fiery test, when they are tried,
  My work may stand, and I may safe abide.

(1635)

meed] reward   still] ever   degree] rank

WILLIAM BROWNE OF TAVISTOCK
1590?–1645?

294 from *Britannia's Pastorals* (294–296)

SHALL I tell you whom I love?
  Hearken then a while to me;
And if such a woman move
  As I now shall versify,
Be assured 'tis she or none
That I love, and love alone.

Nature did her so much right
  As she scorns the help of art.
In as many virtues dight
  As e'er yet embraced a heart.
So much good so truly tried,
Some for less were deified.

Wit she hath without desire
  To make known how much she hath,
And her anger flames no higher
  Than may fitly sweeten wrath.
Full of pity as may be,
Though perhaps not so to me.

Reason masters every sense,
  And her virtues grace her birth:
Lovely as all excellence.
  Modest in her most of mirth:
Likelihood enough to prove
Only worth could kindle love.

Such she is; and if you know
  Such a one as I have sung,
Be she brown, or fair, or so,
  That she be but somewhile young,
Be assured 'tis she or none
That I love, and love alone.

(1616)

dight] clothed Likelihood] Promise That] Provided that somewhile] (1) at times; (2) formerly

295 [*Morning*]

THE Muses' friend, gray-eyed Aurora, yet
Held all the meadows in a cooling sweat,
The milk-white gossamers not upwards snowed,
Nor was the sharp and useful steering goad
Laid on the strong-necked ox; no gentle bud
The sun had dried; the cattle chewed the cud
Low levelled on the grass; no fly's quick sting
Enforced the stonehorse in a furious ring
To tear the passive earth, nor lash his tail
About his buttocks broad; the slimy snail
Might on the wainscot (by his many mazes'
Winding meanders and self-knitting traces)
Be followed, where he stuck his glittering slime,
Not yet wiped off. It was so early time
The careful smith had in his sooty forge
Kindled no coal; nor did his hammers urge
His neighbours' patience: owls abroad did fly,
And day as then might plead his infancy.
Yet of fair Albion all the western swains
Were long since up, attending on the plains,
When Nereus' daughter with her mirthful host
Should summon them, on their declining coast.
  But since her stay was long, for fear the sun
Should find them idle, some of them begun
To leap and wrestle; others threw the bar.
Some from the company removèd are,
To meditate the songs they meant to play,
Or make a new round for next holiday:
Some tales of love their lovesick fellows told;
Others were seeking stakes to pitch their fold.
This, all alone was mending of his pipe;
That, for his lass sought fruits most sweet, most ripe.
Here, from the rest, a lovely shepherd's boy
Sits piping on a hill, as if his joy
Would still endure, or else that age's frost
Should never make him think what he had lost.
Yonder a shepherdess knits by the springs,
Her hands still keeping time to what she sings:

Aurora] goddess of dawn (Greek mythology) stonehorse] stallion urge] demand as then] still swains] shepherds Nereus] father of sea nymphs (Greek mythology) host] i.e. of nereids coast] side (of Earth) bar] log (used as trial of strength) pitch] secure with poles still] always

Or seeming, by her song, those fairest hands
Were comforted in working. Near the sands
Of some sweet river sits a musing lad
That moans the loss of what he sometime had,
His love by death bereft: when fast by him
An aged swain takes place, as near the brim
Of 's grave as of the river; showing how
That as those floods which pass along right now
Are followed still by others from their spring,
And in the sea have all their burying,
Right so our times are known, our ages found
(Nothing is permanent within this round):
One age is now, another that succeeds,
Extirping all things which the former breeds;
Another follows that doth new times raise,
New years, new months, new weeks, new hours, new days;
Mankind thus goes like rivers from their spring,
And in the earth have all their burying.
Thus sate the old man counselling the young,
Whilst underneath a tree which overhung
The silver stream (as some delight it took
To trim his thick boughs in the crystal brook)
Were set a jocund crew of youthful swains,
Wooing their sweetings with delicious strains.
Sportive *oreades* the hills descended,
The *hamadryades* their hunting ended,
And in the high woods left the long-lived harts
To feed in peace, free from their wingèd darts:
Floods, mountains, valleys, woods, each vacant lies
Of nymphs that by them danced their hay-de-guys;
For all those powers were ready to embrace
The present means, to give our shepherds grace.

(1616)

296 [*The Golden Age*]

OH! the Golden Age
Met all contentment in no surplusage
Of dainty viands, but as we do still,
Drank the pure water of the crystal rill,
Fed on no other meats than those they fed,
Labour the salad that their stomachs bred.

295 round] Earth   Extirping] Exterminating   *oreades*] mountain-nymphs   *hamadryades*] wood-nymphs   hay-de-guys] country dance

Nor sought they for the down of silver swans,
Nor those sow-thistle locks each small gale fans;
But hides of beasts, which when they lived they kept,
Served them for bed and cov'ring when they slept.
If any softer lay, 'twas (by the loss
Of some rock's warmth) on thick and spungy moss,
Or on the ground; some simple wall of clay
Parting their beds from where their cattle lay.
And on such pallets one man clippèd then
More golden slumbers than this age again.
That time, physicians thrived not; or if any,
I dare say all; yet then were thrice as many
As now professed, and more: for every man
Was his own patient and physicïan.
None had a body then so weak and thin,
Bankrupt of nature's store, to feed the sin
Of an insatiate female, in whose womb
Could nature all her past and all to come
Infuse, with virtues of all drugs beside,
She might be tired, but never satisfied.
To please which orc her husband's weakened piece
Must have his cullis mixed with ambergris,
Pheasant and partridge into jelly turned,
Grated with gold, seven times refined and burned,
With dust of orient pearl, richer the east
Yet ne'er beheld: oh Epicurean feast!
This is his breakfast, and his meal at night
Possets no less provoking appetite,
Whose dear ingredients valued are at more
Than all his ancestors were worth before,
When such as we by poor and simple fare
More able lived, and died not without heir
Sprung from our own loins and a spotless bed,
Of any other power unseconded.

(1616)

297 [*Epitaph for Marie, Countess of Pembroke*]

UNDERNEATH this sable hearse
Lies the subject of all verse:
Sidney's sister, Pembroke's mother:
Death, ere thou hast slain another,

clippèd] embraced virtues] properties orc] devouring monster piece] weapon cullis] broth orient] excellent

Fair and learn'd and good as she,
Time shall throw a dart at thee.

Marble piles let no man raise
To her name for after days;
Some kind woman born as she,
Reading this, like Niobe
Shall turn marble, and become
Both her mourner and her tomb.

(1623)

298 *Vision V*

A ROSE, as fair as ever saw the north,
Grew in a little garden all alone;
A sweeter flower did nature ne'er put forth,
Nor fairer garden yet was never known:
The maidens danced about it morn and noon,
And learnèd bards of it their ditties made;
The nimble fairies by the pale-faced moon
Watered the root and kissed her pretty shade.
But well-a-day, the gardener careless grew;
The maids and fairies both were kept away,
And in a drought the caterpillars threw
Themselves upon the bud and every spray.
  God shield the stock! if heaven send no supplies,
  The fairest blossom of the garden dies.

(wr. before 1629?)

299

LOVE who will, for I'll love none,
  There's fools enough beside me;
Yet if each woman have not one,
  Come to me where I hide me,
And if she can the place attain,
For once I'll be her fool again.

It is an easy place to find,
  And women sure should know it;
Yet thither serves not every wind,
  Nor many men can show it:
It is the storehouse, where doth lie
All women's truth and constancy.

If the journey be so long,
No woman will adventure;
But dreading her weak vessel's wrong,
The voyage will not enter:
Then may she sigh and lie alone,
In love with all, yet loved of none.

(wr. before 1629)

300 *Sonnet*

FOR her gait if she be walking,
Be she sitting I desire her
For her state's sake, and admire her
For her wit if she be talking.
Gait and state and wit approve her;
For which all and each I love her.

Be she sullen, I commend her
For a modest. Be she merry,
For a kind one her prefer I.
Briefly everything doth lend her
So much grace and so approve her,
That for everything I love her.

(1894)

HENRY FARLEY

fl. 1621

301 *The Bounty of Our Age*

TO see a strange outlandish fowl,
A quaint baboon, an ape, an owl,
A dancing bear, a giant's bone,
A foolish engine move alone,
A morris dance, a puppet play,
Mad Tom to sing a roundelay,
A woman dancing on a rope,
Bull baiting also at the Hope,
A rhymer's jests, a juggler's cheats,
A tumbler showing cunning feats,

Or players acting on the stage:
There goes the bounty of our age;
  But unto any pious motion
  There's little coin and less devotion.

(1621)

ROBERT HERRICK
1591–1674

from *Hesperides* (302–342)

302 *The Argument of His Book*

I SING of brooks, of blossoms, birds, and bowers:
Of April, May, of June, and July-flowers.
I sing of May-poles, hock-carts, wassails, wakes,
Of bridegrooms, brides, and of their bridal cakes.
I write of youth, of love, and have access
By these to sing of cleanly-wantonness.
I sing of dews, of rains, and piece by piece
Of balm, of oil, of spice, and amber-Greece.
I sing of time's trans-shifting; and I write
How roses first came red, and lilies white.
I write of groves, of twilights, and I sing
The court of Mab, and of the fairy king.
I write of hell; I sing (and ever shall)
Of heaven, and hope to have it after all.

(1648)

303 *Another [to His Book]*

WHO with thy leaves shall wipe, at need,
The place where swelling piles do breed:
May every ill that bites or smarts
Perplex him in his hinder-parts.

(1648)

302 *Argument*] Theme July-flowers] gillyflowers hock-carts] ceremonial last harvest-wagons wassails] feasts wakes] fairs or festival vigils amber-Greece] ambergris (waxlike raw material of perfume) trans-shifting] changing; metamorphosis Mab] the fairies' midwife

304 *When He Would Have His Verses Read*

In sober mornings, do not thou rehearse
The holy incantation of a verse;
But when that men have both well drunk, and fed,
Let my enchantments then be sung, or read.
When laurel spirts i' th' fire, and when the hearth
Smiles to itself, and gilds the roof with mirth;
When up the thyrse is raised, and when the sound
Of sacred orgies flies, around, around.
When the rose reigns, and locks with ointments shine,
Let rigid Cato read these lines of mine.

(1648)

305 *To Perilla*

Ah, my Perilla! Dost thou grieve to see
Me, day by day, to steal away from thee?
Age calls me hence, and my grey hairs bid come,
And haste away to mine eternal home;
'Twill not be long, Perilla, after this,
That I must give thee the supremest kiss.
Dead when I am, first cast in salt, and bring
Part of the cream from that religious spring;
With which, Perilla, wash my hands and feet;
That done, then wind me in that very sheet
Which wrapped thy smooth limbs (when thou didst
implore
The gods' protection, but the night before).
Follow me weeping to my turf, and there
Let fall a primrose, and with it a tear;
Then lastly, let some weekly strewings be
Devoted to the memory of me:
Then shall my ghost not walk about, but keep
Still in the cool and silent shades of sleep.

(1648)

rehearse] recite thyrse] a javelin twined with ivy (H.) orgies] songs to Bacchus (H.) Cato] 'Censorius', a severe Roman traditionalist

305 supremest] last cream] foam strewings] i.e. of flowers

306 *Upon the Loss of His Mistresses*

I HAVE lost, and lately, these
Many dainty mistresses:
Stately Julia, prime of all;
Sapho next, a principal;
Smooth Anthea, for a skin
White, and heaven-like crystalline;
Sweet Electra, and the choice
Myrha, for the lute, and voice
Next, Corinna, for her wit,
And the graceful use of it;
With Perilla: all are gone;
Only Herrick's left alone,
For to number sorrow by
Their departures hence, and die.

(1648)

307 *His Request to Julia*

JULIA, if I chance to die
Ere I print my poetry,
I most humbly thee desire
To commit it to the fire:
Better 'twere my book were dead,
Than to live not perfected.

(1648)

308 *Delight in Disorder*

A SWEET disorder in the dress
Kindles in clothes a wontonness:
A lawn about the shoulders thrown
Into a fine distraction;
An erring lace, which here and there
Enthrals the crimson stomacher;
A cuff neglectful, and thereby
Ribbands to flow confusèdly;
A winning wave (deserving note)
In the tempestuous petticoat;

308 lawn] veil fine distraction] refined confusion; pure passion stomacher] front piece of dress Ribbands] Ribbons winning] charming (of rhetoric)

A careless shoestring, in whose tie
I see a wild civility:
Do more bewitch me, than when art
Is too precise in every part.

(1648)

309 *To Dianeme*

SWEET, be not proud of those two eyes,
Which star-like sparkle in their skies;
Nor be you proud that you can see
All hearts your captives, yours yet free.
Be you not proud of that rich hair,
Which wantons with the love-sick air;
Whenas that ruby which you wear,
Sunk from the tip of your soft ear,
Will last to be a precious stone,
When all your world of beauty's gone.

(1648)

310 *Corinna's Going a Maying*

GET up, get up for shame; the blooming morn
Upon her wings presents the god unshorn.
See how Aurora throws her fair
Fresh-quilted colours through the air:
Get up, sweet slug-a-bed, and see
The dew-bespangling herb and tree.
Each flower has wept, and bowed toward the east,
Above an hour since; yet you not dressed,
Nay! not so much as out of bed?
When all the birds have matins said,
And sung their thankful hymns, 'tis sin,
Nay, profanation to keep in,
Whenas a thousand virgins on this day
Spring, sooner than the lark, to fetch in May.
Rise; and put on your foliage, and be seen
To come forth, like the spring-time, fresh and green;
And sweet as Flora. Take no care
For jewels for your gown, or hair:

309 Whenas] Seeing that

310 blooming] bright; full of promise god unshorn] sun's rays Aurora] goddess of morning Flora] Roman vegetation goddess

  Fear not; the leaves will strew
  Gems in abundance upon you:
Besides, the childhood of the day has kept,
Against you come, some orient pearls unwept:
  Come, and receive them while the light
  Hangs on the dew-locks of the night;
  And Titan on the eastern hill
  Retires himself, or else stands still
Till you come forth. Wash, dress, be brief in praying:
Few beads are best, when once we go a Maying.
Come, my Corinna, come; and coming, mark
How each field turns a street; each street a park
  Made green, and trimmed with trees: see how
  Devotion gives each house a bough
  Or branch: each porch, each door, ere this,
  An ark, a tabernacle is
Made up of whitethorn neatly interwove;
As if here were those cooler shades of love.
  Can such delights be in the street
  And open fields, and we not see it?
  Come, we'll abroad; and let's obey
  The proclamation made for May:
And sin no more, as we have done, by staying;
But my Corinna, come, let's go a Maying.
There's not a budding boy or girl, this day,
But is got up, and gone to bring in May.
  A deal of youth, ere this, is come
  Back, and with whitethorn laden home.
  Some have despatched their cakes and cream
  Before that we have left to dream;
And some have wept, and wooed, and plighted troth,
And chose their priest, ere we can cast off sloth:
  Many a green gown has been given;
  Many a kiss, both odd and even:
  Many a glance too has been sent
  From out the eye, love's firmament:
Many a jest told of the keys' betraying
This night, and locks picked, yet w' are not a Maying.
Come, let us go, while we are in our prime;
And take the harmless folly of the time.
  We shall grow old apace, and die
  Before we know our liberty.

Gems] Shoots, buds   orient] lustrous   Titan] the sun   beads] prayers   tabernacle] booth (Lev. 23; 40–2)   proclamation] Charles I's 'declaration . . . concerning lawful sports'   green gown] grass-stained dress

Our life is short; and our days run
As fast away as does the sun:
And as a vapour, or a drop of rain,
Once lost, can ne'er be found again:
So when or you or I are made
A fable, song, or fleeting shade,
All love, all liking, all delight
Lies drowned with us in endless night.
Then while time serves, and we are but decaying,
Come, my Corinna, come, let's go a Maying.

(1648)

311 *To His Dying Brother, Master William Herrick*

LIFE of my life, take not so soon thy flight,
But stay the time till we have bade goodnight.
Thou hast both wind and tide with thee; thy way
As soon dispatched is by the night, as day.
Let us not then so rudely henceforth go
Till we have wept, kissed, sighed, shook hands, or so.
There's pain in parting, and a kind of hell,
When once true lovers take their last farewell.
What? shall we two our endless leaves take here
Without a sad look, or a solemn tear?
He knows not love, that hath not this truth proved,
Love is most loath to leave the thing beloved.
Pay we our vows, and go: yet when we part,
Then, even then, I will bequeath my heart
Into thy loving hands: for I'll keep none
To warm my breast, when thou my pulse art gone.
No, here I'll last, and walk, a harmless shade,
About this urn, wherein thy dust is laid,
To guard it so as nothing here shall be
Heavy, to hurt those sacred seeds of thee.

(1648)

312 *The Lily in a Crystal*

YOU have beheld a smiling rose
When virgins' hands have drawn
O'er it a cobweb-lawn;
And here, you see, this lily shows,

310 or . . . or] either . . . or

312 cobweb-lawn] fine linen

Tombed in a crystal stone,
More fair in this transparent case
Than when it grew alone,
And had but single grace.

You see how cream but naked is,
Nor dances in the eye
Without a strawberry;
Or some fine tincture, like to this,
Which draws the sight thereto
More by that wantoning with it
Than when the paler hue
No mixture did admit.

You see how amber through the streams
More gently strokes the sight,
With some concealed delight,
Than when he darts his radiant beams
Into the boundless air:
Where either too much light his worth
Doth all at once impair,
Or set it little forth.

Put purple grapes or cherries in-
To glass, and they will send
More beauty to commend
Them, from that clean and subtile skin,
Than if they naked stood,
And had no other pride at all
But their own flesh and blood,
And tinctures natural.

Thus lily, rose, grape, cherry, cream,
And strawberry do stir
More love, when they transfer
A weak, a soft, a broken beam,
Than if they should discover
At full their proper excellence,
Without some scene cast over,
To juggle with the sense.

Thus let this crystalled lily be
A rule, how far to teach,
Your nakedness must reach;
And that, no further than we see

case] (1) container; (2) body   tincture] (1) (cosmetic) colour; (2) spiritual principle (alchemy)   proper] individual   scene] curtain, veil

Those glaring colours laid
By art's wise hand, but to this end
They should obey a shade,
Lest they too far extend.

So though you're white as swan, or snow,
And have the power to move
A world of men to love:
Yet, when your lawns and silks shall flow,
And that white cloud divide
Into a doubtful twi-light, then,
Then will your hidden pride
Raise greater fires in men.

(1648)

313 *To Live Merrily, and to Trust to Good Verses*

Now is the time for mirth,
Nor cheek or tongue be dumb;
For with the flowery earth
The golden pomp is come.

The golden pomp is come;
For now each tree does wear
(Made of her pap and gum)
Rich beads of amber here.

Now reigns the rose, and now
The Arabian dew besmears
My uncontrollèd brow,
And my retorted hairs.

Homer, this health to thee,
In sack of such a kind
That it would make thee see,
Though thou wert ne'er so blind.

Next Virgil I'll call forth,
To pledge this second health
In wine whose each cup's worth
An Indian commonwealth.

colours] (1) tints; (2) rhetorical figures pride] (1) glory; (2) difficulty

313 retorted] twisted back

A goblet next I'll drink
  To Ovid, and suppose,
Made he the pledge, he'd think
  The world had all *one nose.*

Then this immensive cup
  Of aromatic wine,
Catullus, I quaff up
  To that terse Muse of thine.

Wild I am now with heat;
  O Bacchus! Cool thy rays!
Or frantic I shall eat
  Thy thyrse, and bite the bays.

Round, round, the roof does run;
  And being ravished thus,
Come, I will drink a tun
  To my Propertius.

Now, to Tibullus, next,
  This flood I drink to thee;
But stay: I see a text,
  That this presents to me:

'Behold, Tibullus lies
  Here burnt, whose small return
Of ashes scarce suffice
  To fill a little urn.'

Trust to good verses then;
  They only will aspire,
When pyramids, as men,
  Are lost in the funeral fire.

And when all bodies meet
  In Lethe to be drowned,
Then only numbers sweet
  With endless life are crowned.

(1648)

Ovid, Catullus] Latin poets   Made ... pledge] If he drank   *nose*] (1) bouquet; (2) Naso, Ovid's family name   immensive] immeasurable   thyrse] thyrsus, ornamented staff   Propertius, Tibullus] Latin poets   Lethe] river of forgetfulness (ancient mythology)   numbers] verses

314 *To the Virgins, To Make Much of Time*

GATHER ye rosebuds while ye may,
  Old Time is still a flying;
And this same flower that smiles today,
  Tomorrow will be dying.

The glorious lamp of heaven, the sun,
  The higher he's a getting;
The sooner will his race be run,
  And nearer he's to setting.

That age is best which is the first,
  When youth and blood are warmer;
But being spent, the worse, and worst
  Times, still succeed the former.

Then be not coy, but use your time,
  And while ye may, go marry;
For having lost but once your prime,
  You may for ever tarry.

(1648)

315 *His Poetry His Pillar*

ONLY a little more
  I have to write,
  Then I'll give o'er,
And bid the world goodnight.

'Tis but a flying minute
  That I must stay,
  Or linger in it;
And then I must away.

O time that cutst down all!
  And scarce leav'st here
  Memorial
Of any men that were.

How many lie forgot
  In vaults beneath?
  And piecemeal rot
Without a fame in death?

Behold this living stone
  I rear for me,
  Ne'er to be thrown
Down, envious time, by thee.

Pillars let some set up,
  If so they please:
  Here is my hope
And my pyrámidès.

(1648)

316 *A Meditation for His Mistress*

You are a tulip seen today,
But, dearest, of so short a stay
That where you grew, scarce man can say.

You are a lovely July-flower,
Yet one rude wind or ruffling shower
Will force you hence—and in an hour.

You are a sparkling rose in the bud,
Yet lost, ere that chaste flesh and blood
Can show where you or grew, or stood.

You are a full-spread fair-set vine,
And can with tendrils love entwine;
Yet dried, ere you distil your wine.

You are like balm enclosèd (well)
In amber, or some crystal shell;
Yet lost ere you transfuse your smell.

You are a dainty violet,
Yet withered, ere you can be set
Within the virgin's coronet.

You are the queen all flowers among,
But die you must, fair maid, ere long;
As he, the maker of this song.

(1648)

316 July-flower] gillyflower or ... or] either ... or distil] produce set] (1) put in place; (2) planted; grafted

317 *The Hock-Cart, or Harvest Home:*
To the Right Honourable Mildmay, Earl of Westmorland

COME sons of summer, by whose toil
We are the lords of wine and oil:
By whose tough labours and rough hands
We rip up first, then reap our lands.
Crowned with the ears of corn, now come,
And, to the pipe, sing harvest home.
Come forth, my lord, and see the cart
Dressed up with all the country art.
See, here a malkin, there a sheet,
As spotless pure as it is sweet:
The horses, mares, and frisking fillies
(Clad, all, in linen, white as lilies).
The harvest swains and wenches bound
For joy, to see the hock-cart crowned.
About the cart, hear how the rout
Of rural younglings raise the shout;
Pressing before, some coming after,
Those with a shout, and these with laughter.
Some bless the cart; some kiss the sheaves;
Some prank them up with oaken leaves;
Some cross the fill-horse; some with great
Devotion stroke the home-borne wheat;
While other rustics, less attent
To prayers than to merriment,
Run after with their breeches rent.
Well, on, brave boys, to your lord's hearth,
Glittering with fire; where, for your mirth,
Ye shall see first the large and chief
Foundation of your feast, fat beef,
With upper storeys, mutton, veal
And bacon (which makes full the meal)
With several dishes standing by,
As here a custard, there a pie,
And here all tempting frumenty.
And for to make the merry cheer,
If smirking wine be wanting here,
There's that which drowns all care, stout beer;

Mildmay] i.e. Mildmay Fane (*c.*1600–66) malkin] pole bound with cloth; effigy or scarecrow swains] male servants; farm labourers cross . . . fill-horse] bless the cart-horse (playing on 'cross' = bestride) attent] attentive bacon] pork frumenty] wheat boiled in milk

Which freely drink, to your lord's health,
Then to the plough, the commonwealth;
Next to your flails, your fanes, your fats;
Then to the maids with wheaten hats:
To the rough sickle, and crooked scythe,
Drink, frolic boys, till all be blithe.
Feed, and grow fat; and as ye eat
Be mindful that the labouring neat
(As you) may have their fill of meat.
And know, besides, ye must revoke
The patient ox unto the yoke,
And all go back unto the plough
And harrow (though they're hanged up now).
And you must know your lord's word's true,
Feed him ye must, whose food fills you;
And that this pleasure is like rain,
Not sent ye for to drown your pain,
But for to make it spring again.

(1648)

318 *To Anthea, Who May Command Him Anything*

BID me to live, and I will live
  Thy protestant to be;
Or bid me love, and I will give
  A loving heart to thee.

A heart as soft, a heart as kind,
  A heart as sound and free
As in the whole world thou canst find,
  That heart I'll give to thee.

Bid that heart stay, and it will stay,
  To honour thy decree;
Or bid it languish quite away,
  And 't shall do so for thee.

Bid me to weep, and I will weep,
  While I have eyes to see;
And having none, yet I will keep
  A heart to weep for thee.

fanes] i.e. winnowing fans   fats] barrels   revoke] summon back

318 protestant] (1) suitor; (2) Protestant

Bid me despair, and I'll despair,
  Under that cypress tree;
Or bid me die, and I will dare
  E'en death, to die for thee.

Thou art my life, my love, my heart,
  The very eyes of me;
And hast command of every part,
  To live and die for thee.

(1648)

319 *To Meadows*

YE have been fresh and green,
  Ye have been filled with flowers;
And ye the walks have been
  Where maids have spent their hours.

You have beheld how they
  With wicker arks did come
To kiss, and bear away
  The richer cowslips home.

You've heard them sweetly sing,
  And seen them in a round:
Each virgin, like a spring,
  With honeysuckles crowned.

But now, we see, none here,
  Whose silvery feet did tread,
And with dishevelled hair
  Adorned this smoother mead.

Like unthrifts, having spent
  Your stock, and needy grown,
You're left here to lament
  Your poor estates, alone.

(1648)

319 round] round dance

320 *Oberon's Feast*

SHAPCOT, to thee the faery state
I with discretion dedicate;
Because thou prizest things that are
Curious, and unfamiliar.
Take first the feast: these dishes gone,
We'll see the faery court anon.

A little mushroom table spread,
After short prayers they set on bread:
A moon-parched grain of purest wheat,
With some small glittering grit, to eat
His choice bits with; then in a trice
They make a feast less great than nice.
But all this while his eye is served,
We must not think his ear was sterved:
But that there was in place, to stir
His spleen, the chirring grasshopper;
The merry cricket, puling fly,
The piping gnat for minstrelsy.
And now, we must imagine first
The elves present to quench his thirst
A pure seed-pearl of infant dew,
Brought and besweetened in a blue
And pregnant violet; which done,
His kitling eyes begin to run
Quite through the table, where he spies
The horns of papery butterflies,
Of which he eats, and tastes a little
Of that we call the cuckoo's spittle.
A little fuzzball pudding stands
By, yet not blessed by his hands,
That was too coarse; but then forthwith
He ventures boldly on the pith
Of sugared rush, and eats the sag
And well bestrutted bee's sweet bag;
Gladding his palate with some store
Of emmet's eggs: what would he more,
But beards of mice, a newt's stewed thigh,
A bloated earwig, and a fly;

Oberon] King of the fairies *Shapcot*] Thomas Shapcot, a lawyer friend parched] dried grit] husked grain spleen] seat of emotions pregnant] big; full kitling] diminutive fuzzball] puffball fungus sag] hanging down bestrutted] (1) bulging; (2) intoxicated store] plenty

With the red-capped worm that's shut
Within the concave of a nut,
Brown as his tooth. A little moth,
Late fattened in a piece of cloth:
With withered cherries; mandrakes' ears;
Moles' eyes; to these, the slain stag's tears;
The unctuous dewlaps of a snail;
The broke heart of a nightingale
O'ercome in music; with a wine
Ne'er ravished from the flattering vine,
But gently pressed from the soft side
Of the most sweet and dainty bride,
Brought in a dainty daisy, which
He fully quaffs up to bewitch
His blood to height; this done, commended
Grace by his priest: *The feast is ended.*

(1648)

321 *To Daffadils*

FAIR daffadils, we weep to see
  You haste away so soon:
As yet the early-rising sun
  Has not attained his noon.
    Stay, stay,
  Until the hasting day
    Has run
  But to the evensong,
And, having prayed together, we
  Will go with you along.

We have short time to stay as you,
  We have as short a spring;
As quick a growth to meet decay
  As you, or any thing.
    We die,
  As your hours do, and dry
    Away,
  Like to the summer's rain,
Or as the pearls of morning's dew
  Ne'er to be found again.

(1648)

320 music] i.e. a musical contest side] loins bride] bridewort?

322 *Her Legs*

FAIN would I kiss my Julia's dainty leg,
Which is as white and hairless as an egg.

(1648)

323 *To the Most Fair and Lovely Mistress Anne Soame, Now Lady Abdie*

SO smell those odours that do rise
From out the wealthy spiceries:
So smells the flower of blooming clove,
Or roses smothered in the stove:
So smells the air of spicèd wine,
Or essences of jessimine:
So smells the breath about the hives,
When well the work of honey thrives;
And all the busy factors come
Laden with wax and honey home:
So smell those neat and woven bowers,
All overarched with orange flowers
And almond blossoms, that do mix
To make rich these aromatics:
So smell those bracelets and those bands
Of amber chafed between the hands,
When thus enkindled they transpire
A noble perfume from the fire.
The wine of cherries, and to these
The cooling breath of respasses;
The smell of morning's milk and cream;
Butter of cowslips mixed with them.
Of roasted warden, or baked pear,
These are not to be reckoned here,
Whenas the meanest part of her
Smells like the maiden pómander.
Thus sweet she smells, or what can be
More liked by her, or loved by me.

(1648)

323 *Anne Soame*] H.'s cousin stove] drying cabinet for sweetmeats jessimine] jasmine factors] workers amber] i.e. ambergris respasses] raspis; raspberries warden] baking pear Whenas] Seeing that maiden] fresh

324 *To Dianeme*

SHOW me thy feet; show me thy legs, thy thighs;
Show me those fleshy principalities;
Show me that hill (where smiling love doth sit)
Having a living fountain under it.
Show me thy waist; then let me therewithal,
By the assention of thy lawn, see all.

(1648)

325 *Upon the Nipples of Julia's Breast*

HAVE ye beheld (with much delight)
A red rose peeping through a white?
Or else a cherry (double graced)
Within a lily's centre placed?
Or ever marked the pretty beam
A strawberry shows, half drowned in cream?
Or seen rich rubies blushing through
A pure smooth pearl, and orient too?
So like to this, nay all the rest,
Is each neat niplet of her breast.

(1648)

326 *To His Peculiar Friend Master Thomas Shapcott, Lawyer*

I'VE paid thee what I promised; that's not all:
Besides I give thee here a verse that shall
(When hence thy circum-mortal-part is gone)
Archlike, hold up thy name's inscription.
Brave men can't die; whose candid actions are
Writ in the poet's endless calendar;
Whose vellum and whose volume is the sky,
And the pure stars the praising poetry.

Farewell.

(1648)

324 assention] (1) ascension; (2) assent lawn] veil

325 orient] lustrous; resplendent niplet] small nipple

327 *To Blossoms*

FAIR pledges of a fruitful tree,
 Why do ye fall so fast?
 Your date is not so past
But you may stay yet here a while,
 To blush and gently smile,
  And go at last.

What, were ye born to be
 An hour or half's delight,
 And so to bid goodnight?
'Twas pity nature brought ye forth
 Merely to show your worth,
  And lose you quite.

But you are lovely leaves, where we
 May read how soon things have
 Their end, though ne'er so brave;
And after they have shown their pride,
 Like you a while, they glide
  Into the grave.

(1648)

328 *To Julia*

JULIA, when thy Herrick dies,
Close thou up thy poet's eyes;
And his last breath, let it be
Taken in by none but thee.

(1648)

329 *Art above Nature: To Julia*

WHEN I behold a forest spread
With silken trees upon thy head,
And when I see that other dress
Of flowers set in comeliness:
When I behold another grace
In the ascent of curious lace,

327 brave] splendid

Which like a pinnacle doth show
The top, and the topgallant too:
Then, when I see thy tresses bound
Into an oval, square, or round,
And knit in knots far more than I
Can tell by tongue, or true-love tie;
Next, when those lawny films I see
Play with a wild civility,
And all those airy silks to flow,
Alluring me, and tempting so:
I must confess, mine eye and heart
Dotes less on nature, than on art.

(1648)

330 *A Hymn to the Graces*

WHEN I love (as some have told,
Love I shall when I am old),
O ye Graces! make me fit
For the welcoming of it.
Clean my rooms, as temples be,
To entertain that deity.
Give me words wherewith to woo,
Suppling and successful too;
Winning postures; and withal,
Manners each way musical:
Sweetness to allay my sour
And unsmooth behaviour.
For I know you have the skill
Vines to prune, though not to kill,
And of any wood ye see,
You can make a Mercury.

(1648)

331 *His Prayer to Ben Jonson*

WHEN I a verse shall make,
Know I have prayed thee,
For old religion's sake,
Saint Ben to aid me.

top . . . topgallant] fighting platforms above the highest masts true-love] (1) true-love knot; (2) true love lawny] lawn-like; soft as fine linen

330 Suppling] Softening any . . . Mercury] ('Every block will not make a Mercury' was a proverb) Mercury] Roman god of eloquence

331 religion's] duty's; sworn friendship's

Make the way smooth for me,
When I, thy Herrick,
Honouring thee, on my knee
Offer my lyric.

Candles I'll give to thee,
And a new altar;
And thou 'Saint Ben' shalt be
Writ in my psalter.

(1648)

332 *The Nightpiece, To Julia*

HER eyes the glow-worm lend thee,
The shooting stars attend thee;
And the elves also,
Whose little eyes glow
Like the sparks of fire, befriend thee.

No will-o' the-wisp mislight thee,
Nor snake or slow-worm bite thee;
But on, on thy way
Not making a stay,
Since ghost there's none to affright thee.

Let not the dark thee cumber;
What though the moon does slumber?
The stars of the night
Will lend thee their light,
Like tapers clear without number.

Then Julia let me woo thee,
Thus, thus to come unto me;
And when I shall meet
Thy silvery feet,
My soul I'll pour into thee.

(1648)

333 *The Funeral Rites of the Rose*

THE rose was sick, and smiling died;
And (being to be sanctified)
About the bed there sighing stood
The sweet and flowery sisterhood.

332 *Nightpiece*] Work of art describing a night-scene will-o' the-wisp] wandering phosphorescence

Some hung the head, while some did bring
(To wash her) water from the spring.
Some laid her forth, while other wept,
But all a solemn fast there kept.
The holy sisters some among
The sacred dirge and trental sung.
But ah! what sweets smelt everywhere,
As heaven had spent all perfumes there.
At last, when prayers for the dead
And rites were all accomplishèd,
They, weeping, spread a lawny loom,
And closed her up, as in a tomb.

(1648)

334 *Upon Julia's Clothes*

WHENAS in silks my Julia goes,
Then, then (methinks) how sweetly flows
That liquefaction of her clothes.

Next, when I cast mine eyes and see
That brave vibration each way free,
Oh how that glittering taketh me!

(1648)

335 *To His Book*

MAKE haste away, and let one be
A friendly patron unto thee,
Lest rapt from hence I see thee lie
Torn for the use of pastery;
Or see thy injured leaves serve well
To make loose gowns for Mackerel;
Or see the grocers in a trice
Make hoods of thee to serve out spice.

(1648)

dirge] Latin antiphon in Office of the Dead   trental] elegy; set of thirty requiem masses   lawny] veil-like   loom] web (poetic)

334 liquefaction] (1) liquefying; (2) melting of the soul in ardour   brave] splendid   vibration] movement causing heavenly bodies to shine

335 gowns] i.e. wrapping papers   Mackerel] (1) fish; (2) type name for bawd

336 *An Ode for Him [Ben Jonson]*

AH Ben!
Say how, or when
Shall we thy guests
Meet at those lyric feasts
Made at the Sun,
The Dog, the Triple Tun?
Where we such clusters had
As made us nobly wild, not mad;
And yet each verse of thine
Outdid the meat, outdid the frolic wine.

My Ben,
Or come again,
Or send to us
Thy wits' great overplus;
But teach us yet
Wisely to husband it,
Lest we that talent spend,
And having once brought to an end
That precious stock, the store
Of such a wit the world should have no more.

(1648)

337 *A Request to the Graces*

PONDER my words, if so that any be
Known guilty here of incivility:
Let what is graceless, discomposed, and rude,
With sweetness, smoothness, softness, be endued.
Teach it to blush, to curtsy, lisp, and show
Demure, but yet, full of temptation too.
Numbers ne'er tickle, or but lightly please,
Unless they have some wanton carriages.
This if ye do, each piece will here be good,
And graceful made, by your neat sisterhood.

(1648)

the Sun . . . Tun] taverns frolic] verse-capping game Or . . . Or] Either . . . Or store] plenty

337 *Numbers*] Verses *carriages*] (1) bearings; (2) deportment

338 *An Hymn to Love*

I WILL confess
With cheerfulness,
Love is a thing so likes me
That let her lay
On me all day,
I'll kiss the hand that strikes me.

I will not, I,
Now blubbering, cry,
It (ah!) too late repents me,
That I did fall
To love at all;
Since love so much contents me.

No, no, I'll be
In fetters free;
While others they sit wringing
Their hands for pain,
I'll entertain
The wounds of love with singing.

With flowers and wine,
And cakes divine,
To strike me I will tempt thee;
Which done, no more
I'll come before
Thee and thine altars empty.

(1648)

339 *To His Honoured and Most Ingenious Friend Master Charles Cotton*

FOR brave comportment, wit without offence,
Words fully flowing, yet of influence,
Thou art that man of men, the man alone
Worthy the public admiration:
Who with thine own eyes readst what we do write,
And giv'st our numbers euphony and weight:

entertain] accept

339 brave] splendid

Tellst when a verse springs high; how understood;
To be, or not, born of the royal blood.
What state above, what symmetry below,
Lines have, or should have, thou the best canst show.
For which, my Charles, it is my pride to be
Not so much known, as to be loved of thee.
Long may I live so, and my wreath of bays
Be less another's laurel, than thy praise.

(1648)

340 *On Himself*

WEEP for the dead, for they have lost this light;
And weep for me, lost in an endless night.
Or mourn, or make a marble verse for me,
Who writ for many, *Benedicite*.

(1648)

341 *The Vision*

METHOUGHT I saw, as I did dream in bed,
A crawling vine about Anacreon's head:
Flushed was his face; his hairs with oil did shine;
And as he spake, his mouth ran o'er with wine.
Tippled he was; and tippling lisped withal;
And lisping reeled, and reeling like to fall.
A young enchantress close by him did stand,
Tapping his plump thighs with a myrtle wand:
She smiled; he kissed; and kissing, culled her too;
And being cup-shot, more he could not do.
For which, methought, in pretty anger she
Snatched off his crown, and gave the wreath to me:
Since when, methinks, my brains about do swim,
And I am wild and wanton like to him.

(1648)

339 state] stateliness

341 culled] fondled

342 *His Tears to Thamasis*

I SEND, I send here my supremest kiss
To thee my silver-footed Thamasis.
No more shall I reiterate thy Strand,
Whereon so many stately structures stand;
Nor in the summer's sweeter evenings go
To bathe in thee, as thousand others do.
No more shall I along thy crystal glide
In barge with boughs and rushes beautified,
With soft smooth virgins for our chaste disport,
To Richmond, Kingstone, and to Hampton Court:
Never again shall I with finny oar
Put from or draw unto the faithful shore;
And landing here, or safely landing there,
Make way to my belovèd Westminster:
Or to the golden Cheapside, where the earth
Of Julia Herrick gave to me my birth.
May all clean nymphs and curious water dames,
With swanlike state, float up and down thy streams:
No drought upon thy wanton waters fall,
To make them lean and languishing at all.
No ruffling winds come hither to dis-ease
Thy pure and silver-wristed naiadës.
Keep up your state ye streams; and as ye spring,
Never make sick your banks by surfeiting.
Grow young with tides, and though I see ye never,
Receive this vow, *so fare ye well for ever.*

(1648)

from *Noble Numbers* (343–348)

343 *What God Is*

GOD is above the sphere of our esteem,
And is the best known, not defining him.

(1648)

Thamasis] *Thames* supremest] last reiterate] repeatedly walk (Latinism) Strand] (1) shore of the Thames; (2) street linking Westminster to the City Richmond . . . Court] palaces upriver Cheapside] goldsmiths' quarter curious] fastidious state] stateliness dis-ease] (1) disturb; (2) infect

344 *His Litany, to the Holy Spirit*

In the hour of my distress,
When temptations me oppress,
And when I my sins confess,
  Sweet Spirit comfort me!

When I lie within my bed,
Sick in heart, and sick in head,
And with doubts discomforted,
  Sweet Spirit comfort me!

When the house doth sigh and weep,
And the world is drowned in sleep,
Yet mine eyes the watch do keep:
  Sweet Spirit comfort me!

When the artless doctor sees
No one hope but of his fees,
And his skill runs on the lees:
  Sweet Spirit comfort me!

When his potion and his pill,
His, or none, or little skill,
Meet for nothing but to kill:
  Sweet Spirit comfort me!

When the passing-bell doth toll,
And the Furies in a shoal
Come to fright a parting soul:
  Sweet Spirit comfort me!

When the tapers now burn blue,
And the comforters are few,
And that number more than true:
  Sweet Spirit comfort me!

When the priest his last hath prayed,
And I nod to what is said,
'Cause my speech is now decayed:
  Sweet Spirit comfort me!

When (God knows) I'm tossed about,
Either with despair or doubt,
Yet before the glass be out,
  Sweet Spirit comfort me!

runs . . . lees] is exhausted   Furies] avengers of the gods (ancient mythology)

When the tempter me pursueth
With the sins of all my youth,
And half damns me with untruth:
   Sweet Spirit comfort me!

When the flames and hellish cries
Fright mine ears, and fright mine eyes,
And all terrors me surprise:
   Sweet Spirit comfort me!

When the judgement is revealed,
And that opened which was sealed,
When to thee I have appealed:
   Sweet Spirit comfort me!

(1648)

345 *A Thanksgiving to God, for His House*

LORD, thou hast given me a cell
      Wherein to dwell;
And little house, whose humble roof
      Is weather-proof;
Under the spars of which I lie
      Both soft and dry;
Where thou my chamber for to ward
      Hast set a guard
Of harmless thoughts, to watch and keep
      Me, while I sleep.
Low is my porch, as is my fate,
      Both void of state;
And yet the threshold of my door
      Is worn by the poor,
Who thither come, and freely get
      Good words, or meat:
Like as my parlour, so my hall
      And kitchen's small:
A little buttery, and therein
      A little bin,
Which keeps my little loaf of bread
      Unchipped, unflayed:
Some brittle sticks of thorn or briar
      Make me a fire,

opened . . . sealed] (Rev. 8: 1)

345 unflayed] safe from mice

Close by whose living coal I sit,
And glow like it.
Lord, I confess too, when I dine,
The pulse is thine,
And all those other bits that be
There placed by thee:
The worts, the purslain, and the mess
Of water-cress,
Which of thy kindness thou hast sent;
And my content
Makes those, and my beloved beet,
To be more sweet.
'Tis thou that crownst my glittering hearth
With guiltless mirth;
And giv'st me wassail bowls to drink,
Spiced to the brink.
Lord, 'tis thy plenty-dropping hand
That soils my land,
And giv'st me, for my bushel sown,
Twice ten for one:
Thou mak'st my teeming hen to lay
Her egg each day,
Besides my healthful ewes to bear
Me twins each year;
The while the conduits of my kine
Run cream (for wine).
All these, and better thou dost send
Me, to this end,
That I should render, for my part,
A thankful heart;
Which, fired with incense, I resign,
As wholly thine;
But the acceptance, that must be,
My Christ, by thee.

(1648)

346 *Another Grace for a Child*

HERE a little child I stand,
Heaving up my either hand:
Cold as paddocks though they be,
Here I lift them up to thee,
For a benison to fall
On our meat, and on us all. *Amen.*

(1648)

345 wassail] spiced ale soils] (1) manures; (2) absolves

347 *The White Island, or Place of the Blest*

In this world, the world of dreams,
While we sit by sorrows' streams,
Tears and terrors are our themes
Reciting;

But when once from hence we fly,
More and more approaching nigh
Unto young eternity
Uniting,

In that whiter island, where
Things are evermore sincere,
Candour here, and lustre there
Delighting:

There no monstrous fancies shall
Out of hell an horror call,
To create (or cause at all)
Affrighting.

There in calm and cooling sleep
We our eyes shall never steep;
But eternal watch shall keep,
Attending

Pleasures such as shall pursue
Me immortalized, and you;
And fresh joys, as never too
Have ending.

(1648)

348 *Good Friday:* Rex Tragicus, *or, Christ Going to His Cross*

Put off thy robe of purple, then go on
To the sad place of executïon:
Thine hour is come, and the tormentor stands
Ready to pierce thy tender feet and hands.
Long before this, the base, the dull, the rude,
The inconstant and unpurgèd multitude

sincere] pure; unmixed Candour] Brilliant whiteness; Sweetness of temper
Attending] Considering; Expecting

Yawn for thy coming: some ere this time cry
'How he defers, how loath he is to die!'
Amongst this scum, the soldier with his spear,
And that sour fellow with his vinegar,
His spunge, and stick, do ask why thou dost stay.
So do the scurf and bran too: go thy way,
Thy way, thou guiltless man, and satisfy
By thine approach each their beholding eye.
Not as a thief shalt thou ascend the mount,
But like a person of some high account:
The cross shall be thy stage, and thou shalt there
The spacious field have for thy theatre.
Thou art that Roscius, and that marked-out man,
That must this day act the tragedian,
To wonder and affrightment: thou art he
Whom all the flux of nations comes to see;
Not those poor thieves that act their parts with thee:
Those act without regard, when once a king,
And God, as thou art, comes to suffering.
No, no, this scene from thee takes life and sense,
And soul and spirit, plot and excellence.
Why then begin, great king! Ascend thy throne,
And thence proceed to act thy passïon
To such a height, to such a period raised,
As hell, and Earth, and heaven may stand amazed.
God and good angels guide thee; and so bless
Thee in thy several parts of bitterness
That those who see thee nailed unto the tree
May, though they scorn thee, praise and pity thee.
And we, thy lovers, while we see thee keep
The laws of action, will both sigh and weep,
And bring our spices to embalm thee dead:
That done, we'll see thee sweetly burièd.

(1648)

scurf . . . bran] scum Roscius] (famous ancient Roman actor) affrightment] sudden terror flux] flood; stream of people regard] notice passïon] (1) narrative of Christ's sufferings; (2) passionate speech period] (1) acme; (2) death; (3) peroration parts] (1) portions; (2) roles laws of action] tragic decorum

WILLIAM CAVENDISH, DUKE OF NEWCASTLE
1592–1676

349

Love's Matrimony

THERE is no happy life
But in a wife,
The comforts are so sweet
When they do meet:
'Tis plenty, peace, a calm
Like dropping balm;
Love's weather is so fair,
Perfumèd air;
Each word such pleasure brings
Like soft-touched strings;
Love's passion moves the heart
On either part.
Such harmony together,
So pleased in either,
No discords, concords still,
Sealed with one will.
  By love, God man made one,
Yet not alone:
Like stamps of king and queen
It may be seen,
Two figures but one coin;
So they do join,
Only they not embrace,
We face to face.

(1928; wr. *c.*1645?)

350

Love's Sun

OH, can we love and live? Pray, let us die
If living cannot meet. I'll tell you why:
When dead we may both of us turn to air,
So meet in higher regions that is fair,
Thus have a calm; or, turned to waters sweet,
Posting down rivers, in the sea to meet;

349 still] ever   stamps] designs, impressions

Or else, our subtle motions air, mount higher,
Our heated love inflame us to one fire,
And there we're joined: one sun, your love and mine,
On mortal lovers here ever to shine.

(1956)

HENRY KING
1592–1669

351 *An Elegy upon S[ir] W[alter] R[aleigh]*

I WILL not weep. For 'twere as great a sin
To shed a tear for thee as to have bin
An actor in thy death. Thy life and age
Was but a various scene on fortune's stage,
With whom thou tugg'st and strov'st ev'n out of breath
In thy long toil. Ne'er mastered till thy death;
And then, despite of trains and cruel wit,
Thou didst at once subdue malice and it.
I dare not then so blast thy memory
As say I do lament or pity thee.
Were I to choose a subject to bestow
My pity on, he should be one as low
In spirit as desert: that durst not die,
But rather were content by slavery
To purchase life. Or I would pity those,
Thy most industrious and friendly foes,
Who when they thought to make thee scandal's story
Lent thee a swifter flight to heaven and glory;
That thought by cutting off some withered days
(Which thou couldst spare them) to eclipse thy praise,
Yet gave it brighter foil, made thy ag'd fame
Appear more white and fair than foul their shame,
And did promote an executïon,
Which, but for them, nature and age had done.
Such worthless things as these were only born
To live on pity's alms, too mean for scorn.
Thou diedst an envious wonder, whose high fate
The world must still admire, scarce imitate.

(1657)

air] take the air; expose themselves

351 trains] intrigues   blast] wither; blow on perniciously   white] innocent

352 *An Exequy to His Matchless Never to be Forgotten Friend*

ACCEPT, thou shrine of my dead saint,
Instead of dirges this complaint!
And for sweet flowers to crown thy hearse
Receive a strew of weeping verse
From thy grieved friend, whom thou mightst see
Quite melted into tears for thee.
  Dear loss! Since thy untimely fate
My task hath been to meditate
On thee, on thee: thou art the book,
The library whereon I look,
Though almost blind. For thee (loved clay!)
I languish out, not live the day,
Using no other exercise
But what I practise with mine eyes.
By which wet glasses I find out
How lazily time creeps about
The one that mourns. This, only this
My exercise and business is:
So I compute the weary hours
With sighs dissolvèd into showers.
  Nor wonder if my time go thus
Backward and most preposterous;
Thou has benighted me. Thy set
This eve of blackness did beget,
Who wast my day (though overcast
Before thou hadst thy noontide passed),
And I remember must in tears,
Thou scarce hadst seen so many years
As day tells hours. By thy clear sun
My love and fortune first did run;
But thou wilt never more appear
Folded within my hemisphere;
Since both thy light and motion
Like a fled star is fallen and gone,
And 'twixt me and my soul's dear wish
The Earth now interposèd is,
Which such a strange eclipse doth make
As ne'er was read in almanac.
  I could allow thee for a time
To darken me and my sad clime:

set] setting

Were it a month, a year, or ten,
I would thy exile live till then,
And all that space my mirth adjourn,
So thou wouldst promise to return,
And putting off thy ashy shrowd
At length disperse this sorrow's cloud.
  But woe is me! the longest date
Too narrow is to calculate
These empty hopes. Never shall I
Be so much blest as to descry
A glimpse of thee, till that day come
Which shall the Earth to cinders doom;
And a fierce fever must calcine
The body of this world, like thine
(My little world!). That fit of fire
Once off, our bodies shall aspire
To our souls' bliss: then we shall rise,
And view ourselves with clearer eyes
In that calm region, where no night
Can hide us from each other's sight.
  Meantime thou hast her, earth: much good
May my harm do thee. Since it stood
With heaven's will I might not call
Her longer mine, I give thee all
My short-lived right and interest
In her, whom living I loved best:
With a most free and bounteous grief
I give thee what I could not keep.
Be kind to her; and prithee look
Thou write into thy Domesday Book
Each parcel of this rarity,
Which in thy casket shrined doth lie:
See that thou make thy reck'ning straight,
And yield her back again by weight;
For thou must audit on thy trust
Each grain and atom of this dust,
As thou wilt answer him that lent,
Not gave thee, my dear monument.
  So close the ground, and about her shade
Black curtains draw: my bride is laid.
  Sleep on, my love, in thy cold bed,
Never to be disquieted.
My last good night! Thou wilt not wake
Till I thy fate shall overtake:

calcine] burn to ash   Domesday Book] (1) record of lands; (2) account for doom's day   straight] promptly   laid] (1) buried; (2) impregnated; (3) given as hostage

Till age, or grief, or sickness must
Marry my body to that dust
It so much loves, and fill the room
My heart keeps empty in thy tomb.
Stay for me there: I will not fail
To meet thee in that hollow vale.
And think not much of my delay:
I am already on the way,
And follow thee with all the speed
Desire can make, or sorrows breed.
Each minute is a short degree,
And every hour a step towards thee.
At night when I betake to rest,
Next morn I rise nearer my west
Of life, almost by eight hours' sail,
Than when sleep breathed his drowsy gale.
  Thus from the sun my bottom steers,
And my days' compass downward bears.
Nor labour I to stem the tide,
Through which to thee I swiftly glide.
  'Tis true; with shame and grief I yield:
Thou, like the van, first tookst the field,
And gotten hast the victory
In thus adventuring to die
Before me, whose more years might crave
A just precedence in the grave.
But hark! My pulse, like a soft drum,
Beats my approach, tells thee I come;
And, slow howe'er my marches be,
I shall at last sit down by thee.
  The thought of this bids me go on,
And wait my dissolutïon
With hope and comfort. Dear, forgive
The crime! I am content to live
Divided, with but half a heart,
Till we shall meet and never part.

(1657)

353

The Surrender

My once dear love (hapless that I no more
Must call thee so!), the rich affection's store
That fed our hopes lies now exhaust and spent,
Like sums of treasure unto bankrupts lent.

352 bottom] ship   compass] extent

We that did nothing study but the way
To love each other—with which thoughts the day
Rose with delight to us, and with them set—
Must learn the hateful art, how to forget.
We that did nothing wish that heav'n could give
Beyond ourselves, nor did desire to live
Beyond that wish, all these now cancel must,
As if not writ in faith, but words and dust.
Yet witness those clear vows which lovers make!
Witness the chaste desires that never brake
Into unruly heats; witness that breast
Which in thy bosom anchored his whole rest,
'Tis no default in us. I dare acquite
Thy maiden faith, thy purpose fair and white
As thy pure self. Cross planets did envý
Us to each other, and heaven did untie
Faster than vows could bind. Oh that the stars,
When lovers meet, should stand opposed in wars!
Since then some higher destinies command,
Let us not strive nor labour to withstand
What is past help. The longest date of grief
Can never yield a hope of our relief;
And though we waste ourselves in moist laments,
Tears may drown us, but not our discontents.
Fold back our arms, take home our fruitless loves,
That must new fortunes try, like turtle doves
Dislodgèd from their haunts. We must in tears
Unwind a love knit up in many years.
In this last kiss I here surrender thee
Back to thyself. Lo, thou again art free.
Thou in another, sad as that, resend
The truest heart that lover e'er did lend.
Now turn from each. So fare our severed hearts
As the divorced soul from her body parts.

(1657)

354

Sic Vita

LIKE to the falling of a star;
Or as the flights of eagles are;
Or like the fresh spring's gaudy hue;
Or silver drops of morning dew;

353 acquite] acquit Cross] Adverse resend] send back

Or like a wind that chafes the flood;
Or bubbles which on water stood:
Even such is man, whose borrowed light
Is straight called in, and paid to night.

The wind blows out, the bubble dries:
The spring entombed in autumn lies:
The dew dries up: the star is shot:
The flight is past: and man forgot.

(1657)

355 *Silence: A Sonnet*

PEACE, my heart's blab! Be ever dumb:
Sorrows speak loud without a tongue.
And my perplexèd thoughts, forbear
To breathe yourselves in any ear:
  'Tis scarce a true or manly grief
  Which gads abroad to find relief.

Was ever stomach that lacked meat
Nourished by what another eat?
Can I bestow it, or will woe
Forsake me when I bid it go?
  Then I'll believe a wounded breast
  May heal by shrift, and purchase rest.

But if, imparting it, I do
Not ease myself, but trouble two,
'Tis better I alone possess
My treasure of unhappiness;
  Engrossing that which is my own
  No longer than it is unknown.

If silence be a kind of death,
He kindles grief who gives it breath.
But let it raked in embers lie
On thine own hearth, 'twill quickly die;
  And, spite of fate, that very womb
  Which carries it shall prove its tomb.

(1657)

called in] required to be repaid

355 eat] ate shrift] confession Engrossing] Monopolizing

356 *Sonnet: The Double Rock*

SINCE thou hast viewed some Gorgon, and art grown
 A solid stone,
To bring again to softness thy hard heart
 Is past my art.
Ice may relent to water in a thaw;
But stone made flesh love's chemistry ne'er saw.

Therefore by thinking on thy hardness, I
 Will petrify;
And so within our double quarry's womb
 Dig our love's tomb.
Thus strangely will our difference agree,
And, with ourselves, amaze the world, to see
How both revenge and sympathy consent
To make two rocks each other's monument.

(1657)

357 *The Change*

Il sabio mude conseio: Il loco persevera

WE loved as friends now twenty years and more:
Is it time or reason, think you, to give o'er?
When though two prenticeships set Jacob free
I have not held my Rachel dear at three.
 Yet will I not your levity accuse;
Continuance sometimes is the worse abuse.
In judgement I might rather hold it strange
If like the fleeting world, you did not change:
Be it your wisdom therefore to retract,
When perseverance oft is folly's act.
 In pity I can think that what you do
Hath justice in't, and some religion too;
For of all virtues moral or divine,
We know, but love, none must in heaven shine.
Well did you the presumption then foresee
Of counterfeiting immortality:
Since, had you kept our loves too long alive,
We might invade heaven's prerogative,

chemistry] alchemy

357 *Il . . . persevera*] 'The wise man takes new advice: the madman perseveres'

Or in our progress, like the Jews, comprise
The legend of an earthly paradise.
  Live happy and more prosperous in the next!
You have discharged your old friend by the text.
Farewell, fair shadow of a female faith;
And let this be our friendship's epitaph:
  Affection shares the frailty of our fate,
  When, like ourselves, 'tis old and out of date:
  'Tis just all human loves their period have,
  When friends are frail, and dropping to the grave.

(1657)

358 *The Forfeiture*

My dearest, to let you or the world know
What debt of service I do truly owe
To your unpatterned self were to require
A language only formed in the desire
Of him that writes. It is the common fate
Of greatest duties to evaporate
In silent meaning, as we often see
Fires by their too much fuel smothered be:
Small obligations may find vent and speak,
When greater the unable debtor break.
And such are mine to you, whose favour's store
Hath made me poorer than I was before;
For I want words and language to declare
How strict my bond or large your bounties are.

  Since nothing in my desperate fortune found
Can payment make, nor yet the sum compound,
You must lose all, or else of force accept
The body of a bankrupt for your debt.
Then, love, your bond to execution sue,
And take my self, as forfeited to you.

(1657)

358 unpatterned] unique   break] ruin, bankrupt

FRANCIS QUARLES
1592–1644

from *Argalus and Parthenia*

359

Hos Ego Versiculos

LIKE to the damask rose you see,
Or like the blossom on the tree,
Or like the dainty flower of May,
Or like the morning to the day,
Or like the sun, or like the shade,
Or like the gourd which Jonas had:
  Even such is man whose thread is spun,
  Drawn out and cut, and so is done.

The rose withers, the blossom blasteth,
The flower fades, the morning hasteth:
The sun sets, the shadow flies,
The gourd consumes, and man he dies.
Like to the blaze of fond delight;
Or like a morning clear and bright;
Or like a frost, or like a shower;
Or like the pride of Babel's tower;
Or like the hour that guides the time;
Or like to beauty in her prime:
  Even such is man, whose glory lends
  His life a blaze or two, and ends.

Delights vanish; the morn o'ercasteth,
The frost breaks, the shower hasteth;
The tower falls, the hour spends;
The beauty fades, and man's life ends.

(1628)

Hos . . . Versiculos] 'I made these little verses [but another took the honour]' (Virgil, according to Donatus's *Life* 17. 70)   Jonas] Jonah (Jon. 4: 6)   blasteth] withers   Babel's tower] Gen. 11: 9

from *Divine Fancies* (360–362)

360 *I. xxxiii: On Those that Deserve It*

OH when our clergy at the dreadful day
Shall make their audit, when the judge shall say,
'Give your accounts: what, have my lambs been fed?
Say, do they all stand sound? Is there none dead
By your defaults? Come shepherds, bring them forth,
That I may crown your labours in their worth'.
Oh what an answer will be given by some!
'We have been silenced: canons struck us dumb;
The great ones would not let us feed thy flock
Unless we played the fools, and wore a frock:
We were forbid, unless we'd yield to sign
And cross their brows (they say, *a mark of thine*).
To say the truth, great Judge, they were not fed;
Lord, here they be; but Lord, they be all dead.'
Ah cruel shepherds! Could your conscience serve
Not to be fools, and yet to let them starve?
What if your fiery spirits had been bound
To antic habits; or your heads been crowned
With peacocks' plumes; had ye been forced to feed
Your saviour's dear-bought flock in a fool's weed?
He that was scorned, reviled, endured the curse
Of a base death in your behalves; nay worse,
Swallowed the cup of wrath charged up to the brim;
Durst ye not stoop to play the fools for him?

(1632)

361 *I. lxvii: On Zacheus*

METHINKS I see with what a busy haste
Zacheus climbed the tree; but oh how fast,
How full of speed, canst thou imagine, when
Our saviour called, he powdered down again!
He ne'er made trial if the boughs were sound
Or rotten; nor how far 'twas to the ground:
There was no danger feared; at such a call
He'll venture nothing, that dare fear a fall;

frock] vestment antic] grotesque, fantastic

361 Zacheus] Luke 19: 5: 'Zaccheus haste, come down' powdered] rushed

Needs must he down, by such a spirit driven,
Nor could he fall unless he fell to heaven.
Down came Zacheus, ravished from the tree;
Bird that was shot ne'er dropped so quick as he.

(1632)

362 *I. lxxvii: On the Ploughman*

I HEAR the whistling ploughman all day long,
Sweetening his labour with a cheerful song:
His bed's a pad of straw, his diet coarse.
In both he fares not better than his horse:
He seldom slakes his thirst but from the pump;
And yet his heart is blithe, his visage plump.
His thoughts are ne'er acquainted with such things
As griefs or fears: he only sweats and sings;
Whenas the landed lord, that cannot dine
Without a qualm, if not refreshed with wine;
That cannot judge that controverted case,
'Twixt meat and mouth, without the bribe of sauce;
That claims the service of the purest linen,
To pamper and to shroud his dainty skin in;
Groans out his days in labouring to appease
The rage of either business or disease.
Alas, his silken robes, his costly diet
Can lend a little pleasure, but no quiet:
The untold sums of his descended wealth
Can give his body plenty, but not health:
The one in pains and want possesses all;
T'other in plenty finds no peace at all.
'Tis strange! And yet the cause is easily shown:
T'one's at God's finding; t'other at his own.

(1632)

from *Emblems* (363–364)

363 *Emblem III. vii*

Job 13. 24: Wherefore hidest thou thy face, and holdest me for thine enemy?

WHY dost thou shade thy lovely face? Oh why
Does that eclipsing hand so long deny
The sunshine of thy soul-enlivening eye?

Without that light, what light remains in me?
Thou art my life, my way, my light; in thee
I live, I move, and by thy beams I see.

Thou art my life: if thou but turn away,
My life's a thousand deaths; thou art my way:
Without thee, Lord, I travel not, but stray.

My light thou art: without thy glorious sight,
My eyes are darkened with perpetual night.
My God, thou art my way, my life, my light.

Thou art my way: I wander, if thou fly;
Thou art my light: if hid, how blind am I!
Thou art my life: if thou withdraw, I die.

My eyes are blind and dark, I cannot see;
To whom, or whither, should my darkness flee,
But to the light? and who's that light but thee?

My path is lost, my wandering steps do stray;
I cannot safely go, nor safely stay;
Whom should I seek but thee, my path, my way?

Oh, I am dead: to whom shall I, poor I,
Repair? To whom shall my sad ashes fly,
But life? And where is life but in thine eye?

And yet thou turnst away thy face, and fly'st me;
And yet I sue for grace, and thou deny'st me;
Speak, art thou angry, Lord, or only try'st me?

Unscreen those heavenly lamps, or tell me why
Thou shad'st thy face. Perhaps thou thinkst no eye
Can view those flames, and not drop down and die.

If that be all, shine forth, and draw thee nigher;
Let me behold and die; for my desire
Is, phoenix-like, to perish in that fire.

Death-conquered Laz'rus was redeemed by thee;
If I am dead, Lord, set death's prisoner free;
Am I more spent, or stink I worse than he?

redeemed] ransomed (John 11: 32–44)

If my puffed life be out, give leave to tine
My shameless snuff at that bright lamp of thine;
Oh, what's thy light the less for lighting mine?

If I have lost my path, great shepherd, say,
Shall I still wander in a doubtful way?
Lord, shall a lamb of Israel's sheepfold stray?

Thou art the pilgrim's path, the blind man's eye,
The dead man's life: on thee my hopes rely;
If thou remove, I err, I grope, I die.

Disclose thy sunbeams; close thy wings and stay;
See, see how I am blind and dead, and stray,
O thou that art my light, my life, my way.

Epigram

If heaven's all-quickening eyes vouchsafe to shine
Upon our souls, we slight; if not, we whine:
Our equinoctial hearts can never lie
Secure beneath the tropics of that eye.

(1635)

364 *Emblem IV. iii*

Psalm 17. 5: Stay my steps in thy paths, that my feet do not slide

WHENE'ER the old exchange of profit rings
  Her silver saint's-bell of uncertain gains,
My merchant soul can stretch both legs and wings;
  How I can run, and take unwearied pains!
    The charms of profit are so strong that I,
    Who wanted legs to go, find wings to fly.

If time-beguiling pleasure but advance
  Her lustful trump, and blow her bold alarms,
Oh how my sportful soul can frisk and dance,
  And hug that siren in her twinèd arms!
    The sprightly voice of sinew-strengthening pleasure
    Can lend my bedrid soul both legs and leisure.

tine] kindle

364 saint's-bell] sanctus bell, rung during the Mass   go] walk

If blazing honour chance to fill my veins
With flattering warmth and flash of courtly fire,
My soul can take a pleasure in her pains;
My lofty strutting steps disdain to tire;
My antic knees can turn upon the hinges
Of compliment, and screw a thousand cringes.

But when I come to thee, my God, that art
The royal mine of everlasting treasure,
The real honour of my better part,
And living fountain of eternal pleasure,
How nerveless are my limbs! How faint and slow!
I have nor wings to fly, nor legs to go.

So when the streams of swift-foot Rhine convey
Her upland riches to the Belgic shore,
The idle vessel slides the watery lay,
Without the blast or tug of wind or oar;
Her slippery keel divides the silver foam
With ease: so facile is the way from home!

But when the home-bound vessel turns her sails
Against the breast of the resisting stream,
Oh then she slugs; nor sail nor oar prevails!
The stream is sturdy, and her tide's extreme:
Each stroke is loss, and every tug is vain;
A boat-length's purchase is a league of pain.

Great all in all, that art my rest, my home;
My way is tedious, and my steps are slow:
Reach forth thy helpful hand, or bid me come;
I am thy child, oh teach thy child to go;
Conjoin thy sweet commands to my desire,
And I will venture, though I fall or tire.

Epigram

Fear not, my soul, to lose for want of cunning;
Weep not; heaven is not always got by running:
Thy thoughts are swift, although thy legs be slow;
True love will creep, not having strength to go.

(1635)

antic] ludicrous Belgic] Netherlandish lay] pool slugs] moves slowly go] walk

from *Hosanna* (365–369)

365 *Upon the Day of Our Saviour's Nativity*

THIS day's a riddle; for the God that made
This day, this day from his own creature had
His making too: his flesh and bone and limb
And breath, from her that had her breath from him.
The unbribed judge of man's eternal doom
This day was prisoner in a virgin's womb;
And the Lord Paramount of all the Earth
Was wanting a poor tenement at his birth:
Into the inn this mean guest must not come.
Strange, he that fills all rooms should have no room.
The sun dropped from his sphere, and did decline
His unshorn head to the Earth; his radiant shine
Peeped from the windores of the east, to breathe
New life on people in the shades of death.
Dear sun, since from thy sphere thou once wert sent,
Here is a soul, make it thy firmament.

(1647)

366 *Born in Winter*

PHLEGMATIC winter on a bed of snow
Lay spitting full of rheum: the sun was now
Inned at the Goat, the melancholic Earth
Had her womb bound, and hopeless of the birth
Of one poor flower, the fields, wood, meads, and all
Feared in this snowy sheet a funeral.
Nor only senseless plants were in decay:
Man, who's a plant reversed, was worse than they.
He had a spiritual winter, and bereft
Not of his leaves, but juice, nay, nothing less,
His passive power to live was so abated
He was not to be raised, but new created.
When all things else were perishèd, and when
No flowers were, but in their causes, then
This wondrous flower itself to act did bring,
And winter was the flower of Jesse's spring.

(1647)

doom] judgement tenement] lodging windores] windows sphere] crystalline globe of orbit

366 Inned ... Goat] (1) situated in Capricorn; (2) lodged at the Goat inn but ... causes] except potentially spring] (1) stem (Isa. 11: 1); (2) origin; (3) spring season

367 *Of St Stephen*

SOME names are ominous, wherein wise fate
Writes in fair characters men's future state:
Hippolitus, who scorned incestuous sports,
Was torn with horses, as his name imports.
Stephen was a crown; which showed in time to come
He should put on the crown of martyrdom.
A crown enchased with stones, nay such a one
Earth cannot boast, 'twas all of precious stone:
The storm of stones which at this martyr flew
Recoiled, enrichèd with an orient hue.
The meanest flint which at this saint was thrown
Reflects a ruby, or some richer stone.
The stones, advancèd to a heap, become
At first our martyr's crown, so now his tomb.
Muse, make a pagan wonder: thus set down:
Here lies a man entombèd in his crown.

(1647)

368 *They Gave Him Vinegar and Gall (Matt. 27) and Wine Mingled with Myrrh (Mark 15)*

WHEN one was on the cursèd tree to die,
They gave narcotic drink to stupefy
And dull the motion of the active sense,
So to allay the racking violence
Of his sharp tortures; and the rabbins say
That these compounded potïons were they
Give wine to men ready to quit their breath.
Vinegar is his preparative to death:
He must have nought but vinegar who hath
Trod in the winepress of his father's wrath.
Those lips that once like honeycombs distilled
Are now with gall instead of honey filled.
And he's presented with a draught of gall,
Whose innocence before had none at all.
One of the wise men that to Bethlem went
To do him homage, did him myrrh present.
So they did here, but in a different case:
'Twas there in honour, here in his disgrace.

(1647)

Hippolitus] Hippolytus, Theseus' son (Greek mythology) Stephen . . . crown] 'Stephen' meant crown (Greek *stephanos*) orient] bright

368 Give] Given (in) rabbins] rabbis, doctors of the law distilled] flowed Bethlem] Bethlehem

369 *Crucified*

THOSE hands, which heav'n like to a curtain spread,
Are spread upon the cross; those hands which did
Consolidate the metals in the ground,
One of those metals gave those hands the wound:
See his hands spread, as if he meant to grace
His executioners with his last embrace.
Nay, all the world; for if his fist can hold
The winds, his arms can all the world enfold.
See there Longinus with his ruder spear
Pierce his diviner side, from whence appear
Water and blood, whose white and red present
Th'admitting and confirming sacrament.
See here his feet nailed to the cross; which done,
Those feet with streams of purple did so run
That in one sense it might be understood
Our saviour's feet were swift to shed blood.
His hands and feet thus forcèd to obey
The cruel nails' command, may we not say
The star that out of Jacob shined so far
Was then, or never, made a fixèd star?

(1647)

GEORGE HERBERT
1593–1633

from Walton's *Lives* (370–371)

370 MY God, where is that ancient heat towards thee,
  Wherewith whole shoals of martyrs once did burn,
  Besides their other flames? Doth poetry
Wear Venus' livery? only serve her turn?
Why are not sonnets made of thee? and lays
  Upon thine altar burnt? Cannot thy love
  Heighten a spirit to sound out thy praise
As well as any she? Cannot thy dove

369 Longinus] Longius (the Roman soldier who pierced Jesus' side)   diviner] (1) prophet; (2) water-diviner; (3) divine, theologian   Th'admitting . . . sacrament] i.e. baptism and Eucharist   star . . . Jacob] the star prophesied by Balaam's ass (Num. 24: 17)

Outstrip their Cupid easily in flight?
Or, since thy ways are deep, and still the same,
Will not a verse run smooth that bears thy name?
Why doth that fire which by thy power and might
Each breast does feel no braver fuel choose
Than that which one day worms may chance refuse?

(1670; wr. ?1610)

371 SURE, Lord, there is enough in thee to dry
Oceans of ink; for, as the deluge did
Cover the earth, so doth thy majesty:
Each cloud distills thy praise, and doth forbid
Poets to turn it to another use.
Roses and lilies speak thee; and to make
A pair of cheeks of them is thy abuse.
Why should I women's eyes for crystal take?
Such poor invention burns in their low mind
Whose fire is wild, and doth not upward go
To praise, and on thee, Lord, some ink bestow.
Open the bones, and you shall nothing find
In the best face but filth, when, Lord, in thee
The beauty lies in the discovery.

(1670; wr. ?1610)

from *The Temple* (372–411)

372 Superliminare

THOU, whom the former precepts have
Sprinkled and taught how to behave
Thyself in church, approach and taste
The Church's mystical repast.

Avoid, profaneness; come not here:
Nothing but holy, pure, and clear,
Or that which groaneth to be so,
May at his peril further go.

(1633)

371 discovery] uncovering; revelation

372 Superliminare] Lintel (properly title of the second stanza) Avoid] Withdraw (imperative)

373 *The Altar*

A BROKEN ALTAR, Lord, thy servant rears,
Made of a heart, and cémented with tears:
Whose parts are as thy hand did frame;
No workman's tool hath touched the same.
A HEART alone
Is such a stone
As nothing but
Thy power doth cut.
Wherefore each part
Of my hard heart
Meets in this frame,
To praise thy name:
That, if I chance to hold my peace,
These stones to praise thee may not cease.
O let thy blessed SACRIFICE be mine,
And sanctify this ALTAR to be thine.

(1633)

374 *Redemption*

HAVING been tenant long to a rich lord,
Not thriving, I resolvèd to be bold,
And make a suit unto him, to afford
A new small-rented lease, and cancel the old.
In heaven at his manor I him sought:
They told me there that he was lately gone
About some land, which he had dearly bought
Long since on earth, to take possession.
I straight returned, and knowing his great birth
Sought him accordingly in great resorts:
In cities, theatres, gardens, parks, and courts.
At length I heard a ragged noise and mirth
Of thieves and murderers: there I him espied,
Who straight, 'Your suit is granted', said, and died.

(1633)

frame] shape   frame (11)] (1) structure; fabric; (2) form of words; (3) state of mind

374 *Redemption*] (see endnote)   afford] grant   straight] immediately   resorts] crowded places

375 *Easter*

RISE, heart; thy lord is risen. Sing his praise
Without delays,
Who takes thee by the hand, that thou likewise
With him mayst rise:
That, as his death calcinèd thee to dust,
His life may make thee gold, and much more, just.

Awake, my lute, and struggle for thy part
With all thy art.
The cross taught all wood to resound his name,
Who bore the same.
His stretchèd sinews taught all strings what key
Is best to celebrate this most high day.

Consórt both heart and lute, and twist a song
Pleasant and long:
Or, since all music is but three parts vied
And multiplied,
O let thy blessèd Spirit bear a part,
And make up our defects with his sweet art.

I got me flowers to straw thy way;
I got me boughs off many a tree:
But thou wast up by break of day,
And broughtst thy sweets along with thee.

The sun arising in the east,
Though he give light, and th' east perfúme,
If they should offer to contest
With thy arising, they presume.

Can there be any day but this,
Though many suns to shine endeavour?
We count three hundred, but we miss:
There is but one, and that one ever.

(1633)

calcinèd] burnt; purified (alchemy) Consórt] Harmonize twist] interweave the musical parts of vied] increased by addition (to form triadic chords) straw] strew three hundred] (1) days of year in round number; (2) number denoted by the tau cross (Greek) miss] mistake

376 *Easter Wings*

LORD, who createdst man in wealth and store,
Though foolishly he lost the same,
Decaying more and more,
Till he became
Most poor:
With thee
O let me rise
As larks, harmoniously,
And sing this day thy victories:
Then shall the fall further the flight in me.

My tender age in sorrow did begin:
And still with sicknesses and shame
Thou didst so punish sin
That I became
Most thin.
With thee
Let me combine
And feel this day thy victory:
For, if I imp my wing on thine,
Affliction shall advance the flight in me.

(1633)

377 *Affliction (I)*

WHEN first thou didst entice to thee my heart,
I thought the service brave:
So many joys I writ down for my part,
Besides what I might have
Out of my stock of natural delights,
Augmented with thy gracious benefits.

I lookèd on thy furniture so fine,
And made it fine to me:
Thy glorious household-stuff did me entwine,
And 'tice me unto thee.
Such stars I counted mine: both heav'n and Earth
Paid me my wages in a world of mirth.

store] plenty Decaying] Declining fall] (1) drop in flight; (2) the Fortunate Fall (the doctrine that sin caused Christ's incarnation) imp] graft feathers on an injured wing (falconry)

377 brave] splendid furniture] furnishings household-stuff] vessels, utensils stars] i.e. treasure in the heavens (Luke 12: 33)

What pleasures could I want, whose king I served,
Where joys my fellows were?
Thus argued into hopes, my thoughts reserved
No place for grief or fear.
Therefore my sudden soul caught at the place,
And made her youth and fierceness seek thy face.

At first thou gav'st me milk and sweetnesses;
I had my wish and way:
My days were straw'd with flow'rs and happiness;
There was no month but May.
But with my years sorrow did twist and grow,
And made a party unawares for woe.

My flesh began unto my soul in pain,
Sicknesses cleave my bones;
Consuming agues dwell in ev'ry vein,
And tune my breath to groans.
Sorrow was all my soul; I scarce believed,
Till grief did tell me roundly, that I lived.

When I got health, thou tookst away my life,
And more; for my friends die:
My mirth and edge was lost; a blunted knife
Was of more use than I.
Thus thin and lean without a fence or friend,
I was blown through with ev'ry storm and wind.

Whereas my birth and spirit rather took
The way that takes the town,
Thou didst betray me to a lingering book,
And wrap me in a gown.
I was entangled in the world of strife,
Before I had the power to change my life.

Yet, for I threatened oft the siege to raise,
Not simpering all mine age,
Thou often didst with academic praise
Melt and dissolve my rage.
I took thy sweetened pill, till I came where
I could not go away, nor persevere.

want] need   sudden] hasty; peremptory   for] because   takes the town] is a *succès fou*

Yet lest perchance I should too happy be
In my unhappiness,
Turning my purge to food, thou throwest me
Into more sicknesses.
Thus doth thy power cross-bias me, not making
Thine own gift good, yet me from my ways taking.

Now I am here, what thou wilt do with me
None of my books will show:
I read, and sigh, and wish I were a tree;
For sure then I should grow
To fruit or shade: at least some bird would trust
Her household to me, and I should be just.

Yet, though thou troublest me, I must be meek;
In weakness must be stout.
Well, I will change the service, and go seek
Some other master out.
Ah my dear God! though I am clean forgot,
Let me not love thee, if I love thee not.

(1633)

378 *Prayer (I)*

PRAYER, the Church's banquet, angel's age,
God's breath in man returning to his birth,
The soul in paraphrase, heart in pilgrimage,
The Christian plummet sounding heaven and Earth;
Engine against th' almighty, sinner's tower,
Reversèd thunder, Christ-side-piercing spear,
The six-days world transposing in an hour,
A kind of tune, which all things hear and fear;
Softness, and peace, and joy, and love, and bliss,
Exalted manna, gladness of the best,
Heaven in ordinary, man well dressed,
The Milky Way, the bird of paradise,
Church-bells beyond the stars heard, the soul's blood,
The land of spices; something understood.

(1633)

cross-bias] continually deflect from my inclination (bowls) just] appropriate, useful change the service] leave my present employment

378 banquet] dessert engine] siege weapon manna] food from heaven (Exod. 16: 14) (type of the Eucharist) ordinary] (1) usual mode (ceremonial); (2) daily meal; (3) prayer book

379 *Jordan (I)*

WHO says that fictions only and false hair
Become a verse? Is there in truth no beauty?
Is all good structure in a winding stair?
May no lines pass, except they do their duty
Not to a true, but painted chair?

Is it no verse, except enchanted groves
And sudden arbours shadow coarse-spun lines?
Must purling streams refresh a lover's loves?
Must all be veil'd, while he that reads, divines,
Catching the sense at two removes?

Shepherds are honest people; let them sing:
Riddle who list, for me, and pull for prime:
I envy no man's nightingale or spring;
Nor let them punish me with loss of rhyme,
Who plainly say, 'My God, My King.'

(1633)

380 *Affliction (II)*

KILL me not ev'ry day,
Thou Lord of life; since thy one death for me
Is more than all my deaths can be,
Though I in broken pay
Die over each hour of Methusalem's stay.

If all men's tears were let
Into one common sewer, sea, and brine,
What were they all, compared to thine?
Wherein if they were set,
They would discolour thy most bloudy sweat.

Jordan] River of entry to the Promised Land (place of Christ's baptism; type of Baptism) do . . . duty] pay reverence (to the throne) shadow] darken; obscure; i.e. hide the bad workmanship of Riddle . . . me] So far as I'm concerned, whoever likes can play riddles pull . . . prime] draw for a winning card at primero

380 broken pay] instalments Methusalem's] Methuselah's (who lived 969 years: Gen. 5: 27) discolour] spoil the colour of

Thou art my grief alone,
Thou Lord conceal it not: and as thou art
All my delight, so all my smart:
Thy cross took up in one,
By way of imprest, all my future moan.

(1633)

381 *Church Monuments*

WHILE that my soul repairs to her devotion,
Here I intomb my flesh, that it betimes
May take acquaintance of this heap of dust;
To which the blast of death's incessant motion,
Fed with the exhalation of our crimes,
Drives all at last. Therefore I gladly trust

My body to this school, that it may learn
To spell his elements, and find his birth
Written in dusty heraldry and lines;
Which dissolution sure doth best discern,
Comparing dust with dust, and earth with earth.
These laugh at jet and marble put for signs,

To sever the good fellowship of dust
And spoil the meeting. What shall point out them,
When they shall bow, and kneel, and fall down flat
To kiss those heaps which now they have in trust?
Dear flesh, while I do pray, learn here thy stem
And true descent; that when thou shalt grow fat,

And wanton in thy cravings, thou mayst know
That flesh is but the glass which holds the dust
That measures all our time; which also shall
Be crumbled into dust. Mark here below
How tame these ashes are, how free from lust,
That thou mayst fit thyself against thy fall.

(1633)

took . . . one] purchased all at once   imprest] advance payment

381 blast] breath, puff; infection   elements] (1) letters; (2) the four elements of physical substance   lines] (1) genealogies; (2) engraved lettering   glass] hour glass   fit] (1) prepare; (2) measure   against . . . fall] (1) in preparation for your death; (2) in opposition to sin

382 *The Church Floor*

MARK you the floor? That square and speckled stone,
Which looks so firm and strong,
Is patience:

And the other black and grave, wherewith each one
Is chequered all along,
Humility:

The gentle rising, which on either hand
Leads to the choir above,
Is confidence:

But the sweet cement, which in one sure band
Ties the whole frame, is love
And charity.

Hither sometimes sin steals, and stains
The marble's neat and curious veins;
But all is cleansèd when the marble weeps.
Sometimes death, puffing at the door,
Blows all the dust about the floor;
But while he thinks to spoil the room, he sweeps.
Blest be the architect, whose art
Could build so strong in a weak heart.

(1633)

383 *The Quiddity*

MY God, a verse is not a crown,
No point of honour, or gay suit,
No hawk, or banquet, or renown,
Nor a good sword, nor yet a lute:

It cannot vault, or dance, or play;
It never was in France or Spain;
Nor can it entertain the day
With my great stable or demain:

chequered] (1) varied alternately; (2) treasured up charity] *caritas*, brotherly love
neat] clean; elegant curious] finely wrought

383 *Quiddity*] Essence; subtlety, quibble demain] landed estate

It is no office, art, or news,
Nor the exchange, or busy hall;
But it is that which while I use
I am with thee, and *most take all.*

(1633)

384

Humility

I SAW the virtues sitting hand in hand
In several ranks upon an azure throne,
Where all the beasts and fowl by their command
Presented tokens of submission.
Humility, who sat the lowest there
To execute their call,
When by the beasts the presents tendered were,
Gave them about to all.

The angry lion did present his paw,
Which by consent was given to mansuetude.
The fearful hare her ears, which by their law
Humility did reach to fortitude.
The jealous turkey brought his coral chain:
That went to temperance.
On justice was bestowed the fox's brain,
Killed in the way by chance.

At length, the crow bringing the peacock's plume
(For he would not), as they beheld the grace
Of that brave gift, each one began to fume
And challenge it, as proper to his place,
Till they fell out; which when the beasts espied,
They leapt upon the throne;
And if the fox had lived to rule their side,
They had deposed each one.

Humility, who held the plume, at this
Did weep so fast that the tears trickling down
Spoiled all the train; then saying 'Here it is
For which ye wrangle,' made them turn their frown
Against the beasts: so jointly bandying,
They drive them soon away,
And then amerced them, double gifts to bring
At the next session-day.

(1633)

hall] guildhall *most take all*] the end of the game is what counts (proverb)

384 mansuetude] meekness; gentleness reach] pass coral chain] i.e. wattle brave] splendid challenge] claim train] tail feather bandying] banding together amerced] fined

385 *Affliction (III)*

My heart did heave, and there came forth, 'O God!'
By that I knew that thou wast in the grief,
To guide and govern it to my relief,
    Making a sceptre of the rod:
        Hadst thou not had thy part,
Sure the unruly sigh had broke my heart.

But since thy breath gave me both life and shape,
Thou knowst my tallies; and when there's assigned
So much breath to a sigh, what's then behind?
    Or if some years with it escape,
        The sigh then only is
A gale to bring me sooner to my bliss.

Thy life on earth was grief, and thou art still
Constant unto it, making it to be
A point of honour, now to grieve in me,
    And in thy members suffer ill.
        They who lament one cross,
Thou dying daily, praise thee to thy loss.

(1633)

386 *Christmas*

All after pleasures as I rid one day,
    My horse and I, both tired, body and mind,
    With full cry of affections quite astray,
I took up in the next inn I could find.
There when I came, whom found I but my dear,
    My dearest Lord, expecting till the grief
    Of pleasures brought me to him, ready there
To be all passengers' most sweet relief?
O thou, whose glorious, yet contracted light,
    Wrapped in night's mantle, stole into a manger;
    Since my dark soul and brutish is thy right,
To man of all beasts be not thou a stranger:
    Furnish and deck my soul, that thou mayst have
    A better lodging than a rack or grave.

tallies] record; reckoning; debts   escape] i.e. escape the reckoning (sighs were held to shorten life)   members] (1) parts of the body; (2) members of the Church, Christ's body

386 rid] rode   cry] pursuit (hunting)   took up] stayed   expecting] waiting   passengers'] travellers'   rack] manger

The shepherds sing; and shall I silent be?
My God, no hymn for thee?
My soul's a shepherd too; a flock it feeds
Of thoughts, and words, and deeds.
The pasture is thy word: the streams, thy grace
Enriching all the place.
Shepherd and flock shall sing, and all my powers
Out-sing the day-light hours.
Then we will chide the sun for letting night
Take up his place and right:

We sing one common Lord; wherefore he should
Himself the candle hold.
I will go searching, till I find a sun
Shall stay, till we have done;
A willing shiner, that shall shine as gladly
As frost-nipped suns look sadly.
Then we will sing, and shine all our own day,
And one another pay:
His beams shall cheer my breast, and both so twine,
Till ev'n his beams sing, and my music shine.

(1633)

387 *The World*

LOVE built a stately house; where fortune came,
And spinning fancies, she was heard to say
That her fine cobwebs did support the frame,
Whereas they were supported by the same;
But wisdom quickly swept them all away.

Then pleasure came, who, liking not the fashion,
Began to make balcónies, terraces,
Till she had weakened all by alteration;
But reverend laws and many a proclamation
Reformèd all at length with menaces.

Then entered sin, and with that sycamore
Whose leaves first sheltered man from drought and dew,
Working and winding slyly evermore,
The inward walls and sommers cleft and tore;
But grace shored these, and cut that as it grew.

the candle hold] give light (Prov. 20: 27) pay] content; satisfy

387 sycamore] (species of fig) sommers] supporting beams that] the sycamore

Then sin combined with death in a firm band
To raze the building to the very floor;
Which they effected, none could them withstand.
But love and grace took glory by the hand,
And built a braver palace than before.

(1633)

388 *Vanity (I)*

THE fleet astronomer can bore,
And thread the spheres with his quick-piercing mind:
He views their stations, walks from door to door,
Surveys, as if he had designed
To make a purchase there: he sees their dances,
And knoweth long before
Both their full-eyed aspécts, and secret glances.

The nimble diver with his side
Cuts through the working waves, that he may fetch
His dearly-earnèd pearl, which God did hide
On purpose from the vent'rous wretch;
That he might save his life, and also hers,
Who with excessive pride
Her own destruction and his danger wears.

The subtle chemic can devest
And strip the creature naked, till he find
The callow principles within their nest:
There he imparts to them his mind,
Admitted to their bed-chamber, before
They appear trim and dressed
To ordinary suitors at the door.

What hath not man sought out and found
But his dear God? who yet his glorious law
Embosoms in us, mellowing the ground
With showers and frosts, with love and awe,
So that we need not say, Where's this command?
Poor man, thou searchest round
To find out *death*, but missest *life* at hand.

(1633)

band] alliance; compact

388 spheres] concentric globes carrying the stars and planets stations] points in a planet's orbit where it seems to stand still aspécts] (1) looks; faces; (2) oppositions (astrology) secret glances] acute aspects (e.g. crescent moon) vent'rous] adventurous chemic] alchemist devest] unclothe callow] featherless (bare, simple, essential)

389 *Virtue*

SWEET day, so cool, so calm, so bright,
The bridal of the earth and sky:
The dew shall weep thy fall tonight;
For thou must die.

Sweet rose, whose hue angry and brave
Bids the rash gazer wipe his eye:
Thy root is ever in its grave,
And thou must die.

Sweet spring, full of sweet days and roses,
A box where sweets compacted lie:
My music shows ye have your closes,
And all must die.

Only a sweet and virtuous soul,
Like seasoned timber, never gives;
But though the whole world turn to coal,
Then chiefly lives.

(1633)

390 *The Pearl. Matt. 13: 45*

I KNOW the ways of learning; both the head
And pipes that feed the press, and make it run;
What reason hath from nature borrowèd,
Or of itself, like a good huswife, spun
In laws and policy; what the stars conspire,
What willing nature speaks, what forced by fire;
Both th' old discoveries, and the new-found seas,
The stock and surplus, cause and history:
All these stand open, or I have the keys:
Yet I love thee.

I know the ways of honour: what maintains
The quick returns of courtesy and wit;
In vies of favours whether party gains,
When glory swells the heart, and mouldeth it

bridal] wedding fall] (1) nightfall; (2) cadence, dying fall angry] (1) red; (2) displeased brave] (1) handsome; (2) challenging box] (1) box of fragrances; (2) music box sweets] (1) fragrances; (2) harmonies compacted] (1) compressed (petals); (2) composed closes] cadences coal] i.e. cinder, in the final conflagration

390 head] fount press] (1) olive press (feeding the lamp of Zech. 4: 12); (2) printing press fire] (1) torturer's fire; (2) alchemist's furnace whether] which glory] pride, ambition

To all expressions both of hand and eye,
Which on the world a true-love-knot may tie,
And bear the bundle, wheresoe'er it goes;
How many drams of spirit there must be
To sell my life unto my friends or foes:
Yet I love thee.

I know the ways of pleasure, the sweet strains,
The lullings and the relishes of it;
The propositions of hot blood and brains;
What mirth and music mean; what love and wit
Have done these twenty hundred years and more;
I know the projects of unbridled store:
My stuff is flesh, not brass; my senses live,
And grumble oft that they have more in me
Than he that curbs them, being but one to five:
Yet I love thee.

I know all these, and have them in my hand:
Therefore not sealèd, but with open eyes
I fly to thee, and fully understand
Both the main sale and the commodities,
And at what rate and price I have thy love,
With all the circumstances that may move:
Yet through these labyrinths, not my grovelling wit,
But thy silk twist let down from heav'n to me,
Did both conduct and teach me how by it
To climb to thee.

(1633)

391 *Affliction (IV)*

BROKEN in pieces all asunder,
Lord, hunt me not,
A thing forgot,
Once a poor creature, now a wonder,
A wonder tortured in the space
Betwixt this world and that of grace.

bear . . . bundle] carry the parcel of favours, like a servant strains] musical or love passages lullings] (1) caresses; (2) soft sounds (music) relishes] (1) tastes; zests; (2) ornaments (music) propositions] (1) offers; (2) first statements of contrapuntal subjects (music) store] wealth he] rational will sealèd] (1) sealèd; (2) seelèd: with eyes sewn shut (falconry) commodities] advantages silk twist] thread, cord (?Josh. 2:18)

391 *Affliction*] (see endnote)

My thoughts are all a case of knives,
Wounding my heart
With scattered smart,
As watering pots give flowers their lives.
Nothing their fury can control,
While they do wound and pink my soul.

All my attendants are at strife,
Quitting their place
Unto my face:
Nothing performs the task of life:
The elements are let loose to fight,
And while I live, try out their right.

Oh help, my God! let not their plot
Kill them and me,
And also thee,
Who art my life: dissolve the knot,
As the sun scatters by his light
All the rebellions of the night.

Then shall those powers which work for grief
Enter thy pay,
And day by day
Labour thy praise, and my relief;
With care and courage building me,
Till I reach heav'n, and much more, thee.

(1633)

392 *Unkindness*

LORD, make me coy and tender to offend:
In friendship first I think, if that agree,
Which I intend,
Unto my friend's intent and end.
I would not use a friend as I use Thee.

If any touch my friend, or his good name,
It is my honour and my love to free
His blasted fame
From the least spot or thought of blame.
I could not use a friend as I use Thee.

392 *Unkindness*] (1) Unkindness; (2) Unnaturalness coy] reserved blasted] withered

My friend may spit upon my curious floor:
Would he have gold? I lend it instantly;
But let the poor,
And thou within them, starve at door.
I cannot use a friend as I use Thee.

When that my friend pretendeth to a place,
I quit my interest, and leave it free:
But when thy grace
Sues for my heart, I thee displace,
Nor would I use a friend as I use Thee.

Yet can a friend what thou hast done fulfil?
Oh write in brass, *My God upon a tree*
His blood did spill
Only to purchase my good-will.
Yet use I not my foes as I use Thee.

(1633)

393

Life

I MADE a posy, while the day ran by:
Here will I smell my remnant out, and tie
My life within this band.
But time did beckon to the flowers, and they
By noon most cunningly did steal away,
And withered in my hand.

My hand was next to them, and then my heart:
I took, without more thinking, in good part
Time's gentle admonition:
Who did so sweetly death's sad taste convey,
Making my mind to smell my fatal day;
Yet sug'ring the suspicïon.

Farewell dear flowers: sweetly your time ye spent,
Fit, while ye lived, for smell or ornament,
And after death for cures.
I follow straight without complaints or grief,
Since if my scent be good, I care not if
It be as short as yours.

(1633)

curious] elegant pretendeth] aspires place] office

393 posy] (1) bouquet; (2) motto; poetry remnant] remaining years band] string, ribbon cures] medicinal use

394

Mortification

HOW soon doth man decay!
When clothes are taken from a chest of sweets
To swaddle infants, whose young breath
Scarce knows the way,
Those clouts are little winding sheets,
Which do consign and send them unto death.

When boys go first to bed,
They step into their voluntary graves;
Sleep binds them fast; only their breath
Makes them not dead:
Successive nights, like rolling waves,
Convey them quickly, who are bound for death.

When youth is frank and free,
And calls for music, while his veins do swell,
All day exchanging mirth and breath
In company,
That music summons to the knell,
Which shall befriend him at the hour of death.

When man grows staid and wise,
Getting a house and home, where he may move
Within the circle of his breath,
Schooling his eyes,
That dumb inclosure maketh love
Unto the coffin that attends his death.

When age grows low and weak,
Marking his grave, and thawing ev'ry year,
Till all do melt and drown his breath
When he would speak,
A chair or litter shows the bier,
Which shall convey him to the house of death.

Man, ere he is aware,
Hath put together a solemnity,
And dressed his hearse, while he has breath
As yet to spare:
Yet Lord, instruct us so to die
That all these dyings may be life in death.

(1633)

sweets] perfumes clouts] swaddling clothes bound] (1) destined; (2) confined knell] passing bell (sounded before death) attends] awaits chair] i.e. sign of infirmity hearse] bier

395 *Jordan (II)*

WHEN first my lines of heav'nly joys made mention,
Such was their lustre, they did so excel,
That I sought out quaint words and trim invention;
My thoughts began to burnish, sprout, and swell,
Curling with metaphors a plain intention,
Decking the sense as if it were to sell.

Thousands of notions in my brain did run,
Offering their service, if I were not sped;
I often blotted what I had begun:
This was not quick enough, and that was dead.
Nothing could seem too rich to clothe the sun,
Much less those joys which trample on his head.

As flames do work and wind when they ascend,
So did I weave myself into the sense.
But while I bustled, I might hear a friend
Whisper, 'How wide is all this long pretence!
There is in love a sweetness ready penned:
Copy out only that, and save expense.'

(1633)

396 *The Quip*

THE merry world did on a day
With his train-bands and mates agree
To meet together where I lay,
And all in sport to jeer at me.

First, beauty crept into a rose,
Which when I plucked not, sir, said she,
Tell me, I pray, whose hands are those?
But thou shalt answer, Lord, for me.

Then money came, and chinking still,
What tune is this, poor man? said he:
I heard in music you had skill.
But thou shalt answer, Lord, for me.

quaint] artful invention] poetic idea burnish] (1) grow fat; spread themselves; (2) shine Curling] Adorning; Twisting sped] successful quick] lively sun] Son (and alluding to the woman 'clothed with the sun', Rev. 12: 1) joys] Joys of Mary (in one, coronation, she trampled the moon) wide] astray pretence] ostentation, display

396 train-bands] citizen soldiers

Then came brave glory puffing by
In silks that whistled, who but he?
He scarce allowed me half an eye.
But thou shalt answer, Lord, for me.

Then came quick wit and conversation,
And he would needs a comfort be,
And, to be short, make an oration.
But thou shalt answer, Lord, for me.

Yet when the hour of thy design
To answer these fine things shall come,
Speak not at large; say, I am thine:
And then they have their answer home.

(1633)

397 *The Dawning*

AWAKE, sad heart, whom sorrow ever drowns;
  Take up thine eyes, which feed on earth;
Unfold thy forehead gathered into frowns:
  Thy Saviour comes, and with him mirth:
          Awake, awake;
And with a thankful heart his comforts take.
  But thou dost still lament, and pine, and cry;
  And feel his death, but not his victory.

Arise sad heart; if thou do not withstand,
  Christ's resurrection thine may be:
Do not by hanging down break from the hand,
  Which as it riseth, raiseth thee:
          Arise, arise;
And with his burial-linen dry thine eyes:
  Christ left his grave-clothes, that we might, when grief
  Draws tears, or blood, not want a handkerchief.

(1633)

half an eye] the merest glance of acknowledgement home] thoroughly

397 *Dawning*] i.e. of Easter morning

398 *Dialogue*

SWEETEST Saviour, if my soul
Were but worth the having,
Quickly should I then control
Any thought of waving.
But when all my care and pains
Cannot give the name of gains
To thy wretch so full of stains,
What delight or hope remains?

What, child, is the balance thine,
Thine the poise and measure?
If I say, Thou shalt be mine,
Finger not my treasure.
What the gains in having thee
Do amount to, only he,
Who for man was sold, can see;
That transferred th' accounts to me.

But as I can see no merit
Leading to this favour,
So the way to fit me for it
Is beyond my savour.
As the reason then is thine,
So the way is none of mine:
I disclaim the whole design:
Sin disclaims and I resign.

That is all, if that I could
Get without repining;
And my clay, my creature, would
Follow my resigning:
That as I did freely part
With my glory and desért,
Left all joys to feel all smart—
Ah! no more: thou breakst my heart.

(1633)

waving] (1) waiving Christ's offer; (2) wavering balance] scales poise] (1) weight; (2) burden savour] understanding *desért*] (pronounced, and often spelt, 'desárt')

399 *Sin's Round*

SORRY I am, my God, sorry I am,
That my offences course it in a ring.
My thoughts are working like a busy flame,
Until their cockatrice they hatch and bring;
And when they once have perfected their draughts,
My words take fire from my inflamèd thoughts.

My words take fire from my inflamèd thoughts,
Which spit it forth like the Sicilian Hill.
They vent the wares, and pass them with their faults,
And by their breathing ventilate the ill.
But words suffice not, where are lewd intentions:
My hands do join to finish the inventions.

My hands do join to finish the inventions:
And so my sins ascend three stories high,
As Babel grew, before there were dissensions.
Yet ill deeds loiter not, for they supply
New thoughts of sinning: wherefore, to my shame,
Sorry I am, my God, sorry I am.

(1633)

400 *Peace*

SWEET peace, where dost thou dwell? I humbly crave,
Let me once know.
I sought thee in a secret cave,
And asked, if peace were there.
A hollow wind did seem to answer, No:
Go seek elsewhere.

I did; and going did a rainbow note:
Surely, thought I,
This is the lace of peace's coat:
I will search out the matter.
But while I looked, the clouds immediately
Did break and scatter.

399 *Round*] (1) Round dance or song; (2) Vicious circle course it] career about cockatrice] mythical cock-serpent hybrid with lethal breath (Isa. 59: 5) the Sicilian Hill] Etna (the Cyclops' armament workshop) vent] (1) sell; (2) discharge wares] (1) merchandise; (2) genitals ventilate] (1) publicize, expose; (2) give vent to passion lewd] evil Babel] the sinful tower of Gen. 11

Then went I to a garden, and did spy
A gallant flower,
The crown imperial: Sure, said I,
Peace at the root must dwell.
But when I digged, I saw a worm devour
What showed so well.

At length I met a rev'rend good old man,
Whom when for peace
I did demand, he thus began:
There was a prince of old
At Salem dwelt, who lived with good increase
Of flock and fold.

He sweetly lived; yet sweetness did not save
His life from foes.
But after death out of his grave
There sprang twelve stalks of wheat:
Which many wond'ring at, got some of those
To plant and set.

It prospered strangely, and did soon disperse
Through all the earth;
For they that taste it do rehearse
That virtue lies therein,
A secret virtue bringing peace and mirth
By flight of sin.

Take of this grain, which in my garden grows,
And grows for you:
Make bread of it; and that repose
And peace, which ev'rywhere
With so much earnestness you do pursue,
Is only there.

(1633)

401 *The Bunch of Grapes*

JOY, I did lock thee up; but some bad man
Hath let thee out again;
And now, methinks, I am where I began
Sev'n years ago: one vogue and vein,
One air of thoughts usurps my brain.

crown imperial] species of fritillary prince of old] Melchizedek (type of Christ as priest) Salem] 'Peace' (Heb. 7: 2) stalks] i.e. the apostles rehearse] tell virtue] power; quality

401 vogue] tendency

I did towards Canaan draw; but now I am
Brought back to the Red Sea, the sea of shame.

For as the Jews of old by God's command
Travelled, and saw no town;
So now each Christian hath his journeys spanned:
Their story pens and sets us down.
A single deed is small renown.
God's works are wide, and let in future times;
His ancient justice overflows our crimes.

Then have we too our guardian fires and clouds;
Our scripture-dew drops fast:
We have our sands and serpents, tents and shrouds;
Alas! our murmurings come not last.
But where's the cluster? Where's the taste
Of mine inheritance? Lord, if I must borrow,
Let me as well take up their joy, as sorrow.

But can he want the grape, who hath the wine?
I have their fruit and more.
Blessèd be God, who prospered Noah's vine,
And made it bring forth grapes good store.
But much more him I must adore,
Who of the Law's sour juice sweet wine did make,
Ev'n God himself being pressèd for my sake.

(1633)

402

Paradise

I BLESS thee, Lord, because I GROW
Among thy trees, which in a ROW
To thee both fruit and order OW.

What open force, or hidden CHARM
Can blast my fruit, or bring me HARM,
While the enclosure is thine ARM?

Enclose me still for fear I START.
Be to me rather sharp and TART,
Than let me want thy hand and ART.

Canaan] the Promised Land spanned] measured; limited pens] (1) records; (2) confines sets us down] (1) chronicles us; (2) places, lowers us let in] make way for scripture-dew] manna (Num. 11: 9) shrouds] shelters cluster] i.e. grapes (Num. 13: 23, a type of Christ) Noah's vine] i.e. vineyard (Gen. 9: 20) good store] in plenty pressèd] i.e. crucified

When thou dost greater judgements SPARE,
And with thy knife but prune and PARE,
Ev'n fruitful trees more fruitful ARE.

Such sharpness shows the sweetest FREND:
Such cuttings rather heal than REND:
And such beginnings touch their END.

(1633)

403 *Divinity*

As men, for fear the stars should sleep and nod,
    And trip at night, have spheres supplied;
As if a star were duller than a clod,
    Which knows his way without a guide:

Just so the other heav'n they also serve,
    Divinity's transcendent sky:
Which with the edge of wit they cut and carve.
    Reason triumphs, and faith lies by.

Could not that wisdom, which first broached the wine,
    Have thickened it with definitions?
And jagged his seamless coat, had that been fine,
    With curious questions and divisions?

But all the doctrine which he taught and gave
    Was clear as heav'n, from whence it came.
At least those beams of truth, which only save,
    Surpass in brightness any flame.

Love God, and love your neighbour. Watch and pray.
    Do as ye would be done unto.
Oh dark instructions; ev'n as dark as day!
    Who can these Gordian knots undo?

But he doth bid us take his blood for wine.
    Bid what he please; yet I am sure
To take and taste what he doth there design
    Is all that saves, and not obscure.

END] (1) conclusion; (2) purpose

403 spheres] either (1) cosmic spheres in which embedded stars moved; or (2) model globes mapping their positions   clod] blockhead   wine] (from the true vine, broached at Christ's crucifixion)   jagged] fashionably slashed   his . . . coat] Christ's (symbol of simple love)

Then burn thy epicycles, foolish man;
Break all thy spheres, and save thy head.
Faith needs no staff of flesh, but stoutly can
To heav'n alone both go, and lead.

(1633)

404 *The Pilgrimage*

I TRAVELLED on, seeing the hill, where lay
My expectation.
A long it was and weary way.
The gloomy cave of desperation
I left on th' one, and on the other side
The rock of pride.

And so I came to fancy's meadow strowed
With many a flower:
Fain would I here have made abode,
But I was quickened by my hour.
So to care's copse I came, and there got through
With much ado.

That led me to the wild of passion, which
Some call the wold:
A wasted place, but sometimes rich.
Here I was robbed of all my gold,
Save one good angel, which a friend had tied
Close to my side.

At length I got unto the gladsome hill,
Where lay my hope,
Where lay my heart; and climbing still,
When I had gained the brow and top,
A lake of brackish waters on the ground
Was all I found.

With that abashed and struck with many a sting
Of swarming fears,
I fell, and cried, Alas my King!
Can both the way and end be tears?
Yet taking heart I rose, and then perceived
I was deceived:

epicycles] complicating improvements of the simple circular orbits of planets in the Ptolemaic system staff] i.e. 'Jacob's staff': (1) pilgrim's staff; (2) astronomical instrument

404 strowed] strewn quickened ... hour] roused by a sense of life's brevity wold] moorland angel] (1) guardian angel; (2) gold coin

My hill was further: so I flung away,
Yet heard a cry,
Just as I went, 'None goes that way
And lives': If that be all, said I,
After so foul a journey death is fair,
And but a chair.

(1633)

405 *The Collar*

I STRUCK the board, and cried, No more.
I will abroad.
What? shall I ever sigh and pine?
My lines and life are free; free as the road,
Loose as the wind, as large as store.
Shall I be still in suit?
Have I no harvest but a thorn
To let me blood, and not restore
What I have lost with cordial fruit?
Sure there was wine
Before my sighs did dry it; there was corn
Before my tears did drown it.
Is the year only lost to me?
Have I no bays to crown it?
No flowers, no garlands gay? All blasted?
All wasted?
Not so, my heart: but there is fruit,
And thou hast hands.
Recover all thy sigh-blown age
On double pleasures: leave thy cold dispute
Of what is fit, and not. Forsake thy cage,
Thy rope of sands,
Which petty thoughts have made, and made to thee
Good cable, to enforce and draw
And be thy law,
While thou didst wink and wouldst not see.
Away; take heed,
I will abroad,

404 chair] i.e. sedan-chair

405 *Collar*] (1) clerical collar; (2) means of restraint (emblem of discipline); (3) part of rigging; (4) choler, fit of anger board] table; communion table lines] (1) courses, routes; (2) verses road] riding; highway; roadstead store] plenty still] always suit] attendance cordial] restorative corn] grain bays] laurels blasted] withered blown] (1) out of breath; (2) tainted rope of sands] impossibility; frail abstraction (proverb) wink] close the eyes

Call in thy death's head there: tie up thy fears.
He that forbears
To suit and serve his need
Deserves his load.
But as I raved and grew more fierce and wild
At every word,
Me thoughts I heard one calling, *Child!*
And I replied, *My Lord.*

(1633)

406 *The Pulley*

WHEN God at first made man,
Having a glass of blessings standing by,
Let us (said he) pour on him all we can:
Let the world's riches, which dispersèd lie,
Contract into span.

So strength first made a way;
Then beauty flowed, then wisdom, honour, pleasure:
When almost all was out, God made a stay,
Perceiving that alone of all his treasure
Rest in the bottom lay.

For if I should (said he)
Bestow this jewel also on my creature,
He would adore my gifts instead of me,
And rest in nature, not the God of nature:
So both should losers be.

Yet let him keep the rest,
But keep them with repining restlessness:
Let him be rich and weary, that at least,
If goodness lead him not, yet weariness
May toss him to my breast.

(1633)

Me thoughts] It seemed
406 span] width of a hand

407 *Aaron*

HOLINESS on the head,
Light and perfections on the breast,
Harmonious bells below, raising the dead
To lead them unto life and rest:
Thus are true Aarons drest.

Profaneness in my head,
Defects and darkness in my breast,
A noise of passions ringing me for dead
Unto a place where is no rest:
Poor priest thus am I drest.

Only another head
I have, another heart and breast,
Another music, making live not dead,
Without whom I could have no rest:
In him I am well drest.

Christ is my only head,
My alone only heart and breast,
My only music, striking me ev'n dead;
That to the old man I may rest,
And be in him new drest.

So holy in my head,
Perfect and light in my dear breast,
My doctrine tuned by Christ (who is not dead,
But lives in me while I do rest):
Come people; Aaron's drest.

(1633)

408 *The Posy*

LET wits contest,
And with their words and posies windows fill:
Less than the least
Of all thy mercies is my posy still.

Aaron] Moses' brother (type of the priest) on the head] i.e. engraved on the mitre (Exod. 28: 4) light and perfections] (the urim and thummim of the priest's breastplate) bells below] (the gold bells on the hem of the priest's robe) noise] band of musicians music] band striking] (1) making; (2) sounding old man] sinful nature (Col. 3)

Posy] Motto; poetry

This on my ring,
This by my picture, in my book I write:
Whether I sing,
Or say, or dictate, this is my delight.

Invention rest,
Comparisons go play, wit use thy will:
Less than the least
Of all God's mercies is my posy still.

(1633)

409 *The Elixir*

TEACH me, my God and king,
In all things thee to see,
And what I do in anything,
To do it as for thee:

Not rudely, as a beast,
To run into an action;
But still to make thee prepossessed,
And give it his perfection.

A man that looks on glass,
On it may stay his eye;
Or if he pleaseth, through it pass,
And then the heav'n espy.

All may of thee partake:
Nothing can be so mean,
Which with his tincture (for thy sake)
Will not grow bright and clean.

A servant with this clause
Makes drudgery divine:
Who sweeps a room, as for thy laws,
Makes that and th' action fine.

This is the famous stone
That turneth all to gold:
For that which God doth touch and own
Cannot for less be told.

(1633)

409 *Elixir*] Philosopher's stone, transmuting metals or prolonging life (alchemy) make . . . prepossessed] give thee a prior claim his] its tincture] principle whose quality may be infused into materials (alchemy) clause] (1) stipulation in contract; (2) word group ('for thy sake') stone] the philosopher's stone touch] test with touchstone told] counted

410 *A Wreath*

A WREATHÈD garland of deservèd praise,
Of praise deservèd, unto thee I give,
I give to thee, who knowest all my ways,
My crooked winding ways, wherein I live,
Wherein I die, not live: for life is straight,
Straight as a line, and ever tends to thee,
To thee, who art more far above deceit
Than deceit seems above simplicity.
Give me simplicity, that I may live,
So live and like, that I may know thy ways,
Know them and practise them: then shall I give
For this poor wreath, give thee a crown of praise.

(1633)

411 *Love (III)*

LOVE bade me welcome; yet my soul drew back,
Guilty of dust and sin.
But quick-eyed love, observing me grow slack
From my first entrance in,
Drew nearer to me, sweetly questioning
If I lacked anything.

A guest, I answered, worthy to be here:
Love said, 'You shall be he.'
I the unkind, ungrateful? 'Ah my dear,
I cannot look on thee.'
Love took my hand, and smiling did reply,
'Who made the eyes but I?'

'Truth Lord, but I have marred them: let my shame
Go where it doth deserve.'
'And know you not,' says love, 'who bore the blame?'
'My dear, then I will serve.'
'You must sit down,' says love, 'and taste my meat':
So I did sit and eat.

(1633)

411 quick-eyed] living-eyed (divine love, not blindfolded Cupid) slack] slow meat] meal (the heavenly feast of Luke 12: 37)

JAMES HOWELL
1593–1666

412 *Upon the Poet of His Time, Ben Jonson: His Honoured Friend and Father*

AND is thy glass run out? Is that oil spent
Which light to such tough sinewy labours lent?
Well, Ben, I now perceive that all the nine,
Though they their utmost forces should combine,
Cannot prevail 'gainst Night's three daughters, but
One still must spin, one twist, the other cut.
  Yet in despite of distaff, clew, and knife,
Thou in thy strenuous lines hast got a life,
Which, like thy bays, shall flourish every age,
While sock or buskin shall ascend the stage.
        —*sic vaticinatur*

(1663)

THOMAS JAMES
1593?–1635?

413 *Lines on His Companions Who Died in the Northern Seas*

I WERE unkind unless that I did shed,
Before I part, some tears upon our dead;
And when my eyes be dry, I will not cease
In heart to pray their bones may rest in peace:
Their better parts (good souls) I know were given
With an intent they should return to heaven.
Their lives they spent, to the last drop of blood,
Seeking God's glory and their country's good;
And, as a valiant soldier rather dies
Than yields his courage to his enemies,
And stops their way with his hewed flesh, when death
Hath quite deprived him of his strength and breath:
So have they spent themselves; and here they lie,
A famous mark of our discovery.

412 nine] the Muses three daughters] the Fates bays] laurels sock . . . buskin] comic or tragic actor's footwear *sic vaticinatur*] so it is prophesied

We that survive, perchance may end our days
In some employment meriting no praise,
And in a dunghill rot; when no man names
The memory of us, but to our shames.
They have outlived this fear, and their brave ends
Will ever be an honour to their friends.
Why drop ye so, mine eyes? Nay, rather pour
My sad departure in a solemn shower.
The winter's cold, that lately froze our blood:
Now were it so extreme, might do this good,
As make these tears bright pearls, which I would lay
Tombed safely with you, till doom's fatal day;
That in this solitary place, where none
Will ever come to breathe a sigh or groan,
Some remnant might be extant of the true
And faithful love I ever tendered you.
Oh, rest in peace, dear friends! and, let it be
No pride to say, the sometime part of me.
What pain and anguish doth afflict the head,
The heart and stomach, when the limbs are dead!
So grieved, I kiss your graves, and vow to die
A foster-father to your memory.

(1633)

THOMAS CAREW
1594?–1640

414

Song: Persuasions to Enjoy

If the quick spirits in your eye
Now languish, and anon must die;
If every sweet and every grace
Must fly from that forsaken face:
 Then, Celia, let us reap our joys,
 Ere time such goodly fruit destroys.

Or, if that golden fleece must grow
For ever, free from agèd snow;
If those bright suns must know no shade,
Nor your fresh beauties ever fade:

414 quick] living   anon] soon

Then fear not, Celia, to bestow
What, still being gathered, still must grow.
  Thus, either time his sickle brings
  In vain, or else in vain his wings.

(1640)

415 *To My Mistress in Absence*

THOUGH I must live here, and by force
Of your command suffer divorce;
Though I am parted, yet my mind
(That's more myself) still stays behind.
I breathe in you, you keep my heart:
'Twas but a carcass that did part.
Then, though our bodies are disjoined,
As things that are to place confined,
Yet let our boundless spirits meet,
And in love's sphere each other greet.
There let us work a mystic wreath,
Unknown unto the world beneath:
There let our clasped loves sweetly twin;
There let our secret thoughts unseen
Like nets be weaved and intertwined,
Wherewith we'll catch each other's mind;
There, whilst our souls do sit and kiss
Tasting a sweet and subtle bliss
(Such as gross lovers cannot know,
Whose hands and lips meet here below)
Let us look down, and mark what pain
Our absent bodies here sustain,
And smile to see how far away
The one doth from the other stray:
Yet burn and languish with desire
To join, and quench their mutual fire.
There let us joy to see from far
Our emulous flames at loving war,
Whilst both with equal lustre shine,
Mine bright as yours, yours bright as mine.
There seated in those heavenly bowers
We'll cheat the lag and lingering hours,
Making our bitter absence sweet,
Till souls, and bodies both, may meet.

(1640)

still] always

415 lag] lagging, tardy

416 *Song: Eternity of Love Protested*

How ill doth he deserve a lover's name,
Whose pale weak flame
Cannot retain
His heat in spite of absence or disdain,
But doth at once, like paper set on fire,
Burn, and expire!
True love can never change his seat,
Nor did he ever love, that could retreat.

That noble flame, which my breast keeps alive,
Shall still survive
When my soul's fled;
Nor shall my love die when my body's dead:
That shall wait on me to the lower shade,
And never fade;
My very ashes in their urn
Shall like a hallowed lamp for ever burn.

(1640)

417 *Upon a Ribband*

This silken wreath, which circles in mine arm,
Is but an emblem of that mystic charm
Wherewith the magic of your beauties binds
My captive soul, and round about it winds
Fetters of lasting love: this hath entwined
My flesh alone, that hath empaled my mind;
Time may wear out these soft weak bands, but those
Strong chains of brass, fate shall not discompose.
This holy relic may preserve my wrist,
But my whole frame doth by that power subsist:
To that my prayers and sacrifice, to this
I only pay a superstitious kiss;
This but the idol, that's the deity;
Religion there is due, here ceremony.
That I receive by faith, this but in trust;
Here I may tender duty, there I must.
This order as a layman I may bear,
But I become love's priest when that I wear.

417 *Ribband*] Ribbon empaled] fenced in; garlanded bands] bonds

This moves like air; that as the centre stands:
That knot your virtue tied; this, but your hands:
That, nature framed, but this was made by art:
This makes my arm your prisoner, that my heart.

(1640)

418 *Another* [*On the Duke of Buckingham*].

Siste hospes sive indigena sive advena vicissitudinis rerum memor pauca pellege

READER, when these dumb stones have told
In borrowed speech what guest they hold,
Thou shalt confess the vain pursuit
Of human glory yields no fruit
But an untimely grave. If fate
Could constant happiness create,
Her ministers, fortune and worth,
Had here that miracle brought forth:
They fixed this child of honour where
No room was left for hope, or fear,
Of more, or less; so high, so great
His growth was, yet so safe his seat.
Safe in the circle of his friends;
Safe in his loyal heart and ends;
Safe in his native valiant spirit;
By favour safe, and safe by merit;
Safe by the stamp of nature, which
Did strength with shape and grace enrich;
Safe in the cheerful courtesies
Of flowing gestures, speech, and eyes;
Safe in his bounties, which were more
Proportioned to his mind than store;
Yet, though for virtue he becomes
Involved himself in borrowed sums,
Safe in his care, he leaves betrayed
No friend engaged, no debt unpaid.
But though the stars conspire to shower
Upon one head the united power

centre] Earth

418 Siste . . . pellege] Stop, passer-by, stranger or native: mindful of life's mutability read these few

Of all their graces, if their dire
Aspects must other breasts inspire
With vicious thoughts, a murderer's knife
May cut, as here, their darling's life.
Who can be happy then, if nature must,
To make one happy man, make all men just?

(1640)

419 *To Ben Jonson: Upon Occasion of His Ode of Defiance Annexed to His Play of 'The New Inn'*

'TIS true, dear Ben, thy just chastising hand
Hath fixed upon the sotted age a brand
To their swollen pride and empty scribbling due:
It can nor judge nor write; and yet 'tis true
Thy comic Muse from the exalted line
Touched by thy *Alchemist* doth since decline
From that her zenith, and foretells a red
And blushing evening when she goes to bed,
Yet such as shall outshine the glimmering light
With which all stars shall gild the following night.
Nor think it much, since all thy eaglets may
Endure the sunny trial, if we say
This hath the stronger wing, or that doth shine
Tricked up in fairer plumes; since all are thine.
Who hath his flock of cackling geese compared
With thy tuned choir of swans? Or else who dared
To call thy births deformed? But if thou bind
By City custom, or by gavelkind,
In equal shares thy love on all thy race,
We may distinguish of their sex, and place:
Though one hand form them, and though one brain strike
Souls into all, they are not all alike.
Why should the follies then of this dull age
Draw from thy pen such an immodest rage
As seems to blast thy (else-immortal) bays,
When thine own tongue proclaims thy itch of praise?
Such thirst will argue drouth. No, let be hurled
Upon thy works, by the detracting world,
What malice can suggest: let the rout say
The running sands, that (ere thou make a play)

419 City . . . gavelkind] i.e. customs whereby offspring shared an inheritance blast] wither drouth] aridity

Count the slow minutes, might a Goodwin frame,
To swallow, when thou hast done, thy shipwrecked name.
Let them the dear expense of oil upbraid,
Sucked by thy watchful lamp, that hath betrayed
To theft the blood of martyred authors, spilt
Into thy ink, whilst thou growest pale with guilt.
Repine not at the taper's thrifty waste,
That sleeks thy terser poems; nor is haste
Praise, but excuse; and if thou overcome
A knotty writer, bring the booty home,
Nor think it theft if the rich spoils so torn
From conquered authors be as trophies worn.
Let others glut on the extorted praise
Of vulgar breath; trust thou to after days:
Thy laboured works shall live, when time devours
The abortive offspring of their hasty hours.
Thou art not of their rank: the quarrel lies
Within thine own virge. Then let this suffice:
The wiser world doth greater thee confess
Than all men else, than thyself only less.

(1640)

420 *A Song*

Ask me no more where Jove bestows,
When June is past, the fading rose;
For in your beauty's orient deep
These flowers, as in their causes, sleep.

Ask me no more whither doth stray
The golden atoms of the day;
For in pure love heaven did prepare
Those powders to enrich your hair.

Ask me no more whither doth haste
The nightingale when May is past;
For in your sweet dividing throat
She winters and keeps warm her note.

Ask me no more where those stars light
That downwards fall in dead of night;
For in your eyes they sit, and there
Fixèd become, as in their sphere.

Goodwin] notoriously dangerous sands virge] neighbourhood of the king's court

420 Jove] Jupiter (ancient Roman supreme deity) orient deep] resplendent depth causes] i.e. formal causes dividing] fluently melodious Fixèd become] Become fixed stars (instead of meteorites) sphere] place of orbit

Ask me no more if east or west
The phoenix builds her spicy nest;
For unto you at last she flies,
And in your fragrant bosom dies.

(1640)

421

A Fancy

MARK how this polished eastern sheet
Doth with our northern tincture meet;
For though the paper seem to sink,
Yet it receives and bears the ink;
And on her smooth soft brow these spots
Seem rather ornaments than blots,
Like those you ladies use to place
Mysteriously about your face,
Not only to set off and break
Shadows and eye beams, but to speak
To the skilled lover, and relate
Unheard, his sad or happy fate.
Nor do their characters delight
As careless works of black and white;
But 'cause you underneath may find
A sense that can inform the mind,
Divine or moral rules impart,
Or raptures of poetic art:
So what at first was only fit
To fold up silks, may wrap up wit.

(1642)

JOHN CHALKHILL

c.. 1594–1642

422

Coridon's Song

OH, the sweet contentment
The countryman doth find!
    High trolollie lollie loe,
    High trolollie lee;
That quiet contemplation
Possesseth all my mind:
    Then care away,
    And wend along with me.

For courts are full of flattery,
As hath too oft been tried;
    High trolollie lollie loe,
    High trolollie lee;
The city full of wantonness,
And both are full of pride:
    Then care away,
    And wend along with me.

But oh, the honest countryman
Speaks truly from his heart,
    High trolollie lollie loe,
    High trolollie lee;
His pride is in his tillage,
His horses and his cart:
    Then care away,
    And wend along with me.

Our clothing is good sheepskins,
Grey russet for our wives,
    High trolollie lollie loe,
    High trolollie lee.
'Tis warmth and not gay clothing
That doth prolong our lives:
    Then care away,
    And wend along with me.

The ploughman, though he labour hard,
Yet on the holiday,
    High trolollie lollie loe,
    High trolollie lee,
No emperor so merrily
Does pass his time away:
    Then care away,
    And wend along with me.

To recompense our tillage
The heavens afford us showers;
    High trolollie lollie loe,
    High trolollie lee;
And for our sweet refreshments
The earth affords us bowers:
    Then care away,
    And wend along with me.

The cuckoo and the nightingale
Full merrily do sing,
    High trolollie lollie loe,
    High trolollie lee,
And with their pleasant roundelays,
Bid welcome to the spring:
    Then care away,
    And wend along with me.

This is not half the happiness
The countryman enjoys;
    High trolollie lollie loe,
    High trolollie lee.
Though others think they have as much,
Yet he that says so lies:
    Then come away, turn
    Countryman with me.

(1653)

ROBERT DAVENPORT

fl. 1624–1640

423

A Sacrifice

Hark!
Did you not hear the mournful cries
Of a new-slain sacrifice?
Would you know what felt the smart?
'Twas a broken, bleeding heart.
Burning, pure, celestial love
Was the high priest, and borne above
The sharp law that steers our life
Was the sacrifising knife.
The altar, built of precious stones,
Secret sighs, true tears, deep groans,
Grievous groans, fetched far and low,
Such as none but the saints know;
The fire, pure zeal, swift of wing,
Like that which ate up Israel's king.
Hail, holy flame! My heart refine;
Purge it from dross; make it divine;
Bathe it in that high-languaged blood
Which out-speaks Abel's; in that flood

Refine, reform it; fix it far
Above my sins, a shining star.
Take from it folly, give it fear:
Kill it here, and crown it there.

(1921)

JAMES SHIRLEY
1596–1666

424 *Cupid's Call*

Ho! Cupid calls; come lovers, come:
Bring his wanton harvest home.
The west wind blows, the birds do sing,
The Earth's enamelled, 'tis high spring:
  Let hinds whose soul is corn and hay
  Expect their crop another day.

Into love's spring garden walk:
Virgins dangle on their stalk,
Full blown, and playing at fifteen;
Come bring your amorous sickles then!
  See, they are pointing to their beds,
  And call to reap their maidenheads.

Hark, how in yonder shady grove
Sweet Philomel is warbling love,
And with her voice is courting kings;
For since she was a bird, she sings,
  There is no pleasure but in men:
  Oh come and ravish me again.

Virgins that are young and fair
May kiss, and grow into a pair;
Then warm and active use your blood:
No sad thought congeal the flood.
  Nature no medicine can impart
  When age once snows upon your heart.

(1646)

424 hinds] agricultural labourers   Philomel] the nightingale she was changed into after her rape (Greek mythology)   sad] serious

425 *Goodnight*

BID me no more goodnight; because
 'Tis dark, must I away?
Love doth acknowledge no such laws,
 And love 'tis I obey;
Which blind, doth all your light despise,
 And hath no need of eyes
  When day is fled.
 Besides, the sun, which you
 Complain is gone, 'tis true,
  Is gone to bed:
 Oh let us do so too.

(1646)

426 *A Lover that Durst Not Speak to His M*[*istress*]

I CAN no longer hold, my body grows
Too narrow for my soul; sick with repose,
My passions call to be abroad; and where
Should I discharge their weight, but in her ear,
From whose fair eyes the burning arrow came,
And made my heart the trophy to her flame.
 I dare not. How? Cupid is blind, we know;
I never heard that he was dumb till now:
Love, and not tell my mistress? How crept in
That subtle shaft? Is it to love a sin?
Is it ill to feed a longing in my blood?
And was it no fault in her to be so good?
I must not then be silent; yet forbear:
Convey thy passion rather in some tear,
Or let a sigh express how much thy bliss
Depends on her; or breathe it in a kiss,
And mingle souls: loud accents call the eyes
Of envy, and but waken jealousies.
Then silence be my language, which if she
But understand, and speak again to me,
We shall secure our fate, and prove at least
The miracles of love are not quite ceased.
Bar frowns from our discourse, and everywhere
A smile may be his own interpreter.
Thus we may read, in spite of standers by,
Whole volumes in the twinkling of an eye.

(1646)

426 How?] What's this?

427 *The Garden*

THIS garden does not take my eyes,
Though here you show how art of men
Can purchase nature at a price
Would stock old paradise again.

These glories while you dote upon,
I envy not your spring nor pride,
Nay boast the summer all your own,
My thoughts with less are satisfied.

Give me a little plot of ground,
Where might I with the sun agree,
Though every day he walk the round,
My garden he should seldom see.

Those tulips that such wealth display,
To court my eye, shall lose their name,
Though now they listen, as if they
Expected I should praise their flame.

But I would see myself appear
Within the violet's drooping head,
On which a melancholy tear
The discontented morn hath shed.

Within their buds let roses sleep,
And virgin lilies on their stem,
Till sighs from lovers glide and creep
Into their leaves to open them.

In the centre of my ground compose
Of bays and yew my summer room,
Which may, so oft as I repose,
Present my arbour, and my tomb.

No woman here shall find me out,
Or if a chance do bring one hither,
I'll be secure, for round about
I'll moat it with my eye's foul weather.

No bird shall live within my pale,
To charm me with their shames of art;
Unless some wandering nightingale
Come here to sing and break her heart.

Upon whose death I'll try to write
An epitaph in some funeral stone,
So sad, and true, it may invite
Myself to die, and prove mine own.

(1646)

CHRISTOPHER HARVEY
1597–1663

428

Church Festivals

MARROW of time; eternity in brief
Compendiums epitomized; the chief
Contents, the indices, the title-pages
Of all past, present, and succeeding ages;
Sublimate graces, antedated glories;
  The cream of holiness;
    The inventories
  Of future blessedness;
The florilegia of celestial stories;
Spirits of joys; the relishes and closes
Of angels' music; pearls dissolvèd; roses
Perfumèd; sugared honeycombs; delights
  Never too highly prized;
    The marriage rites
  Which, duly solemnized,
Usher espousèd souls to bridal nights;
Gilded sunbeams; refinèd elixirs
And quintessential extracts of stars—
Who loves not you, doth but in vain profess
That he loves God, or heaven, or happiness.

(1640)

LAURENCE PRICE?
fl. 1628–1680?

429 *The Maidens of London's Brave Adventures, Or, a Boon Voyage Intended for the Sea*

COME all you very merry London girls that are disposed to travel,
There is a voyage now at hand, will save your feet from gravel.
If you have shoes, you need not fear for wearing out the leather;
For why, you shall on shipboard go, like loving rogues together.
Some are already gone before, the rest must after follow;
Then come away, and do not stay, your guide shall be Apollo.

Peg, Nell, and Sisse, Kate, Doll, and Besse, Sue, Rachel, and sweet Sara,
Joan, Prudence, and Grace have took their place, with Debora, Jane and Mary,
Fair Winifright, and Bridget bright, sweet Rose and pretty Nanny,
With Ursely neat, and Alice complete, that had the love of many.
All these brave girls, and others more, conducted by Apollo,
Have taken their leaves, and are gone before, and their loves will after follow.

Then why should those that are behind slink back, and dare not venture?
For you shall prove the seamen kind, if once the ships you enter.
You shall be fed with good strong fare, according to the season:
Biscuit, salt beef, and English beer, and pork well boiled with peason.
And since that some are gone before, the rest with joy may follow,
To bear each other company, conducted by Apollo.

When you come to the appointed place, your minds you need not trouble,
For every groat that you got here, you shall have three time double.
For there are gold and silver mines, and treasures much abounding,
As plenty as Newcastle coals, at some parts may be founding.
Then come away, make no delay, all you that mean to follow;
The ships are ready bound to go, conducted by Apollo.

(*c.* 1656)

peason] peas

HENRY REYNOLDS
fl. 1628

430 *The Black Maid to the Fair Boy*

FAIR boy, alas, why fliest thou me,
That languish in such flames for thee?
I'm black, 'tis true; why, so is night,
And lovers in dark shades delight.
The whole world, do but close your eye,
Will be to you as black as I;
Or ope it and view how dark a shade
Is by your own fair body made,
Which follows thee where'er thou go
(Oh who, allowed, would not do so).
Then let me ever live so nigh,
And thou shalt need no shade but I.

(1656)

WILLIAM STRODE
1600–1643

431 *Opposite to Melancholy*

RETURN, my joys, and hither bring
A tongue not made to speak but sing,
A jolly spleen, an inward feast,
A causeless laugh without a jest,
A face which gladness doth anoint,
An arm that springs out of his joint,
A spriteful gait that leaves no print,
And makes a feather of a flint,
A heart that's lighter than the air,
An eye still dancing in his sphere,
Strong mirth which nothing can control,
A body nimbler than the soul,

Black] Dark

431 spriteful] lively still] ever control] overwhelm

Free wandering thoughts not tied to muse
Which think on all things, nothing choose,
Which ere we see them come are gone:
These life itself doth feed upon.

(1658)

432 *On Westwell Downs*

When Westwell Downs I gan to tread,
Where cleanly winds the green did sweep,
Methought a landscape there was spread,
Here a bush and there a sheep:
The pleated wrinkles of the face
Of wave-swollen earth did lend such grace,
As shadowings in imagery
Which both deceive and please the eye.

The sheep sometimes did tread the maze
By often winding in and in,
And sometimes round about they trace
Which milkmaids call a fairy ring:
Such semicircles have they run,
Such lines across so trimly spun,
That shepherds learn whene'er they please
A new geometry with ease.

The slender food upon the down
Is always even, always bare;
Which neither spring nor winter's frown
Can ought improve or ought impair:
Such is the barren eunuch's chin,
Which thus doth evermore begin
With tender down to be o'ercast
Which never comes to hair at last.

Here and there two hilly crests
Amidst them hug a pleasant green,
And these are like two swelling breasts
That close a tender fall between.
Here would I sleep, or read, or pray
From early morn till flight of day;
But hark! A sheep-bell calls me up,
Like Oxford college bells, to sup.

(1907)

431 muse] an abstract subject of meditation

433 *On Fairford Windows*

I KNOW no paint of poetry
Can mend such coloured imagery
In sullen ink; yet, Fairford, I
May relish thy fair memory.
  Such is the echo's fainter sound,
Such is the light when sun is drowned;
So did the fancy look upon
The work before it was begun:
Yet when those shows are out of sight
My weaker colours may delight.
  Those images so faithfully
Report true feature to the eye
As you may think each picture was
Some visage in a looking-glass:
Not a glass-window face, unless
Such as Cheapside hath, where a press
Of painted gallants looking out
Bedeck the casement round about.
But these have holy physnomy:
Each pane instructs the laity
With silent eloquence; for here
Devotion leads the eye, not ear,
To note the catechizing paint,
Whose easy phrase doth so acquaint
Our sense with gospel that the creed
In such a hand the weak may read:
Such types even yet of virtue be,
And Christ, as in a glass, we see.
  Behold two turtles in one cage,
With such a lovely equipage
As they who knew them long may doubt
Some young ones have been stolen out.
  When with a fishing rod the clerk
Saint Peter's draught of fish doth mark,
Such is the scale, the eye, the fin,
You'd think they strive and leap within,
But if the net which holds them break,
He with his angle some would take.
  But would you walk a turn in Paul's?
Look up: one little pane enrolls

mend] improve upon sullen] dull physnomy] physiognomy types] figures of New Testament events turtles] turtledoves clerk] cleric; scholar enrolls] incorporates

A fairer temple; fling a stone,
The church is out of the windows thrown.
  Consider, but not ask your eyes,
And ghosts at midday seem to rise:
The saints there, striving to descend,
Are past the glass, and downward bend.
  'Look there! The devil!' all would cry,
Did they not see that Christ was by.
See where he suffers for thee: see
His body taken from the tree:
Had ever death such life before?
The limber corpse, besullied o'er
With meagre paleness, doth display
A middle state twixt flesh and clay;
His arms and legs, his head and crown,
Like a true lambskin dangling down:
Who can forbear, the grave being nigh,
To bring fresh ointment in his eye?
  The wondrous art hath equal fate,
Unfenced and yet inviolate:
The Puritans were sure deceived,
And thought those shadows moved and heaved,
So held from stoning Christ; the wind
And boistrous tempests were so kind
As on his image not to prey,
Whom both the winds and seas obey.
  At Momus' wish be not amazed;
For if each Christian heart were glazed
With such a window, then each breast
Might be his own evangelist.

(1656)

434 *On a Gentlewoman that Sung and Played upon a Lute*

BE silent, you still music of the spheres,
And every sense make haste to be all ears,
And give devout attention to her airs,
To which the gods do listen as to prayers
Of pious votaries; the which to hear
Tumult would be attentive, and would swear

433 equal] just heaved] breathed Momus'] (god of censure) (Greek mythology)

To keep less noise at Nile, if there she sing,
Or with a happy touch grace but the string.
Among so many auditors, so many throngs
Of gods and men that press to hear her songs,
Oh let me have an unespièd room,
And die with such an anthem o'er my tomb.

(1655)

435 *On a Gentlewoman Walking in the Snow*

I SAW fair Cloris walk alone
Where feathered rain came softly down,
And Jove descended from his tower
To court her in a silver shower:
The wanton snow flew to her breast
Like little birds into their nest,
And overcome with whiteness there
For grief it thawed into a tear;
Thence falling on her garment's hem
For grief it freezed into a gem.

(1656)

from *Posies* (436–438)

436 *Bracelets*

THIS keeps my hands
From Cupid's bands.

(1655)

437 *An Ear-string*

HERE silken twines, there locks you see—
Now tell me which the softer be?

(1655)

438 *A Girdle*

WHENE'ER the waist makes too much haste,
That haste again makes too much waste.

(1655)

436 bands] bonds

439 *Sonnet*

My love and I for kisses played:
She would keep stake, I was content;
But when I won she would be paid:
This made me ask her what she meant.
'Pray, since I see', quoth she, 'your wrangling vein,
Take your own kisses, give me mine again.'

(1672)

440 *A Riddle: On a Kiss*

What thing is that, nor felt nor seen
Till it be given? A present for a queen;
A fine conceit to give and take the like.
The giver yet is further for to seek;
The taker doth possess nothing the more;
The giver he hath nothing less in store;
And given once that nature hath it still,
You cannot keep or leave it if you will.
The workmanship is counted very small,
The labour is esteemèd not at all;
But, to conclude, this gift is such indeed
That if some see it 'twill make their hearts to bleed.

(1907)

441 *Justification*

See how the rainbow in the sky
Seems gaudy through the sun's bright eye,
Hark how an echo answer makes,
Feel how a board is smoothed with wax,
Smell how a glove puts on perfúme,
Taste how their sweetness pills assume:
So, by imputed justice, clay
Seems fair, well spoke, smooth, sweet, each way.
  The eye doth gaze on robes appearing,
  The prompted echo takes our hearing,
  The board our touch, the scent our smell,
  The pill our taste: man, God as well.

(1907)

440 nor . . . nor] neither . . . nor   conceit] idea; device

442 *On the Death of Mistress Mary Prideaux*

WEEP not because this child hath died so young,
But weep because yourselves have lived so long:
Age is not filled by growth of time; for then
What old man lives to see the estate of men?
Who sees the age of grand Methusalem?
Ten years make us as old as hundreds him.
Ripeness is from ourselves; and then we die,
When nature hath obtained maturity.
Summer and winter fruits there be, and all
Not at one time, but being ripe, must fall.
Death did not err: your mourners are beguiled;
She died more like a mother than a child.
Weigh the composure of her pretty parts:
Her gravity in childhood; all her arts
Of womanly behaviour. Weigh her tongue
So wisely measured, not too short nor long;
And to her youth add some few riches more:
She took up now what due was at threescore.
She lived seven years, our age's first degree;
Journeys at first time ended happy be.
Yet, take her stature with the age of man,
They well are fitted: both are but a span.

(1907)

443 *On a Good Leg and Foot*

IF Hercules' tall stature might be guessed
But by his thumb, whereby to make the rest
In due proportion, the best rule that I
Would choose to measure Venus' beauty by
Should be her leg and foot. If husbandmen
Measure their timber by the foot, why then
Not we our wives? Whether we go or stride,
Those native compasses are seldom wide
Of telling true: the round and slender foot
Is a sure index, and a secret note
Of hidden parts; and well this way may lead
Unto the closet of a maidenhead.

Methusalem] (Gen. 5: 27) parts] qualities degree] stage

443 note] token

Here, emblems of our youth, we roses tie,
And here the garter, love's dear mystery;
For want of beauty here the peacock's pride
Lets fall her train, and fearing to be spied
Shuts up her painted witnesses to let
Those eyes from view which are but counterfeit.
Who looks not if this part be good or evil
May meet with cloven feet, and match the devil,
For this doth make the difference between
The more unhallowed creatures and the clean;
Well may you judge her other steps are light,
Her thoughts awry that doth not tread aright.
But then there's true perfection, when we see
Those parts more absolute that hidden be:
Nature ne'er laid a fair foundation
For an unworthy frame to rest upon.
Let others view the top and limbs throughout,
The deeper knowledge is to know the root;
And reading of the face, the weakest know
What beauty is: the learnèd look below,
Who, looking there, do all the rest descry,
As in a pool the moon we use to spy.
  Pardon, sweetheart, the pride of my desire,
  If but to kiss your toe it should aspire.

(1658)

444 *Epitaph on the Monument of Sir William Strode*

TREAD soft, for if you wake this knight alone,
You raise an host: religion's champion,
His country's staff, right's bold distributor,
His neighbour's guard, the poor man's almoner;
  Who dies with works about him, as did he,
  Shall rise attended thus triumphantly.

(1907)

443 let] hinder   match] marry

SIR R. HATTON?

fl. 1631?

445 [*Epithalamium*]

HYMEN hath together tied
The lusty bridegroom and the willing bride,
And unto the gods they pray
To banish hence the long and tedious day.
Sing we then and so invite
The lover's friend, the still and shady night,
While we touch the trembling strings,
To add more feathers to her sable wings.
Haste then, gentle night, for we
Know thou hast rites as well as he.

(1631)

RALPH KNEVET

1601–1671 or 1672

446 *The Habitation*

MAN is no microcosm, and they detract
From his dimensions who apply
This narrow term to his immensity.
Heaven, Earth, and hell in him are packed:
He's a miscellany of goods and evils,
A temper mixed with angels, beasts, and devils.

Yea, the immortal Deity doth deign
To inhabit in a carnal cell:
So precious gems in the dark centre dwell,
So gloomy mines fine gold retain;
But by vicissitudes these essences
The various heart of man wont to possess.

For God no inn-mate will with Satan be:
Angels will not consort with beasts.
If man would pursue his best interests,
What blessed seasons might he see?
But he invites the devil and the beast,
Nor God nor angels will he lodge or feast.

(1936)

447 *The Navigation*

THE modest sinner stood behind,
Who whilome wont with amorous belgards
To captivate each wanton mind;
But now in humble sort she earth regards,
Not daring to lift up her eye,
'Cause she had sinned against heaven high.

Her penitential tears did flow:
Into the deeps of true repentance she
Did launch, while dreary sighs did blow
To drive her bark upon the silver lee;
She doubled the Cape of Good Hope,
And mercy kenned from the maintop.

Then to the God of sea and land,
Who had preserved her from a dismal wrack,
She paid her vows, and with her hand
The precious box of fragrant spikenard brake,
And with this unguent did besmear
The temples of her saviour dear.

(1954)

448 *The Vote*

THE helmet now an hive for bees becomes,
And hilts of swords may serve for spiders' looms;
Sharp pikes may make
Teeth for a rake;
And the keen blade, the arch-enemy of life,
Shall be degraded to a pruning knife;
The rustic spade,
Which first was made
For honest agriculture, shall retake
Its primitive employment, and forsake
The rampires steep
And trenches deep.
Tame conies in our brazen guns shall breed,
Or gentle doves their young ones there shall feed;

Navigation] Voyage whilome wont] formerly was used (Spenserian archaisms) belgards] love glances lee] calm kenned] sighted dismal] fatal

448 *Vote*] Prayer; petition; wish rampires] ramparts

In musket barrels
Mice shall raise quarrels
For their quarters; the ventriloquious drum,
Like lawyers in vacations, shall be dumb;
Now all recruits
(But those of fruits)
Shall be forgot; and th'unarmed soldier
Shall only boast of what he did whilere,
In chimneys' ends,
Among his friends.
If good effects shall happy signs ensue,
I shall rejoice, and my prediction's true.

(1936)

MILDMAY FANE, EARL OF WESTMORLAND
1602–1666

449 *My Country Audit*

BLEST privacy, happy retreat, wherein
I may cast up my reck'nings, audit sin,
Count o'er my debts, and how arrears increase
In nature's book, towards the God of peace:
What through perverseness hath been waived, or done
To my first covenant's contradictïon:
How many promised resolutions broke
Of keeping touch (almost as soon as spoke).
Thus, like that tenant who behind-hand cast
Entreats so oft forbearance, till at last
The sum surmounts his hopes, and then no more
Expects, but mercy to strike off the score,
So here, methinks, I see the landlord's grace
Full of compassion to my drooping case,
Bidding me be of comfort and not grieved:
My rent his son should pay if I believed.

(1648)

recruits] renewals of supplies whilere] erewhile (archaism)

449 broke] broken Expects] Looks forward to case] body instance

450 *A Reveille Matin, or Good Morrow to a Friend*

As the black curtain of the night
Is open drawn
By the grey-fingered dawn,
To let out light
And bid good morrow to the teeming day:
So let all darkened thoughts through sin
Call in
Their powers, that led them in a blindfold way;
And roused up from security,
Bring better fruits unto maturity.

For now the fragrant east,
The spicery o' th' world,
Hath hurled
A rosy tincture o'er the phoenix nest;
And from the last day's urn
Another springs,
And brings
With it a chareter too in its turn.
So then by this new fire
Be goodness hatched, all wickedness expire.

Then as this prince of heat doth rise,
In power and in might seem stronger,
Proclaiming that 'tis night no longer;
By vanquishing the witchcrafts of the skies,
The spelly-vap'rous mists:
So let th' enlightened soul
Control
Our actions, that no further they persist
To follow sense, whereby to invite
Ruin, the sauce t' unruly appetite.

Thus now it's clear,
Out of all question,
The world's unmasked, and all of veiling gone.
Phoebus triumphant o'er our hemisphere:
Let us not therefore in disguise
Seek, or bravado,
To shadow as if under maskerado
So many faults and villanies,

chareter] charioteer　　maskerado] masquerade

Knowing that he who made the light
Cannot himself be destitute of sight.

But though his providence
Did this beget,
That suns that rise should set,
And in appearance vanish hence;
Yet doth he claim for th' interest
Of daylight's bliss,
We slumber not amiss;
Whenas our light is borrowed by the west;
But the choice cabinet of mind adorn
With contemplations may befit next morn.

(1648)

451 *Shamed by the Creature*

THE thankful soil manured and winter dressed
Returns the hind an autumn interest
For all his care and labour; nor denies
To be unclothed, to deck his granaries:
So doth the youthful vine those prunings own,
Whenas her blossoms are to clusters grown;
Nor, to show thanks, doth spare her blood to spill,
That so the planter's vessels she may fill.

This vegetable lecture may indeed
Cast a blush o'er me, whose return for seed
So far falls short, as not for everyone
To bring an ear; but for a whole season none,
No, not that corn again was left in trust
And harrowed up under my barren dust;

But pregnant nature doth so rule and reign
That with wild oats she chokes the better grain,
And where my grateful heart should dye my press
It's all besmearèd with unthankfulness.

Nor can a thought, a word, or act proceed
Out of my clay, that turns not straight to weed;

Whenas] Seeing that   cabinet] i.e. collector's cabinet

451 Whenas] When; Seeing that   again was] again which was

And for my fruits, ere ripeness is begun,
Abortive-like, they wither in the sun
Of self-conceit. Lord, prune once more this vine,
And plough this ground, lest the fig-tree's doom be mine.

(1648)

452 *Occasioned by Seeing a Walk of Bay Trees*

No thunder blasts Jove's plant, nor can
Misfortune warp an honest man;
Shaken he may be, by some one
Or other gust, unleaved by none:
Though tribulation's sharp and keen,
His resolutïons keep green;
And whilst integrity's his wall,
His year's all spring, and hath no fall.

(1648)

453 *In Praise of Fidelia*

Get thee a ship well rigged and tight,
With ordnance store, and manned for fight;
Snug in her timber's mould for th' seas,
Yet large in hold for merchandise:
Spread forth her cloth, and anchors weigh,
And let her on the curled waves play,
Till fortune-towed, she chance to meet
Th' Hesperian home-bound western fleet;
Then let her board 'em, and for price
Take gold ore, sugar canes, and spice.
  Yet when all these sh' hath brought ashore,
  In my Fidelia I'll find more.

(1648)

fig-tree's doom] Luke 13: 7 (F.)

452 *Bay*] Laurel (sacred to Jupiter)   Jove's] Jupiter's

453 store] plenty   Hesperian] western; from the Hesperides   price] trophy

454 *How to Ride Out a Storm*

HE only happy is, and wise,
Can con his barque when tempests rise,
Know how to lay the helm and steer,
Lie on a tack, port, and laveer
Sometimes to weather, then to lee,
As waves give way and winds agree;
Nor boom at all in such a stress,
But by degrees loom less and less;
Ride out a storm with no more loss
Than the endurance of a toss;
For though he cannot well bear sail
In such a fresh and powerful gale,
Yet when there is no other shift,
Thinks 't not amiss to ride adrift;
To shut down ports, and tiers to hale in,
To seal the hatch up with tarpaulin;
To ply the pump, and no means slack,
May clear her bilge, and keep from wrack;
To take in cloth, and in a word,
Unlade, and cut the mast by board:
So spoon before the wind and seas,
Where though she'll roll, she'll go at ease;
And not so strained, as if laid under
The wave that threatens sudden founder;
And whilst the fury and the rage
Leaves little hope for anchorage,
Yet if she can but make a coast
In any time, she'll not be lost,
But in affection's bay will find
A harbour suited to her mind:
Where casting out at first the kedge,
Which gives her ground and privilege
Of stop, she secondly lets fall
That anchor from the stream men call;
The others all a cock-bell set,
One after other down are let
Into the sea, till at the last
She's come to moorage, and there fast,
In hopes to be new sheathed 's inclined

con] direct the steering of   port] port the helm   laveer] tack   boom] make all sail   loom] move up and down   tiers] cannons   wrack] wreck   spoon] run before the wind   anchor . . . call] i.e. stream-anchor (for mooring)   cock-bell] cock-bill; anchor suspended ready for letting go

To lie aside until carined,
That when she shall be paid again,
So graved, she may endure the main.
Thus when his vessel hath outgone
This and that rugged motïon,
His pole star's fixed, and guides him there
Where Charles is not in wain but sphere;
Then he'll another voyage try,
Laden with faith and loyalty,
Which he no sooner parts with, than
Dry ground becomes an ocean.

(1648)

455 *A Happy Life* (Martial X. xlvii)

THAT which creates a happy life
Is substance left, not gained by strife;
A fertile and a thankful mould,
A chimney always free from cold;
Never to be the client, nor
But seldom times the counsellor.
A mind content with what is fit,
Whose strength doth most consist in wit;
A body nothing prone to be
Sick, a prudent simplicity;
Such friends as of one's own rank are;
Homely fare, not sought from far;
The table without art's help spread;
A night in wine not burièd,
Yet drowning cares; a bed that's blest
With true joy, chastity, and rest;
Such short sweet slumber as may give
Less time to die in 't, more to live:
  Thine own estate whate'er commend,
  And wish not for, nor fear, thine end.

(1648)

carined] careened graved] cleaned Charles] Charles I (playing on Charles's Wain, Ursa Major)

455 mould] soil

456 In Obitum Ben Johnson Poetae Eximii

HE who began from brick and lime
The Muses' hill to climb,
And whilom busièd in laying stone
Thirsted to drink of Helicon,
Changing his trowel for a pen,
Wrote straight the temper not of dirt but men,

Now, sithence that he is turned to clay and gone,
Let those remain of th' occupatïon
He honoured once, square him a tomb may say
His craft exceeded far a dauber's way;
Then write upon 't: *He could no longer tarry,*
But was returned again unto the quarry.

(1648)

457 *To Retiredness*

NEXT unto God, to whom I owe
Whate'er I here enjoy below,
I must indebted stand to thee,
Great patron of my liberty;
For in the cluster of affairs,
Whence there are dealing several shares,
As in a trick thou hast conveyed
Into my hand what can be said;
Whilst he who doth himself possess
Makes all things pass him seem far less.

Riches and honours that appear
Rewards to the adventurer,
On either tide of Court or seas,
Are not attained nor held with ease;
But as unconstancy bears sway,
Quickly will fleet and ebb away;
And oft when fortune those confers,
She gives them but for torturers;
When with a mind ambition-free,
These, and much more, come home to me.

In . . . Eximii] On the death of the distinguished poet Ben Jonson began . . . lime] started as a bricklayer whilom] while (archaism) Helicon] haunt of the Muses temper] (1) mortar; (2) temperament sithence] since (archaism) remain] remainder dauber's] (1) unskilful artist's; (2) plasterer's

457 fleet] drift; float

Here I can sit, and sitting under
Some portions of his works of wonder,
Whose all are such, observe by reason
Why every plant obeys its season;
How the sap rises, and the fall,
Wherein they shake off leaves and all;
Then how again they bud and spring,
Are laden for an offering;
Which whilst my contemplation sees,
I am taught thankfulness from trees.

Then turning over nature's leaf
I mark the glory of the sheaf:
For every field's a several page,
Deciphering the Golden Age;
So that without a miner's pains,
Or Indie's reach, here plenty reigns;
Which, watered from above, implies
That our acknowledgements should rise
To him, that thus creates a birth
Of mercies for us out of earth.

Here is no other case in law
But what the sunburnt hat of straw
With crookèd sickle reaps and binds
Up into sheaves to help the hinds;
Whose arguing alone's in this,
Which cop lies well, and which amiss,
How the hock-cart with all its gear
Should be tricked up, and what good cheer
Bacon with Cook's reports express,
And how to make the tenth go less.

There, are no other wars or strifes—
Encouragers, shrill trumpets, fifes,
Or horrid drums—but what excels
All music, nature's minstrels
Piping and chirping: as they sit
Embowered in branches, dance to it;
And if at all those do contest,
It is in this, but which sings best;
And when they have contended long,
I, though unseen, must judge the song.

Deciphering] Portraying; revealing hinds] farm labourers cop] heap of unbound hay or corn hock-cart] cart carrying last load of harvest tenth] tithe

Thus, out of fears, or noise of war,
Crowds, and the clamourings at bar,
The merchant's dread, th' unconstant tides,
With all vexatïons besides,
I hug my quiet, and alone
Take thee for my companion,
And deem, in doing so, I've all
I can true conversation call;
For so my thoughts by this retreat
Grow stronger, like contracted heat.

Whether on nature's book I muse,
Or else some other writes on 't, use
To spend the time in, every line
Is not eccentric but divine;
And though all others downward tend,
These look to heaven, and ascend
From whence they came; where pointed high
They ravish into mystery,
To see the footsteps here are trod
Of mercy by a gracious God.

(1648)

OWEN FELTHAM

1602?–1668

458 *On the Duke of Buckingham Slain by Felton, the 23 Aug. 1628*

SOONER I may some fixèd statue be,
Than prove forgetful of thy death or thee!
Canst thou be gone so quickly? Can a knife
Let out so many titles and a life?
  Now I'll mourn thee! Oh that so huge a pile
Of state should pash thus in so small a while!
Let the rude genius of the giddy train
Brag in a fury that they have stabbed Spain,
Austria, and the skipping French: yea, all
Those home-bred papists that would sell our fall:

other writes] another who writes To . . . trod] 'Nunquam minus solus' (F.) ('Never less alone': Cicero, *De Officiis*, 3. 1. 1)

458 state] dignity pash] smash giddy] inconstant train] set (poetic)

The eclipse of two wise princes' judgments: more,
The waste, whereby our land was still kept poor.
I'll pity yet at least thy fatal end,
Shot like a lightning from a violent hand,
Taking thee hence unsummed. Thou art to me
The great example of mortality.
And when the times to come shall want a name
To startle greatness, here is BUCKINGHAM.
Fallen like a meteor; and 'tis hard to say
Whether it was that went the stranger way,
Thou or the hand that slew thee: thy estate
Was high, and he was resolute above that.
Yet since I hold of none engaged to thee,
Death and that liberty shall make me free.
Thy mists I knew not; if thou hast a fault,
My charity shall leave it in the vault,
There for thine own accounting: 'tis undue
To speak ill of the dead, though it be true.
And this even those that envied thee confess,
Thou hadst a mind, a flowing nobleness,
A fortune, friends, and such proportïon
As call for sorrow, to be thus undone.
  Yet should I speak the vulgar, I should boast
Thy bold assassinate, and wish almost
He were no Christian, that I up might stand,
To praise the intent of his misguided hand.
And sure, when all the patriots in the shade
Shall rank, and their full musters there be made,
He shall sit next to Brutus, and receive
Such bays as heath'nish ignorance can give.
But then the Christian (poising that) shall say,
Though he did good, he did it the wrong way.
They oft decline into the worst of ill,
That act the people's wish without law's will.

(1661)

unsummed] not having reached his full length (falconry) Whether] Which estate] rank mists] doubts undue] inappropriate assassinate] assassin shade] next life Brutus] Julius Caesar's assassin bays] laurels poising] weighing

459 *The Ensuing Copy the Late Printer Hath Been Pleased to Honour, by Mistaking It Among Those of the Most Ingenious and Too Early Lost Sir John Suckling*

WHEN, dearest, I but think on thee,
Methinks all things that lovely be
  Are present, and my soul delighted;
For beauties that from worth arise
Are like the grace of deities,
  Still present with us, though unsighted.

Thus while I sit and sigh the day
With all his spreading lights away,
  Till night's black wings do overtake me;
Thinking on thee, thy beauties then,
As sudden lights do sleeping men,
  So they by their bright rays awake me.

Thus absence dies, and dying proves
No absence can consist with loves
  That do partake of fair perfection;
Since in the darkest night they may
By their quick motion find a way
  To see each other by reflection.

The waving sea can with such flood
Bathe some high palace that hath stood
  Far from the main up in the river:
Oh think not then but love can do
As much, for that's an ocean too,
  That flows not every day, but ever.

(1661)

460 *On a Hopeful Youth*

STAY, passenger, and lend a tear:
Youth and virtue both lie here.
Reading this, know thou hast seen
Virtue tombed at but fifteen.

unsighted] unseen   quick motion] lively inclination, desire
460 passenger] passer-by

And if after thou shalt see
Any young and good as he,
Think his virtues are reviving
For examples of thy living.
Practise those and then thou mayst
Fearless die where now thou stayst.

(1661)

461 *To Phryne*

When thou thy youth shalt view
  Fumed out, and hate thy glass for telling true;
When thy face shall be seen
  Like to an Easter apple gathered green;
When thy whole body shall
  Be one foul wrinkle, lame and shrivelled all
So deep that men therein
  May find a grave to bury shame and sin;
When no clasped youth shall be
  Pouring his bones into thy lap and thee;
When thy own wanton fires
  Shall leave to bubble up thy loose desires:
Then wilt thou sighing lie,
  Repent and smart, and so by two deaths die.

(1661)

462 *Upon a Rare Voice*

When I but hear her sing, I fare
Like one that, raised, holds his ear
To some bright star in the supremest round,
Through which, besides the light that's seen,
There may be heard from heaven within
The rests of anthems that the angels sound.

(1661)

461 *Phryne*] ancient Athenian prostitute

462 round] sphere

THOMAS NABBES

fl. 1632–1640

463

Song

WHAT a dainty life the milkmaid leads!
When over the flowery meads
She dabbles in the dew,
And sings to her cow;
And feels not the pain
Of love or disdain:
She sleeps in the night, though she toils in the day,
And merrily passeth her time away.

(1638; a. 1633 or 1634)

464

The Song

BEAUTY no more the subject be
Of wanton art to flatter thee,
Or in dull figures call thee spring,
Lily, or rose, or other thing:
All which beneath thee are, and grow
Into contempt when thou dost show
The unmatched glory of thy brow.

Chorus

Behold a sphere of virgins move,
None mongst them less than queen of love;
And yet their queen so far excels,
Beauty and she are only parallels.

(1637; a. 1635)

MARTIN PARKER

fl. 1632–1656

465

Upon Defacing of Whitehall

WHAT Booker can prognosticate,
Concerning king's or kingdom's fate?
I think myself to be as wise
As he that gazeth on the skies:
  My skill goes beyond the depths of a pond,
    Or rivers in the greatest rain;
  Whereby I can tell all things will be well,
    When the King enjoys his own again.

There's neither Swallow, Dove, nor Dade
Can soar more high or deeper wade,
Nor show a reason from the stars
Which causeth peace, or civil wars:
  The man in the moon may wear out his shoon
    By running after Charles's Wain,
  But all's to no end; for the times will not mend
    Till the King enjoys his own again.

Though for a time we see Whitehall
With cobwebs hanging on the wall,
Instead of silk and silver brave,
Which formerly it used to have,
  With rich perfúme in every room,
    Delightful to that princely train:
  Which again you shall see, when the time it shall be,
    That the King enjoys his own again.

Full forty years the royal crown
Hath been his father's and his own;
And is there anyone but he
That in the same should sharer be?
  For who better may the sceptre sway
    Than he that hath such right to reign?
  Then let's hope for a peace, for the wars will not cease,
    Till the King enjoys his own again.

Booker] John Booker, an almanac-maker   Swallow, Dove, Dade] almanac-makers
Dade] waterbird

Till then, upon Ararat's hill
My hope shall cast her anchor still,
Until I see some peaceful dove
Bring home the branch she dearly love;
Then will I wait till the waters abate,
Which now disturb my troubled brain:
Else never rejoice till I hear the voice
That the King enjoys his own again.

(1644–6)

JOHN TATHAM
fl. 1632–1664

466 *Ostella forth of Town: To My Heart*

HEART be content, though she be gone;
Let reason govern thee:
Thou hast so much of pleasure known,
'Tis fit a seasoned misery
Should temper thy prosperity.

Absence doth whet the appetite
Which presence dulled before;
There is no pleasure truly great,
Nor sweet of such effectual power,
Till seasoned with a little sour.

He cannot truly prize delight
That ne'er knew misery,
Nor deem the glory of the light
Until by wanting it, he be
Sensible of its purity.

Think this the time of thy lost health,
Which, when restored to thee,
Even from the ruin of thy wealth
It brings a perfect remedy,
To double thy felicity.

(1650)

465 Ararat's hill] (where the Ark beached) voice] words

ROGER WILLIAMS
c.1603–1683

467 [*The Courteous Indian*]

THE courteous pagan shall condemn
  Uncourteous Englishmen
Who live like foxes, bears, and wolves,
  Or lion in his den.

Let none sing blessings to their souls,
  For that they courteous are:
The wild barbarians with no more
  Than nature, go so far.

If nature's sons both wild and tame
  Humane and courteous be,
How ill becomes it sons of God
  To want humanity?

(1643)

EDWARD BENLOWES
1603?–1676

from *Theophila*

468 [*The Pleasures of Retirement*]

WHEN lavish Phoebus pours out melted gold,
And Zephyr's breath does spice unfold,
And we the blue-eyed sky in tissue vest behold,

Then view the mower, who with big-swollen veins
Wieldeth the crookèd scythe, and strains
To barb the flowery tresses of the verdant plains.

Then view we valleys by whose fringèd seams
A brook of liquid silver streams,
Whose water crystal seems, sand gold, and pebbles gems;

Zephyr] the west wind   tissue vest] gauzy clothing   barb] mow; shave

Where bright-scaled gliding fish on trembling line
We strike, when they our hook entwine;
Thence do we make a visit to a grave divine.

With harmless shepherds we sometimes do stay,
Whose plainness does outvie the gay,
While nibbling ewes do bleat and frisking lambs do stray.

With them we strive to recollect and find
Dispersed flocks of our rambling mind;
Internal vigils are to that due work designed.

No puffing hopes, no shrinking fears them fright;
No begging wants on them do light;
They wed content, while sloth feels want and bravery spite.

While swains the burth'ning fleeces shear away,
Oat pipes to pastoral sonnets play,
And all the merry hamlet bells chime holy day.

In neighbouring meads, with ermine mantles proud,
Our eyes and ears discern a crowd
Of wide-horned oxen, trampling grass with lowings loud.

Next close feeds many a strutting-uddered cow;
Hard by, tired cattle draw the plough,
Whose gallèd necks with toil and languishment do bow.

Near which, in restless stalks, waved grain promotes
The skipping grasshopper's hoarse notes;
While round the airy choristers distend their throats.

Dry seas, with golden surges, ebb and flow;
The ripening ears smile as we go,
With boasts to crack the barn, so numberless they show.

When Sol to Virgo progress takes, and fields
With his prolongèd lustre gilds;
When Sirius chinks the ground, the swain his hope then builds.

Soon as the sultry month has mellowed corn,
Gnats shake their spears, and wind their horn;
The hinds do sweat through both their skins, and shopsters scorn.

puffing] inflating; exalting close] field progress] state journey chinks] cracks hinds] farm labourers

Their orchards with ripe fruit impregnèd be,
Fruit that from taste of death is free,
And such as gives delight with choice variety.

Yet who in 's thriving mind improves his state,
And virtue steward makes, his fate
Transcends; he's rich at an inestimable rate.

* * * * *

But hark! 'tis late; the whistlers knock from plough;
The droiling swineherd's drum beats now;
Maids have their curtsies made to th' spongy-teated cow.

Larks roosted are, the folded flocks are pent
In hurdled grates, the tired ox sent
In loose trace home, now Hesper lights his torch in 's tent.

See glimmering light, the Pharos of our cot;
By innocence protected, not
By guards, we thither tend, where evensong's not forgot.

O prayer! thou anchor through the worldly sea!
Thou sovereign rhet'ric, 'bove the plea
Of flesh! that feedst the fainting soul, thou'rt heaven's key.

Blest season, when day's eye is closed, to win
Our heart to clear th' account—when sin
Has passed the audit, ravishments of soul begin.

(1652)

JOSEPH RUTTER
fl. 1635

469 [*Epithalamium*]

HYMEN, god of marriage bed,
Be thou ever honourèd:
Thou, whose torch's purer light
Death's sad tapers did affright,

468 impregnèd] impregnated droiling] drudging grates] cages Hesper] Evening Pharos] lighthouse

And instead of funeral fires
Kindled lovers' chaste desires:
  May their love
  Ever prove
True and constant; let not age
Know their youthful heat to assuage.

Maids, prepare the genial bed:
Then come, night, and hide that red
Which her cheeks, his heart, does burn,
Till the envious day return,
And the lusty bridegroom say,
'I have chased her fears away,
  And instead
  Of virginhead,
Given her a greater good,
Perfectïon and womanhood.'

(1651)

SIR THOMAS BROWNE?
1605–1682

470 [*Signs of Spring*]

THE almond flourisheth, the birch trees flow,
The sad mezereon cheerfully doth blow.
The flowery sons before their fathers seen,
The snails begin to crop the mandrake green.
The vernal sun with crocus gardens fills,
With hyacinths, anemones and daffodils:
The hazel catskins now dilate and fall,
And paronychions peep upon each wall.

(1919)

Know . . . to] Know how to

470 blow] flourish flowery sons] *filius ante patrem*; mede-saffron mandrake] white bryony paronychions] whitlow grass

WILLIAM HABINGTON
1605–1654

471

To Roses in the Bosom of Castara

YE blushing virgins happy are
In the chaste nunnery of her breasts,
For he'd profane so chaste a fair,
Who e'er should call them Cupid's nests.

Transplanted thus, how bright ye grow,
How rich a perfume do ye yield!
In some close garden, cowslips so
Are sweeter than i'th' open field.

In those white cloisters live secure
From the rude blasts of wanton breath,
Each hour more innocent and pure,
Till you shall wither into death.

Then that which living gave you room,
Your glorious sepulchre shall be.
There wants no marble for a tomb,
Whose breast hath marble been to me.

(1634)

472

To a Wanton

IN vain, fair sorceress, thy eyes speak charms,
In vain thou mak'st loose circles with thy arms.
I'm above thy spells. No magic him can move,
In whom Castara hath inspired her love.
As she, keep thou strict sentinel o'er thy ear,
Lest it the whispers of soft courtiers hear;
Read not his raptures, whose invention must
Write journey work, both for his patron's lust
And his own plush: let no admirer feast
His eye on the naked banquet of thy breast.
If this fair precedent, nor yet my want
Of love, to answer thine, make thee recant
Thy sorc'ries, pity shall to justice turn,
And judge thee, witch, in thy own flames to burn.

(1634)

472 journey] hack plush] (1) rich clothing (in reward); (2) sexual pleasure

473 *Upon Castara's Departure*

VOWS are vain. No suppliant breath
Stays the speed of swift-heeled death.
Life with her is gone, and I
Learn but a new way to die.
See the flowers condole, and all
Wither in my funeral.
The bright lily, as if day
Parted with her, fades away.
Violets hang their heads, and lose
All their beauty. That the rose
A sad part in sorrow bears,
Witness all those dewy tears,
Which as pearl, or diamond-like,
Swell upon her blushing cheek.
All things mourn, but oh behold
How the withered marigold
Closeth up now she is gone,
Judging her the setting sun.

(1634)

474 *To Castara, Being to Take a Journey*

WHAT'S death, more than departure? The dead go
Like travelling exiles, compelled to know
Those regions they heard mention of: 'tis the art
Of sorrows says, 'who die do but depart.'
Then weep thy funeral tears, which heaven, to adorn
The beauteous tresses of the weeping morn,
Will rob me of; and thus my tomb shall be
As naked, as it had no obsequy.
Know, in these lines' sad music to thy ear,
My sad Castara, you the sermon hear
Which I preach o'er my hearse. And dead, I tell
My own life's story, ring but my own knell.
  But when I shall return, know 'tis thy breath
  In sighs divided, rescues me from death.

(1634)

474 divided] (1) broken; (2) shared; (3) temporarily separate (music)

475 Solum Mihi Superest Sepulchrum

WELCOME, thou safe retreat!
Where the injured man may fortify
'Gainst the invasions of the great;
Where the lean slave, who the oar doth ply,
Soft as his admiral may lie.

Great statist! 'Tis your doom,
Though your designs swell high and wide,
To be contracted in a tomb!
And all your happy cares provide
But for your heir authórized pride.

Nor shall your shade delight
In the pomp of your proud obsequies.
And should the present flattery write
A glorious epitaph, the wise
Will say, 'The poet's wit here lies.'

How reconciled to fate
Will grow the agèd villager,
When he shall see your funeral state!
Since death will him as warm inter
As you in your gay sepulchre.

The great decree of God
Makes every path of mortals lead
To this dark common period.
For what by ways so e'er we tread,
We end our journey 'mong the dead.

Even I, while humble zeal
Makes fancy a sad truth indite,
Insensible away do steal;
And when I'm lost in death's cold night,
Who will remember, now I write?

(1634)

Solum ... Sepulchrum] 'Only the grave remains to me' (Job 17: 1) statist] statesman contracted] (1) committed legally; (2) shrunken authórized] legally sanctioned state] pomp

THOMAS RANDOLPH
1605–1635

476 *An Ode to Mr Anthony Stafford to Hasten Him into the Country*

COME, spur away,
I have no patience for a longer stay,
But must go down,
And leave the chargeable noise of this great town.
I will the country see,
Where old simplicity,
Though hid in gray,
Doth look more gay
Than foppery in plush and scarlet clad.
Farewell, you city wits that are
Almost at civil war;
'Tis time that I grow wise, when all the world grows mad.

More of my days
I will not spend to gain an idiot's praise,
Or to make sport
For some slight puny of the Inns of Court.
Then, worthy Stafford, say,
How shall we spend the day;
With what delights
Shorten the nights?
When from this tumult we are got secure
Where mirth with all her freedom goes,
Yet shall no finger lose;
Where every word is thought, and every thought is pure.

There from the tree
We'll cherries pluck, and pick the strawberry,
And every day
Go see the wholesome country girls make hay,
Whose brown hath lovelier grace
Than any painted face
That I do know
Hyde Park can show;

chargeable] troublesome puny] freshman

Where I had rather gain a kiss than meet
(Though some of them in greater state
Might court my love with plate)
The beauties of the Cheap, and wives of Lombard Street.

But think upon
Some other pleasures: these to me are none;
Why do I prate
Of women, that are things against my fate?
I never mean to wed
That torture to my bed.
My Muse is she
My love shall be.
Let clowns get wealth, and heirs; when I am gone,
And this great bugbear, grisly death,
Shall take this idle breath,
If I a poem leave, that poem is my son.

Of this, no more;
We'll rather taste the bright Pomona's store:
No fruit shall scape
Our palates, from the damson to the grape.
Then, full, we'll seek a shade
And hear what music's made;
How Philomel
Her tale doth tell,
And how the other birds do fill the choir;
The thrush and blackbird lend their throats,
Warbling melodious notes:
We will all sports enjoy, which others but desire.

Ours is the sky,
Where at what fowl we please our hawk shall fly;
Nor will we spare
To hunt the crafty fox or timorous hare,
But let our hounds run loose
In any ground they'll choose;
The buck shall fall,
The stag and all;
Our pleasures must from their own warrants be,
For to my Muse, if not to me,
I'm sure all game is free;
Heaven, Earth, are all but parts of her great royalty.

Cheap] Cheapside (London's chief commercial street) Lombard Street] business district clowns] boors Pomona] Roman goddess of fruit Philomel] the nightingale tale] story of rape by Tereus, and metamorphosis

And when we mean
To taste of Bacchus' blessings now and then,
And drink by stealth
A cup or two to noble Barkley's health,
I'll take my pipe and try
The Phrygian melody,
Which he that hears
Lets through his ears
A madness to distemper all the brain;
Then another pipe will take
And Doric music make,
To civilize with grave notes our wits again.

(1638)

477 *Upon the Loss of His Little Finger*

ARITHMETIC nine digits, and no more,
Admits of; then I still have all my store.
For what mischance hath ta'en from my left hand,
It seems did only for a cipher stand.
But this I'll say for thee, departed joint,
Thou wert not given to steal, nor pick, nor point
At any in disgrace; but thou didst go
Untimely to thy death only to show
The other members what they once must do:
Hand, arm, leg, thigh, and all must follow too.
Oft didst thou scan my verse, where, if I miss
Henceforth, I will impute the cause to this.
A finger's loss (I speak it not in sport)
Will make a verse a foot too short.
Farewell, dear finger: much I grieve to see
How soon mischance hath made a hand of thee.

(1638)

478 *An Elegy*

LOVE, give me leave to serve thee, and be wise:
To keep thy torch in, but restore blind eyes.
I will a flame into my bosom take
That martyrs court when they embrace the stake:
Not dull and smoky fires, but heat divine,
That burns not to consume, but to refine.

476 Phrygian] voluptuous   Doric] serious (ancient mode)

477 pick] pilfer   made . . . thee] done away with you

I have a mistress for perfections rare
In every eye, but in my thoughts most fair:
Like tapers on the altar shine her eyes;
Her breath is the perfúme of sacrifice.
And wheresoe'er my fancy would begin,
Still her perfection lets religion in.
I touch her like my beads with devout care,
And come unto my courtship as my prayer.
We sit, and talk, and kiss away the hours
As chastely as the morning dews kiss flowers.
Go, wanton lover, spare thy sighs and tears;
Put on the livery which thy dotage wears,
And call it love. Where heresy gets in
Zeal's but a coal to kindle greater sin.
We wear no flesh, but one another greet
As blessèd souls in separation meet.
Were 't possible that my ambitious sin
Durst commit rapes unon a cherubin,
I might have lustful thoughts to her, of all
Earth's heavenly choir the most angelical.
Looking into my breast, her form I find,
That like my guardian angel keeps my mind
From rude attempts; and when affections stir,
I calm all passions with one thought of her.
Thus they whose reasons love, and not their sense,
The spirits love: thus one intelligence
Reflects upon his like, and by chaste loves
In the same sphere this and that angel moves.
Nor is this barren love: one noble thought
Begets another, and that still is brought
To bed of more; virtues and grace increase,
And such a numerous issue ne'er can cease.
Where children, though great blessings, only be
Pleasures reprieved to some posterity.
Beasts love like men, if men in lust delight,
And call that love which is but appetite.
When essence meets with essence, and souls join
In mutual knots, that's the true nuptial twine:
Such, lady, is my love, and such is true;
All other love is to your sex, not you.

(1638)

Still] Ever intelligence] spiritual being reprieved] remitted twine] (1) knot; (2) embrace

479 *On Sir Robert Cotton the Antiquary*

POSTERITY hath many fates bemoaned,
But ages long since past for thee have groaned.
Time's trophies thou didst rescue from the grave,
Who in thy death a second burial have.
Cotton, death's conquest now complete I see,
Who ne'er had vanquished all things but in thee.
(1638)

480 *In Praise of Women in General*

HE is a parricide to his mother's name,
And with an impious hand murders her fame,
That wrongs the praise of women: that dares write
Libels on saints, or with foul ink requite
The milk they lent us. Better sex, command
To your defence my more religious hand
At sword, or pen: yours was the nobler birth,
For you of man were made, man but of earth,
The son of dust; and though your sin did breed
His fall, again you raised him in your seed:
Adam in 's sleep a gainful loss sustained,
That for one rib a better self regained;
Who, had he not your blest creation seen,
An anchorite in paradise had been.
Why in this work did the creation rest,
But that eternal providence thought you best
Of all his six days' labour: beasts should do
Homage to man, but man should wait on you.
You are of comelier sight, of daintier touch,
A tender flesh, a colour bright, and such
As Parians see in marble; skin more fair,
More glorious head, and far more glorious hair,
Eyes full of grace and quickness; purer roses
Blush in your cheeks; a milder white composes
Your stately fronts; your breath more sweet than his
Breathes spice, and nectar drops at every kiss.
Your skins are smooth, bristles on theirs do grow
Like quills of porcupines; rough wool doth flow

Who in] Which in

480 your seed] i.e. Christ Parians] people of Paros (famed for white marble) quickness] liveliness fronts] foreheads

O'er all their faces, you approach more near
The form of angels; they like beasts appear.
If then in bodies where the souls do dwell
You better us, do then our souls excel?
No; we in soul's equal perfection see
There can in them nor male nor female be.
Boast we of knowledge? You have more than we:
You were the first ventured to pluck the tree.
And, that more rhetoric in your tongues doth lie
Let him dispute against that dares deny
Your least commands; and not persuaded be
With Sampson's strength, and David's piety,
To be your willing captives. Virtue sure
Were blind as fortune, should she choose the poor
Rough cottage-man to live in, and despise
To dwell in you, the stately edifice.
Thus you are proved the better sex, and we
Must all repent that in our pedigree
We choose the father's name, where, should we take
The mother's (a more honoured blood), 'twould make
Our generation sure and certain be,
And I'd believe some faith in heraldry!
Thus, perfect creatures, if detraction rise
Against your sex, dispute but with your eyes,
Your hand, your lip, your brow, there will be sent
So subtile and so strong an argument,
Will teach the Stoic his affection too,
And call the Cynic from his tub to woo.
Thus mustering up your beauteous troops, go on:
The fairest is the valiant Amazon.

(1640)

tub] habitation like Diogenes', the first Cynic

SIR WILLIAM DAVENANT
1606–1668

from *Madagascar* (481–482)

481 *To the Queen, Entertained at Night by the Countess of Anglesey*

FAIR as unshaded light; or as the day
In its first birth, when all the year was May;
Sweet as the altar's smoke, or as the new
Unfolded bud, swelled by the early dew;
Smooth as the face of waters first appeared,
Ere tides began to strive, or winds were heard;
Kind as the willing saints, and calmer far
Than in their sleeps forgiven hermits are:
You that are more than our discreeter fear
Dares praise, with such dull art, what make you here?
Here, where the summer is so little seen
That leaves (her cheapest wealth) scarce reach at green,
You come, as if the silver planet were
Misled awhile from her much injured sphere,
And to ease the travails of her beams tonight
In this small lanthorn would contract her light.

(1638)

482 *For the Lady Olivia Porter: A Present, upon a New-year's Day*

GO! Hunt the whiter ermine, and present
His wealthy skin, as this day's tribute sent
To my Endymion's love; though she be far
More gently smooth, more soft than ermines are.
Go! Climb that rock; and when thou there hast found
A star, contracted in a diamond,
Give it Endymion's love; whose glorious eyes
Darken the starry jewels of the skies.
Go! Dive into the southern sea; and when
Thou hast found (to trouble the nice sight of men)
A swelling pearl, and such whose single worth
Boasts all the wonders which the seas bring forth,

silver planet] moon

482 Endymion's] Endymion Porter's

Give it Endymion's love; whose every tear
Would more enrich the skillful jeweller.
How I command! How slowly they obey!
The churlish Tartar will not hunt today;
Nor will that lazy, sallow Indian strive
To climb the rock, nor that dull negro dive.
Thus poets like to kings, by trust deceived,
Give oftener what is heard of, than received.

(1638)

from *Poems on Several Occasions* (483–485)

483 *The Winter Storms*

BLOW! Blow! The winds are so hoarse they cannot blow.
Cold, cold! Our tears freeze to hail, our spittle to snow.
  The waves are all up, they swell as they run.
    Let them rise and rise
    As high as the skies,
  And higher to wash the face of the sun.

Port, port! The pilot is blind! Port at the helm!
Yare, yare! For one foot of shore take a whole realm:
  Alee, or we sink! Does no man know to wind her?
    Less noise and more room!
    We sail in a drum!
  Our sails are but rags, which lightning turns to tinder.

Aloof, aloof! Hey, how those carracks and ships
Fall foul and are tumbled and driven like chips!
  Our boatswain, alas, a silly weak gristle,
    For fear to catch cold
    Lies down in the hold:
  We all hear his sighs, but few hear his whistle.

(1673)

484 *Song*

THE lark now leaves his watery nest,
  And climbing, shakes his dewy wings:
He takes this window for the east;
  And to implore your light, he sings.
Awake, awake, the morn will never rise
Till she can dress her beauty at your eyes.

483 Yare] Quickly   Alee] Put to leeward   Aloof] Luff; put nearer the wind
carrack] ship of burden   chips] shavings   gristle] tender child

The merchant bows unto the seaman's star,
  The ploughman from the sun his season takes;
But still the lover wonders what they are,
  Who look for day before his mistress wakes.
Awake, awake, break through your veils of lawn!
Then draw your curtains, and begin the dawn.

(1638)

485 *Song*

Endymion Porter and Olivia

OLIVIA

  BEFORE we shall again behold
In his diurnal race the world's great eye,
  We may as silent be and cold,
As are the shades where buried lovers lie.

ENDYMION

  Olivia, 'tis no fault of love
To lose ourselves in death; but oh, I fear,
  When life and knowledge is above
Restored to us, I shall not know thee there.

OLIVIA

  Call it not heaven, my love, where we
Ourselves shall see, and yet each other miss:
  So much of heaven I find in thee
As, thou unknown, all else privation is.

ENDYMION

  Why should we doubt, before we go
To find the knowledge which shall ever last,
  That we may there each other know?
Can future knowledge quite destroy the past?

OLIVIA

  When at the bowers in the Elysian shade
I first arrive, I shall examine where
  They dwell, who love the highest virtue made;
For I am sure to find Endymion there.

485 Elysian shade] place of blessed afterlife (Greek myth)

ENDYMION

From this vexed world when we shall both retire,
Where all are lovers, and where all rejoice,
I need not seek thee in the heavenly choir;
For I shall know Olivia by her voice.

(1673)

from Plays and Masques (486–488)

486 O THOU that sleepst like pig in straw,
Thou lady dear, arise:
Open, to keep the sun in awe,
Thy pretty pinking eyes;
And having stretched each leg and arm,
Put on your clean white smock,
And then, I pray, to keep you warm,
A petticoat on dock.
Arise, arise! Why should you sleep,
When you have slept enough?
Long since French boys cried 'Chimney-sweep',
And damsels 'Kitchen-stuff'.
The shops were opened long before,
And youngest prentice goes
To lay at his mistress' chamber door
His master's shining shoes.
Arise, arise; your breakfast stays:
Good water gruel warm,
Or sugar sops, which Galen says
With mace will do no harm.
Arise, arise; when you are up,
You'll find more to your cost,
For morning's draught in caudle cup,
Good nutbrown ale and toast.

(1673)

487 'TIS, in good truth, a most wonderful thing
(I am even ashamed to relate it)
That love so many vexations should bring
And yet few have the wit to hate it.

486 pinking] peeping dock] rump Kitchen-stuff] Vegetables Galen] (ancient medical authority) caudle] warm drink

Love's weather in maids should seldom hold fair:
  Like April's mine shall quickly alter.
I'll give him tonight a lock of my hair,
  To whom next day I'll send a halter.

I cannot abide these malapert males,
  Pirates of love who know no duty;
Yet love with a storm can take down their sails,
  And they must strike to Admiral Beauty.

Farewell to that maid who will be undone
  Who in markets of men (where plenty
Is cried up and down) will die even for one.
  I will live to make fools of twenty.

(1673)

488 [*Viola's Song*]

  WAKE all the dead! What ho! What ho!
How soundly they sleep whose pillows lie low!
They mind not poor lovers who walk above
On the decks of the world in storms of love.
  No whisper now nor glance can pass
  Through wickets or through panes of glass;
For our windows and doors are shut and barred.
Lie close in the church, and in the churchyard.
  In every grave make room, make room!
The world's at an end, and we come, we come.

  The state is now love's foe, love's foe;
Has seized on his arms, his quiver and bow;
Has pinioned his wings, and fettered his feet,
Because he made way for lovers to meet.
  But O sad chance, his judge was old;
  Hearts cruel grow, when blood grows cold.
No man being young his process would draw.
O heavens that love should be subject to law!
  Lovers go woo the dead, the dead!
Lie two in a grave, and to bed, to bed!

(1673)

from *Gondibert*

489 [*The City Morning*]

As day new opening fills the hemisphere,
And all at once: so quickly every street
Does by an instant opening full appear,
When from their dwellings busy dwellers meet.

From wider gates oppressors sally there;
Here creeps the afflicted through a narrow door:
Groans under wrongs he has not strength to bear,
Yet seeks for wealth to injure others more.

And here the early lawyer mends his pace,
For whom the earlier client waited long;
Here greedy creditors their debtors chase,
Who scape by herding in the indebted throng.

The advent'rous merchant whom a storm did wake
(His ships on Adriatic billows tossed)
Does hope of eastern winds from steeples take,
And hastens there a courier to the coast.

Here through a secret postern issues out
The scared adulterer who outslept his time:
Day and the husband's spy alike does doubt,
And with a half-hid face would hide his crime.

There from sick mirth neglectful feasters reel,
Who cares of want in wine's false Lethe steep.
There anxious empty gamesters homeward steal,
And fear to wake, ere they begin to sleep.

Here stooping labourers slowly moving are,
Beasts to the rich, whose strength grows rude with ease,
And would usurp, did not their rulers care,
With toil and tax their furious strength appease.

There th' aged walk, whose needless carefulness
Infects them past the mind's best medicine, sleep;
There some to temples early vows address,
And for th' o'er-busy world most wisely weep.

(1651)

advent'rous] rash; venturesome   Lethe] river of forgetfulness

EDMUND WALLER
1606–1687

490 *Song*

Go, lovely rose!
Tell her that wastes her time and me
That now she knows,
When I resemble her to thee,
How sweet and fair she seems to be.

Tell her that's young,
And shuns to have her graces spied,
That, hadst thou sprung
In deserts where no men abide,
Thou must have uncommended died.

Small is the worth
Of beauty from the light retired;
Bid her come forth,
Suffer herself to be desired,
And not blush so to be admired.

Then die; that she
The common fate of all things rare
May read in thee:
How small a part of time they share
That are so wondrous sweet and fair!

(1645)

491 *To a Fair Lady Playing with a Snake*

Strange! that such horror and such grace
Should dwell together in one place:
A Fury's arm, an angel's face!

'Tis innocence and youth which makes
In Cloris' fancy such mistakes,
To start at love, and play with snakes.

By this and by her coldness barred,
Her servants have a task too hard:
The tyrant has a double guard.

491 Fury's] (minister of divine vengeance) servants] suitors

Thrice happy snake, that in her sleeve
May boldly creep; we dare not give
Our thoughts so unconfined a leave.

Contented in that nest of snow
He lies, as he his bliss did know,
And to the wood no more would go.

Take heed, fair Eve, you do not make
Another tempter of this snake:
A marble one, so warmed, would speak.

(1664)

492 *The Story of Phoebus and Daphne, Applied*

THYRSIS, a youth of the inspirèd train,
Fair Sacharissa loved, but loved in vain.
Like Phoebus sung the no less amorous boy;
Like Daphne she, as lovely, and as coy.
With numbers he the flying nymph pursues,
With numbers such as Phoebus' self might use!
Such is the chase when love and fancy leads,
O'er craggy mountains and through flowery meads;
Invoked to testify the lover's care,
Or form some image of his cruel fair.
Urged with his fury, like a wounded deer,
O'er these he fled; and now approaching near,
Had reached the nymph with his harmonious lay,
Whom all his charms could not incline to stay.
Yet what he sung in his immortal strain,
Though unsuccessful, was not sung in vain;
All but the nymph that should redress his wrong
Attend his passion, and approve his song.
Like Phoebus thus, acquiring unsought praise,
He catched at love, and filled his arm with bays.

(1645)

493 *On a Girdle*

THAT which her slender waist confined
Shall now my joyful temples bind;
No monarch but would give his crown,
His arms might do what this has done.

492 *Daphne*] (nymph loved by Phoebus, but changed into laurel) numbers] verses fury] frenzy bays] laurel

It was my heaven's extremest sphere,
The pale which held that lovely deer.
My joy, my grief, my hope, my love,
Did all within this circle move!

A narrow compass! And yet there
Dwelt all that's good, and all that's fair;
Give me but what this ribband bound:
Take all the rest the sun goes round.

(1645)

494 *Of English Verse*

POETS may boast, as safely vain,
Their works shall with the world remain;
Both, bound together, live or die,
The verses and the prophecy.

But who can hope his lines should long
Last in a daily changing tongue?
While they are new, envy prevails;
And as that dies, our language fails.

When architects have done their part,
The matter may betray their art:
Time, if we use ill-chosen stone,
Soon brings a well-built palace down.

Poets that lasting marble seek
Must carve in Latin or in Greek;
We write in sand: our language grows,
And, like the tide, our work o'erflows.

Chaucer his sense can only boast;
The glory of his numbers lost!
Years have defaced his matchless strain;
And yet he did not sing in vain.

The beauties which adorned that age,
The shining subjects of his rage,
Hoping they should immortal prove,
Rewarded with success his love.

494 numbers] verses rage] inspiration

This was the generous poet's scope;
And all an English pen can hope:
To make the fair approve his flame,
That can so far extend their fame.

Verse, thus designed, has no ill fate,
If it arrive but at the date
Of fading beauty; if it prove
But as long-lived as present love.

(1668)

495 *On St James's Park, As Lately Improved by His Majesty*

Of the first paradise there's nothing found;
Plants set by heaven are vanished, and the ground;
Yet the description lasts: who knows the fate
Of lines that shall this paradise relate?
  Instead of rivers rolling by the side
Of Eden's garden, here flows in the tide;
The sea, which always served his empire, now
Pays tribute to our prince's pleasure too.
Of famous cities we the founders know;
But rivers, old as seas to which they go,
Are nature's bounty; 'tis of more renown
To make a river than to build a town.
  For future shade, young trees upon the banks
Of the new stream appear in even ranks;
The voice of Orpheus, or Amphion's hand,
In better order could not make them stand;
May they increase as fast, and spread their boughs,
As the high fame of their great owner grows!
May he live long enough to see them all
Dark shadows cast, and as his palace tall!
Methinks I see the love that shall be made,
The lovers walking in that amorous shade;
The gallants dancing by the river's side;
They bathe in summer, and in winter slide.
Methinks I hear the music in the boats,
And the loud echo which returns the notes;

scope] aim; goal

495 Orpheus] (his music could influence nature) (Greek myth)   Amphion] (his music could move stones)

While overhead a flock of new-sprung fowl
Hangs in the air, and does the sun control,
Darkening the sky; they hover o'er, and shroud
The wanton sailors with a feathered cloud.
Beneath, a shoal of silver fishes glides,
And plays about the gilded barges' sides;
The ladies, angling in the crystal lake,
Feast on the waters with the prey they take:
At once victorious with their lines, and eyes,
They make the fishes, and the men, their prize.
A thousand Cupids on the billows ride,
And sea-nymphs enter with the swelling tide,
From Thetis sent as spies, to make report,
And tell the wonders of her sovereign's court.
All that can, living, feed the greedy eye,
Or dead, the palate, here you may descry:
The choicest things that furnished Noah's ark,
Or Peter's sheet, inhabiting this park;
All with a border of rich fruit-trees crowned,
Whose loaded branches hide the lofty mound.
Such various ways the spacious alleys lead,
My doubtful Muse knows not what path to tread.
Yonder, the harvest of cold months laid up
Gives a fresh coolness to the royal cup;
There ice, like crystal firm, and never lost,
Tempers hot July with December's frost;
Winter's dark prison, whence he cannot fly,
Though the warm spring, his enemy, draws nigh.
Strange, that extremes should thus preserve the snow,
High on the Alps, or in deep caves below.
  Here, a well-polished Mall gives us the joy
To see our prince his matchless force employ:
His manly posture and his graceful mien,
Vigour and youth in all his motions seen;
His shape so lovely and his limbs so strong
Confirm our hopes we shall obey him long.
No sooner has he touched the flying ball
But 'tis already more than half the Mall;
And such a fury from his arm has got,
As from a smoking culverin 'twere shot.
  Near this my Muse, what most delights her, sees
A living gallery of agèd trees:
Bold sons of Earth, that thrust their arms so high,
As if once more they would invade the sky.

control] overcome   shroud] shelter   Thetis] sea-goddess (Greek myth)
Peter's sheet] (Acts 11: 5)   polished] levelled

In such green palaces the first kings reigned,
Slept in their shades, and angels entertained;
With such old counsellors they did advise,
And, by frequenting sacred groves, grew wise.
Free from the impediments of light and noise,
Man, thus retired, his nobler thoughts employs.
Here Charles contrives the ordering of his states,
Here he resolves his neighbouring princes' fates:
What nation shall have peace, where war be made,
Determined is in this oraculous shade;
The world, from India to the frozen north,
Concerned in what this solitude brings forth.
His fancy, objects from his view receives;
The prospect, thought and contemplation gives.
That seat of empire here salutes his eye,
To which three kingdoms do themselves apply;
The structure by a prelate raised, Whitehall,
Built with the fortune of Rome's capitol;
Both, disproportioned to the present state
Of their proud founders, were approved by fate.
From hence he does that antique pile behold,
Where royal heads receive the sacred gold:
It gives them crowns, and does their ashes keep;
There made like gods, like mortals there they sleep;
Making the circle of their reign complete,
Those suns of empire, where they rise, they set.
When others fell, this, standing, did presage
The crown should triumph over popular rage:
Hard by that house, where all our ills were shaped,
The auspicious temple stood, and yet escaped.
So snow on Ætna does unmelted lie,
Whence rolling flames and scattered cinders fly;
The distant country in the ruin shares;
What falls from heaven the burning mountain spares.
Next, that capacious hall he sees, the room
Where the whole nation does for justice come;
Under whose large roof flourishes the gown,
And judges grave, on high tribunals, frown.
Here, like the people's pastor he does go,
His flock subjected to his view below;
On which reflecting in his mighty mind,
No private passion does indulgence find;
The pleasures of his youth suspended are,
And made a sacrifice to public care.

a prelate] Wolsey   antique pile] Westminster Abbey   that house] the Houses of Parliament   capacious hall] Westminster Hall

Here, free from court compliances, he walks,
And with himself, his best adviser, talks:
How peaceful olive may his temples shade,
For mending laws, and for restoring trade;
Or, how his brows may be with laurel charged,
For nations conquered, and our bounds enlarged.
Of ancient prudence here he ruminates,
Of rising kingdoms and of falling states;
What ruling arts gave great Augustus fame,
And how Alcides purchased such a name.
His eyes, upon his native palace bent,
Close by, suggest a greater argument.
His thoughts rise higher when he does reflect
On what the world may from that star expect
Which at his birth appeared, to let us see
Day, for his sake, could with the night agree;
A prince, on whom such different lights did smile,
Born the divided world to reconcile!
Whatever heaven, or high extracted blood
Could promise, or foretell, he will make good;
Reform these nations, and improve them more
Than this fair park, from what it was before.

(1661)

496 *Of Loving at First Sight*

NOT caring to observe the wind,
Or the new sea explore,
Snatched from myself, how far behind
Already I behold the shore!

May not a thousand dangers sleep
In the smooth bosom of this deep?
No; 'tis so rockless and so clear
That the rich bottom does appear,
Paved all with precious things, not torn
From shipwrecked vessels, but there born.

Sweetness, truth, and every grace
Which time and use are wont to teach
The eye may in a moment reach,
And read distinctly in her face.

495 Augustus] Octavian, first Roman emperor Alcides] Hercules native palace] St James's

Some other nymphs, with colours faint
And pencil slow, may Cupid paint,
And a weak heart in time destroy;
She has a stamp, and prints the boy:
Can, with a single look, inflame
The coldest breast, the rudest tame.

(1640)

497 *Upon Ben Jonson*

MIRROR of poets! Mirror of our age,
Which, her whole face beholding on thy stage,
Pleased and displeased with her own faults, endures
A remedy like those whom music cures.
Thou hast alone those various inclinations
Which nature gives to ages, sexes, nations,
So tracèd with thy all-resembling pen
That whate'er custom has imposed on men,
Or ill-got habit (which deforms them so
That scarce a brother can his brother know)
Is represented to the wondering eyes
Of all that see, or read, thy comedies.
Whoever in those glasses looks, may find
The spots returned, or graces, of his mind;
And by the help of so divine an art,
At leisure view, and dress, his nobler part.
Narcissus, cozened by that flattering well,
Which nothing could but of his beauty tell,
Had here, discovering the deformed estate
Of his fond mind, preserved himself with hate.
But virtue too, as well as vice, is clad
In flesh and blood so well that Plato had
Beheld, what his high fancy once embraced,
Virtue with colours, speech, and motion graced.
The sundry postures of thy copious Muse
Who would express, a thousand tongues must use;
Whose fate's no less peculiar than thy art;
For as thou couldst all characters impart,
So none could render thine, which still escapes,
Like Proteus, in variety of shapes;

pencil] brush stamp] printing press

497 Narcissus] A mythic youth enamoured of his own reflection cozened] deceived colours] (1) tints; (2) figures of rhetoric Proteus] ancient sea-god with ability to change shape

Who was nor this, nor that, but all we find,
And all we can imagine, in mankind.

(1638)

498 *The Fall*

SEE how the willing earth gave way,
To take the impression where she lay!
See how the mould, as loth to leave
So sweet a burden, still doth cleave
Close to the nymph's stained garment! Here
The coming spring would first appear,
And all this place with roses strow,
If busy feet would let them grow.
Here Venus smiled to see blind chance
Itself before her son advance,
And a fair image to present,
Of what the boy so long had meant.
'Twas such a chance as this, made all
The world into this order fall;
Thus the first lovers, on the clay
Of which they were composèd, lay;
So, in their prime, with equal grace,
Met the first patterns of our race.
Then blush not, fair, or on him frown,
Or wonder how you both came down;
But touch him, and he'll tremble straight:
How could he then support your weight?
How could the youth, alas, but bend,
When his whole heaven upon him leaned?
If aught by him amiss were done,
'Twas that he let you rise so soon.

(1645)

499 *Of the Last Verses in the Book*

WHEN we for age could neither read nor write,
The subject made us able to indite;
The soul, with nobler resolutions decked,
The body stooping, does herself erect.
No mortal parts are requisite to raise
Her that, unbodied, can her maker praise.

498 But touch] Merely touch

The seas are quiet when the winds give o'er;
So, calm are we when passions are no more!
For then we know how vain it was to boast
Of fleeting things, so certain to be lost.
Clouds of affection from our younger eyes
Conceal that emptiness which age descries.
The soul's dark cottage, battered and decayed,
Lets in new light through chinks that time has made
Stronger by weakness: wiser men become,
As they draw near to their eternal home;
Leaving the old, both worlds at once they view,
That stand upon the threshold of the new.

(1686)

WILLIAM WOOD
1606–post 1637

500 [*The Sea's Abundant Progeny*]

THE king of waters, the sea-shouldering whale,
The snuffing grampus, with the oily seal,
The storm-presaging porpoise, herring-hog,
Line-shearing shark, the catfish, and sea dog,
The scale-fenced sturgeon, wry-mouthed halibut,
The flouncing salmon, codfish, greedigut:
Cole, haddock, hake, the thornback, and the skate,
Whose slimy outside makes him seld in date,
The stately bass, old Neptune's fleeting post,
That tides it out and in from sea to coast.
Consorting herrings, and the bony shad,
Big-bellied alewives, mackerels richly clad
With rainbow colours, th' frostfish and the smelt,
As good as ever lady Gustus felt.
The spotted lamprons, eels, the lamperies,
That seeks fresh water brooks with Argus eyes:
These watery villagers with thousands more
Do pass and repass near the verdant shore.
The luscious lobster, with the crabfish raw,
The brinish oyster, mussel, periwig,

500 flouncing] plunging thornback] ray seld] seldom fleeting] swimming post] express messenger alewives] herring-like fish frostfish] tomcod Gustus] Taste (Latin) lamprons] river lampreys Argus] keen periwig] shellfish

And tortoise sought for by the Indian squaw,
Which to the flats dance many a winter's jig,
To dive for cockles and to dig for clams,
Whereby her lazy husband's guts she crams.

(1634)

SIR RICHARD FANSHAWE
1608–1666

501 *The Fall*

THE bloody trunk of him who did possess
Above the rest a hapless happy state,
This little stone doth seal, but not depress,
And scarce can stop the rolling of his fate.

Brass tombs which justice hath denied to his fault,
The common pity to his virtues pays,
Adorning an imaginary vault,
Which from our minds time strives in vain to rase.

Ten years the world upon him falsely smiled,
Sheathing in fawning looks the deadly knife
Long aimèd at his head; that so beguiled
It more securely might bereave his life;

Then threw him to a scaffold from a throne:
Much doctrine lies under this little stone.

(1648)

502 [*The Golden Age*]

FAIR Golden Age! when milk was th' only food,
And cradle of the infant world the wood
(Rocked by the winds); and th' untouched flocks did bear
Their deer young for themselves! None yet did fear
The sword or poison: no black thoughts begun
T' eclipse the light of the eternal sun;
Nor wandering pines unto a foreign shore
Or war or riches (a worse mischief) bore.

502 pines] ships (poetic)   Or] Either

That pompous sound, idol of vanity,
Made up of title, pride, and flattery,
Which they call honour whom ambition blinds,
Was not as yet the tyrant of our minds,
But to buy real goods with honest toil
Amongst the woods and flocks, to use no guile,
Was honour to those sober souls that knew
No happiness but what from virtue grew.
Then sports and carols amongst brooks and plains
Kindled a lawful flame in nymphs and swains.
Their hearts and tongues concurred: the kiss and joy
Which were most sweet, and yet which least did cloy,
Hymen bestowed on them. To one alone
The lively roses of delight were blown;
The thievish lover found them shut, on trial,
And fenced with prickles of a sharp denial.
Were it in cave or wood, or purling spring,
Husband and lover signified one thing.
  Base present age! which dost with thy impure
Delights the beauty of the soul obscure,
Teaching to nurse a dropsy in the veins;
Bridling the look, but giv'st desire the reins.

(1647)

JOHN MILTON
1608–1674

503

On Shakespeare

WHAT needs my Shakespeare, for his honoured bones,
The labour of an age in pilèd stones,
Or that his hallowed relics should be hid
Under a star-ypointing pyramid?
Dear son of memory, great heir of fame,
What needst thou such weak witness of thy name?
Thou in our wonder and astonishment
Hast built thyself a livelong monument.
For whilst to the shame of slow-endeavouring art
Thy easy numbers flow, and that each heart
Hath from the leaves of thy unvalued book,
Those Delphic lines with deep impression took,

swains] shepherds (poetic)

503 unvalued] invaluable Delphic] oracular (Apollo's oracle was at Delphi)

Then thou our fancy of itself bereaving,
Dost make us marble with too much conceiving;
And so sepúlchred in such pomp dost lie,
That kings for such a tomb would wish to die.

(1632)

from *Poems* (1645) (504–507)

504 *On the University Carrier Who Sickened in the Time of his Vacancy, being Forbid to Go to London, by Reason of the Plague*

HERE lies old Hobson, death hath broke his girt,
And here alas hath laid him in the dirt;
Or else, the ways being foul, twenty to one
He's here stuck in a slough, and overthrown.
'Twas such a shifter, that if truth were known,
Death was half glad when he had got him down;
For he had any time this ten years full
Dodged with him, betwixt Cambridge and the Bull.
And surely, death could never have prevailed,
Had not his weekly course of carriage failed;
But lately finding him so long at home,
And thinking now his journey's end was come,
And that he had ta'en up his latest inn,
In the kind office of a chamberlain
Showed him his room where he must lodge that night,
Pulled off his boots, and took away the light:
If any ask for him, it shall be said,
Hobson has supped, and 's newly gone to bed.

(1645)

505 *L'Allegro*

HENCE, loathèd melancholy,
  Of Cerberus and blackest midnight born,
In Stygian cave forlorn
  'Mongst horrid shapes, and shrieks, and sights unholy;

504 *Vacancy*] Temporary cessation from business girt] girth (variant) shifter] twister Bull] Bull Inn, Bishopsgate course] habit chamberlain] attendant in charge of bedchambers

505 *L'Allegro*] The Joyful Man horrid] rough; dreadful

Find out some uncouth cell,
  Where brooding darkness spreads his jealous wings,
And the night-raven sings:
  There under ebon shades, and low-browed rocks
As ragged as thy locks,
  In dark Cimmerian desert ever dwell.
But come, thou goddess fair and free,
In heaven yclept Euphrosynë,
And by men, heart-easing mirth,
Whom lovely Venus at a birth
With two sister Graces more
To ivy-crownèd Bacchus bore;
Or whether (as some sager sing)
The frolic wind that breathes the spring,
Zephyr with Aurora playing,
As he met her once a-Maying,
There on beds of violets blue
And fresh-blown roses washed in dew,
Filled her with thee, a daughter fair,
So buxom, blithe, and debonair.
Haste thee nymph, and bring with thee
Jest and youthful jollity,
Quips and cranks, and wanton wiles,
Nods, and becks, and wreathèd smiles
Such as hang on Hebe's cheek
And love to live in dimple sleek;
Sport that wrinkled care derides,
And laughter holding both his sides.
Come, and trip it as you go
On the light fantastic toe,
And in thy right hand lead with thee
The mountain nymph, sweet liberty;
And if I give thee honour due,
Mirth, admit me of thy crew
To live with her, and live with thee,
In unreprovèd pleasures free;
To hear the lark begin his flight,
And singing startle the dull night
From his watch-tower in the skies,
Till the dappled dawn doth rise;
Then to come in spite of sorrow,

uncouth] lonely   night-raven] owl or heron   yclept] called (poetic)   Euphrosynë] mirth (one of the Graces)   Bacchus] Roman god of wine   Aurora] Roman goddess of dawn   buxom] compliant   debonair] pleasant, gentle   cranks] wordplays   becks] come-ons   Hebe's] Roman goddess of youth   fantastic] making extravagantly conceived gestures

And at my window bid good morrow,
Through the sweet-briar, or the vine,
Or the twisted eglantine;
While the cock with lively din
Scatters the rear of darkness thin,
And to the stack, or the barn door,
Stoutly struts his dames before,
Oft listening how the hounds and horn
Cheerly rouse the slumbering morn
From the side of some hoar hill,
Through the high wood echoing shrill.
Sometime walking not unseen
By hedgerow elms on hillocks green,
Right against the eastern gate
Where the great sun begins his state,
Robed in flames and amber light,
The clouds in thousand liveries dight;
While the ploughman near at hand
Whistles o'er the furrowed land,
And the milkmaid singeth blithe,
And the mower whets his scythe,
And every shepherd tells his tale
Under the hawthorn in the dale.
Straight mine eye hath caught new pleasures
Whilst the landscape round it measures:
Russet lawns and fallows grey
Where the nibbling flocks do stray,
Mountains on whose barren breast
The labouring clouds do often rest;
Meadows trim with daisies pied,
Shallow brooks and rivers wide.
Towers and battlements it sees
Bosomed high in tufted trees,
Where perhaps some beauty lies,
The cynosure of neighbouring eyes.
Hard by, a cottage chimney smokes
From betwixt two agèd oaks,
Where Corydon and Thyrsis met
Are at their savoury dinner set
Of herbs and other country messes,
Which the neat-handed Phillis dresses;
And then in haste her bower she leaves,

hoar] grey with frost or dew   state] progress   dight] dressed   tells his tale] (1) counts his tally of sheep; (2) tells his story   Straight] At once   pied] variegated   cynosure] centre of attention (literally, Ursa Minor constellation)   Corydon, Thyrsis, Phillis] (type names for rustics)

With Thestylis to bind the sheaves;
Or if the earlier season lead
To the tanned haycock in the mead,
Sometimes with secure delight
The upland hamlets will invite,
When the merry bells ring round,
And the jocund rebecks sound
To many a youth and many a maid,
Dancing in the chequered shade;
And young and old come forth to play
On a sunshine holiday,
Till the livelong daylight fail.
Then to the spicy nut-brown ale,
With stories told of many a feat:
How Faëry Mab the junkets eat,
She was pinched and pulled she said,
And by the friar's lantern led
Tells how the drudging goblin sweat
To earn his cream-bowl duly set,
When in one night, ere glimpse of morn,
His shadowy flail hath threshed the corn
That ten day-labourers could not end;
Then lies him down the lubber fiend,
And, stretched out all the chimney's length,
Basks at the fire his hairy strength;
And crop-full out of doors he flings,
Ere the first cock his matin rings.
Thus done the tales, to bed they creep,
By whispering winds soon lulled asleep.
Towered cities please us then,
And the busy hum of men,
Where throngs of knights and barons bold,
In weeds of peace high triumphs hold,
With store of ladies, whose bright eyes
Rain influence, and judge the prize
Of wit, or arms, while both contend
To win her grace, whom all commend.
There let Hymen oft appear
In saffron robe, with taper clear,
And pomp, and feast, and revelry,
With mask, and antique pageantry:
Such sights as youthful poets dream
On summer eves by haunted stream.

Thestylis] (type name for harvester) secure] carefree (Latinism) rebecks] fiddles lubber] drudge chimney's] fireplace's Basks] Exposes to a flood of warmth Hymen] ancient god of marriage

Then to the well-trod stage anon,
If Jonson's learned sock be on,
Or sweetest Shakespeare fancy's child
Warble his native wood-notes wild,
And ever against eating cares
Lap me in soft Lydian airs,
Married to immortal verse
Such as the meeting soul may pierce
In notes, with many a winding bout
Of linkèd sweetness long drawn out,
With wanton heed, and giddy cunning,
The melting voice through mazes running;
Untwisting all the chains that tie
The hidden soul of harmony,
That Orpheus' self may heave his head
From golden slumber on a bed
Of heaped Elysian flowers, and hear
Such strains as would have won the ear
Of Pluto, to have quite set free
His half-regained Eurydicë.
These delights, if thou canst give,
Mirth with thee I mean to live.

(1645)

506 *Il Penseroso*

HENCE, vain deluding joys,
  The brood of folly without father bred;
How little you bestead,
  Or fill the fixèd mind with all your toys:
Dwell in some idle brain,
  And fancies fond with gaudy shapes possess,
As thick and numberless
  As the gay motes that people the sunbeams,
Or likest hovering dreams
  The fickle pensioners of Morpheus' train.
But hail thou goddess, sage and holy,
Hail divinest melancholy,
Whose saintly visage is too bright
To hit the sense of human sight,

sock] comic actor's slipper wood-notes] ?natural song Lydian] i.e. relaxing bout] turn Orpheus'] Apollo's son (his music nearly freed Eurydicë from death) Elysian] of the idyllic after-life in the Elysian Fields (ancient mythology) Pluto] king of the ancient land of death Eurydicë] Orpheus' love

506 *Il Penseroso*] The Pensive Man bestead] help pensioners] retainers Morpheus'] (Roman god of dreams) hit] fit

And therefore to our weaker view
O'erlaid with black, staid wisdom's hue:
Black, but such as in esteem
Prince Memnon's sister might beseem,
Or that starred Ethiop queen that strove
To set her beauty's praise above
The sea-nymphs, and their powers offended.
Yet thou art higher far descended:
Thee bright-haired Vesta long of yore,
To solitary Saturn bore;
His daughter she (in Saturn's reign,
Such mixture was not held a stain).
Oft in glimmering bowers and glades
He met her, and in secret shades
Of woody Ida's inmost grove,
Whilst yet there was no fear of Jove.
Come pensive nun, devout and pure,
Sober, steadfast, and demure,
All in a robe of darkest grain,
Flowing with majestic train,
And sable stole of cypress lawn
Over thy decent shoulders drawn.
Come, but keep thy wonted state,
With even step, and musing gait,
And looks commercing with the skies,
Thy rapt soul sitting in thine eyes:
There held in holy passion still
Forget thyself to marble, till
With a sad leaden downward cast
Thou fix them on the earth as fast.
And join with thee calm peace, and quiet,
Spare fast, that oft with gods doth diet,
And hears the Muses in a ring
Ay round about Jove's altar sing.
And add to these retirèd leisure,
That in trim gardens takes his pleasure;
But first, and chiefest, with thee bring
Him that yon soars on golden wing,
Guiding the fiery-wheelèd throne,
The cherub contemplatïon;
And the mute silence hist along,

Memnon's] (ancient king of Ethiopia) sister] Himera ('yearning') queen] Cassiopeia Vesta] Saturn's daughter (Roman goddess of home) Saturn] Roman god of time and winter mixture] sexual relation Jove] Jupiter (Roman supreme deity, after he usurped Saturn's throne) grain] colour (poetic) cypress] dark; funereal state] stateliness sad] sober yon] yonder

'Less Philomel will deign a song,
In her sweetest, saddest plight,
Smoothing the rugged brow of night,
While Cynthia checks her dragon yoke,
Gently o'er the accustomed oak:
Sweet bird that shunn'st the noise of folly,
Most musical, most melancholy!
Thee chauntress oft the woods among
I woo to hear thy evensong;
And missing thee, I walk unseen
On the dry smooth-shaven green,
To behold the wandering moon
Riding near her highest noon,
Like one that had been led astray
Through the heaven's wide pathless way;
And oft, as if her head she bowed,
Stooping through a fleecy cloud.
Oft on a plat of rising ground,
I hear the far-off curfew sound
Over some wide-waterèd shore,
Swinging slow with sullen roar;
Or if the air will not permit,
Some still removèd place will fit,
Where glowing embers through the room
Teach light to counterfeit a gloom,
Far from all resort of mirth,
Save the cricket on the hearth,
Or the bellman's drowsy charm,
To bless the doors from nightly harm;
Or let my lamp at midnight hour
Be seen in some high lonely tower,
Where I may oft outwatch the Bear,
With thrice great Hermes, or unsphere
The spirit of Plato to unfold
What worlds or what vast regions hold
The immortal mind that hath forsook
Her mansion in this fleshly nook;
And of those demons that are found
In fire, air, flood, or under ground,
Whose power hath a true consent
With planet or with element.

Philomel] the nightingale plight] (1) state of mind; (2) state, after Tereus raped her (Greek mythology) Cynthia] Roman moon goddess yoke] team Stooping] Descending plat] piece; place outwatch the Bear] stay awake all night Hermes] Hermes Trismegistus (Egyptian god of wisdom) unsphere] summon consent] concord, correspondence

Sometime let gorgeous tragedy
In sceptred pall come sweeping by,
Presenting Thebes, or Pelops' line,
Or the tale of Troy divine.
Or what (though rare) of later age
Ennobled hath the buskined stage.
But, O sad virgin, that thy power
Might raise Musaeus from his bower,
Or bid the soul of Orpheus sing
Such notes as warbled to the string
Drew iron tears down Pluto's cheek,
And made hell grant what love did seek.
Or call up him that left half-told
The story of Cambuscan bold,
Of Camball, and of Algarsife,
And who had Canace to wife,
That owned the virtuous ring and glass,
And of the wondrous horse of brass,
On which the Tartar king did ride;
And if aught else great bards beside
In sage and solemn tunes have sung,
Of tourneys and of trophies hung;
Of forests and enchantments drear,
Where more is meant than meets the ear,
Thus night oft see me in thy pale career,
Till civil-suited morn appear,
Not tricked and frounced as she was wont,
With the Attic boy to hunt,
But kerchiefed in a comely cloud,
While rocking winds are piping loud,
Or ushered with a shower still,
When the gust hath blown his fill,
Ending on the rustling leaves,
With minute drops from off the eaves.
And when the sun begins to fling
His flaring beams, me goddess bring
To archèd walks of twilight groves,
And shadows brown that Sylvan loves
Of pine, or monumental oak,
Where the rude axe with heavèd stroke,

pall] robe Pelops' line] the family of Agamemnon and many other figures of Attic tragedy buskined] trod by the tragic actor's boot Musaeus] legendary Greek poet, Orpheus' pupil him] Chaucer (in The Squire's Tale) virtuous] powerful magically pale] dim tricked] adorned frounced] curled; frizzed Attic boy] Cephalus, grandson of Aeolus the wind god still] quiet Sylvan] Silvanus, Roman woodland god

Was never heard the nymphs to daunt,
Or fright them from their hallowed haunt.
There in close covert by some brook,
Where no profaner eye may look,
Hide me from day's garish eye,
While the bee with honied thigh,
That at her flowery work doth sing,
And the waters murmuring
With such consort as they keep,
Entice the dewy-feathered sleep;
And let some strange mysterious dream,
Wave at his wings in airy stream,
Of lively portraiture displayed,
Softly on my eyelids laid.
And as I wake, sweet music breathe
Above, about, or underneath,
Sent by some spirit to mortals good,
Or the unseen genius of the wood.
But let my due feet never fail
To walk the studious cloister's pale,
And love the high embowèd roof,
With antique pillars' massy proof,
And storied windows richly dight,
Casting a dim religious light.
There let the pealing organ blow
To the full-voiced choir below
In service high and anthems clear,
As may with sweetness, through mine ear,
Dissolve me into ecstasies,
And bring all heaven before mine eyes.
And may at last my weary age
Find out the peaceful hermitage,
The hairy gown and mossy cell,
Where I may sit and rightly spell
Of every star that heaven doth shew,
And every herb that sips the dew;
Till old experience do attain
To something like prophetic strain.
These pleasures melancholy give,
And I with thee will choose to live.

(1645)

consort] orchestra; harmony of sounds genius] local spirit pale] enclosure embowèd] vaulted massy] massive proof] impenetrability storied] historiated; showing scenes from the redemptive history dight] adorned spell / Of] study

507

Sonnet VII

HOW soon hath time the subtle thief of youth
Stolen on his wing my three and twentieth year!
My hasting days fly on with full career,
But my late spring no bud or blossom showeth.
Perhaps my semblance might deceive the truth,
That I to manhood am arrived so near,
And inward ripeness doth much less appear,
That some more timely-happy spirits endueth.
Yet be it less or more, or soon or slow,
It shall be still in strictest measure even
To that same lot, however mean or high,
Toward which time leads me, and the will of heaven;
All is, if I have grace to use it so,
As ever in my great task-master's eye.

(1645)

from *A Masque presented at Ludlow Castle, 1634* (508–511)

[*Comus*]

508

[*Comus' Summons*]

THE star that bids the shepherd fold,
Now the top of heaven doth hold,
And the gilded car of day,
His glowing axle doth allay
In the steep Atlantic stream,
And the slope sun his upward beam
Shoots against the dusky pole,
Pacing toward the other goal
Of his chamber in the east.
Meanwhile, welcome joy, and feast,
Midnight shout, and revelry,
Tipsy dance, and jollity.
Braid your locks with rosy twine
Dropping odours, dropping wine.
Rigour now is gone to bed,
And advice with scrupulous head,
Strict age, and sour severity,
With their grave saws in slumber lie.

semblance] appearance   even / To] level with

508 fold] pen his sheep   allay] cool   slope] declining   pole] sky (Lantinism)

We that are of purer fire
Imitate the starry choir,
Who in their nightly watchful spheres
Lead in swift round the months and years.
The sounds and seas with all their finny drove
Now to the moon in wavering morris move,
And on the tawny sands and shelves
Trip the pert fairies and the dapper elves;
By dimpled brook and fountain-brim
The wood-nymphs decked with daisies trim
Their merry wakes and pastimes keep:
What hath night to do with sleep?
Night hath better sweets to prove,
Venus now wakes, and wakens love.
Come let us our rites begin,
'Tis only daylight that makes sin
Which these dun shades will ne'er report;
Hail goddess of nocturnal sport,
Dark-veiled Cotytto, to whom the secret flame
Of midnight torches burns; mysterious dame
That ne'er art called but when the dragon womb
Of Stygian darkness spits her thickest gloom,
And makes one blot of all the air:
Stay thy cloudy ebon chair,
Wherein thou rid'st with Hecat', and befriend
Us thy vowed priests, till utmost end
Of all thy dues be done, and none left out,
Ere the blabbing eastern scout
The nice morn on th' Indian steep
From her cabined loophole peep,
And to the tell-tale sun descry
Our concealed solemnity.
Come, knit hands, and beat the ground,
In a light fantastic round.

(1637)

sounds] straits morris] morris dance shelves] sandbanks wakes] revels prove] experience Which] What Cotytto] Thracian goddess with licentious rites Stygian] of the Styx (river of the ancient underworld) spits] (1) emits; (2) delves Hecat'] Hecate; Diana nice] over-refined steep] mountain slope cabined loophole] tiny window; porthole solemnity] ceremony round] ring-dance

509 [*Chastity*]

I MEAN that too, but yet a hidden strength
Which if heaven gave it, may be termed her own:
'Tis chastity, my brother, chastity:
She that has that is clad in cómplete steel,
And like a quivered nymph with arrows keen
May trace huge forests and unharboured heaths,
Infamous hills and sandy perilous wilds,
Where through the sacred rays of chastity
No savage fierce, bandit, or mountaineer
Will dare to soil her virgin purity;
Yea there, where very desolation dwells
By grots and caverns shagged with horrid shades,
She may pass on with unblenched majesty,
Be it not done in pride or in presumption.
Some say no evil thing that walks by night
In fog, or fire, by lake, or moorish fen,
Blue meagre hag, or stubborn unlaid ghost
That breaks his magic chains at curfew time,
No goblin or swart faëry of the mine,
Hath hurtful power o'er true virginity.
Do ye believe me yet, or shall I call
Antiquity from the old schools of Greece
To testify the arms of chastity?
Hence had the huntress Dian her dread bow,
Fair silver-shafted queen for ever chaste,
Wherewith she tamed the brinded lioness
And spotted mountain pard, but set at nought
The frivolous bolt of Cupid: gods and men
Feared her stern frown, and she was queen o' the woods.
What was that snaky-headed Gorgon shield
That wise Minerva wore, unconquered virgin,
Wherewith she freezed her foes to cóngealed stone?
But rigid looks of chaste austerity,
And noble grace that dashed brute violence
With sudden adoration and blank awe.
So dear to heaven is saintly chastity
That when a soul is found sincerely so,
A thousand liveried angels lackey her,

unharboured] wild, shelterless shagged] overgrown (Spenserian) unblenched] undismayed moorish] boggy stubborn] i.e. resistant to exoricism Antiquity . . . Greece] Greek philosophers brinded] tawny, striped darker pard] panther Gorgon shield] shield with Medusa's head Minerva] Roman goddess of chastity liveried] uniformed

Driving far off each thing of sin and guilt,
And in clear dream and solemn vision
Tell her of things that no gross ear can hear,
Till oft convérse with heavenly habitants
Begin to cast a beam on the outward shape,
The unpolluted temple of the mind,
And turns it by degrees to the soul's essence,
Till all be made immortal; but when lust,
By unchaste looks, loose gestures, and foul talk,
But most by lewd and lavish act of sin,
Lets in defilement to the inward parts,
The soul grows clotted by contagion,
Embodies, and imbrutes, till she quite lose
The divine property of her first being.
Such are those thick and gloomy shadows damp
Oft seen in charnel-vaults and sepulchres,
Lingering, and sitting by a new-made grave,
As loth to leave the body that it loved,
And linked itself by carnal sensuality
To a degenerate and degraded state.

(1637)

510 [*Sabrina's Song*]

By the rushy-fringèd bank,
Where grows the willow and the osier dank,
My sliding chariot stays,
Thick set with agate, and the azurn sheen
Of turkis blue, and emerald green
That in the channel strays,
Whilst from off the waters fleet
Thus I set my printless feet
O'er the cowslip's velvet head,
That bends not as I tread,
Gentle swain at thy request
I am here.

(1637)

lavish] loose, licentious   Embodies] Grows material   imbrutes] grows bestial

510 azurn] azure (M.'s coinage)   turkis] turquoise

511 [*The Spirit's Epilogue*]

To the ocean now I fly,
And those happy climes that lie
Where day never shuts his eye,
Up in the broad fields of the sky:
There I suck the liquid air
All amidst the gardens fair
Of Hesperus, and his daughters three
That sing about the golden tree:
Along the crispèd shades and bowers
Revels the spruce and jocund spring,
The Graces, and the rosy-bosomed Hours
Thither all their bounties bring,
That there eternal summer dwells,
And west winds with musky wing
About the cedarn alleys fling
Nard and cassia's balmy smells.
Iris there with humid bow
Waters the odorous banks that blow
Flowers of more mingled hue
Than her purfled scarf can show,
And drenches with Elysian dew
(List mortals if your ears be true)
Beds of hyacinth and roses,
Where young Adonis oft reposes,
Waxing well of his deep wound
In slumber soft, and on the ground
Sadly sits the Assyrian queen;
But far above in spangled sheen
Celestial Cupid, her famed son advanced,
Holds his dear Psyche sweet entranced
After her wandering labours long,
Till free consent the gods among
Make her his eternal bride,
And from her fair unspotted side
Two blissful twins are to be born,
Youth and joy; so Jove hath sworn.
But now my task is smoothly done;
I can fly or I can run

liquid] clear, bright Hesperus] evening (Latin mythology) daughters] the Hisperides; Hesperus' grandchildren crispèd] crinkled Hours] *Horae* (seasons: Latin mythology) cedarn] of cedar-trees (coinage) Nard] Spikenard (aromatic plant) cassia's] (cinnamonlike bark) Iris] the rainbow blow] bloom purfled] variegated Elysian] paradisiac Adonis] ancient vegetation god Assyrian queen] Venus (first worshipped by Assyrians)

Quickly to the green Earth's end,
Where the bowed welkin slow doth bend,
And from thence can soar as soon
To the corners of the moon.
Mortals that would follow me,
Love virtue, she alone is free,
She can teach ye how to climb
Higher than the sphery chime;
Or if virtue feeble were,
Heaven itself would stoop to her.

(1637)

512 *Lycidas*

YET once more, O ye laurels, and once more
Ye myrtles brown, with ivy never sere,
I come to pluck your berries harsh and crude,
And with forced fingers rude
Shatter your leaves before the mellowing year.
Bitter constraint and sad occasion dear
Compels me to disturb your season due;
For Lycidas is dead, dead ere his prime,
Young Lycidas, and hath not left his peer:
Who would not sing for Lycidas? He knew
Himself to sing, and build the lofty rhyme.
He must not float upon his watery bier
Unwept, and welter to the parching wind,
Without the meed of some melodious tear.
Begin then, sisters of the sacred well,
That from beneath the seat of Jove doth spring;
Begin, and somewhat loudly sweep the string.
Hence with denial vain and coy excuse;
So may some gentle Muse
With lucky words favour my destined urn,
And as he passes turn,
And bid fair peace be to my sable shroud.
For we were nursed upon the self-same hill,
Fed the same flock; by fountain, shade, and rill.
Together both, ere the high lawns appeared

bowed welkin] sky's curved vault corners] horns (Latinism) sphery chime] music of the spheres

512 never sere] evergreen crude] unripe dear] (1) important; (2) dire Lycidas] pastoral type-name knew] knew how welter] writhe tear] i.e. elegy sisters] Muses lucky] unsought sable] mournful lawns] clearings

Under the opening eyelids of the morn,
We drove a-field, and both together heard
What time the grey-fly winds her sultry horn,
Battening our flocks with the fresh dews of night
Oft till the star that rose, at evening, bright
Toward heaven's descent had sloped his westering wheel.
Meanwhile the rural ditties were not mute,
Tempered to the oaten flute;
Rough satyrs danced, and fauns with cloven heel
From the glad sound would not be absent long,
And old Damaetas loved to hear our song.
  But oh the heavy change, now thou art gone,
Now thou art gone, and never must return!
Thee shepherd, thee the woods and desert caves,
With wild thyme and the gadding vine o'ergrown,
And all their echoes mourn.
The willows and the hazel copses green
Shall now no more be seen,
Fanning their joyous leaves to thy soft lays.
As killing as the canker to the rose,
Or taint-worm to the weanling herds that graze,
Or frost to flowers that their gay wardrobe wear
When first the white-thorn blows:
Such, Lycidas, thy loss to shepherd's ear.
  Where were ye nymphs when the remorseless deep
Closed o'er the head of your loved Lycidas?
For neither were ye playing on the steep,
Where your old bards, the famous Druids, lie,
Nor on the shaggy top of Mona high,
Nor yet where Deva spreads her wizard stream;
Ay me, I fondly dream!
Had ye been there . . . for what could that have done?
What could the Muse herself that Orpheus bore,
The Muse herself for her enchanting son
Whom universal nature did lament,
When by the rout that made the hideous roar,
His gory visage down the stream was sent,
Down the swift Hebrus to the Lesbian shore.
  Alas! What boots it with uncessant care
To tend the homely slighted shepherd's trade,

grey-fly] may-fly   battening] fattening   star] the evening star   Damaetas] (pastoral type-name; Milton's tutor)   gadding] straggling   canker] insect larva   taint-worm] intestinal worm   weanling herds] newly weaned calves   steep] mountain slope   Mona] Anglesey   Deva] the Dee   Muse] Calliope   enchanting] spellbinding (Orpheus' music influenced even inanimate nature)   rout] Bacchantes (Thracian women who dismembered Orpheus)   boots] avails

And strictly meditate the thankless Muse;
Were it not better done as others use,
To sport with Amaryllis in the shade,
Or with the tangles of Neaera's hair?
Fame is the spur that the clear spirit doth raise
(That last infirmity of noble mind)
To scorn delights and live laborious days;
But the fair guerdon when we hope to find,
And think to burst out into sudden blaze,
Comes the blind Fury with th' abhorrèd shears,
And slits the thin-spun life. 'But not the praise,'
Phoebus replied, and touched my trembling ears:
'Fame is no plant that grows on mortal soil,
Nor in the glistering foil
Set off to the world, nor in broad rumour lies,
But lives and spreads aloft by those pure eyes
And perfect witness of all-judging Jove;
As he pronounces lastly on each deed,
Of so much fame in heaven expect thy meed.'
  O fountain Arethuse, and thou honoured flood,
Smooth-sliding Mincius, crowned with vocal reeds,
That strain I heard was of a higher mood;
But now my oat proceeds,
And listens to the herald of the sea
That came in Neptune's plea.
He asked the waves, and asked the felon winds,
What hard mishap hath doomed this gentle swain,
And questioned every gust of rugged wings
That blows from off each beakèd promontory:
They knew not of his story,
And sage Hippotades their answer brings,
That not a blast was from his dungeon strayed,
The air was calm, and on the level brine
Sleek Panope with all her sisters played.
It was that fatal and perfidious bark,
Built in the eclipse and rigged with curses dark,
That sunk so low that sacred head of thine.
  Next Camus, reverend sire, went footing slow,

use] are accustomed Amaryllis] (pastoral type-name) Neaera's] (erotic type-name in Neolatin elegy) last] longest surviving the blind Fury] Atropos (one of the Fates, acting like a Fury) Phoebus] Apollo, ancient Greek god of poetry foil] metal sheet used to enhance a precious stone Arethuse] (nymph of Diana; pastoral Muse) Mincius] (near Mantua, Virgil's birthplace) herald] Triton in . . . plea] to plead Neptune innocent of King's death felon] fierce; wild swain] shepherd Hippotades] Aeolus, god of winds Panope] a sea-nymph Camus] the river Cam; Cambridge University

His mantle hairy, and his bonnet sedge,
Inwrought with figures dim, and on the edge
Like to that sanguine flower inscribed with woe.
'Ah; who hath reft,' quoth he, 'my dearest pledge?'
Last came, and last did go,
The pilot of the Galilean lake;
Two massy keys he bore of metals twain,
(The golden opes, the iron shuts amain).
He shook his mitred locks, and stern bespake,
'How well could I have spared for thee, young swain,
Enow of such as for their bellies' sake
Creep and intrude and climb into the fold!
Of other care they little reckoning make
Than how to scramble at the shearers' feast,
And shove away the worthy bidden guest;
Blind mouths! that scarce themselves know how to hold
A sheep-hook, or have learned aught else the least
That to the faithful herdman's art belongs!
What recks it them? What need they? They are sped;
And when they list, their lean and flashy songs
Grate on their scrannel pipes of wretched straw,
The hungry sheep look up, and are not fed,
But swollen with wind and the rank mist they draw
Rot inwardly, and foul contagion spread;
Besides what the grim wolf with privy paw
Daily devours apace, and nothing said;
But that two-handed engine at the door
Stands ready to smite once, and smite no more.
  Return Alpheus, the dread voice is past
That shrunk thy streams; return Sicilian Muse,
And call the vales, and bid them hither cast
Their bells and flowrets of a thousand hues.
Ye valleys low where the mild whispers use
Of shades and wanton winds and gushing brooks,
On whose fresh lap the swart star sparely looks,
Throw hither all your quaint enamelled eyes,
That on the green turf suck the honied showers,
And purple all the ground with vernal flowers.

hairy] (1) hirsute, like some river plants; (2) furry (like academic gown) inwrought] embroidered; inscribed (?coinage) flower] hyacinth (inscribed 'io', alas) pledge] child pilot] ?St Peter massy] massive amain] forcibly Enow] Enough What . . . them] What does it matter to them sped] satisfied list] please flashy] watery; vapid scrannel] ?thin (dialectal) wolf] Jesuits engine] instrument of retribution Alpheus] (river-god enamoured of Arethusa) (Greek mythology) use] resort swart star] Sirius (associated with heat) enamelled] variegated in colour

Bring the rathe primrose that forsaken dies,
The tufted crow-toe and pale jessamine,
The white pink and the pansy freaked with jet,
The glowing violet,
The musk-rose and the well-attired woodbine,
With cowslips wan that hang the pensive head,
And every flower that sad embroidery wears:
Bid amaranthus all his beauty shed,
And daffadillies fill their cups with tears,
To strew the laureate hearse where Lycid lies.
For so to interpose a little ease
Let our frail thoughts dally with false surmise.
Ay me! Whilst thee the shores and sounding seas
Wash far away, where'er thy bones are hurled:
Whether beyond the stormy Hebrides,
Where thou perhaps under the whelming tide
Visitst the bottom of the monstrous world;
Or whether thou, to our moist vows denied,
Sleepst by the fable of Bellerus old,
Where the great vision of the guarded mount
Looks toward Namancos and Bayona's hold;
Look homeward angel now, and melt with ruth.
And, O ye dolphins, waft the hapless youth.
   Weep no more, woeful shepherds weep no more,
For Lycidas your sorrow is not dead,
Sunk though he be beneath the watery floor;
So sinks the day-star in the ocean bed,
And yet anon repairs his drooping head,
And tricks his beams, and with new spangled ore
Flames in the forehead of the morning sky:
So Lycidas sunk low, but mounted high,
Through the dear might of him that walked the waves;
Where other groves, and other streams along,
With nectar pure his oozy locks he laves,
And hears the unexpressive nuptial song,
In the blest kingdoms meek of joy and love.
There entertain him all the saints above,
In solemn troops and sweet societies
That sing, and singing in their glory move,

rathe] early (Spenserian)   crow-toe] wild hyacinth   jessamine] jasmine   freaked] flecked, streaked   woodbine] bindweed   wan] pale   amaranthus] unfading flower of paradise   whelming] covering   monstrous] inhabited by sea-monsters   moist vows] tearful supplications   Bellerus] Roman name for Land's End   Namancos, Bayona] Spanish Catholic strongpoints   angel] Michael   day-star] sun   repairs] restores   tricks] adjusts   ore] gold   him] Christ (Matt. 14: 25)   oozy] slimy   unexpressive] ineffable   nuptial] of the Lamb's marriage (Rev. 19: 7)

And wipe the tears for ever from his eyes.
Now Lycidas the shepherds weep no more;
Henceforth thou art the genius of the shore,
In thy large recompense, and shalt be good
To all that wander in that perilous flood.
  Thus sang the uncouth swain to the oaks and rills;
While the still morn went out with sandals grey,
He touched the tender stops of various quills,
With eager thought warbling his Doric lay:
And now the sun had stretched out all the hills,
And now was dropped into the western bay;
At last he rose, and twitched his mantle blue:
Tomorrow to fresh woods, and pastures new.

(1638)

513 *Sonnet XIII. To Mr H. Lawes, on His Airs*

HARRY, whose tuneful and well-measured song
  First taught our English music how to span
  Words with just note and accent, not to scan
  With Midas ears, committing short and long;
Thy worth and skill exempts thee from the throng,
  With praise enough for envy to look wan;
  To after age thou shalt be writ the man
  That with smooth air couldst humour best our tongue.
Thou honourst verse, and verse must lend her wing
  To honour thee, the priest of Phoebus' choir
  That tun'st their happiest lines in hymn, or story.
Dante shall give fame leave to set thee higher
  Than his Casella, whom he wooed to sing
  Met in the milder shades of Purgatory.

(1648)

genius] local deity recompense] compensation; atonement uncouth] unknown stops] finger-holes quills] reeds of the shepherd's pipe (Spenserian) Doric] (dialect of ancient Greek pastoral poets)

513 *Lawes*] Henry Lawes, member of the King's Music span] measure accent] i.e. musical accent Midas] Phrygian king, given ass ears for preferring Pan's music to Apollo's committing] mixing up wan] pale

514 *On the New Forcers of Conscience under the Long Parliament*

BECAUSE you have thrown off your prelate lord,
And with stiff vows renounced his liturgy
To seize the widowed whore plurality
From them whose sin ye envied, not abhorred,
Dare ye for this adjure the civil sword
To force our consciences that Christ set free,
And ride us with a classic hierarchy
Taught ye by mere A. S. and Rutherford?
Men whose life, learning, faith and pure intent
Would have been held in high esteem with Paul
Must now be named and printed heretics
By shallow Edwards and Scotch What-d'ye-call;
But we do hope to find out all your tricks,
Your plots and packing worse than those of Trent,
That so the Parliament
May with their wholesome and preventive shears
Clip your phylacteries, though balk your ears,
And succour our just fears
When they shall read this clearly in your charge
New *Presbyter* is but old *Priest* writ large.

(1673)

515 *On the Lord General Fairfax at the Siege of Colchester*

FAIRFAX, whose name in arms through Europe rings,
Filling each mouth with envy or with praise,
And all her jealous monarchs with amaze
And rumours loud that daunt remotest kings,
Thy firm unshaken virtue ever brings
Victory home, though new rebellions raise
Their hydra heads, and the false North displays
Her broken league, to imp their serpent wings,

plurality] holding more than one living   civil sword] lay authority   classic] Presbyterian   Paul] St Paul, Apostle of the Gentiles   Edwards] Thomas Edwards, Puritan preacher   Trent] the Counter-Reformation Council of Trent   phylacteries] hypocritical displays of piety   balk] miss   charge] indictment

515 virtue] valour   league] the Solemn League and Covenant   imp] repair

Oh yet a nobler task awaits thy hand;
For what can war, but endless war still breed,
Till truth and right from violence be freed,
And public faith cleared from the shameful brand
Of public fraud. In vain doth valour bleed
While avarice and rapine share the land.

(1694)

516 *To the Lord General Cromwell*

CROMWELL, our chief of men, who through a cloud
Not of war only, but detractions rude,
Guided by faith and matchless fortitude
To peace and truth thy glorious way hast ploughed,
And on the neck of crownèd fortune proud
Hast reared God's trophies and his work pursued,
While Darwen stream with blood of Scots imbrued,
And Dunbar field resounds thy praises loud,
And Worcester's laureate wreath; yet much remains
To conquer still; peace hath her victories
No less renowned than war, new foes arise
Threatening to bind our souls with secular chains:
Help us to save free conscience from the paw
Of hireling wolves whose gospel is their maw.

(1694)

517 [*Sonnet XVI*]

WHEN I consider how my light is spent,
Ere half my days, in this dark world and wide,
And that one talent which is death to hide
Lodged with me useless, though my soul more bent
To serve therewith my maker, and present
My true account, lest he returning chide,
'Doth God exact day-labour, light denied?'
I fondly ask; but patience to prevent

public fraud] financial corruption under the Long Parliament

516 Darwen] river where battle of Preston was fought Dunbar . . . Worcester's] battles fatal to Royalist hopes wolves] i.e. 'Churchwolves', pluralists

517 useless] (1) purposeless; (2) without attracting interest day-labour] work for daily wages fondly] foolishly prevent] forestall

That murmur soon replies, 'God doth not need
Either man's work or his own gifts; who best
Bear his mild yoke, they serve him best, his state
Is kingly. Thousands at his bidding speed
And post o'er land and ocean without rest:
They also serve who only stand and wait.'

(1673)

518 [*Sonnet XVII*]

LAWRENCE, of virtuous father virtuous son,
Now that the fields are dank, and ways are mire,
Where shall we sometimes meet, and by the fire
Help waste a sullen day; what may be won
From the hard season gaining? Time will run
On smoother, till Favonius reinspire
The frozen earth, and clothe in fresh attire
The lily and rose, that neither sowed nor spun.
What neat repast shall feast us, light and choice,
Of Attic taste, with wine, whence we may rise
To hear the lute well touched, or artful voice
Warble immortal notes and Tuscan air?
He who of those delights can judge, and spare
To interpose them oft, is not unwise.

(1673)

519 [*Sonnet XVIII*]

CYRIACK, whose grandsire on the royal bench
Of British Themis, with no mean applause
Pronounced and in his volumes taught our laws,
Which others at their bar so often wrench:
Today deep thoughts resolve with me to drench
In mirth that after no repenting draws:
Let Euclid rest and Archimedes pause,
And what the Swede intend, and what the French.

Thousands] (Ps. 68: 17) wait] (1) attend; (2) await

518 Favonius] west wind (Horatian) reinspire] breathe again on (Latinism) neither . . . spun] (Matt. 6: 28) neat] tasteful Attic] frugal, simple spare . . . oft] (1) afford . . . oft; (2) refrain . . . too oft

519 Themis] goddess of justice (ancient mythology) others . . . bar] other judges resolve] (imperative) drench] drown after . . . draws] leaves no hangover

To measure life learn thou betimes, and know
  Toward solid good what leads the nearest way;
  For other things mild heaven a time ordains,
And disapproves that care, though wise in show,
  That with superfluous burden loads the day,
  And when God sends a cheerful hour, refrains.

(1673)

520 *To Mr Cyriack Skinner upon His Blindness*

CYRIACK, this three years' day these eyes, though clear
  To outward view, of blemish or of spot,
  Bereft of light their seeing have forgot,
  Nor to their idle orbs doth sight appear
Of sun or moon or star throughout the year,
  Or man or woman. Yet I argue not
  Against heaven's hand or will, nor bate a jot
  Of heart or hope; but still bear up and steer
Right onward. What supports me dost thou ask?
  The conscience, friend, to have lost them overplied
  In liberty's defence, my noble task,
Of which all Europe talks from side to side.
  This thought might lead me through the world's vain mask
  Content though blind, had I no better guide.

(1694)

521 [*Sonnet XIX*]

METHOUGHT I saw my late espousèd saint
  Brought to me like Alcestis from the grave,
  Whom Jove's great son to her glad husband gave,
  Rescued from death by force though pale and faint.
Mine as whom washed from spot of childbed taint
  Purification in the old Law did save,
  And such as yet once more I trust to have
  Full sight of her in heaven without restraint,

520 this . . . day] for three years   bate . . . Of] reduce in the slightest   heart] courage   bear up] face the weather (nautical)   conscience] consciousness   mask] masquerade

521 saint] soul in heaven   Alcestis] Euripides' character, who dies for Admetus   Jove's . . . son] Hercules   childbed] childbirth   old Law] (Lev. 12: 4–8)

Came vested all in white, pure as her mind:
Her face was veiled, yet to my fancied sight
Love, sweetness, goodness in her person shined
So clear as in no face with more delight.
But oh as to embrace me she inclined
I waked, she fled, and day brought back my night.

(1673)

from *Paradise Lost* (522–538)

522

[*Invocation*]

Of man's first disobedience, and the fruit
Of that forbidden tree, whose mortal taste
Brought death into the world, and all our woe,
With loss of Eden, till one greater man
Restore us, and regain the blissful seat,
Sing heavenly Muse, that on the secret top
Of Oreb, or of Sinai, didst inspire
That shepherd, who first taught the chosen seed,
In the beginning how the heavens and Earth
Rose out of chaos; or if Sion hill
Delight thee more, and Siloa's brook that flowed
Fast by the oracle of God, I thence
Invoke thy aid to my advent'rous song,
That with no middle flight intends to soar
Above the Aonian mount, while it pursues
Things unattempted yet in prose or rhyme.
And chiefly thou O Spirit, that dost prefer
Before all temples the upright heart and pure,
Instruct me, for thou knowst; thou from the first
Wast present, and with mighty wings outspread
Dove-like satst brooding on the vast abyss
And mad'st it pregnant: what in me is dark
Illumine, what is low raise and support;
That to the highth of this great argument
I may assert eternal providence,
And justify the ways of God to men.

(1667)

vested] clothed

522 first] (1) earliest; (2) most important fruit] (1) consequence; (2) fruit mortal] death-dealing Eden] Paradise greater man] Jesus restore] put in a state of grace Muse] Urania Oreb] Mt Horeb (where 'That shepherd' Moses saw the burning bush) Sinai] Mt Sinai (where he received the Law) Sion hill] site of the temple at Jerusalem Siloa's] (spring nearby) Aonian mount] Helicon (sacred to the pagan Muses) Dove-like] (as at Luke 3: 22) vast] (1) huge; (2) waste argument] theme

523 [*Satan's Summons*]

He scarce had ceased when the superior fiend
Was moving toward the shore; his ponderous shield
Ethereal temper, massy, large, and round,
Behind him cast; the broad circumference
Hung on his shoulders like the moon, whose orb
Through optic glass the Tuscan artist views
At evening from the top of Fesole,
Or in Valdarno, to descry new lands,
Rivers or mountains in her spotty globe.
His spear, to equal which the tallest pine
Hewn on Norwegian hills, to be the mast
Of some great ammiral, were but a wand
He walked with to support uneasy steps
Over the burning marl, not like those steps
On heaven's azure, and the torrid clime
Smote on him sore besides, vaulted with fire;
Natheless he so endured, till on the beach
Of that inflamèd sea he stood and called
His legions, angel forms, who lay entranced
Thick as autumnal leaves that strew the brooks
In Vallombrosa, where the Etrurian shades
High overarched imbower; or scattered sedge
Afloat, when with fierce winds Orion armed
Hath vexed the Red Sea coast, whose waves o'erthrew
Busiris and his Memphian chivalry,
While with perfidious hatred they pursued
The sojourners of Goshen, who beheld
From the safe shore their floating carcasses
And broken chariot wheels: so thick bestrewn
Abject and lost lay these, covering the flood,
Under amazement of their hideous change.

(1667)

He] Beelzebub superior fiend] Satan Ethereal temper] Hardened in celestial fire massy] massive optic glass] telescope artist] scientist (Galileo) Fesole] Fiesole (overlooking the Arno) ammiral] flagship marl] ground Natheless] Nevertheless (archaic) vexed] tossed Busiris] the Pharaoh (Exod. 14) Memphian] Egyptian sojourners of Goshen] the Israelites amazement stupefaction

524 [*Mulciber*]

THE ascending pile
Stood fixed her stately highth, and straight the doors
Opening their brazen folds discover wide
Within, her ample spaces, o'er the smooth
And level pavement; from the archèd roof
Pendent by subtle magic many a row
Of starry lamps and blazing cressets fed
With naphtha and asphaltus yielded light
As from a sky. The hasty multitude
Admiring entered, and the work some praise
And some the architect: his hand was known
In heaven by many a towered structure high,
Where sceptred angels held their residence,
And sat as princes, whom the súpreme king
Exalted to such power, and gave to rule,
Each in his hierarchy, the orders bright.
Nor was his name unheard or unadored
In ancient Greece; and in Ausonian land
Men called him Mulciber; and how he fell
From heaven, they fabled, thrown by angry Jove
Sheer o'er the crystal battlements; from morn
To noon he fell, from noon to dewy eve,
A summer's day; and with the setting sun
Dropped from the zenith like a falling star
On Lemnos the Aegaean isle: thus they relate,
Erring; for he with this rebellious rout
Fell long before; nor aught availed him now
To have built in heaven high towers; nor did he scape
By all his engines, but was headlong sent
With his industrious crew to build in hell.

(1667)

525 [*Occupations of Hell*]

THUS saying rose
The monarch, and prevented all reply;
Prudent, lest from his resolution raised
Others among the chief might offer now
(Certain to be refused) what erst they feared;

straight] immediately naphtha] oil asphaltus] pitch Ausonian land] Italy Mulciber] Vulcan; Roman god of fire and metallurgy engines] devices

525 prevented] forestalled erst] at first (archaism)

And so refused might in opinion stand
His rivals, winning cheap the high repute
Which he through hazard huge must earn. But they
Dreaded not more the adventure than his voice
Forbidding, and at once with him they rose:
Their rising all at once was as the sound
Of thunder heard remote. Towards him they bend
With awful reverence prone; and as a god
Extol him equal to the highest in heaven;
Nor failed they to express how much they praised,
That for the general safety he despised
His own; for neither do the spirits damned
Lose all their virtue; lest bad men should boast
Their specious deeds on Earth, which glory excites,
Or close ambition varnished o'er with zeal.
Thus they their doubtful consultations dark
Ended rejoicing in their matchless chief;
As, when from mountain tops the dusky clouds
Ascending, while the north wind sleeps, o'erspread
Heaven's cheerful face, the louring element
Scowls o'er the darkened landscape snow or shower:
If chance the radiant sun with farewell sweet
Extend his evening beam, the fields revive,
The birds their notes renew, and bleating herds
Attest their joy, that hill and valley rings.
Oh shame to men! Devil with devil damned
Firm concord holds; men only disagree
Of creatures rational, though under hope
Of heavenly grace, and God proclaiming peace,
Yet live in hatred, enmity, and strife
Among themselves, and levy cruel wars,
Wasting the earth, each other to destroy;
As if (which might induce us to accord)
Man had not hellish foes enow besides,
That day and night for his destruction wait.
  The Stygian council thus dissolved; and forth
In order came the grand infernal peers:
Midst came their mighty paramount, and seemed
Alone the antagonist of heaven, nor less
Than hell's dread emperor with pomp supreme
And God-like imitated state; him round
A globe of fiery seraphim enclosed

awful] full of awe prone] grovelling close] secret element] sky
chance] by chance that hill] so that hill accord] agree enow] enough
Stygian] hellish (from Styx, a river of Hades) paramount] overlord, supremo
globe] throng

With bright emblazonry and horrent arms.
Then of their session ended they bid cry
With trumpets' regal sound the great result:
Toward the four winds four speedy cherubim
Put to their mouths the sounding alchemy
By herald's voice explained: the hollow abyss
Heard far and wide, and all the host of hell
With deafening shout returned them loud acclaim.
Thence more at ease their minds and somewhat raised
By false presumptuous hope, the rangèd powers
Disband, and wandering, each his several way
Pursues, as inclinatïon or sad choice
Leads him perplexed, where he may likeliest find
Truce to his restless thoughts, and entertain
The irksome hours, till this great chief return.
Part on the plain, or in the air sublime
Upon the wing, or in swift race contend,
As at the Olympian games or Pythian fields;
Part curb their fiery steeds, or shun the goal
With rapid wheels, or fronted brígades form.
As when to warn proud cities war appears
Waged in the troubled sky, and armies rush
To battle in the clouds, before each van
Prick forth the airy knights, and couch their spears
Till thickest legions close; with feats of arms
From either end of heaven the welkin burns.
Others with vast Typhoean rage more fell
Rend up both rocks and hills, and ride the air
In whirlwind; hell scarce holds the wild uproar.
As when Alcides, from Oechalia crowned
With conquest, felt the envenomed robe, and tore
Through pain up by the roots Thessalian pines,
And Lichas from the top of Oeta threw
Into the Euboic sea. Others more mild,
Retreated in a silent valley, sing
With notes angelical to many a harp
Their own heroic deeds and hapless fall
By doom of battle; and complain that fate
Free virtue should enthral to force or chance.
Their song was partial, but the harmony

emblazonry] heraldic devices horrent] bristling alchemy] brass raised] encouraged rangèd] drawn up in ranks powers] armies sublime] uplifted (archaic) or . . . or] either . . . or Pythian fields] games held at Delphi goal] turning post of the chariot race fronted] arranged in line of battle Typhoean] fiery (from Typhon the flame-breathing monster) Alcides] Hercules Lichas] his guiltless attendant Euboic] Euboean partial] (1) biassed; (2) polyphonic

(What could it less when spirits immortal sing?)
Suspended hell, and took with ravishment
The thronging audience. In discourse more sweet
(For eloquence the soul, song charms the sense),
Others apart sat on a hill retired,
In thoughts more elevate, and reasoned high
Of providence, foreknowledge, will and fate,
Fixed fate, free will, foreknowledge absolute,
And found no end, in wandering mazes lost.
Of good and evil much they argued then,
Of happiness and final misery,
Passion and apathy, and glory and shame,
Vain wisdom all, and false philosophy;
Yet with a pleasing sorcery could charm
Pain for a while or anguish, and excite
Fallacious hope, or arm the obdured breast
With stubborn patience as with triple steel.
Another part in squadrons and gross bands,
On bold adventure to discover wide
That dismal world, if any clime perhaps
Might yield them easier habitation, bend
Four ways their flying march, along the banks
Of four infernal rivers that disgorge
Into the burning lake their baleful streams:
Abhorrèd Styx the flood of deadly hate;
Sad Acheron of sorrow, black and deep;
Cocytus, named of lamentation loud
Heard on the rueful stream; fierce Phlegethon
Whose waves of torrent fire inflame with rage.
Far off from these a slow and silent stream,
Lethe the river of oblivion, rolls
Her watery labyrinth, whereof who drinks,
Forthwith his former state and being forgets,
Forgets both joy and grief, pleasure and pain.
Beyond this flood a frozen continent
Lies dark and wild, beat with perpetual storms
Of whirlwind and dire hail, which on firm land
Thaws not, but gathers heap, and ruin seems
Of ancient pile; all else deep snow and ice,
A gulf profound as that Serbonian bog
Betwixt Damiata and Mount Casius old,
Where armies whole have sunk: the parching air

apathy] absence of passion   obdured] hardened   gross] large   baleful] evil   Styx] 'Hateful'   Acheron] 'Sorrowful'   pile] stronghold   Serbonian] at Serbonis, an Egyptian lake   Damiata] Damietta, east of the Nile   parching] drying

Burns frore, and cold performs the effect of fire.
Thither by harpy-footed Furies haled,
At certain revolutions all the damned
Are brought, and feel by turns the bitter change
Of fierce extremes, extremes by change more fierce,
From beds of raging fire to starve in ice
Their soft ethereal warmth, and there to pine
Immovable, infixed, and frozen round,
Periods of time, thence hurried back to fire.
They ferry over this Lethean sound
Both to and fro, their sorrow to augment,
And wish and struggle, as they pass, to reach
The tempting stream, with one small drop to lose
In sweet forgetfulness all pain and woe,
All in one moment, and so near the brink;
But fate withstands, and to oppose the attempt
Medusa with Gorgonian terror guards
The ford, and of itself the water flies
All taste of living wight, as once it fled
The lip of Tantalus. Thus roving on
In confused march forlorn, the adventurous bands
With shuddering horror pale and eyes aghast
Viewed first their lamentable lot, and found
No rest: through many a dark and dreary vale
They passed, and many a region dolorous,
O'er many a frozen, many a fiery alp,
Rocks, caves, lakes, fens, bogs, dens, and shades of death,
A universe of death, which God by curse
Created evil, for evil only good,
Where all life dies, death lives, and nature breeds,
Perverse, all monstrous, all prodigious things,
Abominable, inutterable, and worse
Than fables yet have feigned or fear conceived,
Gorgons and Hydras and Chimeras dire.

(1667)

frore] freezing cold harpy-footed] with claws like the Harpies (mythological agencies of vengeance) Furies] avenging goddesses (Roman mythology) revolutions] recurrent periods starve] benumb; freeze Medusa] Gorgon with petrifying glance (Roman mythology) Tantalus] (punished by thirst for impiety: Greek mythology) prodigious] unnatural Gorgons] serpentheaded monsters (Greek mythology) Hydras] monsters with multiple regenerating heads Chimeras] composite monsters

526 [*Satan's Journey*]

INTO this wild abyss,
The womb of nature and perhaps her grave,
Of neither sea, nor shore, nor air, nor fire,
But all these in their pregnant causes mixed
Confusedly, and which thus must ever fight,
Unless the almighty maker them ordain
His dark materials to create more worlds,
Into this wild abyss the wary fiend
Stood on the brink of hell and looked a while,
Pondering his voyage; for no narrow frith
He had to cross. Nor was his ear less pealed
With noises loud and ruinous (to compare
Great things with small) than when Bellona storms,
With all her battering engines bent to raze
Some capital city; or less than if this frame
Of heaven were falling, and these elements
In mutiny had from her axle torn
The steadfast Earth. At last his sail-broad vans
He spreads for flight, and in the surging smoke
Uplifted spurns the ground; thence many a league
As in a cloudy chair ascending rides
Audacious; but that seat soon failing, meets
A vast vacuity: all unawares
Fluttering his pennons vain plumb down he drops
Ten thousand fathom deep, and to this hour
Down had been falling, had not by ill chance
The strong rebuff of some tumultuous cloud
Instinct with fire and nitre hurried him
As many miles aloft; that fury stayed,
Quenched in a boggy Syrtis, neither sea
Nor good dry land; nigh foundered on he fares,
Treading the crude consistence, half on foot,
Half flying; behoves him now both oar and sail.
As when a gryphon through the wilderness
With wingèd course o'er hill or moory dale
Pursues the Arimaspian, who by stealth
Had from his wakeful custody purloined
The guarded gold: so eagerly the fiend

Of neither . . . mixed] not consisting of elements but of their component qualities fiend] Satan frith] firth pealed] dinned ruinous] falling Bellona] (Roman goddess of war) vans] wings (poetic) pennons] plumes (Latinism) Instinct] Inflamed Syrtis] dangerous sandbank off Tripoli gryphon] gold-guarding monster, half lion half eagle Arimaspian] (one-eyed people: Greek legend)

O'er bog or steep, through straight, rough, dense, or rare,
With head, hands, wings or feet pursues his way,
And swims or sinks, or wades, or creeps, or flies . . .

(1667)

527 [*Invocation to Light*]

HAIL, holy Light, offspring of heaven first-born,
Or of the eternal co-eternal beam
May I express thee unblamed? since God is light,
And never but in unapproachèd light
Dwelt from eternity, dwelt then in thee,
Bright effluence of bright essence increate.
Or hearst thou rather pure ethereal stream,
Whose fountain who shall tell? Before the sun,
Before the heavens thou wert, and at the voice
Of God, as with a mantle didst invest
The rising world of waters dark and deep,
Won from the void and formless infinite.
Thee I revisit now with bolder wing,
Escaped the Stygian pool, though long detained
In that obscure sojourn, while in my flight
Through utter and through middle darkness borne
With other notes than to the Orphean lyre
I sung of chaos and eternal night,
Taught by the heavenly Muse to venture down
The dark descent, and up to reascend,
Though hard and rare: thee I revisit safe,
And feel thy sovereign vital lamp; but thou
Revisitst not these eyes, that roll in vain
To find thy piercing ray, and find no dawn;
So thick a drop serene hath quenched their orbs,
Or dim suffusion veiled. Yet not the more
Cease I to wander where the Muses haunt
Clear spring, or shady grove, or sunny hill,
Smit with the love of sacred song; but chief
Thee Sion and the flowery brooks beneath
That wash thy hallowed feet, and warbling flow,
Nightly I visit; nor sometimes forget
Those other two equalled with me in fate,

express] image effluence] emanation increate] uncreated hearst] do you prefer (Latinism) ethereal] spiritual invest] cover infinite] i.e. chaos Stygian pool] hell utter] outer other notes] i.e. epic (Orpheus' were lyric) Muse] Urania drop serene] *gutta serena*, an eye disease dim suffusion] *suffusio nigra*, cataract Sion] i.e. Hebrew poetry

So were I equalled with them in renown,
Blind Thamyris and blind Maeonides,
And Tiresias and Phineus prophets old.
Then feed on thoughts, that voluntary move
Harmonious numbers; as the wakeful bird
Sings darkling, and in shadiest covert hid
Tunes her nocturnal note. Thus with the year
Seasons return, but not to me returns
Day, or the sweet approach of even or morn,
Or sight of vernal bloom, or summer's rose,
Or flocks, or herds, or human face divine;
But cloud instead and ever-during dark
Surrounds me, from the cheerful ways of men
Cut off, and for the book of knowledge fair
Presented with a universal blank
Of nature's works to me expunged and razed,
And wisdom at one entrance quite shut out.
So much the rather thou celestial Light
Shine inward, and the mind through all her powers
Irradiate; there plant eyes, all mist from thence
Purge and disperse, that I may see and tell
Of things invisible to mortal sight.

(1667)

528 [*Paradise*]

In narrow room nature's whole wealth, yea more,
A heaven on Earth, for blissful paradise
Of God the garden was, by him in the east
Of Eden planted; Eden stretched her line
From Auran eastward to the royal towers
Of great Seleucia, built by Grecian kings,
Or where the sons of Eden long before
Dwelt in Telassar: in this pleasant soil
His far more pleasant garden God ordained;
Out of the fertile ground he caused to grow
All trees of noblest kind for sight, smell, taste;
And all amid them stood the tree of life,

Thamyris] (Thracian bard blinded by the Muses: Greek myth) Maeonides] Homer Tiresias] (blind augur of Thebes: Greek myth) Phineus] blind Thracian king (compensated with gifts of prophecy) numbers] rhythms bird] nightingale darkling] in the dark (not poetic) blank] (1) blank page; (2) void

528 Auran] Hauran (Ezek. 27: 23) Seleucia] (seat of Seleucus Nicator, Alexander's general) Telassar] destroyed city (Is. 37: 11–12)

High eminent, blooming ambrosial fruit
Of vegetable gold; and next to life
Our death the tree of knowledge grew fast by,
Knowledge of good bought dear by knowing ill.
Southward through Eden went a river large,
Nor changed his course, but through the shaggy hill
Passed underneath ingulfed; for God had thrown
That mountain as his garden mould high raised
Upon the rapid current, which through veins
Of porous earth with kindly thirst up drawn,
Rose a fresh fountain, and with many a rill
Watered the garden; thence united fell
Down the steep glade, and met the nether flood,
Which from his darksome passage now appears,
And now divided into four main streams
Runs diverse, wandering many a famous realm
And country whereof here needs no account;
But rather to tell how, if art could tell,
How from that sapphire fount the crispèd brooks,
Rolling on orient pearl and sands of gold,
With mazy error under pendant shades
Ran nectar, visiting each plant, and fed
Flowers worthy of paradise which not nice art
In beds and curious knots, but nature boon
Poured forth profuse on hill and dale and plain,
Both where the morning sun first warmly smote
The open field, and where the unpierced shade
Embrowned the noontide bowers; thus was this place
A happy rural seat of various view:
Groves whose rich trees wept odorous gums and balm,
Others whose fruit burnished with golden rind
Hung amiable, Hesperian fables true,
If true, here only, and of delicious taste;
Betwixt them lawns, or level downs, and flocks
Grazing the tender herb, were interposed,
Or palmy hillock, or the flowery lap
Of some irriguous valley spread her store,
Flowers of all hue, and without thorn the rose;

blooming] causing to flourish ambrosial] fragrant, perfumed; immortal vegetable gold] living gold (quasi-alchemic term) a river] the Tigris kindly thirst] natural attraction crispèd] curled in short waves Rolling] Moving smoothly error] devious course nice] over-fastidious curious] artificial knots] patterned flowerbeds boon] bountiful Embrowned] Duskened (poetic) amiable] desirable Hesperian] like those of the guarded fruit of the Hesperides (Greek myth) lawns] clearings irriguous] well-watered store] plenty

Another side, umbrageous grots and caves
Of cool recess, o'er which the mantling vine
Lays forth her purple grape, and gently creeps
Luxuriant; meanwhile murmuring waters fall
Down the slope hills, dispersed, or in a lake,
That to the fringèd bank with myrtle crowned
Her crystal mirror holds, unite their streams.
The birds their choir apply; airs, vernal airs,
Breathing the smell of field and grove, attune
The trembling leaves, while universal Pan
Knit with the Graces and the Hours in dance
Led on the eternal spring. Not that fair field
Of Enna, where Proserpine gathering flowers
Herself a fairer flower by gloomy Dis
Was gathered, which cost Ceres all that pain
To seek her through the world; nor that sweet grove
Of Daphne by Orontes, and the inspired
Castalian spring, might with this paradise
Of Eden strive; nor that Nyseian isle
Girt with the river Triton, where old Cham,
Whom gentiles Ammon call and Libyan Jove,
Hid Amalthea and her florid son
Young Bacchus from his stepdame Rhea's eye;
Nor where Abássin kings their issue guard,
Mount Amara, though this by some supposed
True paradise under the Ethiop line
By Nilus' head, enclosed with shining rock,
A whole day's journey high, but wide remote
From this Assyrian garden, where the fiend
Saw undelighted all delight, all kind
Of living creatures new to sight and strange:
Two of far nobler shape erect and tall,
Godlike erect, with native honour clad
In naked majesty seemed lords of all,
And worthy seemed, for in their looks divine
The image of their glorious maker shone,
Truth, wisdom, sanctitude severe and pure,

umbrageous] shady apply] attend to assiduously Pan] 'All'; ancient god of nature Knit] Clasping hands Graces] daughters of Zeus (beauty and cyclic pattern of nature) Hours] *Horae* (seasons) Proserpine] Ceres' daughter (taken off to Hades by Pluto) Dis] Pluto Ceres] (Roman goddess of harvest) Daphne] (grove with an oracle ('inspired') and spring) Orontes] (near Antioch) Nyseian isle] Nysa, near Tunis Cham] Ham (Noah's son) Libyan Jove] Jupiter Ammon (later transformed to Aries) Amalthea] Amaltheia (beloved of Ammon king of Libya) florid] ruddy Rhea] Ammon's wife (daughter of the sky-god Uranus) Abássin] Abyssinian Ethiop line] equator Nilus'] river Nile

Severe but in true filial freedom placed;
Whence true authority in men; though both
Not equal, as their sex not equal seemed;
For contemplation he and valour formed,
For softness she and sweet attractive grace,
He for God only, she for God in him:
His fair large front and eye sublime declared
Absolute rule; and hyacinthine locks
Round from his parted forelock manly hung
Clustering, but not beneath his shoulders broad:
She as a veil down to the slender waist
Her unadornèd golden tresses wore
Dishevelled, but in wanton ringlets waved
As the vine curls her tendrils; which implied
Subjection, but required with gentle sway,
And by her yielded, by him best received,
Yielded with coy submission, modest pride,
And sweet reluctant amorous delay.
Nor those mysterious parts were then concealed,
Then was not guilty shame, dishonest shame
Of nature's works, honour dishonourable—
Sin-bred, how have ye troubled all mankind
With shows instead, mere shows of seeming pure,
And banished from man's life his happiest life,
Simplicity and spotless innocence.

(1667)

529 [*Unfallen Love*]

HAIL, wedded love, mysterious law, true source
Of human offspring, sole propriety
In paradise of all things common else.
By thee adulterous lust was driven from men
Among the bestial herds to range, by thee
Founded in reason, loyal, just, and pure,
Relations dear, and all the charities
Of father, son, and brother first were known.
Far be it that I should write thee sin or blame,
Or think thee unbefitting holiest place,
Perpetual fountain of domestic sweets,
Whose bed is undefiled and chaste pronounced,

large front] broad forehead sublime] uplifted Absolute] Consummate; independent; confident sway] inclination coy] modest

529 mysterious] symbolic propriety] ownership charities] loves, affections sweets] delights

Present or past, as saints and patriarchs used.
Here Love his golden shafts employs, here lights
His constant lamp, and waves his purple wings,
Reigns here and revels; not in the bought smile
Of harlots, loveless, joyless, unendeared,
Casual fruition, nor in court amours,
Mixed dance, or wanton mask, or midnight ball,
Or serenade, which the starved lover sings
To his proud fair, best quitted with disdain.
These lulled by nightingales embracing slept,
And on their naked limbs the flowery roof
Showered roses, which the morn repaired. Sleep on
Blest pair; and O yet happiest if ye seek
No happier state, and know to know no more.

(1667)

530 [*Raphael's Descent*]

NOR delayed the wingèd saint
After his charge received; but from among
Thousand celestial ardours, where he stood
Veiled with his gorgeous wings, up springing light
Flew through the midst of heaven; the angelic choirs
On each hand parting, to his speed gave way
Through all the empýreal road; till at the gate
Of heaven arrived, the gate self-opened wide
On golden hinges turning, as by work
Divine the sovereign architect had framed.
From hence, no cloud or, to obstruct his sight,
Star interposed, however small he sees,
Not unconform to other shining globes,
Earth and the garden of God, with cedars crowned
Above all hills. As when by night the glass
Of Galileo, less assured, observes
Imagined lands and regions in the moon;
Or pilot from amidst the Cyclades
Delos or Samos first appearing kens
A cloudy spot. Down thither prone in flight
He speeds, and through the vast ethereal sky
Sails between worlds and worlds, with steady wing

mask] masked dance or revel   starved] (1) starved of love; (2) perished with cold   repaired] renewed

530 saint] angel   charge] commission   ardours] flames; fervours   glass] telescope   Cyclades] circular archipelago in the Aegean   kens] distinguishes

Now on the polar winds, then with quick fan
Winnows the buxom air; till, within soar
Of towering eagles, to all the fowls he seems
A phoenix, gazed by all, as that sole bird
When to enshrine his relics in the sun's
Bright temple, to Aegyptian Thebes he flies.
  At once on the eastern cliff of paradise
He lights, and to his proper shape returns,
A seraph winged; six wings he wore, to shade
His lineaments divine; the pair that clad
Each shoulder broad came mantling o'er his breast
With regal ornament; the middle pair
Girt like a starry zone his waist, and round
Skirted his loins and thighs with downy gold
And colours dipped in heaven; the third his feet
Shadowed from either heel with feathered mail
Sky-tinctured grain. Like Maia's son he stood,
And shook his plumes, that heavenly fragrance filled
The circuit wide.

(1667)

531 [*Ascent of Species*]

  To whom the wingèd hierarch replied:
'O Adam, one almighty is, from whom
All things proceed, and up to him return,
If not depraved from good, created all
Such to perfection, one first matter all,
Indued with various forms, various degrees
Of substance, and in things that live, of life;
But more refined, more spirituous, and pure,
As nearer to him placed or nearer tending
Each in their several active spheres assigned,
Till body up to spirit work, in bounds
Proportioned to each kind. So from the root
Springs lighter the green stalk, from thence the leaves
More airy, last the bright consummate flower
Spirits odorous breathes: flowers and their fruit
Man's nourishment, by gradual scale sublimed
To vital spirits aspire, to animal,

fan] wing (poetic) buxom] yielding towering] rising high; or 'touring' (wheeling) phoenix] mythic unique bird, periodically renewed from its own ashes lineaments] figure regal] purple zone] belt grain] in grain; fast dyed Maia's son] Mercury, Roman ambassador-god that heavenly] so that heavenly

531 hierarch] Raphael first matter] material of creation consummate] perfected scale] cosmic ladder sublimed] (1) raised; (2) sublimated (alchemy) vital spirits] fluids sustaining life animal (spirits)] fluids controlling sensation and motion

To intellectual, give both life and sense,
Fancy and understanding, whence the soul
Reason receives, and reason is her being,
Discursive, or intuitive; discourse
Is oftest yours, the latter most is ours,
Differing but in degree, of kind the same.
Wonder not then, what God for you saw good
If I refuse not, but convert, as you,
To proper substance; time may come when men
With angels may participate, and find
No inconvenient diet, nor too light fare;
And from these corporal nutriments perhaps
Your bodies may at last turn all to spirit,
Improved by tract of time, and winged ascend
Ethereal, as we, or may at choice
Here or in heavenly paradises dwell;
If ye be found obedient, and retain
Unalterably firm his love entire
Whose progeny you are.'

(1667)

532 [*Invocation to Urania*]

DESCEND from heaven, Urania, by that name
If rightly thou art called, whose voice divine
Following, above the Olympian hill I soar,
Above the flight of Pegasean wing.
The meaning, not the name I call; for thou
Nor of the Muses nine, nor on the top
Of old Olympus dwellst, but heavenly born,
Before the hills appeared, or fountain flowed,
Thou with eternal Wisdom didst converse,
Wisdom thy sister, and with her didst play
In presence of the almighty Father, pleased
With thy celestial song. Up led by thee
Into the heaven of heavens I have presumed,
An earthly guest, and drawn empyreal air,
Thy tempering; with like safety guided down
Return me to my native element,
Lest from this flying steed unreined (as once

proper] distinctive   tract] lapse   Ethereal] Spiritual

532 Urania] Celestial (the Christian Muse)   Olympian hill] Mt. Olympus (home of the pagan gods)   Pegasean] of Pegasus (mythic winged horse, emblem of inspiration)   Wisdom] daughter of God (Prov. 8)   drawn empyreal air] breathed upper air (fatal to mortals)   native element] Earth

Bellerophon, though from a lower clime),
Dismounted, on the Aleian field I fall
Erroneous there to wander and forlorn.
Half yet remains unsung, but narrower bound
Within the visible diurnal sphere;
Standing on Earth, not rapt above the pole,
More safe I sing with mortal voice, unchanged
To hoarse or mute, though fallen on evil days,
On evil days though fallen, and evil tongues;
In darkness, and with dangers compassed round,
And solitude; yet not alone, while thou
Visitst my slumbers nightly, or when morn
Purples the east: still govern thou my song,
Urania, and fit audience find, though few.
But drive far off the barbarous dissonance
Of Bacchus and his revellers, the race
Of that wild rout that tore the Thracian bard
In Rhodope, where woods and rocks had ears
To rapture, till the savage clamour drowned
Both harp and voice; nor could the Muse defend
Her son. So fail not thou, who thee implores;
For thou art heavenly, she an empty dream.

(1667)

533 [*Creation*]

AND God said, 'Let the waters generate
Reptile with spawn abundant, living soul;
And let fowl fly above the Earth, with wings
Displayed on the open firmament of heaven.'
And God created the great whales, and each
Soul living, each that crept, which plenteously
The waters generated by their kinds,
And every bird of wing after his kind;
And saw that it was good, and blessed them, saying,
'Be fruitful, multiply, and in the seas
And lakes and running streams the waters fill;
And let the fowl be multiplied on the Earth.'

Bellerophon] 'Monster-killer' (who tried to fly Pegasus to heaven) clime] (1) region; (2) climb Aleian] Cilician Erroneous] (1) Wandering; (2) straying from wisdom diurnal sphere] firmament pole] sky In darkness] i.e. blind Thracian bard] Orpheus (dismembered during a Bacchic orgy) Rhodope] mountain range in Thrace she] the Muse Calliope

533 Reptile] Crawling creature soul] animate existence his kind] its nature; its species

Forthwith the sounds and seas, each creek and bay
With fry innumerable swarm, and shoals
Of fish that with their fins and shining scales
Glide under the green wave, in schools that oft
Bank the mid sea: part single or with mate
Graze the sea weed their pasture, and through groves
Of coral stray, or sporting with quick glance
Show to the sun their waved coats dropped with gold,
Or in their pearly shells at ease attend
Moist nutriment, or under rocks their food
In jointed armour watch; on smooth the seal
And bended dolphins play; part huge of bulk
Wallowing unwieldy, enormous in their gait
Tempest the ocean: there leviathan,
Hugest of living creatures, on the deep
Stretched like a promontory sleeps or swims,
And seems a moving land, and at his gills
Draws in, and at his trunk spouts out a sea.
Meanwhile the tepid caves and fens and shores
Their brood as numerous hatch, from the egg that soon
Bursting with kindly rupture forth disclosed
Their callow young, but feathered soon and fledge
They summed their pens, and soaring the air sublime
With clang despised the ground, under a cloud
In prospect; there the eagle and the stork
On cliffs and cedar tops their eyries build:
Part loosely wing the region, part more wise
In common, ranged in figure wedge their way,
Intelligent of seasons, and set forth
Their airy caravan high over seas
Flying, and over lands with mutual wing
Easing their flight; so steers the prudent crane
Her annual voyage, borne on winds: the air
Floats, as they pass, fanned with unnumbered plumes.
From branch to branch the smaller birds with song
Solaced the woods, and spread their painted wings
Till even, nor then the solemn nightingale
Ceased warbling, but all night tuned her soft lays;

Bank] Form a shelf just under the surface waved] (1) undulating; (2) divided wavy (heraldry) dropped] (1) speckled; (2) spotted (heraldry) attend] await smooth] smooth water (nautical) bended] (1) curving (stock Latin epithet); (2) banded (heraldry) Tempest] Violently disturb kindly] natural callow] unfeathered fledge] fit for flight summed . . . pens] completed their plumage (falconry) sublime] aloft clang] harsh resonant cry despised] looked down on Intelligent] Cognizant caravan] convoy with . . . wing] supporting one another (traditional belief) Floats] Undulates unnumbered] innumerable painted] variegated in colour (Virgilian)

Others on silver lakes and rivers bathed
Their downy breast: the swan with archèd neck
Between her white wings mantling proudly, rows
Her state with oary feet: yet oft they quit
The dank, and rising on stiff pennons, tower
The mid aërial sky; others on ground
Walked firm: the crested cock whose clarion sounds
The silent hours, and the other whose gay train
Adorns him, coloured with the florid hue
Of rainbows and starry eyes. The waters thus
With fish replenished, and the air with fowl,
Evening and morn solemnized the fifth day.
  The sixth, and of creation last, arose
With evening harps and matin, when God said,
'Let the earth bring forth soul living in her kind,
Cattle and creeping things, and beast of the earth,
Each in their kind.' The earth obeyed, and straight
Opening her fertile womb teemed at a birth
Innumerous living creatures, perfect forms,
Limbed and full grown: out of the ground up rose
As from his lair the wild beast where he wons
In forest wild, in thicket, brake, or den;
Among the trees in pairs they rose, they walked,
The cattle in the fields and meadows green:
Those rare and solitary, these in flocks
Pasturing at once, and in broad herds upsprung.
The grassy clods now calved, now half appeared
The tawny lion, pawing to get free
His hinder parts, then springs as broke from bonds,
And rampant shakes his brinded mane; the ounce,
The libbard, and the tiger, as the mole
Rising, the crumbled earth above them threw
In hillocks; the swift stag from underground
Bore up his branching head; scarce from his mould
Behemoth biggest born of earth upheaved
His vastness; fleeced the flocks and bleating rose,
As plants; ambiguous between sea and land
The river horse and scaly crocodile.
At once came forth whatever creeps the ground,

mantling] forming a mantle   state] dignity   dank] pool   tower] soar into   other] peacock   matin] (1) morning; (2) Office of Matins   Cattle] Livestock   straight] immediately   teemed] bore   Innumerous] Innumerable   wons] lives   rare] spread out   broad] large (Homeric)   brinded] brindled   ounce] lynx   libbard] leopard   mould] soil   Behemoth] Elephant (Job 40: 15)   ambiguous] (1) doubting; (2) of doubtful category   river horse] hippopotamus

Insect or worm: those waved their limber fans
For wings, and smallest lineaments exact
In all the liveries decked of summer's pride
With spots of gold and purple, azure and green;
These as a line their long dimension drew,
Streaking the ground with sinuous trace: not all
Minims of nature; some of serpent kind
Wondrous in length and corpulence involved
Their snaky folds, and added wings. First crept
The parsimonious emmet, provident
Of future, in small room large heart enclosed,
Pattern of just equality perhaps
Hereafter, joined in her popular tribes
Of commonalty; swarming next appeared
The female bee that feeds her husband drone
Deliciously, and builds her waxen cells
With honey stored: the rest are numberless,
And thou their natures knowst, and gavest them names,
Needless to thee repeated; nor unknown
The serpent subtlest beast of all the field,
Of huge extent sometimes, with brazen eyes
And hairy mane terrific, though to thee
Not noxious, but obedient at thy call.
Now heaven in all her glory shone, and rolled
Her motions, as the great first mover's hand
First wheeled their course; earth in her rich attire
Consummate lovely smiled; air, water, earth,
By fowl, fish, beast, was flown, was swam, was walked
Frequent; and of the sixth day yet remained:
There wanted yet the master work, the end
Of all yet done: a creature who not prone
And brute as other creatures, but endued
With sanctity of reason, might erect
His stature, and upright with front serene
Govern the rest, self-knowing, and from thence
Magnanimous to correspond with heaven,
But grateful to acknowledge whence his good
Descends, thither with heart and voice and eyes
Directed in devotion, to adore
And worship God supreme, who made him chief
Of all his works.

(1667)

worm] serpent, grub, maggot, caterpillar Minims] Smallest forms corpulence] bulk involved] coiled emmet] ant commonalty] democracy terrific] terrible motions] movements (of the spheres) Frequent] Abundantly front] forehead Magnanimous] Great-souled

534 [*Higher Argument*]

No more of talk where God or angel guest
With man, as with his friend, familiar used
To sit indulgent, and with him partake
Rural repast, permitting him the while
Venial discourse unblamed: I now must change
Those notes to tragic: foul distrust, and breach
Disloyal on the part of man, revolt,
And disobedience; on the part of heaven
Now alienated, distance and distaste,
Anger and just rebuke, and judgment given,
That brought into this world a world of woe,
Sin and her shadow death, and misery
Death's harbinger: sad task, yet argument
Not less but more heroic than the wrath
Of stern Achilles on his foe pursued
Thrice fugitive about Troy wall; or rage
Of Turnus for Lavinia disespoused,
Or Neptune's ire or Juno's, that so long
Perplexed the Greek and Cytherea's son;
If answerable style I can obtain
Of my celestial patroness, who deigns
Her nightly visitation unimplored,
And díctates to me slumbering, or inspires
Easy my unpremeditated verse:
Since first this subject for heroic song
Pleased me long choosing, and beginning late;
Not sedulous by nature to indite
Wars, hitherto the only argument
Heroic deemed, chief mastery to dissect
With long and tedious havoc fabled knights
In battles feigned, the better fortitude
Of patience and heroic martyrdom
Unsung; or to describe races and games,
Or tilting furniture, emblazoned shields,
Impreses quaint, caparisons and steeds;

familiar] intimate; on a family footing Venial] Permissible breach] (1) break-up of friendship; (2) violation argument] theme his foe] Hector rage] passion disespoused] deprived of her suitor Turnus (killed by Aeneas) Neptune's] i.e. Homer's sea-god Poseidon Juno's] wife of Jupiter Perplexed the Greek] Tormented Odysseus Cytherea's son] Aeneas answerable] (1) equivalent; (2) accountable patroness] Urania, heavenly Muse mastery] art, skill feigned] fictional tilting furniture] tournament armour Impreses] Heraldic devices or mottoes quaint] ingenious; pretty; cute caparisons] horse armour

Bases and tinsel trappings, gorgeous knights
At joust and tournament; then marshalled feast
Served up in hall with sewers, and seneschals:
The skill of artifice or office mean,
Not that which justly gives heroic name
To person or to poem. Me of these
Nor skilled nor studious, higher argument
Remains, sufficient of itself to raise
That name, unless an age too late, or cold
Climate, or years damp my intended wing
Depressed, and much they may, if all be mine,
Not hers who brings it nightly to my ear.

(1667)

535 [*Uncloistered Virtue*]

To whom with healing words Adam replied.
'Daughter of God and man, immortal Eve,
For such thou art, from sin and blame entire:
Not diffident of thee do I dissuade
Thy absence from my sight, but to avoid
The attempt itself, intended by our foe.
For he who tempts, though in vain, at least asperses
The tempted with dishonour foul, supposed
Not incorruptible of faith, not proof
Against temptation: thou thyself with scorn
And anger wouldst resent the offered wrong,
Though ineffectual found; misdeem not then,
If such affront I labour to avert
From thee alone, which on us both at once
The enemy, though bold, will hardly dare,
Or daring, first on me the assault shall light.
Nor thou his malice and false guile contemn:
Subtle he needs must be, who could seduce
Angels; nor think superfluous others' aid.
I from the influence of thy looks receive
Access in every virtue, in thy sight
More wise, more watchful, stronger, if need were
Of outward strength; while shame, thou looking on,
Shame to be overcome or over-reached
Would utmost vigour raise, and raised unite.

Bases] Cloth housings for horses sewers] waiters seneschals] stewards artifice] mechanic art

535 entire] unblemished diffident] distrustful asperses] spatters faith] fidelity Access] Increase

Why shouldst not thou like sense within thee feel
When I am present, and thy trial choose
With me, best witness of thy virtue tried.'
  So spake domestic Adam in his care
And matrimonial love; but Eve, who thought
Less attribúted to her faith sincere,
Thus her reply with accent sweet renewed.
  'If this be our condition, thus to dwell
In narrow circuit straitened by a foe,
Subtle or violent, we not endued
Single with like defence, wherever met,
How are we happy, still in fear of harm?
But harm precedes not sin; only our foe
Tempting affronts us with his foul esteem
Of our integrity: his foul esteem
Sticks no dishonour on our front, but turns
Foul on himself; then wherefore shunned or feared
By us?—Who rather double honour gain
From his surmise proved false, find peace within,
Favour from heaven, our witness from the event.
And what is faith, love, virtue unassayed
Alone, without exterior help sustained?
Let us not then suspect our happy state
Left so imperfect by the maker wise,
As not secure to single or combined;
Frail is our happiness, if this be so,
And Eden were no Eden thus exposed.'
  To whom thus Adam fervently replied.
'O woman, best are all things as the will
Of God ordained them: his creating hand
Nothing imperfect or deficient left
Of all that he created, much less man,
Or aught that might his happy state secure,
Secure from outward force; within himself
The danger lies, yet lies within his power:
Against his will he can receive no harm.
But God left free the will, for what obeys
Reason, is free, and reason he made right,
But bid her well beware, and still erect,
Lest by some fair appearing good surprised
She díctate false, and misinform the will
To do what God expressly hath forbid.
Not then mistrust, but tender love enjoins

domestic] concerned for the family sincere] pure affronts] (1) insults; (2) sets face to face front] forehead no Eden] no pleasure (Hebrew) still erect] (1) always alert; (2) upright

That I should mind thee oft, and mind thou me.
Firm we subsist, yet possible to swerve,
Since reason not impossibly may meet
Some specious object by the foe suborned,
And fall into deception unaware,
Not keeping strictest watch, as she was warned.
Seek not temptation then, which to avoid
Were better, and most likely if from me
Thou sever not: trial will come unsought.
Wouldst thou approve thy constancy, approve
First thy obedience; the other who can know,
Not seeing thee attempted, who attest?
But if thou think trial unsought may find
Us both securer than thus warned thou seemst,
Go; for thy stay, not free, absents thee more:
Go in thy native innocence, rely
On what thou hast of virtue, summon all,
For God towards thee hath done his part, do thine.'
  So spake the patriarch of mankind, but Eve
Persisted: yet submiss, though last, replied.
  'With thy permission then, and thus forewarned
Chiefly by what thy own last reasoning words
Touched only, that our trial, when least sought,
May find us both perhaps far less prepared,
The willinger I go, nor much expect
A foe so proud will first the weaker seek;
So bent, the more shall shame him his repulse.'
  Thus saying, from her husband's hand her hand
Soft she withdrew . . .

(1667)

536 [*The Tempter Disarmed*]

SINCE first break of dawn the fiend,
Mere serpent in appearance, forth was come,
And on his quest, where likeliest he might find
The only two of mankind, but in them
The whole included race, his purposed prey.
In bower and field he sought, where any tuft
Of grove or garden-plot more pleasant lay,
Their tendance or plantation for delight,

mind] admonish; pay heed to sever] separate approve] demonstrate securer] more over-confident submiss] submissively

536 Mere serpent] Plain serpent, real serpent tendance] object of care

By fountain or by shady rivulet
He sought them both, but wished his hap might find
Eve separate: he wished, but not with hope
Of what so seldom chanced, when to his wish,
Beyond his hope, Eve separate he spies,
Veiled in a cloud of fragrance, where she stood,
Half spied, so thick the roses bushing round
About her glowed; oft stooping to support
Each flower of slender stalk, whose head though gay
Carnation, purple, azure, or specked with gold
Hung drooping unsustained; them she upstays
Gently with myrtle band, mindless the while
Herself, though fairest unsupported flower,
From her best prop so far, and storm so nigh.
Nearer he drew, and many a walk traversed
Of stateliest covert, cedar, pine, or palm,
Then voluble and bold, now hid, now seen
Among thick-woven arborets and flowers
Embordered on each bank, the hand of Eve:
Spot more delicious than those gardens feigned
Or of revived Adonis, or renowned
Alcinous, host of old Laertes' son;
Or that, not mystic, where the sapient king
Held dalliance with his fair Egyptian spouse.
Much he the place admired, the person more.
As one who long in populous city pent,
Where houses thick and sewers annoy the air,
Forth issuing on a summer's morn to breathe
Among the pleasant villages and farms
Adjoined, from each thing met conceives delight,
The smell of grain, or tedded grass, or kine,
Or dairy, each rural sight, each rural sound;
If chance with nymph-like step fair virgin pass,
What pleasing seemed, for her now pleases more,
She most, and in her look sums all delight.
Such pleasure took the serpent to behold
This flowery plat, the sweet recess of Eve
Thus early, thus alone; her heavenly form
Angelic, but more soft and feminine,

hap] chance band] bond mindless] heedless voluble] (1) gliding easily, undulating; (2) glib arborets] shrubs Embordered] (1) Set as a border; (2) furnished with a bordure or hem (heraldry) hand] handiwork feigned] fictional Or . . . or] Either . . . or revived] restored to life Adonis] vegetation god (Greek mythology) Laertes' son] Odysseus mystic] mythological sapient king] Solomon Egyptian spouse] the Pharaoh's daughter (1 Kgs. 3: 1) annoy] pollute tedded] spread to dry kine] cows for her] because of her plat] patch of ground

Her graceful innocence, her every air
Of gesture or least action overawed
His malice, and with rapine sweet bereaved
His fierceness of the fierce intent it brought:
That space the evil one abstracted stood
From his own evil, and for the time remained
Stupidly good, of enmity disarmed,
Of guile, of hate, of envy, of revenge . . .

(1667)

537 [*The Flood*]

'ONE man except, the only son of light
In a dark age, against example good,
Against allurement, custom, and a world
Offended; fearless of reproach and scorn,
Or violence, he of their wicked ways
Shall them admonish, and before them set
The paths of righteousness, how much more safe
And full of peace, denouncing wrath to come
On their impenitence; and shall return
Of them derided, but of God observed
The one just man alive; by his command
Shall build a wondrous ark, as thou beheldst,
To save himself and household from amidst
A world devote to universal rack.
No sooner he with them of man and beast
Select for life shall in the ark be lodged
And sheltered round, but all the cataracts
Of heaven set open on the Earth shall pour
Rain day and night, all fountains of the deep
Broke up shall heave the ocean to usurp
Beyond all bounds, till inundation rise
Above the highest hills; then shall this mount
Of paradise by might of waves be moved
Out of his place, pushed by the hornèd flood,
With all his verdure spoiled and trees adrift,
Down the great river to the opening gulf,
And there take root an island salt and bare,
The haunt of seals and orcs, and sea-mews' clang.
To teach thee that God áttributes to place
No sanctity, if none be thither brought

537 denouncing] proclaiming devote] doomed rack] destruction cataracts] flood-gates (Gen. 7: 11) heave] raise great river] Euphrates (Gen. 15: 18) gulf] Persian Gulf orcs] sea-monsters sea-mew] gull clang] scream

By men who there frequent, or therein dwell.
And now what further shall ensue, behold.'
He looked, and saw the ark hull on the flood,
Which now abated; for the clouds were fled,
Driven by a keen north wind, that blowing dry
Wrinkled the face of deluge, as decayed;
And the clear sun on his wide watery glass
Gazed hot, and of the fresh wave largely drew,
As after thirst, which made their flowing shrink
From standing lake to tripping ebb, that stole
With soft foot towards the deep, who now had stopped
His sluices, as the heaven his windows shut.
The ark no more now floats, but seems on ground
Fast on the top of some high mountain fixed.
And now the tops of hills as rocks appear;
With clamour thence the rapid currents drive
Towards the retreating sea their furious tide.
Forthwith from out the ark a raven flies,
And after him, the surer messenger,
A dove sent forth once and again to spy
Green tree or ground whereon his foot may light;
The second time returning, in his bill
An olive leaf he brings, pacific sign:
Anon dry ground appears, and from his ark
The ancient sire descends with all his train;
Then with uplifted hands, and eyes devout,
Grateful to heaven, over his head beholds
A dewy cloud, and in the cloud a bow
Conspicuous with three listed colours gay,
Betokening peace from God, and Covenant new.

(1667)

538 [*Exile*]

So spake our mother Eve, and Adam heard
Well pleased, but answered not; for now too nigh
The archangel stood, and from the other hill
To their fixèd station, all in bright array
The cherubim descended; on the ground
Gliding meteorous, as evening mist
Risen from a river o'er the marish glides,

hull] drift drew] drank tripping] moving rapidly Anon] Soon Grateful] (1) Thankful; (2) Pleasing listed] arranged in bands

538 meteorous] meteoric (like an exhalation, or *ignis fatuus*) marish] marsh

And gathers ground fast at the labourer's heel
Homeward returning. High in front advanced,
The brandished sword of God before them blazed
Fierce as a comet; which with torrid heat,
And vapour as the Lybian air adust,
Began to parch that temperate clime; whereat
In either hand the hastening angel caught
Our lingering parents, and to the eastern gate
Led them direct, and down the cliff as fast
To the subjected plain; then disappeared.
They looking back, all the eastern side beheld
Of paradise, so late their happy seat,
Waved over by that flaming brand, the gate
With dreadful faces thronged and fiery arms:
Some natural tears they dropped, but wiped them soon;
The world was all before them, where to choose
Their place of rest, and providence their guide:
They hand in hand, with wandering steps and slow,
Through Eden took their solitary way.

(1667)

from *Paradise Regained* (539–543)

539

[*In the Wilderness*]

So spake our morning star, then in his rise,
And looking round on every side beheld
A pathless desert, dusk with horrid shades;
The way he came not having marked, return
Was difficult, by human steps untrod;
And he still on was led, but with such thoughts
Accompanied of things past and to come
Lodged in his breast, as well might recommend
Such solitude before choicest society.
Full forty days he passed, whether on hill
Sometimes, anon in shady vale, each night
Under the covert of some ancient oak,
Or cedar, to defend him from the dew,
Or harboured in one cave, is not revealed;
Nor tasted human food, nor hunger felt
Till those days ended, hungered then at last
Among wild beasts: they at his sight grew mild,

adust] scorched   subjected] (1) underlying; (2) obedient

539 star] Jesus (Rev. 22: 16)   horrid] bristling

Nor sleeping him nor waking harmed; his walk
The fiery serpent fled and noxious worm,
The lion and fierce tiger glared aloof.
But now an agèd man in rural weeds,
Following, as seemed, the quest of some stray ewe,
Or withered sticks to gather, which might serve
Against a winter's day when winds blow keen,
To warm him wet returned from field at eve,
He saw approach, who first with curious eye
Perused him, then with words thus uttered spake.

(1671)

540 [*The Banquet*]

He spake no dream, for as his words had end,
Our Saviour lifting up his eyes, beheld
In ample space under the broadest shade
A table richly spread in regal mode,
With dishes piled, and meats of noblest sort
And savour, beasts of chase, or fowl of game,
In pastry built, or from the spit, or boiled,
Grisamber-steamed; all fish from sea or shore,
Freshet, or purling brook, of shell or fin,
And exquisitest name, for which was drained
Pontus and Lucrine bay and Afric coast.
Alas how simple, to these cates compared,
Was that crude apple that diverted Eve!
And at a stately sideboard by the wine
That fragrant smell diffused, in order stood
Tall stripling youths rich-clad, of fairer hue
Than Ganymede or Hylas, distant more
Under the trees now tripped, now solemn stood
Nymphs of Diana's train, and naiades
With fruits and flowers from Amalthea's horn,
And ladies of the Hesperides, that seemed
Fairer than feigned of old, or fabled since
Of faëry damsels met in forest wide
By knights of Logres or of Lyonesse,

noxious worm] harmful serpent

540 Grisamber-steamed] ambergris (used to scent food) Freshet] Rill Pontus] the Black Sea Lucrine bay] oyster-bed near Naples cates] delicacies Ganymede] Jupiter's cupbearer (ancient mythology) Hylas] Hercules' page tripped] glided smoothly naiades] river-nymphs Amalthea's horn] cornucopia; horn of plenty Hesperides] nymphs guarding golden apples in their mythic garden feigned] told in myth Logres . . . Lyonesse] partly mythic Arthurian lands

Lancelot or Pelleas, or Pellenore;
And all the while harmonious airs were heard
Of chiming strings or charming pipes, and winds
Of gentlest gale Arabian odours fanned
From their soft wings, and Flora's earliest smells.
Such was the splendour, and the tempter now
His invitation earnestly renewed.
  'What doubts the Son of God to sit and eat?
These are not fruits forbidden, no interdict
Defends the touching of these viands pure,
Their taste no knowledge works, at least of evil,
But life preserves, destroys life's enemy,
Hunger, with sweet restorative delight.
All these are spirits of air, and woods, and springs,
Thy gentle ministers, who come to pay
Thee homage, and acknowledge thee their Lord:
What doubtst thou, Son of God? Sit down and eat.'
  To whom thus Jesus temperately replied:
'Saidst thou not that to all things I had right?
And who withholds my power that right to use?
Shall I receive by gift what of my own,
When and where likes me best, I can command?
I can at will, doubt not, as soon as thou,
Command a table in this wilderness,
And call swift flights of angels ministrant
Arrayed in glory on my cup to attend:
Why shouldst thou then obtrude this diligence,
In vain, where no acceptance it can find;
And with my hunger what hast thou to do?
Thy pompous delicacies I contemn,
And count thy specious gifts no gifts but guiles.'

(1671)

541 [*Parthian Powers*]

HE looked and saw what numbers numberless
The city gates outpoured, light-armèd troops
In coats of mail and military pride;
In mail their horses clad, yet fleet and strong,
Prancing their riders bore, the flower and choice
Of many provinces from bound to bound;

540 Lancelot . . . Pelleas] knights of the Round Table   Pellenore] father of Percival (tempted with a banquet)   Flora's] Roman flower-goddess   Defends] Forbids pompous] splendid

From Arachosia, from Candaor east,
And Margiana to the Hyrcanian cliffs
Of Caucasus and dark Iberian dales,
From Atropatia and the neighbouring plains
Of Adiabene, Media, and the south
Of Susiana to Balsara's haven.
He saw them in their forms of battle ranged,
How quick they wheeled, and flying behind them shot
Sharp sleet of arrowy showers against the face
Of their pursuers, and overcame by flight;
The field all iron cast a gleaming brown,
Nor wanted clouds of foot, nor on each horn
Cuirassiers all in steel for standing fight,
Chariots or elephants endorsed with towers
Of archers, nor of labouring pioneers
A multitude with spades and axes armed
To lay hills plain, fell woods, or valleys fill,
Or where plain was raise hill, or overlay
With bridges rivers proud, as with a yoke;
Mules after these, camels and dromedaries,
And wagons fraught with útensils of war.
Such forces met not, nor so wide a camp,
When Agrican with all his northern powers
Besieged Albracca, as romances tell;
The city of Gallaphrone, from thence to win
The fairest of her sex, Angelica
His daughter, sought by many prowest knights,
Both paynim, and the peers of Charlemagne.

(1671)

542 [*Rome*]

HE brought our Saviour to the western side
Of that high mountain, whence he might behold
Another plain, long but in breadth not wide,
Washed by the southern sea, and on the north
To equal length backed with a ridge of hills

Arachosia] east Parthia (now Afghanistan and Pakistan) Candaor] Kendahar Margiana] Khorasan Hyrcanian] (province south-east of the Caspian) Iberian] Georgian Atropatia] (northern province of Media, now Iran) Adiabene] Assyria Susiana] Ilam Balsara's] Basra's horn] wing Cuirassiers] Lightly armoured cavalry endorsed] (1) confirmed; (2) on their backs (Latin wordplay) Agrican] (Tartar king in Boiardo's *Orlando Innamorato*) Gallaphrone] king of Cathay prowest] most valiant (Spenserian) paynim] pagan (Spenserian)

542 Another plain] Latium (Lazio)

That screened the fruits of the earth and seats of men
From cold Septentrion blasts; thence in the midst
Divided by a river, of whose banks
On each side an imperial city stood,
With towers and temples proudly elevate
On seven small hills, with palaces adorned,
Porches and theatres, baths, aqueducts,
Statues and trophies, and triumphal arcs,
Gardens and groves presented to his eyes
Above the height of mountains interposed.
By what strange parallax or optic skill
Of vision multiplied through air, or glass
Of telescope, were curious to inquire;
And now the tempter thus his silence broke.
  'The city which thou seest no other deem
Than great and glorious Rome, queen of the Earth
So far renowned, and with the spoils enriched
Of nations: there the Capitol thou seest
Above the rest lifting his stately head
On the Tarpeian rock, her citadel
Impregnable, and there Mount Palatine
The imperial palace, compass huge, and high
The structure, skill of noblest architects,
With gilded battlements, conspicuous far,
Turrets and terraces, and glittering spires.
Many a fair edifice besides, more like
Houses of gods (so well I have disposed
My airy microscope) thou mayst behold
Outside and inside both, pillars and roofs,
Carved work, the hand of famed artificers,
In cedar, marble, ivory or gold.
Thence to the gates cast round thine eye, and see
What conflux issuing forth or entering in,
Praetors, proconsuls to their provinces
Hasting or on return, in robes of state;
Lictors and rods the ensigns of their power,
Legions and cohorts, turms of horse and wings;
Or embassies from regions far remote
In various habits on the Appian road,
Or on the Aemilian, some from farthest south,

Septentrion] the north wind   imperial city] Rome   arcs] arches
parallax] alteration; displacement   hand] handiwork   conflux] crowd
Praetors] Magistrates   proconsuls] governors   Lictors] Functionaries
ensigns] symbols   turms] tenth parts of a wing   wings] large troops
Appian road] (from Rome to Brindisi)   Aemilian] (Rimini to Piacenza)

Syene, and where the shadow both way falls,
Meroe Nilotic isle, and more to west
The realm of Bocchus to the Blackmoor sea;
From the Asian kings and Parthian among these,
From India and the golden Chersoness,
And utmost Indian isle Taprobane,
Dusk faces with white silken turbans wreathed;
From Gallia, Gades, and the British west,
Germans and Scythians, and Sarmatians north
Beyond Danubius to the Tauric pool.
All nations now to Rome obedience pay,
To Rome's great emperor, whose wide domain
In ample territory, wealth and power,
Civility of manners, arts, and arms,
And long renown thou justly mayst prefer
Before the Parthian; these two thrones except,
The rest are barbarous, and scarce worth the sight,
Shared among petty kings too far removed:
These having shown thee, I have shown thee all
The kingdoms of the world, and all their glory.
This emperor hath no son, and now is old,
Old, and lascivious, and from Rome retired
To Capreae an island small but strong
On the Campanian shore, with purpose there
His horrid lusts in private to enjoy,
Committing to a wicked favourite
All public cares, and yet of him suspicious,
Hated of all, and hating; with what ease,
Endued with regal virtues as thou art,
Appearing, and beginning noble deeds,
Mightst thou expel this monster from his throne
Now made a sty, and in his place ascending
A victor people free from servile yoke!
And with my help thou mayst; to me the power
Is given, and by that right I give it thee.
Aim therefore at no less than all the world;
Aim at the highest: without the highest attained
Will be for thee no sitting, or not long
On David's throne, be prophesied what will.'

(1671)

Syene] Aswan Meroe] (island in the Nile, near the equator) realm of Bocchus] Mauretania Blackmoor sea] Mediterranean, off Morocco and Algeria Chersoness] Ophir (Malay peninsula) Taprobane] Sumatra Gallia] France Gades] Cadiz British west] Brittany Scythians] south Russian tribe Sarmatians] (barbarians from Poland and west Russia) Tauric pool] Sea of Azov emperor] Tiberius Capreae] Capri favourite] Sejanus

543 [*Athens*]

'Look once more ere we leave this specular mount;
Westward, much nearer by south-west, behold
Where on the Aegean shore a city stands
Built nobly, pure the air, and light the soil,
Athens the eye of Greece, mother of arts
And eloquence, native to famous wits
Or hospitable, in her sweet recess,
City or suburban, studious walks and shades:
See there the olive-grove of Academe,
Plato's retirement, where the Attic bird
Trills her thick-warbled notes the summer long,
There flowery hill Hymettus with the sound
Of bees' industrious murmur oft invites
To studious musing; there Ilissus rolls
His whispering stream; within the walls then view
The schools of ancient sages: his who bred
Great Alexander to subdue the world,
Lyceum there, and painted Stoa next;
There thou shalt hear and learn the secret power
Of harmony in tones and numbers hit
By voice or hand, and various-measured verse,
Aeolian charms and Dorian lyric odes,
And his who gave them breath, but higher sung,
Blind Melesigenes thence Homer called,
Whose poem Phoebus challenged for his own.
Thence what the lofty grave tragedians taught
In chorus or iambic, teachers best
Of moral prudence, with delight received
In brief sententious precepts, while they treat
Of fate, and chance, and change in human life;
High actions and high passions best describing:
Thence to the famous orators repair,
Those ancient, whose resistless eloquence
Wielded at will that fierce democraty,
Shook the Arsenal, and fulmined over Greece

specular] lookout; viewpoint recess] retirement, seclusion, privacy Academe] gymnasium Plato] ancient Greek philosopher Attic bird] nightingale Ilissus] (small river flowing from Hymettus south of Athens) his . . . Alexander] Aristotle (Alexander's tutor) Lyceum] a park (home of Aristotle's Peripatetic School) Stoa] northern colonnade of the Agora (where the Stoic Zeno taught) Aeolian] in the Aeolic dialect charms] songs (Latinism) Dorian] in Doric Melesigenes] 'Born near the Meles river' Homer] 'Blind' iambic] meter of the dialogue democraty] democracy Arsenal] naval dockyard at Piraeus fulmined] emitted thunder and lightning

To Macedon, and Artaxerxes' throne;
To sage philosophy next lend thine ear,
From heaven descended to the low-roofed house
Of Socrates: see there his tenement,
Whom well inspired the oracle pronounced
Wisest of men; from whose mouth issued forth
Mellifluous streams that watered all the schools
Of Academics old and new, with those
Surnamed Peripatetics, and the sect
Epicurean, and the Stoic severe:
These here revolve, or, as thou lik'st, at home,
Till time mature thee to a kingdom's weight;
These rules will render thee a king complete
Within thyself, much more with empire joined.'
  To whom our Saviour sagely thus replied:
'Think not but that I know these things, or think
I know them not; not therefore am I short
Of knowing what I ought: he who receives
Light from above, from the fountain of light,
No other doctrine needs, though granted true;
But these are false, or little else but dreams,
Conjectures, fancies, built on nothing firm.
The first and wisest of them all professed
To know this only, that he nothing knew;
The next to fabling fell and smooth conceits;
A third sort doubted all things, though plain sense;
Others in virtue placed felicity,
But virtue joined with riches and long life;
In corporal pleasure he, and careless ease;
The Stoic last in philosophic pride,
By him called virtue; and his virtuous man,
Wise, perfect in himself, and all possessing,
Equal to God, oft shames not to prefer,
As fearing God nor man, contemning all
Wealth, pleasure, pain or torment, death and life,
Which when he lists, he leaves, or boasts he can;
For all his tedious talk is but vain boast,
Or subtle shifts conviction to evade.
Alas what can they teach, and not mislead;
Ignorant of themselves, of God much more,
And how the world began, and how man fell
Degraded by himself, on grace depending?

Macedon] Macedonia (whose king Philip waged war on Athens) Artaxerxes'] the Persian king's Peripatetics] Aristotelians sect Epicurean] school of Epicurus The first] Socrates The next] Plato third sort] the Sceptics Others] Aristotelians he] Epicurus

Much of the soul they talk, but all awry,
And in themselves seek virtue, and to themselves
All glory arrogate, to God give none,
Rather accuse him under usual names,
Fortune and Fate, as one regardless quite
Of mortal things. Who therefore seeks in these
True wisdom, finds her not, or by delusion
Far worse, her false resemblance only meets,
An empty cloud. However many books
Wise men have said are wearisome, who reads
Incessantly, and to his reading brings not
A spirit and judgment equal or superior
(And what he brings, what needs he elsewhere seek),
Uncertain and unsettled still remains,
Deep-versed in books and shallow in himself,
Crude or intoxicate, collecting toys,
And trifles for choice matters, worth a sponge;
As children gathering pebbles on the shore.
Or if I would delight my private hours
With music or with poem, where so soon
As in our native language can I find
That solace? All our Law and story strewed
With hymns, our psalms with artful terms inscribed,
Our Hebrew songs and harps in Babylon,
That pleased so well our victor's ear, declare
That rather Greece from us these arts derived;
Ill imitated, while they loudest sing
The vices of their deities, and their own
In fable, hymn, or song, so personating
Their gods ridiculous, and themselves past shame.
Remove their swelling epithets thick-laid
As varnish on a harlot's cheek, the rest,
Thin-sown with aught of profit or delight,
Will far be found unworthy to compare
With Sion's songs, to all true tastes excelling,
Where God is praised aright, and godlike men,
The holiest of holies, and his saints;
Such are from God inspired, not such from thee;
Unless where moral virtue is expressed
By light of nature not in all quite lost.
Their orators thou then extollst, as those
The top of eloquence, statists indeed,
And lovers of their country, as may seem;

Crude] Powerless to digest   worth a sponge] (1) worth little; (2) deserving to be expunged   story] history   with . . . inscribed] explicitly using artistic conventions   Babylon] (Ps. 137)   Sion's songs] Hebrew poetry   statists] statesmen

But herein to our prophets far beneath,
As men divinely taught, and better teaching
The solid rules of civil government
In their majestic unaffected style
Than all the oratory of Greece and Rome.
In them is plainest taught, and easiest learnt,
What makes a nation happy, and keeps it so,
What ruins kingdoms, and lays cities flat;
These only with our Law best form a king.'

(1671)

from *Samson Agonistes* (544–545)

544 [*Samson's Complaint*]

... CHIEF of all,
O loss of sight, of thee I most complain!
Blind among enemies, oh worse than chains,
Dungeon, or beggary, or decrepit age!
Light the prime work of God to me is extinct,
And all her various objects of delight
Annulled, which might in part my grief have eased,
Inferior to the vilest now become
Of man or worm; the vilest here excel me,
They creep, yet see, I dark in light exposed
To daily fraud, contempt, abuse and wrong,
Within doors or without, still as a fool
In power of others, never in my own;
Scarce half I seem to live, dead more than half.
Oh dark, dark, dark, amid the blaze of noon,
Irrecoverably dark, total eclipse
Without all hope of day!
O first-created beam, and thou great word,
'Let there be light, and light was over all',
Why am I thus bereaved thy prime decree?
The sun to me is dark
And silent as the moon,
When she deserts the night
Hid in her vacant interlunar cave.
Since light so necessary is to life,
And almost life itself, if it be true
That light is in the soul,

544 *Agonistes*] Contestant; champion   prime] first; most important   worm] reptile; insect   still] always   silent] not shining (scientific)   vacant] at leisure   interlunar] between moons

She all in every part, why was the sight
To such a tender ball as the eye confined?
So obvious and so easy to be quenched,
And not as feeling through all parts diffused,
That she might look at will through every pore?
Then had I not been thus exiled from light;
As in the land of darkness yet in light,
To live a life half dead, a living death,
And buried; but oh yet more miserable!
Myself my sepulchre, a moving grave,
Buried, yet not exempt
By privilege of death and burial
From worst of other evils, pains and wrongs,
But made hereby obnoxious more
To all the miseries of life,
Life in captivity
Among inhuman foes.

(1671)

545 CHORUS: ALL is best, though we oft doubt
What the unsearchable dispose
Of highest wisdom brings about,
And ever best found in the close.
Oft he seems to hide his face,
But unexpectedly returns
And to his faithful champion hath in place
Bore witness gloriously; whence Gaza mourns
And all that band them to resist
His uncontrollable intent.
His servants he with new acquist
Of true experience from this great event
With peace and consolation hath dismissed,
And calm of mind all passion spent.

(1671)

obvious] exposed obnoxious] liable to harm

545 doubt] fear, suspect dispose] order in place] at hand Gaza] (the Philistine city whose temple Samson has destroyed) acquist] acquisition

SIR JOHN SUCKLING

1609–1642

546

Song

WHY so pale and wan, fond lover?
    Prithee why so pale?
Will, when looking well can't move her,
    Looking ill prevail?
    Prithee why so pale?

Why so dull and mute, young sinner?
    Prithee why so mute?
Will, when speaking well can't win her,
    Saying nothing do 't?
    Prithee why so mute?

Quit, quit, for shame, this will not move,
    This cannot take her;
If of herself she will not love,
    Nothing can make her,
    The devil take her.

(1638)

547

Sonnet I

DOST see how unregarded now
  That piece of beauty passes?
There was a time when I did vow
    To that alone;
  But mark the fate of faces:
That red and white works now no more on me
Than if it could not charm, or I not see.

And yet the face continues good,
  And I have still desires,
Am still the self-same flesh and blood,
    As apt to melt
  And suffer from those fires;
Oh! Some kind power unriddle where it lies,
Whether my heart be faulty, or her eyes?

She every day her man doth kill,
And I as often die;
Neither her power, then, nor my will
Can questioned be;
What is the mystery?
Sure beauty's empires, like to greater states,
Have certain periods set, and hidden fates.

(1646)

548

Sonnet II

OF thee, kind boy, I ask no red and white
To make up my delight,
No odd becoming graces,
Black eyes, or little know-not-whats, in faces:
Make me but mad enough, give me good store
Of love for her I court,
I ask no more,
'Tis love in love that makes the sport.

There's no such thing as that we beauty call,
It is mere cozenage all;
For though some long ago
Liked certain colours mingled so and so,
That doth not tie me now from choosing new;
If I a fancy take
To black and blue,
That fancy doth it beauty make.

'Tis not the meat, but 'tis the appetite
Makes eating a delight,
And if I like one dish
More than another, that a pheasant is;
What in our watches, that in us is found,
So to the height and nick
We up be wound,
No matter by what hand or trick.

(1646)

548 mere cozenage] pure deception

549 [*The Constant Lover*]

OUT upon it, I have loved
  Three whole days together,
And am like to love three more,
  If it hold fair weather.

Time shall moult away his wings
  Ere he shall discover
In the whole wide world again
  Such a constant lover.

But pox upon 't, no praise
  There is due at all to me:
Love with me had made no stay,
  Had it any been but she.

Had it any been but she
  And that very very face,
There had been at least ere this
  A dozen dozen in her place.

(1659)

550 *Against Fruition* [*I*]

STAY here, fond youth, and ask no more, be wise:
Knowing too much long since lost paradise;
The virtuous joys thou hast, thou wouldst should still
Last in their pride; and wouldst not take it ill
If rudely from sweet dreams (and for a toy)
Thou wert waked? He wakes himself that does enjoy.

Fruition adds no new wealth, but destroys,
And while it pleases much the palate, cloys;
Who thinks he shall be happier for that,
As reasonably might hope he should grow fat
By eating to a surfeit: this once past,
What relishes? Even kisses lose their taste.

Urge not 'tis necessary: alas, we know
The homeliest thing which mankind does is so;
The world is of a vast extent, we see,
And must be peopled; children then must be;
So must bread too; but since there are enough
Born to the drudgery, what need we plough?

Women enjoyed (whatsoe'er before they've been)
Are like romances read, or sights once seen:
Fruition's dull, and spoils the play much more
Than if one read or knew the plot before;
'Tis expectation makes a blessing dear:
It were not heaven, if we knew what it were.

And as in prospects we are there pleased most
Where something keeps the eye from being lost,
And leaves us room to guess, so here restraint
Holds up delight, that with excess would faint.
They who know all the wealth they have, are poor:
He's only rich that cannot tell his store.

(1646)

551 [*Love's Clock*]

THAT none beguilèd be by time's quick flowing,
Lovers have in their hearts a clock still going;
For though time be nimble, his motions
Are quicker
And thicker
Where love hath his notions:

Hope is the mainspring on which moves desire,
And these do the less wheels, fear, joy, inspire;
The balance is thought, evermore
Clicking
And striking,
And ne'er giving o'er;

Occasion's the hand which still's moving round,
Till by it the critical hour may be found,
And when that falls out, it will strike
Kisses,
Strange blisses,
And what you best like.

(1646)

551 less] smaller

552 [*Love's Offence*]

IF, when Don Cupid's dart
Doth wound a heart,
    We hide our grief
    And shun relief,
The smart increaseth on that score;
For wounds unsearched but rankle more.

Then if we whine, look pale,
And tell our tale,
    Men are in pain
    For us again;
So, neither speaking doth become
The lover's state, nor being dumb.

When this I do descry,
Then thus think I,
    Love is the fart
    Of every heart:
It pains a man when 'tis kept close,
And others doth offend, when 'tis let loose.

(1646)

553 [*A Summons to Town*]

SIR,
Whether these lines do find you out
Putting or clearing off a doubt
(Whether Predestinatïon,
Or reconciling three in one,
Or the unriddling how men die,
And live at once eternally,
Now take you up), know 'tis decreed
You straight bestride the College steed:
Leave Socinus and the Schoolmen
(Which Jack Bond swears do but fool men),
And come to town; 'tis fit you show
Yourself abroad, that men may know
(Whate'er some learned men have guessed)
That oracles are not yet ceased.

553 Socinus] F.P. Sozzini (1539–1604), a Unitarian   Schoolmen] Scholastic theologians   Jack Bond] a friend of S.'s

There you shall find the wit and wine
Flowing alike, and both divine;
Dishes with names not known in books,
And less amongst the College cooks,
With sauce so pregnant that you need
Not stay till hunger bids you feed.
The sweat of learned Jonson's brain,
And gentle Shakespeare's easier strain,
A hackney-coach conveys you to,
In spite of all that rain can do;
And for your eighteen pence you sit
The lord and judge of all fresh wit.
News in one day as much we've here
As serves all Windsor for a year,
And which the carrier brings to you,
After it's here been found not true.
Then think what company's designed
To meet you here: men so refined,
Their very common talk at board
Makes wise or mad a young court lord,
And makes him capable to be
Umpire in his father's company.
Where no disputes nor forced defence
Of a man's person for his sense
Take up the time, all strive to be
Masters of truth, as victory;
And where you come, I'd boldly swear
A synod might as easily err.

(1646)

ANONYMOUS

*fl. c.*1639–1641

554 *The Zealous Puritan*

My brethren, all attend,
And list to my relation:
This is the day, mark what I say,
Tends to your renovation;
Stay not among the wicked,
Lest that with them you perish,
But let us to New England go,
And the pagan people cherish.

Then for the truth's sake come along, come along,
Leave this place of superstition:
Were it not for we that the brethren be,
You would sink into perdition.

There you may teach our hymns,
Without the law's controlment:
We need not fear the bishops there,
Nor spiritual courts' enrolment.
Nay, the surplice shall not fright us,
Nor superstitious blindness;
Nor scandals rise, when we disguise,
And our sisters kiss in kindness.
Then for the truth's sake, etc.

For company I fear not,
There goes my cousin Hannah;
And Rueben so persuades to go
My cousin Joyce, Susanna,
With Abigail and Faith;
And Ruth no doubt comes after;
And Sarah kind will not stay behind,
My cousin Constance' daughter.
Then for the truth's sake, etc.

Tom Tyler is prepared,
And the Smith as black as a coal;
Ralph Cobler too with us will go,
For he regards his soul;
The Weaver, honest Simon,
With Prudence, Jacob's daughter,
And Sarah, she, and Barbary,
Professeth to come after.
Then for the truth's sake, etc.

When we that are elected
Arrive in that fair country,
Even by our faith, as the brethren saith,
We will not fear our entry:
The Psalms shall be our music,
Our time spent in expounding,
Which in our zeal we will reveal
To the brethren joy abounding;
Then for the truth's sake, etc.

(1639)

controlment] restraint   enrolment] record   Professeth] Vow

555 *On Francis Drake*

Sir Drake, whom well the world's end knew,
Which thou didst compass round,
And whom both poles of heaven once saw,
Which north and south do bound,
The stars above would make thee known,
If men here silent were;
The sun himself cannot forget
His fellow traveller.

(1640)

556 *On Sir Walter Rawleigh at His Execution*

Great heart, who taught thee so to die,
Death yielding thee the victory?
Where tookst thou leave of life? If there,
How couldst thou be so freed from fear?
But sure thou diedst and quitst the state
Of flesh and blood before thy fate.
Else what a miracle were wrought,
To triumph both in flesh and thought!
I saw in every stander by
Pale death, life only in thine eye:
The example that thou leftst was then,
We look for when thou diest again.
Farewell! Truth shall thy story say:
We died, thou only livedst that day.

(1640)

557 *On His Mistress Going from Home: Song*

So does the sun withdraw his beams
From off the northern coasts and streams,
When clouds and frosts ensue,
And leaves the melancholy slaves
Stupid and dull as near their graves
Till he their joys renew.
Those that in Greenland followed game
Too long, and found, when back they came,
Their shipping gone, believèd they must die
Ere succour came; but yet more blest than I.

How soon our happiness does fly,
Like sounds which with their echoes die,
And leave us in a trance,
Bewailing we had e'er enjoyed
The blessing, since 'tis still destroyed
By some unhappy chance.
Why should the spiteful stars agree
To vex and mock mortality?
For thus, like traitors which in darkness lie,
We're only brought into the light to die.

In dreams things are not as they seem.
Else, what's fruition but a dream
When the possession's past?
Alas, to say 'we were', 'we had'
Is poor content, and even as bad
As if we'd ne'er had taste.
Fire in great frosts, small time possessed,
Produces pain instead of rest:
So does the short enjoyment of such bliss,
And till restored, continual torment is.

(1672)

558

If all the world were paper,
And all the sea were ink,
And all the trees were bread and cheese,
How should we do for drink?

If all the world were sand-o,
Oh, then what should we lack-o?
If, as they say, there were no clay,
How should we take tobacco?

If all our vessels ran-a
If none but had a crack-a;
If Spanish apes ate all the grapes,
How should we do for sack-a?

If friars had no bald pates,
Nor nuns had no dark cloisters;
If all the seas were beans and peas,
How should we do for oysters?

still] ever

558 oysters] (1) sea food; (2) female pudenda

If there had been no projects,
  Nor none that did great wrongs;
If fiddlers shall turn players all,
  How should we do for songs?

If all things were eternal,
  And nothing their end bringing;
If this should be, then how should we
  Here make an end of singing?

(1641)

559 *The Character of a Roundhead*

WHAT creature's this with his short hairs,
His little band and huge long ears,
  That this new faith hath founded?
The Puritans were never such,
The Saints themselves had ne'er so much;
  Oh, such a knave's a roundhead.

What's he that doth the bishops hate,
And count their calling reprobate,
  'Cause by the Pope propounded,
And says a zealous cobbler's better
Than he that studieth every letter?
  Oh, such a knave's a roundhead.

What's he that doth high treason say,
As often as his yea and nay,
  And wish the king confounded,
And dare maintain that Master Pym
Is fitter for the crown than him?
  Oh, such a rogue's a roundhead.

What's he that if he chance to hear
A piece of London's Common-Prayer,
  Doth think his conscience wounded;
And goes five miles to preach and pray,
And lies with's sister by the way?
  Oh, such a rogue's a roundhead.

projects] speculative schemes

559 band] collar, ruff   Saints] Puritans, sectarians

What's he that met a holy sister,
And in a haycock gently kissed her?
  Oh! then his zeal abounded:
Close underneath a shady willow,
Her bible served her for her pillow,
  And there they got a roundhead.

(1641)

GERRARD WINSTANLEY
1609?–1639

560 *The Diggers' Song*

YOU noble Diggers all, stand up now, stand up now;
  You noble Diggers all, stand up now,
The waste land to maintain, seeing Cavaliers by name
Your digging does disdain, and persons all defame.
    Stand up now, stand up now.

Your houses they pull down; stand up now, stand up now;
  Your houses they pull down; stand up now.
Your houses they pull down to fright poor men in town,
But the gentry must come down, and the poor shall wear the crown.
    Stand up now, Diggers all.

With spades and hoes and ploughs, stand up now, stand up now;
  With spades and hoes and ploughs, stand up now,
Your freedom to uphold, seeing Cavaliers are bold
To kill you if they could, and rights from you to hold.
    Stand up now, Diggers all.

Their self-will is their law; stand up now, stand up now;
  Their self-will is their law; stand up now.
Since tyranny came in they count it now no sin
To make a gaol a gin, to starve poor men therein.
    Stand up now, stand up now.

The gentry are all round; stand up now, stand up now;
  The gentry are all round; stand up now.
The gentry are all round; on each side they are found,
This wisdom's so profound, to cheat us of our ground.
    Stand up now, stand up now.

560 gin] contrivance, scheme

The lawyers they conjoin; stand up now, stand up now;
  The lawyers they conjoin, stand up now.
To arrest you they advise, such fury they devise,
The devil in them lies and hath blinded both their eyes.
    Stand up now, stand up now.

The clergy they come in; stand up now, stand up now;
  The clergy they come in; stand up now.
The clergy they come in, and say it is a sin
That we should now begin, our freedom for to win.
      Stand up now, Diggers all.

The tithes they yet will have; stand up now, stand up now;
  The tithes they yet will have; stand up now.
The tithes they yet will have, the lawyers their fees crave,
And this they say is brave, to make the poor their slave.
      Stand up now, Diggers all.

'Gainst lawyers and 'gainst priests, stand up now, stand up now;
  'Gainst lawyers and 'gainst priests, stand up now.
For tyrants they are both, even flat against their oath,
To grant us they are loath, free meat and drink and cloth.
    Stand up now, Diggers all.

The club is all their law; stand up now, stand up now;
  The club is all their law; stand up now.
The club is all their law, to keep men in awe,
But they no vision saw, to maintain such a law.
    Stand up now, Diggers all.

The Cavaliers are foes; stand up now, stand up now;
  The Cavaliers are foes; stand up now.
The Cavaliers are foes; themselves they do disclose
By verses not in prose, to please the singing boys.
    Stand up now, Diggers all.

To conquer them by love, come in now, come in now;
  To conquer them by love, come in now;
To conquer them by love, as it does you behove;
For he is king above: no power is like to love.
    Glory here, Diggers all.

(1650)

conjoin] cooperate   advise] ponder, consider   brave] splendid

THOMAS BEEDOME

d. 1640?

561 *The Question and Answer*

WHEN the sad ruins of that face
In its own wrinkles buried lies,
And the stiff pride of all its grace,
By time undone, falls slack and dies:
    Wilt thou not sigh, and wish in some vexed fit
    That it were now as when I courted it?

And when thy glass shall it present
Without those smiles which once were there,
Showing, like some stale monument,
A scalp departed from its hair,
    At thyself frighted wilt not start and swear
    That I belied thee, when I called thee fair?

Yes, yes, I know thou wilt, and so
Pity the weakness of thy scorn,
That now hath humbled thee to know,
Though fair it was, it is forlorn:
    Love's sweets thy agèd corpse embalming not,
    What marvel if thy carcass, beauty, rot?

Then shall I live, and live to be
Thy envy, thou my pity; say
Whene'er thou see me, or I thee
(Being nighted from thy beauty's day),
    'Tis he, and had my pride not withered me,
    I had, perhaps, been still as fresh as he.

Then shall I smile, and answer: 'True; thy scorn
Left thee thus wrinkled, slacked, corrupt, forlorn.'

(1641)

nighted] benighted

562

The Petition

HEAR me, my God, and hear me soon,
Because my morning toucheth noon,
Nor can I look for their delight,
Because my noon lays hold on night:
I am all circle, my morn, night, and noon
Are individable; then hear me soon.

Thou art all time, my God, and I
Am part of that eternity:
Yet, being made, I want that might
To be as thou art, infinite:
As in thy flesh, so be thou Lord to me,
That is, both infinite and eternity.

But I am dust; at most, but man,
That dust extended to a span:
A span indeed, for in thy hand,
Stretched or contracted, Lord, I stand.
Contract and stretch me too, that I may be
Straitened on Earth, to be enlarged to thee.

But I am nothing; then how can
I call myself, or dust, or man?
Yet thou from nothing all didst frame,
That all things might exalt thy name;
Make me but something, then, my God, to thee:
Then shall thy praise be all in all to me.

(1641)

RICHARD FLECKNOE

fl. 1640–1678?

563

The Ant

LITTLE thinkest thou, poor ant, who there
  With so much toil and so much time
A grain or two to the cell dost bear,
  There's greater work in the world than thine.

562 individable] indivisible   or] either

In the small republic too at home,
  Where thou'rt perhaps some magistrate,
Little thinkest thou when thou dost come
  There's greater in the world than that.

Nor is it such wonder now in thee,
  No more of the world nor things dost know:
That all thy thoughts of the ground should be,
  And mind on things so poor and low.

But that man so base mind should bear
  To fix it on a clod of ground,
As there no greater business were,
  Nor greater worlds for to be found!

He so much of the man does want
  As metamorphosed quite again;
Whilst thou'rt but man turned grovelling ant:
  Such grovellers seem but ants turned men.

(1653)

564 [*Invocation of Silence*]

STILLBORN silence! thou that art
Flood-gate of the deeper heart!
Offspring of a heavenly kind,
Frost of the mouth, and thaw of the mind.
Secrecy's confidant, and he
Who makes religion mystery!
Admiration's speaking'st tongue!
Leave thy desert shades among
Reverend hermits' hallowed cells,
Where retired devotion dwells!
With thy enthusiasms come,
Seize our tongues and strike us dumb!

(1653)

SIDNEY GODOLPHIN
1610–1643

565 ### [*Meditation on the Nativity*]

LORD, when the wise men came from far,
Led to thy cradle by a star,
Then did the shepherds too rejoice,
Instructed by thy angel's voice;
Blest were the wise men in their skill,
And shepherds in their harmless will.

Wise men in tracing nature's laws
Ascend unto the highest cause;
Shepherds with humble fearfulness
Walk safely, though their light be less:
Though wise men better know the way,
It seems no honest heart can stray.

There is no merit in the wise
But love (the shepherd's sacrifice):
Wise men, all ways of knowledge past,
To th' shepherds' wonder come at last;
To know can only wonder breed,
And not to know is wonder's seed.

A wise man at the altar bows
And offers up his studied vows,
And is received; may not the tears,
Which spring too from a shepherd's fears,
And sighs upon his frailty spent,
Though not distinct, be eloquent?

'Tis true, the object sanctifies
All passions which within us rise,
But since no creature comprehends
The cause of causes, end of ends,
He who himself vouchsafes to know
Best pleases his creator so.

skill] reason; knowledge; science

When then our sorrows we apply
To our own wants and poverty,
When we look up in all distress
And our own misery confess,
Sending both thanks and prayers above:
Then, though we do not know, we love.

(1906)

566 *Song*

OR love me less, or love me more
  And play not with my liberty;
Either take all, or all restore;
  Bind me at least, or set me free;
Let me some nobler torture find
  Than of a doubtful wavering mind:
Take all my peace; but you betray
  Mine honour too this cruel way.

'Tis true that I have nursed before
  That hope of which I now complain,
And, having little, sought no more,
  Fearing to meet with your disdain:
The sparks of favour you did give,
  I gently blew to make them live;
And yet have gained by all this care
  No rest in hope, nor in despair.

I see you wear that pitying smile
  Which you have still vouchsafed my smart,
Content thus cheaply to beguile
  And entertain a harmless heart;
But I no longer can give way
  To hope, which doth so little pay,
And yet I dare no freedom owe
  Whilst you are kind, though but in show.

Then give me more, or give me less,
  Do not disdain a mutual sense,
Or your unpitying beauties dress
  In their own free indifference.
But show not a severer eye,
  Sooner to give me liberty;
For I shall love the very scorn
  Which for my sake you do put on.

(1801)

566 still] ever   owe] own

567

Constancy

LOVE unreturned, howe'er the flame
Seem great and pure, may still admit
Degrees of more, and a new name
And strength acceptance gives to it.

Till then, by honour there's no tie
Laid on it, that it ne'er decay;
The mind's last act by constancy
Ought to be sealed, and not the way.

Did aught but love's perfection bind
Who should assign at what degree
Of love, faith ought to fix the mind,
And in what limits we are free.

So hardly in a single heart
Is any love conceived,
That fancy still supplies one part,
Supposing it received.

When undeceived, such love retires,
'Tis but a model lost:
A draught of what might be expires,
Built but at fancy's cost.

Yet if the ruin one tear move,
From pity, not love, sent,
Though not a palace, it will prove
The most wished monument.

(1906)

568

FAIR friend, 'tis true your beauties move
  My heart to a respect,
Too little to be paid with love,
  Too great for your neglect.

I neither love nor yet am free,
  For though the flame I find
Be not intense in the degree
  'Tis of the purest kind.

567 way] particular manner of the act   So hardly] With such difficulty

It little wants of love, but pain:
  Your beauty takes my sense;
And lest you should that price disdain,
  My thoughts, too, feel the influence.

'Tis not a passion's first access
  Ready to multiply,
But like love's calmest state it is
  Possessed with victory.

It is like love to truth reduced,
  All the false values gone,
Which were created and induced
  By fond imagination.

'Tis either fancy or 'tis fate
  To love you more than I:
I love you at your beauty's rate;
  Less were an injury.

Like unstamped gold, I weigh each grace,
  So that you may collect
The intrinsic value of your face
  Safely from my respect.

And this respect would merit love,
  Were not so fair a sight
Payment enough: for who dare move
  Reward for his delight?

(1640)

SAMUEL HARDING

fl. 1640

569 NOBLEST bodies are but gilded clay:
      Put away
  But the precious shining rind,
The inmost rottenness remains behind.
  Kings, on earth though gods they be,
  Yet in death are vile as we;
  He, a thousands' king before,
  Now is vassal unto more.

Vermin now insulting lie,
And dig for diamonds in each eye;
Whilst the sceptre-bearing hand
Cannot their inroads withstand.
Here doth one in odours wade
By the regal unction made,
While another dares to gnaw
On that tongue, his people's law.
Fools! ah, fools are we, who so contrive,
And do strive,
In each gaudy ornament,
Who shall his corpse in the best dish present.

(1640)

WILLIAM CARTWRIGHT
1611–1643

570

To Chloe, Who Wished Herself Young Enough for Me

CHLOE, why wish you that your years
Would backwards run till they meet mine;
That perfect likeness, which endears
Things unto things, might us combine?
Our ages so in date agree
That twins do differ more than we.

There are two births: the one when light
First strikes the new awakened sense,
The other when two souls unite;
And we must count our life from thence:
When you loved me and I loved you,
Then both of us were born anew.

Love then to us did new souls give,
And in those souls did plant new powers;
Since when another life we live:
The breath we breathe is his, not ours.
Love makes those young whom age doth chill,
And whòm he finds young, keeps young still.

Love, like that angel that shall call
  Our bodies from the silent grave,
Unto one age doth raise us all:
  None too much, none too little have.
Nay, that the difference may be none,
He makes two not alike, but one.

And now, since you and I are such,
  Tell me what's yours, and what is mine?
Our eyes, our ears, our taste, smell, touch,
  Do, like our souls, in one combine;
So by this, I as well may be
Too old for you as you for me.

(1651)

571 *On the Great Frost (1634)*

SHOW me the flames you brag of, you that be
Armed with those two fires, wine and poetry:
You're now benumbed, spite of your gods and verse,
And may your metaphors for prayers rehearse,
Whiles you that called snow 'fleece' and 'feathers' do
Wish for true fleeces, and true feathers too.
  Waters have bound themselves, and cannot run,
Suffering what Xerxes' fetters would have done;
Our rivers are one crystal; shores are fit
Mirrors, being now not like to glass, but it;
Our ships stand all as planted: we may swear
They are not borne up only, but grow there.
Whiles waters thus are pavements, firm as stone,
And without faith are each day walked upon:
What parables called folly heretofore
Were wisdom now, *To build upon the shore.*
There's no one dines among us with washed hands:
Water's as scarce here as in Africk sands,
And we expect it not but from some god
Opening a fountain, or some prophet's rod—
Who need not seek out where he may unlock
A stream: whate'er he strook would be true rock.
When heaven drops some smaller showers, our sense
Of grief's increased, being but deluded thence;
For whiles we think those drops to entertain,
They fall down pearl, which came down half-way rain.

571 spite of] despite   Whiles] While   Xerxes'] Xerxes I (who punished the Hellespont with fetters)   strook] struck

Greenland's removal now the poor man fears,
Seeing all waters frozen but his tears.
We suffer day continual, and the snow
Doth make our little night become noon now.
We hear of some encrystalled, such as have
That which procured their death become their grave.
Bodies, that destitute of soul yet stood,
Dead, and not fallen; drowned, and without a flood.
Nay we, who breathe still, are almost as they,
And only may be styled a softer clay;
We stand like statues, as if cast, and fit
For life, not having but expecting it:
Each man's become the Stoic's wise one hence;
For can you look for passion where's no sense?
—Which we have not, resolved to our first stone,
Unless it be one sense to feel we've none.
Our very smiths now work not—nay, what's more,
Our Dutchmen write but five hours and give o'er.
We dare provoke fate now: we know what is
That last cold, death, only by suffering this.
All fires are Vestal now, and we as they
Do in our chimneys keep a lasting day;
Boasting within doors this domestic sun,
Adorèd too with our religïon.
We laugh at fire-briefs now, although they be
Commended to us by his Majesty;
And 'tis no treason, for we cannot guess
Why we should pay them for their happiness.
Each hand would be a Scaevola's: let Rome
Call that a pleasure henceforth, not a doom.
A fever is become a wish: we sit
And think fallen angels have one benefit;
Nor can the thought be impious, when we see
Weather that Bowker durst not prophesy:
Such as may give new epochas, and make
Another SINCE in his bold almanac;
Weather may save his doom, and by his foe
Be thought enough for his to undergo.
We now think Alabaster true, and look
A sudden trump should antedate his book;
For, whiles we suffer this, ought we not fear
The world shall not survive to a fourth year?

Vestal] perpetually lit, like the Roman goddess Vesta's altar fire   fire-briefs] recommendations for charity to sufferers from fire   Scaevola's] Gaius Mucius' (who burnt his hand to show bravery)   Bowker] John Booker   epochas] epochs   Alabaster] William Alabaster, a cabalist

And sure we may conclude weak nature old
And crazèd now, being she's grown so cold.
  But frost's not all our grief: we that so sore
Suffer its stay, fear its departure more;
For when that leaves us, which so long hath stood,
'Twill make a new accompt *From the second Flood.*

(1651)

572 *A Dream Broke*

As Nilus' sudden ebbing here
Doth leave a scale, and a scale there,
And somewhere else perhaps a fin,
Which by his stay had fishes been,
So dreams, which overflowing be,
Departing leave half things, which we
For their imperfectness can call
But joys in the fin, or in the scale.
If, when her tears I haste to kiss,
They dry up and deceive my bliss,
May not I say the waters sink,
And cheat my thirst when I would drink?
If, when her breasts I go to press,
Instead of them I grasp her dress,
May I not say the apples then
Are set down and snatched up again?
Sleep was not thus death's brother meant:
'Twas made an ease, no punishment.
As, then, that's finished by the sun
Which Nile did only leave begun,
My fancy shall run o'er sleep's themes,
And so make up the web of dreams;
In vain, fleet shades, ye do contest:
Awaked howe'er, I'll think the rest.

(1651)

573 *No Platonique Love*

Tell me no more of minds embracing minds,
  And hearts exchanged for hearts;
That spirits spirits meet, as winds do winds,
  And mix their subtlest parts;

571 accompt] account

572 ease] relief

That two unbodied essences may kiss,
And then like angels twist and feel one bliss.

I was that silly thing that once was wrought
To practise this thin love:
I climbed from sex to soul, from soul to thought;
But thinking there to move,
Headlong I rolled from thought to soul, and then
From soul I lighted at the sex again.

As some strict down-looked men pretend to fast,
Who yet in closets eat,
So lovers who profess they spirits taste
Feed yet on grosser meat;
I know they boast they souls to souls convey:
Howe'er they meet, the body is the way.

Come, I will undeceive thee: they that tread
Those vain aërial ways
Are like young heirs and alchemists misled
To waste their wealth and days;
For searching thus to be for ever rich
They only find a medicine for the itch.

(1651)

574 *A Song of Dalliance*

HARK, my Flora: Love doth call us
To that strife that must befall us;
He has robbed his mother's myrtles,
And hath pulled her downy turtles.
See, our genial posts are crowned,
And our beds like billows rise;
Softer combat's nowhere found,
And who loses, wins the prize.

Let not dark nor shadows fright thee;
Thy limbs of lustre they will light thee;
Fear not any can surprise us,
Love himself doth now disguise us.
From thy waist thy girdle throw:
Night and darkness both dwell here;
Words or actions who can know,
Where there's neither eye nor ear?

wrought] worked up   lighted] alighted   closets] private rooms for devotion

574 pulled] plundered; plucked   turtles] turtle-doves

Show thy bosom, and then hide it;
License touching and then chide it;
Give a grant, and then forbear it;
Offer something, and forswear it:
Ask where all our shame is gone;
  Call us wicked wanton men:
Do as turtles, kiss and groan;
  Say, 'We ne'er shall meet again.'

I can hear thee curse, yet chase thee;
Drink thy tears, yet still embrace thee.
Easy riches is no treasure:
She that's willing, spoils the pleasure.
Love bids learn the restless fight,
  Pull and struggle whilst ye twine:
Let me use my force tonight,
  The next conquest shall be thine.

(1656)

ANNE BRADSTREET
1612–1672

575 *To My Dear and Loving Husband*

If ever two were one, then surely we.
If ever man were loved by wife, then thee;
If ever wife was happy in a man,
Compare with me, ye women, if you can.
I prize thy love more than whole mines of gold,
Or all the riches that the east doth hold.
My love is such that rivers cannot quench,
Nor ought but love from thee give recompense.
Thy love is such I can no way repay:
The heavens reward thee manifold, I pray.
Then while we live, in love let's so persévere
That, when we live no more, we may live ever.

(1678)

576 *Upon the Burning of Our House July 10th, 1666*

In silent night, when rest I took,
For sorrow near I did not look:
I wakened was with thundering noise
And piteous shrieks of dreadful voice.
That fearful sound of 'Fire!' and 'Fire!'
Let no man know is my desire.
I, starting up, the light did spy,
And to my God my heart did cry
To strengthen me in my distress
And not to leave me succourless;
Then, coming out, beheld a space
The flame consume my dwelling place.
And when I could no longer look,
I blessed his name that gave and took,
That laid my goods now in the dust.
Yea, so it was, and so 'twas just.
It was his own, it was not mine;
Far be it that I should repine:
He might of all justly bereft,
But yet sufficient for us left.
When by the ruins oft I passed,
My sorrowing eyes aside did cast,
And here and there the places spy
Where oft I sat and long did lie:
Here stood that trunk, and there that chest,
There lay that store I counted best.
My pleasant things in ashes lie,
And them behold no more shall I.
Under thy roof no guest shall sit,
Nor at thy table eat a bit.
No pleasant tale shall e'er be told,
Nor things recounted done of old.
No candle e'er shall shine in thee,
Nor bridegroom's voice e'er heard shall be.
In silence ever shalt thou lie:
Adieu, adieu, all's vanity.
Then straight I 'gin my heart to chide,
'And did thy wealth on Earth abide?
Didst fix thy hope on mouldering dust?
The arm of flesh didst make thy trust?
Raise up thy thoughts above the sky,
That dunghill mists away may fly.
Thou hast an house on high erect,

Framed by that mighty architect,
With glory richly furnishèd,
Stands permanent, though this be fled.
It's purchasèd, and paid for too,
By him who hath enough to do.
A price so vast as is unknown
Yet by his gift is made thine own.'
There's wealth enough, I need no more:
Farewell, my pelf, farewell my store.
The world no longer let me love,
My hope and treasure lies above.

(1867)

577 from *Contemplations*

SHALL I then praise the heavens, the trees, the earth,
Because their beauty and their strength last longer?
Shall I wish there, or never to had birth,
Because they're bigger, and their bodies stronger?
Nay, they shall darken, perish, fade, and die,
And when unmade, so ever shall they lie;
But man was made for endless immortality.

Under the cooling shadow of a stately elm
Close sat I by a goodly river's side,
Where gliding streams the rocks did overwhelm:
A lonely place, with pleasures dignified.
I, once that loved the shady woods so well,
Now thought the rivers did the trees excel,
And if the sun would ever shine, there would I dwell.

While on the stealing stream I fixed mine eye,
Which to the longed-for ocean held its course,
I marked, nor crooks nor rubs that there did lie
Could hinder ought, but still augment its force.
'O happy flood,' quoth I, 'that holds thy race
Till thou arrive at thy belovèd place;
Nor is it rocks or shoals that can obstruct thy pace,

'Nor is it enough that thou alone mayst slide,
But hundred brooks in thy clear waves do meet,
So hand in hand along with thee they glide
To Thetis' house, where all embrace and greet.

Close] Secretly   crooks] (1) bends; (2) fiends' claws   rubs] (1) obstacles; (2) difficulties   Thetis' house] the sea

Thou emblem true of what I count the best,
Oh could I lead my rivulets to rest,
So may we press to that vast mansion, ever blest.'

(1650)

SAMUEL BUTLER
1612–1680

from *Hudibras* (578–579)

578 [*The Presbyterian Knight*]

WHEN civil fury first grew high,
And men fell out, they knew not why;
When hard words, jealousies, and fears
Set folks together by the ears
And made them fight, like mad or drunk,
For Dame Religion as for punk,
Whose honesty they all durst swear for,
Though not a man of them knew wherefore;
When gospel-trumpeter, surrounded
With long-eared rout, to battle sounded,
And pulpit, drum ecclesiastic,
Was beat with fist instead of a stick:
Then did sir knight abandon dwelling,
And out he rode a coloneling.
  A wight he was whose very sight would
Entitle him Mirror of Knighthood;
That never bent his stubborn knee
To anything but chivalry,
Nor put up blow but that which laid
'Right Worshipful' on shoulder-blade;
Chief of domestic knights and errant,
Either for cartel or for warrant;
Great on the bench, great in the saddle,
That could as well bind o'er as swaddle:
Mighty he was at both of these
And styled of war as well as peace.
(So some rats of amphibious nature
Are either for the land or water.)

punk] prostitute wight] man (archaic) put up] suffered tamely cartel] written challenge swaddle] (1) bind; (2) beat (colloquial)

But here our authors make a doubt
Whether he were more wise, or stout.
Some hold the one, and some the other;
But howsoe'er they make a pother,
The difference was so small, his brain
Outweighed his rage but half a grain;
Which made some take him for a tool
That knaves do work with, called a fool,
And offer to lay wagers that,
As Montaigne, playing with his cat,
Complains she thought him but an ass,
Much more she would Sir Hudibras
(For that's the name our valiant knight
To all his challenges did write).
But they're mistaken very much:
'Tis plain enough he was no such.
We grant, although he had much wit,
He was very shy of using it;
As being loath to wear it out,
And therefore bore it not about,
Unless on holidays, or so,
As men their best apparel do.
Beside, 'tis known he could speak Greek
As naturally as pigs squeak;
That Latin was no more difficile
Than to a blackbird 'tis to whistle.
Being rich in both, he never scanted
His bounty unto such as wanted,
But much of either would afford
To many that had not one word.
For Hebrew roots, although they're found
To flourish most in barren ground,
He had such plenty as sufficed
To make some think him circumcised;
And truly so perhaps he was,
'Tis many a pious Christian's case.
He was in logic a great critic,
Profoundly skilled in analytic:
He could distinguish and divide
A hair 'twixt south and southwest side;
On either which he would dispute,
Confute, change hands, and still confute:
He'd undertake to prove, by force
Of argument, a man's no horse.

difficile] troublesome, hard   analytic] logic

He'd prove a buzzard is no fowl,
And that a lord may be an owl,
A calf an alderman, a goose a justice,
And rooks committee-men and trustees.
He'd run in debt by disputation,
And pay with ratiocination.
All this by syllogism, true
In mood and figure, he would do.
  For rhetoric, he could not ope
His mouth but out there flew a trope;
And when he happened to break off
In the middle of his speech, or cough,
He had hard words ready to show why,
And tell what rules he did it by.
Else, when with greatest art he spoke,
You'd think he talked like other folk;
For all a rhetorician's rules
Teach nothing but to name his tools.
His ordinary rate of speech
In loftiness of sound was rich,
A Babylonish dialect,
Which learned pedants much affect.
It was a parti-coloured dress
Of patched and piebald languages:
'Twas English cut on Greek and Latin,
Like fustian heretofore on satin.
It had an odd promiscuous tone,
As if he'd talked three parts in one;
Which made some think, when he did gabble,
They'd heard three labourers of Babel,
Or Cerberus himself pronounce
A leash of languages at once.
This he as volubly would vent,
As if his stock would ne'er be spent;
And truly, to support that charge,
He had supplies as vast and large.
For he could coin or counterfeit
New words with little or no wit:
Words so debased and hard, no stone
Was hard enough to touch them on.
And when with hasty noise he spoke 'em,
The ignorant for current took 'em;

buzzard] worthless person owl] wise fool calf] dolt goose] simpleton rooks] swindlers trustees] (appointed to sell royalist estates) mood . . . figure] correct logical form fustian . . . satin] slashed fustian Cerberus] three-headed watchdog of the classical underworld leash] set of three (sporting) touch] test

That, had the orator, who once
Did fill his mouth with pebble-stones
When he harangued, but known his phrase,
He would have used no other ways.
  In mathematics he was greater
Than Tycho Brahe or Erra Pater;
For he, by geometric scale,
Could take the size of pots of ale;
Resolve by sines and tangents, straight,
If bread or butter wanted weight;
And wisely tell what hour of the day
The clock does strike, by algebra.
  Beside, he was a shrewd philosopher,
And had read every text and gloss over:
Whate'er the crabbed'st author hath,
He understood by implicit faith;
Whatever sceptic could inquire for,
For every why he had a wherefore;
Knew more than forty of them do,
As far as words and terms could go:
All which he understood by rote,
And, as occasion served, would quote,
No matter whether right or wrong;
They might be either said or sung.
His notions fitted things so well
That which was which he could not tell,
But oftentimes mistook the one
For th' other, as great clerks have done.
He could reduce all things to acts,
And knew their natures by abstracts;
Where entity and quiddity,
The ghosts of defunct bodies, fly;
Where truth in person does appear,
Like words congealed in northern air.
He knew what's what, and that's as high
As metaphysic wit can fly.
In school-divinity as able
As he that hight Irrefragable;
Profound in all the nominal
And real ways beyond them all;
And with as delicate a hand
Could twist as tough a rope of sand,

That] So that   the orator] Demosthenes   Brahe] the Danish astronomer   Erra Pater] William Lilly, the astrologer   acts] essences (Scholastic term)   he . . . hight] Alexander Hales   Irrefragable] Invincible   rope of sand] incoherence

And weave fine cobwebs, fit for skull
That's empty when the moon is full;
Such as take lodgings in a head
That's to be let unfurnishèd.
He could raise scruples dark and nice,
And after solve 'em in a trice;
As if divinity had catched
The itch, of purpose to be scratched,
Or, like a mountebank, did wound
And stab herself with doubts profound,
Only to show with how small pain
The sores of faith are cured again;
Although by woeful proof we find
They always leave a scar behind.
He knew the seat of paradise,
Could tell in what degree it lies;
And, as he was disposed, could prove it
Below the moon, or else above it;
What Adam dreamt of when his bride
Came from her closet in his side;
Whether the devil tempted her
By a High Dutch interpreter;
If either of them had a navel;
Who first made music malleable;
Whether the serpent at the Fall
Had cloven feet, or none at all:
All this without a gloss or comment
He would unriddle in a moment,
In proper terms, such as men smatter
When they throw out, and miss the matter.
  For his religion, it was fit
To match his learning and his wit:
'Twas Presbyterian true blue,
For he was of that stubborn crew
Of errant saints whom all men grant
To be the true Church Militant:
Such as do build their faith upon
The holy text of pike and gun;
Decide all controversies by
Infallible artillery,
And prove their doctrine orthodox
By apostolic blows and knocks;
Call fire and sword and desolation

High Dutch] (the Adamic language, thought Goropius Becanus) malleable] hammerable (Pythagorean musicology was based on hammer sounds) feet, or none] (Gen. 3: 14) errant] (1) arrant, thorough-going; (2) wandering

A godly, thorough reformation,
Which always must be carried on,
And still be doing, never done;
As if religion were intended
For nothing else but to be mended.
A sect whose chief devotion lies
In odd, perverse antipathies;
In falling out with that or this,
And finding somewhat still amiss;
More peevish, cross, and splenetic
Than dog distract or monkey sick;
That with more care keep holy day
The wrong, than others the right way;
Compound for sins they are inclined to
By damning those they have no mind to;
Still so perverse and opposite
As if they worshipped God for spite.
The selfsame thing they will abhor
One way, and long another for.
Free will they one way disavow,
Another, nothing else allow;
All piety consists therein
In them, in other men all sin.
Rather than fail, they will defy
That which they love most tenderly;
Quarrel with minced pies, and disparage
Their best and dearest friend, plum porridge;
Fat pig and goose itself oppose,
And blaspheme custard through the nose.

(1678)

579 [*Arms and the Man*]

THERE was an ancient sage philosopher
That had read Alexander Ross over,
And swore the world, as he could prove,
Was made of fighting and of love:
Just so romances are, for what else
Is in them all, but love and battles?
Of the first of these we've no great matter
To treat of, but a world of the latter;
In which to do the injured right
We mean, in what concerns just fight.

579 philosopher] Empedocles Ross] early anthropologist

Certes our authors are to blame,
For to make some well-sounding name
A pattern fit for modern knights
To copy out in frays and fights
(Like those that a whole street do raze,
To build a palace in the place).
They never care how many others
They kill, without regard of mothers,
Or wives, or children, so they can
Make up some fierce, dead-doing man
Composed of many ingredient valours,
Just like the manhood of nine tailors.
So a wild Tartar when he spies
A man that's handsome, valiant, wise,
If he can kill him, thinks to inherit
His wit, his beauty, and his spirit;
As if just so much he enjoyed
As in another is destroyed.
For when a giant's slain in fight,
And mowed o'erthwart, or cleft downright,
It is a heavy case, no doubt,
A man should have his brains beat out
Because he's tall and has large bones,
As men kill beavers for their stones.
But, as for our part, we shall tell
The naked truth of what befell,
And as an equal friend to both
The knight and bear, but more to troth,
With neither faction shall take part,
But give to each his due desert,
And never coin a formal lie on't,
To make the knight o'ercome the giant.
This being professed we hope's enough,
And now go on where we left off.

(1678)

RICHARD CRASHAW

1612?–1649

580 *Upon Bishop Andrewes's Picture before His 'Sermons'*

THIS reverend shadow cast that setting sun
Whose glorious course through our horizon run
Left the dim face of this dull hemisphere
All one great eye, all drowned in one great tear.
Whose fair illustrious soul led his free thought
Through learning's universe, and (vainly) sought
Room for her spacious self, until at length
She found the way home: with an holy strength
Snatched herself hence, to heaven; filled a bright place
Mongst those immortal fires; and on the face
Of her great maker fixed her flaming eye,
There still to read true pure divinity.
And now that grave aspéct hath deigned to shrink
Into this less appearance: if you think
'Tis but a dead face art doth here bequeath,
Look on the following leaves and see him breathe.

(1631)

581 *Wishes: To His (Supposed) Mistress*

WHOE'ER she be,
That not impossible she
That shall command my heart and me;

Where'er she lie,
Locked up from mortal eye
In shady leaves of destiny

Till that ripe birth
Of studied fate stand forth,
And teach her fair steps to our Earth;

Till that divine
Idea take a shrine
Of crystal flesh, through which to shine;

581 teach] guide

Meet you her, my wishes,
Bespeak her to my blisses,
And be ye called my absent kisses.

I wish her beauty
That owes not all his duty
To gaudy tire or glistering shoe-tie;

Something more than
Taffeta or tissue can,
Or rampant feather, or rich fan;

More than the spoil
Of shop, or silkworm's toil,
Or a bought blush, or a set smile;

A face that's best
By its own beauty dressed,
And can alone command the rest;

A face made up
Out of no other shop
Than what nature's white hand sets ope;

A cheek where youth
And blood, with pen of truth,
Write what the reader sweetly ru'th;

A cheek where grows
More than a morning rose:
Which to no box his being owes;

Lips where all day
A lover's kiss may play,
Yet carry nothing thence away;

Looks that oppress
Their richest tires, but dress
And clothe their simplest nakedness;

Eyes that displaces
The neighbour diamond, and outfaces
The sunshine by their own sweet graces;

tire] attire oppress] overpower

Tresses that wear
Jewels but to declare
How much themselves more precious are;

Whose native ray
Can tame the wanton day
Of gems, that in their bright shades play—

Each ruby there,
Or pearl that dare appear,
Be its own blush, be its own tear;

A well-tamed heart,
For whose more noble smart
Love may be long choosing a dart;

Eyes that bestow
Full quivers on love's bow,
Yet pay less arrows than they owe;

Smiles that can warm
The blood, yet teach a charm,
That chastity shall take no harm;

Blushes that bin
The burnish of no sin,
Nor flames of aught too hot within;

Joys that confess
Virtue their mistress,
And have no other head to dress;

Fears, fond and flight
As the coy bride's, when night
First does the longing lover right;

Tears quickly fled
And vain, as those are shed
For a dying maidenhead;

Days that need borrow
No part of their good morrow
From a forespent night of sorrow;

bin] be fond] foolish flight] quick coy] reluctant

Days that, in spite
Of darkness, by the light
Of a clear mind are day all night;

Nights sweet as they,
Made short by lover's play
Yet long by the absence of the day;

Life that dares send
A challenge to his end,
And, when it comes, say, 'Welcome, friend.'

Sydnaean showers
Of sweet discourse, whose powers
Can crown old winter's head with flowers;

Soft silken hours,
Open suns, shady bowers;
'Bove all, nothing within that lours;

Whate'er delight
Can make day's forehead bright,
Or give down to the wings of night;

In her whole frame
Have nature all the name,
Art and ornament the shame;

Her flattery,
Picture and poesy:
Her counsel her own virtue be;

I wish her store
Of worth may leave her poor
Of wishes; and I wish—no more.

Now if time knows
That her whose radiant brows
Weave them a garland of my vows;

Her whose just bays
My future hopes can raise,
A trophy to her present praise;

Sydnaean] i.e. as in Sir Philip Sidney's *Arcadia* bays] laurels

Her that dares be
What these lines wish to see:
I seek no further: it is she.

'Tis she, and here
Lo! I unclothe and clear
My wishes' cloudy character.

May she enjoy it
Whose merit dare apply it,
But modesty dares still deny it.

Such worth as this is
Shall fix my flying wishes,
And determine them to kisses.

Let her full glory,
My fancies, fly before ye:
Be ye my fictions, but her story.

(1641)

582 *Upon the Body of Our Blessed Lord, Naked and Bloody*

THEY'VE left thee naked, Lord—oh that they had!
  This garment too I would they had denied.
Thee with thyself they have too richly clad,
  Opening the purple wardrobe in thy side.
Oh never could there be garment too good
For thee to wear, but this of thine own blood.

(1646)

583 *A Hymn to the Name and Honour of the Admirable Saint Teresa*

Foundress of the reformation of the Discalced Carmelites, both men and women: a woman for angelical height of speculation, for masculine courage of performance, more than a woman: who, yet a child, outran maturity, and durst plot a martyrdom

LOVE, thou art absolute sole lord
Of life and death. To prove the word,
We'll now appeal to none of all
Those thy old soldiers, great and tall,

583 *Discalced*] Barefoot

Ripe men of martyrdom, that could reach down
With strong arms their triumphant crown;
Such as could with lusty breath
Speak loud into the face of death
Their great Lord's glorious name; to none
Of those whose spacious bosoms spread a throne
For love at large to fill: spare blood and sweat,
And see him take a private seat,
Making his mansion in the mild
And milky soul of a soft child.
  Scarce has she learned to lisp the name
Of martyr, yet she thinks it shame
Life should so long play with that breath
Which spent can buy so brave a death.
She never undertook to know
What death with love should have to do;
Nor has she e'er yet understood
Why, to show love, she should shed blood;
Yet though she cannot tell you why,
She can love, and she can die.
  Scarce has she blood enough to make
A guilty sword blush for her sake;
Yet has she a heart dares hope to prove
How much less strong is death than love.
  Be love but there, let poor six years
Be posed with the maturest fears
Man trembles at, you straight shall find
Love knows no nonage, nor the mind.
'Tis love, not years or limbs that can
Make the martyr, or the man.
  Love touched her heart, and lo it beats
High, and burns with such brave heats,
Such thirsts to die, as dares drink up
A thousand cold deaths in one cup.
Good reason, for she breathes all fire:
Her weak breast heaves with strong desire
Of what she may with fruitless wishes
Seek for amongst her mother's kisses.
  Since 'tis not to be had at home,
She'll travel to a martyrdom:
No home for hers confesses she
But where she may a martyr be.
  She'll to the Moors, and trade with them
For this unvalued diadem.

brave] splendid   unvalued] invaluable

She'll offer them her dearest breath,
With Christ's name in't, in change for death.
She'll bargain with them, and will give
Them God: teach them how to live
In him, or, if they this deny,
For him she'll teach them how to die.
So shall she leave amongst them sown
Her Lord's blood, or at least her own.
  Farewell then, all the world, adieu!
Teresa is no more for you.
Farewell, all pleasures, sports, and joys
(Never till now esteemèd toys),
Farewell whatever dear may be,
Mother's arms or father's knee;
Farewell house and farewell home:
She's for the Moors, and martyrdom!
  Sweet, not so fast! Lo, thy fair spouse
Whom thou seekst with so swift vows
Calls thee back, and bids thee come
To embrace a milder martyrdom.
  Blest powers forbid thy tender life
Should bleed upon a barbarous knife;
Or some base hand have power to rase
Thy breast's chaste cabinet, and uncase
A soul kept there so sweet: oh no,
Wise heaven will never have it so:
Thou art love's victim, and must die
A death more mystical and high.
Into love's arms thou shalt let fall
A still surviving funeral.
His is the dart must make the death
Whose stroke shall taste thy hallowed breath:
A dart thrice dipped in that rich flame
Which writes thy spouse's radiant name
Upon the roof of heaven, where aye
It shines, and with a sovereign ray
Beats bright upon the burning faces
Of souls which in that name's sweet graces
Find everlasting smiles. So rare,
So spiritual, pure, and fair
Must be the immortal instrument
Upon whose choice point shall be sent
A life so loved; and that there be
Fit executioners for thee,

rase] slash   cabinet] treasury   uncase] strip; disembody

The fairest and first-born sons of fire,
Blest seraphim, shall leave their choir
And turn love's soldiers, upon thee
To exercise their archery.
  Oh how oft shalt thou complain
Of a sweet and subtle pain,
Of intolerable joys,
Of a death, in which who dies
Loves his death, and dies again,
And would forever so be slain,
And lives, and dies, and knows not why
To live, but that he thus may never leave to die.
  How kindly will thy gentle heart
Kiss the sweetly killing dart,
And close in his embraces keep
Those delicious wounds, that weep
Balsam to heal themselves with. Thus
When these thy deaths so numerous
Shall all at last die into one,
And melt thy soul's sweet mansïon,
Like a soft lump of incense hasted
By too hot a fire and wasted
Into perfúming clouds, so fast
Shalt thou exhale to heaven at last
In a resolving sigh; and then
—Oh what? Ask not the tongues of men.
Angels cannot tell; suffice,
Thyself shall feel thine own full joys,
And hold them fast forever. There
So soon as thou shalt first appear,
The moon of maiden stars, thy white
Mistress, attended by such bright
Souls as thy shining self, shall come
And in her first ranks make thee room,
Where mongst her snowy family
Immortal welcomes wait for thee.
  Oh what delight, when revealed life shall stand
And teach thy lips heaven with his hand,
On which thou now mayst to thy wishes
Heap up thy consecrated kisses.
What joys shall seize thy soul, when she,
Bending her blessed eyes on thee,
Those second smiles of heaven, shall dart
Her mild rays through thy melting heart!
  Angels, thy old friends, there shall greet thee,
Glad at their own home now to meet thee.

All thy good works, which went before
And waited for thee at the door,
Shall own thee there, and all in one
Weave a constellatïon
Of crowns, with which the king thy spouse
Shall build up thy triumphant brows.
All thy old woes shall now smile on thee,
And thy pains sit bright upon thee;
All thy sorrows here shall shine,
All thy sufferings be divine.
Tears shall take comfort and turn gems,
And wrongs repent to diadems.
Even thy deaths shall live, and new
Dress the soul that erst they slew.
Thy wounds shall blush to such bright scars
As keep account of the lamb's wars.
Those rare works where thou shalt leave writ
Love's noble history, with wit
Taught thee by none but him, while here
They feed our souls, shall clothe thine there.
Each heavenly word by whose hid flame
Our hard hearts shall strike fire, the same
Shall flourish on thy brows, and be
Both fire to us and flame to thee;
Whose light shall live bright in thy face
By glory, in our hearts by grace.
Thou shalt look round about and see
Thousands of crowned souls throng to be
Themselves thy crown. Sons of thy vows,
The virgin births with which thy sovereign spouse
Made fruitful thy fair soul, go now
And with them all about thee bow
To him. 'Put on', he'll say, 'Put on,
My rosy love, that thy rich zone
Sparkling with the sacred flames
Of thousand souls whose happy names
Heaven keeps upon thy score. (Thy bright
Life brought them first to kiss the light
That kindled them to stars.)' And so
Thou with the lamb, thy Lord, shalt go,
And wheresoe'er he sets his white
Steps, walk with him those ways of light
Which who in death would live to see
Must learn in life to die like thee.

(1646)

584 *Mr Crashaw's Answer for Hope*

DEAR hope! Earth's dowry, and heaven's debt!
The entity of those that are not yet.
Subtlest but surest being! Thou by whom
Our nothing has a definition!
    Substantial shade, whose sweet allay
    Blends both the noons of night and day!
Fates cannot find out a capacity
    Of hurting thee.
From thee their lean dilemma, with blunt horn,
Shrinks, as the sick moon from the wholesome morn.
  Rich hope! Love's legacy, under lock
Of faith, still spending and still growing stock!
Our crown-land lies above, yet each meal brings
A seemly portion for the sons of kings.
    Nor will the virgin joys we wed
    Come less unbroken to our bed,
Because that from the bridal cheek of bliss
    Thou stealst us down a distant kiss.
Hope's chaste stealth harms no more joy's maidenhead
Than spousal rites prejudge the marriage bed.
  Fair hope, our earlier heaven! By thee
Young time is taster to eternity;
Thy generous wine with age grows strong, not sour.
Nor does it kill thy fruit to smell thy flower.
    Thy golden, growing head never hangs down
    Till in the lap of love's full noon
It falls, and dies. Oh no! It melts away
    As does the dawn into the day:
As lumps of sugar loose themselves, and twine
Their supple essence with the soul of wine.
  Fortune? Alas, above the world's low wars
Hope walks, and kicks the curled heads of conspiring stars.
Her keel cuts not the waves where these winds stir:
Fortune's whole lottery is one blank to her.
    Her shafts and she fly far above,
    And forage in the fields of light and love.
Sweet hope! Kind cheat! Fair fallacy, by thee
We are not where nor what we be,
But what and where we would be. Thus art thou
Our absent presence and our future now.
  Faith's sister! Nurse of fair desire!
Fear's antidote! A wise and well-stayed fire!

still] ever   loose] (1) dissolve; loosen; (2) lose

Temper 'twixt chill despair and torrid joy!
Queen regent in young love's minority!
    Though the vexed chemic vainly chases
    His fugitive gold through all her faces;
Though love's more fierce, more fruitless fires assay
    One face more fugitive than all they,
True hope's a glorious hunter, and her chase
The God of nature in the fields of grace.

(1646)

585 *A Letter from Mr Crashaw to the Countess of Denbigh, Against Irresolution and Delay in Matters of Religion*

WHAT heaven-besiegèd heart is this
Stands trembling at the gate of bliss:
Holds fast the door, yet dares not venture
Fairly to open and to enter?
Whose definition is a doubt
'Twixt life and death, 'twixt in and out.
Ah, linger not, loved soul! A slow
And late consent was a long no.
Who grants at last, a great while tried,
And did his best, to have denied.
  What magic bolts, what mystic bars
Maintain the will in these strange wars?
What fatal yet fantastic bands
Keep the free heart from his own hands?
Say, lingering fair, why comes the birth
Of your brave soul so slowly forth?
Plead your pretences (O you strong
In weakness), why you choose so long
In labour of yourself to lie,
Not daring quite to live nor die.
    So, when the year takes cold, we see
  Poor waters their own prisoners be:
  Fettered and locked up fast they lie
  In a cold self-captivity.
Th'astonished nymphs their flood's strange fate deplore,
To find themselves their own severer shore.
    Love, that lends haste to heaviest things,
  In you alone hath lost his wings.

vexed] perplexed   chemic] alchemist   chase] quarry

585 bands] bonds

Look round and read the world's wide face,
The field of nature or of grace:
Where can you fix, to find excuse
Or pattern for the pace you use?
Mark with what faith fruits answer flowers,
And know the call of heaven's kind showers:
Each mindful plant hastes to make good
The hope and promise of his bud.
Seed-time's not all; there should be harvest too.
Alas! and has the year no spring for you?
Both winds and waters urge their way,
And murmur if they meet a stay.
Mark how the curl'd waves work and wind,
All hating to be left behind.
Each big with business thrusts the other,
And seems to say, 'Make haste, my brother'.
The airy nation of neat doves,
That draw the chariot of chaste loves,
Chide your delay: yea, those dull things,
Whose ways have least to do with wings,
Make wings at least of their own weight,
And by their love control their fate.
So lumpish steel, untaught to move,
Learned first his lightness by his love.
Whate'er love's matter be, he moves
By th' even wings of his own doves:
Lives by his own laws, and does hold
In grossest metals his own gold.
All things swear friends to fair and good,
Yea suitors; man alone is wooed,
Tediously wooed, and hardly won:
Only not slow to be undone.
As if the bargain had been driven
So hardly betwixt Earth and heaven,
Our God would thrive too fast, and be
Too much a gainer by it, should we
Our purchased selves too soon bestow
On him, who has not loved us so.
When love of us called him to see
If we'd vouchsafe his company,
He left his father's court, and came
Lightly as a lambent flame
Leaping upon the hills, to be
The humble king of you and me.

urge] force neat] shining; elegant

Nor can the cares of his whole crown,
When one poor sigh sends for him down,
Detain him, but he leaves behind
The late wings of the lazy wind,
Spurns the tame laws of time and place,
And breaks through all ten heavens to our embrace.
Yield to his siege, wise soul, and see
Your triumph in his victory.
Disband dull fears, give faith the day:
To save your life, kill your delay.
'Tis cowardice that keeps this field,
And want of courage not to yield.
Yield then, oh yield, that love may win
The fort at last, and let life in.
Yield quickly, lest perhaps you prove
Death's prey, before the prize of love.
This fort of your fair self, if't be not won,
He is repulsed indeed, but you're undone.

(1652)

586 *Blessed Be the Paps which Thou Hast Sucked (Luke 11)*

Suppose he had been tabled at thy teats,
Thy hunger feels not what he eats;
He'll have his teat ere long, a bloody one,
The mother then must suck the Son.

(1646)

587 *She Began to Wash His Feet with Tears and Wipe Them with the Hairs of Her Head (Luke 7)*

Her eyes' flood licks his feet's fair stain,
Her hair's flame licks up that again.
This flame thus quenched hath brighter beams;
This flood thus stainèd fairer streams.

(1646)

586 tabled] provided with meals

588 *To Our Blessed Lord: Upon the Choice of His Sepulchre*

How life and death in thee
Agree!
Thou hadst a virgin womb,
And tomb.
A Joseph did betroth
Them both.

(1646)

589 Caritas Nimia, *or The Dear Bargain*

Lord, what is man? Why should he cost thee
So dear? What had his ruin lost thee?
Lord, what is man, that thou hast overbought
So much a thing of nought?

Love is too kind, I see, and can
Make but a simple merchant man.
'Twas for such sorry merchandise
Bold painters have put out his eyes.

Alas, sweet Lord, what were 't to thee
If there were no such worms as we?
Heaven ne'er the less still heaven would be,
Should mankind dwell
In the deep hell.
What have his woes to do with thee?

Let him go weep
O'er his own wounds;
Seraphims will not sleep,
Nor spheres let fall their faithful rounds.

Still would the youthful spirits sing,
And still thy spacious palace ring.
Still would those beauteous ministers of light
Burn all as bright,

Joseph] (1) St Joseph; (2) St Joseph of Arimathaea

589 Caritas Nimia] Too much love overbought] paid too much for merchandise] salesmanship rounds] planets

And bow their flaming heads before thee;
Still thrones and dominations would adore thee;
Still would those ever-wakeful sons of fire
Keep warm thy praise
Both nights and days,
And teach thy loved name to their noble lyre.

Let froward dust, then, do its kind,
And give itself for sport to the proud wind.
Why should a piece of peevish clay plead shares
In the eternity of thy old cares?
Why shouldst thou bow thy awful breast to see
What mine own madnesses have done with me?

Should not the king still keep his throne,
Because some desperate fool's undone?
Or will the world's illustrious eyes
Weep for every worm that dies?

Will the gallant sun
E'er the less glorious run?
Will he hang down his golden head
Or e'er the sooner seek his western bed,
Because some foolish fly
Grows wanton, and will die?

If I were lost in misery,
What was it to thy heaven and thee?
What was it to thy precious blood
If my foul heart called for a flood?

What if my faithless soul and I
Would needs fall in
With guilt and sin:
What did the lamb, that he should die?
What did the lamb, that he should need,
When the wolf sins, himself to bleed?

If my base lust
Bargained with death and well-beseeming dust,
Why should the white
Lamb's bosom write
The purple name
Of my sin's shame?

froward] perverse kind] nature

Why should his unstained breast make good
My blushes with his own heart-blood?

O my saviour, make me see
How dearly thou hast paid for me;
That, lost again, my life may prove,
As then in death, so now in love.

(1648)

LORD FAIRFAX
1612–1671

590

On the Fatal Day January 30, 1648

OH! let that day from time be blotted quite
Out of belief! In after-age be waived,
That in deep'st silence th' act concealèd might;
That so the kingdom's credit might be saved.
But if the power divine permitteth this—
His will's the law, and ours must acquiesce.

Curae loquuntur leves: ingentes stupent.

(1909; wr. 1648/9)

591

Shortness of Life

IN rosy morn I saw Aurora red,
But, when the sun his beams had fully spread,
Vanished; then saw a frost, and then a dew,
Twixt time so short as scarce a time I knew.
This stranger seemed, when in more raisèd thought
I saw death come (how soon a life he'd caught!)
Where, in the turning of an eye, he'd done
Far speedier execution than the sun.

(1909)

592

Upon the New Building at Appleton

THINK not, O man that dwells herein,
This house was made to stay at, but as an inn,
Which for accommodations fitly stands
In the way to mansions that's not made with hands.

590 *Curae . . . stupent*] Slight troubles speak; the great are struck dumb (Seneca *Hippolytus* 607)

But if a time here thou take thy rest,
Yet think on this, eternity's the best.

(1909; wr. 1650?)

JAMES GRAHAM, MARQUIS OF MONTROSE
1612–1650

593 *On Himself, upon Hearing What Was His Sentence*

LET them bestow on every airt a limb;
Open all my veins, that I may swim
To thee my saviour, in that crimson lake;
Then place my parboiled head upon a stake;
Scatter my ashes, throw them in the air:
Lord (since thou knowst where all these atoms are)
I'm hopeful, once thou'lt recollect my dust,
And confident thou'lt raise me with the just.

(1711)

THOMAS KILLIGREW?
1612–1683

594 *Epilogue to 'The Parson's Wedding'*

WHEN boys played women's parts, you'd think the stage
Was innocent in that untempting age.
No; for your amorous fathers then, like you,
Amongst those boys had playhouse misses too;
They set those bearded beauties on their laps:
Men gave 'em kisses, and the ladies claps.
But they, poor hearts, could not supply our room.
They went but females to the tiring-room,
While we, in kindness to ourselves and you,
Can hold out women to our lodgings too.
Now, to oppose the humour of that age,
We have this day expelled our men the stage.

airt] point of the compass

594 tiring-room] dressing-room

Why cannot we as well perform their parts?
No, 'twould not take: the tender ladies' hearts
Would then their former charity give o'er;
The madams in disguise would steal no more
To the young actors' chambers in masked faces,
To leave love offerings of points and laces.
Nor can we act their parts: alas! too soon
You'd find the cheat in the empty pantaloon.
Well; though we are not women's men, at least
We hope to have you gallants constant guests;
Which if you grant, and fill our house each day,
We will return your kindnesses this way:
We'll build up a new theatre to gain you,
And turn this to a house to entertain you.

(1672)

JOHN CLEVELAND
1613–1658

595 from *The Rebel Scot*

How? 'Providence', and yet a Scottish crew?
Then Madam Nature wears black patches too:
What, shall our nation be in bondage thus
Unto a land that truckles under us?
Ring the bells backward! I am all on fire:
Not all the buckets in a country choir
Shall quench my rage. A poet should be feared
When angry, like a comet's flaming beard.
And where's the stoic can his wrath appease,
To see his country sick of Pym's disease:
By Scotch invasion to be made a prey
To such pigwidgin myrmidons as they?
But that there's charm in verse, I would not quote
The name of Scot without an antidote;
Unless my head were red, that I might brew
Invention there, that might be poison too.
Were I a drowsy judge whose dismal note
Disgorgeth halters as a juggler's throat

points] laces

595 Providence] (battle cry of New Model Army) Pym's] John Pym (Parliamentary leader) pigwidgin] ?petty, picayune myrmidons] hired ruffians dismal] dire

Doth ribbons; could I in Sir Empiric's tone
Speak pills in phrase, and quack destruction;
Or roar like Marshall, that Geneva bull,
Hell and damnaẗion a pulpit full;
Yet to express a Scot, to play that prize,
Not all those mouth-grenadoes can suffice.
Before a Scot can properly be cursed,
I must like Hocus swallow daggers first.
Come, keen iambics, with your badgers' feet,
And, badger-like, bite till your teeth do meet.
Help, ye tart satirists, to imp my rage
With all the scorpions that should whip this age.
Scots are like witches: do but whet your pen,
Scratch till the blood come; they'll not hurt you then.
Now as the martyrs were enforced to take
The shapes of beasts, like hypocrites, at stake,
I'll bait my Scot so; yet not cheat your eyes:
A Scot within a beast is no disguise.
No more let Ireland brag her harmless nation
Fosters no venom, since the Scots plantation;
Nor can ours feigned antiquity maintain:
Since they came in, England hath wolves again.

*   *   *   *   *

He that saw hell in his melancholy dream,
And in the twilight of his fancy's theme,
Scared from his sins, repented in a fright,
Had he viewed Scotland, had turned proselyte:
A land where one may pray with cursed intent,
'O may they never suffer banishment!'
Had Cain been Scot, God would have changed his doom,
Not forced him wander but confined him home.
Like Jews they spread, and as infection fly,
As if the devil had ubiquity.
Hence 'tis, they live at rovers, and defy
This or that place, rags of geography.
They're citizens of the world; they're all in all;
Scotland's a nation epidemical.
And yet they ramble not to learn the mode
How to be dressed, or how to lisp abroad,
To return knowing in the Spanish shrug,
Or which of the Dutch States a double jug

Empiric's] 'Quack's'   Marshall] Stephen Marshall (Puritan preacher)   play . . . prize] act that part   grenadoes] grenades   Hocus] any conjurer   imp] supplement by engrafting   scorpions] weighted scourges   Scot . . . beast] i.e. Pict tattooed like a beast   Fosters no venom] i.e. has no snakes   doom] judgement   at rovers] aimlessly   States] i.e. leaders

Resembles most, in belly, or in beard
(The card by which the mariners are steered).
No, the Scots-errant fight, and fight to eat;
Their ostrich stomachs make their swords their meat:
Nature with Scots as tooth-drawers hath dealt,
Who use to hang their teeth upon their belt.
Yet wonder not at this their happy choice;
The serpent's fatal still to paradise.
Sure England hath the haemorrhoids, and these
On the north postern of the patient seize,
Like leeches: thus they physically thirst
After our blood, but in the cure shall burst.
Let them not think to make us run o'th' score
To purchase villeinage as once before,
When an Act passed to stroke them on the head,
Call them good subjects, buy them gingerbread.
Nor gold, nor Acts of Grace; 'tis steel must tame
The stubborn Scot: a prince that would reclaim
Rebels by yielding, doth like him (or worse)
Who saddled his own back to shame his horse.
  Was it for this you left your leaner soil,
Thus to lard Israel with Egypt's spoil?
They are the gospel's lifeguard; but for them,
The garrison of New Jerusalem,
What would the brethren do? The Cause! The Cause!
Sack-possets, and the Fundamental Laws!
Lord! What a goodly thing is want of shirts!
How a Scotch stomach, and no meat, converts!
They wanted food and raiment; so they took
Religion for their seamstress and their cook.
Unmask them well; their honours and estate,
As well as conscience, are sophisticate.
Shrive but their titles, and their money poise:
A laird and twenty pence pronounced with noise,
When construed, but for a plain yeoman go,
And a good sober twopence; and well so.
Hence then you proud imposters; get you gone,
You Picts in gentry and devotïon:
You scandal to the stock of verse, a race
Able to bring the gibbet in disgrace!
Hyperbolus by suffering did traduce
The ostracism, and shamed it out of use.
The Indian that heaven did forswear,

card] chart o'th' score] into debt villeinage] subjection The Cause . . . Fundamental Laws] Puritan slogans Shrive] Investigate poise] weigh Picts] painted Hyperbolus] (Athenian demagogue, murdered in exile)

Because he heard the Spaniards were there,
Had he but known what Scots in hell had been,
He would Erasmus-like have hung between.
My Muse hath done. A voider for the nonce!
I wrong the devil, should I pick the bones.
That dish is his; for when the Scots decease,
Hell like their nation feeds on barnacles.
  A Scot, when from the gallow-tree got loose,
  Drops into Styx, and turns a solan goose.

(1647)

596 *Epitaph on the Earl of Strafford*

HERE lies wise and valiant dust,
Huddled up 'twixt fit and just:
Strafford, who was hurried hence
'Twixt treason and convenïence.
He spent his time here in a mist:
A papist, yet a Calvinist.
His prince's nearest joy, and grief.
He had, yet wanted, all relief.
The prop and ruin of the state;
The people's violent love, and hate:
One in extremes loved and abhorred.
Riddles lie here; or in a word,
Here lies blood; and let it lie
Speechless still, and never cry.

(1647)

597 *The Antiplatonic*

FOR shame, thou everlasting wooer,
Still saying grace and ne'er fall to her!
Love that's in contemplation placed
Is Venus drawn but to the waist.
Unless your flame confess its gender,
And your parley cause surrender,
You're salamanders of a cold desire,
That live untouched amid the hottest fire.

voider] tray for clearing up   Styx] river of hell   solan goose] (supposed to grow on Orkney barnacle-trees)

596 wanted] lacked

597 Still] Always

What though she be a dame of stone,
The widow of Pygmalion;
As hard and unrelenting, she,
As the new-crusted Niobe;
Or, what doth more of statue carry,
A nun of the Platonic quarry?
Love melts the rigour which the rocks have bred:
A flint will break upon a feather bed.

For shame you pretty female elves,
Cease for to candy up yourselves;
No more, you sectaries of the game,
No more of your calcining flame.
Women commence by Cupid's dart,
As a king's hunting dubs a hart.
Love's votaries enthral each other's soul,
Till both of them live but upon parole.

Virtue's no more in womankind
But the green-sickness of the mind:
Philosophy, their new delight,
A kind of charcoal appetite.
There is no sophistry prevails,
Where all-convincing love assails,
But the disputing petticoat will warp,
As skilful gamesters are to seek at sharp.

The soldier, that man of iron,
Whom ribs of horror all environ,
That's strung with wire instead of veins,
In whose embraces you're in chains:
Let a magnetic girl appear,
Straight he turns Cupid's cuirassier.
Love storms his lips and takes the fortress in,
For all the bristled turnpikes of his chin.

(1651)

widow] (in mythology, the statue Pygmalion's love brought to life returned to stone after his death) new-crusted] newly changed to weeping stone Niobe] (in mythology punished by bereavement) candy up] sweeten, preserve in syrup calcining] (1) reducing; (2) refining (alchemy) commence] take their degrees green-sickness] anaemic disease of adolescent girls, causing morbid appetites gamesters] fencers to seek at sharp] found wanting in real duels turnpikes] spiked barriers

HENRY MORE
1614–1687

from *Psychozoia, or, the Life of the Soul*

598

[*Contrition*]

No light to guide but the moon's pallid ray,
And that even lost in misty troubled air:
No tract to take, there was no beaten way;
No cheering strength, but that which might appear
From Dian's face; her face then shined not clear,
And when it shineth clearest, little might
She yieldeth; yet the goddess is severe.
Hence wrathful dogs do bark at her dead light:
Christ help the man thus closed and prisoned in drad night!

O'erwhelmed with irksome toil of strange annoys,
In stony stound like senseless stake I stood,
Till the vast thumps of massy hammers' noise,
That on the groaning steel laid on such load,
Empierced mine ears in that sad stupid mood.
I weening then some harbour to be nigh,
In sorry pace thitherward slowly yode,
By ear directed more than by mine eye;
But here, alas, I found small hospitality.

Four grisly blacksmiths stoutly did their task
Upon an anvil formed in conic wise.
They neither minded who nor what I ask,
But with stern grimy look do still avise
Upon their works; but I my first emprise
Would not forsake, and therefore venture in.
Or none hath list to speak, or none espies
Or hears: the heavy hammers never lin,
And but a blue faint light in this black shop did shine.

There I into a darksome corner creep,
And lay my weary limbs on dusty floor,
Expecting still when soft down-sliding sleep
Should seize mine eyes, and strength to me restore;

tract] track drad] dread (archaism) annoys] annoyances stound] stupor massy] massive weening] supposing harbour] shelter yode] went (archaic) avise] ponder emprise] purpose; adventure lin] cease still] always

But when with hovering wings she 'proached, e'ermore
The mighty souses those foul knaves laid on,
And those huge bellows that aloud did roar,
Chased her away, that she was ever gone
Before she came, on pitchy plumes for fear yflown.

The first of those rude rascals Lypon hight,
A foul great stooping slouch with heavy eyes
And hanging lip; the second ugly sight
Pale Phobon with his hedgehog hairs' disguise.
Aelpon is the third: he the false skies
No longer trusts. The fourth of furious fashion
Phrenition hight, fraught with impatiences;
The bellows be yclept deep Suspiration:
Each knave these bellows blow in mutual circulation.

There is a number of these lonesome forges
In Bacha vale (this was in Bacha vale):
There be no inns but these, and these but scourges;
Instead of ease they work much deadly bale
To those that in this lowly trench do trail
Their feeble loins. Ah me! Who here would fare?
Sad ghosts oft cross the way with visage pale,
Sharp thorns and thistles wound their feeten bare;
Yet happy is the man that here doth bear a share.

When I in this sad vale no little time
Had measurèd, and oft had taken inn,
And by long penance paid for mine ill crime,
Methought the sun itself began to shine,
And that I'd passed Diana's discipline.
But day was not yet come, 'twas perfect night:
I Phoebus' head from Ida hill had seen;
For Ida hill doth give to men the sight
Of Phoebus' form, before Aurora's silver light.

But Phoebus' form from that high hill's not clear
Nor figure perfect. It's envelopèd
In purple cloudy veil; and if it appear
In rounder shape with scowling drearyhead,

souses] blows yflown] flown (Spenserian) Lypon] Sorrow (Greek) hight] was called Phobon] Fear (Greek) Aelpon] Hopeless (Greek) Phrenition] Fury (Greek) yclept] called (archaistic) Bacha] Weeping (Hebrew) trench] valley feeten] feet Ida hill] (in classical myth, site of the judgement of Paris) Aurora's] dawn's drearyhead] gloominess

A glowing face it shows, ne rays doth shed
Of light's serenity. Yet duller eyes
With gazing on this ireful sight be fed
Best to their pleasing; small things they will prize
That never better saw, nor better can devize.

On Ida hill there stands a castle strong;
They that built call it Pantheothen.
Hither resort a rascal rabble throng
Of miscreant wights; but if that wiser men
May name that fort, Pandaemoniothen
They would it clepe. It is the strong'st delusion
That ever demon wrought; the safest pen
That e'er held silly sheep for their confusion.
Ill life and want of love, hence springs each false conclusion.

That rabble rout that in this castle won
Is Ireful-ignorance, Unseemly-zeal,
Strong-self-conceit, Rotten-religion,
Contentious-reproach-gainst-Michael-
If-he-of-Moses'-body-aught-reveal-
Which-their-dull-sconces-cannot-easily-reach,
Love-of-the-carcass, An-inept-appeal-
To-uncertain-papers, A-false-formal-fetch-
Of-feignèd-sighs, Contempt-of-poor-and-sinful-wretch.

(1642)

RICHARD BAXTER
1615–1691

599 from *The Covenant and Confidence of Faith*

Now it belongs not to my care,
Whether I die or live;
To love and serve thee is my share,
And this thy grace must give.
If life be long I will be glad,
That I may long obey;
If short—yet why should I be sad,
That shall have the same pay?

598 ne] nor (archaistic) devize] imagine Pantheothen] All from God (Greek) miscreant] heretical; vile wights] men Pandaemoniothen] All from the devil (Greek) clepe] call (archaic) won] dwell (Spenserian)

If death shall bruise this springing seed
  Before it come to fruit,
The will with thee goes for the deed:
  Thy life was in the root.
Long life is a long grief and toil,
  And multiplieth faults;
In long wars he may have the foil
  That scapes in short assaults.

Would I long bear my heavy load,
  And keep my sorrows long?
Would I long sin against my God,
  And his dear mercy wrong?
How much is sinful flesh my foe,
  That doth my soul pervert
To linger here in sin and woe,
  And steals from God my heart!

Christ leads me through no darker rooms
  Than he went through before;
He that into God's kingdom comes
  Must enter by this door.
Come, Lord, when grace has made me meet
  Thy blessèd face to see;
For if thy work on Earth be sweet,
  What will thy glory be!

Then I shall end my sad complaints
  And weary, sinful days;
And join with the triumphant saints
  That sing Jehovah's praise.
My knowledge of that life is small,
  The eye of faith is dim;
But it's enough that Christ knows all,
  And I shall be with him.

(1681)

foil] defeat

SIR JOHN DENHAM
1615–1669

600 Preface to *The Progress of Learning*

My early mistress, now my ancient Muse,
That strong Circean liquor cease to infuse,
Wherewith thou didst intoxicate my youth:
Now stoop with disenchanted wings to truth;
As the dove's flight did guide Aeneas, now
May thine conduct me to the golden bough;
Tell, like a tall old oak, how learning shoots
To heaven her branches, and to hell her roots.

(1668)

601 *A Song*

Morpheus, the humble god, that dwells
In cottages and smoky cells,
Hates gilded roofs and beds of down;
And, though he fears no prince's frown,
Flies from the circle of a crown.

Come, I say, thou powerful god,
And thy leaden charming rod,
Dipped in the Lethean Lake,
O'er his wakeful temples shake,
Lest he should sleep and never wake.

Nature, alas, why art thou so
Obligèd to thy greatest foe?
Sleep that is thy best repast,
Yet of death it bears a taste,
And both are the same thing at last.

(1642)

Circean] bewitching (from Circe the mythic enchantress)

601 Morpheus] son of sleep (Latin mythology) Lethean] of forgetfulness (mythology) repast] (1) food; (2) repose

SIR JOHN DENHAM

from *Cooper's Hill*

602 [*The Thames*]

HERE should my wonder dwell, and here my praise;
But my fixed thoughts my wandering eye betrays,
Viewing a neighbouring hill, whose top of late
A chapel crowned, till in the common fate
The adjoining abbey fell (may no such storm
Fall on our times, where ruin must reform).
Tell me, my Muse, what monstrous dire offence,
What crime could any Christian king incense
To such a rage? Was it luxury, or lust?
Was he so temperate, so chaste, so just?
Were these their crimes? They were his own much more;
But wealth is crime enough to him that's poor,
Who having spent the treasures of his crown
Condemns their luxury to feed his own.
And yet this act, to varnish o'er the shame
Of sacrilege, must bear devotion's name.
No crime so bold but would be understood
A real, or at least a seeming, good.
Who fears not to do ill, yet fears the name,
And, free from conscience, is a slave to fame.
Thus he the church at once protects, and spoils;
But princes' swords are sharper than their styles.
And thus to the ages past he makes amends:
Their charity destroys, their faith defends.
Then did religion in a lazy cell,
In empty, airy contemplations dwell,
And, like the block, unmovèd lay; but ours,
As much too active, like the stork devours.
Is there no temperate region can be known,
Betwixt their frigid, and our torrid, zone?
Could we not wake from that lethargic dream,
But to be restless in a worse extreme?
And for that lethargy was there no cure,
But to be cast into a calenture?
Can knowledge have no bound, but must advance
So far, to make us wish for ignorance;
And rather in the dark to grope our way,
Than led by a false guide to err by day?
Who sees these dismal heaps but would demand
What barbarous invader sacked the land?
But when he hears no Goth, no Turk did bring
This desolation, but a Christian king;

styles] (1) styli, writing instruments; (2) titles   calenture] type of fever

When nothing but the name of zeal appears
'Twixt our best actions and the worst of theirs,
What does he think our sacrilege would spare,
When such the effects of our devotions are?
Parting from thence 'twixt anger, shame, and fear—
Those for what's past, and this for what's too near—
My eye, descending from the hill, surveys
Where Thames amongst the wanton valleys strays.
Thames, the most loved of all the Ocean's sons,
By his old sire to his embraces runs,
Hasting to pay his tribute to the sea,
Like mortal life to meet eternity;
Though with those streams he no resemblance hold,
Whose foam is amber, and their gravel gold;
His genuine, and less guilty, wealth t'explore,
Search not his bottom, but survey his shore,
O'er which he kindly spreads his spacious wing,
And hatches plenty for the ensuing spring.
Nor then destroys it with too fond a stay,
Like mothers which their infants overlay;
Nor with a sudden and impetuous wave,
Like profuse kings, resumes the wealth he gave.
No unexpected inundations spoil
The mowers' hopes, nor mock the ploughman's toil;
But godlike his unwearied bounty flows:
First loves to do, then loves the good he does.
Nor are his blessings to his banks confined,
But free and common as the sea or wind,
When he to boast or to disperse his stores,
Full of the tributes of his grateful shores,
Visits the world, and in his flying towers
Brings home to us, and makes both Indies ours;
Finds wealth where 'tis, bestows it where it wants;
Cities in deserts, woods in cities plants;
So that to us no thing, no place is strange,
While his fair bosom is the world's exchange.
Rome only conquered half the world, but trade
One commonwealth of that and her hath made,
And, though the sun his beam extends to all,
Yet to his neighbour sheds most liberal:
Lest God and nature partial should appear,
Commerce makes everything grow everywhere.
Oh could I flow like thee, and make thy stream
My great example, as it is my theme!
Though deep, yet clear, though gentle, yet not dull,
Strong without rage, without o'erflowing full.

(1642–68)

JOSEPH BEAUMONT
1616–1699

603

The Hourglass

ONCE as I in my study sat and saw
The faithful hourglass, with what speed it ran
(Much faster than my dull invention),
Methought I might from thence some emblem draw.

I and the sand near kindred had, my dust
Will prove it so; and for the tender glass
My brittle constitutïon may pass.
Time measureth my life, and run it must;

But here's the difference: that its hour will run,
Whilst my poor life hath not one minute sure.
The glass, if used with care, may long endure:
My most uncertain life may break alone.

When that is out, straight turnèd up again
Its life renewèd is, and runs afresh;
But when my dust is out, this helpless flesh
Must in its ruin to time's end remain.

Yet then at length my fate shall happier be:
My dust once turnèd up from my long grave
Runs not by slight vain hours, but stout and brave
Triúmphs o'er time by sure eternity.

(1914)

604

Love's Mystery

THE bright enamoured youth above
I asked, 'What kind of thing is love?'
I asked the saints; they could not tell,
Though in their bosoms it doth dwell.
I asked the lower angels; they
Lived in its flames, but could not say.
I asked the seraphs: these at last confessed
'We cannot tell how God should be expressed.'

'Can you not tell, whose amorous eyes
Flame in love's sweetest ecstasies?
Can you not tell, whose pure thoughts move
On wings all featherèd with love?
Can you not tell, who breathe and live
No life but what great love doth give?
Grant love a god, sweet seraphs, who should know
The nature of this deity, but you?'

'And who, bold mortal, more than we
Should know that love's a mystery?
Hid under his own flaming wing
Lies love, a secret open thing;
And there lie we, all hid in light,
Which gives us, and denies us, sight.
We see what dazzles and inflames our eyes,
And makes them mighty love's burnt sacrifice.'

(1914)

605 *The Cheat*

SWEET beguilings,
Cruel smilings,
Tickling souls to death;
Tedious leisures,
Bitter pleasures,
Smooth yet cragged path;

Heavy lightness,
Whose sad slightness
Cheers, yet breaks the bearer;
Dainty treasons,
Whose quaint reasons
Teach yet fool the hearer;

Glorious troubles,
Mighty bubbles,
Horror fairly brimmed,
Bane in honey,
Brass in money,
Nothing neatly trimmed

605 quaint] clever, ingenious

Are the prizes
Life devises
To warm fond desires,
Which, by growing
Hot, are blowing
Their own funeral fires.

(1914)

606 *Whiteness, or Chastity*

TELL me, where doth whiteness grow?
Not on beds of Scythian snow;
Nor on alabaster hills;
Nor in Canaan's milky rills;
Nor the dainty living land
Of a young queen's breast or hand;
Nor on cygnets' lovely necks;
Nor in lap of virgin wax;
Nor upon the soft and sleek
Pillows of the lily's cheek;
Nor the precious smiling heirs
Of the morning's pearly tears;
Nor the silver-shaming grace
Of the moon's unclouded face:
No; all these candours
Are but the handsome slanders
Cast on the name of genuine whiteness, which
Doth thee alone, fair chastity, enrich.

(1749)

607 *The Gentle Check*

ONE half of me was up and dressed,
The other still in lazy rest
(For yet my prayers I had not said),
When I close at her matins heard
A dainty-tonguèd bird,
Who little thought how she did me upbraid.

606 candours] (1) whitenesses; (2) innocences

But guilt caught hold of every note,
And through my breast the anthem shot:
My breast heard more than did my ear,
For now the tune grew sharp, and chode
Me into thoughts of God,
To whom most due my earlier accents were.

How shall I blush enough? To see
Poor birds prevent my praise to thee!
Dear Lord, my Muse for pardon pants,
And every tardy guilty tone
Doth languish to a groan:
Alas, today she sings not, but recants.

Forgive, forgive my lazy rhyme
Which in its music keeps not time.
If thy sweet patience lets me borrow
Another morn of life, I give
My promise here to strive
Before the lark to be at heaven tomorrow.

(1914; wr. 1652)

608 *The Garden*

THE garden's quit with me. As yesterday
I walked in that, today that walks in me:
Through all my memory
It sweetly wanders, and has found a way
To make me honestly possess
What still another's is.

Yet this gain's dainty sense doth gall my mind
With the remembrance of a bitter loss.
Alas, how odd and cross
Are Earth's delights, in which the soul can find
No honey, but withal some sting
To check the pleasing thing!

For now I'm haunted with the thought of that
Heaven-planted garden, where felicity
Flourished on every tree.
Lost, lost it is; for at the guarded gate
A flaming sword forbiddeth sin
(That's I) to enter in.

607 chode] chid recants] (1) abjures error; (2) repeats (music)

O paradise! When I was turnèd out
Hadst thou but kept the serpent still within,
My banishment had been
Less sad and dangerous; but round about
This wide world runneth raging he
To banish me from me:

I feel that through my soul he death hath shot,
And thou, alas, hast lockèd up life's tree.
Oh miserable me!
What help were left, had Jesus's pity not
Showed me another tree, which can
Enliven dying man.

That tree, made fertile by his own dear blood,
And by his death with quickening virtue fraught.
I now dread not the thought
Of barricadoed Eden, since as good
A paradise I planted see
On open Calvary.

(1914; wr. 1652)

609 *The Gnat*

ONE night, all tirèd with the weary day
And with my tedious self, I went to lay
My fruitless cares
And needless fears
Asleep.
The curtains of the bed and of mine eyes
Being drawn, I hoped no trouble would surprise
The rest which now
Gan on my brow
To creep.

When lo! A little fly, less than its name
(It was a gnat), with angry murmur came.
About she flew
And louder grew,
Whilst I
Fain would have scorned the silly thing, and slept
Out all its noise; I resolute silence kept,
And laboured so
To overthrow
The fly.

608 barricadoed] barred, shut up

But still with sharp alarms vexatious she
Or challengèd, or rather mockèd me.
        Angry at last,
        About I cast
            My hand.
'Twas well night would not let me blush, nor see
With whom I fought; and yet, though feeble she,
        Nor her nor my
        Own wrath could I
            Command.

Away she flies, and her own triumph sings;
I being left to fight with idler things,
        A feebler pair,
        Myself and air.
            How true
A worm is man, whom flies their sport can make!
Poor worm; true rest in no bed can he take,
        But one of earth,
        Whence he came forth
            And grew.

For there none but his silent sisters be,
Worms of as true and genuine earth as he,
        Which from the same
        Corruption came;
            And there,
Though on his eyes they feed, though on his heart,
They neither vex nor wake him; every part
        Rests in sound sleep,
        And out doth keep
            All fear.

(1914)

GEORGE DANIEL
1616–1657

610 from *After a Storm, Going a Hawking*

Long bound in ice and horrid hills of snow
Such as the fur-clad Russians ever know,
We are relieved now by a gentle rain,
And take the pleasures of the field again.

The restive horse now knows the dexterous hand
Of his old rider, runs to his command;
The gentle greyhound, in his ease grown high,
Frisks with delight to see his lord apply
The collar to his neck, and hopes again
To triumph in the blood of poor Watt slain.
The generous falcon, heavy with her ease,
Plies her firm feathers, and doth boldly seize
The trembling quarry, or envy the fowl
Half dead with fear: others, more brave, control
The lofty heron's flight, and venture all
Their life and honour with him in the fall;
Undaunted, yet with such a cautious flight
They almost teach a rational to fight.
For can we think it less to see her armed
And haughty foe fall dead? Herself unharmed,
A glorious victor in his blood, and proud
Of conquest, scatters all his plumes abroad.
Such joys the season doth to men present,
And, yet, a peace gives freedom, but content,
In my retirèd cell. I rather choose
More solid recreations, with the Muse
Which I have chosen, and my thoughts revolve
To every chord of passion, and resolve
Sometime the hardest, braver pleasure far,
To give bright reason wing into the sphere
Of truth, her region; where the fool is still
In our protection: give her way to kill
The harpie she has ruffed; for I dare say
She has earned her bells, to bring down such a prey.
  But we are ill falconers, and strive
Against our pleasure. If we keep alive
The bird, we are better pleased, and take her down
With a false quarry; but the lure is known,
And she disdains to stoop, but (madded) tries
Her wing at every lesser bird that flies:
Another such a check, and though you boast
Your care and cunning, she's for ever lost.

(1878)

ease] idleness   Watt] (type-name for hare)   envy] challenge; injure   fowl] bird   control] overmaster   glorious] haughty   harpie] harrier-like hawk   ruffed] struck (falconry)   bells] ornaments   stoop] swoop on her prey

611 *The Landscape*

But here's the piece, made up to sell;
Our mercenary pencil drew
It to the age's fancy new:
The Atlantic groves, where shadows dwell;
Fame, a perched pheasant and the quest of kings,
Keeps her at bay;
Unkennelled fury, deep-mouthed, rings
Liberty lodged, and chases it quite away.
Call this the wild of fancy: see,
The throne is seized; sedition treads
Down truth; and all the loyal heads
Were worth a hand, in charnels be;
The rest are spinning hopes, each in his chosen tree.

(1878)

SIR ROGER L'ESTRANGE
1616–1704

612 *Mr L'Estrange's Verses in the Prison at Lynn*

Beat on, proud billows! Boreas, blow!
Swell, curlèd waves, high as Jove's roof!
Your incivility shall know
That innocence is tempest-proof:
Though surly Nereus roar, my thoughts are calm;
Then strike, affliction, for thy wounds are balm.

That which the world miscalls a jail,
A private closet is to me,
Whilst a good conscience is my bail,
And innocence my liberty:
Locks, bars, loneliness, together met,
Make me no prisoner, but an anchorite.

I, while I wished to be retired,
Into this private room was turned,
As if their wisdoms had conspired
A salamander should be burned;

pencil] brush lodged] gone to its lair (hunting)

612 Boreas] north wind Nereus] the sea (Latin mythology) closet] study anchorite] hermit turned] put

Or like those sophies that would drown a fish,
I am constrained to suffer what I wish.

So he that struck at Jason's life,
  Thinking to make his purpose sure
By a malicious friendly knife,
  Did only wound him to a cure:
Malice, I see, wants wit; for what it meant,
Mischief, oft-times proves favour in the event.

These manacles upon mine arm
  I as my sweetheart's favours wear;
And then to keep mine ankles warm
  I have some iron shackles there.
Contentment cannot smart: stoics we see
Make torments easy by their apathy.

Here sin for want of food doth starve,
  Where tempting objects are not seen,
And these strong walls do only serve
  To keep vice out, and keep me in;
Malice of late grows charitable sure:
I'm not committed, but I'm kept secure.

When once my prince affliction hath,
  Prosperity doth treason seem;
And then, to smooth so rough a path
  I can learn patience e'en from him.
Now not to suffer shows no loyal heart:
When kings want ease, subjects must learn to smart.

What though I cannot see my king
  Either in his person or his coin?
Yet contemplation is a thing
  Will render what I have not, mine:
My king from me what adamant can part,
Whom I do wear engraven in my heart?

My soul's as free as the ambient air,
  Although my baser part's immured,
While loyal thoughts do still repair
  To accompany my solitude;
And though rebellion do my body bind,
My king can only captivate my mind.

sophies] Persian rulers apathy] passionlessness committed] imprisoned

Have you beheld the nightingale,
  A pilgrim turned into a cage,
How still she tells her wonted tale
  In this her private hermitage?
Even there her chanting melody doth prove
That all her bars are trees, her cage a grove.

I am the bird whom they combine
  Thus to deprive of liberty;
And though they do my corpse confine,
  Yet, maugre hate, my soul is free,
And though immured, yet here I'll chirp and sing
Disgrace to rebels, glory to my king.

(1649)

MARTIN LLUELYN
1616–1682

613 *Epithalamium: To Mistress M. A.*

RISE from your virgin sheets, that be
(Fie on them!) a mere nunnery.
Who solitary winters leads
Turns bracelets to religious beads.
The virgin that at Hymen sticks
Should sell her gems for th' crucifix;
For she's a nun, the sages tell,
That lies alone, though in no cell.
She midst her liberties confined,
Her body's cloister to her mind.
Be they immured whose looks are wore
Pale as the relics they adore.
Where cheeks the rose and lily paint,
A bridegroom is the only saint.
  Then as fair roses, to each other laid,
Unite their blushes and are garlands made,
So you, who when you are asunder only shun
One star, will shine a constellation.

(1646)

maugre] in spite of

613 mere] absolute   Hymen] (classical god of marriage)

ANONYMOUS

fl. 1646

614 *The World is Turned Upside Down*

LISTEN to me and you shall hear
News hath not been this thousand year:
Since Herod, Caesar, and many more,
You never heard the like before.
  Holidays are despised,
  New fashions are devised,
Old Christmas is kicked out of Town.
  Yet let's be content,
  And the times lament;
You see the world turned upside down.

The wise men did rejoice to see
Our saviour Christ's nativity:
The angels did good tidings bring,
The shepherds did rejoice and sing.
  Let all honest men
  Take example by them.
Why should we from good laws be bound?
  Yet let's be content, etc.

Command is given, we must obey,
And quite forget old Christmas day:
Kill a thousand men, or a town regain,
We will give thanks and praise amain.
  The wine pot shall clink,
  We will feast and drink,
And then strange motions will abound.
  Yet let's be content, etc.

Our lords and knights, and gentry too,
Do mean old fashions to forego:
They set a porter at the gate,
That none must enter in thereat.
  They count it a sin
  When poor people come in.
Hospitality itself is drowned.
  Yet let's be content, etc.

motions] (1) manners of walking; (2) political movements, disturbances

The serving men do sit and whine,
And think it long ere dinner time:
The butler's still out of the way,
Or else my lady keeps the key;
  The poor old cook
  In the larder doth look,
Where is no goodness to be found.
  Yet let's be content, etc.

To conclude, I'll tell you news that's right:
Christmas was killed at Nasbie fight;
Charity was slain at that same time,
Jack Tell-Troth too, a friend of mine.
  Likewise then did die
  Roast beef and shred pie;
Pig, goose, and capon no quarter found.
  Yet let's be content, etc.

(1646)

ANONYMOUS

615 [*Loving Mad Tom*]

I'LL bark against the Dog-star,
And crow away the morning;
  I'll chase the moon
  Till it be noon,
And I'll make her leave her horning.
But I will find Bonny Maud, Merry Mad Maud,
  And seek whate'er betides her;
    Yet I will love
    Beneath or above
  That dirty Earth that hides her.

I'll crack the poles asunder,
  Strange things I will devise on.
I'll beat my brain against Charles's Wain,
  And I'll grasp the round horizon.
But I'll find, etc.

I'll search the caves of slumber,
  And please her in a night dream;
I'll tumble her into Lawrence's fen,
  And hang myself in a sunbeam;
But I'll find, etc.

614 shred] mince

I'll sail upon a millstone,
And make the sea-gods wonder;
I'll plunge in the deep, till I wake asleep,
And I'll tear the rocks in sunder.
But I'll find, etc.

(1682)

ROWLAND WATKYNS
1616?–1664

616

A Periwig

... ut moveat cornicula risum
Furtivis nudata coloribus.

WELCOME, brave gallant, with those locks so fair.
It is a question who doth own that hair:
The owner, sure, is dead; but when, or how,
Or in what place he died, thou dost not know.
Perhaps he died at Bedlam: then take heed;
Those hairs mad fancies in thy head may breed.
Perchance sad Tyburn was the fatal place,
Where he did end his days for want of grace.
If it be so, they will infect thy brain,
And cause thee to delight in thievish gain.
If from some broken chambermaid they fell,
They'll move to lust, and modest thoughts expel.
Or, if they grew upon a drunken head,
Thou seldom wilt go sober to thy bed.
But if they came from some bad statesman's ground,
A machiavellian knave thou mayst be found.
Thus these dead excrements, if thou them use,
Will but bad thoughts and qualities infuse.
Cast off those looser hairs, which every wind
Will fright away, and show thy vainer mind:
God numbers all our hairs; let no man scoff
At that which God doth take such notice of.
Besides, it is a sinful, shameful part,
To slubber nature's work with sluttish art.

(1662)

616 *ut moveat ...*] (like) the poor crow, stripped of his stolen colours, he may awake laughter (Horace, *Epist.* I. iii. 19) broken] violated excrements] outgrowths slubber] obscure, sully

617 *The Gardener*

'She, supposing him to be the gardener, said unto him' (John 20)

MARY prevents the day; she rose to weep,
And see the bed where Jesus lay asleep.
She found out whom she sought, but doth not know
Her master's face; he is the gardener now.
This gardener Eden's garden did compose,
For which the chiefest plants and flowers he chose.
He took great care to have sweet rivers run
To enrich the ground where he his work begun.
He is the gardener still, and knoweth how
To make the lilies and the roses grow.
He knows the time to set, when to remove
His living plants to make them better prove.
He hath his pruning knife, when we grow wild,
To tame our nature, and make us more mild:
He curbs his dearest children; when 'tis need,
He cuts his choicest vine and makes it bleed.
He weeds the poisonous herbs which clog the ground.
He knows the rotten hearts, he knows the sound.
The blessed virgin was the pleasant bower
This gardener lodged in his appointed hour:
Before his birth his garden was the womb,
In death he in a garden chose his tomb.

(1662)

HUMPHREY WILLIS
fl. 1647

618 from *Time's Whirligig, Or, The Blue-New-Made-Gentleman Mounted*

WHAT age is this? What times are now?
Vice states it so in each man's brow,
  With thousands waiting on her
Clothed all in silks and purple brave,
As if no honest man, but knave,
  Should e'er again have honour.

prevents] goes before

618 *Blue*] (colour worn by the lower orders)   brave] splendid

Whilst virtue (who's so heavenly sweet
That blessed are kings if kiss her feet)
  Goes slighted up and down;
She that laments poor England's woes,
See, see, how naked there she goes,
  Kicked at by every clown.

An honest man! a thing most rare,
Or gentleman that's debonair,
  To live hath much ado;
Then what one said I now avow,
'Tis hard not to write satyrs now:
  I think you think so too.

A gentleman, good sir! Alack,
What's that? A last year's almanac:
  I thought so by his look;
A foolish, useless, worthless thing,
A cast-by now, just as the King,
  Whom upstarts cannot brook.

No, no, we have a people now,
Blue-apron-blades, men that know how
  All nations fill with wonder;
Who're skilled in state affairs so well,
Each man's another Machiavel,
  To keep the gentry under.

Religion's made a tennis ball,
For every fool to play withal;
  Both which we have so many
That we disputed have so long,
'Bout which is right, and which is wrong,
  Till we have hardly any.

The Covenant cried up so just
That all that's honest take it must,
  Or else no brethren seemed,
Is now by those that pressed it most
Cried down as fast in every coast,
  And Antichristian deemed.

(1647)

clown] fool; rustic   satyrs] satires   Covenant] (the National Covenant of 1638, opposing attempts to make the Scottish Church more Anglican)   coast] region

NICHOLAS MURFORD

fl. 1647–1652

619 *The Storm and Calm: Sent from Embden to M. Edw. Ma. and M. Tho. Ly.*

WEARY with reading and with meditation,
Upon my spirit settled a vexation;
Having no compass, nor no card to view
(Sith we did only drive, and overview,
What did our hasty spirits' griefs renew),
I thought in verse to parley once with you.
The sometime-mounting sea is now so calm,
As if it were surprisèd with a qualm;
The wanton sails do beat the quiet mast,
And the sun's heat doth make wood pitch to taste;
Two days before, I gave the land-sight shilling,
Which I to give, as they to take, was willing;
The mariners were almost at a strife
To have me hear what each would say to's wife.
The thievish Irish we had quite giv'n over,
Concerning thoughts that they could us discover:
We anchored with hope's anchor and our own;
Then from the ground they both again were shown.
Now a dissembling voice of wind doth speak;
But presently we cannot hear him squeak.
The sleepy sea that 'fore so boisterous was,
Is now as smooth as the most even glass:
One now would think the water to be dead,
Or with dead sleep to be heavy as lead;
Which not to wake, the stormy folk I cry on:
'Oh 'tis not good to wake a sleeping lion!'
For not long since, in the same ship we were,
When the mad wind I thought would tear her gear,
And carrying by the board a mast, might quail
The stoutest heart; the skeening of a sail,
The shipping of a sea, the deck in water
For full five hours in my conceit was greater;
But all together, in my vainer mind,
Would make a man to fear the raging wind;
And if the wind, which was but God's mere creature,
Oh how much more God, who was the creator!

card] compass-card   Sith] Since   skeening] splitting and unravelling
conceit] imagination

But when the ship was like to overset,
The seamen's eyes were dry, though bodies wet.
Instead of praying, some did curses vent;
Which that they did, I would they might repent.
Titan withdrew his golden locks; our ark
Now in the day must wander in the dark.
One time we think we must for Norway go;
Then for Scotland; then neither is it so;
For we have hopes for Tinmouth, then for Humber:
Thus doubtful fears our doubtful souls encumber.
So dangerous was our voyage that I vow
I love your presence, but wouldn't have it now.
Thus have we here the calm prosperity
And the great storm of fierce adversity;
Which I desire to draw to use: a moral
May here drawn out be for us mortals all.
The first, her sun, will take away our cloak,
Before the other's blustering wind can choke.
In Court, Elisha had need doubly have
Elijah's spirit, who was in the wave
Of soul-trying, yet good adversity,
Which is the heavenly university.
O Lord, give me my portion of these,
Or either, as thou think fit, and dost please.

(1650)

ABRAHAM COWLEY
1618–1667

from *Miscellanies* (620–622)

620 *The Motto*

Tentanda via est qua me quoque possim
Tollere humo victorque virum volitare per ora.

WHAT shall I do to be for ever known,
And make the age to come my own?
I shall like beasts or common people die,
Unless you write my elegy;
Whilst others great, by being born, are grown,
Their mother's labour, not their own.

620 *Tentanda . . . ora*] (see endnote)

In this scale gold, in the other fame does lie,
The weight of that, mounts this so high.
These men are fortune's jewels, moulded bright,
Brought forth with their own fire and light.
If I her vulgar stone for either look,
Out of myself it must be strook.
Yet I must on; what sound is 't strikes mine ear?
Sure I fame's trumpet hear.
It sounds like the last trumpet; for it can
Raise up the buried man.
Unpassed Alps stop me, but I'll cut through all,
And march, the Muses' Hannibal.
Hence all the flattering vanities that lay
Nets of roses in the way.
Hence the desire of honours or estate,
And all that is not above fate.
Hence love himself, that tyrant of my days,
Which intercepts my coming praise.
Come my best friends, my books, and lead me on;
'Tis time that I were gone.
Welcome, great Stagirite, and teach me now
All I was born to know.
Thy scholar's victories thou dost far outdo:
He conquered th' Earth, the whole world you.
Welcome learn'd Cicero, whose blest tongue and wit
Preserves Rome's greatness yet.
Thou art the first of orators; only he
Who best can praise thee, next must be.
Welcome the Mantuan swan, Virgil the wise,
Whose verse walks highest, but not flies;
Who brought green poesy to her perfect age,
And made that art, which was a rage.
Tell me, ye mighty three, what shall I do
To be like one of you?
But you have climbed the mountain's top, there sit
On the calm flourishing head of it,
And whilst with wearied steps we upward go,
See us and clouds below.

(1656)

strook] struck Hannibal] (Carthaginian general who crossed the Alps to defeat the Romans) Stagirite] Aristotle scholar's] Alexander the Great's world] universe rage] inspired frenzy

621

The Grasshopper

HAPPY insect, what can be
In happiness compared to thee?
Fed with nourishment divine,
The dewy morning's gentle wine!
Nature waits upon thee still,
And thy verdant cup does fill;
'Tis filled wherever thou dost tread,
Nature self's thy Ganymede.
Thou dost drink and dance and sing,
Happier than the happiest king!
All the fields which thou dost see,
All the plants, belong to thee;
All that summer hours produce,
Fertile made with early juice.
Man for thee does sow and plough;
Farmer he, and landlord thou!
Thou dost innocently joy,
Nor does thy luxury destroy;
The shepherd gladly heareth thee,
More harmonious than he.
Thee country hinds with gladness hear,
Prophet of the ripened year!
Thee Phoebus loves, and does inspire;
Phoebus is himself thy sire.
To thee of all things upon Earth,
Life is no longer than thy mirth.
Happy insect, happy thou,
Dost neither age nor winter know.
But when thou'st drunk and danced and sung
Thy fill the flowery leaves among
(Voluptuous and wise withal,
Epicurean animal!),
Sated with thy summer feast,
Thou retir'st to endless rest.

(1656)

still] ever Nature self's] Nature itself is Ganymede] (cupbearer of the gods) (ancient mythology) hinds] rustics

622 *Ode: Of Wit*

TELL me, oh tell, what kind of thing is wit,
Thou who master art of it?
For the first matter loves variety less;
Less women love 't, either in love or dress.
A thousand different shapes it bears,
Comely in thousand shapes appears.
Yonder we saw it plain; and here 'tis now,
Like spirits in a place, we know not how.

London, that vents of false ware so much store,
In no ware deceives us more.
For men led by the colour and the shape,
Like Zeuxis' birds fly to the painted grape:
Some things do through our judgement pass
As through a multiplying glass;
And sometimes, if the object be too far,
We take a falling meteor for a star.

Hence 'tis a wit, that greatest word of fame,
Grows such a common name;
And wits by our creation they become
Just so, as titular bishops made at Rome.
'Tis not a tale, 'tis not a jest
Admired with laughter at a feast,
Nor florid talk, which can that title gain:
The proofs of wit for ever must remain.

'Tis not to force some lifeless verses meet
With their five gouty feet.
All everywhere, like man's, must be the soul,
And reason the inferior powers control.
Such were the numbers which could call
The stones into the Theban wall.
Such miracles are ceased, and now we see
No towns or houses raised by poetry.

Yet 'tis not to adorn, and gild each part:
That shows more cost than art.
Jewels at nose and lips but ill appear;
Rather than all things wit, let none be there.

vents] sells   store] plenty   ware] (1) goods; (2) women   multiplying] magnifying   control] dominate   numbers] verses, rhythms (Amphion's)

Several lights will not be seen,
If there be nothing else between.
Men doubt, because they stand so thick in the sky,
If those be stars which paint the galaxy.

'Tis not when two like words make up one noise;
Jests for Dutch men and English boys;
In which who finds out wit, the same may see
In an'grams and acrostics poetry.
Much less can that have any place
At which a virgin hides her face;
Such dross the fire must purge away: 'tis just
The author blush, there where the reader must.

'Tis not such lines as almost crack the stage
When Bajazet begins to rage;
Nor a tall metaphor in the bombast way;
Nor the dry chips of short-lunged Seneca;
Nor upon all things to obtrude,
And force some odd similitude.
What is it then, which like the power divine
We only can by negatives define?

In a true piece of wit all things must be,
Yet all things there agree;
As in the ark, joined without force or strife,
All creatures dwelt, all creatures that had life;
Or as the primitive forms of all
(If we compare great things with small),
Which without discord or confusion lie
In that strange mirror of the deity.

But love that moulds one man up out of two
Makes me forget and injure you:
I took you for myself, sure, when I thought
That you in anything were to be taught.
Correct my error with thy pen;
And if any ask me then
What thing right wit and height of genius is,
I'll only show your lines, and say ''Tis this.'

(1656)

Several] Separate   Bajazet] Bajazeth in Marlowe's *Tamburlaine*   mirror . . . deity] i.e. mirror of ideas

from *The Mistress* (623–626)

623 *The Wish*

WELL then; I now do plainly see
This busy world and I shall ne'er agree;
The very honey of all earthly joy
Does of all meats the soonest cloy,
And they, methinks, deserve my pity,
Who for it can endure the stings,
The crowd, the buzz, and murmurings
Of this great hive, the City.

Ah, yet, e'er I descend to th' grave
May I a small house and large garden have!
And a few friends, and many books, both true,
Both wise, and both delightful too!
And since love ne'er will from me flee,
A mistress, moderately fair,
And good as guardian angels are,
Only beloved, and loving me!

O fountains, when in you shall I
Myself, eased of unpeaceful thoughts, espy?
O fields! O woods! When, when shall I be made
The happy tenant of your shade?
Here's the spring-head of pleasure's flood,
Where all the riches lie that she
Has coined and stamped for good.

Pride and ambition here
Only in far-fetched metaphors appear;
Here nought but winds can hurtful murmurs scatter,
And nought but Echo flatter.
The gods, when they descended, hither
From heaven did always choose their way;
And therefore we may boldly say
That 'tis the way, too, thither.

How happy here should I
And one dear she live and, embracing, die!
She who is all the world, and can exclude,
In deserts, solitude.
I should have then this only fear,
Lest men, when they my pleasures see,
Should hither throng to live like me,
And so make a city here.

(1668)

624 *The Thief*

THOU robst my days of business and delights,
  Of sleep thou robst my nights;
  Ah, lovely thief, what wilt thou do?
  What, rob me of heaven too?
  Thou even my prayers dost steal from me;
  And I with wild idolatry
Begin, to God, and end them all to thee.

Is it a sin to love, that it should thus
  Like an ill conscience torture us?
  Whate'er I do, where'er I go
  (None guiltless e'er was haunted so),
  Still, still, methinks thy face I view,
  And still thy shape does me pursue,
As if, not you me, but I had murdered you.

From books I strive some remedy to take,
  But thy name all the letters make;
  Whate'er 'tis writ, I find that there,
  Like points and commas everywhere.
  Me blest for this let no man hold;
  For I, as Midas did of old,
Perish by turning everything to gold.

What do I seek, alas, or why do I
  Attempt in vain from thee to fly?
  For, making thee my deity,
  I gave thee then ubiquity.
  My pains resemble hell in this:
  The divine presence there too is,
But to torment men, not to give them bliss.

(1647)

625 *Against Fruition*

NO; thou'rt a fool, I'll swear, if e'er thou grant:
Much of my veneration thou must want,
When once thy kindness puts my ignorance out;
For a learned age is always least devout.
Keep still thy distance, for at once to me
Goddess and woman too thou canst not be;

625 want] lack

Thou'rt queen of all that sees thee, and as such
Must neither tyrannize nor yield too much:
Such freedom give as may admit command,
But keep the forts and magazines in thine hand.
Thou'rt yet a whole world to me, and dost fill
My large ambition; but 'tis dangerous still,
Lest I like the Pellaean prince should be,
And weep for other worlds, having conquered thee:
When love has taken all thou hast away,
His strength by too much riches will decay.
Thou in my fancy dost much higher stand
Than women can be placed by nature's hand;
And I must needs, I'm sure, a loser be,
To change thee, as thou'rt there, for very thee.
Thy sweetness is so much within me placed
That shouldst thou nectar give, 'twould spoil the taste.
Beauty at first moves wonder and delight:
'Tis nature's juggling trick to cheat the sight;
We admire it, whilst unknown, but after more
Admire ourselves for liking it before.
Love, like a greedy hawk, if we give way,
Does over-gorge himself with his own prey;
Of very hopes a surfeit he'll sustain,
Unless by fears he cast them up again:
His spirit and sweetness dangers keep alone;
If once he lose his sting, he grows a drone.

(1647)

626 *Against Hope*

HOPE, whose weak being ruined is,
Alike if it succeed and if it miss;
Whom good or ill does equally confound,
And both the horns of fate's dilemma wound!
Vain shadow, which dost vanish quite
Both at full noon and perfect night!
The stars have not a possibility
Of blessing thee;
If things then from their end we happy call,
'Tis hope is the most hopeless thing of all.

Hope, thou bold taster of delight,
Who whilst thou shouldst but taste, devour'st it quite!

625 Pellaean prince] Alexander the Great very] mere alone] only

Thou bringst us an estate, yet leavest us poor
By clogging it with legacies before!
  The joys which we entire should wed
  Come deflowered virgins to our bed;
Good fortunes without gain imported be,
  Such mighty custom's paid to thee.
For joy, like wine, kept close does better taste:
If it take air before, its spirits waste.

  Hope, fortune's cheating lottery!
Where for one prize an hundred blanks there be;
Fond archer, hope, who takest thy aim so far
That still or short or wide thine arrows are!
  Thin, empty cloud, which the eye deceives
  With shapes that our own fancy gives!
A cloud which gilt and painted now appears,
But must drop presently in tears!
When thy false beams o'er reason's light prevail,
By *ignes fatui* for north stars we sail.

  Brother of fear, more gaily clad!
The merrier fool o' th' two, yet quite as mad:
Sire of repentance, child of fond desire,
That blowst the chemic's and the lover's fire!
  Leading them still insensibly on
  By the strange witchcraft of 'Anon!'
By thee the one does changing nature through
  Her endless labyrinths pursue,
And the other chases woman, whilst she goes
More ways and turns than hunted nature knows.

(1646)

from *Essays*

627

Solitude

HAIL, old patrician trees, so great and good!
  Hail ye plebeian underwood!
  Where the poetic birds rejoice,
And for their quiet nests and plenteous food
  Pay with their grateful voice.

626 still or] always either   chemic's] alchemist's

Hail, the poor Muses' richest manor seat!
  Ye country houses and retreat,
  Which all the happy gods so love
That for you oft they quit their bright and great
  Metropolis above.

Here nature does a house for me erect,
  Nature the wisest architect,
  Who those fond artists does despise
That can the fair and living trees neglect,
  Yet the dead timber prize.

Here let me, careless and unthoughtful lying,
  Hear the soft winds above me flying,
  With all their wanton boughs' dispute,
And the more tuneful birds to both replying;
  Nor be myself too mute.

A silver stream shall roll his waters near,
  Gilt with the sunbeams here and there,
  On whose enamelled bank I'll walk,
And see how prettily they smile, and hear
  How prettily they talk.

Ah wretched and too solitary he
  Who loves not his own company!
  He'll feel the weight of 't many a day
Unless he call in sin or vanity
  To help to bear 't away.

O solitude, first state of human kind!
  Which blest remained till man did find
  Even his own helper's company.
As soon as two, alas, together joined,
  The serpent made up three.

Though God himself through countless ages thee
  His sole companion chose to be:
  Thee, sacred solitude alone,
Before the branchy head of number's tree
  Sprang from the trunk of one.

Thou (though men think thine an unactive part)
  Dost break and tame th' unruly heart,
  Which else would know no settled pace;
Making it move, well managed by thy art,
  With swiftness and with grace.

Thou the faint beams of reason's scattered light
  Dost like a burning-glass unite;
  Dost multiply the feeble heat,
And fortify the strength, till thou dost bright
  And noble fires beget.

Whilst this hard truth I teach, methinks I see
  The monster London laugh at me.
  I should at thee, too, foolish city,
If it were fit to laugh at misery;
  But thy estate I pity.

Let but thy wicked men from out thee go,
  And all the fools that crowd thee so,
  Even thou who dost thy millions boast,
A village less than Islington wilt grow,
  A solitude almost.

(1668)

from *Sylva*

628 *To His Mistress*

TYRIAN dye why do you wear,
You whose cheeks best scarlet are?
  Why do you fondly pin
  Pure linens o'er your skin,
  Your skin that's whiter far;
Casting a dusky cloud before a star?

Why bears your neck a golden chain?
Did nature make your hair in vain,
  Of gold most pure and fine?
  With gems why do you shine?
  They, neighbours to your eyes,
Show but like Phosphor, when the sun doth rise.

I would have all my mistress' parts
Owe more to nature than to arts;
  I would not woo the dress,
  Or one whose nights give less
  Contentment than the day.
She's fair, whose beauty only makes her gay.

628 Phosphor] the morning star

For 'tis not buildings make a court,
Or pomp, but 'tis the king's resort:
  If Jupiter down pour
  Himself, and in a shower
  Hide such bright majesty,
Less than a golden one it cannot be.

(1636)

from *Davideis* (629–630)

629 [*Number, Weight, and Measure*]

TELL me, O Muse (for thou or none canst tell
The mystic powers that in blest numbers dwell,
Thou their great nature knowst, nor is it fit
This noblest gem of thine own crown to omit),
Tell me from whence these heavenly charms arise;
Teach the dull world t' admire what they despise.
  As first a various unformed hint we find
Rise in some godlike poet's fertile mind,
Till all the parts and words their places take,
And with just marches verse and music make,
Such was God's poem, this world's new essay;
So wild and rude in its first draught it lay;
Th' ungoverned parts no correspondence knew,
And artless war from thwarting motions grew;
Till they to number and fixed rules were brought
By the eternal mind's poetic thought.
Water and air he for the tenor chose,
Earth made the base, the treble flame arose;
To th' active moon a quick brisk stroke he gave,
To Saturn's string a touch more soft and grave.
The motions straight and round and swift and slow
And short and long were mixed and woven so,
Did in such artful figures smoothly fall,
As made this decent measured dance of all.
And this is music: sounds that charm our ears
Are but one dressing that rich science wears.
Though no man hear 't, though no man it rehearse,
Yet will there still be music in my verse.
In this great world so much of it we see;

resort] visit, repair

629 base] (1) lowest musical part; (2) foundation   rehearse] recite

The lesser, man, is all o'er harmony.
Storehouse of all proportions! Single choir!
Which first God's breath did tunefully inspire!
From hence blest music's heavenly charms arise,
From sympathy which them and man allies.
Thus they our souls, thus they our bodies win,
Not by their force, but party that's within.
Thus the strange cure on our spilt blood applied,
Sympathy to the distant wound does guide.
Thus when two brethren strings are set alike,
To move them both, but one of them we strike:
Thus David's lyre did Saul's wild rage control,
And tuned the harsh disorders of his soul.

(1656)

630 [*Gabriel's Appearance*]

When Gabriel (no blest spirit more kind or fair)
Bodies and clothes himself with thickened air.
All like a comely youth in life's fresh bloom
(Rare workmanship, and wrought by heavenly loom!),
He took for skin a cloud most soft and bright
That e'er the midday sun pierced through with light;
Upon his cheeks a lively blush he spread,
Washed from the morning beauties' deepest red.
An harmless flaming meteor shone for hair,
And fell adown his shoulders with loose care.
He cuts out a silk mantle from the skies,
Where the most sprightly azure pleased the eyes.
This he with starry vapours spangles all,
Took in their prime ere they grow ripe and fall.
Of a new rainbow, ere it fret or fade,
The choicest piece took out, a scarf is made.
Small streaming clouds he does for wings display,
Not virtuous lovers' sighs more soft than they.
These he gilds o'er with the sun's richest rays,
Caught gliding o'er pure streams on which he plays.
Thus dressed the joyful Gabriel posts away,
And carries with him his own glorious day
Through the thick woods; the gloomy shades a while
Put on fresh looks, and wonder why they smile.

inspire] breathe into

630 meteor] comet, or aurora   sprightly] spiritual   fret] decay

The trembling serpents close and silent lie,
The birds obscene far from his passage fly.
A sudden spring waits on him as he goes,
Sudden as that by which creation rose.
Thus he appears to David: at first sight
All Earth-bred fears and sorrows take their flight.
In rushes joy divine, and hope, and rest;
A sacred calm shines through his peaceful breast.

(1656)

from *The Civil War* (631–632)

631 [*Powers of Darkness*]

THE imperial host before proud Gloucester lay;
From all parts conquest did her beams display.
Fear, sadness, guilt, despair at London meet,
And in black smokes fly thick through every street.
Their best towns lost, no army left to fight!
Charles strong in power, invincible in right!
If he march up, what shall these wretches do?
They're troubled all, and hell was troubled too.
Beneath the silent chambers of the Earth,
Where the sun's fruitful beams give metals birth,
Where he the growth of fatal gold does see,
Gold, which above more influence has than he;
Beneath the dens where unfledged tempests lie,
And infant winds their tender voices try;
Beneath the mighty ocean's wealthy caves;
Beneath th' eternal fountain of all waves,
Where their vast court the mother waters keep,
And undisturbed by moons in silence sleep,
There is a place, deep, wondrous deep below,
Which genuine night and horror does o'erflow.
No bound controls th' unwearied space but hell,
Endless as those dire pains which in it dwell.
Here no dear glimpse of the sun's lovely face
Strikes through the solid darkness of the place.
No dawning morn does her kind reds display;
One slight, weak beam would here be thought the day.
No gentle stars with their fair drops of light
Offend the tyrannous and unquestioned night.
Here rebel minds in envious torments lie;
Must here forever live, forever die.

630 obscene] inauspicious (Latinism)

Here Lucifer the mighty captive reigns,
Proud midst his woes, and tyrant in his chains.
Once general of a gilded host of sprites,
Like Hesper leading on the spangled nights;
But down like lightning, which him strook, he came,
And roared at his first plunge into the flame.
Myriads of spirits fell wounded round him there;
With dropping lights thick shone the singèd air.
Since then the dismal solace of their woe
Has only been weak mankind to undo.
Round the fond Earth their thin-wrought nets they throw:
Worlds of mad souls come crowding down below.
But their dear sin, the sin themselves dare boast,
The sin they love in man, and punish most,
Is proud rebellion, their great son and sire,
Which kindled first, now blows th' eternal fire:
A tall and dreadful fiend, with double face,
One virgin-like and full of painted grace.
Fair seemed her hue, and modest seemed her guise,
Her eyn cast up towards heaven in holy wise.
From her false mouth kind words did always fly,
'Religion, reformation, liberty!'
Oft sung she psalms, and oft made zealous prayers,
All long and loud, to cheat the unknowing ears.
Her other face was grisly black of hue,
And from her staring eyes fierce lightning flew.
Her wicked mouth spoke proud and bitter things;
Blasphemed God's Church, and cursed anointed kings.
Thousand wild lies from her bold lips there came:
Her words were bullets and her breath was flame.
Thus as she went, she enraged the beastly rout,
And hurled unbounded ruin all about.
Like a rough wind, all rest and peace she hates,
And joys in the earthquakes of well-grounded states.

(1973)

632 [*London Subverted by the Furies*]

HE spoke, and what he spoke was soon obeyed;
Haste to their London prey the Furies made.
The gaping ground with natural joy made room
For this old monstrous burden of her womb.

Hesper] evening (ancient mythology)

632 He] Satan

In a long dismal line through Earth they arise;
Th' affrighted night shuts close her trembling eyes.
It was the noon of Cynthia's silent course,
And sleep all senses bound with gentle force.
The subtle fiends themselves through London spread;
Softly, as dreams, they steal into every head:
There unawares the powers of soul surprise,
Whilst each at rest, unarmed and fearless, lies.
The will they poison, and the reason wound;
Leave the pale conscience blinded, gagged, and bound;
All ornaments of nature, art, or grace,
Like zealots in fair churches, they deface.
The rebel passions they below unchain,
And licence that wild multitude to reign.
Their business done, home fled the night and they;
But scarce could nature's self drive on the day.
Pale as his sister's looks, the sun arose;
The sullen morn a night-like garment chose.
What strange, wild madness this ill morning brought!
So soon, in minds prepared, hell's poison wrought!
Up rose the mighty traitors, in whose breasts
The guilt of all our ills so tamely rests:
By sleeping now they advanced our ruin more
Than by long watchings they'd done oft before.
Straight, like thick fumes, into their brains arise
Thousand rich slanders, thousand useful lies.
A thousand arts and thousand sleights they frame
To avert the dangers of sweet peace's name.
To Westminster they haste, and fondly there
Talk, plot, conspire, vote, covenant, and declare.
New fears, new hopes, pretences new they show,
Whilst o'er the wondering town their nets they throw.
Up rose their priests (the viperous brood that dare
With their own mouths their beauteous mother tear);
Their walking noisy diligence ne'er will cease:
They roar and sigh and pray and eat 'gainst peace.
Up rose the base mechanics and the rout,
And cried, 'No peace', the astonished streets throughout.
Here, injured Church, thy strong avengement see:
The same noise plucks down peace, that plucked down thee.
All strive who first shall go, who most shall give,
Gloucester and stiff-necked Massey to relieve.
Their only sons the frantic women send,
Earnest, as if in labour for their end.

dismal] dire   Cynthia's] the moon's   fondly] foolishly   mechanics] labourers and manual tradesmen

The wives (what's that, alas?), the maidens too,
The maids themselves bid their own dear ones go.
The greedy tradesmen scorn their idol gain,
And send forth their glad servants to be slain.
The bald and grey-haired gownmen quite forsook
Their sleepy furs, black shoes, and City look:
All o'er in iron and leather clad they come;
Poor men that trembled erst at Finsbury's drum!
Forth did this rage all trades, all ages, call;
Religions, more than e'er before were all.
  Three thousand hot-brained Calvinists there came,
Wild men that blot their great Reformer's name.
God's image, stamped on monarchs, they deface,
And above the throne their thundering pulpits place.

(1973)

RICHARD LOVELACE
1618–1656 or 1657

from *Lucasta* (1649) (633–641)

633 *Song: To Lucasta, Going beyond the Seas*

IF to be absent were to be
    Away from thee,
  Or that when I am gone
  You or I were alone,
Then, my Lucasta, might I crave
Pity from blustering wind or swallowing wave.

But I'll not sigh one blast or gale
    To swell my sail,
  Or pay a tear to assuage
  The foaming blue god's rage;
For whether he will let me pass
Or no, I'm still as happy as I was.

632 gownmen] aldermen   erst] before   Finsbury's] Finsbury Fields' (exercise ground of the trained bands)

Though seas and land betwixt us both,
Our faith and troth,
Like separated souls,
All time and space controls:
Above the highest sphere we meet
Unseen, unknown, and greet as angels greet.

So then we do anticipate
Our after-fate,
And are alive i' th' skies,
If thus our lips and eyes
Can speak like spirits unconfined
In heaven, their earthy bodies left behind.

(1649)

634

Song: To Lucasta, Going to the Wars

TELL me not, sweet, I am unkind,
That from the nunnery
Of thy chaste breast and quiet mind
To war and arms I fly.

True: a new mistress now I chase,
The first foe in the field;
And with a stronger faith embrace
A sword, a horse, a shield.

Yet this inconstancy is such
As you too shall adore;
I could not love thee, dear, so much,
Loved I not honour more.

(1649)

635

Song: To Amarantha, That She Would Dishevel Her Hair

AMARANTHA sweet and fair,
Ah, braid no more that shining hair!
As my curious hand or eye,
Hovering round thee let it fly.

Let it fly as unconfined
As its calm ravisher the wind,
Who hath left his darling th' east,
To wanton o'er that spicy nest.

Every tress must be confessed
But neatly tangled at the best,
Like a clue of golden thread
Most excellently ravellèd.

Do not then wind up that light
In ribands, and o'ercloud in night;
Like the sun in 's early ray,
But shake your head and scatter day.

See, 'tis broke! Within this grove,
The bower and the walks of love,
Weary lie we down and rest,
And fan each other's panting breast.

Here we'll strip and cool our fire
In cream below, in milk baths higher;
And when all wells are drawn dry,
I'll drink a tear out of thine eye.

Which our very joys shall leave
That sorrows thus we can deceive;
Or our very sorrows weep,
That joys so ripe, so little keep.

(1649)

636 *Song: The Scrutiny*

Why should you swear I am forsworn,
Since thine I vowed to be?
Lady, it is already morn,
And 'twas last night I swore to thee
That fond impossibility.

Have I not loved thee much and long,
A tedious twelve hours' space?
I must all other beauties wrong,
And rob thee of a new embrace,
Could I still dote upon thy face.

635 ribands] ribbons

Not but all joy in thy brown hair
By others may be found;
But I must search the black and fair
Like skilful mineralists that sound
For treasure in unploughed-up ground.

Then if, when I have loved my round,
Thou prov'st the pleasant she,
With spoils of meaner beauties crowned
I laden will return to thee,
Even sated with variety.

(1649)

637 *The Grasshopper: To My Noble Friend, Mr Charles Cotton: Ode*

O THOU that swingst upon the waving hair
Of some well-fillèd oaten beard,
Drunk every night with a delicious tear
Dropped thee from heaven, where now th'art reared,

The joys of earth and air are thine entire,
That with thy feet and wings dost hop and fly;
And when thy poppy works thou dost retire
To thy carved acron bed to lie.

Up with the day, the sun thou welcom'st then,
Sportst in the gilt plats of his beams,
And all these merry days mak'st merry men,
Thyself, and melancholy streams.

But ah, the sickle! Golden ears are cropped;
Ceres and Bacchus bid good night;
Sharp frosty fingers all your flowers have topped,
And what scythes spared, winds shave off quite.

Poor verdant fool! And now green ice! Thy joys,
Large and as lasting as thy perch of grass,
Bid us lay in 'gainst winter rain, and poise
Their floods with an o'erflowing glass.

mineralists] mineralogists

637 acron bed] acorn-bed gilt plats] (1) plaits; (2) flat (gold) ornaments; (3) leaves
Ceres and Bacchus] (Roman divinities of harvest and wine)

Thou best of men and friends! We will create
  A genuine summer in each other's breast;
And spite of this cold time and frozen fate
  Thaw us a warm seat to our rest.

Our sacred hearths shall burn eternally
  As Vestal flames: the north wind, he
Shall strike his frost-stretched wings, dissolve and fly
  This Etna in epitome.

Dropping December shall come weeping in,
  Bewail the usurping of his reign;
But when in showers of old Greek we begin,
  Shall cry he hath his crown again.

Night as clear Hesper shall our tapers whip
  From the light casements where we play,
And the dark hag from her black mantle strip,
  And stick there everlasting day.

Thus richer than untempted kings are we,
  That asking nothing, nothing need:
Though lord of all what seas embrace, yet he
  That wants himself is poor indeed.

(1649)

638 *To My Worthy Friend Mr Peter Lely: On that Excellent Picture of His Majesty and the Duke of York, Drawn by Him at Hampton Court*

SEE! What a clouded majesty! And eyes
Whose glory through their mist doth brighter rise!
See! What an humble bravery doth shine,
And grief triumphant breaking through each line:
How it commands the face! So sweet a scorn
Never did happy misery adorn!
So sacred a contempt that others show
To this (o' th' height of all the wheel) below,
That mightiest monarchs by this shaded book
May copy out their proudest, richest look.

Vestal flames] fire of the Roman hearth goddess Hesper] the evening star (mythology) wants] lacks

638 bravery] splendour

Whilst the true eaglet this quick lustre spies,
And, by his sun's, enlightens his own eyes;
He cares his cares, his burthen feels, then straight
Joys, that so lightly he can bear such weight;
Whilst either either's passïon doth borrow,
And both do grieve the same victorious sorrow.
These, my best Lely, with so bold a spirit
And soft a grace, as if thou didst inherit
For that time all their greatness, and didst draw
With those brave eyes your royal sitters saw.
Not as of old, when a rough hand did speak
A strong aspéct, and a fair face, a weak;
When only a black beard cried 'villain', and
By hieroglyphics we could understand;
When crystal typified in a white spot,
And the bright ruby was but one red blot:
Thou dost the things orientally the same,
Not only paintst its colour, but its flame;
Thou sorrow canst design without a tear,
And, with the man, his very hope or fear,
So that th'amazèd world shall henceforth find
None but my Lely ever drew a mind.

(1649)

639 *Elinda's Glove: Sonnet*

THOU snowy farm with thy five tenements!
Tell thy white mistress here was one
That called to pay his daily rents;
But she a gathering flowers and hearts is gone,
And thou left void to rude possessïon.

But grieve not, pretty ermine cabinet,
Thy alabaster lady will come home;
If not, what tenant can there fit
The slender turnings of thy narrow room,
But must ejected be by his own doom?

Then give me leave to leave my rent with thee:
Five kisses, one unto a place;
For though the lute's too high for me,
Yet servants knowing minikin nor base
Are still allowed to fiddle with the case.

(1649)

quick] living orientally] resplendently

639 farm] land held on lease (legal) tenements] freehold properties; houses (legal) cabinet] lodging; treasure-chamber doom] judgement minikin] (1) treble string of lute; (2) woman

640 *To Althea, from Prison: Song*

WHEN love with unconfinèd wings
  Hovers within my gates,
And my divine Althea brings
  To whisper at the grates;
When I lie tangled in her hair,
  And fettered to her eye,
The gods that wanton in the air
  Know no such liberty.

When flowing cups run swiftly round,
  With no allaying Thames,
Our careless heads with roses bound,
  Our hearts with loyal flames;
When thirsty grief in wine we steep,
  When healths and draughts go free,
Fishes that tipple in the deep
  Know no such liberty.

When, like committed linnets, I
  With shriller throat shall sing
The sweetness, mercy, majesty
  And glories of my king;
When I shall voice aloud how good
  He is, how great should be,
Enlargèd winds that curl the flood
  Know no such liberty.

Stone walls do not a prison make,
  Nor iron bars a cage;
Minds innocent and quiet take
  That for an hermitage:
If I have freedom in my love,
  And in my soul am free,
Angels alone that soar above
  Enjoy such liberty.

(1649)

641 La Bella Bona Roba

I CANNOT tell who loves the skeleton
Of a poor marmoset, nought but bone, bone.
Give me a nakedness with her clothes on:

641 La . . . Roba] The Beautiful Prostitute   marmoset] wanton

Such whose white satin upper coat of skin,
Cut upon velvet rich incarnadine,
Has yet a body, and of flesh, within.

Sure it is meant good husbandry in men,
Who do incorporate with airy lean,
To repair their sides, and get their rib again.

Hard hap unto that huntsman that decrees
Fat joys for all his sweat, whenas he sees,
After his assay, nought but his keeper's fees.

Then, love, I beg, when next thou takest thy bow,
Thy angry shafts, and dost heart-chasing go,
Pass rascal deer, strike me the largest doe.

(1649)

from *Lucasta* (1659–60) (642–643)

642 *To Lucasta*

Like to the sentinel stars, I watch all night;
For still the grand round of your light
And glorious breast
Awakes in me an east,
Nor will my rolling eyes e'er know a west.

Now on my down I'm tossed as on a wave,
And my repose is made my grave;
Fluttering I lie,
Do beat myself and die,
But for a resurrection from your eye.

Ah my fair murderess! Dost thou cruelly heal,
With various pains to make me well?
Then let me be
Thy cut anatomy,
And in each mangled part my heart you'll see.

(1660)

incarnadine] flesh-coloured incorporate] copulate; form one body with again] back (from Eve) keeper's fees] portion assigned to the gamekeeper rascal] lean

642 anatomy] dissected body

643 *To a Lady with Child that Asked an Old Shirt*

AND why an honoured ragged shirt, that shows,
Like tattered ensigns, all its body's blows?
Should it be swathed in a vest so dire,
It were enough to set the child on fire;
Dishevelled queens should strip them of their hair,
And in it mantle the new rising heir:
Nor do I know ought worth to wrap it in,
Except my parchment upper-coat of skin;
And then expect no end of its chaste tears,
That first was rolled in down, now furs of bears.
But since to ladies it hath a custom been
Linen to send, that travail and lie in,
To the nine seamstresses, my former friends,
I sued; but they had nought but shreds and ends.
At last, the jolliest of the three times three
Rent the apron from her smock, and gave it me;
'Twas soft and gentle, subtly spun no doubt.
Pardon my boldness, madam; here's the clout.

(1660)

SIR EDWARD SHERBURNE
1618–1702

644 *And She Washed His Feet with Her Tears, and Wiped Them with the Hairs of Her Head*

THE proud Egyptian queen, her Roman guest
(To express her love in height of state, and pleasure)
With pearl dissolved in gold, did feast:
Both food, and treasure.

And now, dear Lord, thy lover, on the fair
And silver tables of thy feet, behold!
Pearl in her tears, and in her hair,
Offers thee gold.

(1651)

643 ensigns] insignia

645 *Weeping and Kissing*

A KISS I begged; but, smiling, she
  Denied it me:
When straight, her cheeks with tears o'erflown,
  Now kinder grown,
What smiling she'd not let me have,
  She weeping gave.
Then you, whom scornful beauties awe,
  Hope yet relief;
For love (who tears from smiles) can draw
  Pleasure from grief.

(1651)

SIMON FORD
1619?–1699

646 from *London's Resurrection*

  HAIL, glorious day; mayst thou be writ in gold,
Which sawst the sceptered hand the trowel hold,
To lay that stone whence the Exchange became
Anew entitled to its royal name!
Henceforth, proud pillar, to thy readers' view
Tell thine own story, and thy founder's too.
  Fruitful example! From the royal hand
Each artist now takes pattern and command.
Hark, how the clattering tools' confusèd sound
Divides the ear! The pickaxe rends the ground
To load the spade, its loads bestowed between
The sifting ridder and the searching screen.
The saw the file, the axe the grindstone whets:
The knotty tree this hews, the other eats.
The arm the plane, and maul the chisel drives;
Through heart of oak the groaning auger dives.
The glowing steel the weighty sledge's stroke
Beats into form; which quenched doth hiss and smoke.
  Room, next, for miracles, profaned by use:
The issues of the famed Vitruvian Muse,

646 glorious day] 23 October 1667   ridder] riddle   screen] large sieve   maul] mallet   Vitruvian] architectural

And that grave architect's whose ominous hand
Drew learned lines on Syracusan sand;
Whose dying gore did the choice figures drown,
And 's dying weight in *their* room stamped his *own*!
  Here twisted screws, whiles planted on the ground
They worm themselves through a like wreathèd round,
Prop tottering roofs. Versatile rundles there
By equal helps their fellows' burdens bear,
Transferred by clasping ropes; whence greatest weights
By a small force are wound to greatest heights.
The balance engine next, whose loaded end
The tenth part of its burden makes t' ascend.
Nor is 't less wondrous that the vastest beams,
On cylinders supporting both extremes,
Tough levers roll, whiles every lifting hand
One interjection jointly doth command.
  Thus goes the building on. Confusèd grounds
Just verdicts part; and, whiles they fix the bounds
To public streets by the imperious line,
Surveyors like unbounded sovereigns reign;
Each house clasps with its neighbour; and the square
Each front unto its fellow wall doth pair.
And sister piles, whiles thus they intermarry,
Like sister faces, uniformly vary.
  Lady enchantress of the ravished ear,
Ne'er did thy art effect what chance doth here!
Whiles building noises by the pleasèd mind
Are into all harmonious notes combined,
Orpheus to us would grate, Apollo jar:
Hammers and trowels sweeter music are.
By this one spell each melancholy breast
Is of its legion-devil dispossessed;
And where yet falling London's doleful knell
Doth in retentive apprehensions dwell,
By sympathetic cure these joyful sounds
With glad ideas heal the fancy's wounds.
  The fields are busy too. Bold miners found
In paunchèd hills a London under ground.
The realm of silence and eternal night
Is startled at the approach of noise and light.
Twin stones long claspèd in their mother bed,
Now severed, yield with foreign rocks to wed.

architect] Archimedes (killed at Syracuse while drawing a geometrical diagram)
Versatile] (1) Pivoting; (2) versatile rundles] pulleys balance engine] hoist
enchantress] St Cecilia legion-devil] (Mark 5: 8–9) fancy's] imagination's
paunchèd] (1) big-bellied; (2) stabbed

Each polished marble to a mirror grows,
Mocks its own workman, and retorts his blows.
  Here, the green robe pulled off, the unbowelled ground
Affords a clay which with chopped stubble bound
First, the sun fastens; then the brittle cakes
The rapid furnace to just hardness bakes:
An hardness that outstands the fiercest showers
Which heaven from its opened sluices pours;
Which winter frosts can't mellow; and the flame
Itself, that did beget it, cannot tame.
Scarce flint or marble lasts so long in prime:
This brittle stone grinds out the teeth of time.
With this th' immortal queen built Babel's spires,
And with burnt walls beguilèd future fires.
  There, the wood's glories fall, and where the eye
Of heaven scarce pierced, now mortal sight doth pry.
The shades by horror hallowed, the early dawn
Admitted doth illústrate and profane.
The reverend oaks presumptuous axes wound,
Measuring their lengths upon the furrowed ground,
Whiles rattling Echo (as great talkers do)
Reports at distance every blow for two.
The ring-dove sees her lofty nest o'erthrown,
And turtles that their love's bewrayèd, moan;
The magpie scolds whiles her arched roof doth fall;
And sharking rooks, their camp dislodgèd, brawl;
The hare forsakes her form; the rousèd deer
Their branched heads now above their thickets rear;
And all the game tall forests used to shield
Becomes a facile prey in the open field.
The traveller too, who setting forth designed
The crownèd hills, as certain guides, to mind,
At his return, admires the shavèd coast,
And finds his way, with his directors, lost.
  Yea, foreign realms contribute: Spain brings steel,
Libanus cedar sends, and Denmark deal;
A checkered gift the sunburnt India gives,
Whence th' whitest tooth and blackest wood arrives;
Our Ireland oak, on which no spider builds
(Arachne sure hanged on that timber), yields.
Marbles come varied by their native grains:
This, untrod snow with purer brightness stains;

retorts] turns back; returns   unbowelled] disembowelled   queen] Semiramis   illústrate] illuminate   bewrayèd] betrayed   sharking] thieving   form] lair   mind] remember; attend to   admires] wonders at   coast] region; countryside   directors] landmarks   Arachne] (changed to a spider after her suicide, by Minerva)

That's pitchy black, a lump of solid night;
There, bloody veins creep through a lovely white;
Some in its speckled face, heaven's portrait bears,
An azure sky bespangled o'er with stars;
And some (on which Medusa's head did fall),
Wherein her snakes seem still to hiss and crawl.
  Nay (would you think 't? or fame, my author lies),
London by th' great in foreign lands doth rise.
Whiles the Dutch artist takes his module hence,
And sends us houses ready-framed from thence,
The laden sea foams, and the tuggèd oar
Plies hard to tow a floating town to shore;
And the eastern wind (now a repairer grown),
Blows up our buildings as it fired them down.
Whence (sounds the moral oft, when tales are lame)
Some doubt new London may prove Amsterdam.

(1669)

RICHARD LEIGH
fl. 1649–1675

647 *On a Fair Lady, Looking in the Glass*

THE sun, beholding so as he does pass
This floating face in water's liquid glass,
The glitt'ring circle with delight surveys;
And heav'ns on their own bright reflection gaze,
Seeming to view with an admiring beam
Another sun, and heav'ns, in the stream,
As she with only looking on portrays
The glorious image darted from her rays;
Surprised to see what on a sudden there
Has started up, so young, so fresh, so fair.
Her shadow with such curious art does gild
The shining mirror with a new light filled
That well may she with just amazement eye
What only can pretend with her to vie.
Her other self, like her, surprised does show:
Her features mocks, and mocks her wonder too.
The amorous glance, in striving to excel,
Does seem to court her ever here to dwell.

646 by th' great] wholesale   artist] architect

Proud of the transient shape it does present,
Could gladly wish it fixed, and permanent;
Fixed, as those statues we in gardens place,
Viewing in fountains still their carvèd face.
  Could it, alas, her portrait but retain!
It would endure no other figure's stain.
What her stamp seals, as sacred to her smile,
No soiling look profanely would defile.
Or should there any beauties be, that dare
Their spots, or graces, by this glass compare,
Her eyes, before theirs, thus it would prefer,
In flattering them by truly showing her.
  Nor would the sweet impression stamped in air
So lovely have appeared, or half so fair,
Did not the same resemblance polish give,
And lustre add, to what should it receive.
She, dressing by her glass, her glass has dressed,
And richly with her airy shape possessed.
But when too soon the fair unkind retires,
The short-lived beauty that shined here expires;
And as the beamy glance does disappear,
And vanishes, we know not how, not where,
Leaving no print behind, no feeble ray,
That might discover where it once did stay.
The brittle sphere, all darkened thus, will mourn
The frail glory lost, it did return;
And of her radiant likeness then complain
That, naked as it was, 'tis left again.

(1675)

648 *Greatness in Little*

IN spotted globes, that have resembled all
Which we or beasts possess to one great ball,
Dim little specks for thronging cities stand,
Lines wind for rivers, blots bound sea and land.
Small are those spots which in the moon we view,
Yet glasses these like shades of mountains shew;
As what an even brightness does retain,
A glorious level seems, and shining plain.
Those crowds of stars in the populous sky,
Which art beholds as twinkling worlds on high,
Appear to naked, unassisted sight
No more than sparks or slender points of light.

The sun, a flaming universe alone,
Bigger than that about which his fires run;
Enlightening ours, his globe but part does gild,
Part by his lustre or Earth's shades concealed;
His glory dwindled so, as what we spy
Scarce fills the narrow circle of the eye.
What new Americas of light have been
Yet undiscovered there, or yet unseen,
Art's near approaches awfully forbid,
As in the majesty of nature hid.
Nature, who with like state, and equal pride,
Her great works does in height and distance hide,
And shuts up her minuter bodies all
In curious frames, imperceptibly small.
Thus still *incognito*, she seeks recess
In greatness half-seen, or dim littleness.
  Ah, happy littleness! that art thus blest,
That greatest glories aspire to seem least.
Even those installed in a higher sphere,
The higher they are raised, the less appear,
And in their exaltation emulate
Thy humble grandeur and thy modest state.
Nor is this all thy praise, though not the least,
That greatness is thy counterfeit at best.
Those swelling honours, which in that we prize,
Thou dost contain in thy more thrifty size;
And hast that pomp, magnificence does boast,
Though in thy stature and dimensions lost.
Those rugged little bodies whose parts rise
And fall in various inequalities,
Hills in the risings of their surface show,
As valleys in their hollow pits below.
Pompous these lesser things, but yet less rude
Than uncompact and looser magnitude.
What skill is in the frame of insects shown!
How fine the threads in their small textures spun!
How close those instruments and engines knit,
Which motion and their slender sense transmit!
Like living watches, each of these conceals
A thousand springs of life and moving wheels.
Each ligature a labyrinth seems, each part
All wonder is, all workmanship and art.
  Rather let me this little greatness know,
Than all the mighty acts of great ones do:

state] splendour, stateliness   still] ever   close] secret

These engines understand, rather than prove
An Archimedes, and the Earth remove.
These atom worlds found out, I would despise
Columbus and his vast discoveries.

(1675)

WILLIAM CHAMBERLAYNE
1619–1689

from *Pharonnida*

649 [*The Bad Landlord*]

'In yonder fields' (with that directs her eye
To a black fen, whose heavy earth did lie
Low in a dark and dirty vale) 'is placed
Amarus's castle, which though now defaced
More by the owner's covetous neglect
Than time's rough strokes, that strength, which did protect
Once its inhabitants, being now but made
Use of when want doth with weak prayers invade
The gates, being thought sufficient if they keep
The poor at bay, or, whilst his stiff hinds sleep,
Their labouring beasts secure. But I, alas,
Blush to discover that this miser was
Father to my dead Vanlore, and to her
Whose living virtues kind heaven did confer
As blessings on my brother; but the sun
Ne'er saw two sweeter streams of virtue run
From such a bitter fountain. This accurst
And wretched man (so hated that he durst
Scarce look abroad, fearing oppression would
Be paid with vengeance, if he ever should
Fall into the hands of those whose faces he
Ground with extortion till the injury
Fear clothed like justice), venturing once to view
A manor, whose intemperate lord outgrew
In debts the compass of a bond, besides
His common guard of clowns, fellows whose hides

prove . . . remove] move the Earth, as Archimedes said he could, given a suitable lever

649 Amarus's] Bitter's hinds] retainers, farm labourers discover] reveal clowns] rustics

Served for defensive armour, he commands
His son's attendance; who, since from his hands
Racked tenants hoped for ease, he thought that they
Would for that hope with reverent duty pay.
But vain mistakes betray opinion to
A fatal precipice, which they might view
I' the objects of each glance; one side affords
Large plains, whose flocks—the wealth of several lords,
By him contracted—but the spoils appears
Of beggared orphans, pickled in their tears:
Farms for whose loss poor widows wept, and fields,
Which being confined to strict enclosure, yields
To his crammed chests the starving poor man's food;
For private ends robbing their public good,
With guilt enclosed those ways which now had brought
Him by some cottages, whose owners bought
Poor livelihoods at a laborious rate
From his racked lands; for which pursuing hate
Now follows him in curses; for in that
They yet take vengeance; till arriving at
The thicker-peopled villages, where, more bold
By number made, the fire of hate takes hold
On clamorous women, whose vexed husbands thirst
I' the fever of revenge; to these, when first
They kindled had the flame, swiftly succeeds
More active men, such as resolved their deeds,
Spite of restrictive law, should set them free
From the oppressors of their liberty.'

(1659)

ALEXANDER BROME
1620–1666

650 *Plain Dealing*

WELL well, 'tis true
I am now fallen in love,
And 'tis with you;
And now I plainly see,
While you're enthroned by me above,
You all your arts and powers improve
To tyrant over me,

649 Racked] Oppressed with excessive rents

And make my flames the incentives of your scorn,
While you rejoice and feast your eyes to see me thus forlorn.

But yet be wise,
And don't believe that I
Did think your eyes
More bright than stars can be,
Or that your face angels outvies
In their celestial liveries;
'Twas all but poetry.
I could have said as much by any she:
You are not beauteous of yourself, but are made so by me.

Though we, like fools,
Fathom the Earth and sky,
And drain the schools
For names to express you by;
Out-rant the loud'st hyperboles
To dub you saints and deities
By Cupid's heraldry,
We know you're flesh and blood as well as men,
And when we will can mortalize, and make you so again.

Yet since my fate
Has drawn me to this sin
Which I did hate,
I'll not my labour lose,
But will love on, as I begin,
To the purpose now my hand is in,
Spite of those arts you use;
And let you know the world is not so bare:
There's things enough to love, besides such toys as ladies are.

I'll love good wine,
I'll love my book and Muse,
Nay all the nine,
I'll love my real friend,
I'll love my horse, and could I choose
One that would not my love abuse,
To her my heart should bend.
I'll love all those that laugh, and those that sing,
I'll love my country, prince and laws, and those that love the king.

(1655)

incentives] (1) provocation; (2) kindling material schools] lecture rooms

651 *The Resolve*

TELL me not of a face that's fair,
  Nor lip and cheek that's red,
Nor of the tresses of her hair,
  Nor curls in order laid;
Nor of a rare seraphic voice,
  That like an angel sings;
Though if I were to take my choice,
  I would have all these things.
But if that thou wilt have me love
  And it must be a she,
The only argument can move
  Is, that she will love me.

The glories of your ladies be
  But metaphors of things,
And but resemble what we see
  Each common object brings.
Roses out-red their lips and cheeks,
  Lilies their whiteness stain:
What fool is he that shadows seeks
  And may the substance gain?
Then if thou'lt have me love a lass,
  Let it be one that's kind;
Else I'm a servant to the glass
  That's with canary lined.

(1661)

652 *Epithalamy*

NAY fie, Platonics, still adoring
  The fond chimeras of your brain?
Still on that empty nothing poring?
  And only follow what you feign?
Live in your humour, 'tis a curse
So bad, 'twere pity wish a worse.
We'll banish such conceits as those,
Since he that has enjoyment knows
More bliss than Plato could suppose.

stain] obscure the lustre of

652 humour] eccentricity

Cashiered wooers, whose low merit
  Could ne'er arrive at nuptial bliss,
Turn schismatics in love, whose spirit
  Would have none hit 'cause they do miss.
But those reproaches that they vent
Do only blaze their discontent;
Condemned men's words no truth can show,
And hunters when they prove too slow
Cry 'Hares are dry meat, let 'em go.'

The enamoured youth, whose flaming breast
  Makes goddesses and angels all,
In 's contemplation finds no rest,
  For all his joys are sceptical.
At his fruition flings away
His Cloris and his 'welladay',
And gladly joins to fill our choir,
Who to such happiness aspire
As all must envy or admire.

(1661)

653 *The Pastoral: On the King's Death*

WHERE England's Damon used to keep,
  In peace and awe, his flocks,
Who fed, not fed upon, his sheep,
There wolves and tigers now do prey,
There sheep are slain, and goats do sway;
  There reigns the subtle fox,
    While the poor lambkins weep.

The laurelled garland which before
  Circled his brows about,
The spotless coat which once he wore,
The sheep-hook which he used to sway,
And pipe whereon he loved to play,
  Are seized on by the rout,
    And must be used no more.

653 sway] rule (poetic); wield, as emblem of sovereignty

Poor swain, how thou lamentst to see
  Thy flocks o'erruled by those
That serve thy cattle all like thee,
Where hateful vice usurps the crown,
And loyalty is trodden down;
  Down scrip and sheephook goes,
    When foxes shepherds be.

(1661; wr. 1648)

654 *The Riddle*

    No more, no more,
  We are already pined
    And sore and poor,
  In body and in mind.
  And yet our sufferings have been
    Less than our sin.
Come long-desirèd peace, we thee implore,
And let our pains be less, or power more.

    Lament, lament,
  And let thy tears run down,
    To see the rent
  Between the robe and crown;
  Yet both do strive to make it more
    Than 'twas before:
War like a serpent has its head got in,
And will not end so soon as 't did begin.

    One body jars,
  And with itself does fight;
    War meets with wars
  And might resisteth might.
  And both sides say they love the king,
    And peace will bring.
Yet since these fatal civil broils begun,
Strange riddle! both have conquered, neither won.

    One God, one king,
  One true religion still:
    In everything
  One law both should fulfil;

swain] shepherd   cattle] animals   scrip] shepherd's or pilgrim's satchel

654 pined] anguished; tortured   jars] is in conflict   still] always

All these both sides does still pretend
That they defend.
Yet to increase the King and kingdom's woes,
Which side soever wins, good subjects lose.

The king doth swear
That he doth fight for them;
And they declare
They do the like for him;
Both say they wish and fight for peace,
Yet wars increase.
So, between both, before our wars be gone,
Our lives and goods are lost, and we're undone.

Since 'tis our curse
To fight we know not why,
'Tis worse and worse
The longer thus we lie;
For war itself is but a nurse,
To make us worse.
Come blessèd peace we once again implore,
And let our pains be less, or power more.

(1661; wr. 1644)

ROBERT HEATH
fl. 1650

655 ### *Seeing Her Dancing*

ROBES loosely flowing, and aspéct as free,
A careless carriage decked with modesty;
A smiling look, but yet severe:
Such comely graces 'bout her were.
Her steps with such an evenness she wove
As she could hardly be perceived to move;
Whilst her silk sails displayed, she
Swam like a ship with majesty.
As when with steadfast eyes we view the sun,
We know it goes, though see no motïon:
So undiscerned she moved that we
Perceived she stirred, but did not see.

(1650)

656 *On Clarastella Walking in Her Garden*

SEE how Flora smiles to see
This approaching deity!
Where each herb looks young and green
In presence of their coming queen!
Ceres with all her fragrant store
Could never boast so sweet a flower;
While thus in triumph she doth go
The greater goddess of the two.
  Here the violet bows to greet
Her with homage to her feet;
There the lily pales with white
Got by her reflexèd light;
Here a rose in crimson dye
Blushes through her modesty;
There a pansy hangs his head,
About to shrink into his bed,
Because so quickly she passed by,
Not returning suddenly;
Here the currants red and white
In yon green bush, at her sight
Peep through their shady leaves, and cry
'Come eat me', as she passes by;
There a bed of camomile,
When she presseth it, doth smell
More fragrant than the perfumed east,
Or the phoenix' spicy nest;
Here the pinks in rows do throng
To guard her as she walks along.
There the flexive turnsole bends,
Guided by the rays she sends
From her bright eyes, as if thence
It sucked life by influence;
Whilst she, the prime and chiefest flower
In all the garden, by her power
And only life-inspiring breath,
Like the warm sun redeems from death
Their drooping heads, and bids them live
To tell us she their sweets did give.

(1650)

Ceres] (harvest goddess) (Latin mythology) reflexèd] reflected flexive] bending turnsole] heliotrope sweets] perfumes

657 *On the Unusual Cold and Rainy Weather in the Summer, 1648*

WHY puts our grand-dame Nature on
Her winter coat, ere summer's done?
What, hath she got an ague fit?
And thinks to make us hovering sit
Over her lazy embers? Else why should
Old Hyems freeze our vernal blood?
Or, as we each day grow older,
Doth the world wax wan and colder?
'Tis so: see how naked charity
Starves in this frozen age! Whilst we
Have no other heat but glow-worm zeal,
Whose warmth we see but cannot feel.
All changed are Ceres' golden hairs
To clouded grey, and nought appears
In Flora's dress: our hopes do die,
And o' th' sudden blasted lie.
Heaven's glorious lamps do waste away,
The elements themselves decay,
And the mixed bodies mutiny
By a rebellious sympathy,
Whilst the distempered world grows pale
And sickening threatens death to all.
So in an instant waters swept
The old world's monsters, whilst they wept
Its funeral; but the new world's sins
Are so deep dyed no flood can rinse:
Nothing but lightning and heaven's fire
Can purge our pestilential air.

(1650)

Hyems] Winter Starves] Dies of cold Ceres'] harvest's Flora's] the flower-goddess' (Latin mythology) blasted] withered

LUCY HUTCHINSON
1620–post 1675

658 *Verses Written by Mrs Hutchinson in the Small Book Containing Her Own Life, and Most Probably Composed by Her During Her Husband's Retirement from Public Business to His Seat at Owthorpe*

ALL sorts of men through various labours press
To the same end, contented quietness;
Great princes vex their labouring thoughts to be
Possessed of an unbounded sovereignty;
The hardy soldier doth all toils sustain
That he may conquer first, and after reign;
The industrious merchant ploughs the angry seas
That he may bring home wealth, and live at ease;
Which none of them attain; for sweet repose
But seldom to the splendid palace goes:
A troop of restless passions wander there,
And private lives are only free from care.
Sleep to the cottage bringeth happy nights,
But to the court, hung round with flaring lights
Which th' office of the vanished day supply,
His image only comes to close the eye,
But gives the troubled mind no ease of care;
While country slumbers undisturbèd are,
Where, if the active fancy dreams present,
They bring no horrors to the innocent.
Ambition doth incessantly aspire,
And each advance leads on to new desire;
Nor yet can riches av'rice satisfy,
For want and wealth together multiply;
Nor can voluptuous men more fullness find,
For enjoyed pleasures leave their stings behind.
He's only rich who knows no want; he reigns
Whose will no severe tyranny constrains;
And he alone possesseth true delight
Whose spotless soul no guilty fears affright.
This freedom in the country life is found,
Where innocence and safe delights abound:
Here man's a prince; his subjects ne'er repine
When on his back their wealthy fleeces shine;

If for his appetite the fattest die,
Those who survive will raise no mutiny;
His table is with home-got dainties crowned,
With friends, not flatterers, encompassed round;
No spies nor traitors on his trencher wait,
Nor is his mirth confined to rules of state;
An armèd guard he neither hath nor needs,
Nor fears a poisoned morsel when he feeds.
Bright constellations hang above his head,
Beneath his feet are flowery carpets spread;
The merry birds delight him with their songs,
And healthful air his happy life prolongs.
At harvest merrily his flocks he shears,
And in cold weather their warm fleeces wears;
Unto his ease he fashions all his clothes;
His cup with uninfected liquor flows.
The vulgar breath doth not his thoughts elate,
Nor can he be o'erwhelmèd by their hate;
Yet, if ambitiously he seeks for fame,
One village feast shall gain a greater name
Than his who wears the imperial diadem,
Whom the rude multitude do still condemn.
Sweet peace and joy his blest companions are:
Fear, sorrow, envy, lust, revenge, and care,
And all that troop which breeds the world's offence,
With pomp and majesty, are banished thence.
What court, then, can such liberty afford?
Or where is man so uncontrolled a lord?

(Wr. 1660–3?)

THOMAS PHILIPOTT

*c.*1620–1682

659 *To Sir Henry Newton, upon His Re-edifying the Church of Charleton in Kent*

SIR,
You need no Parian or Egyptian stone
To build a tomb for you: your name alone
Shall stand, your monument, which shall outvie
Those fading trophies in stability.

658 still] ever uncontrolled] unchecked

You have the basis of no structures fixed
On widows' ruins, or the mortar mixed
With orphans' tears: you wish the melting skies
May wet your fields, and not your tenants' eyes
Moisten it with their dew. You build no shrine
To lavish riot, where sin's made divine
And idolized; you sacrifice no wealth
At Bacchus' altar, nor give up your health
An offering to 't, or to evacuate rheum
Do you exhale whole manors into fume.
No, sir, you have employed your coin so well
That God himself will be accountable
For what you've spent, you've laid your treasure in
So inaccessible a magazine.
No sacrilegious robber shall purloin,
Or rust embase the value of your coin:
You've built a house where God himself will dwell,
And stand himself there his own sentinel.
Let others sit and brood upon that ore
Which they've collected from the Indian shore,
And put themselves to the expense of care
For a wild unthrift; you make God your heir.

(1646)

ANDREW MARVELL
1621–1678

660 *The Definition of Love*

My love is of a birth as rare
As 'tis for object strange and high:
It was begotten by despair
Upon impossibility.

Magnanimous despair alone
Could show me so divine a thing,
Where feeble hope could ne'er have flown
But vainly flapped its tinsel wing.

fume] i.e. tobacco smoke embase] lower in value

660 tinsel] gauzy, interwoven with gold; glittering

And yet I quickly might arrive
Where my extended soul is fixed;
But fate does iron wedges drive,
And always crowds itself betwixt.

For fate with jealous eye does see
Two perfect loves, nor lets them close:
Their union would her ruin be,
And her tyrannic power depose.

And therefore her decrees of steel
Us as the distant poles have placed,
(Though love's whole world on us doth wheel)
Not by themselves to be embraced,

Unless the giddy heaven fall,
And Earth some new convulsion tear;
And, us to join, the world should all
Be cramped into a planisphere.

As lines so loves oblique may well
Themselves in every angle greet:
But ours so truly parallel,
Though infinite, can never meet.

Therefore the love which us doth bind
But fate so enviously debars
Is the conjunction of the mind
And opposition of the stars.

(1681)

661 *To His Coy Mistress*

HAD we but world enough, and time,
This coyness, Lady, were no crime.
We would sit down, and think which way
To walk, and pass our long love's day.

extended] (1) directed; held out; (2) occupying space (like matter) fixed] directed; attached as . . . poles] i.e. as far apart as possible giddy] whirling cramped . . . planisphere] compressed into flat projections of the hemispheres, with the poles meeting oblique] (1) not perpendicular; (2) lacking moral rectitude (see endnote) truly parallel] (1) perfectly parallel; (2) faithfully constant in equidistance; (3) like lines of latitude conjunction] (1) union; (2) astronomical position in the same sign opposition] (1) contrariety; (2) astronomical position in opposite signs

661 world] life coyness] shy reserve love's day] (1) day of settlement; (2) day devoted to lovemaking

Thou by the Indian Ganges' side
Shouldst rubies find: I by the tide
Of Humber would complain. I would
Love you ten years before the Flood:
And you should, if you please, refuse
Till the conversion of the Jews.
My vegetable love should grow
Vaster than empires, and more slow.
An hundred years should go to praise
Thine eyes, and on thy forehead gaze.
Two hundred to adore each breast;
But thirty thousand to the rest.
An age at least to every part,
And the last age should show your heart:
For, Lady, you deserve this state;
Nor would I love at lower rate.
But at my back I always hear
Time's wingèd chariot hurrying near;
And yonder all before us lie
Deserts of vast eternity.
Thy beauty shall no more be found;
Nor, in thy marble vault, shall sound
My echoing song: then worms shall try
That long-preserved virginity:
And your quaint honour turn to dust;
And into ashes all my lust.
The grave's a fine and private place,
But none, I think, do there embrace.
Now, therefore, while the youthful glue
Sits on thy skin like morning dew,
And while thy willing soul transpires
At every pore with instant fires,
Now let us sport us while we may;
And now, like amorous birds of prey,
Rather at once our time devour,
Than languish in his slow-chapped power.
Let us roll all our strength, and all
Our sweetness, up into one ball:
And tear our pleasures with rough strife
Thorough the iron grates of life.

Humber] (a river near the poet at Hull) conversion . . . Jews] (a proverbial impossibility or apocalyptic event) vegetable] growing try] (1) test; (2) attempt, solicit quaint] (1) dainty; fastidious; nice; (2) pudenda glue] i.e. life (see endnote) dew] (see endnote) slow-chapped] (1) slowly struck (as of clocks); (2) slow-jawed (as of Saturn the devourer) grates] cages; spaces between the bars of a grating; portcullis (see endnote)

Thus, though we cannot make our sun
Stand still, yet we will make him run.

(1681)

662 *The Coronet*

When for the thorns with which I long, too long,
With many a piercing wound,
My saviour's head have crowned,
I seek with garlands to redress that wrong:
Through every garden, every mead,
I gather flowers (my fruits are only flowers),
Dismantling all the fragrant towers
That once adorned my shepherdess's head.
And now when I have summed up all my store,
Thinking (so I myself deceive)
So rich a chaplet thence to weave
As never yet the king of glory wore:
Alas, I find the serpent old
That, twining in his speckled breast,
About the flowers disguised does fold,
With wreaths of fame and interest.
Ah, foolish man, that wouldst debase with them,
And mortal glory, heaven's diadem!
But thou, who only couldst the serpent tame,
Either his slippery knots at once untie,
And disentangle all his winding snare;
Or shatter too with him my curious frame,
And let these wither, so that he may die,
Though set with skill and chosen out with care:
That they, while thou on both their spoils dost tread,
May crown thy feet, that could not crown thy head.

(1681)

run] (as in Eccles. 1: 5)

662 long] (1) wish for; (2) for a long time garlands] (1) wreaths; (2) miscellanies of poems towers] head-dresses store] i.e. of flower-virtues twining in] interlacing fold] wind wreaths] coils, windings (i.e. ulterior motives) diadem] martyr's crown; glory curious] (1) artful; (2) concupiscent frame] (1) structure; (2) nature; (3) protection against cold (horticulture) so that] provided that set] (1) ornamented; (2) formed into fruit (of blossoms) both . . . spoils] i.e. spoils of victory, and the serpent's slough

663 *An Horatian Ode upon Cromwell's Return from Ireland*

THE forward youth that would appear
Must now forsake his Muses dear,
  Nor in the shadows sing
  His numbers languishing.
'Tis time to leave the books in dust,
And oil the unusèd armour's rust;
  Removing from the wall
  The corslet of the hall.
So restless Cromwell could not cease
In the inglorious arts of peace,
  But through adventurous war
  Urgèd his active star.
And, like the three-forked lightning, first
Breaking the clouds where it was nursed,
  Did thorough his own side
  His fiery way divide.
For 'tis all one to courage high
The emulous or enemy;
  And with such to inclose
  Is more than to oppose
Then burning through the air he went,
And palaces and temples rent;
  And Caesar's head at last
  Did through his laurels blast.
'Tis madness to resist or blame
The force of angry heaven's flame:
  And, if we would speak true,
  Much to the man is due,
Who, from his private gardens, where
He lived reservèd and austere,
  As if his highest plot
  To plant the bergamot,
Could by industrious valour climb
To ruin the great work of time,
  And cast the kingdoms old
  Into another mould.

Cromwell's . . . Ireland] (see endnote) forward] (1) eager, zealous; (2) bold; presumptuous appear] come before the public numbers languishing] love poems cease] rest own side] (1) Parliamentary leadership cadres; (2) the cloud with such . . . more] (1) to cramp such a man is more intolerable to him; (2) to contain such an enemy is more prudent Caesar's] i.e. Charles I's blast] strike with lightning (traditionally supposed to avoid laurel) bergamot] 'the pear of kings'

Though justice against fate complain,
And plead the ancient rights in vain:
  But those do hold or break
  As men are strong or weak.
Nature, that hateth emptiness,
Allows of penetration less:
  And therefore must make room
  Where greater spirits come.
What field of all the civil wars,
Where his were not the deepest scars?
  And Hampton shows what part
  He had of wiser art,
Where, twining subtile fears with hope,
He wove a net of such a scope
  That Charles himself might chase
  To Caresbrook's narrow case:
That thence the royal actor born
The tragic scaffold might adorn:
  While round the armèd bands
  Did clap their bloody hands.
He nothing common did or mean
Upon that memorable scene;
  But with his keener eye
  The axe's edge did try:
Nor called the gods with vulgar spite
To vindicate his helpless right;
  But bowed his comely head
  Down as upon a bed.
This was that memorable hour
Which first assured the forcèd power.
  So when they did design
  The capitol's first line,
A bleeding head where they begun
Did fright the architects to run;
  And yet in that the state
  Foresaw its happy fate.
And now the Irish are ashamed
To see themselves in one year tamed:

men] (1) leaders like Charles and Cromwell; (2) subjects emptiness] i.e. a vacuum penetration] simultaneous occupation of the same space by two objects (philosophical) Hampton] i.e. Hampton Court subtile] (1) keen; (2) finely fashioned chase] (1) hurry (intr.); (2) drive Caresbrook's] (see endnote) narrow case] i.e. grave (narrow house) case] container; house clap] i.e. (1) in applause; (2) to drown out Charles's speech mean] (1) intend; (2) base scene] platform; stage keener] (1) sharper (exploiting senses of *acies*, eyesight, edge); (2) more far-sighted than his accusers try] (1) judge; (2) experience assured] secured forcèd] artificial; maintained with effort capitol's] (see endnote)

So much one man can do,
That does both act and know.
They can affirm his praises best,
And have, though overcome, confessed
How good he is, how just,
And fit for highest trust:
Nor yet grown stiffer with command,
But still in the republic's hand:
How fit he is to sway
That can so well obey.
He to the Commons' feet presents
A kingdom, for his first year's rents:
And, what he may, forbears
His fame, to make it theirs:
And has his sword and spoils ungirt,
To lay them at the public's skirt.
So when the falcon high
Falls heavy from the sky,
She, having killed, no more does search
But on the next green bough to perch,
Where, when he first does lure,
The falc'ner has her sure.
What may not then our isle presume
While victory his crest does plume?
What may not others fear
If thus he crown each year?
A Caesar, he, ere long to Gaul,
To Italy an Hannibal,
And to all states not free
Shall climactéric be.
The Pict no shelter now shall find
Within his party-coloured mind,
But from this valour sad
Shrink underneath the plaid:
Happy, if in the tufted brake
The English hunter him mistake,
Nor lay his hounds in near
The Caledonian deer.
But thou, the wars' and fortune's son,
March indefatigably on,

still] as yet sway] (1) govern; (2) control (i.e. be controlled) kingdom] i.e. Ireland what he may] as far as possible Caesar . . . Hannibal] i.e. invaders of Gaul and Italy climactéric] fatal; epoch-making Pict] (1) Scot; (2) painted (Lat. *pictus*) party-coloured] factious (punning on 'party-coloured' and the tattooed Picts) sad] (1) firm; (2) violent mistake] i.e. because of his particoloured camouflage lay in] put into cover (hunting) Caledonian] Scottish

And for the last effect
Still keep thy sword erect:
Besides the force it has to fright
The spirits of the shady night,
The same arts that did gain
A power must it maintain.

(1681; wr. 1650?)

from *Upon Appleton House*

664 *To My Lord Fairfax*

At the demolishing, this seat
To Fairfax fell as by escheat.
And what both nuns and founders willed
'Tis likely better thus fulfilled.
For if the virgin proved not theirs,
The cloister yet remainèd hers.
Though many a nun there made her vow,
'Twas no religious house till now.

From that blest bed the hero came,
Whom France and Poland yet does fame:
Who, when retirèd here to peace,
His warlike studies could not cease;
But laid these gardens out in sport
In the just figure of a fort;
And with five bastions it did fence,
As aiming one for every sense.

When in the east the morning ray
Hangs out the colours of the day,
The bee through these known alleys hums,
Beating the *dian* with its drums.
Then flowers their drowsy eyelids raise,
Their silken ensigns each displays,
And dries its pan yet dank with dew,
And fills its flask with odours new.

effect] (1) impression; (2) purpose sword erect] i.e. blade up in pagan superstition, not hilt up (an image of the cross, disliked by Puritans) spirits] i.e. those who fell in Cromwell's wars, besides the king

664 *Appleton House . . . Fairfax*] (see endnote) demolishing] dissolution escheat] reversion through lack of a successor virgin] (see endnote) religious] (1) godly; (2) belonging to a religious order hero] i.e. either the Lord General, or his grandfather Sir Thomas Fairfax fence] fortify *dian*] reveillé pan] i.e. flintlock powder pan flask] i.e. powder flask

These, as their governor goes by,
In fragrant volleys they let fly;
And to salute their governess
Again as great a charge they press:
None for the virgin nymph; for she
Seems with the flowers a flower to be.
And think so still! though not compare
With breath so sweet or cheek so fair.

Well shot, ye firemen! Oh how sweet
And round your equal fires do meet,
Whose shrill report no ear can tell,
But echoes to the eye and smell.
See how the flowers, as at parade,
Under their colours stand displayed:
Each regiment in order grows,
That of the tulip, pink, and rose.

But when the vigilant patrol
Of stars walks round about the pole,
Their leaves, that to the stalks are curled,
Seem to their staves the ensigns furled.
Then in some flower's belovèd hut
Each bee as sentinel is shut,
And sleeps so too: but, if once stirred,
She runs you through, nor asks the word.

O thou, that dear and happy isle
The garden of the world ere while,
Thou paradise of foür seas,
Which heaven planted us to please,
But, to exclude the world, did guard
With watery if not flaming sword;
What luckless apple did we taste,
To make us mortal, and thee waste?

Unhappy! shall we never more
That sweet militïa restore,
When gardens only had their towers,
And all the garrisons were flowers;
When roses only arms might bear,
And men did rosy garlands wear?

charge] (1) quantity of powder; (2) attack   nymph] i.e. Mary Fairfax   compare] rival   firemen] gunners   round] (1) copiously; from all sides; (2) round (as of shot)   fires] salvoes   word] password   isle] Britain   flaming sword] i.e. the angelic guard on Eden after the Fall

Tulips, in several colours barred,
Were then the Switzers of our guard.

The gardener had the soldier's place,
And his more gentle forts did trace.
The nursery of all things green
Was then the only magazine.
The winter quarters were the stoves,
Where he the tender plants removes.
But war all this doth overgrow:
We ordnance plant and powder sow.

And yet there walks one on the sod
Who, had it pleasèd him and God,
Might once have made our gardens spring
Fresh as his own and flourishing.
But he preferred to the Cinque Ports
These five imaginary forts;
And, in those half-dry trenches, spanned
Power which the ocean might command.

For he did, with his utmost skill,
Ambition weed, but conscience till—
Conscience, that heaven-nursèd plant,
Which most our earthy gardens want.
A prickling leaf it bears, and such
As that which shrinks at every touch;
But flowers eternal and divine,
That in the crowns of saints do shine.

The sight does from these bastions ply,
The invisible artillery;
And at proud Cawood Castle seems
To point the battery of its beams,
As if it quarrelled in the seat
The ambition of its prelate great.
But o'er the meads below it plays,
Or innocently seems to graze.

And now to the abyss I pass
Of that unfathomable grass,
Where men like grasshoppers appear,
But grasshoppers are giants there:

Switzers] Swiss papal guard (whose uniform was striped red and yellow) stoves] hot houses overgrow] (1) overcome; (2) overgrow Cinque Ports] (see endnote) spanned] confined earthy] earthly want] lack; need Cawood Castle] (the Archbishop of York's seat, two miles away) quarrelled] challenged; faulted men . . . grasshoppers] (alluding to Num. (13: 33)

They, in their squeaking laugh, contemn
Us as we walk more low than them;
And, from the precipices tall
Of the green spires, to us do call.

To see men through this meadow dive,
We wonder how they rise alive.
As, under water, none does know
Whether he fall through it or go.
But, as the mariners that sound,
And show upon their lead the ground,
They bring up flowers so to be seen,
And prove they've at the bottom been.

No scene that turns with engines strange
Does oftener than these meadows change.
For when the sun the grass hath vexed,
The tawny mowers enter next;
Who seem like Israelites to be,
Walking on foot through a green sea.
To them the grassy deeps divide,
And crowd a lane to either side.

With whistling scythe and elbow strong
These massacre the grass along:
While one, unknowing, carves the rail,
Whose yet unfeathered quills her fail.
The edge all bloody from its breast
He draws, and does his stroke detest,
Fearing the flesh untimely mowed
To him a fate as black forebode.

But bloody Thestylis, that waits
To bring the mowing camp their cates,
Greedy as kites has trussed it up,
And forthwith means on it to sup:
When on another quick she lights,
And cries, 'He called us Israelites;
But now, to make his saying true,
Rails rain for quails, for manna, dew.'

go] make progress sound] take soundings show . . . ground] i.e. show traces of the bottom scene] stage; scenery Israelites . . . sea] i.e. crossing the Red Sea at the Exodus crowd] force along] flat rail] corncrake; landrail ('the king of quails') cates] food quick] (1) live; (2) quickly He . . . us] i.e. (1) God identified us typologically as; (2) Marvell likened us to Rails . . . dew] i.e. alluding to the Israelites' miraculous provisioning in the wilderness

Unhappy birds! what does it boot
To build below the grass's root,
When lowness is unsafe as height
And chance o'ertakes what scapeth spite?
And now your orphan parents' call
Sounds your untimely funeral.
Death-trumpets creak in such a note,
And 'tis the sourdine in their throat.

Or sooner hatch or higher build:
The mower now commands the field,
In whose new traverse seemeth wrought
A camp of battle newly fought:
Where, as the meads with hay, the plain
Lies quilted o'er with bodies slain:
The women that with forks it fling,
Do represent the pillaging.

And now the careless victors play,
Dancing the triumphs of the hay;
Where every mower's wholesome heat
Smells like an Alexander's sweat,
Their females fragrant as the mead
Which they in fairy circles tread:
When at their dance's end they kiss,
Their new-made hay not sweeter is.

When after this 'tis piled in cocks,
Like a calm sea it shows the rocks;
We wondering in the river near
How boats among them safely steer.
Or, like the desert Memphis sand,
Short pyramids of hay do stand.
And such the Roman camps do rise
In hills for soldiers' obsequies.

This scene again withdrawing brings
A new and empty face of things,
A levelled space, as smooth and plain
As cloths for Lilly stretched to stain.

orphan] bereaved (Latinism) sourdine] muting device in a trumpet Or] Either traverse] (1) passing through; (2) screen, curtain (theatre); (3) parapet (fortification) triumphs] celebrations hay] i.e. (1) harvest; (2) serpentine country dance sweat] (1) sweat (Alexander's reputedly was perfume); (2) sweet cocks] conical heaps Short] (1) Low; (2) Ephemeral Roman camps] British camps; tumuli withdrawing] removing cloths] canvases Lilly] Sir Peter Lely, the portraitist

The world when first created sure
Was such a table rase and pure.
Or rather such is the *toril*
Ere the bulls enter at Madril.

For to this naked equal flat,
Which Levellers take pattern at,
The villagers in common chase
Their cattle, which it closer rase;
And what below the scythe increased
Is pinched yet nearer by the beast.
Such, in the painted world, appeared
Davenant with the universal herd.

They seem within the polished grass
A landskip drawn in looking-glass;
And shrunk in the huge pasture show
As spots, so shaped, on faces do.
Such fleas, ere they approach the eye,
In multiplying glasses lie.
They feed so wide, so slowly move,
As constellations do above.

Then, to conclude these pleasant acts,
Denton sets ope its cataracts,
And makes the meadow truly be
(What it but seemed before) a sea.
For, jealous of its lord's long stay,
It tries t' invite him thus away.
The river in itself is drowned,
And isles the astonished cattle round.

Let others tell the paradox,
How eels now bellow in the ox;
How horses at their tails do kick,
Turned as they hang to leeches quick;

table rase] *tabula rasa*, blank tablet *toril*] bullring Madril] Madrid equal] (1) level; (2) of the same political rank in . . . chase] drive, using it as common pasture rase] crop increased] grew Such . . . herd] i.e. like the painting of Creation in William Davenant's *Gondibert* II. vi. 60 landskip] landscape picture in looking-glass] in a camera obscura; reduced in size Such . . . eye] So fleas, before coming into focus multiplying glasses] magnifying glasses lie] (1) are placed; (2) deceive Denton] (a Fairfax estate on the Wharfe River) astonished] bewildered in the ox] i.e. inside, swallowed by the ox Turned . . . quick] Changed by the water into live leeches (a popular error)

How boats can over bridges sail;
And fishes do the stables scale.
How salmons trespassing are found;
And pikes are taken in the pound.

But I, retiring from the flood,
Take sanctuary in the wood;
And, while it lasts, myself embark
In this yet green, yet growing ark,
Where the first carpenter might best
Fit timber for his keel have pressed,
And where all creatures might have shares,
Although in armies, not in pairs.

The double wood of ancient stocks,
Linked in so thick an union locks,
It like two pedigrees appears,
On th' one hand Fairfax, th' other Vere's:
Of whom though many fell in war,
Yet more to heaven shooting are:
And, as they nature's cradle decked,
Will in green age her hearse expect.

(1681)

665 *The Garden*

How vainly men themselves amaze
To win the palm, the oak, or bays,
And their uncessant labours see
Crowned from some single herb or tree,
Whose short and narrow vergèd shade
Does prudently their toils upbraid,
While all flow'rs and all trees do close
To weave the garlands of repose.

Fair quiet, have I found thee here,
And innocence thy sister dear!
Mistaken long, I sought you then
In busy companies of men.

taken] (1) caught; (2) arrested pound] (1) pond; (2) enclosure for animals embark] (1) go on board; (2) enclose in bark first carpenter] Noah (Gen. 6) pressed] impressed, commandeered pedigrees] family trees

665 amaze] perplex; madden vergèd] (1) limited; (2) extended (towards the horizon) toils] (1) tasks; (2) snares upbraid] (1) censure; (2) braid up

Your sacred plants, if here below,
Only among the plants will grow.
Society is all but rude,
To this delicious solitude.

No white nor red was ever seen
So am'rous as this lovely green.
Fond lovers, cruel as their flame,
Cut in these trees their mistress' name.
Little, alas, they know, or heed,
How far these beauties hers exceed!
Fair trees! wheres'e'er your barks I wound,
No name shall but your own be found.

When we have run our passion's heat,
Love hither makes his best retreat.
The gods, that mortal beauty chase,
Still in a tree did end their race.
Apollo hunted Daphne so,
Only that she might laurel grow:
And Pan did after Syrinx speed,
Not as a nymph, but for a reed.

What wondrous life in this I lead!
Ripe apples drop about my head;
The luscious clusters of the vine
Upon my mouth do crush their wine;
The nectarine and curious peach
Into my hands themselves do reach;
Stumbling on melons, as I pass,
Ensnared with flowers, I fall on grass.

Meanwhile the mind, from pleasures less,
Withdraws into its happiness:
The mind, that ocean where each kind
Does straight its own resemblance find;
Yet it creates, transcending these,
Far other worlds, and other seas,
Annihilating all that's made
To a green thought in a green shade.

but rude, / To] merely uncivil, compared to am'rous] lovely Fond] (1) Doting; (2) Foolish run . . . heat] (1) run its course; (2) spent its ardour Still] Always race] (1) pursuit; (2) lineage Apollo] ancient Greek god of poetry and the sun Daphne] daughter of the River Peneus Pan] ancient Greek god of shepherds (and Apollo's rival in music) Syrinx] Arcadian nymph, metamorphosed to a reed curious] delicate; choice straight] at once Annihilating . . . To] i.e. Reducing creation to nothing, compared to

Here at the fountain's sliding foot,
Or at some fruit-tree's mossy root,
Casting the body's vest aside,
My soul into the boughs does glide:
There like a bird it sits, and sings,
Then whets, and combs its silver wings;
And, till prepared for longer flight,
Waves in its plumes the various light.

Such was that happy garden-state,
While man there walked without a mate:
After a place so pure, and sweet,
What other help could yet be meet!
But 'twas beyond a mortal's share
To wander solitary there:
Two paradises 'twere in one
To live in paradise alone.

How well the skilful gardener drew
Of flowers and herbs this dial new;
Where from above the milder sun
Does through a fragrant zodiac run;
And, as it works, the industrious bee
Computes its time as well as we.
How could such sweet and wholesome hours
Be reckoned but with herbs and flowers!

(1681)

666 *On a Drop of Dew*

SEE how the orient dew,
Shed from the bosom of the morn
Into the blowing roses,
Yet careless of its mansion new,
For the clear region where 'twas born
Round in itself incloses;
And in its little globe's extent
Frames as it can its native element.
How it the purple flower does slight,
Scarce touching where it lies,

sliding] transitory; inconstant vest] garment whets] preens share] lot dial] sundial

666 orient] (1) shining; (2) eastern blowing] blossoming Yet] Still mansion] temporary lodging For] As a substitute for Round ... incloses] Incloses itself round, in itself native element] upper air

But gazing back upon the skies,
Shines with a mournful light:
Like its own tear,
Because so long divided from the sphere.
Restless it rolls and unsecure,
Trembling lest it grow impure,
Till the warm sun pity its pain,
And to the skies exhale it back again.
So the soul, that drop, that ray
Of the clear fountain of eternal day—
Could it within the human flower be seen—
Remembering still its former height,
Shuns the sweet leaves and blossoms green,
And, recollecting its own light,
Does, in its pure and circling thoughts, express
The greater heaven in an heaven less.
In how coy a figure wound,
Every way it turns away:
So the world excluding round,
Yet receiving in the day:
Dark beneath, but bright above,
Here disdaining, there in love.
How loose and easy hence to go,
How girt and ready to ascend:
Moving but on a point below,
It all about does upwards bend.
Such did the manna's sacred dew distil,
White and entïre, though congealed and chill;
Congealed on Earth: but does, dissolving, run
Into the glories of th' almighty sun.

(1681)

667 *The Mower against Gardens*

LUXURIOUS man, to bring his vice in use,
  Did after him the world seduce,
And from the fields the flowers and plants allure,
  Where nature was most plain and pure.
He first enclosed within the garden's square
  A dead and standing pool of air,

sphere] i.e. heavenly sphere   exhale] give off in vapour   recollecting] (1) remembering; (2) collecting again   less] smaller   coy] (1) disdainful; (2) secluded, inaccessible   manna's] food miraculously sent to the Israelites in the wilderness

667 Luxurious] Voluptuous   bring . . . use] practise; establish as customary

And a more luscious earth for them did knead,
  Which stupefied them while it fed.
The pink grew then as double as his mind;
  The nutriment did change the kind.
With strange perfúmes he did the roses taint;
  And flowers themselves were taught to paint.
The tulip, white, did for complexion seek,
  And learned to interline its cheek:
Its onion root they then so high did hold,
  That one was for a meadow sold.
Another world was searched, through oceans new,
  To find the Marvel of Peru.
And yet these rarities might be allowed
  To man, that sovereign thing and proud,
Had he not dealt between the bark and tree,
  Forbidden mixtures there to see.
No plant now knew the stock from which it came;
  He grafts upon the wild the tame:
That the uncertain and adulterate fruit
  Might put the palate in dispute.
His green seraglio has its eunuchs too,
  Lest any tyrant him outdo.
And in the cherry he does nature vex,
  To procreate without a sex.
'Tis all enforced, the fountain and the grot,
  While the sweet fields do lie forgot;
Where willing nature does to all dispense
  A wild and fragrant innocence:
And fauns and fairies do the meadows till,
  More by their presence than their skill.
Their statues, polished by some ancient hand,
  May to adorn the gardens stand:
But howsoe'er the figures do excel,
  The gods themselves with us do dwell.

(1681)

luscious] pleasant; cloying   kind] nature; species   onion root] bulb   Marvel of Peru] *Mirabilis Jalapa*, an imported bloom   dealt . . . tree] (1) engaged in grafting; (2) engaged in underhand dealings or in interference between husband and wife (proverb)   Forbidden mixtures] Prohibited unions (like those of Deut. 22: 9)   vex] trouble in respect of a solution   procreate . . . sex] i.e. 'inoculate' or graft   enforced] (1) constrained, unnatural; (2) raped

668 *Damon the Mower*

HARK how the mower Damon sung,
With love of Juliana stung!
While everything did seem to paint
The scene more fit for his complaint.
Like her fair eyes the day was fair,
But scorching like his am'rous care.
Sharp like his scythe his sorrow was,
And withered like his hopes the grass.

'Oh what unusual heats are here,
Which thus our sunburned meadows sear!
The grasshopper its pipe gives o'er;
And hamstringed frogs can dance no more.
But in the brook the green frog wades;
And grasshoppers seek out the shades.
Only the snake, that kept within,
Now glitters in its second skin.

'This heat the sun could never raise,
Nor dog star so inflame the days.
It from an higher beauty grow'th,
Which burns the fields and mower both:
Which mads the dog, and makes the sun
Hotter than his own Phaëton.
Not July causeth these extremes,
But Juliana's scorching beams.

'Tell me where I may pass the fires
Of the hot day, or hot desires.
To what cool cave shall I descend,
Or to what gelid fountain bend?
Alas! I look for ease in vain,
When remedies themselves complain.
No moisture but my tears do rest,
Nor cold but in her icy breast.

'How long wilt thou, fair shepherdess,
Esteem me and my presents less?
To thee the harmless snake I bring,
Disarmèd of its teeth and sting;

Juliana] Gillian (Latinized) heats] hot season dog star] Sirius (supposed cause of summer malaises) Phaëton] Phaethon, Apollo's son (burnt for mishandling the sun chariot)

To thee chameleons, changing hue,
And oak leaves tipped with honey dew.
Yet thou, ungrateful, hast not sought
Nor what they are, nor who them brought.

'I am the mower Damon, known
Through all the meadows I have mown.
On me the morn her dew distils
Before her darling daffodils;
And, if at noon my toil me heat,
The sun himself licks off my sweat;
While, going home, the evening sweet
In cowslip-water bathes my feet.

'What, though the piping shepherd stock
The plains with an unnumbered flock?
This scythe of mine discovers wide
More ground than all his sheep do hide.
With this the golden fleece I shear
Of all these closes every year.
And though in wool more poor than they,
Yet am I richer far in hay.

'Nor am I so deformed to sight,
If in my scythe I lookèd right;
In which I see my picture done,
As in a crescent moon the sun.
The deathless fairies take me oft
To lead them in their dances soft;
And, when I tune myself to sing,
About me they contract their ring.

'How happy might I still have mowed,
Had not Love here his thistles sowed!
But now I all the day complain,
Joining my labour to my pain;
And with my scythe cut down the grass,
Yet still my grief is where it was:
But, when the iron blunter grows,
Sighing, I whet my scythe and woes.'

While thus he threw his elbow round,
Depopulating all the ground,
And, with his whistling scythe, does cut
Each stroke between the earth and root,

cowslip-water] cosmetic decoction closes] enclosed fields

The edgèd steel by careless chance
Did into his own ankle glance;
And there among the grass fell down,
By his own scythe, the mower mown.

'Alas!' said he, 'these hurts are slight
To those that die by love's despite.
With shepherd's-purse, and clown's-all-heal,
The blood I staunch, and wound I seal.
Only for him no cure is found,
Whom Juliana's eyes do wound.
'Tis death alone that this must do:
For death thou art a mower too.'

(1681)

669 *The Mower's Song*

My mind was once the true survey
Of all these meadows fresh and gay,
And in the greenness of the grass
Did see its hopes as in a glass;
When Juliana came, and she
What I do to the grass, does to my thoughts and me.

But these, while I with sorrow pine,
Grew more luxuriant still and fine,
That not one blade of grass you spied
But had a flower on either side;
When Juliana came, and she
What I do to the grass, does to my thoughts and me.

Unthankful meadows, could you so
A fellowship so true forgo,
And in your gaudy May-games meet,
While I lay trodden under feet?
When Juliana came, and she
What I do to the grass, does to my thoughts and me.

But what you in compassion ought
Shall now by my revenge be wrought:
And flow'rs, and grass, and I and all,
Will in one common ruin fall.
For Juliana comes, and she
What I do to the grass, does to my thoughts and me.

clown's-all-heal] clown's-wound wort (supposed to heal scythe wounds)

669 survey] description; view greenness] i.e. colour of hope ought] owed

And thus, ye meadows, which have been
Companions of my thoughts more green,
Shall now the heraldry become
With which I will adorn my tomb;
For Juliana comes, and she
What I do to the grass, does to my thoughts and me.

(1681)

670 *Bermudas*

WHERE the remote Bermudas ride
In the ocean's bosom unespied,
From a small boat that rowed along
The listening winds received this song.
'What should we do but sing his praise
That led us through the watery maze,
Unto an isle so long unknown,
And yet far kinder than our own?
Where he the huge sea-monsters wracks,
That lift the deep upon their backs,
He lands us on a grassy stage,
Safe from the storms, and prelate's rage.
He gave us this eternal spring,
Which here enamels everything,
And sends the fowls to us in care,
On daily visits through the air.
He hangs in shades the orange bright,
Like golden lamps in a green night,
And does in the pom'granates close
Jewels more rich than Ormus shows.
He makes the figs our mouths to meet,
And throws the melons at our feet;
But apples plants of such a price,
No tree could ever bear them twice.
With cedars, chosen by his hand,
From Lebanon, he stores the land,
And makes the hollow seas that roar
Proclaim the ambergris on shore.
He cast (of which we rather boast)
The gospel's pearl upon our coast,

Bermudas] i.e. refuge of Puritan exiles kinder] (1) more hospitable; (2) more natural daily visits] i.e. as to Elijah (1 Kgs. 17: 6) Ormus] Hormuz, on the Persian Gulf, a centre of the jewel trade apples] (1) pineapples; (2) the forbidden fruit of paradise Lebanon] i.e. source of cedarwood for the Temple ambergris] fragrant secretion of the sperm whale gospel's pearl] the pearl of great price (Matt. 13: 45–6), or that cast before swine (Matt. 7: 6)

And in these rocks for us did frame
A temple, where to sound his name.
Oh let our voice his praise exalt,
Till it arrive at heaven's vault:
Which thence (perhaps) rebounding, may
Echo beyond the Mexique Bay.'
Thus sung they, in the English boat,
An holy and a cheerful note,
And all the way, to guide their chime,
With falling oars they kept the time.

(1681; wr. after 1653)

671 *On Mr Milton's 'Paradise Lost'*

WHEN I beheld the poet blind, yet bold,
In slender book his vast design unfold:
Messiah crowned, God's reconciled decree,
Rebelling angels, the forbidden tree,
Heaven, hell, Earth, chaos, all; the argument
Held me a while misdoubting his intent,
That he would ruin (for I saw him strong)
The sacred truths to fable and old song
(So Sampson groped the temple's posts in spite),
The world o'erwhelming to revenge his sight.
  Yet as I read, soon growing less severe,
I liked his project, the success did fear:
Through that wide field how he his way should find
O'er which lame faith leads understanding blind;
Lest he perplexed the things he would explain,
And what was easy he should render vain.
  Or if a work so infinite he spanned,
Jealous I was that some less skilful hand
(Such as disquiet always what is well,
And by ill imitating would excel)
Might hence presume the whole creation's day
To change in scenes, and show it in a play.
  Pardon me, mighty poet, nor despise
My causeless, yet not impious, surmise.
But I am now convinced that none will dare
Within thy labours to pretend a share.
Thou hast not missed one thought that could be fit,
And all that was improper dost omit;

671 Messiah] Christ reconciled decree] i.e. decree of reconciliation ruin] reduce Sampson] Samson (alluding to Milton's *Samson Agonistes*, 1671) pretend] claim

So that no room is here for writers left,
But to detect their ignorance or theft.
  That majesty which through thy work doth reign
Draws the devout, deterring the profane;
And things divine thou treatst of in such state
As them preserves, and thee, inviolate.
At once delight and horror on us seize,
Thou singst with so much gravity and ease;
And above human flight dost soar aloft,
With plume so strong, so equal, and so soft.
The bird named from that paradise you sing
So never flags, but always keeps on wing.
  Where couldst thou words of such a compass find?
Whence furnish such a vast expense of mind?
Just heaven thee, like Tiresias, to requite,
Rewards with prophecy thy loss of sight.
  Well mightst thou scorn thy readers to allure
With tinkling rhyme, of thine own sense secure;
While the Town-Bays writes all the while and spells,
And like a pack-horse tires without his bells.
Their fancies like our bushy points appear:
The poets tag them; we for fashion wear.
I too, transported by the mode, offend,
And while I meant to *praise* thee must *commend.*
Thy verse created like thy theme sublime,
In number, weight, and measure, needs not rhyme.

(1674)

EDMUND PRESTWICH

fl. 1651

672 *How to Choose a Mistress*

First I would have a face exactly fair:
Not long, nor yet precisely circular;
A smooth high brow, where neither age, nor yet
A froward peevishness, hath wrinkles set;

detect] reveal   plume] (1) feather; wing; (2) pen   equal] just; even   Tiresias] (blind prophet of ancient Greek legend)   Town-Bays] City laureate (Dryden)   spells] writes with difficulty   bushy points] ornamented laces or pendent tags   tag] supply with rhymes   must *commend*] i.e. must use *commend*, to rhyme

672 froward] perverse

And under that a pair of clear black eyes
To be the windows of the edifice,
Not sunk into her head, nor starting out,
Not fixed, nor rolling wantonly about,
But gently moving, as to whet the sight
By some fresh object, not the appetite;
Their orbs both equal, and divided by
A well-proportioned nose's ivory;
The nostrils open, fit to try what air
Would best preserve the mansion, what impair;
The colour in her cheek so mixed, the eye
Cannot distinguish where the red doth lie,
Or white, but every part thereof, as loath
To yield in either, equally hath both;
The mouth but little, whence proceeds a breath
Which might revive one in the gates of death,
And envy strike in the Panchayan groves
When their spiced tops a gentle east wind moves;
The lips ruddy, as blushing to be known
Kissing each other, by the lookers-on;
And these not to perpetual talk disposed,
Nor always in a lumpish silence closed,
But every word her innocence brings forth
Sweetened by a discreet and harmless mirth;
The teeth even and white; a dimpled chin;
And all these clothèd with the purest skin;
Then, as good painters ever use to place
The darker shadow to the fairer face,
A sad brown hair, whose amorous curls may tie
The prisoners fast, ta'en captive by her eye.
Thus would I have her face; and for her mind,
I'd have it clothed in virtue, not behind
The other's beauty; for a house thus dressed
Should be provided of a noble guest.
Then would I have a body so refined,
Fit to support this face, enclose this mind.
When all these graces I in one do prove,
Then may death blind me if I do not love.
Yet there is one thing more must needs concur;
She must love me as well as I love her.

(1651)

Panchayan] of a sacred island of Arabia Felix sad] dark prove] experience

HENRY VAUGHAN

1622–1695

from *Olor Iscanus*

673 *Translation of Boethius 'Consolation of Philosophy' II. v*

HAPPY that first white age! when we
Lived by the Earth's mere charity:
No soft luxurious diet then
Had effeminated men,
No other meat nor wine had any
Than the coarse mast or simple honey,
And by the parents' care laid up
Cheap berries did the children sup.
No pompous wear was in those days,
Of gummy silks or scarlet bays;
Their beds were on some flowery brink
And clear spring-water was their drink.
The shady pine in the sun's heat
Was their cool and known retreat;
For then 'twas not cut down, but stood
The youth and glory of the wood.
The daring sailor with his slaves
Then had not cut the swelling waves,
Nor for desire of foreign store
Seen any but his native shore.
No stirring drum had scarred that age,
Nor the shrill trumpet's active rage:
No wounds by bitter hatred made
With warm blood soiled the shining blade;
For how could hostile madness arm
An age of love to public harm?
When common justice none withstood,
Nor sought rewards for spilling blood.
  Oh that at length our age would raise
Into the temper of those days!
But (worse then Aetna's fires!) debate
And avarice inflame our state.
Alas! who was it that first found
Gold hid of purpose under ground;

white] innocent   mere] pure, absolute   mast] nuts   pompous] splendid
gummy] sticky   bays] laurel wreaths   raise] rise

That sought out pearls, and dived to find
Such precious perils for mankind!

(1651)

from *Silex Scintillans: Silex I* (674–682)

674

The Pursuit

LORD! what a busy, restless thing
Hast thou made man!
Each day and hour he is on wing,
Rests not a span;
Then having lost the sun and light,
By clouds surprised
He keeps a commerce in the night
With air disguised.
Hadst thou given to this active dust
A state untired,
The lost son had not left the husk
Nor home desired:
That was thy secret, and it is
Thy mercy too;
For when all fails to bring to bliss,
Then, this must do.
Ah! Lord! and what a purchase will that be
To take us sick, that sound would not take thee?

(1650)

675

Vanity of Spirit

QUITE spent with thoughts I left my cell, and lay
Where a shrill spring tuned to the early day.
I begged here long, and groaned to know
Who gave the clouds so brave a bow,
Who bent the spheres, and circled in
Corruption with this glorious ring,
What is his name, and how I might
Descry some part of his great light.

I summoned nature: pierced through all her store,
Broke up some seals, which none had touched before;
Her womb, her bosom and her head
Where all her secrets lay a bed

lost son] i.e. prodigal son (Luke 15: 11–32)

675 *Vanity*] Emptiness (Eccles. 1: 14)

I rifled quite; and, having passed
Through all the creatures, came at last
To search my self, where I did find
Traces, and sounds of a strange kind.

Here of this mighty spring, I found some drills,
With echoes beaten from the eternal hills;
Weak beams and fires flashed to my sight,
Like a young east, or moon-shine night,
Which showed me in a nook cast by
A piece of much antiquity,
With hieroglyphics quite dismembered,
And broken letters scarce remembered.

I took them up, and (much joyed) went about
T' unite those pieces, hoping to find out
The mystery; but this near done,
That little light I had was gone:
It grieved me much. 'At last,' said I,
'Since in these veils my eclipsèd eye
May not approach thee (for at night
Who can have commerce with the light?)
I'll disapparel, and to buy
But one half glance, most gladly die.'

(1650)

676 *The Retreat*

HAPPY those early days! when I
Shined in my angel-infancy.
Before I understood this place
Appointed for my second race,
Or taught my soul to fancy aught
But a white, celestial thought;
When yet I had not walked above
A mile or two from my first love,
And looking back (at that short space)
Could see a glimpse of his bright face;
When on some gilded cloud or flower
My gazing soul would dwell an hour,

drills] streams piece] work of art dismembered] mutilated disapparel] unveil; undress (?coinage)

676 *Retreat*] (1) Devotional withdrawal; (2) backward movement second race] spiritual life (Heb. 12: 1) white] innocent

And in those weaker glories spy
Some shadows of eternity;
Before I taught my tongue to wound
My conscience with a sinful sound,
Or had the black art to dispense
A several sin to every sense,
But felt through all this fleshly dress
Bright shoots of everlastingness.
  Oh how I long to travel back
And tread again that ancient track!
That I might once more reach that plain
Where first I left my glorious train,
From whence the enlightened spirit sees
That shady city of palm trees;
But (ah!) my soul with too much stay
Is drunk, and staggers in the way.
Some men a forward motion love,
But I by backward steps would move,
And when this dust falls to the urn
In that state I came return.

(1650)

677 *The Morning Watch*

OH joys! Infinite sweetness! with what flowers,
And shoots of glory, my soul breaks and buds!
    All the long hours
    Of night and rest,
    Through the still shrouds
    Of sleep and clouds,
  This dew fell on my breast;
    Oh how it bloods
And spirits all my Earth! Hark! in what rings
And hymning circulations the quick world
    Awakes and sings;
    The rising winds
    And falling springs,
    Birds, beasts, all things
  Adore him in their kinds.
    Thus all is hurled

shoots] ?(1) sudden rushes; (2) sproutings   shady city] Jericho (Deut. 34: 1–4)

677 *Watch*] Observance, prayer   shoots] sudden advances; shoots of growth   shrouds] shelters; shadows; vaults   bloods] raises the blood of   circulations] (1) rotations; (2) refining distillations (alchemy)   quick] living   hurled] whirled

In sacred hymns and order, the great chime
And symphony of nature. Prayer is
The world in tune,
A spirit voice,
And vocal joys
Whose echo is heaven's bliss.
Oh let me climb
When I lie down! The pious soul by night
Is like a clouded star, whose beams though said
To shed their light
Under some cloud
Yet are above,
And shine and move
Beyond that misty shroud.
So in my bed,
That curtained grave, though sleep, like ashes, hide
My lamp and life, both shall in thee abide.

(1650)

678 *Corruption*

SURE, it was so. Man in those early days
Was not all stone and earth:
He shined a little, and by those weak rays
Had some glimpse of his birth.
He saw heaven o'er his head, and knew from whence
He came (condemnèd) hither,
And, as first love draws strongest, so from hence
His mind sure progressed thither.
Things here were strange unto him: sweat and till,
All was a thorn, or weed;
Nor did those last, but (like himself) died still
As soon as they did seed.
They seemed to quarrel with him; for that act
That felled him, foiled them all:
He drew the curse upon the world, and cracked
The whole frame with his fall.
This made him long for home, as loath to stay
With murmurers and foes;
He sighed for Eden, and would often say
'Ah! what bright days were those!'
Nor was heaven cold unto him; for each day
The valley or the mountain

chime] harmonious system symphony] harmony, concord

678 till] ploughing still] always that act] i.e. eating the forbidden fruit

Afforded visits, and still paradise lay
  In some green shade or fountain.
Angels lay ledger here; each bush and cell,
  Each oak and highway knew them:
Walk but the fields, or sit down at some well,
  And he was sure to view them.
Almighty love! where art thou now? Mad man
  Sits down, and freezeth on,
He raves, and swears to stir nor fire nor fan,
  But bids the thread be spun.
I see, thy curtains are close-drawn; thy bow
  Looks dim too in the cloud;
Sin triumphs still, and man is sunk below
  The centre and his shroud;
All's in deep sleep and night; thick darkness lies
  And hatcheth o'er thy people;
But hark! what trumpet's that! what angel cries
  'Arise! Thrust in thy sickle.'

(1650)

679 *Unprofitableness*

How rich, O Lord! how fresh thy visits are!
'Twas but just now my bleak leaves hopeless hung
  Sullied with dust and mud;
Each snarling blast shot through me, and did share
Their youth and beauty, cold showers nipped and wrung
  Their spiciness and blood;
But since thou didst in one sweet glance survey
Their sad decays, I flourish, and once more
  Breathe all perfumes and spice;
I smell a dew like myrrh, and all the day
Wear in my bosom a full sun; such store
  Hath one beam from thy eyes.
But, ah, my God! what fruit hast thou of this?
What one poor leaf did ever I yet fall
  To wait upon thy wreath?
Thus thou all day a thankless weed dost dress,
And when th' hast done, a stench or fog is all
  The odour I bequeath.

(1650)

ledger] resident as ambassadors   centre] Earth   his shroud] its shadow   hatcheth o'er] (1) covers; (2) matures   Thrust . . . sickle] i.e. so as to gather the vine of the Earth (Rev. 14: 18)

679 bleak] wan, discoloured   share] shear   myrrh] incense

680 *Son-days*

BRIGHT shadows of true rest! some shoots of bliss;
Heaven once a week;
The next world's gladness prepossessed in this;
A day to seek
Eternity in time; the steps by which
We climb above all ages; lamps that light
Man through his heap of dark days; and the rich
And full redemption of the whole week's flight.

The pulleys unto headlong man; time's bower;
The narrow way;
Transplanted paradise; God's walking hour;
The cool o' the day;
The creatures' jubilee; God's parle with dust;
Heaven here; man on those hills of myrrh and flowers;
Angels descending; the returns of trust;
A gleam of glory, after six-days-showers.

The Church's love-feasts; time's prerogative
And interest
Deducted from the whole; the combs and hive
And home of rest.
The milky way chalked out with suns; a clue
That guides through erring hours; and in full story
A taste of heaven on Earth; the pledge and cue
Of a full feast; and the out courts of glory.

(1650)

681 *Retirement (I)*

WHO on yon throne of azure sits,
Keeping close house
Above the morning-star,
Whose meaner shows
And outward útensils these glories are
That shine and share

shoots] sudden rushes prepossessed] taken possession of in advance jubilee] fiftieth year; year of remission of debts parle] truce-talk myrrh] perfume love-feasts] communal meals; eucharists prerogative] God-given privilege clue] thread laid through a maze out courts] outer courts

681 útensils] household goods; sacred furnishings

Part of his mansion; he one day
When I went quite astray
Out of mere love
By his mild dove
Did show me home, and put me in the way.

Let it suffice at length thy fits
And lusts (said he)
Have had their wish and way:
Press not to be
Still thy own foe, and mine; for to this day
I did delay,
And would not see, but chose to wink—
Nay, at the very brink
And edge of all,
When thou wouldst fall,
My love-twist held thee up, my unseen link.

I know thee well; for I have framed
And hate thee not:
Thy spirit too is mine;
I know thy lot,
Extent and end, for my hands drew the line
Assignèd thine.
If then thou wouldst unto my seat,
'Tis not the applause and feat
Of dust and clay
Leads to that way,
But from those follies a resolved retreat.

Now here below, where yet untamed
Thou dost thus rove,
I have a house as well
As there above,
In it my name and honour both do dwell,
And shall until
I make all new; there nothing gay
In perfumes or array:
Dust lies with dust
And hath but just
The same respect, and room, with every clay.

dove] i.e. the Holy Spirit put ... way] gave me directions fits] caprices; humours twist] cord, thread lot] fate rove] (1) digress; wander; (2) practise piracy

A faithful school where thou mayst see
In heraldry
Of stones and speechless earth
Thy true descent;
Where dead men preach, who can turn feasts and mirth
To funerals and Lent.
There dust, that out of doors might fill
Thy eyes and blind thee still,
Is fast asleep;
Up then, and keep
Within those doors (my doors): dost hear? *I will.*

(1650)

682 *The World (I)*

I SAW eternity the other night
Like a great ring of pure and endless light,
All calm as it was bright,
And round beneath it, time in hours, days, years
Driven by the spheres
Like a vast shadow moved, in which the world
And all her train were hurled:
The doting lover in his quaintest strain
Did there complain,
Near him, his lute, his fancy, and his flights,
Wit's sour delights,
With gloves and knots, the silly snares of pleasure;
Yet his dear treasure
All scattered lay, while he his eyes did pour
Upon a flower.
The darksome statesman hung with weights and woe
Like a thick midnight-fog moved there so slow
He did nor stay, nor go;
Condemning thoughts (like sad eclipses) scowl
Upon his soul,
And clouds of crying witnesses without
Pursued him with one shout.
Yet digged the mole, and lest his ways be found
Worked under ground,
Where he did clutch his prey (but one did see
That policy):
Churches and altars fed him, perjuries
Were gnats and flies,

682 spheres] celestial globes carrying the planets (and so determining time) hurled] whirled knots] tassels pour] (1) discharge tears; (2) study earnestly, ponder (pore) one] God gnats and flies] trivial

It rained about him blood and tears; but he
Drank them as free.
The fearful miser on a heap of rust
Sat pining all his life there, did scarce trust
His own hands with the dust;
Yet would not place one piece above, but lives
In fear of thieves.
Thousands there were as frantic as himself
And hugged each one his pelf;
The downright epicure placed heaven in sense
And scorned pretence,
While others slipped into a wide excess
Said little less;
The weaker sort slight, trivial wares enslave
Who think them brave;
And poor, despisèd truth sat counting by
Their victory.
Yet some, who all this while did weep and sing,
And sing and weep, soared up into the ring,
But most would use no wing.
O fools (said I) thus to prefer dark night
Before true light,
To live in grots and caves, and hate the day
Because it shows the way,
The way which from this dead and dark abode
Leads up to God,
A way where you might tread the sun, and be
More bright than he.
But as I did their madness so discuss
One whispered thus,
'This ring the bride-groom did for none provide
But for his bride.'

John ii 16–17
All that is in the world, the lust of the flesh, the lust of the eyes, and the pride of life, is not of the father but is of the world.

And the world passeth away, and the lusts thereof, but he that doth the will of God abideth for ever.

(1650)

piece] coin brave] splendid bride] i.e. the Church (Eph. 5: 24)

from *Silex II* (683–688)

683

Ascension Hymn

DUST and clay
Man's ancient wear!
Here you must stay,
But I elsewhere;
Souls sojourn here, but may not rest;
Who will ascend must be undressed.

And yet some
That know to die
Before death come,
Walk to the sky
Even in this life; but all such can
Leave behind them the old man.

If a star
Should leave the sphere,
She must first mar
Her flaming wear,
And after fall; for in her dress
Of glory she cannot transgress.

Man of old
Within the line
Of Eden could
Like the sun shine
All naked, innocent and bright,
And intimate with heaven, as light;

But since he
That brightness soiled,
His garments be
All dark and spoiled,
And here are left as nothing worth,
Till the refiner's fire breaks forth.

Then comes he!
Whose mighty light
Made his clothes be
Like heaven, all bright:

know] know how old man] fallen nature (Col. 3: 9) transgress] (1) go outside the sphere's limit; (2) sin line] boundary refiner's] i.e. God's (Mal. 3: 2)

The fuller whose pure blood did flow
To make stained man more white than snow.

He alone
And none else can
Bring bone to bone
And rebuild man,
And by his all-subduing might
Make clay ascend more quick than light.

(1655)

684 ¶

THEY are all gone into the world of light!
And I alone sit ling'ring here;
Their very memory is fair and bright,
And my sad thoughts doth clear.

It glows and glitters in my cloudy breast
Like stars upon some gloomy grove,
Or those faint beams in which this hill is dressed,
After the sun's remove.

I see them walking in an air of glory,
Whose light doth trample on my days:
My days, which are at best but dull and hoary,
Mere glimmering and decays.

O holy hope! and high humility,
High as the heavens above!
These are your walks, and you have showed them me
To kindle my cold love.

Dear, beauteous death! the jewel of the just,
Shining nowhere but in the dark;
What mysteries do lie beyond thy dust,
Could man outlook that mark?

He that hath found some fledged bird's nest may know
At first sight, if the bird be flown;
But what fair well or grove he sings in now,
That is to him unknown.

fuller] i.e. Christ (Mal. 3: 2) quick] (1) rapid; (2) alive

684 trample on] traverse outlook] look beyond well] spring, pool

And yet, as angels in some brighter dreams
  Call to the soul when man doth sleep:
So some strange thoughts transcend our wonted themes,
    And into glory peep.

If a star were confined into a tomb
  Her captive flames must needs burn there;
But when the hand that locked her up gives room,
    She'll shine through all the sphere.

O Father of eternal life, and all
  Created glories under thee!
Resume thy spirit from this world of thrall
    Into true liberty.

Either disperse these mists, which blot and fill
  My perspective (still) as they pass,
Or else remove me hence unto that hill
    Where I shall need no glass.

(1655)

685 *The Dwelling-Place*

John 1: 38, 39

  WHAT happy, secret fountain,
  Fair shade, or mountain,
Whose undiscovered virgin glory
Boasts it this day, though not in story,
Was then thy dwelling? Did some cloud
Fixed to a tent descend and shroud
My distressed Lord? or did a star
Beckoned by thee, though high and far,
In sparkling smiles haste gladly down
To lodge light, and increase her own?
My dear, dear God! I do not know
What lodged thee then, nor where, nor how;
But I am sure thou dost now come
Oft to a narrow, homely room,
Where thou too hast but the least part,
My God, I mean my sinful heart.

(1655)

the sphere] space   resume] take to himself again   perspective] telescope or other viewing glass

685 story] historical record   lodge] give lodging to

686 *Childhood*

I CANNOT reach it; and my striving eye
Dazzles at it, as at eternity.
  Were now that chronicle alive,
Those white designs which children drive,
And the thoughts of each harmless hour
With their content too in my power,
Quickly would I make my path even,
And by mere playing go to heaven.
    Why should men love
A wolf, more than a lamb or dove?
Or choose hell-fire and brimstone streams
Before bright stars and God's own beams?
Who kisseth thorns will hurt his face,
But flowers do both refresh and grace,
And sweetly living (*fie on men!*)
Are, when dead, medicinal then.
If seeing much should make staid eyes,
And long experience should make wise;
Since all that age doth teach is ill,
Why should I not love childhood still?
Why, if I see a rock or shelf,
Shall I from thence cast down my self,
Or, by complying with the world,
From the same precipice be hurled?
Those observations are but foul
Which make me wise to lose my soul.

And yet the practice worldlings call
Business and weighty action all,
Checking the poor child for his play,
But gravely cast themselves away.
  Dear, harmless age! the short, swift span,
Where weeping virtue parts with man;
Where love without lust dwells, and bends
What way we please, without self-ends.

An age of mysteries! which he
Must live twice, that would God's face see;
Which angels guard, and with it play:
Angels! which foul men drive away.

dazzles] loses the power of distinct vision   white] innocent   drive] carry on; prolong   shelf] ledge of rock   practice] scheming, sharp practice   self-ends] selfish purposes

How do I study now, and scan
Thee, more than ere I studied man,
And only see through a long night
Thy edges, and thy bordering light!
Oh for thy centre and mid-day!
For sure that is the narrow way.

(1655)

687 *The Waterfall*

WITH what deep murmurs through time's silent stealth
Doth thy transparent, cool and watery wealth
    Here flowing fall,
    And chide, and call,
As if his liquid, loose retínue stayed
Ling'ring, and were of this steep place afraid,
    The common pass
    Where, clear as glass,
    All must descend
    Not to an end:
But quickened by this deep and rocky grave,
Rise to a longer course more bright and brave.

Dear stream! dear bank, where often I
Have sat, and pleased my pensive eye,
Why, since each drop of thy quick store
Runs thither, whence it flowed before,
Should poor souls fear a shade or night,
Who came (sure) from a sea of light?
Or since those drops are all sent back
So sure to thee that none doth lack,
Why should frail flesh doubt any more
That what God takes he'll not restore?
O useful element and clear!
My sacred wash and cleanser here,
My first consigner unto those
Fountains of life where the lamb goes!
What sublime truths and wholesome themes
Lodge in thy mystical, deep streams!
Such as dull man can never find
Unless that Spirit lead his mind,

narrow way] i.e. to salvation (Matt. 7: 14)

687 quickened] (1) made to flow more quickly; (2) restored to life   sacred wash] i.e. water of baptism (Rev. 7: 17)

Which first upon thy face did move,
And hatched all with his quickening love.
As this loud brook's incessant fall
In streaming rings restagnates all,
Which reach by course the bank, and then
Are no more seen, just so pass men.
O my invisible estate,
My glorious liberty, still late!
Thou art the channel my soul seeks,
Not this with cataracts and creeks.

(1655)

688 *Quickness*

FALSE life! a foil and no more, when
Wilt thou be gone?
Thou foul deception of all men
That would not have the true come on.

Thou art a moon-like toil; a blind
Self-posing state;
A dark contést of waves and wind;
A mere tempestuous debate.

Life is a fixed, discerning light,
A knowing joy;
No chance, or fit: but ever bright
And calm and full, yet doth not cloy.

'Tis such a blissful thing that still
Doth vivify
And shine and smile, and hath the skill
To please without eternity.

Thou art a toilsome mole, or less,
A moving mist;
But life is, what none can express,
A quickness, which my God hath kissed.

(1655)

restagnates] remains stagnant by course] naturally creeks] inlets

688 foil] (1) means of reflecting light deceptively; (2) contrast (to heaven) moon-like] inconstant Self-posing] Self-perplexing fit] transitory state

MARGARET CAVENDISH, DUCHESS OF NEWCASTLE
1623–1673

689 [*Imagination*]

I LANGUAGE want, to dress my fancies in:
The hairs uncurled, the garments loose and thin;
Had they but silver lace to make them gay,
Would be more courted than in poor array.
Or had they art, might make a better show;
But they are plain, yet cleanly do they go.
The world in bravery doth take delight,
And glistering shows do more attract the sight,
And everyone doth honour a rich hood
As if the outside made the inside good;
And everyone doth bow, and give the place,
Not for the man's sake, but the silver lace.
Let me entreat in my poor book's behalf
That all may not adore the golden calf.
Consider, pray, gold hath no life therein,
And life in nature is the richest thing.
So fancy is the soul in poetry,
And if not good, a poem ill must be.
Be just, let fancy have the upper place,
And then my verses may perchance find grace.
If flattering language all the passions rule,
Then sense, I fear, will be a mere dull fool.

(1653)

690 [*Courting the Faerie Queen*]

SIR Charles into my chamber coming in,
When I Queen Mab within my fancy viewed,
'I pray', said he, 'when Queen Mab you do see,
Present my service to Her Majesty,
And tell her I have heard fame's loud report,
Both of her beauty and her stately court.'
When I Queen Mab within my fancy viewed,
My thoughts bowed low, fearing I should be rude;
Kissing her garment thin, which fancy made,
Kneeling upon a thought, like one that prayed,

In whispers soft I did present
His humble service, which in mirth was sent.
Thus by imagination I have been
In Faerie Court, and seen the Faerie Queen.
For why, imagination runs about
In every place, yet none can trace it out.

(1653)

691 *Her Descending Down*

THE stately palace in which the queen dwells,
Whose fabric is built of hodmandod shells;
The hangings thereof a rainbow that's thin,
Which seems wondrous fine, if one enter in;
The chambers are made of amber that's clear,
Which gives a sweet smell, if fire be near;
Her bed a cherry-stone, carved throughout,
And with a butterfly's wing hung about;
Her sheets are made of a dove's eyes' skin,
Her pillow a violet bud laid therein;
The large doors are cut of transparent glass,
Where the queen may be seen as she doth pass.
The doors are locked fast with silver pins:
The queen's asleep, and now our day begins.
Her time in pleasure passes thus away,
And shall do so, until the world's last day.

(1653)

692 *Of Stars*

WE find in the East Indies stars there be
Which we in our horizon did ne'er see;
Yet we do take great pains in glasses clear,
To see what stars do in the sky appear;
But yet the more we search, the less we know,
Because we find our work doth endless grow.
For who doth know, but stars we see by night
Are suns which to some other worlds give light?
But could our outward senses pace the sky
As well as can imaginations high,
If we were there, as little may we know
As those which stay, and never do up go.
Then let not man in fruitless pains life spend:
The most we know is, nature death will send.

(1653)

691 hodmandod] snail

693 *Of Many Worlds in This World*

JUST like unto a nest of boxes round,
Degrees of sizes within each box are found,
So in this world may many worlds more be,
Thinner, and less, and less still by degree;
Although they are not subject to our sense,
A world may be no bigger than twopence.
Nature is curious, and such work may make
That our dull sense can never find, but scape.
For creatures small as atoms may be there,
If every atom a creature's figure bear.
If four atoms a world can make, then see
What several worlds might in an ear-ring be.
For millions of these atoms may be in
The head of one small, little, single pin.
And if thus small, then ladies well may wear
A world of worlds as pendents in each ear.

(1653)

694 *A Discourse of Melancholy*

A SAD and solemn verse doth please the mind,
With chains of passions doth the spirits bind.
As pencilled pictures drawn presents the night,
Whose darker shadows give the eye delight,
Melancholy aspécts invite the eye,
And always have a seeming majesty.
By its converting qualities there grows
A perfect likeness, when itself it shows.
Then let the world in mourning sit and weep,
Since only sadness we are apt to keep.
In light and toyish things we seek for change;
The mind grows weary, and about doth range.
What serious is, there constancies will dwell;
Which shows that sadness mirth doth far excel.
Why should men grieve when they do think of death,
Since they no settlement can have in mirth?
The grave, though sad, in quiet still they keep:
Without disturbing dreams they lie asleep,
No rambling thoughts to vex their restless brains,
Nor labour hard, to scorch and dry their veins.

694 pencilled] painted with brush still] ever

No care to search for that they cannot find,
Which is an appetite to every mind.
Then wish, good man, to die in quiet peace,
Since death in misery is a release.

(1653)

695 *A Landscape*

STANDING upon a hill of fancies high,
Viewing about with curiosity's eye,
Saw several landscapes under my thoughts to lie.
  Some champians of delights where there did feed
Pleasures, as wethers fat, and ewes to breed;
And pastures of green hopes, wherein cows went,
Of probability give milk of sweet content.
Some fields, though ploughed with care, unsowed did lie,
Wanting the fruitful seed, industry.
In other fields full crops of joys there growed,
Where some ripe joy's fruition down had mowed.
Some blasted with ill accidents looked black,
Others blown down with sorrow strong lay flat.
  Then did I view inclosures close to lie,
Hearts hedged about with thoughts of secrecy.
Fresh meadow of green youth did pleasant seem:
Innocency, as cowslips, grew therein.
Some ready with old age to cut for hay,
Some hay cocked high for death to take away.
Clear rivulets of health ran here and there,
No mind of sickness in them did appear.
No stones or gravel stopped their passage free,
No weeds of pain, or slimy gouts could see.
  Woods did present my view on the left side,
Where trees of high ambition grew great pride.
There shades of envy were made of dark spite,
Which did eclipse the fame of honour's light.
Faults stood so close, not many beams of praise
Could enter in: spite stopped up all the ways.
But leaves of prattling tongues, which ne'er lie still,
Sometimes speak truth, although most lies they tell.
  Then did I a garden of beauty view,
Where complexions of roses and lilies grew;

695 champians] open country   blown . . . strong] 'As ripe corn will doe with the wind' (C.)   close] secret   gravel] (1) coarse sand; (2) aggregations of urinary crystals   gouts] (1) streams, sluices; (2) diseases

And violets of blue veins there growed,
Upon the banks of breasts most perfect showed.
Lips of fresh gilliflowers grew up high,
Which oft the sun did kiss as he passed by.
Hands of Narcissus perfect white were set,
The palms were curious tulips, finely streaked.
   And by this garden a lovely orchard stood,
Wherein grew fruit of pleasure rare and good.
All coloured eyes grew there, as bullace grey,
And damsons black, which do taste best, some say.
Others there were of the pure bluest grape,
And pear-plum faces of an oval shape.
Cheeks of apricots made red with heat,
And cherry lips, which most delight to eat.
When I had viewed this landscape round about,
I fell from fancy's hill, and so wit's sight went out.

(1653)

696 *The Hunting of the Hare*

BETWIXT two ridges of ploughed land lay Wat,
Pressing his body close to earth lay squat.
His nose upon his two forefeet close lies,
Glaring obliquely with his great grey eyes.
His head he always sets against the wind:
If turn his tail, his hairs blow up behind,
Which he too cold will grow; but he is wise,
And keeps his coat still down, so warm he lies.
Thus resting all the day, till sun doth set,
Then riseth up, his relief for to get,
Walking about until the sun doth rise;
Then back returns, down in his form he lies.
At last poor Wat was found, as he there lay,
By huntsmen with their dogs which came that way.
Seeing, gets up, and fast begins to run,
Hoping some ways the cruel dogs to shun.
But they by nature have so quick a scent
That by their nose they trace what way he went;
And with their deep, wide mouths set forth a cry
Which answered was by echoes in the sky.
Then Wat was struck with terror and with fear,
Thinks every shadow still the dogs they were;

bullace] semi-wild plum   pear-plum] variety of plum

696 grow] cause to become   still] ever   relief] food   form] lair

And running out some distance from the noise
To hide himself, his thoughts he new employs.
Under a clod of earth in sandpit wide,
Poor Wat sat close, hoping himself to hide.
There long he had not sat but straight his ears
The winding horns and crying dogs he hears:
Starting with fear up leaps, then doth he run,
And with such speed, the ground scarce treads upon.
Into a great thick wood he straightway gets,
Where underneath a broken bough he sits;
At every leaf that with the wind did shake
Did bring such terror, made his heart to ache.
That place he left; to champian plains he went,
Winding about, for to deceive their scent,
And while they snuffling were, to find his track,
Poor Wat, being weary, his swift pace did slack.
On his two hinder legs for ease did sit:
His forefeet rubbed his face from dust and sweat.
Licking his feet, he wiped his ears so clean
That none could tell that Wat had hunted been.
But casting round about his fair great eyes,
The hounds in full career he near him spies;
To Wat it was so terrible a sight,
Fear gave him wings, and made his body light.
Though weary was before, by running long,
Yet now his breath he never felt more strong.
Like those that dying are, think health returns,
When 'tis but a faint blast which life out burns.
For spirits seek to guard the heart about,
Striving with death; but death doth quench them out.
Thus they so fast came on, with such loud cries,
That he no hopes hath left, nor help espies.
With that the winds did pity poor Wat's case,
And with their breath the scent blew from the place.
Then every nose is busily employed,
And every nostril is set open wide;
And every head doth seek a several way
To find what grass or track the scent on lay.
Thus quick industry, that is not slack,
Is like to witchery, brings lost things back.
For though the wind had tied the scent up close,
A busy dog thrust in his snuffling nose,
And drew it out, with it did foremost run;
Then horns blew loud, for the rest to follow on.

close] secret champian] unenclosed

The great slow hounds, their throats did set a base,
The fleet swift hounds as tenors next in place;
The little beagles they a treble sing,
And through the air their voice a round did ring;
Which made a consort as they ran along:
If they but words could speak, might sing a song:
The horns kept time, the hunters shout for joy,
And valiant seem, poor Wat for to destroy.
Spurring their horses to a full career,
Swim rivers deep, leap ditches without fear;
Endanger life and limbs, so fast will ride,
Only to see how patiently Wat died.
For why, the dogs so near his heels did get
That they their sharp teeth in his breech did set.
Then tumbling down, did fall with weeping eyes,
Gives up his ghost, and thus poor Wat he dies.
Men hooping loud such acclamations make
As if the devil they did prisoner take,
When they do but a shiftless creature kill,
To hunt, there needs no valiant soldier's skill.
But man doth think that exercise and toil,
To keep their health, is best, which makes most spoil;
Thinking that food and nourishment so good,
And appetite, that feeds on flesh and blood.
When they do lions, wolves, bears, tigers see
To kill poor sheep, straight say, they cruel be;
But for themselves all creatures think too few,
For luxury, wish God would make them new.
As if that God made creatures for man's meat,
And gave them life and sense, for man to eat;
Or else for sport, or recreation's sake,
Destroy those lives that God saw good to make;
Making their stomachs graves, which full they fill
With murthered bodies that in sport they kill.
Yet man doth think himself so gentle, mild,
When of all creatures he's most cruel wild;
And is so proud, thinks only he shall live,
That God a godlike nature did him give,
And that all creatures for his sake alone
Was made for him to tyrannize upon.

(1653)

breech] rump   shiftless] helpless

PATRICK CARY
1623 or 1624–1656/7

697 [*A Fig for the Lower House*]

AND now a fig for the lower House;
The army I do set at nought:
I care not for them both a louse;
For spent is my last groat, boys,
  For spent is my last groat.

Delinquent I'd not fear to be,
Though gainst the cause and Noll I'd fought;
Since England's now a state most free
For who's not worth a groat, boys,
  For who's not worth a groat.

I'll boldly talk, and do, as sure
By pursuivants ne'er to be sought;
'Tis a protection most secure,
Not to be worth a groat, boys,
  Not to be worth a groat.

I should be soon let loose again
By some mistake if I were caught;
For what can any hope to gain
From one not worth a groat, boys,
  From one not worth a groat?

Nay, if some fool should me accuse,
And I unto the bar were brought,
The judges audience would refuse,
I being not worth a groat, boys,
  I being not worth a groat.

Or, if some raw one should be bent
To make me in the air to vault,
The rest would cry 'He's innocent:
He is not worth a groat, boys,
  He is not worth a groat.'

House] i.e. of Parliament Delinquent] Royalist Noll] Oliver Cromwell
pursuivant] warrant-officer raw] uncivilized; brutal

Ye rich men that so fear the state,
This privilege is to be bought:
Purchase it then at any rate;
Leave not yourselves a groat, boys,
  Leave not yourselves a groat.

The Parliament which now does sit
(That all may have it as they ought)
Intends to make them for it fit,
And leave no man a groat, boys
  And leave no man a groat.

Who writ this song would little care
Although at th' end his name were wrought;
Committee-men their search may spare,
For spent is his last groat, boys,
  For spent is his last groat.

(1771; wr. between 1642 and 1651)

MATTHEW STEVENSON
fl. 1654–1685

698 from *An Elegy upon Old Freeman*

[*'Used hardly by the Committee, for lying in the cathedral and in church porches, praying the Common Prayer by heart'*]

HERE in this homely cabinet
Resteth a poor old anchoret;
Upon the ground he laid, all weathers,
Not as most men, gooselike on feathers.
For so indeed it came to pass,
The lord of lords his landlord was.
He lived, instead of wainscot rooms,
Like the possessed, among the tombs,
As by some spirit thither led,
To be acquainted with the dead.
Each morning from his bed so hallowed
He rose, took up his cross, and followed.
To every porch he did repair,
To vent himself in common prayer;

697 rate] price

Wherein he was alone devout,
When preaching jostled praying out.
In such procession, through the City,
Maugre the devil and Committee,
He daily went; for which he fell,
Not into Jacob's, but Bridewell.

(1654)

ANONYMOUS
fl. before 1655

699 [*Prayer to Hymen*]

WHEN I was young, unapt for use of man,
I married was unto a champion,
Youthful and full of vigour as of blood,
That unto Hymen's rights full stiffly stood;
But, see the luck, this gallant younker dies,
And in his place an aged father lies,
Weak, pithless, dry, who suffers me all night
Untouched to lie, now full of years and might.
Whenas my former man, God rest his sprite,
Girl as I was, tired me with sweet delight,
But what I did refuse now fain would use
But cannot have, O Hymen, if you can,
Give me those years again, or else the man.

(1956)

700

WHEN I am dead and thou wouldst try
The truth of love's great mystery,
When thou a sparkle dost espy
Dancing before thy brighter eye,
Oh do not doubt that sparkle came
From the fervour of my heart's flame;
Which thus to prove, open the urn
Wherein my restless ashes burn,
Then rake that dust, and thou shalt see
The fire remain that burns for thee.

(1956)

Maugre] In spite of Bridewell] prison

699 Whenas] Seeing that

700 prove] test

ANONYMOUS

701

[*Jinny*]

As oft I do record
The pleasures I have had
At yonder slide-thrift board
With many a lively lad,
It makes me merry and glad,
Though it puts me to mickle pain:
I would I had sold mine old white nag,
Gin Jinny were here again.

She baked and brewed to sell
To those that passèd by;
Good fellows loved her well.
Good faith! and so did I;
For oh! when I was dry,
Her liquor I might have ta'en.
I would I had tread my shoon awry,
Gin Jinny were here again.

A man might for his money
Have had two pots of ale,
Or tasted of a coney
The head or eke the tail.
You never need to fail,
So she were in the vein.
Alas, alas! all flesh is frail;
Would Jinny were here again.

Full oft have she and I
All in the buttery played
At trey-trip with a die,
And sent away the maid.
She was o' the dealing trade:
She'd gi'e ye two for one;
And yet she was no fulsome jade.
Would Jinny were here again.

I ligged me down for woe,
And I wept mine eyn out clean.
I would poor Jockey's eyn
My Jinny had never seen,

slide-thrift] shuffle-board   Gin] If   trey-trip] game at dice   ligged] laid

For oh! as I do ween,
She was my beauty's queen.
I would that, aye, poor Jockey might die,
Gin Jinny were here again.

(1959)

702 GENTLY, gently prithee, time,
Do not make such haste away:
To be hasty is a crime,
Then where love entreats to stay.
Stay, stay prithee stay, make not such cruel haste,
Lest presents brought too late may be disgraced.

Humbly, humbly you poor lines,
Kiss the virgin's gentle hands:
She in whom so great worth shines
Such obedience commands.
And tell her, though the year be scarce a youth,
Your master's duty is at perfect growth.

Ever, ever may true joy
In that breast sleep still and sure,
And let Venus' gentle boy
Give no wound but what he'll cure,
Till, as thou enjoyst and conquerest all hearts,
Love know, and recompense, all thy deserts.

(1959)

703 HERE'S a jolly couple! Oh the jolly jolly couple!
The spring and the winter are married,
The rose and the hawthorn so crabbed and so supple
To the bonfire of love are miscarried.
They roast, they fry:
Their flames rise high.
Let us sing, let us dance about them;
Hold hand in hand a round.
Such a pair are not found:
The world cannot stand without them.

Oh the pretty tulip! Oh the pretty pretty tulip!
So fresh to be looked on and gaudy!
She is to the stomach as cooling as a julep;
She deserves a fit warmth, is not bawdy.
Short peace, long rest
Be in their nest.

Let us sing, let us dance about them;
Hold hand in hand a round.
Such a pair are not found:
The world cannot stand without them.

(1959)

704

I LOVE thee for thy fickleness
And great inconstancy,
For hadst thou been a constant lass
Then thou hadst ne'er loved me.

I love thee for thy wantonness
And for thy drollery,
For if thou hadst not loved to sport
Then thou hadst ne'er loved me.

I love thee for thy ugliness
And for thy foolery,
For if thou hadst been fair or wise
Then thou hadst ne'er loved me.

I love thee for thy poverty
And for thy want of coin,
For if thou hadst been worth a groat
Then thou hadst ne'er been mine.

Then let me have thy heart awhile
And thou shalt have my money:
I'll part with all the wealth I have
To enjoy a lass so bonny.

(1959)

705

[*Milla*]

MILLA, the glory of whose beauteous rays
Gained heaven her wonder and the Earth's best praise,
Whom Thirsis met, was fair, and lovely too;
He liked her well, but knew not how to woo.

They arm in arm into the garden walked,
Where all the day she endless riddles talked:
Her speech and actions wisely had an end,
Yet wist he not whereto they did intend.

She grieves to see his youth no better taught;
To gather him a posy he her besought.
With that her light green gown she then up tucked,
And may for him, and thyme for her she plucked;

Which when she brought he took her by the middle.
He kissed her oft, but could not read her riddle.
'Ah, fool!' quoth she; with that burst out in laughter,
Blushed, ran away, and scorned him ever after.

(1959)

706

My mistress loves no woodcocks
Yet loves to pick the bones;
My mistress loves no jewels
Yet loves the precious stones;
My mistress loves no hunting
Yet loves to hear the horn;
My mistress loves no tables
Yet loves to see men lorn;
My mistress loves no wrestling
Yet loves to take a fall;
My mistress loves not some things,
And yet she loveth all;
My mistress loves a spender
Yet loves she not a waster;
My mistress loves no cuckold,
And yet she loves my master.

(1959)

707

Seest thou those diamonds which she wears
On that rich carcanet,
And those on her dishevelled hairs,
Fair pearls in order set?
Believe, young man, all these were tears
Of sundry lovers, sent
In bubbles, hyacinths, and rue,
All embling discontent,
Which when not warmèd by her view,
Through cold neglect each one
Congealed to pearl or stone;

706 woodcocks] fools tables] gambling tables

707 carcanet] jewelled necklace bubbles] (1) containers of bubble-glass; (2) dupes embling] embleming

Which now, the spoils of love, upon her
She wears as trophies of her honour.
Oh then beware, fond man, and thus surmise:
She that will wear thy tears would wear thine eyes.

(1959)

708 [*Silly Boy*]

SILLY boy, wert you but wise,
Thou hadst no need of eyes;
But wanting them as well as wit,
How canst thou find the way to hit?
Away, you wag! Away, away, away!
Leave off your cunning play;
You shall not feel my heart.
Poor knave! He does inquire about.
And now his hand hath found it out.
Oh, there he sticks his dart!

(1959)

709 *A Mess of Nonsense*

UPON a dark, light, gloomy, sunshine day,
As I in August walked to gather may,
It was at noon near ten o'clock at night;
The sun being set did shine exceeding bright.
I with mine eyes began to hear a noise,
And turned my ears about to see the voice,
When from a cellar seven storeys high
With loud low voice Melpomene did cry:
'What sober madness hath possessed your brains?
And, men of no place, shall your easy pains
Be thus rewarded? Passing Smithfield bars,
Cast up thy blear-eyed eyes down to the stars,
And see the Dragon's head in quartile move.
Now Venus is with Mercury in love;
Mars patient rages in a fustian fume,
And Jove will be revenged or quit the room;
Mild Juno, beauteous Saturn, Martia free,
At ten leagues' distance now assembled be.
Then shut your eyes and see bright Iris mount
Five hundred fathoms deep by just account,

709 Melpomene] Muse of tragedy bars] barriers Iris] the rainbow

And with a noble ignominious train
Pass flying to the place where Mars was slain.'
Thus silently she spake, whilst I, mine eyes
Fixed on the ground, advancèd to the skies,
And then, not speaking any word, replied:
'Our noble family is near allied
To that renownèd peasant George a Green,
Stout Wakefield pinner, he that stood between
Achilles and the fierce Eacides,
And them withstood with most laborious ease;
Yet whilst that Boreas and kind Auster lie
Together, and at once the same way fly,
And that unmovèd wandering fixèd star
That bloody peace foretells, and patient war,
And scares the Earth with fiery apparitions,
And plants in men both good and bad conditions,
  I ever will with my weak able pen
  Subscribe myself your servant
    Francis Ben.'

(1655)

WILLIAM HAMMOND
fl. 1655–1685

710 *On the Same [Death of My Dear Brother, Mr. H.S., Drowned]: The Boat*

How well the brittle boat doth personate
      Man's frail estate!
Whose concave, filled with lightsome air, did scorn
      The proudest storm.
Man's fleshy boat bears up; whilst breath doth last,
      He fears no blast.
Poor floating bark, whilst on yon mount you stood,
      Rain was your food:
Now the same moisture, which once made thee grow,
      Doth thee o'erflow.
Rash youth hath too much sail; his giddy path
      No ballast hath;

Eacides] Aeacides; Achilles   Boreas] north wind   Auster] south wind

710 *Brother*] Brother-in-law

He thinks his keel of wit can cut all waves,
And pass those graves;
Can shoot all cataracts, and safely steer
The fourscorth year.
But stoop thine ear, ill-counselled youth, and hark,
Look on this bark.
His emblem, whom it carried, both defied
Storms, yet soon died;
Only this difference: that sunk downward, this
Weighed up to bliss.

(1655)

711 *To the Same [My Dear Sister, Mrs S.]: The Tears*

YOU modern wits, who call this world a star,
Who say the other planets too worlds are,
And that the spots that in the midst are found
Are to the people there islands and ground;
And that the water which surrounds the Earth
Reflects to each, and gives their shining birth;
The brightness of these tears had you but seen
Fallen from her eyes, no argument had been,
To contradict that water here displays
To them, as they to us, sidereous rays.
Her tears have, than the stars, a better right
And a more clear propriety to light.
For stars receive their borrowed beams from far;
These bring their own along with them, and are
Born in the sphere of light. Others may blind
Themselves with weeping much, because they spend
The brightness of their eyes upon their tears;
But hers are inexhaustible; she spares
Beams to her tears, as tapers lend their light;
And should excess of tears rob her of sight,
Two of these moist sparks might restore 't. Our eyes
An humour watery crystalline comprise:
Why may not then two crystal drops restore
That sight a crystal humour gave before?
Love dews his locks here, woos each drop to fall
A pupil in his eye, and sight recall;
And I hope fortune passing through this rain
Will, at last, see to recompense her pain.

(1655)

711 sidereous] starry, sidereal propriety] fitness, property

JOHN COLLOP
1625–post 1676

712

The Praise of a Yellow Skin; or, An Elizabeth in Gold

THE sun, when he enamels day,
No other colour doth display.
Lilies, ashamed thou shouldst outvie,
Themselves from white to yellow die.
Thy arms are wax, nay honey too
Colour and sweetness hath from you.
But when thy neck doth but appear,
I think I view an Indie there.
Can passion reason then befool,
Where such an empress beareth rule?
Thy yellow breasts are hills of fire
To heat, not snow to quench desire.
Ransack Peru and Tagus shore,
And then vie treasure: thou'lt be poor.
Let wretches delve for yellow ore:
A golden skin I ask, no more.
  Sure Jove descending in a yellow shower
To rival me, thus gilt my Danaë over.

(1656)

THOMAS STANLEY
1625–1678

713

The Glow-worm

STAY, fairest Chariessa, stay and mark
This animated gem, whose fainter spark
Of fading light its birth had from the dark.

A star thought by the erring passenger,
Which falling from its native orb dropped here,
And makes the Earth, its centre, now its sphere.

Elizabeth] (1) coin; (2) Queen Elizabeth die] (1) dye; (2) die vie] match in competition

713 passenger] traveller orb] cosmic sphere

Should many of these sparks together be,
He that the unknown light far off should see
Would think it a terrestrial galaxy.

Take it up, fair saint; see how it mocks thy fright:
The paler flame doth not yield heat, though light,
Which thus deceives thy reason through thy sight.

But see how quickly it, taken up, doth fade,
To shine in darkness only being made;
By th' brightness of thy light turned to a shade,

And burnt to ashes by thy flaming eyes,
On the chaste altar of thy hand it dies,
As to thy greater light a sacrifice.

(1651)

714 *Celia Singing*

ROSES in breathing forth their scent,
Or stars their borrowed ornament;
Nymphs in the watery sphere that move,
Or angels in their orbs above;
The wingèd chariot of the light,
Or the slow silent wheels of night;
The shade which from the swifter sun
Doth in a circular motion run;
Or souls that their eternal rest do keep,
Make far more noise than Celia's breath in sleep.

But if the angel which inspires
This subtle frame with active fires
Should mould this breath to words, and those
Into a harmony dispose,
The music of this heavenly sphere
Would steal each soul out at the ear,
And into plants and stones infuse
A life that cherubins would choose;
And with new powers invert the laws of fate,
Kill those that live, and dead things animate.

(1651)

715 *To Celia Pleading Want of Merit*

DEAR, urge no more that killing cause
Of our divorce;
Love is not fettered by such laws,
Nor bows to any force:
Though thou deniest I should be thine,
Yet say not thou deserv'st not to be mine.

Oh rather frown away my breath
With thy disdain,
Or flatter me with smiles to death;
By joy or sorrow slain,
'Tis less crime to be killed by thee,
Than I thus cause of mine own death should be.

Thyself of beauty to divest
And me of love,
Or from the worth of thine own breast
Thus to detract, would prove
In us a blindness, and in thee
At best a sacrilegious modesty.

But, Celia, if thou wilt despise
What all admire,
Nor rate thyself at the just price
Of beauty or desire,
Yet meet my flames and thou shalt see
That equal love knows no disparity.

(1651)

716 *Love Deposed*

YOU that unto your mistress' eyes
Your hearts do sacrifice,
And offer sighs or tears at love's rich shrine,
Renounce with me
The idolatry,
Nor this infernal power esteem divine.

The brand, the quiver, and the bow,
Which we did first bestow,
And he as tribute wears from every lover,
I back again
From him have ta'en,
And the imposter now unveiled discover.

I can the feeble child disarm,
Untie his mystic charm,
Divest him of his wings, and break his arrow;
We will obey
No more his sway,
Nor live confined to laws or bounds so narrow.

And you, bright beauties, that inspire
The boy's pale torch with fire,
We safely now your subtle power despise,
And, unscorched, may
Like atoms play
And wanton in the sunshine of your eyes.

Nor think hereafter by new arts
You can bewitch our hearts,
Or raise this devil by your pleasing charm;
We will no more
His power implore,
Unless like Indians, that he do no harm.

(1651)

717 *The Relapse*

OH turn away those cruel eyes,
The stars of my undoing;
Or death in such a bright disguise
May tempt a second wooing.

Punish their blindly impious pride,
Who dare contemn thy glory;
It was my fall that deified
Thy name, and sealed thy story.

Yet no new sufferings can prepare
A higher praise to crown thee;
Though my first death proclaim thee fair,
My second will unthrone thee.

Lovers will doubt thou canst entice
No other for thy fuel,
And if thou burn one victim twice,
Both think thee poor and cruel.

(1651)

718 *The Grasshopper*

GRASSHOPPER thrice happy! who
Sipping the cool morning dew
Queenlike chirpest all the day
Seated on some verdant spray;
Thine is all whate'er Earth brings,
Or the hours with laden wings;
Thee the ploughman calls his joy,
'Cause thou nothing dost destroy:
Thou by all art honoured; all
Thee the spring's sweet prophet call;
By the Muses thou admired,
By Apollo art inspired,
Ageless, ever singing, good,
Without passion, flesh or blood;
Oh how near thy happy state
Comes the gods to imitate!

(1651)

719 [*The Pythagoric Letter*]

THE Pythagoric letter, two ways spread,
Shows the two paths in which man's life is led:
The right-hand track to sacred virtue tends;
Though steep and rough at first, in rest it ends;
The other broad and smooth, but from its crown,
On rocks the traveller is tumbled down.
He who to virtue by harsh toils aspires,
Subduing pains, worth and renown acquires;
But who seeks slothful luxury, and flies
The labour of great acts, dishonoured dies.

(1660)

720 *On a Violet in Her Breast*

SEE how this violet which before
  Hung sullenly her drooping head,
As angry at the ground that bore

719 *Pythagoric*] Pythagorean   letter] i.e. Upsilon (Y)

The purple treasure which she spread,
Doth smilingly erected grow,
Transplanted to those hills of snow.

And whilst the pillows of thy breast
Do her reclining head sustain,
She swells with pride to be so blest,
And doth all other flowers disdain,
Yet weeps that dew which kissed her last,
To see her odours so surpassed.

Poor flower! How far deceived thou wert,
To think the riches of the morn,
Or all the sweets she can impart,
Could these or sweeten or adorn;
Since thou from them dost borrow scent,
And they to thee lend ornament.

(1647–8)

ANONYMOUS
fl. 1656

721 *On the Bible*

BEHOLD this little volume here enrolled:
'Tis the Almighty's present to the world.
Hearken Earth, Earth: each senseless thing can hear
His maker's thunder, though it want an ear.
God's word is senior to his work; nay, rather,
If rightly weighed, the world may call it father.
God spake, 'twas done; this great foundatïon
Was but the maker's exhalatïon,
Breathed out in speaking. The least work of man
Is better than his word; but if we scan
God's word aright, his works far short do fall:
The word is God, the works are creatures all.
The sundry pieces of this general frame
Are dimmer letters, all which spell the same
Eternal word. But these cannot express
His greatness with such easy readiness,
And therefore yield. For heaven shall pass away,
The sun, the moon, the stars, shall all obey

To light one general bonfire; but his word,
His builder-up, his all-destroying sword
Yet still survives: no jot of that can die,
Each tittle measures immortality.
Once more this mighty word his people greets,
Thus lapped and thus swathed up in paper sheets.
Read here God's image with a zealous eye,
The legible and written deity.

(1656)

722 *How to Choose a Mistress*

HER for a mistress would I fain enjoy
That hangs out lip and pouts at every toy;
Speaks like a wag, is bold, dares stoutly stand,
And bids love welcome with a wanton hand:
If she be modest wise and chaste of life,
Hang her she's good for nothing but a wife.

(1656)

723 *Fortune's Legacy*

BLIND fortune, if thou wants a guide,
I'll show thee how thou shalt divide,
Distribute unto each his due:
Justice is blind and so are you.
To the usurer this doom impart,
May scriveners break, and then his heart;
His debtors all to beggary call,
Or, what's as bad, turn courtiers all.
Unto the tradesmen that sell dear,
A long vacation all the year;
Revenge us too for their deceits
By sending wives light as their weights.
But fortune how wilt recompense
The Frenchmen's daily insolence?
That they may know no greater pain,
May they return to France again.
To lovers, that will not believe
Their sweet mistakes, thy blindness give.
And, lest the players should grow poor,
Give them *Aglauras* more and more.

723 doom] judgement scriveners] brokers break] go bankrupt *Aglauras*] plays like Sir John Suckling's *Aglaura* (1638)

To Physicians, if thou please,
Give them another new disease.
To scholars give, if thou canst do 't,
A benefice without a suit.
To court lords grant monopolies,
And to their wives communities:
So, fortune, thou shalt please them all,
When lords do rise and ladies fall.
Give to the lawyers, I beseech,
As much for silence as for speech.
Give ladies' ushers strength of back,
And unto me a cup of sack.

(1656)

HENRY HALSWELL
fl. 1656

724 *Upon Mr Hopton's Death*

GRIEF'S prodigals, where are you? Unthrifts, where?
Whose tears and sighs extemporary are,
Poured out, not spent; who never ask a day
Your debt of sorrow on the grave to pay,
But as if one hour's mourning could suffice,
Dare think it now no sin to have dry eyes.
Away, profane not Hopton's death, nor shame
His grave with grief not worthy of that name:
Sorrow conceived and vented both together,
Like prayers of Puritans, or in foul weather
The sailors' forced devotion, when in fear
They pray this minute, and the next they swear.
No, I must meet with men, men that do know
How to compute their tears and weigh their woe;
That can set down in an exact account
To what the loss of Hopton doth amount;
Tell you particulars, how much of truth,
Of unmatched virtue and untainted youth,
Is gone with him; and, having summed all, look
Like bankrupt merchants on their table-book,

communities] common ownerships of (1) goods; (2) their persons

724 table-book] memorandum-book

With eyes confounded and amazed, to find
The poor and blank remainder left behind.

(1656)

SIR ROBERT HOWARD
1626–1698

725 *To the Unconstant Cynthia: a Song*

TELL me once, dear, how it does prove
That I so much forsworn could be?
I never swore always to love,
I only vowed still to love thee;
  And art thou now what thou wert then,
  Unsworn unto by other men?

In thy fair breast and once-fair soul,
I thought my vows were writ alone;
But others' oaths so blurred the scroll
That I no more could read my own.
  And am I still obliged to pay
  When you had thrown the bond away?

Nor must we only part in joy:
Our tears as well must be unkind;
Weep you, that could such truth destroy,
And I, that could such falseness find.
  Thus we must unconcerned remain
  In our divided joys and pain.

Yet we may love, but on this different score:
You what I am, I what you were before.

(1660)

725 still (l. 4)] ever

ROBERT WILD
fl. 1656?

726 *An Epitaph on Some Bottles of Sack and Claret Laid in Sand*

ENTER and see this tomb, sirs, do not fear:
No spirits but of sack will fright you here;
Weep o'er this tomb, your waters here may have
Wine for their sweet companion in this grave.
A dozen Shakespeares here interred do lie,
Two dozen Jonsons full of poetry.
Unhappy grapes, could not one pressing do,
But now at last you must be buried too?
'Twere commendable sacrilege, no doubt,
Could I come at your graves to steal you out.
Sleep on but scorn to die, immortal liquor,
The burying of thee thus shall make thee quicker.
Meanwhile thy friends pray loud that thou mayst have
A speedy resurrection from thy grave.

(1656)

HUGH CROMPTON
fl. 1657

727 *Epigram VII: Winifred*

SHE is facetious, of a gentle nature,
Well educated, of a seemly stature,
Pleasant and lovely, full of witty knacks.
She has all perfections, and there's none she lacks:
She's young, she's old, she is both stale and new,
She is a virgin and a woman too.
She is religious; nay, I'll tell you more:
She is a lady and she is a whore.

(1658)

726 quicker] (1) livelier; (2) quicker acting

728 *Epigram LXVII: Time, the Interpreter*

WHAT serious students with their busied brains
Could ne'er unlock; what philosophic pains
Tried, and fell short of; what strong art ne'er wist;
What was a theme too hard for th' alchemist;
What mighty Merlin in his operation,
Foresight, prediction, and prognostication
Could not unroll, time has now detected.
Yet still he is despised and disrespected:
There's no man crowns him with a wreath of praise
Composed of laurel triumph, though his ways
Are rules of truth; while error boldly draws
Worlds of applause to her insatiate claws.
Infected animals, how are ye blinded
With misty judgements? How inticed and winded
With strange belief? How nimble, and how prone
To build on rottenness? Rely upon
Deluding motives? Making declination
From the firm basis of true revelation.
Purge your opinions, you unbridled youths;
For time, not artists, will declare our truths.

(1658)

HENRY BOLD
1627–1683

729 CHLORIS, forbear awhile,
  Do not o'erjoy me;
Urge not another smile
  Lest it destroy me.
That beauty pleases most,
  And is best taking,
Which soon is won, soon lost,
  Kind yet forsaking.
I love a coming lady, faith! I do;
But now and then I'd have her scornful too.

winded] turned aside   artists] scientists

729 coming] forward

O'ercloud those eyes of thine,
Bo-peep thy features;
Warm with an April shine,
Scorch not thy creatures:
Still to display thy ware,
Still to be fooling,
Argues how rude you are
In Cupid's schooling.
Disdain begets a suit, scorn draws us nigh:
'Tis cause I would and cannot, makes me try.

Fairest, I'd have thee wise:
When gallants view thee
And court, do thou despise;
Fly, they'll pursue thee.
Fasts move an appetite,
Make hunger greater;
Who's stinted of delight
Falls to 't the better.
Be kind and coy by turns, be calm and rough!
And buckle now and then, and that's enough.

(1656)

JOHN HALL
1627–1656

730 *The Call*

ROMIRA, stay,
And run not thus like a young roe away;
No enemy
Pursues thee, foolish girl, 'tis only I:
I'll keep off harms,
If thou'll be pleased to garrison mine arms.
What, dost thou fear
I'll turn a traitor? May these roses here
To paleness shred,
And lilies stand disguisèd in new red,
If that I lay
A snare wherein thou wouldst not gladly stay.

729 Still] Always buckle] (1) submit; (2) come to close quarters

See, see, the sun
Does slowly to his azure lodging run;
Come, sit but here,
And presently he'll quit our hemisphere:
So, still among
Lovers, time is too short or else too long;
Here will we spin
Legends for them that have love-martyrs been;
Here on this plain
We'll talk Narcissus to a flower again.
Come here, and choose
On which of these proud plats thou would repose;
Here mayst thou shame
The rusty violets, with the crimson flame
Of either cheek,
And primroses white as thy fingers seek;
Nay, thou mayst prove
That man's most noble passion is to love.

(1646)

731 *An Epicurean Ode*

SINCE that this thing we call the world
By chance on atoms is begot,
Which though in daily motions hurled
Yet weary not,
How doth it prove
Thou art so fair, and I in love?

Since that the soul doth only lie
Immersed in matter, chained in sense,
How can, Romira, thou and I
With both dispense,
And thus ascend
In higher flights than wings can lend?

Since man's but pasted up of earth,
And ne'er was cradled in the skies,
What *terra lemnia* gave thee birth?
What diamond, eyes?
Or thou alone,
To tell what others were, came down?

(1646)

still] ever plats] patches of grass prove] test by experience

731 *terra lemnia*] the place where Vulcan fell from heaven

ANONYMOUS

fl. before 1658

732 *On the Death of Mr Persall's Little Daughter in the Beginning of the Spring, at Amsterdam*

SAY not, because no more you see
In the fair arms of her mother tree
  This infant bloom, the wind of time
  Has nipped the flower before the prime;
Or whate'er autumn promised to make good
In early fruit is withered in the bud;

But, as when roses breathe away
Their sweet consenting souls, none say
  The still deflowers those virgin leaves,
  But them extracts, exalts, receives,
Even so has heaven's almighty chemic here
Drawn this pure spirit to its proper sphere.

Sad parents, then, recall your griefs:
Your little one now truly lives,
  Your pretty messenger of love,
  Your new intelligence above;
Since God created such immortal flowers
To grow in his own paradise, not ours.

(1658)

733 *On Melancholy*

STAND off, physician! Let me frolic
With my humour melancholic.
  'Tis pleasure—it is pain likewise;
  'Tis hell, and yet a paradise.
'Tis white and black—'tis all upon
Checkered imagination.
  'Tis an odd-conceited theme;
  'Tis nature's rambling, idle dream;
Her cheating optic glass, which lies,
Falsely abstracts, and multiplies.

chemic] alchemist, chemist   intelligence] (1) spirit; (2) agency for exchange of information

733 optic glass] telescope

The man of Rhodes, whose stature was
Nine hundred camels' load of brass,
  This mighty Phoebus can't compare
  With the meláncholy I bear,
In hands, feet, nose—fancy makes him
Bigger by far in every limb.

Another wasteful humour straight
Brings him down to a half-ounce weight,
  Then, like some bird (a pretty folly!)
  Flies aloft, winged with melancholy!
He's air, or some thin exhalation
Next degree to annihilation.

'Tis thraldom, freedom, 'tis express
Good company, and loneliness;
  It laughs and cries all in one breath;
  'Tis wealth or want, 'tis life or death.
A Bedlam trance, 'tis what you will,
'Tis as you'd have it, well or ill.
  A fickle contradicting mood,
  Arising from distempered blood.

Stand off, physician! 'Tis, I'm sure,
As a disease, so its own cure.

(1658)

734 *On Bond the Usurer*

HERE lies a Bond under this tomb,
Sealed and delivered to—God knows whom.

(1658)

735 *A Question*

I ASK thee whence those ashes were
Which shrine themselves in plaits of hair?
Unknown to me; sure, each morn, dies
A phoenix for a sacrifice.

I ask whence are those airs that fly
From birds in sweetest harmony?
Unknown to me; but sure the choice
Of accents echoed from her voice.

733 exhalation] vapour   express] unmistakably   Bedlam trance] fit

I ask thee whence those active fires
Take light, which glide through burnished air?
Unknown to me; unless there flies
A flash of lightning from her eyes.

I ask thee whence those ruddy blooms
Pierce on her cheeks, on scarlet gowns?
Unknown to me; sure that which flies
From fading roses her cheek dyes.

I'll ask thee of the lily, whence
It gained that type of innocence?
Unknown to me; sure nature's deck
Was ravished from her snowy neck.

(1658)

ANONYMOUS

fl. before 1660

736 *The Lark*

SWIFT through the yielding air I glide
While night's sable shades abide,
Yet in my flight, though ne'er so fast,
I tune and time the wild wind's blast;

And e'er the sun be come about
Teach the young lark her lesson out;
Who, early as the day is born,
Sings his shrill *Ave* to the rising morn.

Let never mortal lose the pain
To imitate my airy strain,
Whose pitch, too high for human ears,
Was set me by the tuneful spheres.

I carol to the faerie king,
Wake him a mornings when I sing,
And when the sun stoops to the deep,
Rock him again and his fair queen asleep.

(1669; wr. before 1660)

736 pain] labour

ANONYMOUS
fl. 1661

737

Carol, for Candlemas Day

CHRISTMAS hath made an end,
  Welladay, welladay;
Which was my dearest friend,
  More is the pity:
For with an heavy heart
Must I from thee depart
To follow plough and cart
  All the year after.

Lent is fast coming on,
  Welladay, welladay;
That loves not any one,
  More is the pity;
For I doubt both my cheeks
Will look thin eating leeks:
Wise is he then that seeks
  For a friend in a corner.

All our good cheer is gone,
  Welladay, welladay;
And turnèd to a bone,
  More is the pity:
In my good master's house
I shall eat no more souse:
Then give me one carouse,
  Gentle kind butler.

It grieves me to the heart,
  Welladay, welladay,
From my friend to depart,
  More is the pity:
Christmas, I mean 'tis thee
That thus forsaketh me;
Yet till one hour I see
  Will I be merry.

(1661)

souse] pigs' feet and ears

JOHN BUNYAN
1628–1688

from *The Pilgrim's Progress*

738

[*Valiant's Song*]

WHO would true valour see,
Let him come hither;
One here will constant be,
Come wind, come weather.
There's no discouragement
Shall make him once relent
His first avowed intent
To be a pilgrim.

Whoso beset him round
With dismal stories
Do but themselves confound:
His strength the more is.
No lion can him fright,
He'll with a giant fight,
But he will have a right
To be a pilgrim.

Hobgoblin nor foul fiend
Can daunt his spirit;
He knows he at the end
Shall life inherit.
Then fancies fly away,
He'll fear not what men say,
He'll labour night and day
To be a pilgrim.

(1684)

N. HOOKES
1628–1712

739 *To Amanda Walking in the Garden*

AND now what monarch would not gardener be,
My fair Amanda's stately gait to see?
How her feet tempt! how soft and light she treads,
Fearing to wake the flowers from their beds!
Yet from their sweet green pillows everywhere,
They start and gaze about to see my fair.
Look at yon flower yonder, how it grows,
Sensibly! how it opes its leaves and blows,
Puts its best Easter clothes on, neat and gay:
Amanda's presence makes it holiday!
Look how on tiptoe that fair lily stands
To look on thee, and court thy whiter hands
To gather it! I saw in yonder crowd—
That tulip bed of which Dame Flora's proud—
A short dwarf flower did enlarge its stalk,
And shoot an inch to see Amanda walk.
Nay, look, my fairest! look how fast they grow
Into a scaffold-method spring! as though,
Riding to Parliament, were to be seen
In pomp and state some royal amorous queen.
The gravelled walks, though even as a die,
Lest some loose pebble should offensive lie,
Quilt themselves o'er with downy moss for thee;
The walls are hanged with blossomed tapestry
To hide their nakedness when looked upon;
The maiden fig-tree puts Eve's apron on;
The broad-leaved sycamore, and every tree,
Shakes like the trembling asp, and bends to thee,
And each leaf proudly strives, with fresher air
To fan the curlèd tresses of thy hair.
Nay, and the bee, too, with his wealthy thigh,
Mistakes his hive, and to thy lips doth fly,
Willing to treasure up his honey there,
Where honeycombs so sweet and plenty are.
Look how that pretty modest columbine
Hangs down its head, to view those feet of thine!
See the fond motion of the strawberry
Creeping on th' earth, to go along with thee!

blows] blooms   scaffold-method] stage-scenery

The lovely violet makes after too,
Unwilling yet, my dear, to part with you;
The knot-grass and the daisies catch thy toes,
To kiss my fair one's feet before she goes;
All court and wish me lay Amanda down,
And give my dear a new green-flowered gown.
  Come, let me kiss thee falling, kiss at rise,
  Thou in the garden, I in paradise.

(1653)

GEORGE VILLIERS, DUKE OF BUCKINGHAM
1628–1687

740 *The Cabin-Boy*

NAY, he could sail a yacht both nigh and large,
Knew how to trim a boat, and steer a barge;
Could say his compass, to the nation's joy,
And swear as well as any cabin-boy.
But not one lesson of the ruling art
Could this dull blockhead ever get by heart.
Look over all the universal frame,
There's not a thing the will of man can name
In which this ugly, perjured rogue delights,
But ducks and loitering, buttered buns and whites.

(1705)

741 *An Epitaph upon Thomas, Lord Fairfax*

  UNDER this stone doth lie
  One born for victory,
Fairfax the valiant, and the only he
Who e'er for that alone a conqueror would be.
Both sexes' virtues were in him combined:
He had the fierceness of the manliest mind
And all the meekness too of womankind.
He never knew what envy was, nor hate;
His soul was filled with worth and honesty,
And with another thing besides, quite out of date,
    Called modesty.

740 *Cabin-Boy*] (Charles II) nigh] close to the wind large] with a favourable wind ducks] i.e. in St James's Park buttered buns] whores and mistresses

He ne'er seemed impudent but in the field, a place
Where impudence itself dares seldom show its face.
Had any stranger spied him in a room
With some of those whom he had overcome,
And had not heard their talk, but only seen
Their gesture and their mien,
They would have sworn he had the vanquished been;
For as they bragged, and dreadful would appear,
Whilst they their own ill luck in war repeated,
His modesty still made him blush to hear
How often he had them defeated.

Through his whole life the part he bore
Was wonderful and great,
And yet it so appeared in nothing more
Than in his private last retreat;
For 'tis a stranger thing to find
One man of such a glorious mind
As can despise the power he hath got,
Than millions of the polls and braves,
Those despicable fools and knaves
Who such a pudder make
Through dullness and mistake
In seeking after power, and get it not.

When all the nation he had won,
And with expence of blood had bought
Store great enough, he thought,
Of fame and of renown,
He then his arms laid down
With full as little pride
As if he'd been of the enemy's side,
Or one of them could do, that were undone.
He neither wealth nor places sought:
For others, not himself, he fought.
He was content to know,
For he had found it so,
That when he pleased to conquer he was able;
And left the spoil and plunder to the rabble.

He might have been a king,
But that he understood
How much it is a meaner thing
To be unjustly great, than honourably good.

polls] passmen   braves] bravos   pudder] muddle

This from the world did admiration draw,
And from his friends both love and awe,
Remembering what he did in fight before.
    Nay his foes loved him too,
    As they were bound to do,
Because he was resolved to fight no more.
So blest of all he died; but far more blest were we
If we were sure to live till we could see
A man as great in war, as just in peace, as he.

(1689?; wr. 1671?)

CHARLES COTTON
1630–1687

742

Song: Montrose

ASK not why sorrow shades my brow,
  Nor why my sprightly looks decay:
Alas! What need I beauty now,
  Since he that loved it died today?

Can ye have ears, and yet not know
  Mirtillo, brave Mirtillo's slain?
Can ye have eyes, and they not flow,
  Or hearts that do not share my pain?

He's gone! he's gone! and I will go;
  For in my breast such wars I have,
And thoughts of him perplex me so
  That the whole world appears my grave.

But I'll go to him, though he lie
  Wrapped in the cold, cold arms of death;
And under yon sad cypress tree
  I'll mourn, I'll mourn away my breath.

(1689; wr. 1650?)

742 Mirtillo] pastoral type-name

743

Morning Quatrains

THE cock has crowed an hour ago,
'Tis time we now dull sleep forgo;
Tired nature is by sleep redressed,
And labour's overcome by rest.

We have outdone the work of night,
'Tis time we rise to attend the light,
And ere he shall his beams display,
To plot new business for the day.

None but the slothful or unsound
Are by the sun in feathers found,
Nor, without rising with the sun,
Can the world's business e'er be done.

Hark! Hark! the watchful chanticleer
Tells us the day's bright harbinger
Peeps o'er the eastern hills, to awe
And warn night's sovereign to withdraw.

The morning curtains now are drawn,
And now appears the blushing dawn;
Aurora has her roses shed,
To strew the way Sol's steeds must tread.

Xanthus and Aethon harnessed are,
To roll away the burning car,
And, snorting flame, impatient bear
The dressing of the charioteer.

The sable cheeks of sullen night
Are streaked with rosy streams of light,
Whilst she retires away in fear,
To shade the other hemisphere.

The merry lark now takes her wings,
And longed-for day's loud welcome sings,
Mounting her body out of sight,
As if she meant to meet the light.

chanticleer] cock   Aurora] Morning (Latin mythology)   Xanthus] horse given to Juno by Neptune   Aethon] horse of Apollo   sullen] dull

Now doors and windows are unbarred,
Each-where are cheerful voices heard,
And round about goodmorrows fly,
As if day taught humanity.

The chimneys now to smoke begin,
And the old wife sits down to spin,
Whilst Kate, taking her pail, does trip
Mulls' swollen and stradling paps to strip.

Vulcan now makes his anvil ring,
Dick whistles loud, and Maud doth sing,
And Silvio with his bugle horn
Winds an imprime unto the morn.

Now through the morning doors behold
Phoebus arrayed in burning gold,
Lashing his fiery steeds, displays
His warm and all-enlightening rays.

Now each one to his work prepares,
All that have hands are labourers,
And manufactures of each trade
By opening shops are open laid.

Hob yokes his oxen to the team,
The angler goes unto the stream,
The woodman to the purlieus hies,
And labouring bees to load their thighs.

Fair Amarillis drives her flocks,
All night safe folded from the fox,
To flowery downs, where Collin stays
To court her with his roundelays.

The traveller now leaves his inn
A new day's journey to begin,
As he would post it with the day,
And early rising makes good way.

Mulls'] Cows' Vulcan] god of blacksmiths (Latin mythology) imprime] dislodging of a deer (hunting) manufactures] goods purlieus] fringes of the forest roundelays] simple songs with refrains post] travel quickly with relays of horses

The slick-faced schoolboy satchel takes,
And with slow pace small riddance makes;
For why, the haste we make, you know,
To knowledge and to virtue's slow.

The fore-horse jingles on the road,
The wagoner lugs on his load,
The field with busy people snies,
And city rings with various cries.

The world is now a busy swarm,
All doing good, or doing harm;
But let's take heed our acts be true,
For heaven's eye sees all we do.

None can that piercing sight evade,
It penetrates the darkest shade;
And sin, though it could scape the eye,
Would be discovered by the cry.

(1689)

744 *Evening Quatrains*

THE day's grown old, the fainting sun
Has but a little way to run;
And yet his steeds, with all his skill,
Scarce lug the chariot down the hill.

With labour spent and thirst oppressed,
Whilst they strain hard to gain the west,
From fetlocks hot drops melted light,
Which turn to meteors in the night.

The shadows now so long do grow
That brambles like tall cedars show,
Molehills seem mountains, and the ant
Appears a monstrous elephant.

A very little little flock
Shades thrice the ground that it would stock;
Whilst the small stripling following them
Appears a mighty Polypheme.

riddance] progress snies] teems

744 Polypheme] cyclops

These being brought into the fold,
And by the thrifty master told,
He thinks his wages are well paid,
Since none are either lost or strayed.

Now lowing herds are each-where heard;
Chains rattle in the villains' yard;
The cart's on tail set down to rest,
Bearing on high the cuckold's crest.

The hedge is stripped, the clothes brought in,
Nought's left without should be within;
The bees are hived, and hum their charm;
Whilst every house does seem a swarm.

The cock now to the roost is prest
For he must call up all the rest;
The sow's fast pegged within the sty,
To still her squeaking progeny.

Each one has had his supping mess,
The cheese is put into the press,
The pans and bowls clean scalded all,
Reared up against the milk-house wall.

And now on benches all are sat
In the cool air to sit and chat,
Till Phoebus, dipping in the west,
Shall lead the world the way to rest.

(1689)

JOHN DANCER

fl. 1660–1707

745 *The Variety*

THOU sayst I swore I loved thee best,
And that my heart lived in thy breast;
And now thou wonderst much that I
Should what I swore then, now deny,

744 told] counted villains' yard] farmyard cuckold's crest] 'horns' of the shafts prest] ready supping mess] suppable food; broth

And upon this thou taxest me
With faithlessness, inconstancy;
Thou hast no reason so to do:
Who can't dissemble ne'er must woo.

That so I loved thee, 'tis confessed;
But 'twas because I judged thee best,
For then I thought that thou alone
Wast virtue's, beauty's paragon:
But now that the deceit I find,
To love thee still were to be blind;
And I must needs confess to thee
I love in love variety.

Alas! Should I love thee alone,
In a short time I should love none;
Who on one well-loved feeds, yet,
Once being cloyed, of all, loathes it.
Wouldst thou be subject to a fate
To make me change my love to hate?
Blame me not, then, since 'tis for love
Of thee, that I inconstant prove.

And yet in truth 'tis constancy,
For which I am accused by thee;
To nature those inconstant are,
Who fix their love on one that's fair;
Why did she, but for our delight,
Present such numbers to our sight?
'Mongst all the earthly kings, there's none
Contented with one crown alone.

(1660)

CLEMENT PAMAN
fl. 1660

746 *On Christmas Day: To My Heart*

Today,
Hark! Heaven sings;
Stretch, tune, my heart!
(For hearts have strings
May bear their part)
And though thy lute were bruised i' the fall,
Bruised hearts may reach an humble pastoral.

Today
Shepherds rejoice,
And angels do
No more: thy voice
Can reach that too:
Bring then at least thy pipe along,
And mingle consort with the angels' song

Today,
A shed that's thatched
(Yet straws can sing)
Holds God; God matched
With beasts; beasts bring
Their song their way: for shame then, raise
Thy notes! Lambs bleat, and oxen bellow praise.

Today,
God honoured man
Not angels: yet
They sing; and can
Raised man forget?
Praise is our debt today, now shall
Angels (man's not so poor) discharge it all?

Today,
Then, screw thee high,
My heart, up to
The angels' key;
Sing 'Glory', do:
What if thy strings all crack and fly?
On such a ground, music 'twill be to die.

(Wr. 1660)

JOHN DRYDEN
1631–1700

Prologues to plays (747–749)

747

from *Oedipus*

WHEN Athens all the Graecian state did guide,
And Greece gave laws to all the world beside,
Then Sophocles with Socrates did sit,
Supreme in wisdom one, and one in wit;

747 Sophocles] author of *Oedipus Rex*

And wit from wisdom differed not in those
But as 'twas sung in verse or said in prose.
Then *Oedipus* on crowded theatres
Drew all admiring eyes and listening ears:
The pleased spectator shouted every line,
The noblest, manliest, and the best design!
And every critic of each learned age
By this just model has reformed the stage.
Now, should it fail (as heaven avert our fear!),
Damn it in silence, lest the world should hear.
For, were it known this poem did not please,
You might set up for perfect savages:
Your neighbours would not look on you as men,
But think the nation all turned Picts again.
Faith, as you manage matters, 'tis not fit
You should suspect yourselves of too much wit.
Drive not the jest too far, but spare this piece,
And for this once be not more wise than Greece.
See twice! Do not pell-mell to damning fall,
Like true born Britains, who ne'er think at all:
Pray be advised; and though at Mons you won,
On pointed cannon do not always run.
With some respect to ancient wit proceed;
You take the four first Councils for your creed.
But when you lay tradition wholly by,
And on the private spirit alone rely,
You turn fanatics in your poetry.
If, notwithstanding all that we can say,
You needs will have your pennyworths of the play,
And come resolved to damn, because you pay,
  Record it, in memorial of the fact,
  The first play buried since the Woollen Act.

(1679)

748

from *The Silent Woman*
To the University of Oxford

WHAT Greece, when learning flourished, only knew
(Athenian judges), you this day renew.
Here too are annual rites to Pallas done,
And here poetic prizes lost or won.
Methinks I see you crowned with olives sit,
And strike a sacred horror from the pit.

747 poem] work   Britains] ancient Britons   Woollen Act] 1678 Act making wool mandatory for shrouds

A day of doom is this of your decree,
Where even the best are but by mercy free:
A day which none but Jonson durst have wished to see.
Here they who long have known the useful stage
Come to be taught themselves to teach the age.
As your commissioners our poets go,
To cultivate the virtue which you sow:
In your Lyceum first themselves refined,
And delegated thence to human kind.
But as ambassadors, when long from home,
For new instructions to their princes come,
So poets who your precepts have forgot
Return, and beg they may be better taught:
Follies and faults elsewhere by them are shown,
But by your manners they correct their own.
The illiterate writer, empiric like, applies
To minds diseased, unsafe, chance remedies:
The learned in schools, where knowledge first began,
Studies with care the anatomy of man;
Sees virtue, vice, and passions in their cause,
And fame from science, not from fortune, draws.
So poetry, which is in Oxford made
An art, in London only is a trade.
There haughty dunces whose unlearned pen
Could ne'er spell grammar, would be reading men.
Such build their poems the Lucretian way,
So many huddled atoms make a play;
And if they hit in order by some chance,
They call that nature, which is ignorance.
To such a fame let mere town wits aspire,
And their gay nonsense their own cits admire.
Our poet, could he find forgiveness here,
Would wish it rather than a *Plaudit* there.
He owns no crown from those Praetorian bands,
But knows that right is in this senate's hands.
Not impudent enough to hope your praise,
Low at the Muses' feet his wreath he lays,
And where he took it up resigns his bays.
Kings make their poets whom themselves think fit,
But 'tis your suffrage makes authentic wit.

(1684; a. 1673)

Lyceum] Athenian garden where Aristotle taught empiric] quack Lucretian way] the random manner described in *De Rerum Naturae* cits] citizens *Plaudit*] call for applause (Latin) bays] laurels

749 from *Love Triumphant*

As, when some treasurer lays down the stick,
Warrants are signed for ready money thick,
And many desperate debentures paid,
Which never had been, had his lordship stayed,
So now this poet, who forsakes the stage,
Intends to gratify the present age.
One warrant shall be signed for every man:
All shall be wits that will, and beaux that can;
Provided still this warrant be not shown,
And you be wits but to yourselves alone.
Provided too you rail at one another;
For there's no one wit will allow a brother.
Provided also that you spare this story,
Damn all the plays that e'er shall come before ye.
If one by chance prove good in half a score,
Let that one pay for all, and damn it more.
For if a good one scape among the crew,
And you continue judging as you do,
Every bad play will hope for damning too.
You might damn this, if it were worth your pains;
Here's nothing you will like: no fustian scenes;
And nothing too of—you know what he means;
No *doubles entendres*, which you sparks allow,
To make the ladies look they know not how,
Simply as 'twere; and knowing both together,
Seeming to fan their faces in cold weather.
But here's a story which no books relate,
Coined from our own old poet's addle-pate.
The fable has a moral too, if sought;
But let that go, for upon second thought,
He fears but few come hither to be taught.
Yet if you will be profited, you may;
And he would bribe you, too, to like his play:
He dies, at least to us, and to the stage,
And what he has, he leaves this noble age.
He leaves you, first, all plays of his inditing,
The whole estate which he has got by writing.
The beaux may think this nothing but vain praise:
They'll find it something, the testator says;
For half their love is made from scraps of plays.
To his worst foes, he leaves his honesty;
That they may thrive upon 't as much as he.

still] always   sparks] fops

He leaves his manners to the roaring boys,
Who come in drunk, and fill the house with noise.
He leaves to the dire critics of his wit
His silence and contempt of all they writ.
To Shakespeare's critic, he bequeaths the curse,
To find his faults, and yet himself make worse:
A precious reader in poetic schools,
Who by his own examples damns his rules.
Last, for the fair, he wishes you may be,
From your dull critics the lampooners, free:
Though he pretends no legacy to leave you,
An old man may at least good wishes give you.
Your beauty names the play; and may it prove
To each an omen of triumphant love.

(1694)

from *Absalom and Achitophel* (750–751)

750 [*Monmouth*]

In pious times, ere priestcraft did begin,
Before polygamy was made a sin;
When man on many multiplied his kind;
Ere one to one was, cursedly, confined;
When nature prompted, and no law denied,
Promiscuous use of concubine and bride;
Then, Israel's monarch, after heaven's own heart,
His vigorous warmth did variously impart
To wives and slaves, and, wide as his command,
Scattered his maker's image through the land.
Michal, of royal blood, the crown did wear,
A soil ungrateful to the tiller's care:
Not so the rest; for several mothers bore
To godlike David, several sons before.
But since like slaves his bed they did ascend,
No true succession could their seed attend.
Of all this numerous progeny was none
So beautiful, so brave as Absolon:
Whether inspired by some diviner lust
His father got him with a greater gust,
Or that his conscious destiny made way
By manly beauty to imperial sway.

750 Israel's monarch] Charles II   Michal] Catherine of Braganza   gust] (1) liking; (2) violent rush   imperial sway] royal power

Early in foreign fields he won renown
With kings and states allied to Israel's crown:
In peace the thoughts of war he could remove,
And seemed as he were only born for love.
Whate'er he did was done with so much ease,
In him alone 'twas natural to please.
His motions all accompanied with grace;
And paradise was opened in his face.
With secret joy, indulgent David viewed
His youthful image in his son renewed:
To all his wishes nothing he denied,
And made the charming Annabel his bride.
What faults he had (for who from faults is free?)
His father could not or he would not see.
Some warm excesses, which the law forbore,
Were cónstrued youth that purged by boiling o'er;
And Ammon's murder, by a specious name,
Was called a just revenge for injured fame.
Thus praised and loved the noble youth remained,
While David, undisturbed, in Sion reigned.
But life can never be sincerely blest:
Heaven punishes the bad, and proves the best.

(1681)

751 [*Shaftesbury*]

OF these the false Achitophel was first:
A name to all succeeding ages cursed;
For close designs and crooked counsels fit;
Sagacious, bold, and turbulent of wit;
Restless, unfixed in principles and place;
In power unpleased, impatient of disgrace:
A fiery soul, which, working out its way,
Fretted the pygmy body to decay,
And o'er-informed the tenement of clay.
A daring pilot in extremity;
Pleased with the danger, when the waves went high
He sought the storms; but, for a calm unfit,
Would steer too nigh the sands, to boast his wit.
Great wits are sure to madness near allied,
And thin partitions do their bounds divide;

accompanied] consorted Annabel] Anne, Countess of Buccleuch Ammon's] ?Sir John Coventry's sincerely] wholly

751 Achitophel] Anthony Ashley Cooper, Earl of Shaftesbury close] secret tenement] lodging

Else, why should he, with wealth and honour blest,
Refuse his age the needful hours of rest?
Punish a body which he could not please;
Bankrupt of life, yet prodigal of ease?
And all to leave what with his toil he won
To that unfeathered, two-legged thing, a son,
Got while his soul did huddled notions try,
And born a shapeless lump, like anarchy.
In friendship false, implacable in hate;
Resolved to ruin or to rule the state.
To compass this, the triple bond he broke,
The pillars of the public safety shook,
And fitted Israel for a foreign yoke.
Then, seized with fear, yet still affecting fame,
Usurped a patriot's all-atoning name.
So easy still it proves in factious times,
With public zeal to cancel private crimes:
How safe is treason, and how sacred ill,
Where none can sin against the people's will!
Where crowds can wink, and no offence be known,
Since in another's guilt they find their own.
Yet fame deserved no enemy can grudge:
The statesman we abhor, but praise the judge.
In Israel's courts ne'er sat an abbethdin
With more discerning eyes, or hands more clean:
Unbribed, unsought, the wretched to redress;
Swift of despatch, and easy of access.
Oh, had he been content to serve the crown
With virtues only proper to the gown,
Or had the rankness of the soil been freed
From cockle that oppressed the noble seed!
David, for him his tuneful harp had strung,
And heaven had wanted one immortal song.
But wild ambition loves to slide, not stand;
And fortune's ice prefers to virtue's land:
Achitophel, grown weary to possess
A lawful fame and lazy happiness,
Disdained the golden fruit to gather free,
And lent the crowd his arm to shake the tree.

(1681)

Got] Conceived huddled] muddled triple bond] Triple Alliance, with Holland and Sweden abbethdin] Jewish judge wanted] lacked

from *Mac Flecknoe*

752 [*Shadwell's Claims*]

ALL human things are subject to decay,
And, when fate summons, monarchs must obey;
This Fleckno found, who, like Augustus, young
Was called to empire, and had governed long:
In prose and verse was owned without dispute
Through all the realms of Nonsense absolute.
This aged prince now flourishing in peace,
And blest with issue of a large increase,
Worn out with business, did at length debate
To settle the succession of the state;
And pondering which of all his sons was fit
To reign, and wage immortal war with wit,
Cried, ''Tis resolved; for nature pleads that he
Should only rule, who most resembles me:
Sh —— alone my perfect image bears,
Mature in dullness from his tender years.
Sh —— alone of all my sons is he
Who stands confirmed in full stupidity.
The rest to some faint meaning make pretence,
But Sh —— never deviates into sense.
Some beams of wit on other souls may fall,
Strike through and make a lucid interval;
But Sh ——'s genuine night admits no ray,
His rising fogs prevail upon the day;
Besides, his goodly fabric fills the eye,
And seems designed for thoughtless majesty:
Thoughtless as monarch oaks that shade the plain,
And, spread in solemn state, supinely reign.
Heywood and Shirley were but types of thee,
Thou last great prophet of tautology . . .'

(1681)

753 from *Religio Laici, or, A Layman's Faith*

DIM as the borrowed beams of moon and stars
To lonely, weary, wandering travellers
Is reason to the soul; and as on high
Those rolling fires discover but the sky,

752 Sh ——] Thomas Shadwell (a rival dramatist) Heywood . . . Shirley] Thomas Heywood . . . James Shirley (earlier dramatists)

Not light us here, so reason's glimmering ray
Was lent not to assure our doubtful way,
But guide us upward to a better day.
And as those nightly tapers disappear
When day's bright lord ascends our hemisphere,
So pale grows reason at religion's sight;
So dies, and so dissolves in supernatural light.
Some few, whose lamp shone brighter, have been led
From cause to cause, to nature's secret head,
And found that one first principle must be;
But what, or who, that universal he:
Whether some soul encompassing this ball
Unmade, unmoved, yet making, moving all;
Or various atoms' interfering dance
Leapt into form (the noble work of chance);
Or this great all was from eternity;
Not even the Stagirite himself could see.
And Epicurus guessed as well as he,
As blindly groped they for a future state,
As rashly judged of providence and fate.
But least of all could their endeavours find
What most concerned the good of human kind;
For happiness was never to be found,
But vanished from 'em like enchanted ground.
One thought content the good to be enjoyed:
This, every little accident destroyed;
The wiser madmen did for virtue toil:
A thorny or at best a barren soil;
In pleasure some their glutton souls would steep,
But found their line too short, the well too deep,
And leaky vessels which no bliss could keep.
Thus anxious thoughts in endless circles roll,
Without a centre where to fix the soul:
In this wild maze their vain endeavours end.
How can the less the greater comprehend,
Or finite reason reach infinity?
For what could fathom God were more than he.

(1682)

the Stagirite] Aristotle

754 *To the Memory of Mr Oldham*

FAREWELL, too little and too lately known,
Whom I began to think and call my own;
For sure our souls were near allied, and thine
Cast in the same poetic mould with mine.
One common note on either lyre did strike,
And knaves and fools we both abhorred alike;
To the same goal did both our studies drive,
The last set out the soonest did arrive.
Thus Nisus fell upon the slippery place,
While his young friend performed and won the race.
O early ripe! To thy abundant store
What could advancing age have added more?
It might (what nature never gives the young)
Have taught the numbers of thy native tongue;
But satire needs not those, and wit will shine
Through the harsh cadence of a rugged line.
A noble error, and but seldom made,
When poets are by too much force betrayed.
Thy generous fruits, though gathered ere their prime,
Still showed a quickness; and maturing time
But mellows what we write to the dull sweets of rhyme.
Once more, hail and farewell; farewell thou young,
But ah too short, Marcellus of our tongue;
Thy brows with ivy and with laurels bound,
But fate and gloomy night encompass thee around.

(1684)

from *The Hind and the Panther*

755 [*The Presbyterians*]

MORE haughty than the rest, the wolfish race
Appear with belly gaunt and famished face;
Never was so deformed a beast of grace.
His ragged tail betwixt his legs he wears
Close clapped for shame, but his rough crest he rears,
And pricks up his predestinating ears.
His wild disordered walk, his haggard eyes,
Did all the bestial citizens surprise.

754 *Oldham*] (John Oldham, 1653–83) Nisus] Aeneas' comrade friend] Euryalus (*Aeneid* V) performed] finished numbers] rhythms Still] Ever Marcellus] the great Roman general, who died aged 20

Though feared and hated, yet he ruled awhile
As captain or companion of the spoil.
Full many a year his hateful head had been
For tribute paid, nor since in Cambria seen:
The last of all the litter scaped by chance,
And from Geneva first infested France.
Some authors thus his pedigree will trace;
But others write him of an upstart race,
Because of Wicliff's brood no mark he brings
But his innate antipathy to kings.
These last deduce him from the Helvetian kind
Who near the Leman lake his consort lined.
That fiery Zvynglius first the affection bred,
And meagre Calvin blessed the nuptial bed.
In Israel some believe him whelped long since,
When the proud Sanhedrin oppressed the prince;
Or, since he will be Jew, derive him higher,
When Corah with his brethren did conspire,
From Moyses' hand the sovereign sway to wrest,
And Aaron of his ephod to divest;
Till opening earth made way for all to pass,
And could not bear the burden of a class.

(1687)

756 *A Song for St Cecilia's Day, 1687*

FROM harmony, from heavenly harmony
This universal frame began.
When nature underneath a heap
Of jarring atoms lay,
And could not heave her head,
The tuneful voice was heard from high,
'Arise ye more than dead.'
Then cold and hot and moist and dry,
In order, to their stations leap,
And MUSIC's power obey.
From harmony, from heavenly harmony
This universal frame began:
From harmony to harmony
Through all the compass of the notes it ran,
The diapason closing full in man.

Wicliff's brood] Wycliffe's brood; Lollards   deduce him] trace his descent   lined] filled   Zvynglius] Ulrich Zwingli, the Swiss Reformer   Moyses'] Moses' (Num. 16)   sway] power (poetic)   class] presbytery

756 *Cecilia's*] (the patron saint of music)   jarring] conflicting

What passion cannot MUSIC raise and quell!
    When Jubal struck the corded shell,
  His listening brethren stood around,
    And wondering, on their faces fell
  To worship that celestial sound.
Less than a god they thought there could not dwell
    Within the hollow of that shell
    That spoke so sweetly and so well.
What passion cannot MUSIC raise and quell!

  The TRUMPET'S loud clangour
    Excites us to arms
  With shrill notes of anger
    And mortal alarms.
  The double double double beat
    Of the thundering DRUM
  Cries 'Hark, the foes come;
Charge, charge, 'tis too late to retreat!'

  The soft complaining FLUTE
  In dying notes discovers
  The woes of hopeless lovers,
Whose dirge is whispered by the warbling LUTE.

  Sharp VIOLINS proclaim
Their jealous pangs and desperation,
Fury, frantic indignation,
Depth of pains, and height of passion
  For the fair, disdainful dame.

  But oh! what art can teach
  What human voice can reach
The sacred ORGAN'S praise?
Notes inspiring holy love,
Notes that wing their heavenly ways
  To mend the choirs above.

Orpheus could lead the savage race;
And trees unrooted left their place,
  Sequacious of the lyre;
But bright CECILIA raised the wonder higher:
When to her ORGAN vocal breath was given,
An angel heard, and straight appeared
  Mistaking Earth for heaven.

Jubal] the first musician (Gen. 4: 21) Orpheus] Apollo's son (his music had magical influence)

Grand CHORUS

As from the power of sacred lays
The spheres began to move,
And sung the great creator's praise
To all the bless'd above,
So when the last and dreadful hour
This crumbling pageant shall devour,
The TRUMPET *shall be heard on high,*
The dead shall live, the living die,
And MUSIC *shall untune the sky.*

(1687)

from *Amphitryon*

757 [*Mercury's Song to Phaedra*]

FAIR Iris I love, and hourly I die,
But not for a lip, nor a languishing eye:
She's fickle and false, and there we agree;
For I am as false and as fickle as she:
We neither believe what either can say,
And, neither believing, we neither betray.

'Tis civil to swear, and say things of course;
We mean not the taking for better for worse.
When present, we love; when absent, agree:
I think not of Iris, nor Iris of me:
The legend of love no couple can find
So easy to part or so equally joined.

(1690)

from *Fables Ancient and Modern* (758–759)

758 *Baucis and Philemon, Out of the Eighth Book of Ovid's Metamorphoses*

THUS Achelous ends; his audience hear
With admiration, and admiring, fear
The powers of heaven; except Ixion's son,
Who laughed at all the gods, believed in none.
He shook his impious head, and thus replies:
These legends are no more than pious lies;
You áttribute too much to heavenly sway,
To think they give us forms, and take away.

The rest of better minds, their sense declared
Against this doctrine, and with horror heard.
Then Lelex rose, an old experienced man,
And thus with sober gravity began:
Heaven's power is infinite: earth, air, and sea,
The manufacture mass, the making power obey.
By proof to clear your doubt: in Phrygian ground
Two neighb'ring trees, with walls encompassed round,
Stand on a moderate rise, with wonder shown,
One a hard oak, a softer linden one.
I saw the place and them, by Pittheus sent
To Phrygian realms, my grandsire's government.
Not far from thence is seen a lake, the haunt
Of coots and of the fishing cormorant;
Here Jove with Hermes came, but in disguise
Of mortal men concealed their deities:
One laid aside his thunder, one his rod,
And many toilsome steps together trod;
For harbour at a thousand doors they knocked,
Not one of all the thousand but was locked.
At last a hospitable house they found,
A homely shed: the roof, not far from ground,
Was thatched with reeds, and straw together bound.
There Baucis and Philemon lived, and there
Had lived long married, and a happy pair;
Now old in love, though little was their store,
Inured to want, their poverty they bore,
Nor aimed at wealth, professing to be poor.
For master or for servant here to call
Was all alike, where only two were all.
Command was none, where equal love was paid,
Or rather both commanded, both obeyed.
From lofty roofs the gods repulsed before,
Now stooping, entered through the little door;
The man (their hearty welcome first expressed)
A common settle drew for either guest,
Inviting each his weary limbs to rest.
But ere they sat, officious Baucis lays
Two cushions stuffed with straw, the seat to raise—
Coarse, but the best she had—then rakes the load
Of ashes from the hearth, and spreads abroad
The living coals; and, lest they should expire,
With leaves and barks she feeds her infant fire:
It smokes; and then with trembling breath she blows,
Till in a cheerful blaze the flames arose.

manufacture] hand made   disguise] deception   officious] attentive, kind

With brushwood and with chips she strengthens these,
And adds at last the boughs of rotten trees.
The fire thus formed, she sets the kettle on
(Like burnished gold the little seether shone),
Next took the coleworts which her husband got
From his own ground (a small well-watered spot);
She stripped the stalks of all their leaves; the best
She culled, and then with handy care she dressed.
High o'er the hearth a chine of bacon hung;
Good old Philemon seized it with a prong,
And from the sooty rafter drew it down,
Then cut a slice, but scarce enough for one,
Yet a large portion of a little store,
Which for their sakes alone he wished were more.
This in the pot he plunged without delay,
To tame the flesh, and drain the salt away.
The time between, before the fire they sat,
And shortened the delay by pleasing chat.
  A beam there was, on which a beechen pail
Hung by the handle on a driven nail:
This filled with water, gently warmed, they set
Before their guests; in this they bathed their feet,
And after with clean towels dried their sweat;
This done, the host produced the genial bed,
Sallow the feet, the borders, and the stead,
Which with no costly coverlet they spread,
But coarse old garments; yet such robes as these
They laid alone at feasts, on holidays.
The good old housewife, tucking up her gown,
The table sets; the invited gods lie down.
The trivet-table of a foot was lame,
A blot which prudent Baucis overcame,
Who thrusts beneath the limping leg a shard:
So was the mended board exactly reared;
Then rubbed it o'er with newly-gathered mint,
A wholesome herb that breathed a grateful scent.
Pallas began the feast, where first was seen
The particoloured olive, black and green;
Autumnal cornels next in order served,
In lees of wine well pickled and preserved.
A garden salad was the third supply,
Of endive, radishes, and succory;
Then curds and cream, the flower of country fare,
And new-laid eggs, which Baucis' busy care

seether] boiling utensil (nonce use) dressed] made ready tame] soften genial] nuptial Pallas] Pallas Athene (to whom the olive was sacred)

Turned by a gentle fire, and roasted rear.
All these in earthenware were served to board;
And next in place, an earthen pitcher stored
With liquor of the best the cottage could afford.
This was the table's ornament and pride,
With figures wrought; like pages at his side
Stood beechen bowls, and these were shining clean,
Varnished with wax without, and lined within.
By this the boiling kettle had prepared,
And to the table sent the smoking lard;
On which with eager appetite they dine,
A savoury bit that served to relish wine;
The wine itself was suiting to the rest,
Still working in the must, and lately pressed.
The second course succeeds like that before:
Plums, apples, nuts, and of their wintry store
Dry figs, and grapes, and wrinkled dates were set
In canisters, to enlarge the little treat;
All these a milk-white honeycomb surround,
Which in the midst the country banquet crowned.
But the kind hosts their entertainment grace
With hearty welcome and an open face:
In all they did, you might discern with ease
A willing mind, and a desire to please.
  Meantime the beechen bowls went round, and still
Though often emptied, were observed to fill;
Filled without hands, and of their own accord
Ran without feet, and danced about the board.
Devotion seized the pair, to see the feast
With wine, and of no common grape, increased;
And up they held their hands, and fell to prayer,
Excusing as they could their country fare.
  One goose they had ('twas all they could allow),
A wakeful sentry, and on duty now,
Whom to the gods for sacrifice they vow:
Her, with malicious zeal, the couple viewed;
She ran for life, and limping they pursued;
Full well the fowl perceived their bad intent,
And would not make her master's compliment,
But, persecuted, to the powers she flies,
And close between the legs of Jove she lies.
He with a gracious ear the suppliant heard,
And saved her life; then what he was declared,
And owned the god. 'The neighbourhood,' said he,

rear] lightly   prepared] readied   relish] impart relish to   working] fermenting   still] ever

'Shall justly perish for impiety:
You stand alone exempted; but obey
With speed, and follow where we lead the way;
Leave these accursed, and to the mountain's height
Ascend; nor once look backward in your flight.'
They haste, and what their tardy feet denied,
The trusty staff (their better leg) supplied.
An arrow's flight they wanted to the top,
And there secure, but spent with travel, stop;
Then turn their now no more forbidden eyes.
Lost in a lake the floated level lies:
A watery desert covers all the plains;
Their cot alone, as in an isle, remains:
Wondering with weeping eyes, while they deplore
Their neighbours' fate and country now no more,
Their little shed, scarce large enough for two,
Seems, from the ground increased, in height and bulk to grow.
A stately temple shoots within the skies,
The crotches of their cot in columns rise:
The pavement polished marble they behold,
The gates with sculpture graced, the spires and tiles of gold.
Then thus the sire of gods, with look serene:
'Speak thy desire, thou only just of men;
And thou, O woman, only worthy found
To be with such a man in marriage bound.'
A while they whisper; then to Jove addressed,
Philemon thus prefers their joint request:
'We crave to serve before your sacred shrine,
And offer at your altars rites divine;
And since not any action of our life
Has been polluted with domestic strife,
We beg one hour of death, that neither she
With widow's tears may live to bury me,
Nor weeping I, with withered arms may bear
My breathless Baucis to the sepulchre.'
The godheads sign their suit. They run their race
In the same tenor all the appointed space;
Then, when their hour was come, while they relate
These past adventures at the temple gate,
Old Baucis is by old Philemon seen
Sprouting with sudden leaves of spritely green:
Old Baucis looked where old Philemon stood,
And saw his lengthened arms a sprouting wood;
New roots their fastened feet begin to bind,

crotches] supporting poles

Their bodies stiffen in a rising rind;
Then ere the bark above their shoulders grew,
They give and take at once their last adieu:
At once 'Farewell, O faithful spouse,' they said;
At once the encroaching rinds their closing lips invade.
Even yet, an ancient Tyanaean shows
A spreading oak that near a linden grows;
The neighbourhood confirm the prodigy:
Grave men, not vain of tongue or like to lie.
I saw myself the garlands on their boughs,
And tablets hung for gifts of granted vows;
And offering fresher up, with pious prayer,
The good, said I, are God's peculiar care,
And such as honour heaven shall heavenly honour share.

(1700)

from *Theodore and Honoria, From Boccace*

759 [*Disdain Punished*]

Of all the cities in Romanian lands,
The chief and most renowned Ravenna stands,
Adorned in ancient times with arms and arts,
And rich inhabitants with generous hearts.
But Theodore the brave, above the rest,
With gifts of fortune and of nature blessed,
The foremost place for wealth and honour held,
And all in feats of chivalry excelled.
  This noble youth to madness loved a dame
Of high degree, Honoria was her name,
Fair as the fairest, but of haughty mind,
And fiercer than became so soft a kind;
Proud of her birth (for equal she had none);
The rest she scorned, but hated him alone.
His gifts, his constant courtship, nothing gained;
For she, the more he loved, the more disdained:
He lived with all the pomp he could devise,
At tilts and tournaments obtained the prize,
But found no favour in his lady's eyes;
Relentless as a rock, the lofty maid
Turned all to poison that he did or said;
Nor prayers, nor tears, nor offered vows could move;
The work went backward; and the more he strove

759 *Boccace*] Boccaccio   Romanian] of Romagna   kind] nature; sex   pomp] magnificence

To advance his suit, the further from her love.
  Wearied at length, and wanting remedy,
He doubted oft, and oft resolved to die;
But pride stood ready to prevent the blow,
For who would die to gratify a foe?
His generous mind disdained so mean a fate;
That passed, his next endeavour was to hate.
But vainer that relief than all the rest,
The less he hoped with more desire possessed;
Love stood the siege, and would not yield his breast.
  Change was the next, but change deceived his care:
He sought a fairer, but found none so fair.
He would have worn her out by slow degrees,
As men by fasting starve the untamed disease;
But present love required a present ease.
Looking, he feeds alone his famished eyes,
Feeds lingering death; but looking not he dies.
Yet still he chose the longest way to fate,
Wasting at once his life and his estate.
  His friends beheld, and pitied him in vain,
For what advice can ease a lover's pain?
Absence, the best expedient they could find,
Might save the fortune, if not cure the mind:
This means they long proposed, but little gained,
Yet after much pursuit at length obtained.
  Hard, you may think it was, to give consent,
But, struggling with his own desires, he went,
With large expence, and with a pompous train
Provided, as to visit France or Spain,
Or for some distant voyage o'er the main.
But love had clipped his wings, and cut him short,
Confined within the purlieus of his court:
Three miles he went, nor further could retreat;
His travels ended at his country seat:
To Chassi's pleasing plains he took his way,
There pitched his tents, and there resolved to stay.
  The spring was in the prime, the neighbouring grove
Supplied with birds, the choristers of love:
Music unbought, that ministered delight
To morning walks, and lulled his cares by night.
There he discharged his friends, but not the expence
Of frequent treats and proud magnificence.
He lived as kings retire, though more at large
From public business, yet with equal charge;

wanting] lacking   still] ever   pompous train] magnificent retinue   Chassi's] Chiassi's

With house and heart still open to receive,
As well content as love would give him leave:
He would have lived more free; but many a guest,
Who could forsake the friend, pursued the feast.
It happed one morning, as his fancy led,
Before his usual hour he left his bed,
To walk within a lonely lawn that stood
On every side surrounded by the wood:
Alone he walked, to please his pensive mind,
And sought the deepest solitude to find;
'Twas in a grove of spreading pines he strayed;
The winds within the quivering branches played,
And dancing trees a mournful music made.
The place itself was suiting to his care,
Uncouth and savage as the cruel fair.
He wandered on, unknowing where he went,
Lost in the wood, and all on love intent:
The day already half his race had run,
And summoned him to due repast at noon,
But love could feel no hunger but his own.
While list'ning to the murmuring leaves he stood,
More than a mile immersed within the wood,
At once the wind was laid; the whispering sound
Was dumb; a rising earthquake rocked the ground;
With deeper brown the grove was overspread:
A sudden horror seized his giddy head,
And his ears tinkled, and his colour fled.
Nature was in alarm; some danger nigh
Seemed threatened, though unseen to mortal eye:
Unused to fear, he summoned all his soul
And stood collected in himself, and whole.
Not long; for soon a whirlwind rose around,
And from afar he heard a screaming sound,
As of a dame distressed who cried for aid
And filled with loud laments the secret shade.
A thicket close beside the grove there stood,
With briars and brambles choked, and dwarfish wood;
From thence the noise; which now approaching near
With more distinguished notes invades his ear:
He raised his head, and saw a beauteous maid,
With hair dishevelled, issuing through the shade;
Stripped of her clothes, and even those parts revealed
Which modest nature keeps from sight concealed.
Her face, her hands, her naked limbs were torn

tinkled] tingled

With passing through the brakes and prickly thorn;
Two mastiffs gaunt and grim her flight pursued,
And oft their fastened fangs in blood imbrued:
Oft they came up and pinched her tender side:
'Mercy, oh mercy, heaven,' she ran, and cried;
When heaven was named they loosed their hold again,
Then sprung she forth, they followed her amain.
  Not far behind, a knight of swarthy face
High on a coal-black steed pursued the chase:
With flashing flames his ardent eyes were filled,
And in his hands a naked sword he held;
He cheered the dogs to follow her who fled,
And vowed revenge on her devoted head.
  As Theodore was born of noble kind,
The brutal action roused his manly mind:
Moved with unworthy usage of the maid,
He, though unarmed, resolved to give her aid.
A sapling pine he wrenched from out the ground,
The readiest weapon that his fury found.
Thus furnished for offence, he crossed the way
Betwixt the graceless villain and his prey.
  The knight came thundering on, but from afar
Thus in imperious tone forbade the war:
'Cease, Theodore, to proffer vain relief,
Nor stop the vengeance of so just a grief;
But give me leave to seize my destined prey,
And let eternal justice take the way:
I but revenge my fate; disdained, betrayed,
And suffering death for this ungrateful maid.'
  He said; at once dismounting from the steed;
For now the hell-hounds with superior speed
Had reached the dame, and fastening on her side,
The ground with issuing streams of purple dyed.
Stood Theodore surprised in deadly fright,
With chattering teeth and bristling hair upright;
Yet armed with inborn worth, 'Whate'er,' said he,
'Thou art, who knowst me better than I thee,
Or prove thy rightful cause, or be defied.'
The spectre, fiercely staring, thus replied:
  'Know, Theodore, thy ancestry I claim,
And Guido Cavalcanti was my name.
One common sire our fathers did beget,
My name and story some remember yet;
Thee, then a boy, within my arms I laid,

devoted] doomed; cursed   grief] anger

When for my sins I loved this haughty maid;
Not less adored in life, nor served by me,
Than proud Honoria now is loved by thee.
What did I not her stubborn heart to gain?
But all my vows were answered with disdain;
She scorned my sorrows, and despised my pain.
Long time I dragged my days in fruitless care;
Then loathing life, and plunged in deep despair,
To finish my unhappy life, I fell
On this sharp sword, and now am damned in hell.
'Short was her joy; for soon the insulting maid
By heaven's decree in the cold grave was laid,
And as in unrepenting sin she died,
Doomed to the same bad place, is punished for her pride,
Because she deemed I well deserved to die,
And made a merit of her cruelty.
There, then, we met; both tried and both were cast,
And this irrevocable sentence passed:
That she whom I so long pursued in vain
Should suffer from my hands a lingering pain;
Renewed to life that she might daily die;
I daily doomed to follow, she to fly.
No more a lover but a mortal foe,
I seek her life (for love is none below):
As often as my dogs with better speed
Arrest her flight is she to death decreed.
Then with this fatal sword on which I died
I pierce her opened back or tender side,
And tear that hardened heart from out her breast,
Which, with her entrails, makes my hungry hounds a feast.
Nor lies she long, but as her fates ordain
Springs up to life, and fresh to second pain
Is saved today, tomorrow to be slain.'

(1700)

insulting] exulting scornfully   cast] condemned

KATHERINE PHILIPS
1632–1664

760 *To the Excellent Mrs Anne Owen, upon Her Receiving the Name of Lucasia, and Adoption into Our Society. 28 December 1651*

We are complete, and fate hath now
No greater blessing to bestow:
Nay, the dull world must now confess
We have all worth, all happiness.
Annals of state are trifles to our fame,
Now 'tis made sacred by Lucasia's name.

But as though through a burning-glass
The sun more vigorous doth pass,
It still with general freedom shines;
For that contracts, but not confines:
So though by this her beams are fixèd here,
Yet she diffuses glories everywhere.

Her mind is so entirely bright,
The splendour would but wound our sight,
And must to some disguise submit,
Or we could never worship it;
And we by this relation are allowed
Lustre enough to be Lucasia's cloud.

Nations will own us now to be
A temple of divinity;
And pilgrims shall ten ages hence
Approach our tombs with reverence.
May then that time which did such bliss convey
Be kept with us perpetual holy day!

(1664)

761 *To My Excellent Lucasia, on Our Friendship*

I did not live until this time
Crowned my felicity,
When I could say without a crime,
'I am not thine, but thee.'

This carcase breathed, and walked, and slept,
So that the world believed
There was a soul the motions kept;
But they were all deceived.

For as a watch by art is wound
To motion, such was mine;
But never had Orinda found
A soul till she found thine;

Which now inspires, cures, and supplies,
And guides my darkened breast:
For thou art all that I can prize,
My joy, my life, my rest.

No bridegroom's nor crown-conqueror's mirth
To mine compared can be:
They have but pieces of this Earth,
I've all the world in thee.

Then let our flames still light and shine,
And no false fear control,
As innocent as our design,
Immortal as our soul.

(1664)

762 *L'Amitie: To Mrs M. Awbrey*

SOUL of my soul, my joy, my crown, my friend!
A name which all the rest doth comprehend;
How happy are we now, whose souls are grown,
By an incomparable mixture, one:
Whose well-acquainted minds are now as near
As love, or vows, or friendship can endear.
I have no thought but what's to thee revealed,
Nor thou desire that is from me concealed.
Thy heart locks up my secrets richly set,
And my breast is thy private cabinet.
Thou shedst no tear but what my moisture lent,
And if I sigh, it is thy breath is spent.
United thus, what horror can appear
Worthy our sorrow, anger, or our fear?

Orinda] Katherine Philips control] overwhelm

762 cabinet] treasure-chamber

Let the dull world alone to talk and fight,
And with their vast ambitions nature fright;
Let them despise so innocent a flame,
While envy, pride, and faction play their game;
But we by love sublimed so high shall rise,
To pity kings, and conquerors despise;
Since we that sacred union have engrossed,
Which they and all the factious world have lost.

(1664; wr. 1651)

763 *Orinda to Lucasia*

Observe the weary birds ere night be done,
How they would fain call up the tardy sun:
  With feathers hung with dew,
  And trembling voices too,
They court their glorious planet to appear,
That they may find recruits of spirits there.
  The drooping flowers hang their heads,
  And languish down into their beds,
While brooks more bold and fierce than they,
  Wanting those beams from whence
  All things drink influence,
Openly murmur and demand the day.

Thou, my Lucasia, art far more to me
That he to all the under-world can be;
  From thee I've heat and light,
  Thy absence makes my night.
But ah, my friend, it now grows very long,
The sadness weighty and the darkness strong:
  My tears (its dew) dwell on my cheeks,
  And still my heart thy dawning seeks,
And to thee mournfully it cries
  That if too long I wait
  Even thou mayst come too late,
And not restore my life, but close my eyes.

(1667)

762 sublimed] purified engrossed] formally endorsed

764 *Epitaph: On Her Son H.P. at St Syth's Church, where Her Body also Lies Interred*

WHAT on Earth deserves our trust?
Youth and beauty both are dust.
Long we gathering are with pain,
What one moment calls again.
Seven years' childless marriage past,
A son, a son is born at last:
So exactly limned and fair,
Full of good spirits, mien, and air
As a long life promised;
Yet, in less than six weeks, dead.
Too promising, too great a mind,
In so small room to be confined;
Therefore, as fit in heaven to dwell,
He quickly broke the prison shell.
So the subtle alchemist
Can't with Hermes-seal resist
The powerful spirit's subtler flight,
But 'twill bid him long good night.
And so the sun, if it arise
Half so glorious as his eyes,
Like this infant, takes a shroud,
Buried in a morning cloud.

(1667)

765 *On the Numerous Access of the English to Wait upon the King in Flanders*

HASTEN, great Prince, unto thy British Isles,
Or all thy subjects will become exiles:
To thee they flock, thy presence is their home,
As Pompey's camp, where'er it moved, was Rome.
They that asserted thy just cause go hence,
To testify their joy and reverence;
And they that did not, now, by wonder taught,
Go to confess and expiate their fault;
So that if thou dost stay, thy gasping land
Itself will empty on the Belgic sand;

St Syth's] St Benet's Sherehog (in Syth's Lane)   Hermes-seal] hermetic seal

765 Belgic] Netherlandish

Where the affrighted Dutchman doth profess
He thinks it an invasion, not address.
As we unmonarched were for want of thee,
So till thou come we shall unpeopled be.
None but the close fanatic will remain,
Who by our loyalty his ends will gain;
And he the exhausted land will quickly find
As desolate a place as he designed.
For England, though grown old with woes, will see
Her long denied and sovereign remedy.
So when old Jacob could but credit give
That his prodigious Joseph still did live
(Joseph that was preservèd to restore
Their lives that would have taken his before),
'It is enough', said he: 'to Egypt I
Will go, and see him once before I die.'

(1664)

766 *On the Welsh Language*

IF honour to an ancient name be due,
Or riches challenge it for one that's new,
The British language claims in either sense,
Both for its age and for its opulence.
But all great things must be from us removed,
To be with higher reverence beloved.
So landscapes which in prospects distant lie,
With greater wonder draw the pleasèd eye.
Is not great Troy to one dark ruin hurled,
Once the famed scene of all the fighting world?
Where's Athens now, to whom Rome learning owes,
And the safe laurels that adorned her brows?
A strange reverse of fate she did endure,
Never once greater than she's now obscure.
Even Rome herself can but some footsteps show
Of Scipio's times, or those of Cicero.
And, as the Roman and the Grecian state,
The British fell, the spoil of time and fate.
But though the language hath the beauty lost,
Yet she has still some great remains to boast;
For 'twas in that the sacred bards of old
In deathless numbers did their thoughts unfold.

address] courtship close] secret

766 numbers] verses

In groves, by rivers, and on fertile plains,
They civilized and taught the listening swains,
Whilst with high raptures, and as great success,
Virtue they clothed in music's charming dress.
This Merlin spoke, who in his gloomy cave
Even destiny herself seemed to enslave.
For to his sight the future time was known,
Much better than to others is their own;
And with such state predictions from him fell,
As if he did decree, and not foretell.
This spoke King Arthur, who, if fame be true,
Could have compelled mankind to speak it too.
In this once Boadicca valour taught,
And spoke more nobly than her soldiers fought:
Tell me what hero could do more than she,
Who fell at once for fame and liberty?
Nor could a greater sacrifice belong,
Or to her children's, or her country's wrong.
This spoke Caractacus, who was so brave
That to the Roman fortune check he gave;
And when their yoke he could decline no more,
He it so decently and nobly wore
That Rome herself with blushes did believe
A Briton would the law of honour give,
And hastily his chains away she threw,
Lest her own captive else should her subdue.

(1667)

from *Corneille's Pompey*

767

[*Cornelia's Defiance*]

NOT thither, Caesar, yet;
Till first thy ruin, granted me by fate,
To these loved ashes shall unlock the gate;
And thither (though as dear to Rome as me)
They come not till triumphant over thee.
To Africk I must this rich burden bear,
Where Pompey's sons, Cato and Scipio, are,
Who'll find, I hope (with a brave king allied),
Fortune as well as justice on their side;
And thou shalt see, there with new fury hurled,
Pharsalia's ruins arm another world.

766 swains] shepherds

From rank to rank these ashes I'll expose,
Mixed with my tears, to exasperate thy foes.
My hate shall guide them, too, and they shall fight
With urns instead of eagles in their sight;
That such sad objects may make them intent
On his revenge, and on thy punishment.
Thou to this hero now devout art grown;
But, raising his name, dost exalt thy own.
I must be witness too! And I submit;
But thou canst never move my heart with it.
My loss can never be repaired by fate,
Nor is it possible to exhaust my hate.
This hate shall be my Pompey now, and I
In his revenge will live, and with it die.
But as a Roman, though my hate be such,
I must confess, I thee esteem as much.
Both these extremes justice can well allow:
This does my virtue, that my duty show.
My sense of honour does the first command;
Concern, the last, and they are both constrained.
And as thy virtue, whom none can betray,
Where I should hate, makes me such value pay:
My duty so my anger does create,
And Pompey's widow makes Cornelia hate.
But I from hence shall hasten, and know then,
I'll raise against thee gods as well as men.
Those gods that flattered thee, and me abused,
And in Pharsalia Pompey's cause refused;
Who at his death could thunderbolts refrain,
To expiate that, will his revenge maintain;
If not, his soul will give my zeal such heat,
As I without their help shall thee defeat.
But should all my endeavours prosper ill,
What I can not do, Cleopatra will.
I know thy flame, and that t' obey its force
Thou from Calphurnia study'st a divorce:
Now blinded, thou wouldst this alliance make,
And there's no law of Rome thou dar'st not break.
But know, the Roman youth think it no sin
To fight against the husband of a queen;
And thy offended friends will at the price
Of thy best blood revenge their scorned advice.
  I check thy ruin if I check thy love;
  Adieu; tomorrow will thy honour prove.

(1667)

exasperate] heighten the courage of

768 *Wiston Vault*

AND why this vault and tomb? Alike we must
Put off distinction, and put on our dust.
Nor can the stateliest fabric help to save
From the corruptions of a common grave;
Nor for the resurrection more prepare
Than if the dust were scattered into air.
What then? The ambition's just, say some, that we
May thus perpetuate our memory.
Ah false vain task of art! Ah poor weak man,
Whose monument does more than his merit can!
Who by his friends' best care and love's abused,
And in his very epitaph accused;
For did they not suspect his name would fall,
There would not need an epitaph at all.
But after death too I would be alive,
And shall, if my Lucasia do survive.
I quit these pomps of death, and am content,
Having her heart to be my monument:
Though ne'er stone to me, 'twill stone for me prove
By the peculiar miracles of love.
There I'll inscription have which no tomb gives:
Not 'Here Orinda lies', but 'Here she lives.'

(1664)

THOMAS SHIPMAN
1632–1680

769 from *The Frost, 1654: To Mr W.L.*

THE streams are fettered, and with us as rare
As fountains in Arabian deserts are.
No tears in woman's eyes; their skill is crossed,
And that most ready fountain now is lost.
Our nose-drops freeze to pearls, and jewels there,
Like salvage Indians, we are forced to wear.
Bracelets may now be cheap; our lasses try—
They can spit forth as good as they can buy.

Lucasia] Mrs Anne Owen   Orinda] Katherine Philips

769 salvage] savage (archaic)

Glass furnaces are needless: he's an ass
That will buy any, when he pisses glass.
Surgeons, with all their lancets, do no good:
Our veins are stuffed with coral, not with blood.
To be in the rain, the service now's as hot
As twixt two armies joined: each drop's a shot.
Each hail a bullet, shot with rattling noise;
And snow (white powder) silently destroys.
If now our sheep lie down upon the grass,
You'd swear how each a boronetho was,
And there took rooting; for thus fixed they show
Like snowy hillocks, or like breathing snow.
Fish freeze i' th' deeps, and think 't a happy lot
Now to be caught and put into a pot;
And hares ev'n frozen in their forms do lie,
As they had put themselves into a pie.
  Nature's enslaved, her very breath confined;
Her lungs are stopped and cannot gather wind.
Sometimes she's raging mad, and fiercely blows,
Foaming and frothing all the Earth with snows.
Those downy showers appear (which Boreas brings),
As though the moulting clouds had mewed their wings.
What else is snow but feathered drizzle, blown
From the sky, where their swift pinions late had flown?
No other flights than these now haunt the air,
Till, limed with frost, they're forced to tarry here.
  The air's so thick it does like th' Dead Sea flow,
Where birds, with feathered oars, can scarcely row;
And hollow clouds, rammed full as they can bear,
Discharge hail-shot in volleys through the air.
Those dewdrops that upon the Earth are found,
Right pearls they are, and have the glittering ground.
Wherever any grassy turf is viewed,
It seems a tansy all with sugar strewed.

(1683)

770 *The Kiss, 1656. To Mrs C.*

HOLD not your lips so close; dispense
Treasures, perfúmes, and life from thence.
Squeeze not those full-ripe cherries; this
Becomes a simper, not a kiss.

769 boronetho] 'plant-animal' (S.) Boreas] the north wind mewed] moulted tansy] pudding flavoured with the herb

There's danger to lock up your breath,
It cousin-german is to death.
None bags up wind, the merchant swears,
Unless some wrinkled Laplanders.
What needs this guard? It is small sense
Thus to hedge in a double fence.
Closed lips express but silent blisses,
And at the best are but dumb kisses.
You are with Cupid little kind,
To make him dumb as well as blind.
Such smacks but show a silent state;
Kisses should be articulate.
An open-mouthèd kiss speaks sense:
It is the lover's eloquence.
Let yours speak out, then! There's no bliss
To the pronunciation of a kiss.

(1683)

SAMUEL PORDAGE
1633–1691?

771 [*To Lucia Playing on Her Lute*,] *Another*

When last I heard your nimble fingers play
Upon your lute, nothing so sweet as they
Seemed: all my soul fled ravished to my ear,
That sweetly animating sound to hear.
My ravished heart with play kept equal time,
Fell down with you, with you did ela climb,
Grew sad or lighter, as the tunes you played,
And with your lute a perfect measure made:
If all, so much as I, your music love,
The whole world would at your devotion move,
And, at your speaking lute's surpassing charms,
Embrace a lasting peace, and fling by arms.

(1660)

771 ela] the highest note of the gamut; anything highflown   move] be stirred

ELDRED REVETT

*c.*1635–?

772 *Ode: Hastening His Friend into the Country*

COME, let us down,
Bloat with this smoky town,
And broiled in heat
Of a tumultuous sweat.
Why linger we in coarse flames? Never think
We can burn martyrs here, but out and stink.

Nothing but noise,
The sour-breathed musket's voice,
And with a long blast
The trumpet hoarse at last.
Such still ascending volleys thither fly,
They lay up a new thunder in the sky.

'Tis gross as day
Seen compliment, to stay:
Black patches mend
The faces we attend,
That are but sleeked with size and whited o'er
The hair and rough-cast that was laid before.

That cup, and then
We sleep, to part again.
A fire there reigns,
Hath scorchèd black our veins;
And our Canary faces dashed with wines,
Shot through the windows, blaze the tavern signs.

Let us repair
To the soft winged air,
Which spread a space
Will gently fan the face,
And wipe with the down pennons sweat away,
Leaving them only gilded by the day.

Bloat] Puffed, swollen   sweat] labour; sweating   gross] obvious   pennons] wings (poetic)

Then in some bower
Belies the day's bright hour,
Where sun hath made,
Squeezed in, a curd of shade,
Under a vocal roof of birds we'll lie
That sing us asleep, and are our canopy.

Or underneath
We'll resty fancy breathe,
That else will lie
Tippled in exstasy;
And tune some rhapsody to their wild notes,
That in the leafy belfry chime their throats.

Or harmless sack
Drink from the harvest jack,
Will never flush
Our cheeks with guilty blush;
And view the country girls turn dry the hay,
While their jet eyes frowse it as fast as they.

Glances they throw
To Dick at the next mow.
At night in flocks
Dream fine things in coarse smocks,
And though the sun looks on their faces too full,
Have skins as white as milk, and soft as wool.

(1657)

SIR GEORGE ETHEREGE
1636?–1692?

773 ### *Song*

IF she be not as kind as fair,
But peevish and unhandy,
Leave her—she's only worth the care
Of some spruce Jack-a-dandy.

772 resty] indolent   jack] leathern jug   frowse] ruffle   mow] haystack

I would not have thee such an ass,
  Hadst thou ne'er so much leisure,
To sigh and whine for such a lass
  Whose pride's above her pleasure.

Make much of every buxom girl
  Which needs but little courting;
Her value is above the pearl,
  That takes delight in sporting.

(1664)

774 *The Imperfect Enjoyment*

AFTER a pretty amorous discourse,
She does resist my love with pleasing force,
Moved not with anger but with modesty:
Against her will she is my enemy.
Her eyes the rudeness of her arms excuse,
Those do accept what these seem to refuse;
To ease my passion and to make me blest,
The linen of itself falls from her breast;
Then with her lovely hands she does conceal
Those wonders chance so kindly did reveal.
In vain, alas, her nimble fingers strove
To keep her beauties from my greedy love;
Guarding her breasts, they do her lips expose:
To save a lily she must lose a rose.
What charms are here in every part! What grace!
A hundred hands can't shield each beauteous place.
Now she consents, her force she does recall,
And since I must have part she'll give me all.
Her arms, which did repulse me, now embrace,
And seem to guide me to the fought-for place.
Her love is in her sparkling eyes expressed,
She falls on the bed for pleasure more than rest.
But oh, strange passions! Oh, abortive joy!
My zeal does my devotion quite destroy:
Come to the temple where I should implore
My saint, I worship at the sacred door.
Oh cruel chance! The town which did oppose
My strength so long now yields to my dispose,
When, overjoyed with victory, I fall
Dead at the foot of the surrendered wall.

774 dispose] direction, management

Without the usual ceremony, we
Have both fulfilled the amorous mystery;
The action which we should have jointly done,
Each has unluckily performed alone;
The union which our bodies should enjoy
The union of our eager souls destroy.
Our flames are punished by their own excess—
We'd had more pleasure had our love been less.
She blushed and frowned, perceiving we had done
The sport she thought we had not yet begun.
Alas, said I, condemn yourself, not me;
This is the effect of too much modesty.
Hence with that harmful virtue; the delight
Of both our victories was lost in the fight.
From my defeat your glory does arise,
My weakness proves the vigour of your eyes:
They did consume the victim, ere it came
Unto the altar, with a purer flame.
Phillis, let this same comfort ease your care:
You'd been more happy had you been less fair.

(1672)

WALTER POPE

fl. 1666–1714

775 *The Old Man's Wish*

If I live to grow old (for I find I go down),
Let this be my fate: in a country town
Let me have a warm house, with a stone at the gate,
And a cleanly young girl to rub my bald pate.
  May I govern my passion with an absolute sway,
  And grow wiser and better as my strength wears away,
  Without gout or stone, by a gentle decay.

In a country town, by a murmuring brook,
With the ocean at distance, whereon I may look;
With a spacious plain without hedge or stile,
And an easy pad-nag to ride out a mile.
  May I govern, etc.

775 sway] control pad-nag] ambling nag

With Horace and Petrarch, and two or three more
Of the best wits that lived in the ages before;
With a dish of roast mutton, not venison or teal,
And clean though coarse linen at every meal.
  May I govern, etc.

With a pudding on Sundays, and stout humming liquor,
And remnants of Latin to welcome the vicar,
With a hidden reserve of Burgundy wine,
To drink the king's health in, as oft as I dine.
  May I govern, etc.

When the days are grown short, and it freezes and snows,
May I have a coal fire as high as my nose:
A fire, which once stirred up with a prong
Will keep the room temperate all the night long.
  May I govern, etc.

With a courage undaunted may I face my last day,
And when I am dead, may the better sort say,
In the morning when sober, in the evening when mellow,
'He's gone, and left not behind him his fellow;
  For he governed his passions with an absolute sway,
  And grew wiser and better as his strength wore away,
  Without gout or stone, by a gentle decay.'

(1685)

THOMAS FLATMAN
1637–1688

776 *A Thought of Death*

WHEN on my sick bed I languish,
Full of sorrow, full of anguish,
  Fainting, gasping, trembling, crying,
  Panting, groaning, speechless, dying,
My soul just now about to take her flight
Into the regions of eternal night,
    Oh tell me you
  That have been long below,
    What shall I do?

775 humming] strong

What shall I think, when cruel death appears,
  That may extenuate my fears?
Methinks I hear some gentle spirit say,
  'Be not fearful, come away!
Think with thyself that now thou shalt be free,
And find thy long-expected liberty;
Better thou mayst, but worse thou canst not be
Than in this vale of tears and misery.
Like Caesar, with assurance then come on,
And unamazed attempt the laurel crown
That lies on th' other side death's Rubicon.'

(1660)

777 *The Unconcerned: Song*

Now that the world is all in amaze,
  Drums and trumpets rending heavens,
    Wounds a bleeding, mortals dying,
    Widows and orphans piteously crying;
Armies marching, towns in a blaze,
  Kingdoms and states at sixes and sevens:
    What should an honest fellow do,
    Whose courage and fortunes run equally low?
Let him live, say I, till his glass be run,
  As easily as he may;
    Let the wine and the sand of his glass flow together,
  For life's but a winter's day;
Alas! from sun to sun
    The time's very short, very dirty the weather,
  And we silently creep away.
Let him nothing do, he could wish undone,
And keep himself safe from the noise of a gun.

(1674)

776 extenuate] lessen

THOMAS KEN

1637–1711

778

A Morning Hymn

AWAKE, my soul, and with the sun
Thy daily stage of duty run;
Shake off dull sloth, and early rise
To pay thy morning sacrifice.

Redeem thy misspent time that's past;
Live this day as if 'twere thy last;
T' improve thy talent take due care:
'Gainst the great day thyself prepare.

Let all thy converse be sincere,
Thy conscience as the noonday clear;
Think how all-seeing God thy ways
And all thy secret thoughts surveys.

Influenced by the light divine
Let thy own light in good works shine:
Reflect all heaven's propitious ways,
In ardent love and cheerful praise.

Wake, and lift up thyself, my heart,
And with the angels bear thy part,
Who all night long unwearied sing
Glory to the eternal king.

I wake, I wake, ye heavenly choir;
May your devotion me inspire,
That I like you my age may spend,
Like you may on my God attend.

May I like you in God delight,
Have all day long my God in sight,
Perform like you my maker's will;
Oh may I never more do ill!

Had I your wings, to heaven I'd fly;
But God shall that defect supply,
And my soul, winged with warm desire,
Shall all day long to heaven aspire.

Glory to thee who safe has kept,
And hath refreshed me whilst I slept.
Grant, Lord, when I from death shall wake,
I may of endless light partake.

I would not wake, nor rise again,
Even heaven itself I would disdain,
Wert not thou there to be enjoyed,
And I in hymns to be employed.

Heaven is, dear Lord, where'er thou art:
Oh never, then, from me depart;
For to my soul 'tis hell to be
But for one moment without thee.

Lord, I my vows to thee renew;
Disperse my sins as morning dew;
Guard my first springs of thought and will,
And with thyself my spirit fill.

Direct, control, suggest, this day,
All I design, or do, or say,
That all my powers, with all their might,
In thy sole glory may unite.

(1695)

THOMAS TRAHERNE
1637–1674

779 *Innocence*

I

BUT that which most I wonder at, which most
I did esteem my bliss, which most I boast,
And ever shall enjoy, is that within
  I felt no stain nor spot of sin.

  No darkness then did overshade,
  But all within was pure and bright;
  No guilt did crush nor fear invade,
  But all my soul was full of light.

A joyful sense and purity
  Is all I can remember.
The very night to me was bright,
  'Twas summer in December.

2

A serious meditation did employ
My soul within, which taken up with joy
Did seem no outward thing to note, but fly
  All objects that do feed the eye.

  While it those very objects did
  Admire, and prize, and praise, and love,
  Which in their glory most are hid,
  Which presence only doth remove.

  Their constant daily presence I
    Rejoicing at, did see;
  And that which takes them from the eye
  Of others, offered them to me.

3

No inward inclination did I feel
To avarice or pride: my soul did kneel
In admiration all the day. No lust, nor strife,
  Polluted then my infant life.

  No fraud nor anger in me moved,
  No malice, jealousy, or spite:
  All that I saw I truly loved.
  Contentment only and delight

  Were in my soul. O heaven! what bliss
    Did I enjoy and feel!
  What powerful delight did this
  Inspire! For this I daily kneel.

4

Whether it be that nature is so pure,
And custom only vicious; or that sure
God did by miracle the guilt remove,
  And make my soul to feel his love

  So early; or that 'twas one day
  Wherein this happiness I found,
  Whose strength and brightness so do ray
  That still it seemeth to surround;

Whate'er it is, it is a light
  So endless unto me
That I a world of true delight
Did then and to this day do see.

5

That prospect was the gate of heaven, that day
The ancient light of Eden did convey
Into my soul: I was an Adam there,
  A little Adam in a sphere

Of joys! Oh there my ravished sense
Was entertained in paradise,
And had a sight of innocence.
All was beyond all bound and price.

An antepast of heaven sure!
  I on the Earth did reign.
Within, without me, all was pure.
I must become a child again.

(1903)

780

The Rapture

  SWEET infancy!
O fire of heaven! O sacred light!
  How fair and bright!
  How great am I,
Whom all the world doth magnify!

  O heavenly joy!
O great and sacred blessedness,
  Which I possess!
  So great a joy
Who did into my arms convey?

  From God above
Being sent, the heavens me enflame
  To praise his name.
  The stars do move!
The burning sun doth show his love.

antepast] foretaste

780 move] incline me

Oh how divine
Am I! To all this sacred wealth,
This life and health,
Who raised? Who mine
Did make the same? What hand divine?

(1903)

781 *Insatiableness*

I

No walls confine! Can nothing hold my mind?
Can I no rest nor satisfaction find?
Must I behold eternity,
And see
What things above the heavens be?
Will nothing serve the turn?
Nor Earth, nor seas, nor skies?
Till I what lies
In time's beginning find,
Must I till then for ever burn?

Not all the crowns; not all the heaps of gold
On Earth; not all the tales that can be told,
Will satisfaction yield to me:
Nor tree,
Nor shade, nor sun, nor Eden, be
A joy; nor gems in gold
(Be 't pearl or precious stone),
Nor spring, nor flowers,
Answer my craving powers,
Nor anything that eyes behold.

Till I what was before all time descry,
The world's beginning seems but vanity.
My soul doth there long thoughts extend:
No end
Doth find, or being comprehend;
Yet somewhat sees that is
The óbscure shady face
Of endless space,
All room within, where I
Expect to meet eternal bliss.

2

This busy, vast, enquiring soul
Brooks no control,
No limits will endure,
Nor any rest: it will all see,
Not time alone, but even eternity.
What is it? Endless sure.

'Tis mean ambition to desire
A single world:
To many I aspire,
Though one upon another hurled;
Nor will they all, if they be all confined,
Delight my mind.

This busy, vast enquiring soul
Brooks no control;
'Tis hugely curious too.
Each one of all those worlds must be
Enriched with infinite variety
And worth, or 'twill not do.

'Tis nor delight nor perfect pleasure
To have a purse
That hath a bottom of its treasure,
Since I must thence endless expense disburse.
Sure there's a God (for else there's no delight),
One infinite.

(1932)

CHARLES SACKVILLE, EARL OF DORSET
1638–1706

782 [*Written at Sea, in the First Dutch War*]

To all you ladies now at land,
We men at sea do write;
But first I hope you'll understand
How hard 'tis to indite:
The Muses now, and Neptune too,
We must implore, to write to you.

For though the Muses should be kind,
And fill our empty brains,
Yet when rough Neptune calls the wind
To rouse the azure main,
Our paper, ink, and pen, and we
Roll up and down our ship at sea.

Then, if we write not by each post,
Think not we are unkind,
Nor yet conclude that we are lost
By Dutch or else by wind;
Our tears we'll send a speedier way:
The tide shall bring them twice a day.

With wonder and amaze the king
Will vow his seas grow bold,
Because the tides more water bring
Than they were wont of old;
But you must tell him that our cares
Send floods of grief to Whitehall Stairs.

To pass the tedious hours away,
We throw the merry main,
Or else at serious ombre play;
But why should we in vain
Each other's ruin thus pursue?
We were undone when we left you.

If foggy Opdam did but know
Our sad and dismal story,
The Dutch would scorn so weak a foe,
And leave the port of Goree;
For what resistance can they find
From men that left their hearts behind?

Let wind and weather do their worst,
Be you to us but kind;
Let Frenchmen vapour, Dutchmen curse,
No sorrow shall we find:
'Tis then no matter how things go,
Nor who's our friend, nor who's our foe.

amaze] amazement throw . . . main] play dice ombre] card game foggy] flabby, bloated Opdam] Wassanaer-Opdam, Dutch admiral Goree] (island north of Gambia river) vapour] talk emptily

In justice, you cannot refuse
  To think of our distress,
Since we in hope of honour lose
  Our certain happiness:
All our designs are but to prove
Ourselves more worthy of your love.

Alas! our tears tempestuous grow,
  And cast our hopes away;
While you, unmindful of our woe,
  Sit careless at a play,
And now permit some happier man
To kiss your busk, and wag your fan.

When any mournful tune you hear,
  That dies in every note
As if it sighed for each man's care
  For being so remote,
Think then how oft our love we made
To you, while all those tunes were played.

And now we have told all our love,
  And also all our tears,
We hope our declarations move
  Some pity for our cares;
Let's hear of no unconstancy
We have too much of that at sea.

(1714; wr. ?1664)

783

Song

DORINDA'S sparkling wit, and eyes,
  Uniting cast too fierce a light,
Which blazes high, but quickly dies;
  Pains not the heart, but hurts the sight.

Love is a calmer, gentler joy,
  Smooth are his looks, and soft his pace;
Her Cupid is a blackguard boy
  That runs his link full in your face.

(1701; wr. *c.*1677)

busk] stays

783 Dorinda] Katherine Sedley (James II's mistress)   blackguard] urban vagrant
link] torch

SIR CHARLES SEDLEY
1639?–1701

784 *On a Cock at Rochester*

THOU cursèd cock, with thy perpetual noise,
Mayst thou be capon made, and lose thy voice,
Or on a dunghill mayst thou spend thy blood,
And vermin prey upon thy craven brood;
May rivals tread thy hens before thy face,
Then with redoubled courage give thee chase;
Mayst thou be punished for St Peter's crime,
And on Shrove Tuesday perish in thy prime;
May thy bruised carcass be some beggar's feast,
Thou first and worst disturber of man's rest.

(1692)

785 *Song*

SEE! Hymen comes; how his torch blazes!
  Looser loves, how dim they burn!
No pleasures equal chaste embraces,
  When we love for love return.

When fortune makes the match, he rages,
  And forsakes th' unequal pair;
But when love two hearts engages,
  The kind god is ever there.

Regard not then high blood nor riches,
  You that would his blessings have;
Let untaught love guide all your wishes,
  Hymen should be Cupid's slave.

Young virgins, that yet bear your passions
  Coldly as the flint its fire,
Offer to Hymen your devotions,
  He will warm you with desire.

785 Hymen] god of marriage (ancient mythology)   rages] takes his pleasure

Young men, no more neglect your duty
To the god of nuptial vows:
Pay your long arrears to beauty,
As his chaster law allows.

(1692)

786 *On Fruition*

NONE but a Muse in love can tell
The sweet tumultuous joys I feel,
When on Caelia's breast I lie,
When I tremble, faint, and die;
Mingling kisses with embraces,
Darting tongues and joining faces,
Panting, stretching, sweating, cooing,
All in the ecstasy of doing.

(attrib. to; 1707)

APHRA BEHN
1640–1689

787 *Song: Love Armed*

LOVE in fantastic triumph sat,
Whilst bleeding hearts around him flowed,
For whom fresh pains he did create,
And strange tyrannic power he showed:
From thy bright eyes he took his fire,
Which round about in sport he hurled;
But 'twas from mine he took desire,
Enough to undo the amorous world.

From me he took his sighs and tears,
From thee his pride and cruelty;
From me his languishments and fears,
And every killing dart from thee.
Thus thou and I the god have armed,
And set him up a deity;
But my poor heart alone is harmed,
Whilst thine the victor is, and free.

(1684)

788 *In Imitation of Horace*

WHAT mean those amorous curls of jet?
  For what heart-ravished maid
Dost thou thy hair in order set,
  Thy wanton tresses braid,
And thy vast store of beauties open lay,
That the deluded fancy leads astray?

For pity hide thy starry eyes,
  Whose languishments destroy;
And look not on the slave that dies
  With an excess of joy.
Defend thy coral lips, thy amber breath;
To taste these sweets lets in a certain death.

Forbear, fond charming youth, forbear
  Thy words of melting love:
Thy eyes thy language well may spare,
  One dart enough can move;
And she that hears thy voice and sees thy eyes
With too much pleasure, too much softness, dies.

Cease, cease, with sighs to warm my soul,
  Or press me with thy hand:
Who can the kindling fire control,
  The tender force withstand?
Thy sighs and touches like winged lightning fly,
And are the god of love's artillery.

(1684)

789 *Epitaph on the Tombstone of a Child, the Last of Seven that Died Before*

THIS little, silent, gloomy monument
Contains all that was sweet and innocent:
The softest prattler that e'er found a tongue,
His voice was music and his words a song;
Which now each listening angel smiling hears,
Such pretty harmonies compose the spheres;
Wanton as unfledged Cupids, ere their charms
Had learned the little arts of doing harms;

788 amber] ambergris; perfumed   control] overmaster

Fair as young cherubins, as soft and kind,
And though translated could not be refined;
The seventh dear pledge the nuptial joys had given,
Toiled here on Earth, retired to rest in heaven,
Where they the shining host of angels fill,
Spread their gay wings before the throne, and smile.

(1685)

790 *To Alexis in Answer to His Poem against Fruition: Ode*

Ah hapless sex! who bear no charms
But what like lightning flash and are no more,
False fires sent down for baneful harms,
Fires which the fleeting lover feebly warms,
And given like past debauches o'er,
Like songs that please, though bad, when new,
But learned by heart neglected grew.

In vain did heaven adorn the shape and face
With beauties which by angels' forms it drew;
In vain the mind with brighter glories grace,
While all our joys are stinted to the space
Of one betraying interview:
With one surrender to the eager will
We're short-lived nothing, or a real ill.

Since man with that inconstancy was born,
To love the absent and the present scorn,
Why do we deck, why do we dress
For such a short-lived happiness?
Why do we put attraction on,
Since either way 'tis we must be undone?

They fly if honour take our part,
Our virtue drives 'em o'er the field;
We lose 'em by too much desert,
And oh! they fly us if we yield.
Ye gods! is there no charm in all the fair
To fix this wild, this faithless, wanderer?

789 translated] (1) removed to heaven; (2) transmuted Toiled] Dragged about

Man! our great business and our aim,
For whom we spread our fruitless snares,
No sooner kindles the designing flame
But to the next bright object bears
The trophies of his conquest and our shame:
Inconstancy's the good supreme,
The rest is airy notion, empty dream!

Then, heedless nymph, be ruled by me,
If e'er your swain the bliss desire:
Think like Alexis he may be,
Whose wished possession damps his fire;
The roving youth in every shade
Has left some sighing and abandoned maid,
For 'tis a fatal lesson he has learned,
After fruition ne'er to be concerned.

(1688)

791 *The Disappointment*

One day the amorous Lysander,
By an impatient passion swayed,
Surprised fair Cloris, that loved maid,
Who could defend herself no longer.
All things did with his love conspire:
The gilded planet of the day,
In his gay chariot drawn by fire,
Was now descending to the sea,
And left no light to guide the world,
But what from Cloris' brighter eyes was hurled.

In a lone thicket made for love,
Silent as yielding maid's consent,
She with a charming languishment
Permits his force, yet gently strove:
Her hands his bosom softly meet,
But not to put him back designed,
Rather to draw 'em on inclined;
Whilst he lay trembling at her feet,
Resistance 'tis in vain to show;
She wants the power to say 'Ah! What d'ye do?'

Her bright eyes sweet, and yet severe,
Where love and shame confusedly strive,
Fresh vigour to Lysander give;
And breathing faintly in his ear

She cried, 'Cease, cease . . . your vain desire,
Or I'll call out. . . . What would you do?
My dearer honour even to you
I cannot, must not give. . . . Retire,
Or take this life, whose chiefest part
I gave you with the conquest of my heart.'

But he, as much unused to fear
As he was capable of love,
The blessèd minutes to improve,
Kisses her mouth, her neck, her hair:
Each touch her new desire alarms.
His burning trembling hand he pressed
Upon her swelling snowy breast,
While she lay panting in his arms:
All her unguarded beauties lie
The spoils and trophies of the enemy.

And now without respect or fear
He seeks the object of his vows
(His love no modesty allows),
By swift degrees advancing . . . where
His daring hand that altar seized
Where gods of love do sacrifice:
That awful throne, that paradise
Where rage is calmed and anger pleased:
That fountain where delight still flows,
And gives the universal world repose.

Her balmy lips encountering his,
Their bodies, as their souls, are joined,
Where both in transports unconfined
Extend themselves upon the moss.
Cloris half dead and breathless lay;
Her soft eyes cast a humid light,
Such as divides the day and night,
Or falling stars whose fires decay;
And now no signs of life she shows,
But what in short-breathed sighs returns and goes.

He saw how at her length she lay;
He saw her rising bosom bare;
Her loose thin robes, through which appear
A shape designed for love and play,

alarms] arouses   rage] passion   still] ever

Abandoned by her pride and shame.
She does her softest joys dispence,
Offering her virgin innocence
A victim to love's sacred flame,
While the o'er-ravished shepherd lies
Unable to perform the sacrifice.

Ready to taste a thousand joys,
The too transported hapless swain
Found the vast pleasure turned to pain;
Pleasure which too much love destroys:
The willing garments by he laid,
And heaven all opened to his view;
Mad to possess, himself he threw
On the defenceless lovely maid.
But oh! what envying god conspires
To snatch his power, yet leave him the desire?

Nature's support (without whose aid
She can no human being give),
Itself now wants the art to live;
Faintness its slackened nerves invade:
In vain the enragèd youth essayed
To call its fleeting vigour back;
No motion 'twill from motion take.
Excess of love his love betrayed:
In vain he toils, in vain commands;
The insensible fell weeping in his hand.

In this so amorous cruel strife,
Where love and fate were too severe,
The poor Lysander in despair
Renounced his reason with his life:
Now all the brisk and active fire
That should the nobler part inflame
Served to increase his rage and shame,
And left no spark for new desire;
Not all her naked charms could move
Or calm that rage that had debauched his love.

Cloris returning from the trance
Which love and soft desire had bred,
Her timorous hand she gently laid
(Or guided by design or chance)

wants] lacks nerves] sinews (playing on nerve = penis) motion] (1) change; (2) bidding rage] perturbation

Upon that fabulous Priapus,
That potent god, as poets feign;
But never did young shepherdess,
Gathering of fern upon the plain,
More nimbly draw her fingers back,
Finding beneath the verdant leaves a snake,

Than Cloris her fair hand withdrew,
Finding that god of her desires
Disarmed of all his awful fires,
And cold as flowers bathed in the morning dew.
Who can the nymph's confusion guess?
The blood forsook the hinder place,
And strewed with blushes all her face,
Which both disdain and shame expressed;
And from Lysander's arms she fled,
Leaving him fainting on the gloomy bed.

Like lightning through the grove she hies,
Or Daphne from the Delphic god:
No print upon the grassy road
She leaves, to instruct pursuing eyes.
The wind that wantoned in her hair
And with her ruffled garments played
Discovered in the flying maid
All that the gods e'er made, if fair.
So Venus, when her love was slain,
With fear and haste flew o'er the fatal plain.

The nymph's resentments none but I
Can well imagine or condole;
But none can guess Lysander's soul
But those who swayed his destiny.
His silent griefs swell up to storms,
And not one god his fury spares:
He cursed his birth, his fate, his stars;
But more the shepherdess's charms,
Whose soft bewitching influence
Had damned him to the hell of impotence.

(1684)

Priapus] ancient fertility god feign] invent Delphic god] Apollo her love] Adonis condole] sympathize with

792 *The Cabal at Nickey Nackey's*

A POX of the statesman that's witty,
Who watches and plots all the sleepless night
For seditious harangues to the Whigs of the City,
And maliciously turns a traitor in spite.
Let him wear and torment his lean carrion
  To bring his sham plots about,
  Till at last king, bishop, and baron
For the public *good* he have quite rooted out.

  But we that are no politicians,
But rogues that are 'impudent', 'barefaced', and 'great',
Boldly head the rude rabble in times of sedition,
And bear all down before us in church and in state.
  Your impudence is the best state-trick;
    And he that by law means to rule,
  Let his history with ours be related;
And though we are the knaves, we know who's the fool.

(1684)

ANONYMOUS
fl. 1671

793 *Song*

HANG sorrow, cast away care,
  Come let us drink up our sack;
    They say it is good
    To cherish the blood,
  And eke to strengthen the back.
'Tis wine that makes the thoughts aspire,
  And fills the body with heat;
    Beside 'tis good,
    If well understood,
  To fit a man for the feat:
      Then call,
    And drink up all,
  The drawer is ready to fill.
    A pox of care,
    What need we to spare,
  My father hath made his will.

(1671)

792 *Nickey Nackey's*] Aquilina's (the courtesan in *Venice Preserved*)

794 *'What care I though the world reprove'*

WHAT care I though the world reprove
My bold, my over-daring love:
Ignoble minds themselves exempt
From interest in a brave attempt.

The eagle soaring to behold
The sun arrayed in flames of gold
Regards not though she burns her wings,
Since that rich sight such pleasure brings.

So feel I now my smiling thought
To such a resolution brought
That it contemns all grief and smart,
Since I so high have placed my heart.

And if I die, some worthy spirits
To future times shall sing my merits,
That easily did my life despise,
Yet ne'er forsook my enterprise.

Then shine, bright sun, and let me see
The glory of thy majesty:
I wish to die, so I may have
Thy look my death, thine eye my grave.

(1671)

EDWARD TAYLOR
1642?–1729

795 *Meditation I. vi: Another Meditation at the Same Time [as Meditation I. v: Cant. 2: 1: The Lily of the Valleys]*

AM I thy gold? Or purse, Lord, for thy wealth,
  Whether in mine, or mint, refined for thee?
I'm counted so; but count me o'er thyself,
  Lest gold-washed face and brass in heart I be.
  I fear my touchstone touches when I try
  Me, and my counted gold too overly.

Am I new minted by thy stamp indeed?
  Mine eyes are dim, I cannot clearly see.
Be thou my spectacles that I may read
  Thine image and inscription stamped on me.
  If thy bright image do upon me stand,
  I am a golden angel in thy hand.

Lord, make my soul thy plate; thine image bright
  Within the circle of the same enfoil.
And on its brims in golden letters write
  Thy superscription in an holy style.
  Then I shall be thy money, thou my hoard:
  Let me thy angel be, be thou my Lord.

(1939; wr. 1683)

796 *Meditation I. xx: Phil. 2: 9: God Hath Highly Exalted Him*

VIEW, all ye eyes above, this sight which flings
  Seraphic fancies in chill raptures high:
A turf of clay, and yet bright glory's king
  From dust to glory angel-like to fly.
  A mortal clod immortalized, behold,
  Flies through the skies swifter than angels could.

795 try] (1) assay; (2) judge   angel] (1) coin; (2) messenger   enfoil] (1) cover with metal; (2) set off by contrast

Upon the wings he of the wind rode in,
  His bright sedan, through all the silver skies,
And made the azure cloud his chariot bring
  Him to the mountain of celestial joys.
  The prince of the air durst not an arrow spend,
  While through his realm his chariot did ascend.

He did not in a fiery chariot's shine,
  And whirlwind, like Elias, upward go;
But the golden ladder's jasper rounds did climb
  Unto the heavens high from Earth below.
  Each step trod on a golden stepping stone
  Of deity, unto his very throne.

Methinks I see heaven's sparkling courtiers fly
  In flakes of glory down him to attend;
And hear heart-cramping notes of melody
  Surround his chariot as it did ascend,
  Mixing their music, making every string
  More to enravish as they this tune sing:

'God is gone up with a triumphant shout,
  The Lord with sounding trumpets' melodies.
Sing praise; sing praise; sing praise; sing praises out,
  Unto our king sing praise seraphicwise.
  Lift up your heads, ye lasting doors', they sing,
  'And let the king of glory enter in.'

Art thou ascended up on high, my Lord,
  And must I be without thee here below?
Art thou the sweetest joy the heavens afford?
  Oh that I with thee was! What shall I do?
  Should I pluck feathers from an angel's wing,
  They could not waft me up to thee, my king.

Lend me thy wings, my Lord, I'st fly apace.
  My soul's arms stud with thy strong quills, true faith,
My quills then feather with thy saving grace:
  My wings will take the wind thy word display'th.
  Then I shall fly up to thy glorious throne
  With my strong wings, whose feathers are thine own.

(1939; wr. 1686)

prince of the air] Satan   Elias] Elijah (2 Kgs. 2)   rounds] (1) rungs; (2) celestial spheres   I'st] I'll   stud] (1) supply with uprights; (2) ornament with nails

797 *Meditation I. xxix: John 20: 17: My Father, and Your Father, to My God, and Your God*

My shattered fancy stole away from me
(Wits run a wooling over Eden's park),
And in God's garden saw a golden tree,
Whose heart was all divine, and gold its bark;
Whose glorious limbs and fruitful branches strong
With saints and angels bright are richly hung.

Thou! Thou, my dear dear Lord, art this rich tree,
The tree of life within God's paradise.
I am a withered twig, dried fit to be
A chat cast in thy fire, writh off by vice.
Yet if thy milk-white gracious hand will take me
And graft me in this golden stock, thou'lt make me.

Thou'lt make me then its fruit, and branch to spring;
And though a nipping east wind blow, and all
Hell's nymphs with spite their dog's sticks thereat ding
To dash the graft off, and its fruits to fall,
Yet I shall stand thy graft, and fruits that are
Fruits of the tree of life thy graft shall bear.

I being graffed in thee there up do stand:
In us relations all that mutual are.
I am thy patient, pupil, servant, and
Thy sister, mother, dove, spouse, son, and heir.
Thou art my priest, physician, prophet, king,
Lord, brother, bridegroom, father, everything.

I being graffed in thee am grafted here
Into thy family, and kindred claim
To all in heaven, God, saints, and angels there.
I thy relations my relations name.
Thy father's mine, thy God my God, and I
With saints and angels draw affinity.

My Lord, what is it that thou dost bestow?
The praise on this account fills up, and throngs
Eternity brimful, doth overflow
The heavens vast with rich angelic songs.
How should I blush? How tremble at this thing,
Not having yet my gamut learned to sing?

chat] twig writh] twisted spring] grow ding] beat graffed] grafted

But, Lord, as burnished sunbeams forth out fly
  Let angel-shine forth in my life out flame,
That I may grace thy graceful family,
  And not to thy relations be a shame.
  Make me thy graft, be thou my golden stock.
  Thy glory then I'll make my fruits and crop.

(1939; wr. 1688)

798 *Meditation II. vii: Ps. 105: 17: He Sent a Man before Them, even Joseph, Who Was Sold . . .*

ALL dull, my Lord, my spirits flat and dead,
  All water-soaked and sapless to the skin.
Oh, screw me up, and make my spirits bed
  Thy quickening virtue! For my ink is dim,
  My pencil blunt. Doth Joseph type out thee?
  Heralds of angels sing out, 'Bow the knee.'

Is Joseph's glorious shine a type of thee?
  How bright art thou! He envied was as well,
And so was thou. He's stripped, and picked, poor he,
  Into the pit; and so was thou: they shell
  Thee of thy kernel. He by Judah's sold
  For twenty bits; thirty for thee he'd told.

Joseph was tempted by his mistress vile,
  Thou by the devil; but both shame the foe.
Joseph was cast into the gaol awhile,
  And so was thou: sweet apples mellow so.
  Joseph did from his gaol to glory run:
  Thou from death's pallet rose like morning sun.

Joseph lays in against the famine, and
  Thou dost prepare the bread of life for thine.
He bought with corn for Pharaoh the men and land:
  Thou with thy bread mak'st such themselves consign
  Over to thee, that eat it. Joseph makes
  His brethren bow before him: thine too quake.

Joseph constrains his brethren till their sins
  Do gall their souls; repentance babbles fresh.
Thou treatst sinners till repentance springs,
  Then with him sendst a Benjamin-like mess.
  Joseph doth cheer his humble brethren: thou
  Dost stud with joy the mourning saints that bow.

pencil] brush   type out] foreshadow   picked] (1) thrown; (2) robbed   bits] small silver coins   Benjamin-like] larger than his brothers' (Gen. 43)   mess] feast   stud] support; ornament

Joseph's bright shine the eleven tribes must preach;
And thine apostles, now eleven, thine.
They bear his presents to his friends: thine reach
Thine unto thine; thus now behold a shine.
How hast thou pencilled out, my Lord, most bright
Thy glorious image here, on Joseph's light.

This I bewail in me under this shine
To see so dull a colour in my skin.
Lord, lay thy brightsome colours on me thine.
Scour thou my pipes, then play thy tunes therein.
I will not hang my harp in willows by,
While thy sweet praise, my tunes doth glorify.

(1939; wr. 1694)

799 *Meditation II.xviii: Heb. 13: 10: We Have an Altar*

A BRAN, a chaff, a very barley yawn,
An husk, a shell, a nothing, nay yet worse,
A thistle, briar prickle, pricking thorn,
A lump of lewdness, pouch of sin, a purse
Of naughtiness I am, yea what not, Lord?
And wilt thou be mine altar? And my board?

Mine heart's a park or chase of sins; mine head
'S a bowling alley. Sins play ninehole here.
Fancy's a green: sin, barley breaks in it led.
Judgement's a pingle: blind man's buff's played there.
Sin plays at coursey park within my mind:
My will's a walk in which it airs what's blind.

Sure then I lack atonement. Lord me help.
Thy shittim wood o'erlaid with wealthy brass
Was an atoning altar, and sweet smelt;
But if o'erlaid with pure pure gold it was,
It was an incense altar, all perfúmed
With odours, wherein, Lord, thou thus was bloomed.

light] (1) example; (2) highlight

799 yawn] awn, husk barley breaks] chasing game pingle] (1) keen contest, struggle; (2) paddock coursey park] course-a-park (chasing game) shittim] acacia bloomed] caused to flourish

Did this e'erduring wood, when thus o'erspread
With these e'erlasting metals altarwise,
Type thy eternal plank of Godhead, wed
Unto our mortal chip, its sacrifice?
Thy deity mine altar, manhood thine,
Mine offering on't for all men's sins, and mine?

This golden altar puts such weight into
The sacrifices offered on 't, that it
O'erweighs the weight of all the sins that flow
In thine elect. This wedge and beetle split
The knotty logs of vengeance, too, to shivers;
And from their guilt and shame them clear delivers.

This holy altar by its heavenly fire
Refines our offerings: casts out their dross
And sanctifies their gold by its rich tire
And all their steams with holy odours boss.
Pillars of frankincense and rich perfúme
They 'tone God's nostrils with, off from this loom.

Good news, good sirs, more good than comes within
The canopy of angels: heaven's hall
Allows no better. This atones for sin,
My glorious God, whose grace here thickest falls.
May I my barley yawn, bran, briar claw,
Lay on't, a sacrifice? Or chaff or straw?

Shall I my sin pouch lay on thy gold bench,
My offering, Lord, to thee? I've such alone,
But have no better; for my sins do drench
My very best unto their very bone.
And shall mine offering, by thine altar's fire
Refined and sanctified, to God aspire?

Amen, ev'n so be it. I now will climb
The stairs up to thine altar, and on 't lay
Myself, and services, even for its shrine.
My sacrifice brought thee accept, I pray.
My morn and evening offerings I'll bring,
And on this golden altar incense fling.

Type] Foreshadow   plank] (1) cross; (2) table (Eucharist)   beetle] mallet
tire] covering; accoutrement   boss] swells; ornaments   loom] implement
drench] saturate; tan

Lord, let thy deity mine altar be,
And make thy manhood on 't my sacrifice.
For mine atonement, make them both for me
My altar, to sanctify my gifts likewise,
That so myself and service on 't may bring
Its worth along with them to thee, my King.

The thoughts whereof do make my tunes as fume
From off this altar rise to thee, Most High,
And all their steams, stuffed with thy altar's blooms,
My sacrifice of praise in melody.
Let thy bright angels catch my tune, and sing 't.
That equals David's michtam, which is in 't.

(1939; wr. 1696)

800 *The Preface*

INFINITY, when all things it beheld
In nothing, and of nothing all did build,
Upon what base was fixed the lathe, wherein
He turned this globe, and riggalled it so trim?
Who blew the bellows of his furnace vast?
Or held the mould wherein the world was cast?
Who laid its corner-stone? Or whose command?
Where stand the pillars upon which it stands?
Who laced and filleted the Earth so fine,
With rivers like green ribbons smaragdine?
Who made the seas its selvage, and it locks
Like a gilt ball within a silver box?
Who spread its canopy? Or curtains spun?
Who in this bowling alley bowled the sun?
Who made it always when it rises set
To go at once both down, and up to get?
Who the curtain rods made for this tapestry?
Who hung the twinkling lanthorns in the sky?
Who? Who did this? Or who is he? Why, know
It's only might almighty this did do.
His hand hath made this noble work, which stands
His glorious handiwork not made by hands;
Who spake all things from nothing, and with ease
Can speak all things to nothing, if he please;

michtam] type of psalm

800 riggalled] marked with a ring-groove smaragdine] smaragd-coloured (emerald-like) lanthorns] lanterns

Whose little finger at his pleasure can
Out mete ten thousand worlds with half a span;
Whose might almighty can by half a looks
Root up the rocks and rock the hills by th' roots;
Can take this mighty world up in his hand,
And shake it like a squitchen or a wand;
Whose single frown will make the heavens shake
Like as an aspen leaf the wind makes quake.
Oh, what a might is this, whose single frown
Doth shake the world as it would shake it down!
Which all from nothing fet, from nothing, all:
Hath all on nothing set, lets nothing fall.
Gave all to nothing man indeed, whereby
Through nothing man all might him glorify.
In nothing then embossed the brightest gem,
More precious than all preciousness in them.
But nothing man did throw down all by sin,
And darkenèd that lightsome gem in him;
That now his brightest diamond is grown
Darker by far than any coalpit stone.

(1939)

BENJAMIN TOMPSON
1642–1714

801 *On a Fortification at Boston Begun by Women*

Dux Foemina Facti

A GRAND attempt some Amazonian dames
Contrive whereby to glorify their names:
A ruff for Boston Neck, of mud and turf,
Reaching from side to side, from surf to surf,
Their nimble hands spin up like Christmas pies;
Their pastry by degrees on high doth rise.
The wheel at home counts it an holiday,
Since, while the mistress worketh, it may play.
A tribe of female hands, but manly hearts,
Forsake at home their pasty-crust and tarts,
To knead the dirt: the samplers down they hurl;
Their undulating silks they closely furl.

squitchen] (1) scutcheon (bark used in grafting); (2) 'squitcher' (stick)   fet] fetched

801 Dux . . . facti] The leader is a woman (Virgil, *Aeneid* 1. 364)

The pick-axe one as a commandress holds,
While t' other at her awkness gently scolds.
One puffs and sweats, the other mutters 'Why
Can't you promove your work so fast as I?'
Some dig, some delve, and others' hands do feel
The little wagon's weight with single wheel.
And lest some fainting fits the weak surprise,
They want no sack nor cakes; they are more wise.
These brave essays draw forth male stronger hands,
More like to daubers than to martial bands:
These do the work, and sturdy bulwarks raise;
But the beginners well deserve the praise.

(1676)

EDWARD RAVENSCROFT
*c.*1643–1707

802 *In Derision of a Country Life*

FOND nymphs, from us true pleasure learn:
There is no music in a churn;
The milkmaids sing beneath the cow,
The sheep do bleat, the oxen low.
  If these are comforts for a wife,
  Defend, defend me from a country life.

The team comes home, the ploughman whistles,
The great dog barks, the turkey-cock bristles,
The jackdaws caw, the magpies chatter,
'Quack, quack,' cry the ducks that swim in the water.
  If these are comforts for a wife,
  Defend, defend me from a country life.

Then melancholy crows the cock,
And dull is the sound of the village clock:
The leaden hours pass slow away;
Thus yawning mortals spend the day.
  If these are comforts for a wife,
  Defend, defend me from a country life.

(1698)

801 awkness] ineptitude promove] advance want] lack daubers] plasterers

JAMES WRIGHT
1643–1713

803

Out of Horace

WHAT do I wish? No more than what I have,
The same estate, and quiet to the grave;
That no succeeding hour the fates allow
My life's remains may see me worse than now.
Plenty of books; provision for the year;
A settled mind, unswayed by hope or fear.
Life and estate are all I can invent
To ask of heaven: I'll give myself content.

(1692)

ALEXANDER RADCLIFFE
*c.*1645–after 1696

804

As Concerning Man

TO what intent or purpose was man made,
Who is by birth to misery betrayed?
Man in his tedious course of life runs through
More plagues than all the land of Egypt knew:
Doctors, divines, grave disputations, puns,
Ill-looking citizens and scurvy duns;
Insipid squires, fat bishops, deans and chapters,
Enthusiasts, prophecies, new rants and raptures;
Pox, gout, catarrhs, old sores, cramps, rheums and aches;
Half-witted lords, double-chinned bawds with patches;
Illiterate courtiers, chancery suits for life,
A teasing whore, and a more tedious wife;
Raw Inns of Court men, empty fops, buffoons,
Bullies robust, round aldermen, and clowns;
Gown-men which argue, and discuss, and prate,
And vent dull notions of a future state,
Sure of another world, yet do not know
Whether they shall be saved, or damned, or how.
'Twere better then that man had never been,
Than thus to be perplexed: God save the Queen.

(1682)

804 clowns] rustics

HENRY ALDRICH?
1647–1710

805 *A Catch*

If all be true that I do think,
There are five reasons we should drink:
Good wine; a friend; or being dry;
Or lest we should be, by and by;
Or any other reason why.

(1689)

PHILIP PAIN
c. 1647–*c.* 1667

from *Daily Meditations*

806 *Meditation VIII*

Scarce do I pass a day, but that I hear
Someone or other's dead; and to my ear
Methinks it is no news; but oh, did I
Think deeply on it, what it is to die,
My pulses all would beat, I should not be
Drowned in this deluge of security.

(1668)

JAMES CARKESSE
fl. 1678

807 *His Rule of Behaviour:*
If You Are Civil, I Am Sober

Porter and keepers, when they're civil,
They charm in me the madmen's devil:
The roaring lion turns to lamb,
Lies down and couches wondrous tame;
For though at Bedlam wits ebb and flow
As wandering stars move swift or slow,

My brain's not ruled by the pale moon,
Nor keep the spheres my soul in tune;
But she observes, and changes notes
With the azure of sky-coloured coats.

(1679)

808 *On the Doctors' Telling Him that till He Left off Making Verses He Was Not Fit to be Discharged*

DESIRING his imprisoned Muse to enlarge,
The poet, Mad-quack moved, for his discharge.
He angry answered, 'Parson, 'tis too soon:
As yet I have not cured you of lampoon;
For know, New Bedlam chiefly for the infected
With this new sort of madness was erected:
Bucks both and Rochester, unless they mend,
Hither the king designs forthwith to send.
Shepherd and Dryden too must on 'em wait;
For he's resolved at once to rid the state
Of this poetic, wanton, madlike tribe,
Whose rampant Muse does court and city gibe.
Thus Bedlam may be cured perchance, if it hits,
After despair of physic, by the wits.'
The answer pleased; yet I have cause to fear
The doctor flattered, as 'tis usual here.
But if my brethren come, I've learned this lesson:
In such good company, Bedlam is no prison.

(1679)

'EPHELIA'
fl. 1678–1681

809 *To J. G.*

TELL me you hate, and flatter me no more;
By heaven I do not wish you should adore:
With humbler blessings I content can be,
I only beg that you would pity me

azure . . . coats] i.e. mood of the keepers (who wore blue uniforms)

808 enlarge] free   Bucks] Duke of Buckingham   hits] succeeds   wits] (1) poets; (2) reason

'EPHELIA'

In as much silence as I first designed
To bear the raging torture of my mind.
For when your eyes first made my heart your slave,
I thought t' have hid my fetters in my grave:
Heaven witness for me that I strove to hide
My violent love, and my fond eyes did chide
For glancing at thee; and my blushes hid
With as much care as ever virgin did,
And though I languished in the greatest pain
That e'er despairing lover did sustain,
I ne'er in public did let fall a tear,
Nor breathed a sigh in the reach of any ear.
Yet I in private drew no breath but sighs,
And showers of tears fell from my wretched eyes:
The lilies left my front, the rose my cheeks;
My nights were spent in sobs and sudden shrieks;
I felt my strength insensibly decayed,
And death approach. But ah! then you conveyed
Soft amorous tales into my listening ears,
And gentle vows, and well becoming tears;
Then deeper oaths; nor e'er your siege removed
Till I confessed my flame, and owned I loved.
Your kinder smiles had raised my flames so high
That all at distance might the fire descry:
I took no care my passion to suppress,
Nor hide the love I thought I did possess.
But ah! too late I find your love was such
As gallants pay in course, or scarce so much:
You shun my sight, you feed me with delays,
You slight, affront, a thousand several ways
You do torment with studied cruelty;
And yet alternately you flatter me.
Oh! if you love not, plainly say you hate,
And give my miseries a shorter date:
'Tis kinder than to linger out my fate.
And yet I could with less regret have died
A victim to your coldness, than your pride.

(1679)

front] forehead

810 *To One That Asked Me Why I Loved J. G.*

WHY do I love? Go, ask the glorious sun
Why every day it round the world doth run;
Ask Thames and Tiber why they ebb and flow;
Ask damask roses why in June they blow;
Ask ice and hail the reason why they're cold;
Decaying beauties, why they will grow old.
They'll tell thee fate, that every thing doth move,
Enforces them to this, and me to love.
There is no reason for our love or hate:
'Tis irresistible as death or fate.
'Tis not his face: I've sense enough to see
That is not good, though doted on by me.
Nor is 't his tongue that has this conquest won,
For that at least is equalled by my own.
His carriage can to none obliging be—
'Tis rude, affected, full of vanity,
Strangely ill-natured, peevish and unkind,
Unconstant, false, to jealousy inclined.
His temper could not have so great a power,
'Tis mutable, and changes every hour.
Those vigorous years that women so adore
Are past in him, he's twice my age and more.
And yet I love this false, this worthless, man
With all the passion that a woman can
Dote on his imperfections: though I spy
Nothing to love, I love, and know not why.
Sure 'tis decreed in the dark book of fate
That I should love, and he should be ingrate.

(1679)

811 *First Farewell to J. G.*

FAREWELL, my dearer half, joy of my heart;
Heaven only knows how loath I am to part:
Whole months but hours seem, when you are here;
When absent, every minute is a year:
Might I but always see thy charming face,
I'd live on racks and wish no easier place.
But we must part: your interest says we must;
Fate, me no longer with such treasure trust.

811 interest] business; advantage

I would not tax you with inconstancy,
Yet, Strephon, you are not so kind as I:
No interest, no, nor fate itself has power
To tempt me from the idol I adore.
But, since you needs must go, may Africk be
Kinder to you than Europe is to me:
May all you meet and everything you view
Give you such transport as I met in you.
May no sad thoughts disturb your quiet mind,
Except you'll think of her you left behind.

(1679)

812 *Upon His Leaving His Mistress*

'TIS not that I am weary grown
Of being yours, and yours alone;
But with what face can I incline
To damn you to be only mine?
  You whom some tender power did fashion
  By merit and by inclination,
  The joy at least of one whole nation?

Let meaner spirits of your sex
With humbler aims their thoughts perplex;
And boast, if by their arts they can
Contrive to wake one happy man:
  Whilst moved by an impartial sense,
  Favours like nature you dispense
  With universal influence.

See the kind seed-receiving Earth
To every grain affords a birth:
On her no showers unwelcome fall;
Her willing womb retains them all.
  And shall my Celia be confined?
  No: live up to thy mighty mind,
  And be the mistress of mankind.

(1679)

811 Strephon] type name for pastoral lover   Except] Unless

813 *To Phylocles, Inviting Him to Friendship*

BEST of thy sex! If sacred friendship can
Dwell in the bosom of inconstant man,
As cold, as clear as ice, as snow unstained,
With love's loose crimes unsullied, unprofaned,

Or you a woman with that name dare trust,
And think to friendship's ties we can be just,
In a strict league together we'll combine,
And friendship's bright example shine.

We will forget the difference of sex,
Nor shall the world's rude censure [us] perplex:
Think me all man; my soul is masculine,
And capable of as great things as thine.

I can be gen'rous, just, and brave,
Secret, and silent, as the grave;
And if I cannot yield relief,
I'll sympathize in all thy grief.

I will not have a thought from thee I'll hide,
In all my actions thou shalt be my guide,
In every joy of mine thou shalt have share,
And I will bear a part in all thy care.

Why do I vainly talk of what we'll do?
We'll mix our souls: you shall be me, I you;
And both so one, it shall be hard to say
Which is Phylocles, which Ephelia.

Our ties shall be strong as the chains of fate,
Conquerors and kings our joys shall emulate:
Forgotten friendship, held at first divine,
To its native purity we will refine.

(1679)

814 *Maidenhead: Written at the Request of a Friend*

AT your entreaty I at last have writ
This whimsy, that has nigh nonplussed my wit:
The toy I've long enjoyed, if it may
Be called to enjoy, a thing we wish away;

But yet no more its character can give
Than tell the minutes that I have to live.
'Tis a fantastic ill, a loathed disease,
That can no sex, no age, no person please:
Men strive to gain it, but the way they choose
To obtain their wish, that and the wish doth lose.
Our thoughts are still uneasy, till we know
What 'tis, and why it is desirèd so;
But the first unhappy knowledge that we boast
Is that we know the valued trifle's lost.
Thou dull companion of our active years,
That chillst our warm blood with thy frozen fears:
How is it likely thou shouldst long endure,
When thought itself thy ruin may procure?
Thou short-lived tyrant, that usurpst a sway
O'er womankind; though none thy power obey
Except th' ill-natured, ugly, peevish, proud;
And these indeed thy praises sing aloud.
But what's the reason they obey so well?
Because they want the power to rebel.
But I forget, or have my subject lost.
Alas! thy being's fancy at the most;
Though much desired, 'tis but seldom men
Court the vain blessing from a woman's pen.

(1679)

MARY MOLLINEUX
1648–1695

815

Solitude

How sweet is harmless solitude!
  What can its joys control?
Tumults and noise may not intrude,
  To interrupt the soul,

That here enjoys itself, retired
  From Earth's seducing charms;
Leaving her pomp to be admired
  By such as court their harms.

still] ever   sway] power (poetic)

815 control] overcome

While she on contemplation's wings
  Soars far beyond the sky,
And feeds her thoughts on heavenly things
  Which in her bosom lie.

Great privileges here of old
  The wise men did obtain;
And treasure far surpassing gold
  They digged for not in vain.

The tincture of philosophers
  Here happily they found;
The music of the morning stars
  Here in their hearts did sound.

(1702)

JOHN WILMOT, EARL OF ROCHESTER
1648–1680

816

Love and Life: A Song

ALL my past life is mine no more:
  The flying hours are gone
Like transitory dreams given o'er,
Whose images are kept in store
  By memory alone.

Whatever is to come is not;
  How can it then be mine?
The present moment's all my lot,
And that as fast as it is got,
  Phillis, is wholly thine.

Then talk not of inconstancy,
  False hearts, and broken vows:
If I by miracle can be,
  This livelong minute, true to thee,
  'Tis all that heaven allows.

(1680)

815 tincture] elixir

817 *Against Constancy*

TELL me no more of constancy,
That frivolous pretence,
Of cold age, narrow jealousy,
Disease, and want of sense.

Let duller fools, on whom kind chance
Some easy heart has thrown,
Despairing higher to advance,
Be kind to one alone.

Old men and weak, whose idle flame
Their own defects discovers,
Since changing can but spread their shame,
Ought to be constant lovers;

But we, whose hearts do justly swell
With no vainglorious pride,
Who know how we in love excel,
Long to be often tried.

Then bring my bath, and strew my bed,
As each kind night returns;
I'll change a mistress till I'm dead,
And fate change me for worms.

(1676)

818 *A Satyr against Reason and Mankind*

WERE I (who to my cost already am
One of those strange, prodigious creatures, man)
A spirit free to choose, for my own share,
What case of flesh and blood I pleased to wear,
I'd be a dog, a monkey, or a bear,
Or anything but that vain animal
Who is so proud of being rational.
The senses are too gross, and he'll contrive
A sixth, to contradict the other five,
And before certain instinct, will prefer
Reason, which fifty times for one does err;

818 *Satyr*] Satire   case] body; container

Reason, an *ignis fatuus* in the mind,
Which, leaving light of nature, sense, behind,
Pathless and dangerous wandering ways it takes
Through error's fenny bogs and thorny brakes;
Whilst the misguided follower climbs with pain
Mountains of whimsies, heaped in his own brain;
Stumbling from thought to thought, falls headlong down
Into doubt's boundless sea, where, like to drown,
Books bear him up awhile, and make him try
To swim with bladders of philosophy;
In hopes still to o'ertake the escaping light,
The vapour dances in his dazzling sight
Till, spent, it leaves him to eternal night.
Then old age and experience, hand in hand,
Lead him to death, and make him understand,
After a search so painful and so long,
That all his life he has been in the wrong.
Huddled in dirt the reasoning engine lies,
Who was so proud, so witty, and so wise.
  Pride drew him in, as cheats their bubbles catch,
And made him venture to be made a wretch.
His wisdom did his happiness destroy,
Aiming to know that world he should enjoy.
And wit was his vain, frivolous pretence
Of pleasing others at his own expense;
For wits are treated just like common whores:
First they're enjoyed, and then kicked out of doors.
The pleasure past, a threatening doubt remains
That frights the enjoyer with succeeding pains.
Women and men of wit are dangerous tools,
And ever fatal to admiring fools:
Pleasure allures, and when the fops escape,
'Tis not that they're beloved, but fortunate,
And therefore what they fear at heart, they hate.
  But now, methinks, some formal band and beard
Takes me to task. Come on, sir; I'm prepared.
  'Then, by your favour, anything that's writ
Against this gibing, jingling knack called wit
Likes me abundantly; but you take care,
Upon this point, not to be too severe.
Perhaps my Muse were fitter for this part,
For I profess I can be very smart
On wit, which I abhor with all my heart.
I long to lash it in some sharp essáy,

engine] wit; genius   bubbles] dupes   formal band] clerical dress

But your grand indiscretion bids me stay,
And turns my tide of ink another way.
'What rage ferments in your degenerate mind,
To make you rail at reason and mankind?
Blest, glorious man! to whom alone kind heaven
An everlasting soul has freely given,
Whom his great maker took such care to make
That from himself he did the image take,
And this fair frame in shining reason dressed,
To dignify his nature above beast;
Reason, by whose aspiring influence
We take a flight beyond material sense,
Dive into mysteries, then soaring pierce
The flaming limits of the universe,
Search heaven and hell, find out what's acted there,
And give the world true grounds of hope and fear.'
'Hold, mighty man,' I cry, 'all this we know
From the pathetic pen of Ingelo,
From Patrick's *Pilgrim*, Sibbes' soliloquies,
And 'tis this very reason I despise:
This supernatural gift, that makes a mite
Think he's the image of the infinite,
Comparing his short life, void of all rest,
To the eternal and the ever blest;
This busy, puzzling stirrer-up of doubt,
That frames deep mysteries, then finds 'em out,
Filling with frantic crowds of thinking fools
Those reverend bedlams, colleges and schools;
Borne on whose wings, each heavy sot can pierce
The limits of the boundless universe.
So charming ointments make an old witch fly
And bear a crippled carcass through the sky.
'Tis this exalted power whose business lies
In nonsense and impossibilities;
This made a whimsical philosopher,
Before the spacious world, his tub prefer;
And we have modern cloistered coxcombs who
Retire to think, 'cause they have naught to do.
'But thoughts are given for action's government;
Where action ceases, thought's impertinent.
Our sphere of action is life's happiness,
And he who thinks beyond, thinks like an ass.
Thus, whilst against false reasoning I inveigh,

Ingelo] Nathaniel Ingelo (1621?–83) Patrick's] Simon Patrick's (1626–1707) *Pilgrim*] *The Parable of the Pilgrim* (1664) Sibbes'] Richard Sibbes' (1577–1635), Puritan divine whimsical philosopher] Diogenes the Cynic

I own right reason, which I would obey:
That reason which distinguishes by sense,
And gives us rules of good and ill from thence
That bounds desires with a reforming will,
To keep 'em more in vigour, not to kill.
Your reason hinders, mine helps to enjoy,
Renewing appetites yours would destroy.
My reason is my friend, yours is a cheat;
Hunger calls out, my reason bids me eat;
Perversely, yours your appetite does mock:
This asks for food, that answers "What's o'clock?"
This plain distinction, sir, your doubt secures:
'Tis not true reason I despise, but yours.
  'Thus I think reason righted, but for man,
I'll ne'er recant; defend him if you can.
For all his pride and his philosophy,
'Tis evident beasts are, in their degree,
As wise at least, and better far than he.
Those creatures are the wisest who attain,
By surest means, the ends at which they aim.
If therefore Jowler finds and kills his hares
Better than Meres supplies committee chairs,
Though one's a statesman, the other but a hound,
Jowler, in justice, would be wiser found.
  'You see how far man's wisdom here extends;
Look next if human nature makes amends:
Whose principles most generous are, and just,
And to whose morals you would sooner trust.
Be judge yourself, I'll bring it to the test:
Which is the basest creature, man or beast?
Birds feed on birds, beasts on each other prey,
But savage man alone does man betray.
Pressed by necessity, they kill for food;
Man undoes man to do himself no good.
With teeth and claws by nature armed, they hunt:
Nature's allowance, to supply their want.
But man, with smiles, embraces, friendship, praise,
Inhumanly his fellow's life betrays;
With voluntary pains works his distress,
Not through necessity, but wantonness.
  'For hunger or for love they fight and tear,
Whilst wretched man is still in arms for fear.
For fear he arms, and is of arms afraid,
By fear, to fear, successively betrayed;

Meres] Sir Thomas Meres (1635–1715), MP for Lincoln   still] ever

Base fear, the source whence his best passions came:
His boasted honour, and his dear-bought fame;
That lust of power, to which he's such a slave,
And for the which alone he dares be brave;
To which his various projects are designed;
Which makes him generous, affable, and kind;
For which he takes such pains to be thought wise,
And screws his actions in a forced disguise,
Leading a tedious life in misery
Under laborious, mean hypocrisy.
Look to the bottom of his vast design,
Wherein man's wisdom, power, and glory join:
The good he acts, the ill he does endure,
'Tis all from fear, to make himself secure.
Merely for safety, after fame we thirst,
For all men would be cowards if they durst.
　'And honesty's against all common sense:
Men must be knaves, 'tis in their own defence.
Mankind's dishonest; if you think it fair
Amongst known cheats to play upon the square,
You'll be undone.
Nor can weak truth your reputation save:
The knaves will all agree to call you knave.
Wronged shall he live, insulted o'er, oppressed,
Who dares be less a villain than the rest.
　'Thus, sir, you see what human nature craves:
Most men are cowards, all men should be knaves.
The difference lies, as far as I can see,
Not in the thing itself, but the degree,
And all the subject matter of debate
Is only: Who's a knave of the first rate?'

　All this with indignation have I hurled
At the pretending part of the proud world,
Who, swollen with selfish vanity, devise
False freedoms, holy cheats, and formal lies,
Over their fellow slaves to tyrannize.
　But if in Court so just a man there be
(In Court a just man, yet unknown to me)
Who does his needful flattery direct,
Not to oppress and ruin, but protect
(Since flattery, which way soever laid,
Is still a tax on that unhappy trade);
If so upright a statesman you can find,

screws] forces, constrains

Whose passions bend to his unbiased mind;
Who does his arts and policies apply
To raise his country, not his family,
Nor, whilst his pride owned avarice withstands,
Receives close bribes through friends' corrupted hands—
  Is there a churchman who on God relies;
Whose life, his faith and doctrine justifies?
Not one blown up with vain prelatic pride,
Who, for reproof of sins, does man deride;
Whose envious heart makes preaching a pretence,
With his obstreperous, saucy eloquence,
To chide at kings, and rail at men of sense;
None of that sensual tribe whose talents lie
In avarice, pride, sloth, and gluttony;
Who hunt good livings, but abhor good lives;
Whose lust exalted, to that height arrives
They act adultery with their own wives,
And ere a score of years completed be,
Can from the lofty pulpit proudly see
Half a large parish their own progeny;
Nor doting bishop who would be adored
For domineering at the council board,
A greater fop in business at fourscore,
Fonder of serious toys, affected more,
Than the gay, glittering fool at twenty proves
With all his noise, his tawdry clothes, and loves;
  But a meek, humble man of honest sense,
Who, preaching peace, does practise continence;
Whose pious life's a proof he does believe
Mysterious truths, which no man can conceive.
If upon Earth there dwell such God-like men,
I'll here recant my paradox to them,
Adore those shrines of virtue, homage pay,
And, with the rabble world, their laws obey.
  If such there be, yet grant me this at least:
Man differs more from man, than man from beast.

(1679)

819 *Upon Nothing*

NOTHING, thou elder brother even to shade!
Thou hadst a being ere the world was made,
And, well fixed, art alone of ending not afraid.

Ere time and place were, time and place were not;
When primitive nothing something straight begot;
Then all proceeded from the great united what.

Something, the general attribute of all,
Severed from thee, its sole original,
Into thy boundless self must undistinguished fall;

Yet something did thy mighty power command,
And from thy fruitful emptiness's hand
Snatched men, beasts, birds, fire, water, air, and land.

Matter, the wickedest offspring of thy race,
By form assisted, flew from thy embrace,
And rebel light obscured thy reverend dusky face.

With form and matter, time and place did join;
Body, thy foe, with these did leagues combine,
To spoil thy peaceful realm, and ruin all thy line;

But turncoat time assists the foe in vain,
And bribed by thee destroys their short-lived reign,
And to thy hungry womb drives back thy slaves again.

Though mysteries are barred from laic eyes,
And the divine alone with warrant pries
Into thy bosom, where the truth in private lies,

Yet this of thee the wise may truly say:
Thou from the virtuous nothing dost delay,
And to be part of thee the wicked wisely pray.

Great negative, how vainly would the wise
Inquire, define, distinguish, teach, devise,
Didst thou not stand to point their blind philosophies!

Is or is not, the two great ends of fate,
And true or false, the subject of debate,
That perfect or destroy the vast designs of state—

When they have racked the politician's breast,
Within thy bosom most securely rest,
And, when reduced to thee, are least unsafe and best.

straight] immediately   combine] form in combination

But nothing, why does something s
That sacred monarchs should in c
With persons highly thought, at b

While weighty something modes
From princes' coffers, and from
And nothing there like stately r

Nothing! who dwellst with fo
For whom they reverend sha
Lawn sleeves and furs and

French truth, Dutch prowess, British polic
Hibernian learning, Scotch civility,
Spaniards' dispatch, Danes' wit, are mainly seen in thee;

The great man's gratitude to his best friend,
Kings' promises, whores' vows—towards thee they bend,
Flow swiftly into thee, and in thee ever end.

(1680)

820

Song

GIVE me leave to rail at you
(I ask nothing but my due):
To call you false, and then to say
You shall not keep my heart a day.
But, alas, against my will,
I must be your captive still.
Ah! Be kinder, then; for I
Cannot change, and would not die.

Kindness has resistless charms—
All besides but weakly move—
Fiercest anger it disarms,
And clips the wings of flying love.
Beauty does the heart invade;
Kindness only can persuade:
It gilds the lover's servile chain,
And makes the slave grow pleased and vain.

(1677 in part; 1680)

819 Lawn sleeves] Episcopal dress

Song

LOVE a woman? You're an ass!
'Tis a most insipid passion
To choose out for your happiness
The silliest part of God's creation.

Let the porter and the groom,
Things designed for dirty slaves,
Drudge in fair Aurelia's womb
To get supplies for age and graves.

Farewell, woman! I intend
Henceforth every night to sit
With my lewd, well-natured friend,
Drinking to engender wit.

Then give me health, wealth, mirth, and wine,
And, if busy love entrenches,
There's a sweet, soft page of mine
Does the trick worth forty wenches.

(1680)

822

Song

FAIR Chloris in a pigsty lay;
Her tender herd lay by her.
She slept; in murmuring gruntlings they,
Complaining of the scorching day,
Her slumbers thus inspire.

She dreamt whilst she with careful pains
Her snowy arms employed
In ivory pails to fill out grains,
One of her love-convicted swains
Thus hasting to her cried:

'Fly, nymph! Oh, fly ere 'tis too late
A dear, loved life to save;
Rescue your bosom pig from fate,
Who now expires, hung in the gate
That leads to Flora's cave.

insipid] dull, tasteless, stupid entrenches] encroaches

822 Chloris] (Greek vegetation goddess, metamorphosed to the spring goddess Flora)

'Myself had tried to set him free,
  Rather than brought the news;
But I am so abhorred by thee
That even thy darling's life from me
  I know thou wouldst refuse.'

Struck with the news, as quick she flies
  As blushes to her face;
Not the bright lightning from the skies,
Nor love, shot from her brighter eyes,
  Move half so swift a pace.

This plot, it seems, the lustful slave
  Had laid against her honour,
Which not one god took care to save;
For he pursues her to the cave
  And throws himself upon her.

Now piercèd is her virgin zone;
  She feels the foe within it.
She hears a broken amorous groan,
The panting lover's fainting moan,
  Just in the happy minute.

Frighted she wakes, and waking frigs.
  Nature thus kindly eased
In dreams raised by her murmuring pigs
And her own thumb between her legs,
  She's innocent and pleased.

(1680)

823 *The Platonic Lady*

I COULD love thee till I die,
Wouldst thou love me modestly,
And ne'er press, whilst I live,
For more than willingly I would give:
  Which should sufficient be to prove
  I'd understand the art of love.

I hate the thing is called enjoyment:
Besides it is a dull employment,
It cuts off all that's life and fire
From that which may be termed desire;
  Just like the bee whose sting is gone
  Converts the owner to a drone.

823 enjoyment] orgasm

I love a youth will give me leave
His body in my arms to wreathe;
To press him gently, and to kiss;
To sigh, and look with eyes that wish
  For what, if I could once obtain,
  I would neglect with flat disdain.

I'd give him liberty to toy
And play with me, and count it joy.
Our freedom should be full complete,
And nothing wanting but the feat.
  Let's practise, then, and we shall prove
  These are the only sweets of love.

(1926)

824 *The Mistress: A Song*

An age in her embraces passed
  Would seem a winter's day,
Where life and light with envious haste
  Are torn and snatched away.

But oh, how slowly minutes roll
  When absent from her eyes,
That feed my love, which is my soul:
  It languishes, and dies.

For then no more a soul, but shade,
  It mournfully does move,
And haunts my breast, by absence made
  The living tomb of love.

You wiser men, despise me not
  Whose lovesick fancy raves
On 'shades of souls', and heaven knows what:
  Short ages live in graves.

Whene'er those wounding eyes, so full
  Of sweetness, you did see,
Had you not been profoundly dull,
  You had gone mad like me.

Nor censure us, you who perceive
  My best beloved and me
Sigh and lament, complain and grieve.
  You think we disagree.

Alas! 'Tis sacred jealousy,
Love raised to an extreme:
The only proof 'twixt her and me
We love, and do not dream.

Fantastic fancies fondly move,
And in frail joys believe,
Taking false pleasure for true love;
But pain can ne'er deceive.

Kind jealous doubts, tormenting fears,
And anxious cares, when past,
Prove our hearts' treasure fixed and dear,
And make us blest at last.

(1691)

825 *A Song of a Young Lady: To Her Ancient Lover*

ANCIENT person, for whom I
All the flattering youth defy,
Long be it ere thou grow old,
Aching, shaking, crazy cold;
But still continue as thou art,
Ancient person of my heart.

On thy withered lips and dry,
Which like barren furrows lie,
Brooding kisses I will pour,
Shall thy youthful heat restore.
Such kind showers in autumn fall,
And a second spring recall;
Nor from thee will ever part,
Ancient person of my heart.

Thy nobler part, which but to name
In our sex would be counted shame,
By age's frozen grasp possessed,
From his ice shall be released,
And, soothed by my reviving hand,
In former warmth and vigour stand.
All a lover's wish can reach,
For thy joy my love shall teach;

fancies] imaginations move] are inclined

825 still] ever

And for thy pleasure shall improve
All that art can add to love.
Yet still I love thee without art,
Ancient person of my heart.

(1691)

826 *Verses Put into a Lady's Prayer-Book*

FLING this useless book away,
And presume no more to pray:
Heaven is just, and can bestow
Mercy on none but those that mercy show.
With a proud heart maliciously inclined
Not to increase, but to subdue mankind,
In vain you vex the gods with your petition;
Without repentance and sincere contrition,
You're in a reprobate condition.
Phillis, to calm the angry powers,
And save my soul as well as yours,
Relieve poor mortals from despair,
And justify the gods that made you fair;
And in those bright and charming eyes
  Let pity first appear, then love;
That we by easy steps may rise
  Through all the joys on Earth, to those above.

(1697)

827 [*A Satire on Charles II*]

I' TH' ISLE of Britain long since famous grown
For breeding the best cunts in Christendom,
There reigns—and oh! long may he reign and thrive—
The easiest king and best bred man alive.
Him no ambition moves, to get renown
Like the French fool, who wanders up and down
Starving his people, hazarding his crown.
Peace is his aim, his gentleness is such,
And love he loves, for he loves fucking much.
Nor are his high desires above his strength:
His sceptre and his prick are of a length,
And she may sway the one, who plays with th' other,
And make him little wiser than his brother.

827 French fool] Louis XIV brother] James, Duke of York

Restless he rolls about from whore to whore,
A merry monarch, scandalous and poor.
Poor prince, thy prick like thy buffoons at Court
Will govern thee, because it makes thee sport.
'Tis sure the sauciest that e'er did swive,
The proudest, peremptoriest prick alive.
Though safety, law, religion, life lay on 't,
'Twould break through all to make its way to cunt.
To Carwell, the most dear of all his dears,
The best relief of his declining years,
Oft he bewails his fortunes and her fate,
To love so well and be beloved so late.
For though in her he settles well his tarse,
Yet his dull graceless ballocks hang an arse.
This you'd believe, had I but time to tell you
The pains it cost the poor laborious Nelly
Whilst she employs hands, fingers, mouth, and thighs
Ere she can raise the member she enjoys—
I hate all monarchs, and the thrones they sit on,
From the Hector of France to the cully of Britain.

(1697)

THOMAS HEYRICK
1649–1694

828

On a Sunbeam

THOU beauteous offspring of a sire as fair,
With thy kind influence thou dost all things heat:
Thou gildst the heaven, the sea, the earth and air,
And under massy rocks dost gold beget.
   The opaque dull earth thou dost make fine;
   Thou dost i' th' moon and planets shine;
   And, if astronomy say true,
Our Earth to them doth seem a planet too.

How unaccountable thy journeys prove!
Thy swift course through the universe doth fly,
From lofty heights in distant heavens above,
To all that at the lowly centre lie.

827 Carwell] Louise de Kéroualle, Duchess of Portsmouth   tarse] penis   hang an arse] be sluggish   Nelly] Nell Gwyn   Hector] a bully   cully] fool, dupe

Thy parent sun once in a day
Through heaven doth steer his well-beat way;
Thou of a swifter, subtler breed
Dost every moment his day's course exceed.

Thy common presence makes thee little prized;
Which, if we once had lost, we'd dearly buy:
How would the blind hug what's by us despised!
How welcome wouldst thou in a dungeon be!
Thrice wretched those in mines are bred
That from thy sight are burièd,
When all the stores for which they try
Neither in use nor beauty equal thee.

Could there be found an art to fix thee down
And of condensèd rays a gem to make,
'Twould be the brightest lustre of a crown
And an esteem invaluable take.
New wars would the tired world molest
And new ambition fire men's breast,
More battles fought for it than e'er
Before for love, empire, or treasure, were.

Thou'rt quickly born and dost as quickly die:
Pity so fair a birth to fate should fall!
Now here and now in abject dust dost lie,
One moment 'twixt thy birth and funeral.
Art thou, like angels, only shown,
Then, to our grief, for ever flown?
Tell me, Apollo, tell me where
The sunbeams go, when they do disappear.

(1691)

829 *On an Indian Tomineios, the Least of Birds*

I'M made in sport by nature, when
She's tired with the stupendious weight
Of forming elephants and beasts of state:
Rhinoceros, that love the fen;
The elks, that scale the hills of snow;
And lions couching in their awful den.
These do work nature hard, and then
Her wearied hand in me doth show
What she can for her own diversion do.

828 esteem] worth take] taken

Man is a little world ('tis said),
And I in miniature am drawn,
A perfect creature, but in shorthand shown.
The ruck, in Madagascar bred
(If new discoveries truth do speak),
Whom greatest beasts and armèd horsemen dread,
Both him and me one artist made:
Nature in this delight doth take,
That can so great and little monsters make.

The Indians me a sunbeam name,
And I may be the child of one:
So small I am, my kind is hardly known.
To some a sportive bird I seem,
And some believe me but a fly;
Though me a feathered fowl the best esteem.
Whate'er I am, I'm nature's gem,
And, like a sunbeam from the sky,
I can't be followed by the quickest eye.

I'm the true bird of paradise,
And heavenly dew's my only meat:
My mouth so small, 'twill nothing else admit.
No scales know how my weight to poise,
So light, I seem condensèd air;
And did at the end of the creation rise,
When nature wanted more supplies,
When she could little matter spare,
But in return did make the work more rare.

(1691)

ANONYMOUS
fl. 1681?

830 WOULD you be a man in fashion?
Would you lead a life divine?
Take a little dram of passion
In a lusty dose of wine.
If the nymph has no compassion,
Vain it is to sigh and groan:
Love was but put in for fashion,
Wine will do the work alone.

(1684; wr. before 1681?)

829 ruck] roc (mythical bird)

FRANCIS DANIEL PASTORIUS
1651–1720

831

DELIGHT in books from evening
Till midnight when the cocks do sing,
Till morning when the day doth spring,
Till sunset when the bell doth ring.
Delight in books, for books do bring
Poor men to learn most everything:
The art of true Levelling;
Yea even how to please the king.
Delight in books: they're carrying
Us so far that we know to fling
On waspish men (who taking wing
Surround us) that they cannot sting.

(1968)

NAHUM TATE
1652–1715

832

WHILE shepherds watched their flocks by night,
  All seated on the ground,
The angel of the Lord came down,
  And glory shone around.

'Fear not,' said he, for mighty dread
  Had seized their troubled mind;
'Glad tidings of great joy I bring
  To you and all mankind.

'To you, in David's town, this day
  Is born of David's line
The saviour, who is Christ the Lord,
  And this shall be the sign:

'The heavenly babe you there shall find
  To human view displayed,
All meanly wrapped in swathing bands,
  And in a manger laid.'

Thus spake the seraph; and forthwith
  Appeared a shining throng
Of angels, praising God, who thus
  Addressed their joyful song:

'All glory be to God on high,
  And to the Earth be peace;
Good will henceforth from heaven to men
  Begin and never cease.'

(1700)

833 *The Penance*

NYMPH Fanarett, supposed to be
The gentlest, most indulgent she
(For what offence I cannot say)
A day and night, and half a day,
Banished her shepherd from her sight;
Sure his default could not be light,
Or this compassionate judge had ne'er
Imposed a penance so severe.
And lest she should anon revoke
What in her warmer rage she spoke,
She bound the sentence with an oath,
Protested by her faith and troth,
Nought should compound for his offence
But the full term of abstinence.
  But when his penance-glass were run,
His hours of castigation done,
Should he defer one minute's space
T' appear and be restored to grace,
With sparkling threatening eyes she swore,
That failing would incense her more
Than all his trespasses before.

(1677)

JACOB ALLESTRY
1653–1686

834 WHAT art thou, love? Whence are those charms,
  That thus thou bearst an universal rule?
For thee the soldier quits his arms,
  The king turns slave, the wise man fool.

In vain we chase thee from the field,
  And with cool thoughts resist thy yoke:
Next tide of blood, alas! we yield,
  And all those high resolves are broke.

Can we e'er hope thou shouldst be true,
  Whom we have found so often base?
Cozened and cheated, still we view
  And fawn upon the treacherous face.

In vain our nature we accuse,
  And dote, because she says we must:
This for a brute were an excuse,
  Whose very soul and life is lust.

To get our likeness! What is that?
  Our likeness is but misery;
Why should I toil to propagate
  Another thing as vile as I?

From hands divine our spirits came,
  And gods, that made us, did inspire
Something more noble in our frame,
  Above the dregs of earthly fire.

(1693)

THOMAS D'URFEY
1653?–1723

835 ### *The Fisherman's Song*

Of all the world's enjoyments
  That ever valued were
There's none of our employments
  With fishing can compare:
    Some preach, some write,
    Some swear, some fight,
All golden lucre courting;
  But fishing still bears off the bell
For profit or for sporting.

cozened] deceived

835 still] always   bell] prize

Then who a jolly fisherman, a fisherman will be,
His throat must wet,
Just like his net,
To keep out cold at sea.

The country squire loves running
A pack of well-mouthed hounds;
Another fancies gunning
For wild ducks in his grounds:
This hunts, that fowls,
This hawks, Dick bowls,
No greater pleasure wishing;
But Tom that tells what sport excels
Gives all the praise to fishing.

A good Westphalia gammon
Is counted dainty fare;
But what is 't to a salmon
Just taken from the Ware?
Wheatears and quails,
Cocks, snipes, and rails
Are prized while season's lasting;
But all must stoop to crawfish soup,
Or I've no skill in tasting.

Keen hunters always take to
Their prey with too much pains;
Nay, often break a neck, too,
A penance for no brains:
They run, they leap,
Now high, now deep;
Whilst he that fishing chooses
With ease may do 't, nay more to boot,
May entertain the Muses.

And though some envious wranglers
To jeer us will make bold,
And laugh at patient anglers
Who stand so long in the cold,
They wait on miss,
We wait on this,
And think it easier labour;
And, if you'd know, fish profits too:
Consult our Holland neighbour.

(1700)

JOHN OLDHAM
1653–1683

836 from *A Satyr. The Person of Spenser is Brought in, Dissuading the Author from the Study of Poetry, and Showing how Little It is Esteemed and Encouraged in this Present Age.*

ONE night, as I was pondering of late
On all the miseries of my hapless fate,
Cursing my rhyming stars, raving in vain
At all the powers which over poets reign,
In came a ghastly shape, all pale and thin,
As some poor sinner who by priest had been
Under a long Lent's penance, starved and whipped;
Or parboiled lecher, late from hot-house crept:
Famished his looks appeared, his eyes sunk in,
Like morning-gown about him hung his skin;
A wreath of laurel on his head he wore;
A book, inscribed *The Faerie Queene*, he bore.
  By this I knew him, rose, and bowed, and said,
'Hail, reverend ghost! All hail, most sacred shade!
Why this great visit? Why vouchsafed to me,
The meanest of thy British progeny?
Comest thou, in my uncalled, unhallowed Muse
Some of thy mighty spirit to infuse?
If so, lay on thy hands, ordain me fit
For the high cure and ministry of wit:
Let me, I beg, thy great instructions claim;
Teach me to treat the glorious paths of fame.
Teach me (for none does better know than thou)
How, like thyself, I may immortal grow.'
  Thus did I speak, and spoke it in a strain
Above my common rate and usual vein,
As if inspired by presence of the bard;
Who with a frown thus to reply was heard,
In style of satyr, such wherein of old
He the famed tale of *Mother Hubberd* told:
  'I come, fond idiot, ere it be too late,
Kindly to warn thee of thy wretched fate:
Take heed betimes, repent, and learn of me
To shun the dangerous rocks of poetry;

Satyr] Satire   hot-house] brothel; steam-bath   cure] care; office

Had I the choice of flesh and blood again,
To act once more in life's tumultuous scene,
I'd be a porter, or a scavenger,
A groom, or anything but poet here.
Hast thou observed some hawker of the town,
Who through the streets with dismal scream and tone
Cries "Matches, small coal, brooms, old shoes and boots,
Socks, sermons, ballads, lies, gazettes, and votes"?
So unrecorded to the grave I'd go,
And nothing but the register tell who;
Rather that poor unheard-of wretch I'd be
Than the most glorious name in poetry,
With all its boasted immortality:
Rather than he who sung on Phrygia's shore
The Grecian bullies fighting for a whore,
Or he of Thebes whom fame so much extols
For praising jockeys and Newmarket fools.

* * * * *

'Perhaps, fond fool, thou soothst thyself in dream
With hopes of purchasing a lasting name?
Thou thinkst perhaps thy trifles shall remain,
Like sacred Cowley and immortal Ben?
But who of all the bold adventurers
Who now drive on the trade of fame in verse
Can be ensured in this unfaithful sea,
Where there so many lost and shipwracked be?
How many poems writ in ancient time,
Which thy forefathers had in great esteem,
Which in the crowded shops bore any rate,
And sold like news-books and affairs of state,
Have grown contemptible and slighted since,
As Pordidge, Flecknoe, or *The British prince*?
Quarles, Chapman, Heywood, Withers had applause,
And Wild and Ogilby in former days,
But now are damned to wrapping drugs and wares,
And cursed by all their broken stationers;
And so mayst thou perchance pass up and down,
And please awhile the admiring court and town,
Who after shalt in Duck Lane shops be thrown,
To mould with Sylvester and Shirley there ...'

(1683)

he ... Phrygia's shore] Homer he of Thebes] Pindar Newmarket] i.e. Newmarket racecourse ensured] assured rate] distinction Pordidge ... Ogilby] (see endnote) broken] bankrupt Duck Lane] (centre of second-hand book trade) moul] moulder

from *A Satyr, in Imitation of The Third of Juvenal*

837

[*London*]

Sir, to be short, in this expensive town
There's nothing without money to be done:
What will you give to be admitted there,
And brought to speech of some court minister?
What will you give to have the quarter-face,
The squint and nodding go-by of His Grace?
His porter, groom, and steward must have fees,
And you may see the tombs and Tower for less:
Hard fate of suitors, who must pay, and pray
To livery slaves, yet oft go scorned away!
Whoe'er at Barnet, or St Albans, fears
To have his lodging drop about his ears,
Unless a sudden hurricane befall,
Or such a wind as blew old Noll to hell?
Here we build slight, what scarce outlasts the lease,
Without the help of props and buttresses;
And houses nowadays as much require
To be ensured from falling, as from fire.
There buildings are substantial, though less neat,
And kept with care both wind- and water-tight;
There you in safe security are blest,
And nought but conscience to disturb your rest.
I am for living where no fires affright,
No bells rung backward break my sleep at night;
I scarce lie down and draw my curtains here,
But straight I'm roused by the next house on fire:
Pale and half dead with fear, myself I raise,
And find my room all over in a blaze:
By this it's seized on the third stairs, and I
Can now discern no other remedy
But leaping out at window to get free;
For if the mischief from the cellar came,
Be sure the garret is the last, takes flame.
The movables of P[orda]ge were a bed
For him and 's wife, a piss-pot by its side,
A looking-glass upon the cupboard's head,
A comb-case, candlestick, and pewter spoon,
For want of plate, with desk to write upon;
A box without a lid served to contain

tombs] i.e. Westminster tombs   Tower] Tower of London   Noll] Oliver Cromwell   neat] elegant   curtains] i.e. bed-curtains

Few authors, which made up his Vatican;
And there his own immortal works were laid,
On which the barbarous mice for hunger preyed.
P[ordage] had nothing, all the world does know;
And yet, should he have lost this nothing too,
No one the wretched bard would have supplied
With lodging, house room, or a crust of bread.
But if the fire burn down some great man's house,
All straight are interéssèd in the loss:
The court is straight in mourning sure enough,
The act, commencement, and the term put off;
Then we mischances of the town lament,
And fasts are kept, like judgements to prevent.
Out comes a brief immediately, with speed
To gather charity as far as Tweed.
Nay, while 'tis burning, some will send him in
Timber and stone to build his house again;
Others, choice furniture; here some rare piece
Of Rubens, or Vandyke, presented is;
There a rich suit of Moreclack tapestry,
A bed of damask, or embroidery;
One gives a fine scrutoire or cabinet,
Another a huge massy dish of plate,
Or bag of gold; thus he at length gets more
By kind misfortune than he had before,
And all suspect it for a laid design,
As if he did himself the fire begin.
Could you but be advised to leave the town,
And from dear plays and drinking friends be drawn,
An handsome dwelling might be had in Kent,
Surrey, or Essex, at a cheaper rent
Than what you're forced to give for one half year,
To lie, like lumber, in a garret here;
A garden there, and well that needs no rope,
Engine, or pains to crane its waters up;
Water is there through nature's pipes conveyed,
For which no custom or excise is paid:
Had I the smallest spot of ground, which scarce
Would summer half a dozen grasshoppers,
Not larger than my grave, though hence remote
Far as St Michael's Mount, I would go to 't,
Dwell there content, and thank the Fates to boot.
Here want of rest a nights more people kills

interéssèd] involved; affected with concern act, commencement] degree ceremonies at Oxford and Cambridge respectively Moreclack] Mortlake scrutoire] escritoire massy] massive kind] (1) natural; (2) kind

Than all the college, and the weekly bills;
Where none have privilege to sleep but those
Whose purses can compound for their repose:
In vain I go to bed or close my eyes;
Methinks the place the middle region is,
Where I lie down in storms, in thunder rise;
The restless bells such din in steeples keep,
That scarce the dead can in their churchyards sleep;
Huzzahs of drunkards, bellmen's midnight rhymes,
The noise of shops, with hawkers' early screams,
Besides the brawls of coachmen, when they meet
And stop in turnings of a narrow street,
Such a loud medley of confusion make
As drowsy A[rche]r on the bench would wake.

(1683; wr. 1682)

JOHN NORRIS
1657–1711

838 *The Meditation*

It must be done, my soul, but 'tis a strange,
  A dismal and mysterious change,
When thou shalt leave this tenement of clay,
And to an unknown somewhere wing away;
When time shall be eternity, and thou
Shalt be thou knowst not what, and live thou knowst not how.

Amazing state! No wonder that we dread
  To think of death, or view the dead.
Thou art all wrapped up in clouds, as if to thee
Our very knowledge had antipathy.
Death could not a more sad retínue find:
Sickness and pain before, and darkness all behind.

Some courteous ghost, tell this great secrecy,
  What 'tis you are, and we must be.
You warn us of approaching death, and why
May we not know from you what 'tis to die?

college] i.e. of physicians   bills] i.e. of mortality, listing plague victims   middle region] i.e. of air

838 dismal] fatal, ominous   tenement] dwelling

But you, having shot the gulf, delight to see
Succeeding souls plunge in with like uncertainty.

When life's close knot, by writ from destiny,
  Disease shall cut, or age untie;
When after some delays, some dying strife,
The soul stands shivering on the ridge of life;
With what a dreadful curiosity
Does she launch out into the seas of vast eternity!

So, when the spacious globe was deluged o'er,
  And lower holds could save no more,
On the utmost bough the astonished sinners stood,
And viewed the advances of the encroaching flood.
O'ertopped at length by the element's increase,
With horror they resigned to the untried abyss.

(1687)

839 *My Estate*

How do I pity that proud wealthy clown,
That does with scorn on my low state look down!
  Thy vain contempt, dull earthworm, cease;
  I won't for refuge fly to this,
  That none of fortune's blessings can
  Add any value to the man.
This all the wise acknowledge to be true;
But know I am as rich, more rich, than you.

While you a spot of Earth possess with care
Below the notice of the geographer,
  I by the freedom of my soul
  Possess, nay more, enjoy the whole:
  To the universe a claim I lay.
  Your writings show, perhaps you'll say:
That's your dull way; my title runs more high:
'Tis by the charter of philosophy.

From that a firmer title I derive
Than all your courts of law doth ever give,
  A title that more firm doth stand
  Than does even your very land,
  And yet so generous and free
  That none will e'er bethink it me;
Since my possessions tend to no man's loss,
I all enjoy, yet nothing I engross.

839 clown] peasant   show] make a formal award (legal)   bethink] grudge

Throughout the works divine I cast my eye,
Admire their beauty and their harmony.
  I view the glorious host above,
  And him that made them, praise and love.
  The flowery meads and fields beneath
  Delight me with their odorous breath.
Thus is my joy, by you not understood,
Like that of God when he said all was good.

Nay!—what you'd think less likely to be true—
I can enjoy what's yours much more than you.
  Your meadow's beauty, I survey,
  Which you prize only for its hay.
  There can I sit beneath a tree,
  And write an ode or elegy.
What to you care, does to me pleasure bring:
You own the cage, I in it sit and sing.

(1687)

RICHARD DUKE
1658–1711

840

To Caelia

Mistress of all my senses can invite,
Free as the air, and unconfined as light;
Queen of a thousand slaves that fawn and bow,
And with submissive fear my power allow,
Should I exchange this noble state of life
To gain the vile detested name of wife?
Should I my native liberty betray,
Call him my lord who at my footstool lay?
No: thanks kind heaven that has my soul employed,
With my great sex's useful virtue, pride,
That generous pride, that noble just disdain,
That scorns the slave that would presume to reign.
Let the raw am'rous scribbler of the times
Call me his Caelia in insipid rhymes:
I hate and scorn you all, proud that I am
To revenge my sex's injuries on man.
Compared to all the plagues in marriage dwell,
It were preferment to lead apes in hell.

(1717)

ANNE WHARTON
1659–1685

841 *Elegy on the Earl of Rochester*

DEEP waters silent roll, so grief like mine
Tears never can relieve, nor words define.
Stop, then, stop your vain source, weak springs of grief,
Let tears flow from their eyes whom tears relieve.
They from their heads show the light trouble there;
Could my heart weep, its sorrows 'twould declare:
Weep drops of blood, my heart, thou'st lost thy pride,
The cause of all thy hopes and fears, thy guide.
He would have led thee right in wisdom's way,
And 'twas thy fault whene'er thou wentst astray;
And since thou strayedst when guided and led on,
Thou wilt be surely lost now left alone.
It is thy elegy I write, not his:
He lives immortal and in highest bliss.
But thou art dead, alas! my heart, thou'rt dead:
He lives, that lovely soul for ever fled,
But thou mongst crowds on Earth art burièd.
Great was thy loss, which thou canst ne'er express,
Nor was th' insensible dull nation's less:
He civilized the rude and taught the young,
Made fools grow wise, such artful magic hung
Upon his useful, kind, instructing tongue.
His lively wit was of himself a part,
Not, as in other men, the work of art;
For, though his learning like his wit was great,
Yet sure all learning came below his wit;
As God's immediate gifts are better far
Than those we borrow from our likeness here,
He was—but I want words, and ne'er can tell;
Yet this I know, he did mankind excel.
  He was what no man ever was before;
Nor can indulgent nature give us more,
For to make him she exhausted all her store.

(1685)

ANONYMOUS

fl. 1685–1690

842 *One Writing against His Prick*

BASE metal hanger by your master's thigh!
Eternal shame to all prick's heraldry,
Hide thy despisèd head and do not dare
To peep, no not so much as take the air
But through a button-hole; but pine and die
Confined within the codpiece monastery.
The little childish boy that hardly knows
The way through which his urine flows,
Touched by my mistress her magnetic hand
His little needle presently will stand.
Did she not raise thy drooping head on high
As it lay nodding on her wanton thigh?
Did she not clap her legs about my back,
Her porthole open? Damned prick what is 't you lack?
Henceforth stand stiff and gain your credit lost,
Or I'll ne'er draw thee, but against a post.

(1968)

843 *The Female Wits: A Song by a Lady of Quality*

MEN with much toil, and time, and pain,
  At length at fame arrive,
While we a nearer way obtain
  The palms for which they strive.

We scorn to climb by reason's rules
  To the loud name of wit,
And count them silly, modest fools,
  Who to that test submit.

Our sparkling way a method knows
  More airy and refined,
And should dull reason interpose,
  Our lofty flight 'twould bind.

Then let us on—and still believe;
  A good bold faith will do,
If we ourselves can well deceive,
  The world will follow too.

What matter though the witty few
  Our emptiness do find?
They for their interest will be true,
  'Cause we are brisk and kind.

(1685)

844

OH waly, waly up the bank,
  And waly, waly down the brae,
And waly, waly yon burnside
  Where I and my love wont to gae.
I leaned my back unto an aik,
  I thought it was a trusty tree;
But first it bowed, and syne it brak:
  Sae my true love did lightly me.

Oh waly, waly gin love be bonny,
  A little time while it is new;
But when it's auld, it waxeth cauld,
  And fades awa like morning dew.
Oh wherefore should I busk my head?
  Or wherefore should I kame my hair?
For my true love has me forsook,
  And says he'll never love me mair.

Now Arthur Seat shall be my bed,
  The sheets shall n'er be filed by me;
Saint Anton's well shall be my drink,
  Since my true love has forsaken me.
Martinmas wind, when wilt thou blaw,
  And shake the green leaves off the tree?
O gentle death, when wilt thou come?
  For of my life I am weary.

'Tis not the frost that freezes fell,
  Nor blawing snaw's inclemency;
'Tis not sic cauld that makes me cry,
  But my love's heart grown cauld to me.
When we came in by Glasgow town,
  We were a comely sight to see;
My love was cled in the black velvet,
  And I mysel in cramasie.

844 waly] alas   aik] oak   syne] after   lightly] despise   gin] if   busk] do   kame] comb   filed] soiled   sic] such   cramasie] crimson velvet, satin, etc.

But had I wist, before I kissed,
  That love had been sae ill to win,
I had locked my heart in a case of gold,
  And pinned it with a silver pin.
And oh! if my young babe were born,
  And set upon the nurse's knee,
And I mysel were dead and gane!
  For a maid again I'll never be.

(1724–7)

845 *The Bonny Earl of Murray*

Ye highlands and ye lawlands,
  Oh where have ye been?
They have slain the Earl of Murray,
  And they laid him on the green.

'Now wae be to thee, Huntly!
  And wherefore did you sae;
I bade you bring him wi you,
  But forbade you him to slay.'

He was a braw gallant,
  And he rid at the ring;
And the bonny Earl of Murray,
  Oh, he might have been a king!

He was a braw gallant,
  And he played at the ba;
And the bonny Earl of Murray
  Was the flower amang them a'.

He was a braw gallant,
  And he played at the glove;
And the bonny Earl of Murray,
  Oh he was the Queen's love!

Oh lang will his lady
  Look o'er the Castle Doune,
Ere she see the Earl of Murray
  Come sounding through the town.

(1733)

wist] known

845 rid] rode   ring] suspended target for the rider's lance   glove] target game

846 *Auld Lang Syne*

SHOULD old acquaintance be forgot,
  And never thought upon;
The flames of love extinguishèd,
  And freely past and gone?
Is thy kind heart now grown so cold
  In that loving breast of thine,
That thou canst never once reflect
  On auld lang syne?

Where are thy protestations,
  Thy vows and oaths, my dear,
Thou made to me, and I to thee,
  In register yet clear?
Is faith and truth so violate
  To the immortal gods divine,
That thou canst never once reflect
  On auld lang syne?

Is it Cupid's fears, or frosty cares,
  That makes thy spirits decay?
Or is 't some object of more worth,
  That's stolen thy heart away?
Or some desert, makes thee neglect
  Him, so much once was thine,
That thou canst never once reflect
  On auld lang syne?

Is it worldly cares so desperate,
  That makes thee to despair?
Is 't that makes thee exasperate,
  And makes thee to forbear?
If thou of that were free as I,
  Thou surely should be mine:
If this were true, we should renew
  Kind auld lang syne;

But since that nothing can prevail,
  And all hope is in vain,
From these rejected eyes of mine
  Still showers of tears shall rain;
And though thou hast me now forgot,
  Yet I'll continue thine,
And ne'er forget for to reflect
  On auld lang syne.

Syne] Since   register] tone   exasperate] harsh

If e'er I have a house, my dear,
That truly is called mine,
And can afford but country cheer,
Or ought that's good therein;
Though thou were rebel to the king,
And beat with wind and rain,
Assure thyself of welcome, love,
For auld lang syne.

(1711)

ANNE KILLIGREW
1660–1685

847 *On a Picture Painted by Herself, Representing Two Nymphs of Diana's, One in a Posture to Hunt, the Other Bathing*

We are Diana's virgin train,
Descended of no mortal strain:
Our bows and arrows are our goods,
Our palaces the lofty woods;
The hills and dales at early morn
Resound and echo with our horn;
We chase the hind and fallow deer;
The wolf and boar both dread our spear;
In swiftness we outstrip the wind,
And eye and thought we leave behind;
We fawns and shaggy satyrs awe;
To sylvan powers we give the law:
Whatever does provoke our hate,
Our javelins strike, as sure as fate.
We bathe in springs, to cleanse the soil
Contracted by our eager toil;
In which we shine like glittering beams,
Or crystal in the crystal streams:
Though Venus we transcend in form,
No wanton flames our bosoms warm.
If you ask where such wights do dwell,
In what blest clime, that so excel,
The poets only that can tell.

(1686)

847 wights] creatures

PIERRE ANTOINE MOTTEUX
1660–1718

848 *A Song*

Slaves to London, I'll deceive you;
For the country now I leave you.
Who can bear, and not be mad,
Wine so dear and yet so bad?
Such a noise, an air so smoky:
That to stun ye, this to choke ye?
Men so selfish, false, and rude,
Nymphs so young, and yet so lewd?

If we play, we're sure of losing;
If we love, our doom we're choosing.
At the playhouse tedious sport,
Cant in City, cringe at Court,
Dirt in streets, and dirty bullies,
Jolting coaches, whores, and cullies,
Knaves and coxcombs everywhere:
Who that's wise would tarry here?

Quiet harmless country pleasure
Shall at home engross my leisure.
Farewell, London! I'll repair
To my native country air:
I leave all thy plagues behind me—
But at home my wife will find me?
O ye gods! 'Tis ten times worse!
London is a milder curse.

(1696)

THOMAS SOUTHERNE
1660–1746

849 *Song*

Pursuing beauty, men descry
The distant shore, and long to prove
(Still richer in variety)
The treasures of the land of love.

849 prove] experience; appraise

We women, like weak Indians, stand
  Inviting, from our golden coast,
The wandering rovers to our land;
  But she who trades with 'em is lost.

With humble vows they first begin,
  Stealing, unseen, into the heart;
But by possession settled in,
  They quickly act another part.

For beads and baubles, we resign,
  In ignorance, our shining store,
Discover nature's richest mine;
  And yet the tyrants will have more.

Be wise, be wise, and do not try
  How he can court, or you be won;
For love is but discovery:
  When that is made, the pleasure's done.

(1690)

ANNE FINCH, COUNTESS OF WINCHILSEA
1661–1720

850 from *The Petition for an Absolute Retreat: Inscribed to the Right Honourable Catharine Countess of Thanet, Mentioned in the Poem under the Name of Arminda*

GIVE me, O indulgent fate,
Give me yet, before I die,
A sweet, but absolute retreat,
Mongst paths so lost and trees so high
That the world may ne'er invade,
Through such windings and such shade,
My unshaken liberty.
  No intruders thither come!
Who visit but to be from home;
None who their vain moments pass,
Only studious of their glass:
News, that charm to listening ears;

849 discover] uncover

That common theme for every fop,
From the statesman to the shop,
In those coverts ne'er be spread,
Of who's deceased or who's to wed;
Be no tidings thither brought,
But silent as a midnight thought,
Where the world may ne'er invade,
Be those windings, and that shade.
  Courteous fate! afford me there
A table spread without my care,
With what the neighbouring fields impart,
Whose cleanliness be all its art:
When of old the calf was dressed
(Though to make an angel's feast)
In the plain, unstudied sauce
Nor truffle, nor morillia was;
Nor could the mighty patriarch's board
One far-fetched ortolan afford.
Courteous fate, then give me there
Only plain, and wholesome fare.
Fruits, indeed (would heaven bestow),
All that did in Eden grow,
All but the forbidden tree,
Would be coveted by me:
Grapes, with juice so crowded up,
As breaking through the native cup;
Figs, yet growing, candied o'er
By the sun's attracting power;
Cherries, with the downy peach,
All within my easy reach;
Whilst creeping near the humble ground
Should the strawberry be found
Springing wheresoe'er I strayed,
Through those windings and that shade.
  For my garments, let them be
What may with the time agree:
Warm, when Phoebus does retire,
And is ill supplied by fire;
But when he renews the year,
And verdant all the fields appear,
Beauty everything resumes,
Birds have dropped their winter plumes;
When the lily full displayed
Stands in purer white arrayed

morillia] morels patriarch's] Abraham's (Gen. 18: 7) Phoebus] the sun
supplied] replaced

Than that vest which heretofore
The luxurious monarch wore
When from Salem's gates he drove
To the soft retreat of love,
Lebanon's all-burnished house,
And the dear Egyptian spouse,
Clothe me, fate, though not so gay;
Clothe me light and fresh as May.
In the fountains let me view
All my habit cheap and new,
Such as, when sweet zephyrs fly,
With their motions may comply;
Gently waving, to express
Unaffected carelessness:
No perfúmes have there a part,
Borrowed from the chemist's art;
But such as rise from flowery beds,
Or the falling jasmine sheds!
'Twas the odour of the field,
Esau's rural coat did yield,
That inspired his father's prayer
For blessings of the earth and air:
Of gums or powders had it smelt,
The supplanter, then unfelt,
Easily had been descried
For one that did in tents abide;
For some beauteous handmaid's joy,
And his mother's darling boy.
Let me then no fragrance wear
But what the winds from gardens bear
In such kind, surprising gales
As gathered from Fidentia's vales
All the flowers that in them grew;
Which intermixing as they flew,
In wreathen garlands dropped again
On Lucullus and his men,
Who, cheered by the victorious sight,
Trebled numbers put to flight.
Let me, when I must be fine,
In such natural colours shine;
Wove, and painted by the sun,
Whose resplendent rays to shun,
When they do too fiercely beat,

vest] robe monarch] Solomon chemist's] alchemist's; chemist's odour . . . field] (Gen. 27: 27) gales] breezes Fidentia's] (town in Cisalpine Gaul) Lucullus] Roman general

Let me find some close retreat
Where they have no passage made
Through those windings and that shade.
  Give me there (since heaven has shown
It was not good to be alone)
A partner suited to my mind,
Solitary, pleased and kind,
Who, partially, may something see
Preferred to all the world in me;
Slighting, by my humble side,
Fame and splendour, wealth and pride.
When but two the Earth possessed,
'Twas their happiest days, and best;
They by business, nor by wars,
They by no domestic cares,
From each other e'er were drawn,
But in some grove or flowery lawn
Spent the swiftly flying time,
Spent their own, and nature's, prime
In love, that only passion given
To perfect man, whilst friends with heaven.
Rage, and jealousy, and hate,
Transports of his fallen state
(When by Satan's wiles betrayed)
Fly those windings, and that shade!

(1713)

851 *The Spleen: A Pindaric Poem*

WHAT art thou, spleen, which everything dost ape?
Thou Proteus to abused mankind,
Who never yet thy real cause could find,
Or fix thee to remain in one continued shape.
Still varying thy perplexing form,
Now a Dead Sea thou'lt represent,
A calm of stupid discontent;
Then, dashing on the rocks, wilt rage into a storm.
Trembling sometimes thou dost appear
Dissolved into a panic fear;
On sleep intruding dost thy shadows spread
Thy gloomy terrors round the silent bed,
And crowd with boding dreams the melancholy head;

851 *The Spleen*] Melancholy   Proteus] (protean sea-god, son of Neptune)   Still] Ever

Or, when the midnight hour is told,
And drooping lids thou still dost waking hold,
Thy fond delusions cheat the eyes:
Before them antic spectres dance,
Unusual fires their pointed heads advance,
And airy phantoms rise.
Such was the monstrous vision seen,
When Brutus (now beneath his cares oppressed,
And all Rome's fortunes rolling in his breast,
Before Philippi's latest field,
Before his fate did to Octavius lead)
Was vanquished by the spleen.
Falsely, the mortal part we blame
Of our depressed and ponderous frame,
Which, till the first degrading sin
Let thee, its dull attendant, in,
Still with the other did comply,
Nor clogged the active soul disposed to fly
And range the mansions of its native sky.
Nor, whilst in his own heaven he dwelt,
Whilst man his paradise possessed,
His fertile garden in the fragrant east,
And all united odours smelt,
No armèd sweets, until thy reign,
Could shock the sense, or in the face
A flushed, unhandsome colour place.
Now the jonquil o'ercomes the feeble brain:
We faint beneath the aromatic pain,
Till some offensive scent thy powers appease,
And pleasure we resign for short and nauseous ease.
  In everyone thou dost possess,
New are thy motions and thy dress:
Now in some grove a listening friend
Thy false suggestions must attend,
Thy whispered griefs, thy fancied sorrows hear,
Breathed in a sigh and witnessed by a tear;
Whilst in the light and vulgar crowd
Thy slaves, more clamorous and loud,
By laughters unprovoked, thy influence too confess.
In the imperious wife thou vapours art,
Which from o'erheated passions rise
In clouds to the attractive brain,
Until, descending thence again,

Brutus] (see endnote) latest] last mansions] (1) lodgings; (2) astrological houses attractive] absorptive

Through the o'ercast and showering eyes,
Upon her husband's softened heart,
He the disputed point must yield,
Something resign of the contested field;
Till lordly man, born to imperial sway,
Compounds for peace, to make that right away,
And woman, armed with spleen, does servilely obey.
  The fool, to imitate the wits,
Complains of thy pretended fits,
And dullness, born with him, would lay
Upon thy accidental sway;
Because, sometimes, thou dost presume
Into the ablest heads to come,
That often men of thoughts refined,
Impatient of unequal sense,
Such slow returns where they so much dispense,
Retiring from the crowd, are to thy shades inclined.
O'er me, alas! thou dost too much prevail:
I feel thy force, whilst I against thee rail;
I feel my verse decay, and my cramped numbers fail.
Through thy black jaundice I all objects see
As dark and terrible as thee,
My lines decried, and my employment thought
An useless folly or presumptuous fault:
Whilst in the Muses' paths I stray,
Whilst in their groves and by their secret springs
My hand delights to trace unusual things,
And deviates from the known and common way,
Nor will in fading silks compose
Faintly th' inimitable rose,
Fill up an ill-drawn bird, or paint on glass
The sovereign's blurred and undistinguished face,
The threatening angel, and the speaking ass.
  Patron thou art to every gross abuse:
The sullen husband's feigned excuse,
When the ill humour with his wife he spends,
And bears recruited wit and spirits to his friends.
The son of Bacchus pleads thy power,
As to the glass he still repairs,
Pretends but to remove thy cares,
Snatch from thy shades one gay and smiling hour,
And drown thy kingdom in a purple shower.
When the coquette, whom every fool admires,

sway] sovereignty, power (poetic)   unequal sense] unjust opinion   numbers] verses   recruited] restored, reinvigorated

Would in variety be fair,
And, changing hastily the scene
From light, impertinent, and vain,
Assumes a soft, a melancholy air,
And of her eyes rebates the wandering fires,
The careless posture, and the head reclined;
The thoughtful and composèd face
Proclaiming the withdrawn, the absent mind,
Allows the fop more liberty to gaze,
Who gently for the tender cause inquires:
The cause, indeed, is a defect in sense;
Yet is the spleen alleged, and still the dull pretence.
But these are thy fantastic harms,
The tricks of thy pernicious stage,
Which do the weaker sort engage;
Worse are the dire effects of thy more powerful charms.
By thee religion, all we know
That should enlighten here below,
Is veiled in darkness, and perplexed
With anxious doubts, with endless scruples vexed,
And some restraint implied from each perverted text;
Whilst 'touch not', 'taste not' what is freely given
Is but thy niggard voice, disgracing bounteous heaven.
From speech restrained by thy deceits abused,
To deserts banished, or in cells reclused,
Mistaken vot'ries to the powers divine,
Whilst they a purer sacrifice design,
Do but the spleen obey, and worship at thy shrine.
In vain to chase thee every art we try,
In vain all remedies apply,
In vain the Indian leaf infuse,
Or the parched eastern berry bruise;
Some pass, in vain, those bounds, and nobler liquors use.
Now harmony, in vain, we bring:
Inspire the flute, and touch the string.
From harmony no help is had;
Music but soothes thee, if too sweetly sad,
And if too light, but turns thee gaily mad.
Though the physician's greatest gains,
Although his growing wealth he sees
Daily increased by ladies' fees,
Yet dost thou baffle all his studious pains.
Not skilful Lower thy source could find,
Or through the well-dissected body trace

eastern berry] coffee   Lower] Richard Lower (1631–91)

The secret, the mysterious ways
By which thou dost surprise and prey upon the mind.
Though in the search, too deep for human thought,
With unsuccessful toil he wrought,
Till thinking thee to have catched, himself by thee was caught,
Retained thy prisoner, thy acknowledged slave,
And sunk beneath thy chain to a lamented grave.

(1701)

852 *A Letter to Daphnis, April 2, 1685*

THIS to the crown and blessing of my life,
The much loved husband of a happy wife:
To him whose constant passion found the art
To win a stubborn and ungrateful heart,
And to the world by tenderest proof discovers
They err who say that husbands can't be lovers.
With such return of passion as is due,
Daphnis I love, Daphnis my thoughts pursue;
Daphnis, my hopes, my joys, are bounded all in you:
Even I, for Daphnis' and my promise' sake,
What I in women censure, undertake.
But this from love, not vanity, proceeds;
You know who writes, and I who 'tis that reads.
Judge not my passion by my want of skill:
Many love well, though they express it ill;
And I your censure could with pleasure bear,
Would you but soon return, and speak it here.

(1903; wr. before 1689?)

LORD CUTTS
1661–1707

853 *To a Lady, Who Desired Me Not To Be in Love with Her*

I WILL obey you to my utmost power;
You cannot ask, nor I engage, for more.
But if, when I have tried my utmost skill,
A tide of love drives back my floating will,
When on the naked beach you see me lie,
For pity's sake you must not let me die.

Take pattern by the glorious god of day,
And raise no storms but what you mean to lay;
He, when the charms of his attractive eye
Have stirred up vapours and disturbed the sky,
Lets nature weep and sigh a little while,
And then revives her with a pleasing smile.
If 'tis to try me, use me as you please,
But, when that trial's over, give me ease;
Don't torture one that wishes you no harm:
Prepare to cure me, or forbear to charm.

(1687)

MARY EVELYN?
1665–1685

854 *from* Mundus Muliebris, *Or, The Lady's Dressing-Room Unlocked, and Her Toilette Spread. In Burlesque . . .*

IN pinup ruffles now she flaunts,
About her sleeves are *engageants*;
Of ribbon, various *échelles*;
Gloves trimmed and laced as fine as Nell's,
Twelve dozen Martial, whole and half,
Of jonquil, tuberose, don't laugh
Frangipan, orange, violet,
Narcissus, jassemin, ambrette,
And some of chicken skin for night,
To keep her hands plump, soft, and white;
Mouches for pushes, to be sure,
From Paris the *très fine* procure,
And Spanish paper, lip, and cheek
With spittle sweetly to belick;

854 Mundus Muliebris] Female World ruffles] 'by our forefathers called cuffs' (E.) *engageants*] 'deep double ruffles, hanging down to the wrists' (E.) *échelles*] 'a pectoral or stomacher laced with ribbon, like the rounds of a ladder' (E.) Nell's] Nell Gwyn's (Charles II's mistress) Martial] 'famous French perfumer, emulating the Frangipani of Rome' (E.) tuberose] essence of *Polianthes tuberosa* (playing on 'tuberous', potato-like) jassemin] jasmine ambrette] musk-like seed used in perfumery *Mouches*] 'Flies, or black patches, by the vulgar' (E.) *très fine*] '*langage de beau.* Extremely fine, and delicate' (E.) Spanish paper] 'red colour, which the ladies, etc. in Spain paint their faces withal' (E.)

Nor therefore spare in the next place
The pocket sprunking looking-glass;
Calambac combs in *pulvil* case,
To set and trim the hair and face;
And, that the cheeks may both agree,
Plumpers to fill the cavity.

* * * * *

Besides all these, 'tis always meant
You furnish her appartiment
With Moreclack tapestry, damask bed,
Or velvet richly embroiderèd;
Branches, *brasero, cassolettes*,
A *coffre-fort*, and cabinets,
Vasas of silver, porcelain, store
To set and range about the floor;
The chimney furniture of plate
(For iron's now quite out of date);
Tea-table, screens, trunks, and stand,
Large looking-glass richly japanned,
An hanging shelf, to which belongs
Romances, plays, and amorous songs;
Repeating clocks, the hour to show
When to the play 'tis time to go
In pompous coach, or else sedanned
With equipage along the Strand,
And with her new beau Foppling manned.
A new scene to us next presents,
The dressing-room and implements
Of toilet, plate gilt and embossed,
And several other things of cost;
The table *miroir*, one glue pot,
One for *pomatum*, and what not?
Of washes, unguents, and cosmetics;
A pair of silver candlesticks;
Snuffers and snuff-dish, boxes more,
For powders, patches, waters store,
In silver flasks or bottles, cups
Covered, to open, to wash chaps;

sprunking] 'Dutch term for pruning, tiffing [arranging], trimming, setting out, by the glass' (E.) *Calambac*] 'wood of an agreeable scent, brought from the Indies' (E.) *pulvil*] 'Portugal term for the most exquisite . . . perfumes' (E.) Plumpers] 'light balls, to plump out and fill up the cavities of the cheeks, much used by old court countesses' (E.) Moreclack] Mortlake Branches] Hanging candlesticks *brasero*] brazier *cassolettes*] perfuming pots or censers *coffre-fort*] 'strong box of some precious or hard wood, etc., bound with gilded ribs' (E.) *Vasas*] Vases store] plenty pompous] magnificent equipage] state chaps] jowls

Nor may Hungarian queen's be wanting,
Nor store of spirits against fainting.

(1690)

HENRY HALL?

d. 1713

855 *Upon the King's Return from Flanders, 1695*

REJOICE, you sots, your idol's come again,
To pick your pockets and kidnap your men.
Give him your moneys, and his Dutch your lands.
Ring not your bells, ye fools, but wring your hands.

(1971; wr. 1695?)

MARY ASTELL

1666–1731

856 *In Emulation of Mr Cowley's Poem Called 'The Motto'*

WHAT shall I do? Not to be rich or great,
  Not to be courted and admired,
  With beauty blest, or wit inspired:
Alas! these merit not my care and sweat,
  These cannot my ambition please,
My high born soul shall never stoop to these;
But something I would be that's truly great
In 'tself, and not by vulgar estimate.

If this low world were always to remain,
  If the old philosophers were in the right,
  Who would not, then, with all their might
Study and strive to get themselves a name?
  Who would in soft repose lie down,
Or value ease like being ever known?
But since fame's trumpet has so short a breath,
Shall we be fond of that which must submit to death?

854 Hungarian queen's] distilled water

Nature permits not me the common way,
By serving court, or state, to gain
That so much valued trifle, fame;
Nor do I covet in wit's realm to sway.
But O ye bright illustrious few,
What shall I do to be like some of you?
Whom this misjudging world does underprize,
Yet are most dear in heaven's all-righteous eyes.

How shall I be a Peter or a Paul,
That to the Turk and infidel
I might the joyful tidings tell,
And spare no labour to convert them all?
But ah, my sex denies me this,
And Mary's privilege I cannot wish;
Yet hark! I hear my dearest Saviour say
They are more blessèd who his word obey.

Up then, my sluggard soul! Labour and pray,
For if with love enflamed thou be,
Thy Jesus will be born in thee,
And by thy ardent prayers thou canst make way
For their conversion whom thou mayst not teach,
Yet by a good example always preach;
And though I want a persecuting fire,
I'll be at least a martyr in desire.

(1988; wr. 7 Jan. 1687/8)

ALICIA D'ANVERS
1668?–1725

857

To the University

HAIL, peaceful shade, whose sacred verdant side
Bold Thamesis salutes; hail, noble tide;
Hail, learning's mother; hail, Great Britain's pride.
Hail to thy lovely groves and bowers, wherein
Thy heaven-begotten darlings sit and sing:
Thy firstborn sons, who shall in after-story
Share thy loud fame, as now they bring thee glory.

Peter . . . Paul] i.e. the apostles   want] lack
857 Thamesis] the Thames

Arrived at such a rich maturity,
Those who spell man so well, would blush to be
Took at the mother's breast, or nurse's knee;
Much more in filth to wallow shoulder high,
In tears till his kind nurse had laid him dry.
Actions that give no blush of guilt or shame
To those so young that yet they want a name
(I've heard that brute and infant are the same).
Then beauteous matron, frown not on me for 't,
Though at the triflings of your younger sort
I smile so much; since all I hope to do
Is but to raise your smiles, and others' too,
And please myself, if pardoned first by you.

(1691)

ELIZABETH TIPPER

fl. 1698–1704

858 *To a Young Lady that Desired a Verse of My Being Servant One Day, and Mistress Another*

MORE than a king's my word does rule today:
His subjects his, my betters mine obey;
Quality, fortune, beauty, virtue, wit
Do govern others, but to me submit.
Tomorrow from this dignity I fall,
And am a servant at each beck and call;
Next day I'm free in liberty and power,
And, as before, a mistress every hour.

Changeable is my state, and yet not strange,
When day to night, and light to darkness change.
Yet fate I cannot blame, but justly own
She, in this difference, evenness hath shown;
For when I'm mistress, none I can command,
When servant, curbed by no imperious hand:
This is a riddle, yet here wonder why,
When all the world's a riddle, why not I?

(1698)

858 Tomorrow] 'I teach ladies writing and accounts one day, and keep shop-books the other day, in which business I am a hired servant' (T.)

ELIZABETH THOMAS
1675–1731

859 *A Midnight Thought (on the Death of Mrs E.H. and Her Little Daughter, Cast away under London Bridge, Aug. 5, 1699), Ending with an Address to Clemena*

O SACRED time! how soon thou'rt gone!
How swift thy circling minutes run!
O time! our chiefest worldly good,
If we employ thee as we should.
And yet how few thy value know,
But think thee troublesome and slow!
(Motion and rest fill up our time,
And little, O my soul, is thine!)
We eat, we drink, we sleep, and then
We rise—to do the same again;
And thus like fairies daily tread
The same dull round our predecessors led.

Young Lydia prudent was and fair,
Was all that virtuous women are;
And yet how soon her glass was run,
How short her fatal thread was spun!
How know we our appointed fate,
Whether ordained us soon or late?
Health is uncertain, death is more;
And much we have to do before.

Ah then, my friend, let us be wise:
No more the precious gift despise,
But use it for the end 'twas given,
And prove we're candidates of heaven.
Let others to the play repair,
Be courted and reputed fair:
Whole winter nights at ombre play
To pass the drug of time away,
While we our better parts employ,
And placidly our souls enjoy;
Praising that power did us create,
But more the love redeemed our fate.

drug] drag

Then with the illustrious dead converse,
And sometimes with a friend in verse.
Thus in the culture of the mind
Improve those hours by fate assigned:
So shall we from superfluous time be free;
'Tis want of sense makes superfluity.

(1722)

GEORGE FARQUHAR
1678–1707

860

A Song

How blest are lovers in disguise!
  Like gods they see,
  As I do thee,
Unseen by human eyes.
  Exposed to view,
  I'm hid from you;
I'm altered, yet the same:
  The dark conceals me,
  Love reveals me—
Love which lights me by its flame.

Were you not false, you me would know;
  For though your eyes
  Could not devise,
Your heart had told you so.
  Your heart would beat
  With eager heat,
And me by sympathy would find:
  True love might see
  One changed like me,
False love is only blind.

(1699; a. 1698)

ALEXANDER POPE
1688–1744

861 *Ode on Solitude*

HAPPY the man whose wish and care
A few paternal acres bound,
Content to breathe his native air,
  In his own ground.

Whose herds with milk, whose fields with bread,
Whose flocks supply him with attire,
Whose trees in summer yield him shade,
  In winter fire.

Blest! who can unconcernedly find
Hours, days, and years slide soft away,
In health of body, peace of mind,
  Quiet by day,

Sound sleep by night; study and ease
Together mixed; sweet recreation
And innocence, which most does please,
  With meditation.

Thus let me live, unseen, unknown;
Thus unlamented let me die;
Steal from the world, and not a stone
  Tell where I lie.

(1717)

NOTES AND REFERENCES

The references that follow indicate the source of the preferred text of each item, which is not necessarily the first publication. Where a modern scholarly edition exists, this is generally cited, and may be consulted for further information. The notes attempt only very brief explanations of some of the allusions, together with a few items of biographical information likely to be of interest, or difficult of access elsewhere. Unless otherwise indicated, the place of publication of modern editions may be assumed to be London.

1. Elizabeth, Lady Tanfield: text, inscription, Burford Parish Church, Oxfordshire.

2–10. Fulke Greville, Lord Brooke: texts, *Poems and Dramas of Fulke Greville*, ed. G. Bullough, 2 vols. (Edinburgh and London, 1938) and *The Remains*, ed. G. A. Wilkes (Oxford, 1965). **2.** 'Son' (45) alludes to the mythic Phaethon, who disastrously misguided the sun-chariot. **5.** As the earth's centre (2) was the old location of hell in the macrocosm, so with the microcosm. 'Unprivation' (16) is the opposite of evil, which was 'deprivation of the good' (Philippe de Mornay, *The Trueness of the Christian Religion*, in *The Prose Works of Sir Philip Sidney*, ed. A. Feuillerat, iii (Cambridge, 1912) 231). **6.** Julius Caesar's 'fame' as a would-be king led to his assassination, whereas M. Porcius Cato enjoyed an enduring reputation for wisdom and austere morality. **7.** The 'forbidden tree' (13) is the Tree of Knowledge of Gen. 3: 5; 'clouds' (22) alludes to Ixion's embracing a cloud instead of Juno; the Egyptian darkness (25) of Exod. 10 was allegorized as the blindness of sin. **8.** *Chorus Primus*, lines 65–96: according to Gen. 2: 19, Adam (21) named things truly. **9.** *Of Nobility*, VIII, sts. 330–4. **10.** *Of Peace*, XI, sts. 468–70, 472–3: Augustus (19) increased grain supplies by dredging the Nile canals or 'sluices'. Trajan's useful bridge over the Danube is described by Dio Cassius, lxviii. 13.

11. Anne Howard: text, R. Johnson, *The Crown Garland of Golden Roses* (1631).

12–29. George Chapman: texts, *The Poems*, ed. P. B. Bartlett (New York, 1941), *Chapman's Homer*, ed. A. Nicoll, 2 vols. (1957), and *The Georgics of Hesiod* (1618). **12.** Lines 266–81. **13.** Lines 606–35. **14.** Lines 726–57. **15.** Lines 1106–36. **16.** Epistle to Prince Henry, 46–79. **17.** Bk I, 1–32. **18, 19.** Bk. XII, 243–65, 303–32. **20.** Bk. XIII, 10–43. **21.** Bk. XVII, 168–84. **22.** Bk. XVIII, 469–521. **23.** Bk. XXIV, 414–96. **24.** Lines 531–86: the speaker is William Lord Russell, whose death occasioned the poem; the matter depends on Xylander's translation of Plutarch's *De E apud Delphos* 392. The 'Asterism of Seven' (25) is sometimes identified as the Pleiades, but, in view of 'crown', is more probably Corona (given as seven stars by Palingenius). Bees (33) were a common emblem of thrift (e.g. G. Wither, *Emblems* (1635) ii. 28). **25.** Epistle to Somerset, 157–74, 179–202: Roger Bacon's legendary brazen head spoke omnisciently, but immediately fell and was smashed. **26.** Bk. IX, 673–97: the Homeric Oceanus was a cosmic river encircling the world. **27.** Bk. XI, 1–68. **28.** Bk. XXIV, 222–64. **29.** Bk. II, 214–61.

30. Sir John Harington: text, *The Letters and Epigrams*, ed. N. E. McClure (Philadelphia, Pa, 1930).

31–2. Samuel Daniel: texts, *The Complete Works*, ed. A. B. Grosart, 4 vols. (1885). **32.** *Tethys Festival*, 341–58.

33. Sir John Stradling: text, *Divine Poems in Seven Several Classes* (1625): Classis i, sts. 62–9.

34–55. Michael Drayton: texts, *The Works*, ed. J. W. Hebel *et al.*, 5 vols. (Oxford, 1931–41), and early editions. **34–41.** Texts, 1599, 1600, and 1619: **42–9.** From *Poems Lyric and Pastoral* (1606) and *Odes, with Other Lyric Poesies* (1619): **42.** New Year poems were often numerologically organized: here the 84 lines measure days between New Year day (1 Jan.) and Lady Day (25 March), which began the civil year: Corona Borealis and Australis were sometimes represented as wreaths (45). **44.** Apollo (1) perhaps refers to Ben Jonson's club room at the Devil Tavern. **45.** The patent for an expedition to Virginia was sealed on 6 April 1606, but Drayton follows accounts of earlier voyages in Hakluyt. **49.** For a crime against the gods, Tantalus (13) was punished by tantalizing proximity to inaccessible water and grapes. **50–4.** From *Poly-Olbion* ('The Many-Blessed'): **50.** *Song I*, lines 173–203. **51, 52.** *Song II*, 1–18, 60–71. **53.** *Song III*, 41–64, 110–56. **54.** *Song XIII*, 163–99. **55.** Lines 633–746.

56–9. Joshua Sylvester: texts, *The Divine Weeks and Works of . . . du Bartas*, transl. Joshua Sylvester, ed. S. Snyder, 2 vols. (Oxford, 1979), and *The Complete Works of Joshuah Sylvester*, ed. A. B. Grosart, 2 vols. (1880). **56.** *The Fourth Day of the First Week*, lines 201–76.

60–4. William Shakespeare: texts, *The Oxford Shakespeare* (Oxford, 1986). **60, 61.** *Cymbeline* II. iii. 19–25 and IV. ii. 259–82. **62, 63.** *Tempest* I. ii. 378–90 and I. ii. 400–8. **64.** *Two Noble Kinsmen* I. i. 1–24.

65. King James VI and I: text, *New Poems by James I*, ed. A. F. Westcott (New York, 1911) and *Poems*, ed. J. Craigie, 2 vols. (Edinburgh, 1955–8).

66–7. John Hoskyns: texts, Louise B. Osborn, *The Life, Letters, and Writings* (New Haven and London, 1937).

68–9. Sir William Alexander, Earl of Stirling: texts, *The Poetical Works*, ed. L. E. Kastner and H. B. Charlton, 2 vols., STS (Edinburgh and London, 1921–9).

70–4. Thomas Campian: texts, Fellowes.

75–81. Sir Henry Wotton: texts, *Reliquiae Wottonianae* (1651; rev. and enlarged 1672) and H. J. C. Grierson, *MLR* vi (1911). Wotton, British ambassador on various European embassies of significance, and subsequently Provost of Eton College, wrote the first architectural treatise in English.

82. Sir Francis Hubert: text, *The Poems*, ed. B. Mellor (Hong Kong, 1961), sts. 52–5.

83–96. Sir Robert Ayton: texts, *Poems and Songs*, ed. H. M. Shire (Cambridge, 1961), *The English and Latin Poems*, ed. C. B. Gullans, STS (Edinburgh, 1963), and James Watson's *Choice Collection* (Glasgow, 1706–11).

97–9. Emilia Lanier: texts, *The Poems of Shakespeare's Dark Lady: 'Salve Deus Rex Judaeorum' by Emilia Lanier*, ed. A. L. Rowse (1978). **98.** Lines 1–64. **99.** Lines 761–856.

100–1. Samuel Rowlands: texts, *Uncollected Poems*, ed. F. O. Waage, Jr. (Gainesville, Fla., 1970).

102–3. Thomas Dekker: texts, Bowers, *The Sun's Darling*, III. iv. 1–36 and I. i. 90–109.

104–39. John Donne: texts, *The Elegies and the Songs and Sonnets*, ed. H. Gardner (Oxford, 1965); *The Divine Poems*, ed. H. Gardner (Oxford, 1952); *The Satires, Epigrams and Verse Letters*, ed. W. Milgate (Oxford, 1967); *The Epithalamions, Anniversaries, and Epicedes*, ed. W. Milgate (Oxford, 1978); and *The Complete English Poems*, ed. A. J. Smith (1971). **109.** The seven sleepers' den (4) is the cave where, as Gregory of Tours relates, Christians walled up alive during the Decian persecution (AD 249) slept for 230 years. **113.** St Lucy's day was popularly thought the shortest day of the year, although the winter solstice did not fall on 13 December in Donne's time. One of his patronesses was Lucy Countess of Bedford, whose serious illness in 1612/13 has been connected with the poem. With 'Life, soul, form, spirit' (20) cf. the tetrads in Tycho Brahe's *Magical Calendar* (ed. Maclean, p. 14), such as 'Mens, spiritus, anima, corpus' or 'esse, vivere, scire, intelligere'. **120.** 'Where I begun' (36) implies construction not merely of a circumference, but also of a radius, as in emblems such as Heinsius's SINE FINE. **121.** For 'falls' (8), *1633–69* and some manuscripts have 'falst', perhaps mistaking the grammar, perhaps pursuing a word play with 'falseth' (prove unreliable, play false). **124.** Probably Donne's last poem. James Hamilton, second marquis, d. 2 March 1625 aged 36. **125.** Lines 205–38. **126, 127.** Lines 66–120 and 281–300. Elizabeth Drury's death had been in December 1610. This second anniversary meditation, written at least partly in France, was printed in 1612. **136.** Donne journeyed from Polesworth to Montgomery on 3 April 1613. **137.** Donne travelled to Germany as chaplain to the Earl of Doncaster in May 1619. **138.** Written by Donne on his deathbed, according to Walton; but according to the judge Sir Julius Caesar, during his illness of December 1623. Anyan (18) is either Anian (mod. Annam), the straits thought to divide America from Asia, or Anyouam, at the mouth of the Mozambique Channel.

140–78. Ben Jonson: texts, *Ben Jonson*, ed. I. Donaldson (Oxford, 1985) and *Ben Jonson*, ed. C. H. Herford and P. and E. Simpson, 11 vols. (Oxford, 1925–32). For details of publication of some of the poems earlier than in the collections, see Donaldson's notes. **140.** William Camden (1551–1623), the great antiquary, was J.'s old schoolmaster. The name (4) of Britain (used by James I in his title) had been popularized by Camden's masterpiece *Britannia*. **146.** Sir Henry Cary (1575?–1633), later Viscount Falkland, father of Sir Lucius Cary. In an engagement near the confluence of the Ruhr and the Rhine in 1605, he tried to stop a rout of the English and Dutch troops; Jonson compares his consequent capture to a civil arrest (6) because so few (only three) supported him that his act might superficially have seemed antisocial. His ransom occasioned serious financial losses (11). **147.** Jonson appeared on behalf of William Roe (1585–?) in a lawsuit. **148.** Lucy, Countess of Bedford (1581?–1627), daughter of the poet Sir John Harington, was a patron and friend of Donne, Drayton, and Daniel as well as Jonson (in some of whose masques she danced). **149.** Sir Henry Goodyere (1571–1628), a close friend of Donne, danced in Jonson's masque *Hymenaei* (1606). **150.** Edward Alleyn (1566–1625), the celebrated actor, took leading roles in Marlowe's plays, and appeared in Jonson's Salisbury House entertainment (1608). **152.** Mary, Lady Wroth (*c.*1586–?), wife of Sir Robert Wroth and daughter of Robert Sidney, Earl of Leicester, was herself an outstanding poet and romance writer. **153.** Clement Edmonds (1564?–1622) was the author of *Observations* on Caesar's *Gallic War*. **154.** An attack on Inigo Jones, architect and masque designer, Jonson's collaborator, friend, and eventually enemy. **158.** Lines 121–54. Nicholas Hill (1570?–1610) wrote *Philosophia, Epicurea, Democritiana, Theophrastica, Proposita*

Simpliciter, non Edocta (1601). **169.** Sir Lucius Cary, Viscount Falkland, of Great Tew, was a famous patron of letters. Sir Henry Morison d. 1629, aged about 21. **171.** Printed in the first folio of Shakespeare. **172, 173.** *Cynthia's Revels*, I. ii. 65–75 and V. vi. 1–18. **174.** *The Masque of Queens*, lines 723–30. **175.** *Epicoene*, I. i. 91–102. **176.** *Pleasure Reconciled to Virtue*, 13–36. **177.** *The New Inn*, IV. iv. 4–13. **178.** *The Gypsies Metamorphosed*, lines 1061–1125.

179. Anonymous: text, Doughtie.

180. Thomas Heywood: text, *An Apology for Actors* (1612).

181–2. John Webster. **181.** *The White Devil*, V. iv. 95–104: text, Revels edition (1960). **182.** *The Devil's Law Case*, V. iv. 131–46: text, *The Complete Works*, ed. F. L. Lucas (1927).

183. Anonymous: text, William Camden, *Remains Concerning Britain*, ed. R. D. Dunn (Toronto, 1984).

184. Robert Burton: text, *The Anatomy of Melancholy* (1628), i, ed. T. C. Faulkner *et al.* (Oxford, 1989).

185. Thomas Forde: text, Fellowes.

186. George Sandys: text, *A Paraphrase upon the Divine Poems* (1638): Job 2: 1–9.

187–94. John Taylor: text, *The Works of John Taylor the Water Poet*, Pubs. of the Spenser Soc. (1868) and early editions. **187–9.** Texts, *The Sculler* (1612). **190.** Text, *Water Work* (1614). **191–3.** Texts, *The Nipping or Snipping of Abuses* (1614). **194.** Lines 1–61.

195–203. John Fletcher: texts, Bowers; *The Oxford Shakespeare* (1986); and *Beaumont and Fletcher*, ed. A. Glover and A. R. Waller, 10 vols. (Cambridge, 1905–12). **195, 196.** *The Faithful Shepherdess*, III. i. 429–36 and IV. i. 1–25. **197.** *Henry VIII*, III. i. 3–14. **198.** *The Elder Brother*, III. v. 77–94. **199.** *Love's Cure*, III. ii. 118–25. **200.** *Women Pleased*, III. iv. 49–60. **201, 202.** *The Tragedy of Valentinian*, II. v. 5–24 and V. ii. 13–22. **203.** *Beggar's Bush*, II. i. 143–64.

204–5. Robert Hayman, from the Latin of John Owen (*c.*1564–*c.*1628): texts, *Quodlibets* (1628): *Owen's Epigrams*, III. 161 and I. 131.

206. Thomas Middleton: text, Bowers, *The Nice Valour*, III. iii. 35–53.

207. John Digby, Earl of Bristol: text, B.L. Add. MS 25707.

208. Thomas Morton: text, Meserole.

209. Dudley North, Lord North: text, Blunden and Mellor.

210–15. Richard Corbett: texts, *The Poems*, ed. J. A. W. Bennett and H. R. Trevor-Roper (Oxford, 1955). **210.** William Chourne was a servant of Leonard Hutten, Corbett's future father-in-law. **215.** Arabella Stuart, daughter of the fifth Earl of Lennox, was connected with both Tudor and Stuart royal lines. After a secret marriage she was imprisoned in the Tower.

216–24. Lord Herbert of Cherbury: texts, *The Poems English and Latin*, ed. G. C. Moore Smith (Oxford, 1923).

225–30. Phineas Fletcher: texts, *Giles and Phineas Fletcher, Poetical Works*, ed. F. S. Boas, 2 vols. (1908–9). **225.** *The Locusts*, I. x–xii. **229.** *The Purple Island*, X. xxvii–xxxviii.

231–2. Sir John Beaumont: texts, *Bosworth Field* (1629) and *Jacobean and Caroline Poetry*, ed. T. G. S. Cain (London and New York, 1981).

233–5. Aurelian Townshend: texts, *The Poems and Masques*, ed. C. C. Brown (Reading, 1983) and *Poems and Masks*, ed. E. K. Chambers (Oxford, 1912).

236. William Basse: text, Izaak Walton, *The Compleat Angler*, ed. J. Bevan (Oxford, 1983).

237–8. Francis Beaumont: texts, Bowers, and Francis Beaumont and John Fletcher, *Comedies and Tragedies* (1647). **237.** *The Masque of the Inner Temple*, 321–42. **238.** *The Little French Lawyer*, IV. i.

239–65. William Drummond of Hawthornden: texts, *The Poetical Works*, ed. L. E. Kastner, STS, 2 vols. (Edinburgh and London, 1913) and *Poems and Prose*, ed. R. H. MacDonald (Edinburgh and London, 1976). **252.** Lines 1–178. **260.** Lines 163–336. **262.** John Pym, celebrated parliamentarian, d. 8 December 1643. **263.** Alexander Craig (*c.*1567–*c.*1627) was a bad Scottish poet, whose many fictional loves included Kala. **264.** Marcus Curtius plunged sacrificially into a chasm threatening the Forum (Roman legend).

266–7. Giles Fletcher: texts, *Giles and Phineas Fletcher: Poetical Works*, ed. F. S. Boas, 2 vols. (Cambridge, 1908–9). **266.** Lines 473–519. **267.** Sts. xxx–xli.

268. John Ford: *The Broken Heart*, IV. iii: text, Revels edn.

269–80. Lady Mary Wroth: texts, *The Poems*, ed. J. A. Roberts (Baton Rouge and London, 1983).

281. William Austin: text, *The Poems*, ed. A. Ridler (Oxford, 1983).

282. Sir Francis Kynaston: text, Saintsbury.

283. Richard Brathwait: text, *Barnabee's Journal*, ed. J. Haslewood (1876).

284. Luke Wadding: text, *The Oxford Book of Irish Verse*, ed. D. MacDonagh and L. Robinson (Oxford, 1958).

285–93. George Wither: texts, *The Poetry*, ed. F. Sidgwick, 2 vols. (1902) and *A Collection of Emblems, Ancient and Modern* (1635). **286.** *The Shepherd's Hunting*, iii. 222–61. **288.** Lines 3413–42.

294–300. William Browne of Tavistock: texts, *Poems*, ed. G. Goodwin, 2 vols. (1904) and *Britannia's Pastorals* (1616). **294, 295.** *Song II*, 193–223 and 1–70. **296.** *Song III*, 223–63.

301. Henry Farley: text, Ault.

302–48. Robert Herrick: texts, *The Poetical Works*, ed. L.C. Martin (rev. edn., Oxford, 1968) and *The Complete Poetry*, ed. J. Max Patrick (rev. edn., New York, 1968). **339.** Charles Cotton is probably not the poet but his father (d. 1658).

349–50. William Cavendish, Duke of Newcastle: texts, *The Fancies*, ed. D. Grant (1956).

351–8. Henry King: texts, *The Poems*, ed. M. Crum (Oxford, 1965).

359–69. Francis Quarles: texts, *The Complete Works in Prose and Verse*, ed. A. B. Grosart, 3 vols. (repr. New York, 1967), *Argalus and Parthenia*, ed. D. Freeman (Washington, 1986), and *Hosanna, or, Divine Poems on the Passion of Christ*, ed. J. Horden (Liverpool, 1960). **363, 364.** Quotations from the Fathers omitted.

370–411. George Herbert: texts, *The Works*, ed. F. E. Hutchinson (Oxford, 1941).

412. James Howell: text, *Poems on Several Choice and Various Subjects* (1663).

413. Thomas James: text, *The Strange and Dangerous Voyage of Captain Thomas James, in His Intended Discovery of the Northwest Passage into the South Sea* (1633).

414–21. Thomas Carew: texts, *The Poems*, ed. R. Dunlap (Oxford, 1949).

422. John Chalkhill: text, Izaak Walton, *The Compleat Angler*, ed. J. Bevan (Oxford, 1983). On Chalkhill, see P. J. Croft, *TLS* (27 June 1958).

423. Robert Davenport: text, *A Little Ark*, ed. G. Thorn-Drury (1921).

424–7. James Shirley: texts, *The Poems*, ed. R. L. Armstrong (New York, 1941) and *Poems* (1646).

428. Christopher Harvey: text, *The Complete Poems*, ed. A. B. Grosart (1874): *The Synagogue* 26.

429. Laurence Price: text, *An American Garland*, ed. C. H. Firth (Oxford, 1915).

430. Henry Reynolds: text, *Parnassus Biceps* (1656), ed. G. Thorn-Drury (1927).

431–44. William Strode: texts, *The Poetical Works*, ed. B. Dobell (1907). **431.** Answering Thomas Middleton's 'Melancholy', above. **444.** Sir William Strode d. 27 June 1637.

445. R. Hatton?: text, Cutts.

446–8. Ralph Knevet: texts, *The Shorter Poems*, ed. A. M. Charles (Columbus, Ohio, 1966).

449–57. Mildmay Fane, Earl of Westmorland: texts, *The Poems . . . (1648)*, ed. A. B. Grosart (privately printed, 1879).

458–62. Owen Feltham: texts, *Lusoria: or, Occasional Pieces*, appended to *Resolves* (1661, 1677).

463–4. Thomas Nabbes: texts, *The Works*, ed. A. H. Bullen, vol. i (1887) and early editions. **463.** *Tottenham Court* (1638), I. iii. **464.** *Hannibal and Scipio* (1637), II. v.

465. Martin Parker: text, *The Roxburghe Ballads*, ed. J. W. Ebsworth (Hertford, 1890).

466. John Tatham: text, *Ostella* (1650). Tatham was City poet after John Taylor.

467. Roger Williams: text, Meserole.

468. Edward Benlowes: text, Saintsbury: Canto XIII, sts. 1–16, 82–6.

469. Joseph Rutter: text, *The Shepherd's Holiday* (1635).

470. Sir Thomas Browne: texts, *The Works*, ed. G. Keynes, iii (1964).

471–5. William Habington: texts, *The Poems*, ed. K. Allott (Liverpool, 1948).

476–80. Thomas Randolph: texts, *Poems*, ed. G. Thorn-Drury (1929). **476.** Barkley was George, eighth baron Berkeley (1601–58).

481–9. William Davenant: texts, *The Shorter Poems and Songs from the Plays and Masques*, ed. A. M. Gibbs (Oxford, 1972) and *Gondibert*, ed. D. F. Gladish (Oxford, 1971). **489.** II. i. 14–21.

490–9. Edmund Waller: texts, *The Poems*, ed. G. Thorn-Drury (London and New York, 1893) and early editions.

500. William Wood: text, Meserole.

501–2. Richard Fanshawe: texts, *Shorter Poems and Translations*, ed. N. W. Bawcutt (Liverpool, 1964) and Battista Guarini, *Il Pastor Fido*, ed. J. H. Whitfield

(Edinburgh, 1976). **501.** From Gongora's *En la muerte de don Rodrigo Calderón.* **502.** *The Faithful Shepherd* (1647) IV. ix.

503–45. John Milton: texts, *The Poems*, ed. J. Carey and A. Fowler (1968). **508.** Lines 93–144. **509.** Lines 417–74. **510.** Lines 889–900. **511.** Lines 975–1022. **514.** Adam Stuart and Samuel Rutherford were Presbyterian controversialists. **518.** Henry Lawrence (1600–64) was Chairman of the Council of State. **519.** Cyriack Skinner (b. 1627) was Milton's former pupil; the 'grandsire' was Sir Edward Coke (who opposed extending the royal prerogative). **522, 523, 524.** I. 1–26, 283–313, and 722–51. **525, 526.** II. 466–628 and 910–50. **527.** III. 1–55. **528, 529.** IV. 207–318 and 750–75. **530, 531.** V. 247–87 and 468–503. **532, 533.** VII. 1–39 and 387–516. **534, 535, 536.** IX. 1–47, 290–386, and 412–66. **537.** XI. 808–67. **538.** XII. 624–49. **539.** I. 294–320. **540.** II. 337–91. **541.** III. 310–43. **542, 543.** IV. 25–108 and 236–364. **544.** Lines 66–109. **545.** Lines 1745–58.

546–53. Sir John Suckling: texts, *The Non-Dramatic Works*, ed. T. Clayton (Oxford, 1971).

554–9. Anonymous. **554.** Text, *An American Garland*, ed. C. H. Firth (Oxford, 1915). **555–7.** Texts, *Wits' Recreations* (1640). **558.** Text, Ault. **559.** Text, *Rump Poems and Songs* (1662).

560. Gerrard Winstanley: text, *The Clarke Papers*, ed. C. H. Firth, Camden Soc., vol. ii (1894) and *The Works*, ed. G. H. Sabine (Ithaca, NY, 1941).

561–2. Thomas Beedome: texts, *Poems Divine and Human* (1641).

563–4. Richard Flecknoe: texts, *Miscellania* (1653).

565–8. Sidney Godolphin: texts, *Poems*, ed. W. Dighton (1931) and *Ben Jonson*, ed. I. Donaldson (Oxford, 1985).

569. Samuel Harding: text, *Sicily and Naples* (1640): Act III, Scene ii.

570–4. William Cartwright: texts, *The Plays and Poems*, ed. G. B. Evans (Madison, Wis., 1951).

575–7. Anne Bradstreet: texts, *The Works*, ed. J. Hensley (Cambridge, Mass., 1967). **577.** Lines 140–68.

578–9. Samuel Butler: texts, *Hudibras*, ed. J. Wilders (Oxford, 1967). **578.** I. i. 1–228. **579.** I. ii. 1–44.

580–9. Richard Crashaw: texts, *The Poems*, ed. L. C. Martin (rev. edn.: Oxford, 1927).

590–2. Thomas Fairfax, Lord Fairfax: texts, E. B. Reed, *Transactions of the Connecticut Academy of Arts and Sciences*, xiv (New Haven, 1909), 237–90, Bodl. MSS Fairfax 38 and 40, and B.L. Add. MS 11744.

593. James Graham, Marquis of Montrose: text, *Watson's Choice Collection*, ed. J. Watson (1711) (privately printed, Glasgow, 1869).

594. Thomas Killigrew: text, *Covent Garden Drollery* (1672).

595–7. John Cleveland: texts, *The Poems*, ed. B. Morris and E. Withington (Oxford, 1967). **595.** Lines 1–40, 57–126.

598. Henry More: text, *Philosophical Poems*, ed. G. Bullough (Manchester, 1931), iii. 4–13.

599. Richard Baxter: text, *Poetical Fragments* (1681), lines 25–64.

600–2. Sir John Denham: texts, *The Poetical Works*, ed. T. H. Banks (rev. edn.: Middletown, Conn., 1969) and *Expans'd Hieroglyphics*, ed. B. O Hehir (Berkeley and Los Angeles, 1969). **600.** Preface. **602.** Draft IV, lines 111–96.

603–9. Joseph Beaumont: texts, *The Minor Poems*, ed. E. Robinson (Boston and New York, 1914).

610–11. George Daniel: texts, *The Poems*, ed. A. B. Grosart, 4 vols. (Boston, 1878).

612. Roger L'Estrange: text, B.L. MS Harl. 3511.

613. Martin Lluelyn: text, *Men-Miracles* (1646).

614. Anonymous: text, H. E. Rollins, *Cavalier and Puritan* (New York, 1923).

615. Anonymous: text, *Loving Mad Tom*, ed. J. Lindsay (1927).

616–17. Rowland Watkyns: texts, *Flamma Sine Fumo (1662)*, ed. P. C. Davies (Cardiff, 1968).

618. Humphrey Willis: text, *Time's Whirligig* (1647), lines 1–42.

619. Nicholas Murford: text, *Fragmenta Poetica, 1650*, ed. E. M. Beloe (King's Lynn, 1914).

620–32. Abraham Cowley: texts, *Works*, ed. A. R. Waller, 2 vols. (Cambridge, 1905–6), *The Mistress with Other Select Poems*, ed. J. Sparrow (1926), and *The Civil War*, ed. A. Pritchard (Toronto, 1973). **620.** *Tentanda . . . ora*: Virgil, *Georgics*, iii. 8–9: 'New ways I must attempt, my grovelling name / To raise aloft, and wing my flight to fame.' (tr. Dryden). **629.** I. 439–80. **630.** II. 795–827. **631.** II. 357–420. **632.** III. 1–62.

633–43. Richard Lovelace: texts, *The Poems*, ed. C. H. Wilkinson (rev. edn.: Oxford, 1968).

644–5. Sir Edward Sherburne: texts, *The Poems and Translations*, ed. F. J. van Beeck, SJ (Assen, 1961) and *Salmacis* (1651).

646. Simon Ford: text, *London in Flames: London in Glory*, ed. R. A. Aubin (New Brunswick, NJ, 1943), lines 105–224.

647–8. Richard Leigh: texts, *Poems . . . (1675)*, ed. H. Macdonald (Oxford, 1947).

649. William Chamberlayne: text, Saintsbury: IV. iii. 49–102.

650–4. Alexander Brome: texts, *Poems*, ed. R. R. Dubinski, 2 vols. (Toronto, 1982).

655–7. Robert Heath: texts, *Clarastella; together with Poems Occasional* (1650).

658. Lucy Hutchinson: text, Greer.

659. Thomas Philipott: text, *Poems (1646)*, ed. L. C. Martin (Liverpool, 1950).

660–71. Andrew Marvell: texts, *The Poems and Letters*, ed. H. M. Margoliouth *et al.* (3rd edn.: Oxford, 1971) and *The Complete Poems*, ed. E. S. Donno (1972). **661.** At every point of the Earth's surface except the poles and equator, the axis of the terrestrial sphere is oblique (25) to the horizon; 'glue' (33) as in *MS Bodl. Eng. poet. d. 49*, the 1681 folio (*1681*) reading 'hue'; at 34, *MS* has 'dew', *1681* 'glue'; at 44, *MS* has 'grates', *1681* 'gates'. **663.** Cancelled from most copies of *1681*, and not printed again until 1776. Cromwell returned (title) in May 1650, and entered Scotland on 22 July; if 'And . . . oppose' (19–20) refers to Cromwell, it means 'And with such a man, circumscription is more repugnant than opposition': if to the rivals

(15), 'Containment is more of an achievement than opposition'. Charles I fled to Carisbrooke Castle (52), Isle of Wight, Cromwell allegedly conniving at his escape from Hampton Court to oblige Parliament to act against him. 'Capitol's' (69) alludes to Livy, who tells (*Annals* I. lv. 6) how a man's head was turned up in the foundations of the Temple of Jupiter on the Capitoline Hill—an omen that Rome would be capital of the world. **664.** Lines 273–496. Appleton House is Nun Appleton, a former Cistercian priory that came to the Fairfaxes at the Dissolution. Lord General Fairfax was C.-in-C. of the Parliamentary forces until he resigned in 1650. Marvell was languages tutor to his daughter Mary, then 12–14 years old, from 1650 to 1652. The 'virgin' (5) is Isabel Thwaites, an heiress married by William Fairfax (1518) but earlier immured by her guardian, Prioress of Nun Appleton. The 'Cinque Ports' (77) were five S. E. ports entrusted by Parliament to the Council of State in 1650, just before Fairfax resigned from it. **666.** 'swert' (23) is John Sparrow's emendation from 'sweet' (*1681*).

672. Edmund Prestwich: text, *Hippolitus, Translated out of Seneca. Together with Divers Other Poems* (1651).

673–88. Henry Vaughan: texts, *The Complete Poems*, ed. A. Rudrum (1976) and *The Works*, ed. L. C. Martin (rev. edn: Oxford, 1957).

689–96. Margaret Cavendish, Duchess of Newcastle: texts, *Poems and Fancies* (1653) and Greer. **690.** 'Charles' is Sir Charles Cavendish (1620–43), Cavendish's brother-in-law.

697. Patrick Cary: text, *The Poems*, ed. Sister V. Delany (Oxford, 1978).

698. Matthew Stevenson: text, Marshall.

699–709. Anonymous. **699, 700.** Texts, *Seventeenth-Century Songs*, ed. J. P. Cutts and J. F. Kermode (Reading, 1956). **701–8.** Texts, Cutts. **709.** Text, *Wit's Interpreter* (1671).

710–11. William Hammond: texts, Saintsbury.

712. John Collop: text, *The Poems*, ed. C. Hilberry (Madison, Wis., 1962).

713–20. Thomas Stanley: texts, *The Poems and Translations*, ed. G. M. Crump (Oxford, 1962) and *The History of Philosophy, Part III* (1660).

721–3. Anonymous: texts, *Parnassus Biceps (1656)*, ed. G. Thorn-Drury.

724. Henry Halswell: text, ibid.

725. Sir Robert Howard: text, *Poems* (1660).

726. Robert Wild: text, *Parnassus Biceps (1656)*, ed. G. Thorn-Drury (1927).

727–8. Hugh Crompton: texts, *Pierides* (1658).

729. Henry Bold: text, *Poems, Lyric, Macaronic, Heroic* (1664).

730–1. John Hall: texts, Saintsbury.

732–7. Anonymous. **732, 733.** Texts, Blunden and Mellor. **734, 735.** Texts, *Wit Restored* (1658). **736.** Text, B.L. Add. MS 11608. **737.** Text, Ault.

738. John Bunyan: text, *The Pilgrim's Progress*, ed. J. B. Wharey and R. Sharrock (Oxford, 1960).

739. N. Hookes: text, *Amanda* (1653).

740–1. George Villiers, Duke of Buckingham: texts, *Buckingham: Public and Private Man*, ed. C. Phipps (New York and London, 1985).

742–4. Charles Cotton: texts, *Poems . . . 1630–1687*, ed. J. Beresford (1923) and *Poems*, ed. J. Buxton (1958).

745. John Dancer: text, *Aminta . . . Together with Divers Ingenious Poems* (1660).

746. Clement Paman: text, B.L. Add. MS 18220. Paman was chaplain to Sir Henry North, and later Dean of Elphin in Ireland.

747–59. John Dryden: texts, *The Poems*, ed. J. Kinsley, 4 vols. (Oxford, 1958). **750, 751.** Lines 1–44 and 150–203. **752.** Lines 1–30. **753.** Lines 1–41. **755.** Lines 160–89. **757.** Act IV. **759.** Lines 1–188.

760–8. Katherine Philips: texts, *Poems. By the Incomparable Mrs K. P.* (1664), *Poems by Mrs Katherine Philips, the Matchless Orinda* (1667 and 1669), and Greer. **767.** v. iv. 36–90.

769–70. Thomas Shipman: texts, *Carolina: Or, Loyal Poems* (1683). **769.** Lines 1–42.

771. Samuel Pordage: text, *Poems upon Several Occasions* (1660). Pordage was a noted Behmenist: see Christopher Hill, *The Experience of Defeat* (1984).

772. Eldred Revett: text, *Selected Poems Human and Divine*, ed. D. M. Friedman (Liverpool, 1966).

773–4. Sir George Etherege: texts, *The Poems*, ed. J. Thorpe (Princeton, 1963).

775. Walter Pope: text, *A Choice Collection of 180 Loyal Songs* (1685).

776–7. Thomas Flatman: texts, Saintsbury.

778. Thomas Ken: text, *A Manual of Prayers for . . . Winchester College* (1695).

779–81. Thomas Traherne: texts, *Centuries, Poems, and Thanksgivings*, ed. H. M. Margoliouth, ii (Oxford, 1958).

782–3. Charles Sackville, Earl of Dorset: texts, B.L. Harl. MS 3991 and C. Gildon, *A New Miscellany* (1701).

784–6. Sir Charles Sedley: texts, *The Poetical and Dramatic Works*, ed. V. de S. Pinto (1928). **786.** Attribution doubtful.

787–92. Aphra Behn: texts, *The Works*, ed. M. Summers, vi (1915).

793–4. Anonymous. **793.** Text, *Academy of Compliments* (1671). **794.** Text, Kerr.

795–800. Edward Taylor: texts, *Poems*, ed. D. E. S. Stanford (New Haven, Conn., 1960).

801. Benjamin Tompson: text, Meserole.

802. Edward Ravenscroft: text, *The Italian Husband* (1698), I, i.

803. James Wright: text, Kerr.

804. Alexander Radcliffe: text, Love.

805. Henry Aldrich: text, H. Playford, *The Banquet of Music, III* (1689).

806. Philip Pain: text, *Daily Meditations* (Cambridge, Mass., 1668).

807–8. James Carkesse: texts, *Lucida Intervalla* (1679), ed. M. V. Deporte (Los Angeles, 1979). Carkesse was committed to Finsbury asylum in 1678, and then to Bedlam (Deporte's Introd.; Pepys, *Diary*).

809–14. 'Ephelia': texts, *Female Poems on Several Occasions* (1679) and Greer.

815. Mary Mollineux: text, *The Cavalier Poets*, ed. R. Skelton (1970).

816–27. John Wilmot, Earl of Rochester: texts, *The Poems*, ed. K. Walker (Oxford, 1984) and *The Complete Poems*, ed. D. M. Vieth (New Haven and London, 1968).

828–9. Thomas Heyrick: texts, *Miscellany Poems* (1691). Heyrick was curate of Market Harborough, Leicestershire, and author of many sermons.

830. Anonymous: text, J. Playford, *Choice Airs and Songs . . . The Fifth Book* (1684) and *A Choice Collection of 180 Loyal Songs* (1685).

831. Francis Daniel Pastorius: text, Meserole.

832–3. Nahum Tate: texts, *Supplement to the New Version of the Psalms* (1700) and *Poems* (1677).

834. Jacob Allestry: text, Kerr.

835. Thomas D'Urfey: text, *The Songs*, ed. C. L. Day (Cambridge, Mass., 1933).

836–7. John Oldham: texts, *The Poems*, ed. H. F. Brooks and R. Selden (Oxford, 1987). **836.** Lines 1–51, 85–106: Samuel Pordage (1633–91?) was a playwright and poet; Richard Flecknoe (*fl.* 1640–78?) had already been satirized by Dryden; *The British Princes: An Heroic Poem* (1669) was written by Edward Howard; John Ogilby (1600–76) was a heroic poet. **837.** Lines 279–374.

838–9. John Norris: texts, *The Poems of John Norris of Bemerton*, ed. A. B. Grosart (1871) and *A Collection of Miscellanies* (1687).

840. Richard Duke: text, *Poems on Several Occasions* (1717).

841. Anne Wharton: text, Greer.

842–6. Anonymous. **842.** Text, Love. **843.** Text, *Miscellany . . . Poems*, ed. Aphra Behn (1685). **844.** Text, Percy, *Reliques*. **845.** Text, Ramsay, *Tea-Table Miscellany* (1724–7) and Childe's *Ballads*. **846.** Text, James Watson, *Choice Collection* (Glasgow, 1711).

847. Anne Killigrew: text, Greer.

848. Pierre Antoine Motteux: text, *Love's a Jest* (1696), Act I, lines 1–24.

849. Thomas Southerne: text, *The Works*, ed. R. Jordan and H. Love, i (Oxford, 1988): *Sir Anthony Love*, Act II.

850–2. Anne Finch, Countess of Winchilsea: texts, *The Poems*, ed. M. Reynolds (Chicago, 1903). **850.** Lines 1–125. **851.** Marcus Junius Brutus (21), Caesar's assassin, had an ominous vision before his defeat at Philippi (42 BC) by Octavian.

853. Lord John Cutts: text, *Poetical Exercises Written upon Several Occasions* (1687). Cutts distinguished himself for bravery in William III's wars.

854. Mary Evelyn (and perhaps, in part, John Evelyn her father): text, Greer: lines 85–104, 145–77.

855. Henry Hall: text, *Poems on Affairs of State, vol. 5: 1688–1697*, ed. W. J. Cameron (New Haven and London, 1971). Hall was organist at Hereford.

856. Mary Astell: text, Greer.

857. Alicia D'Anvers: text, Greer.

858. Elizabeth Tipper: text, Greer.

859. Elizabeth Thomas: text, Greer. Clemena is Anne Osborne, Thomas's cousin.

860. George Farquhar: text, *The Works*, ed. S. S. Kenny, i (Oxford, 1988): *Love and a Bottle*, III. i. 112–31.

861. Alexander Pope: text, *Minor Poems*, ed. N. Ault and J. Butt (London and New Haven, 1964).

INDEX OF FIRST LINES

The references are to the numbers of the poems

INDEX OF FIRST LINES

INDEX OF FIRST LINES

INDEX OF FIRST LINES

INDEX OF FIRST LINES

INDEX OF AUTHORS

The references are to the numbers of the poems

INDEX OF AUTHORS